**COMMUNICATION
SYSTEMS**

McGRAW-HILL
ELECTRICAL AND ELECTRONIC ENGINEERING SERIES

FREDERICK EMMONS TERMAN, Consulting Editor
W. W. HARMAN, J. G. TRUXAL, and
R. A. ROHRER, Associate Consulting Editors

ANGELAKOS AND EVERHART: Microwave Communications
ANGELO: Electronic Circuits
ANGELO: Electronics: BJTs, FETs, and Microcircuits
ASELTINE: Transform Method in Linear System Analysis
BELOVE, SCHACHTER, AND SCHILLING: Digital and Analog Systems, Circuits, and Devices:
   An Introduction
BENNETT: Introduction to Signal Transmission
BERANEK: Acoustics
BRACEWELL: The Fourier Transform and Its Application
BRENNER AND JAVID: Analysis of Electric Circuits
CARLSON: Communication Systems: An Introduction to Signals and Noise in Electrical
   Communication
CHEN: The Analysis of Linear Systems
CHEN: Linear Network Design and Synthesis
CHIRLIAN: Analysis and Design of Electronic Circuits
CHIRLIAN: Basic Network Theory
CHIRLIAN: Electronic Circuits: Physical Principles, Analysis, and Design
CHIRLIAN AND ZEMANIAN: Electronics
CLEMENT AND JOHNSON: Electrical Engineering Science
D'AZZO AND HOUPIS: Feedback Control System Analysis and Synthesis
ELGERD: Control Systems Theory
ELGERD: Electric Energy Systems Theory: An Introduction
EVELEIGH: Adaptive Control and Optimization Techniques
EVELEIGH: Introduction to Control Systems Design
FEINSTEIN: Foundations of Information Theory
FITZGERALD, HIGGINBOTHAM, AND GRABEL: Basic Electrical Engineering
FITZGERALD, KINGSLEY, AND KUSKO: Electric Machinery
FRANK: Electrical Measurement Analysis
GEHMLICH AND HAMMOND: Electromechanical Systems
GHAUSI: Principles and Design of Linear Active Circuits
GREINER: Semiconductor Devices and Applications
HAMMOND AND GEHMLICH: Electrical Engineering
HANCOCK: An Introduction to the Principles of Communication Theory
HARMAN: Principles of the Statistical Theory of Communication
HAYT: Engineering Electromagnetics
HAYT AND KEMMERLY: Engineering Circuit Analysis
HILL: Electronics in Engineering
JOHNSON: Transmission Lines and Networks
KRAUS: Antennas
KRAUS AND CARVER: Electromagnetics
KUO: Linear Networks and Systems
LEPAGE: Complex Variables and the Laplace Transform for Engineering
LEVI AND PANZER: Electromechanical Power Conversion
LINVILL AND GIBBONS: Transistors and Active Circuits
LYNCH AND TRUXAL: Introductory System Analysis
LYNCH AND TRUXAL: Principles of Electronic Instrumentation
MCCLUSKEY: Introduction to the Theory of Switching Circuits
MEISEL: Principles of Electromechanical-energy Conversion
MILLMAN AND HALKIAS: Electronic Devices and Circuits

MILLMAN AND HALKIAS: Integrated Electronics: Analog and Digital Circuits and Systems
MILLMAN AND TAUB: Pulse, Digital, and Switching Waveforms
MINORSKY: Theory of Nonlinear Control Systems
MOORE: Traveling-wave Engineering
MURDOCH: Network Theory
OBERMAN: Disciplines in Combinational and Sequential Circuit Design
PETTIT AND MCWHORTER: Electronic Amplifier Circuits
PETTIT AND MCWHORTER: Electronic Switching, Timing, and Pulse Circuits
REZA AND SEELY: Modern Network Analysis
RUSTON AND BORDOGNA: Electric Networks: Functions, Filters, Analysis
SCHILLING AND BELOVE: Electronic Circuits: Discrete and Integrated
SCHWARTZ: Information Transmission, Modulation, and Noise
SCHWARTZ AND FRIEDLAND: Linear Systems
SHOOMAN: Probabilistic Reliability: An Engineering Approach
SISKIND: Direct-current Machinery
SKILLING: Electric Transmission Lines
STEVENSON: Elements of Power System Analysis
STRAUSS: Wave Generation and Shaping
SU: Active Network Synthesis
TAUB AND SCHILLING: Principles of Communication Systems
TERMAN: Electronic and Radio Engineering
TERMAN AND PETTIT: Electronic Measurements
THALER AND PASTEL: Analysis and Design of Nonlinear Feedback Control Systems
TOU: Modern Control Theory
TUTTLE: Electric Networks: Analysis and Synthesis
WEEKS: Antenna Engineering

**McGRAW-HILL
BOOK COMPANY**
New York
St. Louis
San Francisco
Düsseldorf
Johannesburg
Kuala Lumpur
London
Mexico
Montreal
New Delhi
Panama
Paris
São Paulo
Singapore
Sydney
Tokyo
Toronto

A. BRUCE CARLSON

*Associate Professor of Systems Engineering
Rensselaer Polytechnic Institute*

Communication Systems

AN INTRODUCTION TO SIGNALS AND NOISE IN ELECTRICAL COMMUNICATION

SECOND EDITION

This book was set in Times New Roman.
The editors were Kenneth J. Bowman and Michael Gardner;
the cover was designed by Pencils Portfolio, Inc.;
the production supervisor was Leroy A. Young.
The drawings were done by J & R Services, Inc.
Kingsport Press, Inc., was printer and binder.

Library of Congress Cataloging in Publication Data

Carlson, A   Bruce, date
    Communication system.

    (McGraw-Hill electrical and electronic engineering
series)
    Bibliography: p.
    1. Signal theory (Telecommunication) 2. Telecom-
munication. I. Title.
TK512.5.C3 1975   621.38'043   74-9841
ISBN 0-07-009957-X

COMMUNICATION SYSTEMS
An Introduction to
Signals and Noise in
Electrical Communication

1234567890KPKP7987654

To the memory of my father,
ALBIN JOHN CARLSON

CONTENTS

This text, like its first edition, is an introduction to electrical communication systems written at a level appropriate for advanced undergraduates and first-year graduate students. Because electrical communication involves many diverse aspects — from electronic and electromagnetic hardware considerations to the mathematical abstractions of information and detection theory — I have attempted here to chart a middle path by adopting the systems engineering viewpoint, focusing upon those basic concepts, techniques, and problems that characterize information transfer via electrical signals, given the inevitable limitations of physical systems.

The specific subject matter and organization is indicated by the contents and discussed in Sect. 1.6. New features that motivated this edition are as follows.

1. The fundamentals of analog- and digital-signal transmission are first introduced in the context of baseband communication (Chap. 4). Thus, such concepts as channel loss, distortion, bandwidth requirements, signal-to-noise ratios, and errors are presented at a more elementary level, and a standard of comparison is established for the subsequent study of modulation methods.

2. Reflecting the increasing importance of digital communication, coverage of this topic has been expanded and interwoven throughout the text, starting with Chap. 4.

3. Flexibility for the instructor and the student has been enhanced through the use of separate chapters on noise in CW modulation (Chap. 7), sampling and pulse modulation (Chap. 8), information theory (Chap. 9), and digital data systems (Chap. 10), plus three appendixes. This provides considerable lattitude in the selection of topics following Chap. 6. Additionally, optional material of a more advanced nature within each chapter has been designated by the symbol ★.

4. Correlation and spectral density functions are introduced first for deterministic signals (Sect. 2.6) using the general concept of scalar products, thereby paving the way for the treatment of random signals (Sect. 3.5). The supporting signal-space theory of scalar products is given in Appendix A.

5. There are numerous examples chosen particularly to illustrate techniques that most students find troublesome. There are also exercises (usually with answers) interspersed through the text to encourage students to test their grasp of the material.

6. Special effort has been made to serve the needs of two general groups of students: those who are starting a sequence of study in the area of electrical communication; and those who desire a relatively self-contained treatment of the subject. For the former, the optional material provides a link to graduate-level work. For the latter, I have tried to point out the connections with related fields in other disciplines as well as within electrical engineering.

Consistent with the potential heterogeneity of interests, together with a desire to keep prerequisites at a minimum, I have assumed only that the students are modestly adept at circuit analysis (including simple transient and steady-state problems) and have some knowledge of electronics. Prior exposure to linear systems analysis, Fourier transforms, and probability theory is helpful but not essential. With this background, the first eight or nine chapters are easily covered in a one-semester course if the optional sections are omitted. Selected additions or omissions will tailor the text to fit other course lengths or different student backgrounds.

Two types of references have been included: those cited via footnotes give further details on a particular item; those mentioned under the heading Selected Supplementary Reading constitute a brief annotated bibliography of other tutorial treaments and landmark papers. All references have been screened for easy accessibility.

Approximately 370 problems have been provided, including those with the appendixes. They range from basic computations (with answers supplied) to more advanced analysis and design questions. Problems that relate to optional material or that require some ingenuity on the part of the student are identified by the symbol ★. The latter may be considered by the instructor for classroom discussion. An instructor's manual giving complete solutions is available from the publisher on request.

Besides problem solutions, the instructor's manual contains: Selected figures from the text in a form suitable for making projection transparencies; instructions for several lecture-demonstrations; and complete student study guides for those who may wish to teach the subject using individualized or self-paced instruction, i.e., PSI, IPI, etc. Incidentally, I have used self-paced instruction for this course at Rensselaer since 1972, so the study guides are based on considerable experience. The method seems to work very well with the subject matter, and student response has been generally enthusiastic.

I am indebted to many people for their advice and assistance with this second edition. Dr. David G. Gisser of Rensselaer Polytechnic Institute provided several important contributions relating to communication electronics. Other Rensselaer colleagues who helped include Drs. Dean N. Arden, Charles M. Close, Lester A. Gerhardt, and Dean K. Frederick. Dr. John C. Lindenlaub of Purdue University gave many significant suggestions from the very inception of the second edition; he also assisted with the student study guides which he has class-tested at Purdue. Numerous pedagogical improvements were stimulated by the comments of students and graduate teaching assistants in the self-paced course, particularly Messrs. Mounir P. Badawy, Nelson R. Corby, Jeffrey S. Lucash, Michael P. Meyer, and Arthur P. Sarkisian. Finally, for the support so necessary for this project, credit goes to the administration of the School of Engineering at Rensselaer, and to my wife and family.

A. Bruce Carlson

1

INTRODUCTION

"Attention, the Universe! By kingdoms, right wheel!" This prophetic phrase is the first telegraph message on record; it was sent over a 16-kilometer (km) line by Samuel F. B. Morse in 1838. Thus was born a new era in communication, the era of electrical communication.

Today, electrical communication systems are found wherever information is to be conveyed from one point to another. Telephone, radio, and television have become integral parts of everyday life. Long-distance circuits span the globe, carrying text, voice, and images. Radar and telemetry systems play vital roles in navigation, defense, and scientific research. Computers talk to computers via transcontinental data links. The accomplishments are many, and the list is seemingly endless. Certainly, great strides have been made since the days of Morse; equally certain, coming decades will see many new achievements of communication engineering. Indeed, the potential applications are bounded only by man's needs, aspirations, and imagination.

Because of the myriad types of communication systems, a book like this, devoted to the subject of electrical communication, cannot possibly cover every application. The result would be no more than a catalog, and one that would soon be out of date. Nor can we discuss in detail the individual components or hardware items that go to make up a specific system. A typical system consists of numerous and diverse parts whose understanding draws on virtually all the specialties of electrical engineering: energy conversion, network theory, electronics, and electromagnetics, to name a few. Moreover, a part-by-part analysis would miss the essential point that a system is an integrated whole that really does exceed the sum of its parts.

Instead, this book approaches the subject from a more general viewpoint. Recognizing that all communication systems have the same basic function, namely *information transmission*, we shall seek out and isolate the principles and problems of transmitting information in electrical form. These will be examined in detail so as to provide the fundamental analysis and design techniques applicable to any type of electrical communication. In short, this book treats communication systems as *systems*.

The system engineering approach is a powerful one; it is also somewhat abstract, relying heavily on mathematics to cut through to the heart of complex problems. However, it should be kept in mind that the mathematics is only a means to an end, that end being a basic understanding of electrical communication. To that end, the use of abstract mathematical tools and models must be tempered with physical reasoning and engineering judgment.

The purpose of this introductory chapter is twofold: to give a general description of communication systems, enumerating the essential elements, their functions, and associated problems; and to place in perspective the roles of the various disciplines in communication system engineering.

1.1 COMMUNICATION, MESSAGES, AND SIGNALS

To begin with, we define communication as the process whereby information is transferred from one point in space and time, called the *source*, to another point, the *destination* or user. A communication system is the totality of mechanisms that provides the information link between source and destination. An electrical communication system is one that achieves this function primarily, but not exclusively, through the use of electric devices and phenomena.

Clearly, the concept of *information* is central to communication. But what is information? Here we can run into difficulty, for information is a loaded word implying such semantic and philosophical notions as knowledge or meaning. These subjective aspects, fascinating though they may be, are largely irrelevant to the technological problems of communication. Eventually, in our discussion of information theory, a precise mathematical definition of information will be formulated. For the present, however, a slightly different avenue will be followed. Instead of coming to grips with information per se, we shall concentrate on the physical manifestation of the information as produced by the source, i.e., the *message*.

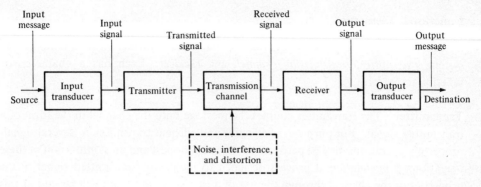

FIGURE 1.1
The elements of a communication system.

There are many kinds of information sources, including men and machines, so messages appear in a variety of forms: a sequence of discrete symbols or letters (e.g., words written on a telegraph blank, the holes punched in an IBM card); a single time-varying quantity (e.g., the acoustic pressure produced by speech or music, the angular position of an aircraft gyro); several functions of time and other variables (e.g., the light intensity and color of a television scene). But whatever the message may be, the purpose of a communication system is to provide an acceptable replica of it at the destination.

As a rule, the message produced by a source is not electrical and hence an input transducer is required. This transducer converts the message to a *signal*, a time-varying electrical quantity such as voltage or current. Similarly, another transducer at the destination converts the output signal to the appropriate message form. While transducer design is an important part of communication engineering, we shall limit our consideration to the strictly electric portion of the system, i.e., that portion where the message appears as an electric signal. Hereafter, the terms *signal* and *message* will be used interchangeably since the signal, like the message, is a physical embodiment of the information.

With these preliminaries out of the way, let us turn our attention to the system, its parts, and its problems.

1.2   THE ELEMENTS OF A COMMUNICATION SYSTEM

Figure 1.1 shows the functional elements of a complete communication system. For convenience we have isolated them as distinct entities, though in actual systems the separation may not be so obvious. Also indicated are some of the unwanted factors that inevitably enter the picture.

Functional Elements

Exclusive of transducers, there are three essential parts in an electrical communication system, *transmitter*, *transmission channel*, and *receiver*. Each has a characteristic function to perform.

Transmitter The transmitter couples the message onto the channel in the form of a transmitted signal. For purposes of effective and efficient transmission, several signal-processing operations may be performed. The commonest and most important of these operations is *modulation*, a process designed to match the transmitted signal to the properties of the channel through the use of a carrier wave. More will be said of this process shortly; later on, the subject will consume four chapters.

Transmission channel The transmission channel or medium is the electrical connection between transmitter and receiver, bridging the distance from source to destination. It may be a pair of wires, a coaxial cable, a radio wave, or even a laser beam. But regardless of type, all electrical transmission media are characterized by *attenuation*, the progressive decrease of signal power with increasing distance. The amount of attenuation can be small or very large. Usually it is large and therefore a factor to be reckoned with.

Receiver The function of the receiver is to extract the desired signal from the channel and deliver it to the output transducer. Since received signals are often very feeble as a result of transmission attenuation, the receiver may have several stages of amplification. However, the key operation performed by the receiver is *demodulation* (or detection), the reverse of the transmitter's modulation process, which restores the signal to its original form.

Contaminations

In the course of signal transmission, certain unwanted and undesirable effects take place. One is attenuation, which reduces the signal *strength*; more serious, however, are distortion, interference, and noise, which appear as alterations of the signal *shape*. While such contaminations are introduced throughout the system, it is a common and convenient practice to blame them all on the channel, treating the transmitter and receiver as being ideal. Figure 1.1 reflects this convention.

Broadly speaking, any unintended signal perturbation may be classified as "noise," and it is sometimes difficult to distinguish the various offenders in a corrupted signal. Nonetheless, there are good reasons and an adequate basis for separating the three effects, as follows.

Distortion   Distortion is signal alteration due to imperfect response of the system to the desired signal itself. Unlike noise and interference, distortion disappears when the signal is turned off. Improved system design or compensating networks can reduce distortion. Theoretically perfect compensation may be possible. Practically, some distortion must be accepted, though the amount can be held within tolerable limits in all but extreme cases.

Interference   Interference is contamination by extraneous signals, usually man-made, of a form similar to the desired signal. The problem is particularly common in broadcasting, where two or more signals may be picked up at the same time by the receiver. The cure for interference is obvious: eliminate, in one way or another, the interfering signal or its source. Again, a perfect solution is possible, if not always practical.

Noise   Finally, saving the worst for last, we come to noise. By noise we mean the random and unpredictable electric signals from natural causes, both internal and external to the system. When such random variations are added to an information-bearing signal, the information may be partially masked or totally obliterated. Of course the same can be said for interference and distortion; what makes noise unique is that it can never be completely eliminated, even in theory. As we shall see, noneliminable noise poses one of the basic problems of electrical communication.

1.3   MODULATION

Most input signals, as they come from the transducer, cannot be sent directly over the channel. Instead, a *carrier wave*, whose properties are better suited to the transmission medium in question, is modified to represent the message. Modulation is the systematic alteration of a carrier wave in accordance with the message (modulating signal) and may also include coding.

It is interesting to note that many nonelectrical forms of communication also involve a modulation process, speech being a good example. When a person speaks, the movements of the mouth take place at rather low rates, on the order of 10 Hz†, and as such cannot effectively produce propagating acoustic waves. Transmission of voice through air is achieved by generating higher-frequency carrier tones in the vocal cords and modulating these tones with the muscular actions of the oral cavity. What the ear hears as speech is thus a modulated acoustic wave, similar in many respects to a modulated electric wave.

---

† The *hertz*, abbreviated Hz, is the unit for frequency in cycles per second. It will be used throughout this book, often with prefixes as follows: 1 kHz=1 kilohertz= 10^3 cps; 1 MHz=1 megahertz=10^6 cps; 1 GHz=1 gigahertz=10^9 cps.

Types of Modulation

To a large extent, the success of a communication system in a given mission depends on the modulation, so much so that the type of modulation is a pivotal decision in system design. Correspondingly, many different modulation techniques have evolved to suit various tasks and system requirements. And as new tasks arise, new techniques will be developed.

Despite the multitude of varieties, it is possible to identify two basic types of modulation, according to the kind of carrier wave: *continuous wave* (CW) *modulation*, for which the carrier is simply a sinusoidal waveform, and *pulse modulation*, for which the carrier is a periodic train of pulses.

CW modulation, being a continuous process, is obviously suited to signals that are continuously varying with time. Usually, the sinusoidal carrier is at a frequency much higher than any of the frequency components contained in the modulating signal. The modulation process is then characterized by *frequency translation*; i.e., the message spectrum (its frequency content) is shifted upward to a new and higher band of frequencies.

Pulse modulation is a discontinuous or discrete process, in the sense that the pulses are present only at certain distinct intervals of time. Hence, pulse modulation is best suited to messages that are discrete in nature. Nonetheless, with the aid of *sampling*, continuously varying signals can be transmitted on pulsed carriers. Often, as in telegraph and teletype, pulse modulation and coding go hand in hand.

As an alternative to the above classification it sometimes is preferable to speak of modulation as being *analog* or *coded* (digital). This is particularly true of the more complex systems employing both CW and pulsed techniques, making distinction by carrier type hazy. The analog-versus-digital distinction is as follows. In analog modulation, the modulated parameter varies in direct proportion to the modulating signal. In coded modulation, a digital transformation takes place whereby the message is converted from one symbolic language to another. If the message is originally a continuous time function, it must be sampled and digitized (quantized) prior to encoding.

But regardless of type — CW or pulsed, analog or coded — modulation must be a *reversible* process, so that the message can be retrieved at the receiver by the complementary operation of demodulation.

Why Modulate?

In his book on modulation theory, Black (1953)† devotes an entire chapter to this question. We have already given a concise answer, namely, that modulation is required to *match* the signal to the transmission medium. However, this match involves several considerations deserving further amplification.

---

† References are indicated in this fashion throughout. Complete citations are listed alphabetically by author in the References at the end of the book.

Modulation for ease of radiation Efficient electromagnetic radiation requires radiating elements (antennas) whose physical dimensions are at least $\frac{1}{10}$ wavelength or so. But many signals, especially audio signals, have frequency components down to 100 Hz or lower, necessitating antennas some 300 km long if radiated directly. Utilizing the frequency-translation property of modulation, these signals can be impressed on a high-frequency carrier, thereby permitting substantial reduction of antenna size. For example, in the FM broadcast band, where carriers are in the 88- to 108-MHz range, antennas need be no more than a meter or so across.

Modulation to reduce noise and interference We have said that it is impossible to eliminate noise from the system. And though it is possible to eliminate interference, it may not be practical. Fortunately, certain types of modulation have the useful property of suppressing both noise and interference. The suppression, however, is not without a price; it generally requires a transmission bandwidth (frequency range) much larger than that of the original signal bandwidth, hence the designation *wideband noise reduction*. This trade-off of bandwidth for noise reduction is one of the most interesting and sometimes frustrating aspects of communication system design.

Modulation for frequency assignment The owner of a radio or television set has the option of selecting one of several stations even when all stations are broadcasting similar program material in the same transmission medium. The selection and separation of any one station is possible because each has a different assigned carrier frequency. Were it not for modulation, only one station could operate in a given area. Two or more stations transmitting directly in the same medium, without modulation, would produce a hopeless jumble of interfering signals.

Modulation for multiplexing Often it is desired to send many signals simultaneously between the same two points. Multiplexing techniques, inherently forms of modulation, permit multiple-signal transmission on one channel such that each signal can be picked out at the receiving end. Applications of multiplexing include data telemetry, FM stereophonic broadcasting, and long-distance telephone. It is quite common, for instance, to have as many as 1,800 intercity telephone conversations multiplexed for transmission on a coaxial cable less than a centimeter in diameter.

Modulation to overcome equipment limitations The design of a system is usually constrained by available equipment, equipment whose performance is often contingent upon the frequencies involved. Modulation can be used to place a signal in that portion of the frequency spectrum where equipment limitations are minimum or where design requirements are more easily met. For this purpose, modulation devices are also found in receivers as well as transmitters.

1.4 FUNDAMENTAL LIMITATIONS IN ELECTRICAL COMMUNICATION

In the design of a communication system, or any system for that matter, the engineer is faced with two general kinds of constraints. On the one hand are the *technological problems*, the engineering facts of life. On the other hand are the *fundamental physical limitations* imposed by the system itself, the laws of nature as they pertain to the task.

Since engineering is, or should be, the art of the possible, both kinds of constraints must be recognized in system design. Nonetheless, there is a difference. Technological problems are problems of feasibility, including such diverse considerations as equipment availability, interaction with existing systems, economic factors, etc., problems that can be solved in theory, though the solution may not be practical. But the fundamental physical limitations are just that; when they are encountered head on, there is no recourse, even in theory. Technological questions notwithstanding, it is these limitations that ultimately dictate what can or cannot be accomplished. The fundamental limitations of information transmission by electrical means are *bandwidth* and *noise*.

The Bandwidth Limitation

Although not explicitly shown in Fig. 1.1, the time element is an integral part of communication systems. Efficient system utilization calls for minimizing transmission time i.e., sending the most information in the least time. Rapid information transmission is achieved by using signals that change rapidly with time. But we are dealing with an electrical system, which always includes energy storage; and it is a well-known physical law that for all but lossless systems, a change in stored energy requires a definite amount of time. Thus, we cannot arbitrarily increase signaling speed, for eventually the system will cease to respond to the signal changes.

A convenient measure of signal speed is its bandwidth, the width of the signal spectrum. Similarly, the rate at which a system can change stored energy is reflected by its usable frequency response, measured in terms of the *system bandwidth*. Transmitting a large amount of information in a small amount of time requires wideband signals to represent the information and wideband systems to accommodate the signals. Bandwidth therefore emerges as a fundamental limitation. When real-time transmission is required, the design must provide for adequate system bandwidth. If the bandwidth is insufficient, it may be necessary to decrease signaling speed and thereby increase transmission time.

Along these same lines it may be remarked that equipment design is not so much a question of *absolute* bandwidth as of *fractional* bandwidth, i.e., absolute bandwidth divided by the center frequency. Modulating a wideband signal onto a high-frequency carrier reduces the fractional bandwidth and thereby simplifies equipment design. This is one reason why TV signals, having a bandwidth of about 6 MHz, are sent on much higher carriers than AM radio, where the bandwidth is about 10 kHz.

Likewise given a fractional bandwidth dictated by equipment considerations, the absolute bandwidth can be increased almost indefinitely by going to higher carrier frequencies. A 5-GHz microwave system can accommodate 10,000 times as much information in a given period as a 500-kHz radio-frequency carrier, while a laser beam of frequency 5×10^{14} Hz has a theoretical information capacity exceeding that of the microwave system by a factor of 10^5, or roughly equivalent to 10 million TV channels. Thus it is that communication engineers are continually seeking new and usable high-frequency carrier sources to compensate for the bandwidth factor.

Figure 1.2 shows those portions of the electromagnetic spectrum now in use or potentially available for electrical communication. Representative applications and transmission media are indicated. As a rough guideline, available bandwidth at any point is about 10 percent of the carrier frequency. Owing to several factors the gap from 10^{11} Hz (100 GHz) to 10^{14} Hz will probably remain a void insofar as communication is concerned.

The Noise Limitation

A measuring instrument having 1 percent resolution can yield more information than an instrument having 10 percent resolution; the difference is one of *accuracy*. Similarly, successful electrical communication depends on how accurately the receiver can determine which signal was actually sent, as distinguished from signals that might have been sent. Perfect signal identification might be possible in the absence of noise and other contaminations, but noise is always present in electrical systems, and superimposed noise perturbations limit our ability to correctly identify the intended signal and thereby limit information transmission.

Why is noise inevitable? Curiously, the answer comes from kinetic theory. Any particle at a temperature other than absolute zero has thermal energy manifested as random motion or thermal agitation. If the particle happens to be an electron, its random motion constitutes a random current. If the random current takes place in a conducting medium, a random voltage known as *thermal noise* or *resistance noise* is produced. While resistance noise is only one of the possible sources in a system, most others are related in one way or another to random electron motion. Moreover, as might be expected from the wave-particle duality, there is thermal noise associated with electromagnetic radiation. Hence, just as we cannot have electrical communication without electrons or electromagnetic waves, we cannot have electrical communication without noise.

Typical noise variations are quite small, on the order of microvolts. If the

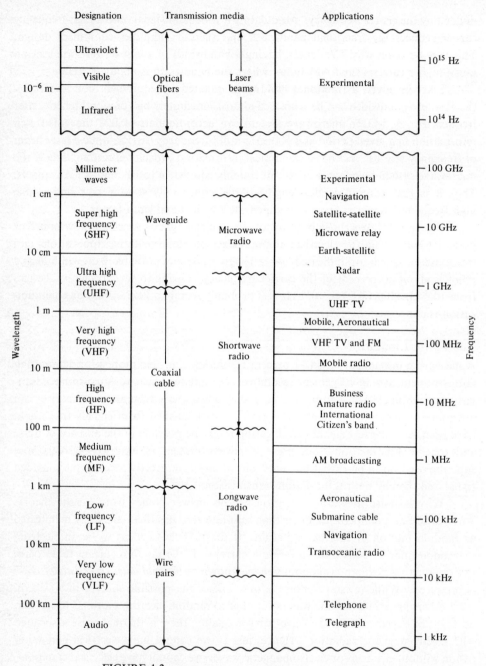

FIGURE 1.2
The electromagnetic spectrum. (Applications shown are illustrative; space limitations prevent a complete listing.)

signal variations are substantially greater, say several volts peak to peak, then the noise may be all but ignored. Indeed, in ordinary systems under ordinary conditions, the *signal-to-noise ratio* is large enough for noise to go unnoticed. But in long-range or minimum-power systems, the received signal may be as small as the noise or smaller. When this happens, the noise limitation becomes very real.

It is important to note that if the signal strength is insufficient, adding more stages of amplification at the receiver is to no avail; the noise will be amplified along with the signal, leaving the signal-to-noise ratio unimproved. Increasing the transmitted power does help, but power cannot be increased indefinitely because of technological problems. (One of the early transatlantic cables was apparently destroyed by high-voltage rupture in an effort to obtain a usable received signal.) Alternately, as mentioned earlier, we can exchange bandwidth for signal-to-noise ratio via modulation and coding techniques. Not surprisingly, the most effective of these techniques generally turns out to be the most difficult and costly to instrument. Also note that swapping bandwidth for signal-to-noise ratio may take us from one limitation to the other.

In the final analysis, given a system of fixed bandwidth and signal-to-noise ratio, there is a definite upper limit on the rate at which information can be transmitted by that system. This upper limit is called the information *capacity* and is one of the central concepts of information theory. Because the capacity is finite, it can truly be said that communication system design is a matter of compromise; a compromise between transmission time, transmitted power, bandwidth, and signal-to-noise ratio; a compromise further constrained by the technological problems.

1.5 A CHRONOLOGY OF ELECTRICAL COMMUNICATION

The organization of this text is dictated by pedagogical considerations and does not necessarily reflect the evolutionary order. But the history of electrical communication is both interesting and informative, if only to provide some feeling for the significant events of the past, when they occurred, and the names associated with them.

A complete history is impossible here, of course, for it would require a book unto itself.† As an alternate, the following selected chronology is presented, listing the more important inventions, discoveries, and papers. The chronology gives little indication of the relative importance and interrelationships of events, but further comments are withheld till later chapters where additional discussion will be more meaningful. The reader may therefore find it helpful to refer back to this section from time to time.

† E.g., Still (1946) or Black (1953, chap. 1); also see *Scientific American*, vol. 227, September 1972, which is devoted entirely to communication in many forms.

Year	Event
1800–1837	**Preliminary developments** Volta discovers the primary battery; the mathematical treatises of Fourier, Cauchy, and Laplace; experiments on electricity and magnetism by Oersted, Ampere, Faraday, and Henry; Ohm's law (1826); early telegraph systems by Gauss and Weber and by Wheatstone and Cooke.
1838–1866	**The birth of telegraphy** Morse perfects his system with the help of Gale, Henry, and Vail; Steinheil finds that the earth can be used for a current path; commercial service initiated (1844); multiplexing techniques devised; William Thomson (Lord Kelvin) calculates the pulse response of a telegraph line (1855); transatlantic cables installed by Cyrus Field and associates.
1845	Kirchhoff's circuit laws enunciated.
1864	"A Dynamical Theory of the Electromagnetic Field," by James Clerk Maxwell, predicts electromagnetic radiation.
1876–1899	**The birth of telephony** Acoustic transducer perfected by Alexander Graham Bell, after earlier attempts by Reis; first telephone exchange, in New Haven, Conn., with eight lines (1878); Edison's carbon-button transducer; cable circuits introduced; Strowger devises automatic step-by step switching (1887); the theory of cable loading by Heaviside, Pupin, and Campbell.
1887–1907	**Wireless telegraphy** Heinrich Hertz verifies Maxwell's theory; demonstrations by Marconi and Popov; Marconi patents a complete wireless telegraph system (1897); the theory of tuning circuits developed by Sir Oliver Lodge; commercial service begins, including ship-to-shore and transatlantic systems.
1892–1899	Oliver Heaviside's publications on operational calculus, circuits, and electromagnetics.
1904–1920	**Electronics applied to radio and telephone** Lee De Forest invents the Audion (triode) based on Fleming's diode; basic filter types devised by G. A. Campbell and others; experiments with AM radio broadcasting; transcontinental telephone line with electronic repeaters completed by the Bell System (1915); multiplexed carrier telephony introduced; E. H. Armstrong perfects the superheterodyne radio receiver (1918); first broadcasting station, KDKA, Pittsburgh.
1920–1928	Landmark papers on the theory of signal transmission and noise by J. R. Carson, H. Nyquist, J. B. Johnson, and R. V. L. Hartley.
1923–1938	**The birth of television** Mechanical image-formation systems demonstrated by Baird and Jenkins; theoretical analysis of bandwidth requirements by Gray, Horton, and Mathes; Farnsworth and Zworykin propose electronic systems; vacuum cathode-ray tubes perfected by DuMont and others; field tests and experimental broadcasting begin.
1931	Teletypewriter service initiated.
1934	H. S. Black develops the negative-feedback amplifier.
1936	"A Method of Reducing Disturbances in Radio Signaling by a System of Frequency Modulation," by Armstrong, states the case for FM radio.
1937	Alec Reeves conceives pulse code modulation.
1938–1945	**World War II** Radar and microwave systems developed; FM used extensively for military communications; improved electronics, hardware, and theory in all areas; Weiner and Kolmogoroff apply statistical methods to signal detection problems.
1948	C. E. Shannon publishes "A Mathematical Theory of Communication."
1948–1951	Transistor devices invented by Bardeen, Brattain, and Shockley.
1950	Time-division multiplexing applied to telephony.
1955	J. R. Pierce proposes satellite communication systems.
1956	First transoceanic telephone cable (36 voice channels).

Year	Event
1958	Long-distance data transmission systems developed for military purposes.
1960	Maiman demonstrates the first laser.
1961	Integrated circuits go into commercial production.
1962	Satellite communication begins with Telstar I.
1962–1966	**The birth of high-speed digital communication** Data transmission service offered commercially; wideband channels designed for digital signaling; pulse code modulation proves feasible for voice and TV transmission; major breakthroughs in the theory and implementation of digital transmission, including error-control coding methods by Bose, Chaudhuri, Wozencraft, and others, and the development of adaptive equalization by Lucky and coworkers.
1963	Solid-state microwave oscillators perfected by Gunn and others.
1964	Fully electronic telephone switching system (No. 1 ESS) goes into service.
1965	Mariner IV transmits pictures from Mars to earth.
1966–1975	**Precursors of the future** Cable TV systems; experimental laser communication links; Picturephone® field trials; developmental work in fiber optics, helical waveguide, digital filtering, charge-coupled devices, and large-scale integrated circuitry.

1.6 PROSPECTUS

This study of communication systems begins with the fundamental physical limitations, their description, and analysis. In Chap. 2 the mathematical tools of signal theory and linear systems are reviewed, emphasizing the frequency-domain approach leading to the concepts of spectrum and bandwidth. By and large this will be familiar territory, based on elementary transform methods and circuit theory. Chapter 3 is a very short course on probability and statistics as applied to particular random signals of interest in communication. Our principal task will be the description of undesired noise, particularly from the spectral viewpoint.

Having developed the necessary tools, we then turn to the stuff of communication engineering, namely, the theory and practice of signal transmission. Chapter 4 introduces basic system parameters and design strategies in the context of baseband transmission, i.e., no modulation. Continuous-wave modulation is dealt with in Chaps. 5 to 7, while Chap. 8 treats sampling theory and pulse modulation. Throughout these chapters, the problem of signal recovery in the presence of noise and interference will be considered. Multiplexing techniques, wideband noise reduction, and threshold effects are examined where applicable. For the most part, system elements and instrumentation will be described as "black boxes" having specified properties, but on occasion the lid is lifted to see what goes on inside and how the various functions are achieved in practice.

Information theory and its implications for electrical communication are surveyed in Chap. 9. Of particular importance is the Hartley-Shannon equation, which expresses in quantitative form the bandwidth and noise limitations on information transmission. In the light of this theory it is possible to draw some conclusion about the relative merits of conventional systems and also get some hints as to how better systems can be designed.

The text concludes, in Chap. 10, with digital data transmission, the most rapidly expanding area in communication engineering. This topic not only involves all the previous material but also gives added meaning to the mathematical theory of communication.

Each chapter contains several exercises designed to clarify and reinforce the concepts and analytic techniques as they are introduced. Students are strongly encouraged to test their grasp of the material by working these exercises. Answers have been provided where appropriate.

Certain optional or more advanced topics are interspersed through the text. Identified by the symbol ★, these sections can be omitted without serious loss of continuity. Other optional material of a supplementary nature has been collected in the three appendices at the back of the book.

Also at the back the reader will find several tables and a list of selected supplementary reading. The former contain most of the mathematical relations and numerical data needed to work the problems at the end of the chapters. The latter serves as an annotated bibliography of books and papers for the benefit of those who wish to pursue a topic in greater depth.

SIGNALS, SPECTRA, AND FILTERS

Electrical communication signals are time-varying quantities, such as voltage or current. The usual description of a signal $v(t)$ is in the *time domain*, where the independent variable is t. But for communications work, it is often more convenient to describe signals in the *frequency domain*, where the independent variable is f. Roughly speaking, we think of the time function as being composed of a number of frequency components, each with appropriate amplitude and phase. Thus, while the signal physically exists in the time domain, we can say that it consists of those components in its frequency-domain description, called the *spectrum*.

Spectral analysis, based on the Fourier series and transform, is a powerful tool in communication engineering. Accordingly, we will concentrate primarily on Fourier theory rather than on other techniques such as Laplace transforms and time-domain analysis. There are several reasons for this emphasis.

First, the frequency domain is essentially a steady-state viewpoint; and for many purposes it is reasonable to restrict attention to the steady-state behavior of a communication system. Indeed, considering the multitude of possible signals that a system may handle, detailed transient solutions for each would be an impossible task. Second, the spectral approach allows us to treat entire classes of signals that have similar properties in the frequency domain. This not only gives insight to analysis but is invaluable for design. It is quite unlikely, for example, that such a significant technique as single-sideband modulation could have been developed without the aid of spectral concepts. Third, many components of a communication system can be classified as linear and time-invariant devices; when this is so, we can describe them by their *frequency-response characteristics* which, in turn, further expedites analysis and design work.

This chapter therefore is devoted to a review† and elaboration of Fourier analysis of signals and frequency-response characteristics of system components, particularly those frequency-selective components known as filters. However, the spectral approach should not be thought of as the only method used by communication engineers. There are some problems where it cannot be applied directly, and some problems where other techniques are more convenient. Thus, each new problem must be approached with an open mind and a good set of analytic tools.

As the first step in much of our work we will write equations representing signals or components. But one must bear in mind that such equations are only mathematical *models* of physical entities, usually imperfect models. In fact, a completely faithful description of the simplest signal or component would be prohibitively complex in mathematical form and consequently useless for engineering purposes. Hence the models we seek are ones that represent, with minimum complexity, those properties that are pertinent to the problem at hand. This sometimes leads to constructing several different models for the same thing, according to need. Then, given a particular problem, the choice of which model to use is based on understanding the physical phenomena involved and the limitations of the mathematics; in short, it is engineering.

2.1 AC SIGNALS AND NETWORKS

Figure 2.1 represents a two-port electrical network or system being driven by an input signal $x(t)$ which produces the output signal $y(t)$. We say that $x(t)$ is a sinusoidal or AC signal if

$$x(t) = A_x \cos(\omega_0 t + \theta_x) \qquad -\infty < t < \infty \qquad (1)$$

where A_x is the *amplitude* (in volts or amperes), ω_0 is the *angular frequency* (in radians per second), and θ_x is the *phase* (in radians or degrees). It is also convenient to introduce the *cyclical frequency* $f_0 = \omega_0/2\pi$ (in cycles per second or hertz) so the *period* (in seconds) is $T_0 = 1/f_0 = 2\pi/\omega_0$. The significance of T_0 is that $x(t)$ repeats itself every T_0 seconds for all time. Obviously, no real signal lasts forever, but Eq. (1) is a convenient and useful representation or model for a sinusoidal signal of finite duration if the duration is much longer than the period.

---

† It is assumed that the reader has some background in transform theory and linear systems analysis. Accordingly, certain proofs and derivations have been omitted.

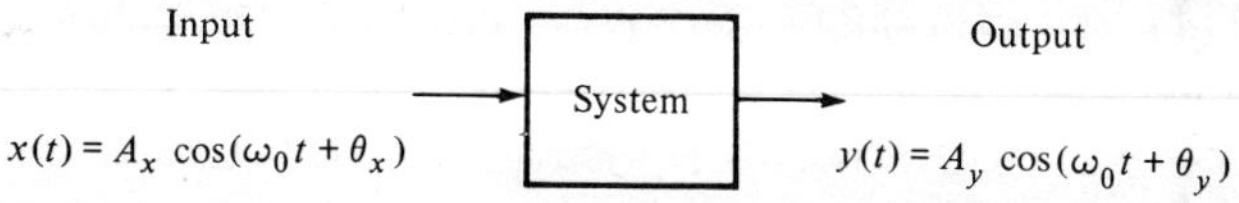

Input

System

Output

$$x(t) = A_x \cos(\omega_0 t + \theta_x)$$

$$y(t) = A_y \cos(\omega_0 t + \theta_y)$$

FIGURE 2.1
System in AC steady-state condition.

Now assume that the network is *linear*, *time-invariant*, and *asymptotically stable*. In essence, this means that superposition applies, there are no time-varying parameters, and the natural behavior decays with time. Under these conditions, the output signal will also be sinusoidal at the same frequency as the input, differing only in amplitude and phase, i.e.,

$$y(t) = A_y \cos (\omega_0 t + \theta_y) \qquad -\infty < t < \infty \qquad (2)$$

Therefore, given the parameters of the input signal and the network's characteristics, we need only solve for A_y and θ_y to completely describe the resulting output signal. This is, of course, the familiar AC steady-state problem.

It is well known that such problems are most easily solved using exponential time functions of the form $e^{j\omega t}$ rather than sinusoidal functions. Take the case, for instance, of a circuit having complex impedance $Z(j\omega)$; if the current through the circuit is $e^{j\omega t}$ then, by the definition of impedance, the resulting voltage is simply $Z(j\omega)e^{j\omega t}$. Similarly, for the two-port network case of Fig. 2.1, we define the network's *transfer function* $H(j\omega)$ such that $y(t) = H(j\omega)e^{j\omega t}$ when $x(t) = e^{j\omega t}$; that is,

$$H(j\omega) \triangleq \frac{y(t)}{x(t)} \qquad \text{when } x(t) = e^{j\omega t} \qquad (3)$$

a definition† we will generalize subsequently. Combining Eq. (3) with the superposition principle, it follows that if $x(t)$ is a linear combination of exponentials, say

$$x(t) = \alpha_1 e^{j\omega_1 t} + \alpha_2 e^{j\omega_2 t} + \cdots \qquad (4a)$$

then

$$y(t) = H(j\omega_1)\alpha_1 e^{j\omega_1 t} + H(j\omega_2)\alpha_2 e^{j\omega_2 t} + \cdots \qquad (4b)$$

where α_1 and α_2 are constants, $H(j\omega_1)$ represents $H(j\omega)$ evaluated at $\omega = \omega_1$, etc.

However, we have not yet solved the AC problem stated at the outset, which now entails converting sinusoids to exponentials. At this point most circuit theory students would probably write $x(t) = \text{Re}\,[A_x e^{j\theta_x} e^{j\omega_0 t}]$ but, preparing the way for future developments, we want an expression more like Eq. (4a). For that purpose we invoke a corollary of Euler's theorem,‡ to wit:

$$\cos \phi = \tfrac{1}{2}(e^{j\phi} + e^{-j\phi}) \qquad (5)$$

† The symbol $\triangleq$ stands for "equals by definition."
‡ Euler's theorem is the most versatile of the trigonometric identities. A short table of these useful relations is given in Table B at the end of the book.

Thus, the sinusoidal input $x(t)$ in Eq. (1) can be rewritten as

$$x(t) = A_x \tfrac{1}{2}[e^{j(\omega_0 t + \theta_x)} + e^{-j(\omega_0 t + \theta_x)}]$$

$$= \frac{A_x}{2} e^{j\theta_x} e^{j\omega_0 t} + \frac{A_x}{2} e^{-j\theta_x} e^{-j\omega_0 t} \tag{6a}$$

and since this has the same form as Eq. (4a), appropriate substitution in Eq. (4b) gives

$$y(t) = H(j\omega_0) \frac{A_x}{2} e^{j\theta_x} e^{j\omega_0 t} + H(-j\omega_0) \frac{A_x}{2} e^{-j\theta_x} e^{-j\omega_0 t} \tag{6b}$$

While this is a correct result, it can be tidied up and made more understandable via the following two steps.

First, since the transfer function is in general a complex quantity, we will express it in the polar form

$$H(j\omega) = |H(j\omega)| e^{j \arg [H(j\omega)]} \tag{7}$$

where $|H(j\omega)|$ is the *magnitude* and $\arg [H(j\omega)]$ is the *angle*.† Second, despite the fact that $H(j\omega)$ is complex, $y(t)$ ought to be a real function of time since $x(t)$ is real; and this will be true if and only if

$$H(-j\omega) = H^*(j\omega)$$

$$= |H(j\omega)| e^{-j \arg [H(j\omega)]} \tag{8}$$

where $H^*(j\omega)$ is the complex conjugate of $H(j\omega)$. The complex-conjugate relationship does, in fact, hold for any real network.

Applying Eqs. (7) and (8) to Eq. (6b) and simplifying yields

$$y(t) = |H(j\omega_0)| \frac{A_x}{2} [e^{j(\omega_0 t + \theta_x + \arg [H(j\omega_0)])} + e^{-j(\omega_0 t + \theta_x + \arg [H(j\omega_0)])}]$$

$$= \underbrace{|H(j\omega_0)| A_x}_{A_y} \cos (\omega_0 t + \underbrace{\theta_x + \arg [H(j\omega_0)]}_{\theta_y}) \tag{9}$$

in which we have identified

$$A_y = |H(j\omega_0)| A_x \qquad \theta_y = \theta_x + \arg [H(j\omega_0)] \tag{10}$$

† That is, if H_r and H_i are the real and imaginary parts of $H(j\omega)$, respectively, then

$$|H(j\omega)| = \sqrt{H_r^2 + H_i^2} \qquad \arg [H(j\omega)] = \arctan \frac{H_i}{H_r}$$

The reader who has difficulties with such manipulations is advised to brush up on the subject of complex numbers.

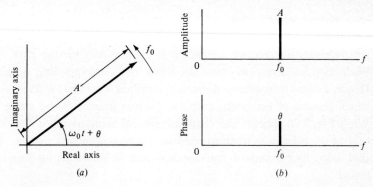

FIGURE 2.2
Representations of $A \cos(\omega_0 t + \theta)$. (a) Phasor diagram; (b) line spectrum.

Thus, we have these very simple equations for the output amplitude and phase of the AC steady-state response, providing we know the network's transfer function. More will be said about the latter after we have looked at the frequency-domain interpretation.

EXERCISE 2.1 Write $H(j\omega_0)$ and $H(-j\omega_0)$ in polar form and show that the imaginary part of Eq. (6b) is not zero when $H(-j\omega_0) \neq H^*(j\omega_0)$.

Phasors and Line Spectra

Besides facilitating network analysis, converting sinusoids to exponentials also underlies the notion of the frequency domain by way of phasor diagrams. To introduce this idea, consider the arbitrary sinusoid

$$v(t) = A \cos(\omega_0 t + \theta) \qquad \omega_0 = 2\pi f_0$$

which can be written as

$$A \cos(\omega_0 t + \theta) = \text{Re}\,[Ae^{j(\omega_0 t + \theta)}]$$
$$= \text{Re}\,[Ae^{j\theta} e^{j\omega_0 t}] \qquad (11)$$

This is called a *phasor representation* because the term inside the brackets may be viewed as a rotating vector in a complex plane whose axes are the real and imaginary parts, as Fig. 2.2a illustrates. The phasor has length A, rotates counterclockwise at a rate f_0 revolutions per second, and at time $t = 0$ makes an angle θ with respect to the positive real axis. At any time t the projection of the phasor on the real axis—i.e., its real part—equals the sinusoid $v(t)$.

Note carefully that only three parameters are needed to specify a phasor: amplitude, relative phase, and rotational frequency. To describe the same phasor in the *frequency domain*, we see that it is defined only for the particular frequency f_0. With this frequency we must associate the corresponding amplitude and phase. Hence, a suitable frequency-domain description would be the *line spectrum* of Fig. 2.2*b*, which consists of two plots, amplitude versus frequency and phase versus frequency. While Fig. 2.2*b* appears simple to the point of being trivial, it does have great conceptual value, especially when applied to more complicated signals. But before taking that step, four standard conventions used in constructing line spectra should be stated.

1 In all our spectral drawings the independent variable will be *cyclical frequency* f in hertz, rather than radian frequency ω, and any specific frequency such as f_0, being a constant, will be identified by a subscript. We will, however, use ω with or without subscripts as a shorthand notation for $2\pi f$ in various equations since that combination occurs so often.

2 Phase angles will be measured with respect to *cosine* waves or, equivalently, with respect to the positive real axis of the phasor diagram. Hence, sine waves need to be converted to cosines via the identity

$$\sin \omega t = \cos (\omega t - 90°) \qquad (12)$$

3 We regard amplitude as always being a *positive* quantity; when negative signs appear, they must be absorbed in the phase, e.g.,

$$-A \cos \omega t = A \cos (\omega t \pm 180°) \qquad (13)$$

and it does not matter whether one takes $+180°$ or $-180°$ since the phasor ends up in the same place either way.

4 Phase angles usually are expressed in degrees even though other angles are inherently in radians—for instance, ωt in Eqs. (12) and (13) is a radian measure while $-90°$ and $\pm 180°$ clearly are in degrees. No confusion should result from this mixed notation since angles expressed in degrees will always carry the appropriate symbol.

Illustrating these conventions and carrying the idea of line spectrum further, suppose a signal consists of a sum of sinusoids, such as

$$w(t) = 2 + 6 \cos (2\pi 10t + 30°) + 3 \sin 2\pi 30t - 4 \cos 2\pi 35t$$

Converting the constant (DC) term to a zero-frequency sinusoid and applying Eqs. (12) and (13) gives

$$w(t) = 2 \cos 2\pi 0t + 6 \cos (2\pi 10t + 30°) + 3 \cos (2\pi 30t - 90°) + 4 \cos (2\pi 35t - 180°)$$

so the spectrum, Fig. 2.3, has amplitude and phase lines at 0, 10, 30, and 35 Hz.

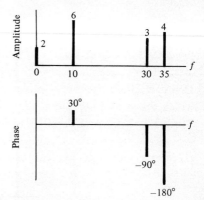

FIGURE 2.3
The line spectrum of
$2 + 6 \cos (2\pi 10t + 30°)$
$+ 3 \sin 2\pi 30t - 4 \cos 2\pi 35t$.

Figures 2.2*b* and 2.3, called *one-sided* or *positive-frequency line spectra*, can be generated for any linear combination of sinusoids. But there is another spectral representation which is only slightly more complicated and turns out to be much more useful. It is based on writing a sinusoid as a sum of two exponentials, similar to Eq. (6*a*), i.e.,

$$A \cos (\omega_0 t + \theta) = \frac{A}{2} e^{j\theta} e^{j\omega_0 t} + \frac{A}{2} e^{-j\theta} e^{-j\omega_0 t} \qquad (14)$$

which we will call the *conjugate-phasor* representation since the two terms are complex conjugates of each other. The corresponding diagram is shown in Fig. 2.4*a*, where there are now two phasors having equal lengths but opposite angles and directions of rotation. Hence, it is the vector sum at any time that equals $v(t)$. Note that the sum always falls on the real axis — as it should since $v(t)$ is real.

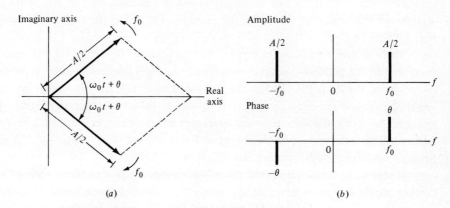

(a)   (b)

FIGURE 2.4
(a) Conjugate-phasor representation of $A \cos (\omega_0 t + \theta)$; (b) two-sided line spectrum.

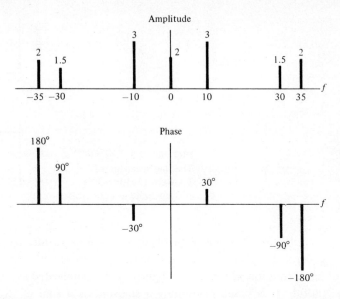

FIGURE 2.5
The two-sided version of Fig. 2.3.

A line spectrum taken from the conjugate-phasor expression must include negative frequencies to allow for the two rotational directions. Thus in the *two-sided line spectrum* of Fig. 2.4*b*, half of the original amplitude is associated with each of the two frequencies $\pm f_0$. The rules for constructing such spectra are quite simple; a little thought will show that the amplitude lines have even symmetry in f, while the phase lines have odd symmetry. The symmetry is a direct consequence of $v(t)$ being a real (noncomplex) function of time. So, for example, Fig. 2.5 is the two-sided version of Fig. 2.3.

There is one significant difference in interpreting the two-sided line spectrum compared to the positive-frequency spectrum. A single line in the latter represents a cosine wave, via Re $[e^{j\omega t}]$. But in the two-sided case, one line by itself represents a single phasor, and the conjugate term is required to get a real function of time. Thus, whenever we speak of some frequency interval in a two-sided spectrum, such as f_1 to f_2, we must include the corresponding negative-frequency interval, $-f_1$ to $-f_2$. A simple notation specifying both intervals is $f_1 \leq |f| \leq f_2$.

It should be emphasized that these line spectra are just pictorial ways of representing certain signals in terms of the form $e^{j\omega t}$. The effect on a signal by a network then reduces to a steady-state AC problem. We also point out that, in some ways, the amplitude spectrum is more important than the phase spectrum. Both parts are required, of course, to unambiguously define a signal in the time domain, but the

amplitude spectrum by itself shows what frequencies are present and in what proportions — that is, it tells us the signal's *frequency content*. The specific advantage of
the two-sided version will become apparent as we go along.

EXERCISE 2.2   Explain why the zero-frequency term results in just one amplitude
line in Fig. 2.5, and state how the figure would be changed if that term were negative.

Transfer Functions and Frequency Response

Just as a signal can be described in the frequency domain by way of its spectrum, a
network or system can be described in terms of its frequency-response characteristics
as determined from the transfer function $H(j\omega)$. Emphasizing the frequency-domain
viewpoint, it is now convenient to introduce a new notation $H(f)$, defined by

$$H(f) \triangleq H(j\omega) \quad \text{with } \omega = 2\pi f \quad (15)$$

which, henceforth, will be called either the frequency-response function or the
transfer function. Although Eq. (15) modestly violates formal mathematical notation,
it simply means that $H(f)$ is identical to $H(j\omega)$ with ω replaced by $2\pi f$. It then follows
from Eq. (8) that, for a real network,

$$H(-f) = H^*(f) \quad (16a)$$

or in polar form,

$$|H(-f)| = |H(f)| \qquad \arg[H(-f)] = -\arg[H(f)] \quad (16b)$$

a property known as *hermitian symmetry*.

For the interpretation of $H(f)$, suppose the input signal is a single phasor

$$x(t) = A_x e^{j\theta_x} e^{j\omega_0 t} \qquad \omega_0 = 2\pi f_0$$

so, from Eq. (4b), the output is

$$y(t) = H(f_0) A_x e^{j\theta_x} e^{j\omega_0 t}$$

$$= \underbrace{|H(f_0)| A_x}_{A_y} \exp j(\underbrace{\theta_x + \arg[H(f_0)]}_{\theta_y}) e^{j\omega_0 t}$$

Hence, just as in the AC case, the input and output signal parameters are related by

$$\frac{A_y}{A_x} = |H(f_0)| \qquad \theta_y - \theta_x = \arg[H(f_0)] \quad (17)$$

so $|H(f_0)|$ is the ratio of amplitudes and $\arg[H(f_0)]$ is the phase difference, both at
the specific frequency f_0. Generalizing, we conclude that $|H(f)|$ gives the system's

amplitude ratio (sometimes called *amplitude response* or *gain*) and arg $[H(f)]$ gives the *phase shift*, both as continuous functions of frequency. Plots of these two versus f give a frequency-domain representation of the system, analogous to the amplitude and phase spectrum of a signal. Moreover, the hermitian symmetry of Eq. (16) means that the amplitude ratio will be an even function of frequency while the phase shift will be an odd function. An illustrative example is presented below after brief consideration of the question of determining $H(f)$ for a particular system.

Given the circuit diagram of a network, finding $H(f)$ is nothing more than a phasor analysis problem, i.e., we assume the input is $e^{j2\pi ft}$ and calculate the output, which will be $H(f)e^{j2\pi ft}$. All the standard electrical engineering tools — Ohm's law for complex impedance, Kirchhoff's laws, etc. — can be brought to bear. Alternatively, if a system is described by a linear differential equation with constant coefficients, of the general form

$$a_n \frac{d^n y}{dt^n} + \cdots + a_1 \frac{dy}{dt} + a_0\, y(t) = b_m \frac{d^m x}{dt^m} + \cdots + b_1 \frac{dx}{dt} + b_0\, x(t) \qquad (18a)$$

then

$$H(f) = \frac{b_m(j2\pi f)^m + \cdots + b_1(j2\pi f) + b_0}{a_n(j2\pi f)^n + \cdots + a_1(j2\pi f) + a_0} \qquad (18b)$$

whose derivation is left as an exercise. A third method, involving the system's impulse response, is presented in Sect. 2.5.

EXERCISE 2.3   Derive Eq. (18b) by substituting $x(t) = e^{j2\pi ft}$ and $y(t) = H(f)e^{j2\pi ft}$ in Eq. (18a) and solving for $H(f)$.

Example 2.1   RC Lowpass Filter

The network of Fig. 2.6a, virtually a classic in communications, is called an RC lowpass filter; $x(t)$ is the input voltage and $y(t)$ is the output voltage under open-circuit (unloaded) conditions. Finding the transfer function is a simple matter since, with $x(t) = e^{j2\pi ft}$, application of the voltage-divider relation yields

$$y(t) = \frac{Z_C}{R + Z_C} e^{j2\pi ft}$$

where the capacitor's impedance is $Z_C = 1/j2\pi fC$. Thus,

$$H(f) = \frac{(1/j2\pi fC)}{R + (1/j2\pi fC)} = \frac{1}{1 + j2\pi RCf}$$

$$= \frac{1}{1 + j(f/B)} \qquad (19)$$

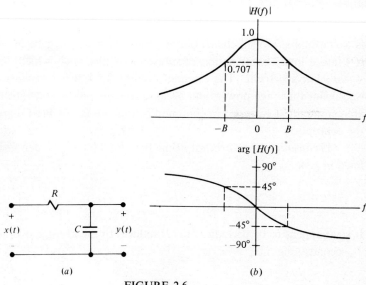

FIGURE 2.6
RC lowpass filter. (a) Circuit; (b) transfer function.

in which we have defined the system parameter

$$B \triangleq \frac{1}{2\pi RC}$$

Conversion to polar form gives the amplitude ratio and phase shift as

$$|H(f)| = \frac{1}{\sqrt{1 + (f/B)^2}} \qquad (20a)$$

$$\arg [H(f)] = -\arctan \frac{f}{B} \qquad (20b)$$

which are plotted in Fig. 2.6b.   ////

EXERCISE 2.4   Suppose the resistor and capacitor are interchanged in Fig. 2.6a. Find the new $H(f)$ and, by sketching $|H(f)|$, justify calling this circuit an RC *highpass* filter.

2.2 PERIODIC SIGNALS AND FOURIER SERIES

A signal $v(t)$ is said to be periodic with repetition period T_0 if, for any integer m,

$$v(t \pm mT_0) = v(t) \qquad -\infty < t < \infty \qquad (1)$$

Since this implies a signal that lasts forever, our earlier remarks about the difference between a signal and its mathematical model are pertinent here. Assuming that Eq. (1) is a reasonable model, then Fourier series expansion can be invoked to decompose $v(t)$ into a linear combination of sinusoids or phasors — which, in turn, leads to the signal's line spectrum. The essential proviso for Fourier expansion is that $v(t)$ have well-defined average power, and because average power and time averages in general are commonly used terms in communications, we take a brief digression to formalize the concepts.

The *average* of an arbitrary time function $v(t)$ will be denoted by $\langle v(t) \rangle$ and defined in general as

$$\langle v(t) \rangle \triangleq \lim_{T \to \infty} \frac{1}{T} \int_{-T/2}^{T/2} v(t)\, dt \qquad (2)$$

If $v(t)$ happens to be periodic, Eq. (2) reduces to the average over any interval exactly T_0 seconds long, i.e.,

$$\langle v(t) \rangle = \frac{1}{T_0} \int_{T_0} v(t)\, dt \qquad (3)$$

where $\int_{T_0}$ stands for integration from t_1 to $t_1 + T_0$ with t_1 an arbitrary constant. Average power is, of course, the time average of instantaneous power; e.g., if $v(t)$ is the voltage across a 1-ohm (Ω) resistance, the instantaneous power is $v^2(t)$ and the average power is $\langle v^2(t) \rangle$. For our purposes it is convenient to assume all resistances are normalized to unity so that, whether $v(t)$ is a periodic voltage or current, its *average power P* will be defined as

$$P \triangleq \langle |v(t)|^2 \rangle = \frac{1}{T_0} \int_{T_0} |v(t)|^2\, dt \qquad (4)$$

The signal $v(t)$ is then said to have well-defined average power if the integral (4) exists and yields a finite quantity. Note also that we have allowed for the possibility of complex signals by writing $|v(t)|^2 = v(t)v^*(t)$ instead of $v^2(t)$.

EXERCISE 2.5 Use Eqs. (3) and (4) to show that if

$$v(t) = A \cos(\omega_0 t + \theta) \qquad \omega_0 = \frac{2\pi}{T_0} \qquad (5a)$$

then

$$\langle v(t) \rangle = 0 \qquad \langle |v(t)|^2 \rangle = \frac{A^2}{2} \qquad (5b)$$

Thus the average power of a sinusoid depends only on its amplitude.

Fourier Series and Line Spectra

The *exponential Fourier series* expansion of a periodic signal $v(t)$ is

$$v(t) = \sum_{n=-\infty}^{\infty} c(nf_0)e^{j2\pi nf_0 t} \qquad f_0 = \frac{1}{T_0} \qquad (6)$$

where $c(nf_0)$ is the nth Fourier coefficient

$$c(nf_0) \triangleq \frac{1}{T_0} \int_{T_0} v(t)e^{-j2\pi nf_0 t} \, dt \qquad (7)$$

Equation (6) states that $v(t)$ can be expressed as a linear combination or weighted sum of phasors at the frequencies $f = nf_0 = 0, \pm f_0, \pm 2f_0, \ldots$, the weighting factors being given by Eq. (7). If $v(t)$ has well-defined average power, then the summation on the right of Eq. (6) converges to $v(t)$ everywhere it is finite and continuous, which would be true of any physical signal. Insofar as engineering purposes are concerned, we may view the series as being identical to $v(t)$.

Actually, one seldom carries out the summation of Eq. (6) to find $v(t)$; instead, given a periodic signal, we use Eq. (7) to find its Fourier coefficients and, from that, the line spectrum. Before addressing that aspect, a few points regarding $c(nf_0)$ are in order. In general, the coefficients are complex quantities, even when the signal is real; therefore, we can write

$$c(nf_0) = |c(nf_0)| e^{j \, \text{arg} \, [c(nf_0)]}$$

If $v(t)$ is a *real* function, then replacing n by $-n$ in Eq. (7) shows that

$$c(-nf_0) = c^*(nf_0) \qquad (8)$$

so again we have conjugate phasors and hermitian symmetry. Finally, note that $c(nf_0)$ does not depend on time since Eq. (7) is a definite integral with t being the variable of integration. It is helpful, however, to regard $c(nf_0)$ as a function of frequency f defined only for the discrete frequencies $f = nf_0$.

Turning to the spectral interpretation, we see from Eq. (6) that a periodic signal contains only those frequency components that are *integer multiples of the fundamental frequency* $f_0 = 1/T_0$ or, in other words, all the frequencies are *harmonics* of the fundamental. Since the coefficient of the nth harmonic is $c(nf_0)$, its amplitude and phase are $|c(nf_0)|$ and arg $[c(nf_0)]$, respectively. Therefore, we have a two-sided line spectrum with $|c(nf_0)|$ giving the amplitude and arg $[c(nf_0)]$ the phase. Some of the important properties of such spectra are listed below.

1 All spectral lines are equally spaced by f_0 since all the frequencies are harmonically related to the fundamental.

2 The DC component equals the *average value* of the signal since setting $n = 0$ in Eq. (7) yields

$$c(0) = \frac{1}{T_0} \int_{T_0} v(t) \, dt = \langle v(t) \rangle \qquad (9)$$

Therefore, calculated values of $c(0)$ may be checked by inspection of $v(t)$ — which is a wise practice since the integration frequently yields an indeterminate form for $c(0)$.

3 If $v(t)$ is *real*, the amplitude spectrum has even symmetry while the phase spectrum has odd symmetry, i.e.,

$$|c(-nf_0)| = |c(nf_0)| \qquad \arg [c(-nf_0)] = -\arg [c(nf_0)] \qquad (10)$$

which follows from Eq. (8).

4 If a real signal has *even symmetry* in time, such that

$$v(-t) = v(t) \qquad (11a)$$

then $c(nf_0)$ is entirely *real* and

$$\arg [c(nf_0)] = 0 \quad \text{or} \quad \pm 180° \qquad (11b)$$

where $\pm 180°$ corresponds to $c(nf_0)$ being negative. Conversely, if a real signal has *odd time symmetry*, i.e.,

$$v(-t) = -v(t) \qquad (12a)$$

then $c(nf_0)$ is entirely *imaginary* and

$$\arg [c(nf_0)] = \pm 90° \qquad (12b)$$

which stems from the fact that $\pm j = e^{\pm j\pi/2} = e^{\pm j90°}$. Proving these symmetry relations is left for the reader.

One final point before taking up an example: When $v(t)$ is real, we can draw upon Eq. (10) and regroup the exponential series in conjugate-phasor pairs of the form

$$c(nf_0)e^{j2\pi nf_0 t} + c^*(nf_0)e^{-j2\pi nf_0 t} = 2|c(nf_0)| \cos (2\pi nf_0 t + \arg [c(nf_0)])$$

so that Eq. (6) becomes

$$v(t) = c(0) + \sum_{n=1}^{\infty} |2c(nf_0)| \cos (2\pi nf_0 t + \arg [c(nf_0)]) \qquad (13)$$

By this process we have arrived at a *trigonometric* Fourier series, and in a sense have come full circle, for $v(t)$ is now described as a sum of sinusoids rather than conjugate phasors. Indeed, Eq. (13) is less versatile than Eq. (6) and certainly lacks the attractive symmetry of the exponential series. We shall, however, have some occasions for its use and for the corresponding positive-frequency line spectrum.

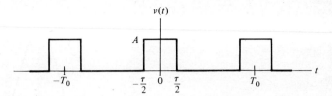

FIGURE 2.7
Rectangular pulse train.

Example 2.2 Rectangular Pulse Train

As an important example of the ideas we have discussed, let us find the line spectrum of the periodic waveform in Fig. 2.7, called a rectangular pulse train. To calculate $c(nf_0)$, we take the range of integration in Eq. (7) as† $[-T_0/2, T_0/2]$ and observe that in this interval

$$v(t) = \begin{cases} A & |t| < \dfrac{\tau}{2} \\[2mm] 0 & |t| > \dfrac{\tau}{2} \end{cases}$$

where τ is the pulse duration and A is the amplitude. Note, incidentally, that this signal model has stepwise *discontinuities* at $t = \pm\tau/2$, etc., and values of $v(t)$ are *undefined* wherever it is discontinuous. This illustrates one of the possible differences between a physical signal and its mathematical model, since a physical signal never has an abrupt stepwise transition. However, this model is useful if the actual transition time is very small compared to the pulse duration, and the undefined values at the discontinuity points have no effect on the calculation of $c(nf_0)$.

Proceeding with that calculation, we have

$$c(nf_0) = \frac{1}{T_0} \int_{-T_0/2}^{T_0/2} v(t) e^{-j2\pi n f_0 t} \, dt$$

$$= \frac{1}{T_0} \int_{-\tau/2}^{\tau/2} A e^{-j2\pi n f_0 t} \, dt$$

$$= \frac{A}{-j2\pi n f_0 T_0} (e^{-j\pi n f_0 \tau} - e^{+j\pi n f_0 \tau})$$

$$= \frac{A}{\pi n} \sin \pi n f_0 \tau$$

where we used the fact that $f_0 T_0 = 1$ and $e^{j\phi} - e^{-j\phi} = 2j \sin \phi$.

† The notation $[-T_0/2, T_0/2]$ stands for $-T_0/2 \le t \le T_0/2$.

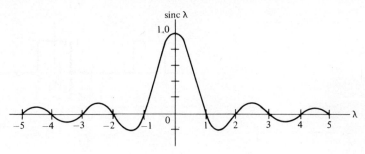

FIGURE 2.8
The function sinc $\lambda = (\sin \pi\lambda)/\pi\lambda$.

To somewhat simplify notation in the above result, we introduce a new function called the *sinc* function† and defined by

$$\text{sinc } \lambda \triangleq \frac{\sin \pi\lambda}{\pi\lambda} \qquad (14)$$

where λ is the independent variable. This function will be quite important owing to its relation to averages of exponentials and sinusoids; in particular, as is easily proved,

$$\frac{1}{T} \int_{-T/2}^{T/2} e^{\pm j2\pi ft}\, dt = \frac{1}{T} \int_{-T/2}^{T/2} \cos 2\pi ft\, dt = \text{sinc } fT \qquad (15)$$

in which T is an arbitrary constant not necessarily related to f. Figure 2.8 shows that sinc λ is an even function having its peak at $\lambda = 0$ and zero crossings at all other integer values of λ, i.e.,

$$\text{sinc } \lambda = \begin{cases} 1 & \lambda = 0 \\ 0 & \lambda = \pm 1,\ \pm 2,\ \ldots \end{cases}$$

Numerical values of sinc λ and sinc$^2 \lambda$ are given in Table C.

Using the sinc function, the series coefficients for the rectangular pulse train become

$$c(nf_0) = Af_0\tau\, \frac{\sin \pi nf_0\tau}{\pi nf_0\tau} = Af_0\tau\, \text{sinc } nf_0\tau \qquad (16)$$

which is independent of time and strictly real — the latter because $v(t)$ happens to be real and even. Therefore, the amplitude spectrum is $|c(nf_0)| = Af_0\tau|\text{sinc } nf_0\tau|$, as shown in Fig. 2.9*a* for the case where $f_0\tau = \frac{1}{4}$. Such plots are facilitated by regarding the continuous function $Af_0\tau|\text{sinc } f\tau|$ as the *envelope* of the lines, indicated by the

† Some authors use the so-called *sampling function*, Sa $(\lambda) \triangleq (\sin \lambda)/\lambda$; note that sinc $\lambda = $ Sa $(\pi\lambda)$.

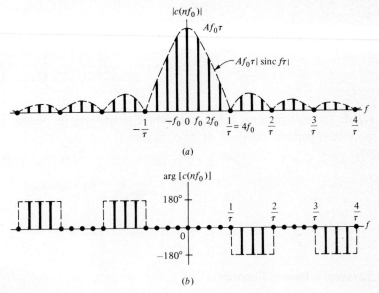

FIGURE 2.9
Spectrum of rectangular pulse train with $f_0 \tau = \frac{1}{4}$. (a) Amplitude; (b) phase.

dashed curve. The spectral lines at $\pm 4f_0$, $\pm 8f_0$, etc., are "missing" since they fall precisely at multiples of $1/\tau$ where the envelope equals zero. The DC component has amplitude $c(0) = Af_0 \tau = A\tau/T_0$ which should be recognized as the average value of $v(t)$ by inspection of Fig. 2.7. Note, incidentally, that τ/T_0 is the ratio of "on" time to period, frequently designated as the *duty cycle* in pulse electronics work.

Figure 2.9b, the phase spectrum, is constructed by observing that $c(nf_0)$ is always real but sometimes negative. Hence, arg $[c(nf_0)]$ takes on the values $0°$ and $\pm 180°$, according to the polarity of sinc $nf_0 \tau$. Both $+180°$ and $-180°$ have been used to preserve the odd symmetry, although this is more or less arbitrary in such cases.

////

EXERCISE 2.6 Sketch the amplitude spectrum of a rectangular pulse train for each of the following cases: $\tau = T_0/5$, $\tau = T_0/2$, $\tau = T_0$. In the last case the pulse train degenerates into a constant for all time; how does this show up in the spectrum?

EXERCISE 2.7 Show that the *square wave* in Fig. 2.10 has

$$c(nf_0) = \begin{cases} A \text{ sinc}\dfrac{n}{2} & n = \pm 1, \pm 3, \ldots \\ 0 & n = 0, \pm 2, \pm 4, \ldots \end{cases} \tag{17}$$

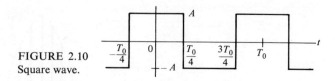

FIGURE 2.10
Square wave.

(*Hint:* The manipulation below is useful for simplifying the answer in this and similar problems, particularly when ϕ_1 or ϕ_2 is zero.)

$$e^{j\phi_1} \pm e^{j\phi_2} = [e^{j(\phi_1-\phi_2)/2} \pm e^{-j(\phi_1-\phi_2)/2}]e^{j(\phi_1+\phi_2)/2}$$

$$= \begin{cases} 2\cos\dfrac{\phi_1-\phi_2}{2}\, e^{j(\phi_1+\phi_2)/2} \\[2ex] 2j\sin\dfrac{\phi_1-\phi_2}{2}\, e^{j(\phi_1+\phi_2)/2} \end{cases} \qquad (18)$$

Parseval's Power Theorem

This famous theorem relates the average power P of a periodic signal to its Fourier series coefficients. To derive the relationship, we start with the definition of P, Eq. (4), write $|v(t)|^2 = v(t)v^*(t)$, replace $v^*(t)$ by its Fourier series, and interchange the order of summation and integration, as follows:

$$P = \frac{1}{T_0}\int_{T_0} v(t) \overbrace{\left[\sum_{n=-\infty}^{\infty} c^*(nf_0)e^{-j2\pi nf_0 t}\right]}^{v^*(t)} dt$$

$$= \sum_{n=-\infty}^{\infty} \underbrace{\left[\frac{1}{T_0}\int_{T_0} v(t)e^{-j2\pi nf_0 t}\, dt\right]}_{c(nf_0)} c_v^*(nf_0)$$

Thus

$$P = \sum_{n=-\infty}^{\infty} c(nf_0)c^*(nf_0) = \sum_{n=-\infty}^{\infty} |c(nf_0)|^2 \qquad (19)$$

The spectral interpretation of this result is extraordinarily simple; i.e., average power can be found by squaring and adding the heights of the amplitude lines. Observe that Eq. (19) does not involve the phase spectrum $\arg[c(nf_0)]$, underscoring our prior comment about the dominant role of the amplitude spectrum relative to a signal's frequency content.

For further interpretation of Eq. (19), recall that the exponential Fourier series expands $v(t)$ as a sum of phasors each of the form $c(nf_0)e^{j2\pi nf_0 t}$. Now it is easily shown that the average power of each of these is

$$\langle |c(nf_0)e^{j2\pi nf_0 t}|^2\rangle = |c(nf_0)|^2$$

Therefore, Parseval's theorem implies *superposition of average power* in that the total average power of $v(t)$ is the sum of the average powers of its phasor components.

Periodic Steady-State Response

In Sect. 2.1 we found the AC steady-state response of a network by expressing the sinusoidal input as a sum of phasors. Those results are readily extended to the case of an arbitrary periodic input signal by the method presented here.

First, expand the input $x(t)$ as

$$x(t) = \sum_{n=-\infty}^{\infty} c_x(nf_0)e^{j2\pi nf_0 t} \qquad (20a)$$

where $c_x(nf_0)$ is found from Eq. (7). Then, since each of the above phasors produces an output of the form $H(nf_0)c_x(nf_0)$ exp $(j2\pi nf_0 t)$, and since superposition is assumed, the total output is

$$y(t) = \sum_{n=-\infty}^{\infty} c_y(nf_0)e^{j2\pi nf_0 t} \qquad (20b)$$

where

$$c_y(nf_0) = H(nf_0)c_x(nf_0) \qquad (21)$$

Therefore, the periodic steady-state response is a periodic signal having the same fundamental frequency as the input, whose Fourier series coefficients $c_y(nf_0)$ equal the respective coefficients of the input signal multiplied by the network's transfer function $H(f)$ evaluated at $f = nf_0$. Moreover, the average power in the output signal is

$$P_y = \sum_{n=-\infty}^{\infty} |c_y(nf_0)|^2 = \sum_{n=-\infty}^{\infty} |H(nf_0)|^2|c_x(nf_0)|^2 \qquad (22)$$

by application of Parseval's theorem.

The frequency-domain interpretation of these results is best seen by converting Eq. (21) to polar form, thus:

$$|c_y(nf_0)| = |H(nf_0)| \, |c_x(nf_0)|$$
$$\arg [c_y(nf_0)] = \arg [c_x(nf_0)] + \arg [H(nf_0)] \qquad (23)$$

Putting this into words, the output amplitude spectrum equals the input amplitude spectrum *times* the network's amplitude ratio, whereas the output phase spectrum equals the input phase spectrum *plus* the network's phase shift at the frequencies in question. The phase relationship is additive instead of multiplicative simply because arguments add when exponentials are multiplied.

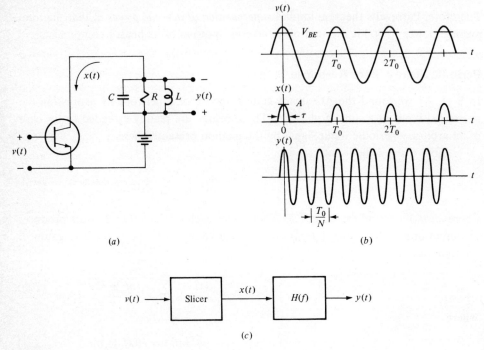

FIGURE 2.11
Frequency multiplier. (*a*) Circuit; (*b*) waveforms; (*c*) block diagram.

Equations (20) to (22) provide a theoretical solution to the periodic steady-state analysis problem. Practically speaking, however, determining the actual *shape* of the output waveform $y(t)$ from Eq. (20*b*) is a tedious process — unless there are only a few significant terms in the sum. The following example falls in this category and demonstrates how the spectral interpretation helps estimate the number of significant terms.

Example 2.3 Frequency Multiplier

Figure 2.11*a* is the circuit diagram of a frequency multiplier, a device often used in communication systems. The input voltage $v(t)$ is a sinusoid at a specified frequency f_0 and the output $y(t)$ is supposed to be a sinusoid at a multiple of the input frequency, say Nf_0. Usually, $N = 2$ or 3, i.e., a *frequency doubler* or *tripler*, and greater multiplication factors are obtained by connecting doublers and triplers in tandem.

The waveforms shown in Fig. 2.11*b* illustrate the essential operations, as follows. The transistor is a silicon *npn* type without base-emitter bias so the current $x(t)$ is negligible unless $v(t)$ exceeds the base-emitter voltage drop V_{BE}. Thus, if the amplitude of $v(t)$ is just slightly greater than V_{BE}, as indicated, $x(t)$ consists of short pulses having period $T_0 = 1/f_0$. From our previous work we know that such a waveform in general will contain *all harmonics* of f_0, and the role of the parallel RLC circuit† is to pick out the Nth harmonic and reject the rest. This implies that the circuit is *tuned* or *resonant* at Nf_0. For analysis purposes these functions can be represented in block-diagram form, per Fig. 2.11c, which we will take as our model of the device.

While conceivably one could exactly calculate the Fourier series coefficients of $x(t)$, there is really no need for such precision. Rather, we will approximate $x(t)$ as a *rectangular* pulse train of amplitude A and duration $\tau \ll T_0$; hence, for small values of n,

$$c_x(nf_0) \approx Af_0\tau \qquad |n| \ll \frac{T_0}{\tau} \qquad (24)$$

where we have used the results of Example 2.2 together with sinc $\lambda \approx 1$ for $|\lambda| \ll 1$. It is likewise assumed that $N \ll T_0/\tau$.

Next we need the transfer function $H(f)$ of the tuned circuit. Noting that its input $x(t)$ is a current and the output $y(t)$ is a voltage, $H(f)$ is identical to the circuit's impedance $Z(j\omega)$ with $\omega = j2\pi f$. Routine analysis gives‡

$$H(f) = \frac{R}{1 + jQ\left(\dfrac{f^2 - f_r^2}{ff_r}\right)} \qquad (25)$$

where

$$f_r \triangleq \frac{1}{2\pi\sqrt{LC}} \qquad Q \triangleq \frac{R}{2\pi f_r L} = R\sqrt{\frac{C}{L}}$$

which are the resonant frequency and quality factor, respectively. It has been assumed in Eq. (25) that $Q > \frac{1}{2}$ so the circuit actually is resonant; as a matter of fact, the present application requires $Q \gg 1$. The corresponding amplitude ratio $|H(f)|$ is plotted in Fig. 2.12a directly above the input amplitude spectrum $|c_x(nf_0)|$, Fig. 2.12b. Negative frequencies have been omitted for convenience, since we know that both functions have even symmetry.

If we recall that $|c_y(nf_0)| = |H(nf_0)|\,|c_x(nf_0)|$, Fig. 2.12 suggests that all the harmonics in $y(t)$ except Nf_0 can be made to have negligible amplitude if

$$f_r = Nf_0 \qquad \text{and} \qquad Q \gg N/2$$

---

† As a rule the resistance R represents losses in L and any coupled load rather than being a distinct circuit element.

‡ See, for instance, Close (1966, chap. 6).

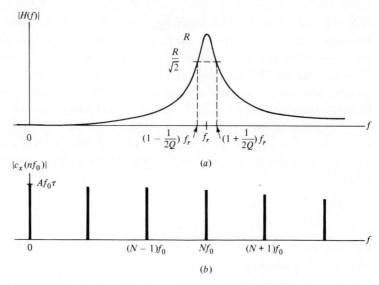

FIGURE 2.12
(*a*) Amplitude ratio of tuned circuit, $Q = 10$; (*b*) amplitude spectrum of input signal.

the condition on Q ensuring that $[1 + (1/2Q)]f_r < (N + 1)f_0$ and $[1 - (1/2Q)f_r] > (N - 1)f_0$ so the tuned circuit "passes" only Nf_0. Therefore, the output amplitude spectrum consists essentially of two terms, $c_y(\pm Nf_0)$, and

$$y(t) \approx H(Nf_0)c_x(Nf_0)e^{j2\pi Nf_0 t} + H(-Nf_0)c_x(-Nf_0)e^{-j2\pi Nf_0 t}$$
$$= 2RAf_0 \tau \cos 2\pi Nf_0 t$$

where we have used Eqs. (24) and (25) and converted the result to sinusoidal form.

////

2.3 NONPERIODIC SIGNALS AND FOURIER TRANSFORMS

We have described a periodic signal as one with a repeating characteristic applied for a long time interval, theoretically infinite. Now we consider nonperiodic signals whose effects are concentrated over a brief period of time. Such signals may be *strictly timelimited*, so $v(t)$ is identically zero outside of a specified interval, or *asymptotically timelimited*, so $v(t) \to 0$ as $t \to \pm\infty$. In either case it is assumed that the signal's total *energy* is well-defined, energy being measured in the same normalized sense as was power in the previous section, namely,

$$E \triangleq \int_{-\infty}^{\infty} |v(t)|^2 \, dt \qquad (1)$$

Implied by this definition is the fact that if E is finite, then both the average value and average power equal zero, an observation pursued more fully in Sect. 2.6. Here we are concerned with the frequency-domain description of nonperiodic energy signals via the Fourier transform.

Fourier Transforms and Continuous Spectra

A periodic signal can be represented by its exponential Fourier series

$$v(t) = \sum_{n=\infty}^{\infty} \overbrace{\left[\frac{1}{T_0} \int_{T_0} v(t) e^{-j2\pi n f_0 t} \, dt\right]}^{c_v(nf_0)} e^{j2\pi n f_0 t} \tag{2}$$

where the integral expression for $c_v(nf_0)$ has been written out in full. According to the *Fourier integral theorem* there is a similar representation for a *nonperiodic* signal, namely,

$$v(t) = \int_{-\infty}^{\infty} \underbrace{\left[\int_{-\infty}^{\infty} v(t) e^{-j2\pi f t} \, dt\right]}_{V(f)} e^{j2\pi f t} \, df \tag{3}$$

The bracketed term is the *Fourier transform* of $v(t)$, symbolized by $V(f)$ or $\mathscr{F}[v(t)]$ and defined as

$$V(f) = \mathscr{F}[v(t)] \triangleq \int_{-\infty}^{\infty} v(t) e^{-j2\pi f t} \, dt \tag{4}$$

which is an integration over all time. The theorem (3) states that $v(t)$ can be found by the *inverse Fourier transform* of $V(f)$,

$$v(t) = \mathscr{F}^{-1}[V(f)] \triangleq \int_{-\infty}^{\infty} V(f) e^{j2\pi f t} \, df \tag{5}$$

which is an integration over all frequency.

Equations (4) and (5) are often referred to as the Fourier integrals or the Fourier transform pair† and, at first glance, they seem to be a closed circle of operations. In a given problem, however, one usually knows either $V(f)$ or $v(t)$ but not both. If $V(f)$ is known, $v(t)$ can be found by carrying out the inverse transform (5), and vice versa when finding $V(f)$ from $v(t)$.

Turning to the frequency-domain picture, a comparison of Eqs. (2) and (3) indicates that $V(f)$ plays the same role for nonperiodic signals that $c_v(nf_0)$ plays for

---

† Somewhat different definitions apply when $\omega = 2\pi f$ is used as the independent variable of the frequency domain.

periodic signals. Thus, $V(f)$ is the *spectrum* of the nonperiodic signal $v(t)$. But $V(f)$ is a continuous function defined for all values of f whereas $c_v(nf_0)$ is defined only for discrete frequencies. Therefore, a nonperiodic signal will have a *continuous spectrum* rather than a line spectrum. Again, comparing Eqs. (2) and (3) helps explain this difference: in the periodic case we return to the time domain by *summing* discrete-frequency phasors while in the nonperiodic case we *integrate* a continuous frequency function.

Like $c_v(nf_0)$, $V(f)$ generally is a complex function so that $|V(f)|$ is the amplitude spectrum and arg $[V(f)]$ is the phase spectrum. Other important properties of $V(f)$, paralleling properties of $c_v(nf_0)$, are listed below.

1 If $v(t)$ is *real*, then $V(-f) = V^*(f)$ and

$$|V(-f)| = |V(f)| \qquad \arg[V(-f)] = -\arg[V(f)] \tag{6}$$

Hence, the spectrum has hermitian symmetry.

2 If $v(t)$ has either even or odd *time symmetry*, then Eq. (4) simplifies to

$$V(f) = \begin{cases} 2\int_0^\infty v(t)\cos \omega t\, dt & v(t)\ \text{even} \\[2mm] -j2\int_0^\infty v(t)\sin \omega t\, dt & v(t)\ \text{odd} \end{cases} \tag{7}$$

where we have written ω in place of $2\pi f$ for notational convenience, a practice frequently used hereafter. It follows from Eq. (7) that if $v(t)$ is also real, then $V(f)$ is purely real or imaginary, respectively.

3 The value of $V(f)$ at $f = 0$ equals the *net area* of $v(t)$, i.e.,

$$V(0) = \int_{-\infty}^{\infty} v(t)\, dt \tag{8}$$

which compares with the periodic case where $c_v(0)$ equals the average value of $v(t)$.

EXERCISE 2.8 Integrals of the general form $\int_{-T}^{T} w(t)\, dt$ simplify when the integrand is symmetrical; specifically, for any constant T,

$$\int_{-T}^{T} w(t)\, dt = \begin{cases} 2\int_0^T w(t)\, dt & \text{if } w(-t) = w(t) \tag{9a} \\[2mm] 0 & \text{if } w(-t) = -w(t) \tag{9b} \end{cases}$$

Use Eq. (9) to derive Eq. (7) from Eq. (4).

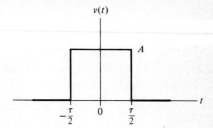

FIGURE 2.13
The rectangular pulse $v(t) = A\Pi(t/\tau)$.

Example 2.4 Rectangular Pulse

In Example 2.2, Sect. 2.2, we found the line spectrum of a rectangular pulse train. Now we will consider the continuous spectrum of the *single* rectangular pulse shown in Fig. 2.13. This is so common a signal model that it deserves a symbol of its own. Let us therefore adopt the notation

$$\Pi\left(\frac{t}{\tau}\right) \triangleq \begin{cases} 1 & |t| < \dfrac{\tau}{2} \\[2mm] 0 & |t| > \dfrac{\tau}{2} \end{cases} \tag{10}$$

which stands for a *rectangular function* with unit height or amplitude having width or duration τ centered at $t = 0$. Thus, $v(t) = A\Pi(t/\tau)$ in Fig. 2.13.

Since $v(t)$ has even symmetry, its Fourier transform is

$$V(f) = 2 \int_0^\infty v(t) \cos \omega t \, dt$$

$$= 2 \int_0^{\tau/2} A \cos \omega t \, dt = \frac{2A}{\omega} \sin \frac{\omega \tau}{2}$$

$$= A\tau \operatorname{sinc} f\tau \tag{11}$$

and $V(0) = A\tau$ which clearly equals the pulse's area. The corresponding spectrum is plotted in Fig. 2.14. This figure should be compared with Fig. 2.7 to illustrate our previous discussion of line spectra and continuous spectra.

It is apparent from $|V(f)|$ that the significant portion of the spectrum is in the range $|f| < 1/\tau$ since $|V(f)| \ll V(0)$ for $|f| > 1/\tau$. We therefore may take $1/\tau$ as a measure of the spectral "width." Now if the pulse duration is reduced (small τ), the frequency width is increased, whereas increasing the duration reduces the spectral width. Thus, short pulses have broad spectra, long pulses have narrow spectra. This phenomenon is called *reciprocal spreading* and is a general property of all signals, pulses or not, because high-frequency components are demanded by rapid time

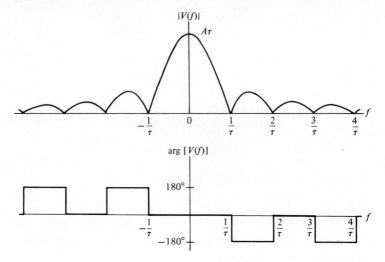

FIGURE 2.14
Spectrum of a rectangular pulse, $V(f) = A\tau \operatorname{sinc} f\tau$.

variations whereas smoother, slower time variations require relatively little high-frequency content.   ////

Example 2.5   Exponential Pulse

Consider a decaying exponential function of the form $v(t) = Ae^{-t/T}$, $t > 0$. To ensure that the energy is finite, we further specify that $v(t) = 0$ for $t < 0$. Introducing the *unit step function* notation

$$u(t) \triangleq \begin{cases} 1 & t > 0 \\ 0 & t < 0 \end{cases} \tag{12}$$

we can write

$$v(t) = Ae^{-t/T}u(t)$$

which will be called an exponential pulse.

The integration for $V(f)$ is a simple problem, resulting in

$$V(f) = \int_0^\infty Ae^{-t/T}e^{-j\omega t}\, dt = \frac{AT}{1 + j2\pi fT}$$

so the amplitude and phase spectra are

$$|V(f)| = \frac{AT}{\sqrt{1 + (2\pi fT)^2}} \qquad \arg[V(f)] = -\arctan 2\pi fT$$

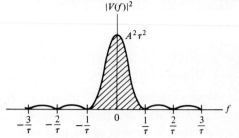

FIGURE 2.15
Energy spectral density of a rectangular
pulse, $|V(f)|^2 = A^2\tau^2 \, \text{sinc}^2 \, f\tau$.

Thus, unlike the previous example, the phase is a smooth curve between $+90°$ ($f = -\infty$) and $-90°$ ($f = +\infty$). Sharp-eyed readers will probably spot similarities between $V(f)$ and the transfer function of an RC lowpass filter, Example 2.1. The similarity is not accidental, and we will explain why in Sect. 2.5. ////

Rayleigh's Energy Theorem

Analogous to Parseval's power theorem, Rayleigh's energy theorem relates the total energy E of a signal to its amplitude spectrum. Actually, the theorem is a special case of an interesting integral relationship

$$\int_{-\infty}^{\infty} v(t)w^*(t) \, dt = \int_{-\infty}^{\infty} V(f)W^*(f) \, df, \qquad (13)$$

where $V(f) = \mathscr{F}[v(t)]$ and $W(f) = \mathscr{F}[w(t)]$. Proof of Eq. (13) follows the same method used to prove Parseval's theorem, Eq. (19), Sect. 2.2. We obtain Rayleigh's theorem by taking $w(t) = v(t)$ so the left-hand side of Eq. (13) is the energy of $v(t)$—by the definition (1)—and hence

$$E = \int_{-\infty}^{\infty} V(f)V^*(f) \, df = \int_{-\infty}^{\infty} |V(f)|^2 \, df \qquad (14)$$

Therefore, integrating the square of the amplitude spectrum $|V(f)|^2$ over all frequency yields the total energy.

The value of Eq. (14) lies not so much in computing E, since the time-domain integration of $|v(t)|^2$ often is easier. Rather, it implies that $|V(f)|^2$ gives the distribution of energy in the frequency domain, and therefore may be termed the *energy spectral density*. By this we mean that the energy in any differential frequency band $f \pm df/2$ equals $|V(f)|^2 \, df$. That interpretation, in turn, lends quantitative support to the notion of spectral width in the sense that most of the energy of a given signal should be contained in the range of frequencies taken to be the spectral width.

By way of illustration, Fig. 2.15 is the energy spectral density of a rectangular pulse whose spectral width was previously claimed to be $|f| < 1/\tau$. The energy in that band is the shaded area in the figure, i.e.,

$$\int_{-1/\tau}^{1/\tau} |V(f)|^2 \, df = \int_{-1/\tau}^{1/\tau} (A\tau)^2 \, \text{sinc}^2 f\tau \, df = 0.92A^2\tau$$

whose evaluation entails numerical methods. But the total signal energy is $E = \int_{-\infty}^{\infty} |v(t)|^2 \, dt = A^2\tau$ (found by inspection!) so the asserted spectral width encompasses more than 90 percent of the total energy.

Transform Theorems

Given below are some of the many other theorems associated with Fourier transforms. They are included not just as manipulation exercises but for two very practical reasons. First, the theorems are invaluable when interpreting spectra, for they express relationships between time-domain and frequency-domain operations. Second, one can build up an extensive catalog of transform pairs by applying the theorems to known pairs — and such a catalog will be useful as we seek new signal models.

In stating the theorems, we indicate a signal and its transform (or spectrum) by lowercase and uppercase letters, e.g., $V(f) = \mathscr{F}[v(t)]$ and $v(t) = \mathscr{F}^{-1}[V(f)]$. This is also denoted more compactly by $v(t) \leftrightarrow V(f)$. Table A at the back of the book lists the theorems and transform pairs covered here, plus a few others.

Linearity (Superposition)

For the constants α and β

$$\alpha v(t) + \beta w(t) \leftrightarrow \alpha V(f) + \beta W(f) \tag{15}$$

This theorem simply states that linear combinations in the time domain become linear combinations in the frequency domain. Although proof of the theorem is trivial, its importance cannot be overemphasized. From a practical viewpoint Eq. (15) greatly facilitates spectral analysis when the signal in question is a linear combination of functions whose individual spectra are known. From a theoretical viewpoint it underscores the applicability of the Fourier transform for the study of linear systems.

Time Delay

If a signal $v(t)$ is delayed in time by t_d seconds, producing the new signal $v(t - t_d)$ the spectrum is modified by a linear phase shift of slope $-2\pi t_d$, that is,

$$v(t - t_d) \leftrightarrow V(f)e^{-j\omega t_d} \tag{16}$$

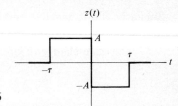

FIGURE 2.16

Translation of a signal in time thus changes the spectral phase but not the amplitude. Note that if t_d is a negative number, the signal is *advanced* in time and the phase shift has *positive* slope. Since time advancement is a physical impossibility, we conclude that in actual signal processing the spectral phase will have negative slope, though not necessarily linear.

Proof of this theorem is accomplished by change of variable $\lambda = t - t_d$ in the transform integral. (Observe that time is indeed a dummy variable in the direct transform, just as frequency is a dummy variable in the inverse transform.) The change-of-variable technique is basic to the proof of most transform theorems, and is demonstrated here:

$$\mathcal{F}[v(t - t_d)] = \int_{-\infty}^{\infty} v(t - t_d)e^{-j\omega t}\, dt$$

$$= \int_{-\infty}^{\infty} v(\lambda)e^{-j\omega(\lambda + t_d)}\, d\lambda$$

$$= \left[\int_{-\infty}^{\infty} v(\lambda)e^{-j\omega\lambda}\, d\lambda\right]e^{-j\omega t_d}$$

The integral in brackets is just $V(f)$, so $\mathcal{F}[v(t - t_d)] = V(f)e^{-j\omega t_d}$.

EXERCISE 2.9   The signal in Fig. 2.16 can be written as

$$z(t) = A\Pi\left(\frac{t + t_d}{\tau}\right) - A\Pi\left(\frac{t - t_d}{\tau}\right) \qquad t_d = \frac{\tau}{2} \qquad (17a)$$

Apply the linearity and time-delay theorems to the results of Example 2.4 to obtain

$$Z(f) = j2A\tau \operatorname{sinc} f\tau \sin \pi f\tau \qquad (17b)$$

Then sketch the amplitude spectrum and compare with Fig. 2.14.

Scale Change

Time delay is equivalent to translation of the time origin. Another geometric operation is scale change, in which the time axis is expanded, compressed, or reversed. Thus, $v(at)$ is a compressed version of $v(t)$ when a is positive and greater than 1.

Similarly, if a is negative and less than 1, $v(at)$ is the expanded image of $v(t)$ reversed in time. Such operations may occur in playback of recorded signals, for example.

The scale-change theorem says that

$$v(at) \leftrightarrow \frac{1}{|a|} V\left(\frac{f}{a}\right) \qquad (18)$$

which formally expresses the property of reciprocal spreading encountered in Example 2.4; for if the signal is compressed in time by the factor a, its spectrum is expanded in frequency by $1/a$, and conversely. The theorem is proved by change of variables, considering positive and negative values of a separately.

Duality

The powerful concept of duality is well known in circuit analysis. In spectral analysis there is also duality, a duality between the time and frequency domains that stems from the similarity of the Fourier transform integrals. The duality theorem says that if

$$v(t) \leftrightarrow V(f)$$

then the transform of the *time* function $V(t)$ is

$$\mathscr{F}[V(t)] = v(-f) \qquad (19)$$

as proved by interchanging t and f in the Fourier transform integrals.

In the form of Eq. (19) this theorem is rather abstract, and it is difficult to visualize its use in generating new transform pairs. The following example should help to clarify the procedure.

Example 2.6   Sinc Pulse

Consider the signal $z(t) = A \operatorname{sinc} 2Wt$, a sinc function in time. (Although the idea of a sinc pulse may seem strange at first, it plays a major role in the study of digital data transmission.) Recalling the transform pair of Example 2.4, $A\Pi(t/\tau) \leftrightarrow A\tau \operatorname{sinc} f\tau$, we apply duality by writing $z(t)$ in the form

$$z(t) = V(t) = \frac{A}{2W} 2W \operatorname{sinc} t2W$$

so

$$Z(f) = v(-f) = \frac{A}{2W} \Pi\left(\frac{-f}{2W}\right)$$

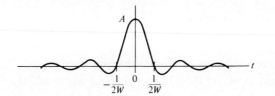

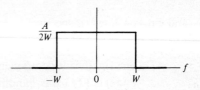

FIGURE 2.17
A sinc pulse and its bandlimited spectrum.

Because the rectangular function has even symmetry, $\Pi(-f/2W) = \Pi(f/2W)$, and we have derived the new transform pair

$$A \operatorname{sinc} 2Wt \leftrightarrow \frac{A}{2W} \Pi\left(\frac{f}{2W}\right) \qquad (20)$$

which is shown in Fig. 2.17. As can be seen, the spectrum of a sinc pulse has clearly defined spectral width W. In fact, the spectrum is zero for $|f| > W$, and the signal is said to be *bandlimited* in W. This is our first encounter with a signal that is strictly bandlimited in frequency. Note that the signal itself is only asymptotically limited in time. $\qquad ////$

Frequency Translation (Modulation)

Duality can be used to generate transform theorems as well as transform pairs. For example, a dual of the time-delay theorem (16) is

$$v(t)e^{j\omega_c t} \leftrightarrow V(f - f_c) \qquad \omega_c = 2\pi f_c \qquad (21)$$

We designate this as *frequency translation* or *complex modulation*, since multiplying a time function by $e^{j\omega_c t}$ causes its spectrum to be translated in frequency by $+f_c$.

To see the effects of frequency translation, let $v(t)$ have the bandlimited spectrum of Fig. 2.18a, where the amplitude and phase are plotted on the same axes using solid

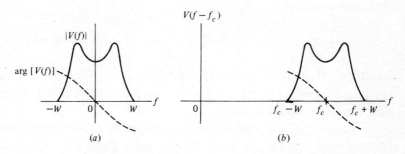

FIGURE 2.18

and broken lines, respectively. Inspection of the translated spectrum $V(f-f_c)$ in Fig. 2.18b reveals the following:

1   The significant components are concentrated around the frequency f_c.
2   Though $V(f)$ was bandlimited in W, $V(f-f_c)$ has a spectral width of $2W$. Translation has therefore doubled spectral width. Stated another way, the negative-frequency portion of $V(f)$ now appears at positive frequencies.
3   $V(f-f_c)$ is not hermitian but does have symmetry with respect to translated origin at $f=f_c$.

These considerations may appear somewhat academic in view of the fact that $v(t)e^{j\omega_c t}$ is not a real time function and cannot occur as a communication signal. However, signals of the form $v(t)\cos(\omega_c t + \theta)$ are common — in fact, they are the basis of carrier modulation — and by direct extension of Eq. (21) we have the following *modulation theorem:*

$$v(t)\cos(\omega_c t + \theta) \leftrightarrow \frac{e^{j\theta}}{2} V(f-f_c) + \frac{e^{-j\theta}}{2} V(f+f_c) \qquad (22)$$

In words, multiplying a signal by a sinusoid translates its spectrum *up and down* in frequency by f_c. All the comments about complex modulation also apply here. In addition, the resulting spectrum is hermitian, which it must be if $v(t)\cos(\omega_c t + \theta)$ is a real function of time. The theorem is easily proved with the aid of Euler's theorem and Eq. (21).

Example 2.7   RF Pulse

Consider the finite-duration sinusoid of Fig. 2.19a, sometimes referred to as an RF pulse when f_c falls in the radio-frequency band. Since

$$z(t) = A\Pi\left(\frac{t}{\tau}\right)\cos\omega_c t \qquad (23a)$$

we have immediately

$$Z(f) = \frac{A}{2}\operatorname{sinc}(f-f_c)\tau + \frac{A}{2}\operatorname{sinc}(f+f_c)\tau \qquad (23b)$$

by setting $v(t) = A\Pi(t/\tau)$ and $V(f) = A\tau\operatorname{sinc}f\tau$ in Eq. (22). The resulting amplitude spectrum is sketched in Fig. 2.19b for the case of $f_c \gg 1/\tau$ so the two translated sinc functions have negligible overlap.

Because this is a sinusoid of finite duration, its spectrum is continuous and contains more than just the frequencies $f = \pm f_c$. Those other frequencies stem from the fact that $z(t) = 0$ for $|t| > \tau/2$, and the smaller τ is, the larger the spectral spread around $\pm f_c$ — reciprocal spreading, again. On the other hand, had we been dealing

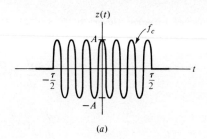

(a)

(b)

FIGURE 2.19
An RF pulse and its amplitude spectrum, $f_c \gg 1/\tau$.

with a sinusoid of *infinite* duration, the frequency-domain representation would be a two-sided *line* spectrum containing only the discrete frequencies $\pm f_c$. ////

Differentiation and Integration

Certain processing techniques involve differentiating or integrating a signal. The frequency-domain effects of these operations are indicated in the theorems below. A word of caution, however: The theorems should not be applied before checking to make sure that the differentiated or integrated signal is Fourier-transformable, i.e., has well-defined energy. And the fact that $v(t)$ has finite energy is not a guarantee that the same is true for its derivative or integral.

To derive the differentiation theorem, we replace $v(t)$ by the inverse transform integral and interchange the order of operations, as follows:

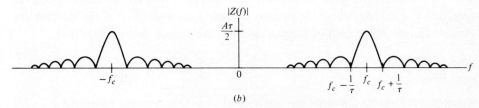

Referring back to the Fourier integral theorem (3) reveals that the bracketed term must be $\mathcal{F}[dv(t)/dt]$, so

$$\frac{d}{dt}v(t) \leftrightarrow j2\pi f V(f)$$

and by iteration

$$\frac{d^n}{dt^n}v(t) \leftrightarrow (j2\pi f)^n V(f) \tag{24}$$

which is the *differentiation theorem*.

Now suppose we generate another time function from $v(t)$ by carrying out the operation $\int_{-\infty}^{t} v(\lambda)\,d\lambda$, where the dummy variable λ is required since the independent variable t is the upper limit of integration. The *integration theorem* says that

$$\int_{-\infty}^{t} v(\lambda)\,d\lambda \leftrightarrow \frac{1}{j2\pi f}V(f) \tag{25}$$

whose proof involves the same method used above. One can also generalize Eq. (25) to multiple integration but the notation is cumbersome.

Inspecting these theorems, we can say that differentiation enhances the high-frequency components of a signal while integration suppresses high-frequency components. Spectral interpretation thus agrees with the time-domain viewpoint that differentiation accentuates time variations while integration smoothes them out.

Example 2.8   Triangular Pulse

To illustrate the integration theorem — and obtain yet another useful transform pair — let us integrate the signal $z(t)$ in Fig. 2.16 and divide it by the constant τ. This produces

$$w(t) = \frac{1}{\tau}\int_{-\infty}^{t} z(\lambda)\,d\lambda = \begin{cases} A\left(1 - \dfrac{|t|}{\tau}\right) & |t| < \tau \\ 0 & |t| > \tau \end{cases}$$

a *triangular* pulse shape shown in Fig. 2.20a. (The reader is strongly encouraged to check this result using the graphical interpretation of integration.) Then, taking $Z(f)$ from Eq. (17b), we have

$$W(f) = \frac{1}{\tau}\frac{1}{j2\pi f}Z(f) = \frac{j2A\tau\,\text{sinc}\,f\tau\,\sin\pi f\tau}{j2\pi f\tau} = A\tau\,\text{sinc}^2 f\tau$$

as sketched in Fig. 2.20b. Comparing this spectrum with Fig. 2.14 shows that the triangular pulse has less high-frequency content than a rectangular pulse with amplitude A and duration τ, even though they both have the same area. The difference is

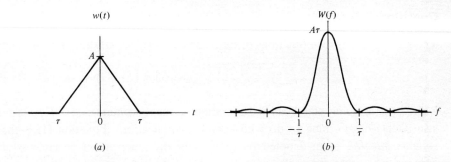

FIGURE 2.20
A triangular pulse and its spectrum.

traced to the fact that the triangular pulse is spread over 2τ seconds and does not have the sharp, stepwise time variations of the rectangular shape.

This transform pair can be written more compactly by defining the *triangular function*

$$\Lambda\left(\frac{t}{\tau}\right) \triangleq \begin{cases} 1 - \dfrac{|t|}{\tau} & |t| < \tau \\ 0 & |t| > \tau \end{cases} \tag{26}$$

Then $w(t) = A\Lambda(t/\tau)$ and

$$A\Lambda\left(\frac{t}{\tau}\right) \leftrightarrow A\tau \, \text{sinc}^2 \, f\tau \tag{27}$$

It so happens that triangular functions can be generated from rectangular functions by another mathematical operation, namely, convolution. And convolution happens to be the next major subject on the agenda, so we will take another look at this example soon.　　　　////

2.4 CONVOLUTION AND IMPULSES

The mathematical operation known as convolution ranks high among the analytic tools used by communication engineers. For one reason, it is a good model of the physical processes that go on in a linear system; for another, it helps to further our understanding of the relationships between the time domain and the frequency domain. In both cases, convolution goes hand in hand with that curious engineering fiction called the impulse or delta function. This section deals with these concepts as they relate to signals; they are applied to linear systems in the next section.

Convolution Integral

The convolution of two functions of the same variable, say $v(t)$ and $w(t)$, is defined as

$$v * w(t) \triangleq \int_{-\infty}^{\infty} v(\lambda)w(t - \lambda) \, d\lambda \qquad (1)$$

where $v * w(t)$ merely stands for the operation on the right-hand side of Eq. (1) and the asterisk ($*$) has nothing to do with complex conjugation. Equation (1) is the *convolution integral*, often denoted by $v * w$ when the independent variable is unambiguous. At other times the notation $[v(t)] * [w(t)]$ is necessary for clarity. Note carefully that the independent variable here is t, the same as the independent variable of the functions being convolved; the integration is always performed with respect to a dummy variable (such as λ) and t is a constant insofar as the integration is concerned.

Calculating $v * w(t)$ is no more difficult than ordinary integration when the two functions are continuous for all t. Often, however, one or both of the functions is defined in a piecewise fashion, and the graphical interpretation of convolution illustrated in Fig. 2.21 becomes especially helpful. Figures 2.21a and b are the functions involved here, but the integrand in Eq. (1) is $v(\lambda)w(t - \lambda)$. Of course, $v(\lambda)$ is nothing more than $v(t)$ with t replaced by λ, Fig. 2.21c. But $w(t - \lambda)$ as a function of λ must be obtained by two steps: first, $w(-\lambda)$ is $w(t)$ reversed in time with t replaced by λ; then, for a given value of t, sliding $w(-\lambda)$ to the right t units yields $w(t - \lambda)$. Figure 2.21d shows $w(t - \lambda)$ for the case of $t = t_1 > 0$, illustrating that the value of t always equals the distance from the origin of $v(\lambda)$ to the shifted origin of $w(-\lambda)$. Finally, $v(\lambda)$ and $w(t - \lambda)$ are multiplied and the area of the product equals $v * w(t)$ for that particular value of t, Fig. 2.21e.

As $v * w(t)$ is evaluated for $-\infty < t < \infty$, the plot of $w(t - \lambda)$ moves from the left to right with respect to $v(\lambda)$, and the actual form of the convolution integration may change depending on the value of t. In Fig. 2.21, for instance, it follows that

$$v * w(t) = 0 \qquad t < 0$$

since $w(t - \lambda)$ does not overlap $v(\lambda)$ and the area of the product is zero. Similarly,

$$v * w(t) = \begin{cases} \int_0^t v(\lambda)w(t - \lambda) \, d\lambda & 0 < t < T \\ \int_{t-T}^t v(\lambda)w(t - \lambda) \, d\lambda & t > T \end{cases}$$

since $v(\lambda) = 0$ for $\lambda < 0$ and $w(t - \lambda) = 0$ for $\lambda < t - T$ and $\lambda > t$. Note in these cases that t appears as a limit of integration. Simple sketches of the functions involved help one discover these different cases.

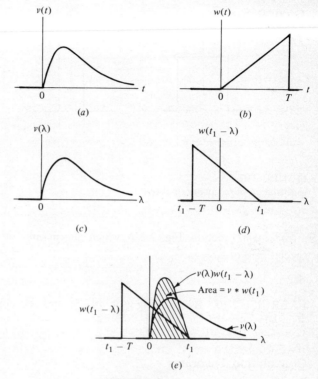

FIGURE 2.21
The graphical interpretation of convolution.

Further study of Fig. 2.21 should reveal that $v * w(t) = w * v(t)$, i.e., we get the same result by reversing v and sliding it past w. This property and several other convolution properties are listed below for reference.

$$v * w = w * v \qquad (2a)$$

$$v * (w * z) = (v * w) * z \qquad (2b)$$

$$(\alpha v + \beta w) * z = \alpha(v * z) + \beta(w * z) \qquad (2c)$$

$$\frac{d}{dt}(v * w) = v * \frac{dw}{dt} = \frac{dv}{dt} * w \qquad (3)$$

Example 2.9   Convolution of Rectangular Pulses

The convolution of two rectangular pulses, Fig. 2.22a, is relatively simple using the graphical interpretation, and the problem breaks up into three cases: $|t| > (\tau_1 + \tau_2)/2$, $(\tau_1 - \tau_2)/2 < |t| < (\tau_1 + \tau_2)/2$, and $|t| < (\tau_1 - \tau_2)/2$, assuming $\tau_1 \geq \tau_2$. The result is

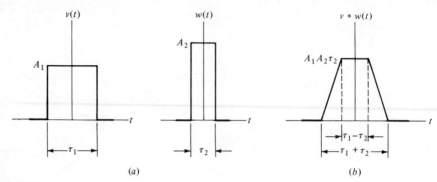

FIGURE 2.22
Convolution of rectangular pulses.

a *trapezoidal* function, Fig. 2.22b, which degenerates into a triangular function in the special case of $\tau_1 = \tau_2$. ////

EXERCISE 2.10 By carrying out all the details, confirm the result asserted in Example 2.9.

Convolution Theorems

Having defined convolution, we now give the theorems pertaining to convolution and transforms, which are two in number, namely,

$$v * w(t) \leftrightarrow V(f)W(f) \tag{4}$$

$$v(t)w(t) \leftrightarrow V * W(f) \tag{5}$$

These theorems state that convolution in the time domain becomes multiplication in the frequency domain, while multiplication in the time domain becomes convolution in the frequency domain. Both of these relationships are important for future work.

The proof of Eq. (4) uses the time-delay theorem, as follows:

$$\mathscr{F}[v * w(t)] = \int_{-\infty}^{\infty} \left[\int_{-\infty}^{\infty} v(\lambda)w(t - \lambda) \, d\lambda \right] e^{-j\omega t} \, dt$$

$$= \int_{-\infty}^{\infty} v(\lambda) \left[\int_{-\infty}^{\infty} w(t - \lambda)e^{-j\omega t} \, dt \right] d\lambda$$

$$= \int_{-\infty}^{\infty} v(\lambda)[W(f)e^{-j\omega \lambda}] \, d\lambda$$

$$= \left[\int_{-\infty}^{\infty} v(\lambda)e^{-j\omega \lambda} \, d\lambda \right] W(f) = V(f)W(f)$$

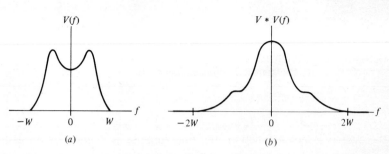

$V(f)$

$V * V(f)$

$-W$ 0 W

$-2W$ 0 $2W$

(a)

(b)

FIGURE 2.23

Equation (5) can be proved by writing out the transform of $v(t)w(t)$ and replacing $w(t)$ by the inversion integral $\mathscr{F}^{-1}[W(f)]$.

EXERCISE 2.11   Use Eq. (4) together with the results of Example 2.9 to obtain the transform of a triangular pulse, Eq. (27), Sect. 2.3.

Example 2.10   The Spectrum of $v^2(t)$

Suppose $v(t)$ is bandlimited in W, with a spectrum as shown in Fig. 2.23a. What then is the spectrum of $v^2(t)$? From Eq. (5) we must convolve $V(f)$ with itself, the result being something like Fig. 2.23b. Without any further specific knowledge of $v(t)$ we reach this important conclusion: when $v(t)$ is bandlimited in W, $v^2(t)$ is bandlimited in $2W$. (Note the difference between this operation and the modulation theorem, both of which double spectral width.) The process may be iterated for $v^3(t)$, etc., with predictable conclusions.   ////

Unit Impulse

Previous examples have demonstrated that convolution is a *smoothing* operation; i.e., the result is "smoother" and "longer" or "wider" than either of the functions involved. But there is one notable exception to this rule, namely, when one of the functions is a *unit impulse* or *Dirac delta function* $\delta(t)$; in that case, providing $v(t)$ is continuous,

$$[v(t)] * [\delta(t)] = v(t) \qquad (6)$$

so convolving with an impulse merely reproduces the other function in its entirety.

Actually, $\delta(t)$ is not a function in the strict mathematical sense; rather, it is a member of that special class known as *generalized functions* or *distributions*. And

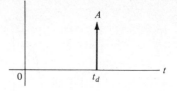

FIGURE 2.24
The graphical representation of $A\delta(t - t_d)$.

because it is not a function, the unit impulse is defined by an assignment rule or process instead of a conventional equation. Specifically, given any ordinary function $v(t)$ that is continuous at $t = 0$, $\delta(t)$ is defined by

$$\int_{t_1}^{t_2} v(t)\, \delta(t)\, dt = \begin{cases} v(0) & t_1 < 0 < t_2 \\ 0 & \text{otherwise} \end{cases} \qquad (7)$$

a rule that assigns a number—either $v(0)$ or 0—to the process on the left-hand side.

Taking $v(t) = 1$ for all t, it follows from Eq. (7) that

$$\int_{-\infty}^{\infty} \delta(t)\, dt = \int_{-\epsilon}^{\epsilon} \delta(t)\, dt = 1 \qquad (8a)$$

which may be interpreted by saying that $\delta(t)$ has *unit area* concentrated at the discrete point $t = 0$ and no net area elsewhere. Carrying this argument further suggests that

$$\delta(t) = 0 \qquad t \neq 0 \qquad (8b)$$

Equations (8a) and (8b) are the more familiar "definitions" of the impulse, and lead to the common graphical representation. For instance, the picture of $A\delta(t - t_d)$ is shown in Fig. 2.24, where the letter A next to the arrowhead means that $A\delta(t - t_d)$ has area or weight A located at $t = t_d$. It should be noted that Eq. (8b) is not an assignment rule, and distribution theory, strictly interpreted, does not specify values for the impulse other than in the integral sense. It is, however, consistent with Eq. (7) and helps us visualize impulse properties under the operation of integration.

Two of the most important integration properties are

$$\int_{-\infty}^{\infty} v(t)\, \delta(t - t_d)\, dt = v(t_d) \qquad (9)$$

$$[v(t)] * [\delta(t - t_d)] = v(t - t_d) \qquad (10)$$

both of which can be derived from Eq. (7). Equation (9) is called the *sampling* property since the indicated operation picks out or samples the values of $v(t)$ at $t = t_d$ where $\delta(t - t_d)$ is "located." On the other hand, convolving $v(t)$ with $\delta(t - t_d)$ is a *replication* property since, according to Eq. (10), it reproduces the entire function $v(t)$ displaced by t_d units. The difference between Eqs. (9) and (10) should be clearly understood: sampling picks out a particular value, i.e., a number, while convolving repeats the function completely.

By definition, the impulse has no mathematical or physical meaning unless it appears under integration. Even so, it is convenient to state three nonintegral relations as simplifications that can be made before integration since they are consistent with what would happen after integration. Specifically, in view of the sampling property (9), we can just as well replace $v(t)$ by $v(t_d)$, so that

$$v(t) \, \delta(t - t_d) = v(t_d) \, \delta(t - t_d) \qquad (11)$$

whose justification stems from integrating both sides over $-\infty < t < \infty$. Similarly one can justify the scale-change relationship

$$\delta(at) = \frac{1}{|a|} \delta(t) \qquad a \neq 0 \qquad (12)$$

which says that, relative to the independent variable t, $\delta(at)$ is an impulse having weight $1/|a|$. The special case of $a = -1$ indicates the even-symmetry property $\delta(t) = \delta(-t)$. Finally, relating the unit impulse to the unit step $u(t)$ defined in Eq. (13), Sect. 2.3, we see from Eq. (7) that

$$\int_{-\infty}^{t} \delta(\lambda) \, d\lambda = \begin{cases} 1 & t > 0 \\ 0 & t < 0 \end{cases}$$

$$= u(t)$$

Differentiating both sides then yields

$$\delta(t) = \frac{du(t)}{dt} \qquad (13)$$

which is not a definition of $\delta(t)$ but a consequence of the assignment rule (7).

Although an impulse does not exist physically, there are numerous conventional functions that have all the properties of $\delta(t)$ in the limit as some parameter ϵ goes to zero. In particular, if the function $\delta_\epsilon(t)$ is such that

$$\lim_{\epsilon \to 0} \int_{-\infty}^{\infty} v(t) \, \delta_\epsilon(t) \, dt = v(0) \qquad (14a)$$

then we say that

$$\lim_{\epsilon \to 0} \delta_\epsilon(t) = \delta(t) \qquad (14b)$$

Two functions satisfying Eq. (14a) are

$$\delta_\epsilon(t) = \frac{1}{\epsilon} \Pi\left(\frac{t}{\epsilon}\right) \qquad (15)$$

$$\delta_\epsilon(t) = \frac{1}{\epsilon} \operatorname{sinc} \frac{t}{\epsilon} \qquad (16)$$

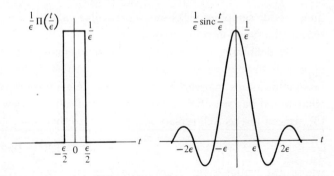

FIGURE 2.25
Two functions that become impulses as $\epsilon \to 0$.

which are plotted in Fig. 2.25. One can easily show that Eq. (15) satisfies Eq. (14a) by expanding $v(t)$ in a Maclaurin series prior to integrating. An argument for Eq. (16) will be given shortly when we consider impulses and transforms.

EXERCISE 2.12   Use Eq. (16) to prove that

$$\lim_{F \to \infty} \int_{-F}^{F} e^{\pm j2\pi ft} \, df = \delta(t) \qquad (17)$$

Impulses in Frequency

Sections 2.2 and 2.3 drew the distinction between periodic power signals and non-periodic energy signals, one class being described by line spectra, the other by continuous spectra. This means that we have something of a quandary if a signal consists of periodic and nonperiodic parts since different frequency-domain representations would be required. This quandary is solved by allowing impulses in the frequency domain as the representation of discrete frequency components. Such impulses are derived by limiting operations on conventional Fourier transform pairs, and may be dubbed *transforms in the limit*. Note, however, that the corresponding time functions are power signals having infinite or undefined energy, and the concept of energy spectral density no longer applies.

As a starting point of this discussion, consider the signal $v(t) = A$, a constant for all time. Referring to Fig. 2.17a, we let $v(t)$ be a *sinc pulse* with $W \to 0$, i.e.,

$$v(t) = \lim_{W \to 0} A \operatorname{sinc} 2Wt = A$$

But we already have the transform pair $A \operatorname{sinc} 2Wt \leftrightarrow (A/2W)\Pi(f/2W)$, so

$$\mathscr{F}[v(t)] = \lim_{W \to 0} \frac{A}{2W} \Pi\left(\frac{f}{2W}\right) = A \, \delta(f)$$

where we have invoked Eq. (15) with t replaced by f and ϵ replaced by $2W$. Therefore,

$$A \leftrightarrow A\delta(f) \qquad (18)$$

and the spectrum of a constant in the time domain is an impulse in the frequency domain at $f = 0$. This result agrees with intuition in that a constant signal has no time variation and its spectral content ought to be confined to $f = 0$. The impulsive form results simply because we use integration to return to the time domain, via the inverse transform, and an impulse is required to concentrate nonzero area at a discrete point in frequency. Checking this argument mathematically gives

$$\mathscr{F}^{-1}[A \, \delta(f)] = \int_{-\infty}^{\infty} A \, \delta(f)e^{j2\pi ft} \, dt = Ae^{j2\pi ft}\bigg|_{f=0} = A$$

which justifies Eq. (18) for our purposes. Note that the impulse has been integrated to obtain a physical quantity, namely, the signal $v(t) = A$.

As an alternate to the above procedure for deriving Eq. (18), we could have begun with a rectangular pulse, $A\Pi(t/\tau)$, and let $\tau \to \infty$ to get a constant for all time. Then, since $\mathscr{F}[A\Pi(t/\tau)] = A\tau \operatorname{sinc} f\tau$, agreement with Eq. (18) requires that

$$\lim_{\tau \to \infty} A\tau \operatorname{sinc} f\tau = A\delta(f)$$

And this supports the earlier assertion Eq. (16) that a sinc function becomes an impulse under appropriate limiting conditions.

To generalize Eq. (18), direct application of the frequency-translation and modulation theorems yields

$$Ae^{j\omega_c t} \leftrightarrow A\delta(f - f_c) \qquad (19)$$

$$A \cos(\omega_c t + \theta) \leftrightarrow \frac{Ae^{j\theta}}{2} \delta(f - f_c) + \frac{Ae^{-j\theta}}{2} \delta(f + f_c) \qquad (20)$$

Thus, the spectrum of a single phasor is an impulse at $f = f_c$ while the spectrum of a sinusoid has two impulses, Fig. 2.26. Going even further in this direction, if $v(t)$ is an arbitrary periodic signal whose exponential Fourier series is

$$v(t) = \sum_{n=-\infty}^{\infty} c_v(nf_0)e^{j2\pi nf_0 t} \qquad (21a)$$

then its Fourier transform is

$$V(f) = \sum_{n=-\infty}^{\infty} c_v(nf_0) \, \delta(f - nf_0) \qquad (21b)$$

where superposition allows one to transform the sum term by term.

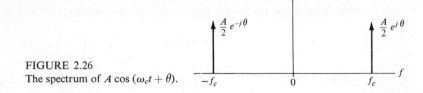

FIGURE 2.26
The spectrum of $A \cos(\omega_c t + \theta)$.

By now it should be obvious from Eqs. (18) to (21) that any two-sided line spectrum can be converted to a "continuous" spectrum using this rule: convert the spectral lines to impulses whose weights equal the line heights. The phase portion of the line spectrum is absorbed by letting the impulse weights be complex numbers, e.g., the weights in Eq. (21b) are $c_v(nf_0) = |c_v(nf_0)| e^{j \, \mathrm{arg}\,[c_v(nf_0)]}$. Hence, with the aid of transforms in the limit, we can represent both periodic and nonperiodic signals by continuous spectra. In addition, the transform theorems developed in Sect. 2.3 can now be applied to periodic signals. That strange beast the impulse function thereby emerges as a key to unifying spectral analysis.

But one may well ask: What is the difference between the line spectrum and the "continuous" spectrum of a periodic signal? Obviously there can be no physical difference; the difference lies in the mathematical conventions. To return to the time domain from the line spectrum, we sum the phasors which the lines represent. To return to the time domain from the continuous spectrum, we integrate the impulses to get phasors.

EXERCISE 2.13 Prove Eq. (20) by carrying out the inverse transform of the right-hand side.

Impulses in Time

The time-domain impulse may seem a trifle farfetched as a signal model, but the next section will show conditions where it is both reasonable and highly useful. Here we are concerned with the transform

$$A\delta(t) \leftrightarrow A \qquad (22)$$

which is derived by Fourier transformation using Eq. (17) to evaluate the integral. Since the transform of the time impulse has *constant amplitude*, its spectrum contains all frequencies in equal proportion.

The reader may have observed that Eq. (22) is the dual of $A \leftrightarrow A\delta(f)$. This dual relationship has its roots in reciprocal spreading, Eqs. (18) and (22) being the two extremes; i.e., a constant signal of infinite duration has "zero" spectral width, whereas an impulse in time has "zero" duration and infinite spectral width.

Applying the time-delay theorem to Eq. (22) yields the more general pair

$$A\delta(t - t_d) \leftrightarrow Ae^{-j\omega t_d} \qquad (23)$$

Problem 2.34 outlines how this pair, together with the differentiation theorem, provides a shortcut method for finding certain other transforms.

2.5   SYSTEM RESPONSE AND FILTERS

Let us return to the input-output or system response problem as posed at the beginning of the chapter, save that now we allow the input $x(t)$ to be more or less arbitrary. We will still assume that the system is linear, time-invariant, and asymptotically stable, and we will add the constraint that there is no stored energy in the system when the input is applied. The system's response $y(t)$ will be formulated using both time-domain and frequency-domain analysis.

Impulse Response and Time-Domain Analysis

In linear system theory, the *impulse response* $h(t)$ of a system is defined as the output that results when the input is a unit impulse, i.e.,

$$h(t) \triangleq y(t) \qquad \text{when } x(t) = \delta(t) \qquad (1)$$

The response to an arbitrary input $x(t)$ is then found by convolving $h(t)$ with $x(t)$, so

$$y(t) = h * x(t) = \int_{-\infty}^{\infty} h(\lambda)x(t - \lambda) \, d\lambda \qquad (2)$$

Often called the *superposition integral*, Eq. (2) is the basis of time-domain system analysis. This method therefore requires knowing the impulse response as well as the ability to carry out the convolution.

Several techniques are available for finding the impulse response of a system, given its mathematical model. If the model is a simple block diagram without feedback loops, $h(t)$ usually can be found from inspection by invoking the definition (1). Other times it is easier to calculate the *step response* $y_u(t)$, defined by

$$y_u(t) \triangleq y(t) \qquad \text{when } x(t) = u(t) \qquad (3a)$$

in which case

$$h(t) = \frac{dy_u(t)}{dt} \qquad (3b)$$

This follows since $y_u(t) = [h(t)] * [u(t)]$ so $dy_u(t)/dt = [h(t)] * [du(t)/dt] = [h(t)] * [\delta(t)] = h(t)$, the pertinent relations being Eqs. (3), (6), and (13), Sect. 2.4. When these methods do not work, the problem is probably a candidate for frequency-domain analysis.

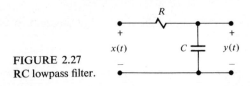

FIGURE 2.27
RC lowpass filter.

Example 2.11 Step, Impulse, and Pulse Response of an RC Lowpass Filter

Again consider the RC lowpass filter, Fig. 2.27. If $x(t)$ is a unit step, Fig. 2.28a, the step response is well known to be

$$y_u(t) = (1 - e^{-t/RC})u(t) \qquad (4a)$$

as plotted in Fig. 2.28b. Differentiation then yields Fig. 2.28c, namely,

$$h(t) = \frac{dy_u(t)}{dt} = \frac{1}{RC}e^{-t/RC}u(t) \qquad (4b)$$

Now consider the response to a rectangular pulse of duration τ starting at $t = 0$, i.e., $x(t) = A\Pi[(t - \tau/2)/\tau]$. Putting $x(t)$ and $h(t)$ in Eq. (2) gives, with the help of the graphical interpretation of convolution,

$$y(t) = \begin{cases} 0 & t < 0 \\ A(1 - e^{-t/RC}) & 0 < t < \tau \\ A(1 - e^{-\tau/RC})e^{-(t-\tau)/RC} & t > \tau \end{cases} \qquad (5)$$

which is sketched in Fig. 2.29 for two values of τ/RC. ////

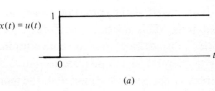

(a)

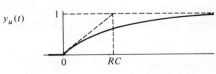

(b)

FIGURE 2.28
Waveforms for RC lowpass filter. (a)
Unit step input; (b) step response $y_u(t)$;
impulse response $h(t) = dy_u(t)/dt$.

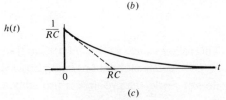

(c)

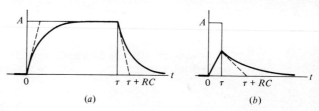

FIGURE 2.29
Rectangular pulse response of an RC lowpass filter. (a) $\tau/RC \gg 1$; (b) $\tau/RC \ll 1$.

Transfer Function and Frequency-Domain Analysis

Linking time-domain analysis to the frequency domain, let the input in the superposition integral (2) be $x(t) = e^{j2\pi ft}$ for $-\infty < t < \infty$. Then,

$$y(t) = \int_{-\infty}^{\infty} h(\lambda)e^{j2\pi f(t-\lambda)}\, d\lambda$$

$$= \left[\int_{-\infty}^{\infty} h(\lambda)e^{-j2\pi f\lambda}\, d\lambda \right] e^{j2\pi ft} \qquad (6)$$

and the expression in brackets is recognized as a Fourier transform integral. To identify that integral, recall that the transfer function $H(f)$ of a system was previously defined such that, when $x(t) = e^{j2\pi ft}$, $y(t) = H(f)e^{j2\pi ft}$—but Eq. (6) has precisely this form if we take

$$H(f) = \mathscr{F}[h(t)] = \int_{-\infty}^{\infty} h(t)e^{-j2\pi ft}\, dt \qquad (7)$$

Therefore, the impulse response and transfer function of a given system constitute a Fourier transform pair, and all the properties of $H(f)$ stated earlier can be derived from Eq. (7).

Equation (7) also explains why the Fourier transform of the exponential pulse, Example 2.5, Sect. 2.3, turned out to have the same frequency dependence as the transfer function of an RC lowpass filter, Example 2.1, Sect. 2.1. In hindsight, this demonstrates the $h(t) \leftrightarrow H(f)$ pair, since Example 2.11 showed that the impulse response of an RC lowpass filter is an exponential pulse.

As for frequency-domain analysis per se, we take the Fourier transform of the superposition integral and apply the convolution theorem, Eq. (4), Sect. 2.4. Thus

$$\mathscr{F}[y(t)] = \mathscr{F}[h * x(t)] = \mathscr{F}[h(t)]\mathscr{F}[x(t)]$$

or

$$Y(f) = H(f)X(f) \qquad (8)$$

as illustrated schematically in Fig. 2.30 along with the time-domain relation. This elegantly simple equation, the basis of frequency-domain analysis, says that the

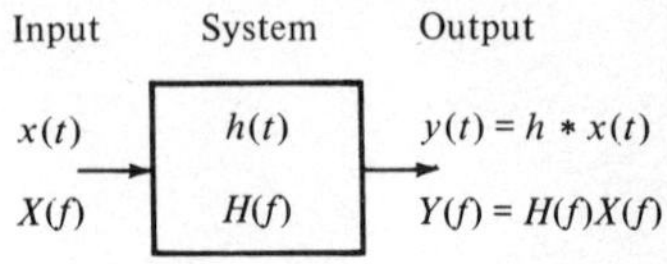

	Input	System	Output
	$x(t)$	$h(t)$	$y(t) = h * x(t)$
	$X(f)$	$H(f)$	$Y(f) = H(f)X(f)$

FIGURE 2.30
Input-output relations for a linear time-invariant system.

output spectrum $Y(f)$ equals the input spectrum $X(f)$ multiplied by the transfer function $H(f)$. The corresponding amplitude and phase spectra are

$$|Y(f)| = |H(f)|\,|X(f)|$$
$$\arg[Y(f)] = \arg[X(f)] + \arg[H(f)]$$

(9)

which should be compared to the periodic steady-state result, Eq. (23), Sect. 2.2. Additionally, if the output $y(t)$ is an energy signal, its energy spectral density and total energy are given by

$$|Y(f)|^2 = |H(f)|^2\,|X(f)|^2 \tag{10}$$

$$E_y = \int_{-\infty}^{\infty} |H(f)|^2\,|X(f)|^2\,df \tag{11}$$

from Rayleigh's energy theorem.

Further interpretation of Eq. (8) is afforded if we take $x(t)$ as a unit impulse; then, since $X(f) = \mathscr{F}[\delta(t)] = 1$,

$$Y(f) = H(f) \qquad \text{when } x(t) = \delta(t) \tag{12}$$

in agreement with the fact that the transfer function is the transform of the impulse response. Viewed from the frequency domain, the spectrum of the input signal has all frequency components in equal proportion in this case, so the output spectrum is shaped entirely by the transfer function $H(f)$.

Finally, one can return to the time domain by taking the inverse transform of Eq. (8), i.e.,

$$y(t) = \mathscr{F}^{-1}[H(f)X(f)] = \int_{-\infty}^{\infty} H(f)X(f)e^{j2\pi ft}\,df \tag{13}$$

Contrasting Eqs. (13) and (8), it appears that the output spectrum is more easily obtained than the output time function, which indeed is the case if $H(f)$ and $X(f)$ are known. The power of frequency-domain analysis rests on the simple relationship of input and output spectra. Furthermore, an experienced communication engineer can often infer all he needs to know from the spectrum. (Much of this chapter has pointed toward making such inferences.) On the other hand, if specific details of the time function are to be investigated, the superposition integral may be easier than Eq. (13) for finding $y(t)$.

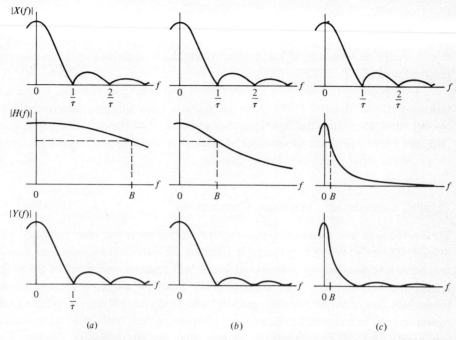

FIGURE 2.31
Frequency-domain analysis of the rectangular pulse response of an RC lowpass filter. (*a*) $B \gg 1/\tau$; (*b*) $B \approx 1/\tau$; (*c*) $B \ll 1/\tau$.

Example 2.12

To illustrate how far one can go just in terms of the frequency domain, suppose a rectangular pulse of duration τ is applied to an RC lowpass filter with $B = 1/2\pi RC$. Our prior studies have shown that most of the pulse's spectral content is in $|f| < 1/\tau$, while the filter responds primarily to frequencies in the range $|f| < B$. Clearly, the shape of the output spectrum — and, hence, the output signal — depends on the relative values of $1/\tau$ and B. Figure 2.31 gives plots of $|X(f)|$, $|H(f)|$, and $|Y(f)| = |H(f)| |X(f)|$ for the three cases $B \gg 1/\tau$, $B \approx 1/\tau$, and $B \ll 1/\tau$.

In the first case, Fig. 2.31*a*, the filter passes all the significant frequency components since $H(f) \approx 1$ for $|f| < 1/\tau$. Therefore, $Y(f) \approx X(f)$ and $y(t) \approx x(t)$, so the output time function should look very much like the input. As a direct check on that conclusion, Fig. 2.29*a* shows the actual waveforms under this condition. In the second case, Fig. 2.31*b*, the shape of the output spectrum depends on both $X(f)$ and $H(f)$ so $y(t)$ will differ substantially from $x(t)$. We then say that the output is *distorted* in the sense that it does not resemble the input, but a more precise statement entails actually going through the time-domain calculations. In the third case, Fig. 2.31*c*, the input spectrum is constant or "flat" over $|f| < B$ so $Y(f) \approx A\tau H(f)$. Since the output spectrum now depends primarily on $H(f)$, the output signal will look like the filter's *impulse response*, i.e., $y(t) \approx A\tau h(t)$. Again, this is confirmed by the time-domain result plotted in Fig. 2.29*b*.

Extrapolating this last case to other filters and other pulse shapes, we state the following rule of thumb: If the input spectrum is essentially constant over the frequency band where the filter has significant response, then the output signal is essentially the impulse response of the filter. Under such conditions, it is quite reasonable to model the input signal as being an impulse.   ////

Parallel, Cascade, and Feedback Connections

More often than not, a communication system comprises many interconnected units or subsystems. When the subsystems in question are described by individual transfer functions, it is possible and desirable to lump them together and speak of the overall system transfer function. The corresponding relations are given below for two subsystems connected in parallel, cascade, and feedback. More complicated configurations can be analyzed by successive application of these basic rules. One essential assumption must be made, however, namely, that any interaction or *loading* effects have been accounted for in the individual transfer functions so that they represent the actual response of the subsystems in the context of the overall system.

Figure 2.32*a* diagrams two subsystems in *parallel*; both units have the same input and their outputs are summed to get the system's output. From superposition it follows that $Y(f) = [H_1(f) + H_2(f)]X(f)$ so the overall transfer function is

$$H(f) = H_1(f) + H_2(f) \qquad \text{Parallel connection} \qquad (14)$$

In the *cascade* connection, Fig. 2.32*b*, the output of the first unit is the input to the second, so $Y(f) = H_2(f)[H_1(f)X(f)]$ and

$$H(f) = H_1(f)H_2(f) \qquad \text{Cascade connection} \qquad (15)$$

The *feedback* connection, Fig. 2.32*c*, differs from the other two in that the output is sent back through $H_2(f)$ and subtracted from the input. Thus, $Y(f) = H_1(f)[X(f) - H_2(f)Y(f)]$ and rearranging yields $Y(f) = \{H_1(f)/[1 + H_1(f)H_2(f)]\}X(f)$ so

$$H(f) = \frac{H_1(f)}{1 + H_1(f)H_2(f)} \qquad \text{Feedback connection} \qquad (16)$$

This case is more properly termed the *negative* feedback connection as distinguished from positive feedback, where the returned signal is added to the input instead of subtracted.

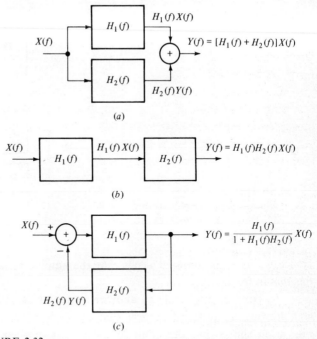

FIGURE 2.32
(a) Parallel connection; (b) cascade connection; (c) feedback connection.

Example 2.13   Zero-Order Hold

The zero-order hold system, Fig. 2.33a, has several applications in electrical communication. Here we take it as an instructive exercise of the parallel and cascade relations. But first we need the individual transfer functions, determined as follows: the upper branch of the parallel section is a straight-through path so, trivially, $H_1(f) = 1$; the lower branch produces pure time delay of T seconds and sign inversion, and lumping them together gives $H_2(f) = -e^{-j2\pi fT}$ by application of the time-delay theorem; using the integration theorem, the integrator in the final block has $H_3(f) = 1/j2\pi f$. Figure 2.33b is the equivalent block diagram in terms of these transfer functions.

Having gotten this far, the rest of the work is easy. We combine the parallel branches in $H_{12}(f) = H_1(f) + H_2(f)$ and use the cascade rule to obtain

$$H(f) = H_{12}(f)H_3(f) = [H_1(f) + H_2(f)]H_3(f)$$

$$= [1 - e^{-j2\pi fT}]\frac{1}{j2\pi f}$$

$$= \frac{e^{j\pi fT} - e^{-j\pi fT}}{j2\pi f}e^{-j\pi fT} = \frac{\sin \pi fT}{\pi f}e^{-j\pi fT}$$

$$= T \operatorname{sinc} fTe^{-j\pi fT} \tag{17}$$

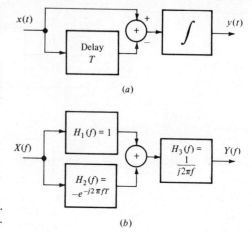

FIGURE 2.33
Block diagrams of zero-order hold.
(*a*) Time domain; (*b*) frequency domain.

Hence we have the unusual result that the amplitude ratio of this system is a *sinc function* in frequency!

To confirm this result by another route, let us calculate the impulse response $h(t)$ drawing upon the definition that $y(t) = h(t)$ when $x(t) = \delta(t)$. Inspection of Fig. 2.33*a* shows that the input to the integrator then is $x(t) - x(t - T) = \delta(t) - \delta(t - T)$, so

$$h(t) = \int_{-\infty}^{t} [\delta(\lambda) - \delta(\lambda - T)] \, d\lambda = \begin{cases} 1 & 0 < t < T \\ 0 & \text{otherwise} \end{cases}$$

$$= \Pi\left(\frac{t - T/2}{T}\right) \tag{18}$$

and the impulse response is a rectangular pulse, Fig. 2.34. The reader should have little trouble identifying Eq. (17) as the transform of Eq. (18).　　////

EXERCISE 2.14   Derive Eq. (17) by letting $x(t) = e^{j2\pi f t}$ in Fig. 2.33*a* and finding $y(t)$.

Real and Ideal Filters

Systems or networks that exhibit frequency-selective characteristics are called *filters*. A lowpass filter (LPF), for instance, passes only "low" frequencies — in the sense that

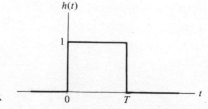

FIGURE 2.34
Impulse response of zero-order hold.

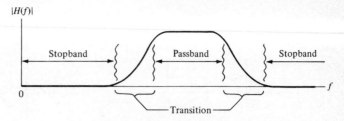

FIGURE 2.35
Passband and stopbands of a typical bandpass filter.

its amplitude ratio $|H(f)|$ is much greater at low frequencies than at high frequencies. The RC lowpass filter and the zero-order hold just discussed illustrate this type of frequency response. Similarly, there are *highpass* filters (HPF), *bandpass* filters (BPF), and *band-rejection* filters. The tuned circuit in the frequency multiplier acts as a BPF.

Ideally, a filter should have a sharp boundary between its *passband* and *stopband* or rejection band. Then the bandwidth of the filter could be unambiguously measured as the width of the passband. However, actual amplitude ratio curves do not have pronounced demarcation points, so the ends of the passband and stopband are ambiguous and there is a *transition* band between them. Figure 2.35 illustrates this characteristic for a typical bandpass filter; note that the negative-frequency portion has been omitted and the various bands are indicated only in terms of positive frequencies, in recognition of the even symmetry of $|H(f)|$ plus the fact that negative frequencies are something of a fiction introduced for analytic convenience.

When dealing with real filters, the bandwidth usually is taken to be the range of *positive frequencies* over which $|H(f)|$ falls no lower than $1/\sqrt{2}$ times the maximum value of $|H(f)|$ in the passband. This particular bandwidth convention — and there are others — is called the *half-power* or *3-decibel (dB) bandwidth*. The name stems from the fact that a sinusoidal input at the band-edge frequency would come out with its average power reduced by $(1/\sqrt{2})^2 = \frac{1}{2}$ compared to a sinusoid at the center of the passband. Converting this ratio to decibels† gives $10 \log_{10} \frac{1}{2} \approx -3$ dB so the power ratio at the edge of the passband is 3 dB below the center.

As an example of this convention, the half-power bandwidth of the RC LPF (Fig. 2.6) is $B = 1/2\pi RC$ since $|H(f)|_{max} = |H(0)| = 1$ and $|H(B)| = 1/\sqrt{2}$; the passband is $0 \le f \le B$. By the same token, the bandwidth of the tuned-circuit BPF in Fig. 2.12 is $B = f_r/Q$ since $|H(f)|_{max} = |H(f_r)| = R$ and $|H(f_r \pm f_r/2Q| = R/\sqrt{2}$. (At this point the reader should take another look at Figs. 2.6 and 2.12 in the light of these comments, especially noting that B is measured in terms of the positive-frequency range.)

† See Table E.

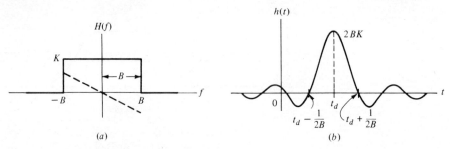

FIGURE 2.36
Ideal lowpass filter. (*a*) Transfer function; (*b*) impulse response.

More sophisticated filter designs have much more selective characteristics than our simple examples, to the point approaching stepwise frequency transitions. In the limit, we define an *ideal* LPF as having the rectangular characteristic

$$H(f) = Ke^{-j\omega t_d}\Pi\left(\frac{f}{2B}\right) \qquad (19)$$

where K is the amplification, t_d is the time delay, and B is the bandwidth. Figure 2.36a plots this transfer function. Note that the bandwidth is unambiguous and the response outside the passband is identically zero. Ideal BPFs and HPFs are similarly defined, and BPFs will come up for further discussion in Chap. 5.

In advanced network theory it is shown that ideal filters cannot be physically realized. We skip the general proof here and give instead an argument based on impulse response. Consider, for example, the impulse response of an ideal LPF. By definition and using Eq. (19),

$$h(t) = \mathcal{F}^{-1}[H(f)] = \mathcal{F}^{-1}\left[Ke^{-j\omega t_d}\Pi\left(\frac{f}{2B}\right)\right]$$

$$= 2BK \text{ sinc } 2B(t - t_d) \qquad (20)$$

which is plotted in Fig. 2.36b. Since $h(t)$ is the response to $\delta(t)$ and $h(t)$ has nonzero values for $t < 0$, *the output appears before the input is applied.* Such a filter is said to be *anticipatory*, and the portion of the output appearing before the input is called a *precursor*. Without doubt, such behavior is physically impossible, and hence the filter must be nonrealizable. Similar results are found for the bandpass and highpass case.

Fictitious though they may be, ideal filters are still conceptually useful in the study of communication systems, and practical filters can be designed that come quite close to being ideal, at least for engineering purposes. In fact, as the number

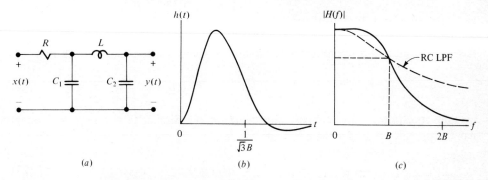

FIGURE 2.37
Third-order Butterworth filter. (*a*) Circuit ($R = 100$, $C_1 = 1/400\pi B$, $C_2 = 3C_1$, $L = 200/3\pi B$); (*b*) impulse response; (*c*) amplitude ratio.

of reactive elements increases without limit, the transfer function can be made arbitrarily close to that of an ideal filter. But at the same time, the filter time delay increases without limit. As a side point we observe that the infinite time delay means the precursors will always appear after the input is applied, which must be true of a real filter.

Example 2.14 Butterworth Lowpass Filter

Figure 2.37*a* is the circuit diagram of a third-order Butterworth filter with 3-dB bandwidth B. Its transfer function and impulse response are

$$H(f) = \left\{ 1 - 2\left(\frac{f}{B}\right)^2 + j\left[2\left(\frac{f}{B}\right) - \left(\frac{f}{B}\right)^3\right]\right\}^{-1}$$

$$h(t) = 2\pi B\left[e^{-2\pi Bt} - \frac{2}{\sqrt{3}}e^{-\pi Bt}\cos\left(\pi\sqrt{3}\,Bt + 30°\right)\right]u(t)$$

as plotted in Fig. 2.37*b* and *c*. The similarity to an ideal LPF is apparent. Figure 2.37*c* also shows that this filter has a narrower transition region than the simple RC LPF.

For the case of M reactive elements, the amplitude ratio of an Mth-order Butterworth is

$$|H(f)| = \left[1 + \left(\frac{f}{B}\right)^{2M}\right]^{-1/2} \tag{21}$$

which is said to be *maximally flat* since the first M derivatives of $|H(f)|$ are zero at $f = 0$. (Incidentally, the RC LPF is a first-order Butterworth.) Other types of filter designs are given in the literature.   ////

Bandlimiting and Timelimiting

Earlier we said that a signal $v(t)$ is *bandlimited* if there is a constant W such that

$$\mathscr{F}[v(t)] = 0 \qquad |f| > W \qquad (22)$$

i.e., the spectrum has no content outside $|f| < W$. Similarly, a *timelimited* signal has the property that, for the constants $t_1 < t_2$,

$$v(t) = 0 \qquad t < t_1 \text{ and } t > t_2 \qquad (23)$$

so the signal "starts" at time t_1 and "ends" at time t_2. Here we consider the meaning of these two definitions.

Ideal filters and bandlimited signals are concepts that go hand in hand. Indeed, passing an arbitrary signal through an ideal LPF produces a bandlimited signal at the output. But it has been seen that the impulse response of an ideal LPF is a sinc pulse existing for all time. We now assert that any signal emerging from an ideal LPF will exist for all time; stated another way, a bandlimited signal cannot be strictly timelimited. Conversely, a strictly timelimited signal cannot be bandlimited. In short, *bandlimiting and timelimiting are mutually incompatible*. A general proof of the assertion is difficult and will not be attempted here.† However, every transform pair encountered in this chapter is consistent therewith; e.g., see Figs. 2.13, 2.14, 2.17, 2.20.

This observation has implications for the signal and system models used in the study of communication systems. Since a signal cannot be simultaneously bandlimited and timelimited, we should either abandon bandlimited signals (and ideal filters) or accept signal models which exist for all time. But a physically real signal *is* strictly timelimited; it starts and it stops, or is turned on and off. On the other hand, the concept of bandlimited spectra is too powerful and appealing for engineering purposes to be dismissed entirely.

Fortunately, resolution of the dilemma is really not so difficult, requiring but a small compromise. Although a strictly timelimited signal is not strictly bandlimited, its spectrum can be *essentially* zero outside a certain frequency range, in the sense that the neglected frequency components contain an inconsequential portion of the total energy; e.g., consider $|f| \gg 1/\tau$ in the spectrum of a rectangular pulse. Similarly, a strictly bandlimited signal can be virtually zero outside a certain time interval; e.g., sinc $2Wt \approx 0$ for $|t| \gg 1/2W$. Therefore, it is not inappropriate to speak of signals that are both bandlimited and timelimited for most practical purposes.

---

† See Wozencraft and Jacobs (1965, app. 5B).

2.6 CORRELATION AND SPECTRAL DENSITY

In Sects. 2.3 and 2.4, two particular cases were observed. Nonperiodic energy signals were represented in the frequency domain by Fourier transforms that are continuous functions of frequency, free of impulses; the signal energy is

$$E = \int_{-\infty}^{\infty} |v(t)|^2 \, dt = \int_{-\infty}^{\infty} v(t)v^*(t) \, dt \tag{1}$$

and the *energy spectral density* $|V(f)|^2$ gives its distribution in frequency; the power averaged over all time is zero since E is finite. On the other hand, periodic power signals were represented in the frequency domain by impulsive spectra resulting from transforms in the limit; the average power is

$$P = \lim_{T \to \infty} \frac{1}{T} \int_{-T/2}^{T/2} |v(t)|^2 \, dt = \lim_{T \to \infty} \frac{1}{T} \int_{-T/2}^{T/2} v(t)v^*(t) \, dt \tag{2}$$

and the concept of energy spectral density does not apply since the total energy must be infinite when $P \neq 0$. However, it may be meaningful to speak of the distribution of power in the frequency domain, as described by a *power spectral density*.

The purpose of this section is to develop more fully the spectral density concept in a form that applies to both of the above cases as well as to the case of *random signals* — the latter anticipating the needs of Chap. 3. This generality is obtained at the price of using the somewhat abstract viewpoint of *signal space*, but the price is a worthwhile long-range investment that pays off now and in our future work. In the interest of getting to useful results as quickly as possible, many of the signal space derivations have been relegated to Appendix A, which the reader can consult for details omitted here.

Scalar Product, Norm, and Orthogonality

Let $v(t)$ and $w(t)$ be two signals of the same *class*, i.e., either energy type or power type. Their *scalar product* is a quantity — possibly complex — denoted† as $\langle v(t), w(t) \rangle$ and defined by

$$\langle v(t), w(t) \rangle \triangleq \begin{cases} \displaystyle\int_{-\infty}^{\infty} v(t)w^*(t) \, dt & \text{Energy signals} \quad (3a) \\[2ex] \displaystyle\lim_{T \to \infty} \frac{1}{T} \int_{-T/2}^{T/2} v(t)w^*(t) \, dt & \text{Power signals} \quad (3b) \end{cases}$$

† This notation is distinguished from $\langle v(t) \rangle$, the *time average* of $v(t)$; the scalar product symbol always has *two* functions separated by a comma.

If $v(t)$ and $w(t)$ happen to be periodic with period T_0, Eq. (3b) simplifies to

$$\langle v(t),w(t)\rangle = \frac{1}{T_0}\int_{T_0} v(t)w^*(t)\, dt \qquad \text{Periodic signals} \qquad (3c)$$

Another scalar product definition will be given in Chap. 3 covering the case of random signals. The value of the scalar product concept is that $\langle v(t),w(t)\rangle$ has certain invariant properties regardless of the specific definition.

Before stating some of those properties, note that the scalar product of $v(t)$ with itself equals either the energy E or power P. Generalizing, the *norm* of $v(t)$ is defined by

$$\|v\| \triangleq \langle v(t),v(t)\rangle^{1/2} \qquad (4)$$

a real nonnegative quantity, not to be confused with the function $|v(t)|$. Therefore

$$\|v\|^2 = \langle v(t), v(t)\rangle = \begin{cases} E & \text{Energy signals} \\ P & \text{Power signals} \end{cases} \qquad (5)$$

as follows from Eqs. (1) to (4).

Schwarz's inequality links Eqs. (3) and (4) in the form

$$|\langle v(t),w(t)\rangle| \le \|v\|\,\|w\| \qquad (6a)$$

which establishes an upper bound on the magnitude of the scalar product. The upper bound is achieved only when the two signals are directly proportional, i.e.,

$$|\langle v(t),w(t)\rangle| = \|v\|\,\|w\| \qquad \text{if } w(t) = \alpha v(t) \qquad (6b)$$

where α is an arbitrary constant. On the other hand, suppose that $v(t)$ and $w(t)$ are *orthogonal*, meaning

$$\langle v(t),w(t)\rangle = 0 \qquad (7)$$

Under this condition

$$\|v + w\|^2 = \|v\|^2 + \|w\|^2 \qquad (8)$$

proof of which is given in Appendix A along with the proof of Eq. (6).

In signal space theory, orthogonal signals are viewed as perpendicular vectors and Eq. (8) becomes equivalent to the pythagorean theorem. Here we interpret $\langle v(t),w(t)\rangle = 0$ as the condition for *superposition of energy or power*. For instance, suppose $v(t)$ and $w(t)$ are orthogonal energy signals with $E_v = \|v\|^2$ and $E_w = \|w\|^2$; then the signal $z(t) = v(t) + w(t)$ has energy $E_z = \|v + w\|^2$ which, from Eq. (8), equals $E_v + E_w$.

It is also useful to enumerate some specific relationships between the functions or waveforms $v(t)$ and $w(t)$ that result in their being orthogonal. Three different conditions under which $\langle v(t),w(t)\rangle = 0$ are:

1 When $v(t)$ and $w(t)$ have *opposite symmetry*, i.e., one is an even function and the other is odd.

2 When $v(t)$ and $w(t)$ are nonoverlapping or *disjoint in time*, i.e., one equals zero when the other is nonzero, and vice versa.

3 When $v(t)$ and $w(t)$ are *disjoint in frequency*, i.e., their spectra do not overlap.

The first two conditions are derived directly from Eq. (3); Eq. (13), Sect. 2.3, leads to the third. Bear in mind, however, that these are not the only relationships giving rise to orthogonality.

As a final point, note that the scalar product measures the degree of *similarity* between two signals. If they are proportional (i.e., similar), then $|\langle v(t),w(t)\rangle|$ is maximum; if they are orthogonal (i.e., dissimilar), then $\langle v(t),w(t)\rangle = 0$.

Correlation Functions

For any two signals of the same type, the *crosscorrelation* of $v(t)$ with $w(t)$ is defined† as

$$R_{vw}(\tau) \triangleq \langle v(t), w(t - \tau)\rangle \qquad (9)$$

a scalar product in which the second signal is displaced or shifted in time τ seconds. The displacement τ is arbitrary and, in fact, the crosscorrelation has τ as its independent variable, the time variable t having been washed out by the scalar product operation. By extension of the arguments just given, $R_{vw}(\tau)$ measures the similarity between $v(t)$ and $w(t - \tau)$ as a function of the displacement τ of $w(t)$ with respect to $v(t)$. Therefore, the crosscorrelation is a more comprehensive measure than the regular scalar product, for it detects any time-shifted similarities that would be ignored by $\langle v(t),w(t)\rangle$.

Now suppose we form the correlation of $v(t)$ with itself, i.e.,

$$R_v(\tau) \triangleq R_{vv}(\tau) = \langle v(t), v(t - \tau)\rangle \qquad (10)$$

which is called the *autocorrelation function*. Physically, autocorrelation has the same interpretation as crosscorrelation save that it compares a signal with itself displaced in time. But this means that $R_v(\tau)$ will tell us something about the *time variation* of $v(t)$, at least in an integrated or averaged sense. For instance, if $|R_v(\tau)|$ is large, then we infer that $v(t - \tau)$ is very similar (proportional) to $\pm v(t)$ for that particular value of τ; conversely, if $R_v(\tau) = 0$ for some value of τ, then we know that $v(t)$ and $v(t - \tau)$ are orthogonal. This interpretation presently is invoked in conjunction with the

---

† The definition $\langle v(t), w(t + \tau)\rangle$ is also used.

spectral density function. First, however, we need to list two mathematical properties of autocorrelation.

Applying Eqs. (5) and (6) to Eq. (10) yields

$$R_v(0) = \langle v(t), v(t) \rangle = \|v\|^2 \qquad (11a)$$

$$|R_v(\tau)| \le R_v(0) \qquad (11b)$$

so that $R_v(\tau)$ has a maximum at $\tau = 0$ where it equals the signal energy or power $\|v\|^2$. It can also be shown from Eqs. (3) and (10) that

$$R_v(-\tau) = R_v^*(\tau) \qquad (12)$$

Thus, if $v(t)$ is *real*, $R_v(\tau)$ is *real* and has *even symmetry*.

Consider now the sum of two signals, say $z(t) = v(t) + w(t)$, whose correlation is $R_z(\tau) = R_v(\tau) + R_{vw}(\tau) + R_{wv}(\tau) + R_w(\tau)$. If the component signals are *orthogonal for all* τ, i.e., if

$$R_{vw}(\tau) = R_{wv}(\tau) = 0 \qquad (13a)$$

then

$$R_z(\tau) = R_v(\tau) + R_w(\tau) \qquad (13b)$$

and, setting $\tau = 0$,

$$\|z\|^2 = \|v\|^2 + \|w\|^2 \qquad (13c)$$

In this case, the signals are said to be *incoherent* and we have superposition of correlation functions as well as superposition of energy or power.

Example 2.15   Autocorrelation of a Sinusoid

Let us calculate the autocorrelation of the periodic power signal

$$z(t) = A \cos(\omega_0 t + \theta) \qquad \omega_0 = 2\pi/T_0$$

While this may be done directly using Eqs. (3c) and (10), it is easier and more instructive to write

$$z(t) = \underbrace{\frac{A}{2} e^{j\theta} e^{j\omega_0 t}}_{v(t)} + \underbrace{\frac{A}{2} e^{-j\theta} e^{-j\omega_0 t}}_{w(t)}$$

This happens to be a better method for the case at hand because $v(t)$ and $w(t - \tau)$ are orthogonal for all τ—since they are disjoint in frequency—and, moreover, $w(t) = v^*(t)$. Thus, $R_{vw}(\tau) = R_{wv}(\tau) = 0$ and $R_w(\tau) = R_v^*(\tau)$, so Eq. (13b) becomes $R_z(\tau) = R_v(\tau) + R_v^*(\tau) = 2 \operatorname{Re}[R_v(\tau)]$. Incidentally, although not all problems can be simplified this much, the student should be alert to such possibilities.

Proceeding with the calculation, we have

$$R_v(\tau) = \frac{1}{T_0} \int_{T_0} \left[\frac{A}{2} e^{j\theta} e^{j\omega_0 t} \right] \left[\frac{A}{2} e^{-j\theta} e^{-j\omega_0(t-\tau)} \right] dt = \frac{A^2}{4} e^{j\omega_0 \tau} \qquad (14)$$

and hence

$$R_z(\tau) = 2 \text{ Re } [R_v(\tau)] = \frac{A^2}{2} \cos \omega_0 \tau \qquad (15)$$

so that $R_z(0) = A^2/2 = \|z\|^2$ as predicted. Note that the autocorrelation of a sinusoid is another sinusoid at the same frequency but in the "τ domain" rather than the time domain. The phase parameter θ has dropped out owing to the averaging effect of correlation. Because of this fact we conclude that the autocorrelation does not uniquely define a signal, e.g., all $z(t) = A \cos (\omega_0 t + \theta)$ have the same $R_z(\tau)$ regardless of θ. ////

EXERCISE 2.15 The autocorrelation of an energy signal is a type of *convolution* since replacing t with λ in Eq. (3a) gives

$$R_v(\tau) = \int_{-\infty}^{\infty} v(\lambda) v^*(\lambda - \tau) \, d\lambda = [v(\tau)] * [v^*(-\tau)] \qquad (16)$$

Use this to show that a rectangular pulse

$$v(t) = A\Pi\left(\frac{t}{T}\right) \qquad (17a)$$

has a triangular autocorrelation

$$R_v(\tau) = A^2 T \Lambda\left(\frac{\tau}{T}\right) \qquad (17b)$$

Underscoring the previously observed nonuniqueness, Eq. (17b) also holds when $v(t) = A\Pi[(t - t_d)/T]$ for any value of t_d.

Spectral Density Functions

In view of our observation that $R_v(\tau)$ gives information about the time-domain behavior of $v(t)$, it seems plausible to investigate the Fourier transform of $R_v(\tau)$ as a possible basis for frequency-domain analysis. Consider, therefore,

$$G_v(f) \triangleq \mathscr{F}[R_v(\tau)] = \int_{-\infty}^{\infty} R_v(\tau) e^{-j2\pi f \tau} \, d\tau \qquad (18a)$$

which is called the *spectral density function* for reasons soon explained. Having made this definition, it follows that $\mathscr{F}^{-1}[G_v(f)]$ equals $R_v(\tau)$, i.e.,

$$R_v(\tau) = \int_{-\infty}^{\infty} G_v(f)e^{-j2\pi f\tau} \, df \qquad (18b)$$

so we have the Fourier transform pair

$$R_v(\tau) \leftrightarrow G_v(f) \qquad (19)$$

where τ takes the place of t. Equation (19) bears the name of the *Wiener-Kinchine theorem*. In the special but important case where $v(t)$ is *real*, $G_v(f)$ is *real* and *even* since $R_v(\tau)$ is real and even.

The fundamental property of $G_v(f)$ is that integrating it over all frequency yields $\|v\|^2$, as is easily proved by setting $\tau = 0$ in Eq. (18b), i.e.,

$$\int_{-\infty}^{\infty} G_v(f) \, df = R_v(0) = \|v\|^2 \qquad (20)$$

To interpret this, and thereby justify the name of $G_v(f)$, we recall that $\|v\|^2$ is the energy or power associated with $v(t)$. Therefore, one can argue that $G_v(f)$ tells how the energy or power is distributed in the frequency domain and deserves being called the spectral density.

Supporting that view, let $v(t)$ be an energy signal and $V(f)$ its spectrum. From Eq. (16), $R_v(\tau) = [v(\tau)] * [v^*(-\tau)]$; so, invoking the convolution theorem,

$$G_v(f) = \mathscr{F}[R_v(\tau)] = \mathscr{F}[v(\tau)]\mathscr{F}[v^*(-\tau)]$$

Clearly, $\mathscr{F}[v(\tau)] = \mathscr{F}[v(t)] = V(f)$, and it is a routine exercise to show that $\mathscr{F}[v^*(-\tau)] = \{\mathscr{F}[v(t)]\}^* = V^*(f)$. Therefore,

$$G_v(f) = V(f)V^*(f) = |V(f)|^2 \qquad (21a)$$

which was identified in Sect. 2.3 as the *energy spectral density*. Inversion of Eq. (21a) gives

$$R_v(\tau) = \mathscr{F}^{-1}[|V(f)|^2] = \int_{-\infty}^{\infty} |V(f)|^2 e^{j2\pi f\tau} \, df \qquad (21b)$$

an alternate expression for the autocorrelation function of an energy signal. Furthermore, with $\tau = 0$,

$$\|v\|^2 = \int_{-\infty}^{\infty} |V(f)|^2 \, df \qquad (21c)$$

which, in retrospect, is just *Rayleigh's energy theorem*. The reader may wish to check the consistency of Eq. (21b) with Eq. (17).

Now consider a periodic power signal expressed in Fourier series form

$$v(t) = \sum_{n=-\infty}^{\infty} c_v(nf_0)e^{j2\pi nf_0t} \qquad f_0 = \frac{1}{T_0}$$

Using Eq. (14) and the fact that all terms in the series are mutually incoherent,

$$R_v(\tau) = \sum_{n=-\infty}^{\infty} |c_v(nf_0)|^2 e^{j2\pi nf_0\tau} \qquad (22a)$$

and Fourier transformation gives

$$G_v(f) = \sum_{n=-\infty}^{\infty} |c_v(nf_0)|^2 \delta(f-nf_0) \qquad (22b)$$

But is this the *power spectral density* of a periodic signal? The answer is clearly affirmative since a periodic signal can be decomposed into terms of the form $c_v(nf_0)e^{j2\pi nf_0t}$ each of which represents an amount of power equal to $|c_v(nf_0)|^2$ located exactly at the frequency $f = nf_0$. The spectral density is impulsive in this case simply because impulses are required to indicate that nonzero units of power are concentrated at discrete frequencies. Finally, integrating Eq. (22b) over all f—or simply setting $\tau = 0$ in Eq. (22a)—gives *Parseval's power theorem*.

To summarize, while we have not explicitly proved that $G_v(f)$ represents the spectral density for other types of signals, we have presented strong evidence in favor of that conclusion based on two cases where there is a firm intuitive notion of what the spectral density should be. Concluding this chapter, spectral density functions are used in conjunction with transfer functions to determine input-output relations. But before doing so, it must be pointed out that $G_v(f)$, like $R_v(\tau)$, does not uniquely represent $v(t)$. True, a given signal has only one spectral density function; however, that spectral density function may apply to other signals. Phase-shifted sinusoids and time-delayed rectangular pulses are simple examples. And in the case of random signals, two or more drastically different waveforms can have the same spectral density—meaning that their averages are the same even though the waveforms are different.

Input-Output Relations

As diagramed in Fig. 2.38, let $x(t)$ be the input to a linear time-invariant system having inpulse response $h(t)$ and transfer function $H(f)$. If it happens that $x(t)$ is an energy signal with spectrum $X(f)$, the output energy spectral density is

$$|Y(f)|^2 = |H(f)|^2 |X(f)|^2$$

or

$$G_y(f) = |H(f)|^2 G_x(f) \qquad (23)$$

since $G_x(f) = |X(f)|^2$ is the energy spectral density of the input, etc.

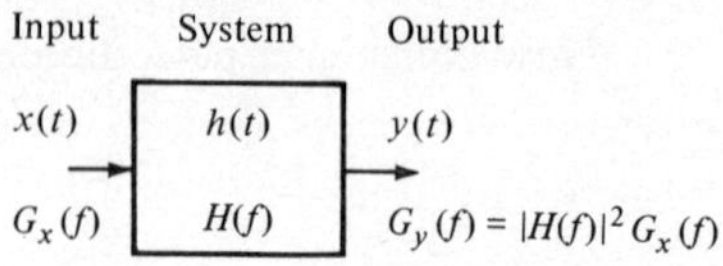

Input	System	Output
$x(t)$	$h(t)$	$y(t)$
$G_x(f)$	$H(f)$	$G_y(f) = \|H(f)\|^2 G_x(f)$

FIGURE 2.38

Although we derived Eq. (23) for energy signals, its form suggests that $|H(f)|^2$ always relates the input and output spectral density functions, irrespective of signal type. This, indeed, is true; Eq. (23) applies for any type of input whose spectral density function exists. The general proof is relatively straightforward but tedious, and will only be outlined here.

First, the autocorrelation $R_y(\tau)$ of the output is found by inserting

$$y(t) = \int_{-\infty}^{\infty} h(\lambda)x(t - \lambda)\, d\lambda$$

into $R_y(\tau) = \langle y(t), y(t - \tau)\rangle$. Upon manipulation, this yields the awesome expression

$$R_y(\tau) = \iint_{-\infty}^{\infty} h(\lambda)h^*(\mu)R_x(\tau + \mu - \lambda)\, d\mu\, d\lambda \tag{24}$$

where μ is another dummy variable. Then, taking the Fourier transform, one finally gets to

$$G_y(f) = \left[\int_{-\infty}^{\infty} h(\lambda)e^{-j2\pi f\lambda}\, d\lambda\right]\left[\int_{-\infty}^{\infty} h^*(\mu)e^{+j2\pi f\mu}\, d\mu\right]G_x(f)$$

so $G_y(f) = H(f)H^*(f)G_x(f)$, as asserted.

To reiterate the significance of this result, given an input signal of almost any type, the corresponding spectral density function at the output of a linear system is found by multiplying the input spectral density by $|H(f)|^2$. Having thus obtained $G_y(f)$, application of Eq. (20) gives the output signal's *energy* or *power* as

$$\|y\|^2 = \int_{-\infty}^{\infty} G_y(f)\, df = \int_{-\infty}^{\infty} |H(f)|^2 G_x(f)\, df \tag{25}$$

Often, especially in those problems involving random signals, $\|y\|^2$ is precisely the information being sought — and Eq. (25) offers the most direct route to that information. Other information about $y(t)$ may be gleaned from

$$R_y(\tau) = \mathscr{F}^{-1}[G_y(f)] = \int_{-\infty}^{\infty} |H(f)|^2 G_x(f)e^{j2\pi f\tau}\, df \tag{26}$$

Note, by the way, that this inverse transform is probably easier to deal with than Eq. (24).

Equation (23) also expedites spectral density calculations, whether or not filtering actually is involved. Suppose, for instance, that $w(t) = dv(t)/dt$, $G_v(f)$ is known, and one desires to find $G_w(f)$. Conceptually, $w(t)$ could be generated by passing $v(t)$ through an ideal differentiator, for which $H(f) = j2\pi f$—see Eq. (24), Sect. 2.3. Therefore, using Eq. (23), if

$$w(t) = \frac{dv(t)}{dt} \qquad (27a)$$

then

$$G_w(f) = (2\pi f)^2 G_v(f) \qquad (27b)$$

Likewise, if

$$w(t) = \int_{-\infty}^{t} v(\lambda)\, d\lambda \qquad (28a)$$

then

$$G_w(f) = (2\pi f)^{-2} G_v(f) \qquad (28b)$$

Further illustrations of the use of Eqs. (23), (25), and (26) are presented in the next chapter, as applied to random signals.

2.7 PROBLEMS

2.1   (Sect. 2.1) Use Eq. (9) to find $y(t)$ when $x(t) = 4 \cos 2\pi 10 t$ and $H(j\omega) = 15 + j(\omega/\pi)$. Ans.: $100 \cos (2\pi 10 t + 53°)$.

2.2   (Sect. 2.1) Find and sketch $|H(f)|$ and arg $[H(f)]$ for each of the following transfer functions:
(a) $(10 + jf)/(1 + jf)$
(b) $(1 + jf)/(10 + jf)$
(c) $(1 - jf)/(1 + jf)$

2.3   (Sect. 2.1) If the capacitor in Fig. 2.6a is replaced by an inductor, show that $H(f) = j(f/B)/[1 + j(f/B)]$ where $B = R/2\pi L$. Sketch the amplitude ratio and phase shift.

2.4   (Sect. 2.1) Referring to Fig. 2.6a, suppose $x(t) = 10 \cos 2\pi f_0 t$ and the filter has $B = 3$ kHz. If $A_y = 2$, what is the value of f_0?

2.5   (Sect. 2.2) Find $\langle v(t) \rangle$ and P for $v(t) = Ae^{j(\omega_0 t + \theta)}$. Ans.: 0, A^2.

2.6   (Sect. 2.2) Find $\langle v(t) \rangle$ and P for the full-rectified sinusoid $v(t) = A|\sin 2\pi t/T_0|$.

2.7   (Sect. 2.2) When $v(-t) = v(t)$, show that

$$c(nf_0) = \frac{2}{T_0} \int_0^{T_0/2} v(t) \cos 2\pi n f_0 t\, dt$$

and use this to prove Eq. (11). Carry out a similar analysis for $v(-t) = -v(t)$.

2.8   (Sect. 2.2) Calculate $c(nf_0)$ for a periodic triangular wave having $v(t) = A(1 - 4|t|/T_0)$, $|t| \leq T_0/2$. (*Hint*: See Prob. 2.7.)

2.9   (Sect. 2.2) Calculate $c(nf_0)$ for the *full-rectified wave* in Prob. 2.6. *Ans.*: $c(nf_0) = 2A/\pi(1 - n^2)$, n even; $c(nf_0) = 0$, n odd.

2.10   (Sect. 2.2) Use Eqs. (16) and (17) to compare the spectrum of a square wave with a rectangular pulse train having $f_0\tau = \frac{1}{2}$.

2.11   (Sect. 2.2) Suppose all frequency components at $|f| > 1/\tau$ are removed from the spectrum of a rectangular pulse train. Use Parseval's theorem to calculate the percentage power that remains when $f_0\tau = \frac{1}{2}$ and when $f_0\tau = \frac{1}{5}$.

2.12   (Sect. 2.2) Referring to Example 2.3, calculate the amplitude of the output sinusoidal component at $2f_0$ when $N = 3$, $f_r = 3f_0$, and $Q = 12$. Compare with the amplitude of the $3f_0$ component.

2.13   (Sect. 2.2) A full-rectified wave (Prob. 2.9) with $f_0 = 60$ Hz is the input to an RC lowpass filter. Find the value of B such that the amplitude of the largest output sinusoidal component is 10 percent of the DC component. *Ans.*: 18.2 Hz.

2.14   (Sect. 2.3) Find $V(f)$ for the *gaussian pulse* $v(t) = Ae^{-\pi(t/\tau)^2}$, and verify the reciprocal-spreading effect by sketching $v(t)$ and $V(f)$ for $\tau = 2$ and $\tau = 1$. *Ans.*: $A\tau e^{-\pi(f\tau)^2}$.

2.15   (Sect. 2.3) Find $V(f)$ for the *cosine pulse* $v(t) = A \cos \pi t/\tau$, $|t| \leq \tau/2$, expressing your answer in terms of the sinc function. Sketch $|V(f)|$.

2.16   (Sect. 2.3) Prove Eq. (13) by replacing $v(t)$ with the integral expression for $\mathscr{F}^{-1}[V(f)]$.

2.17   (Sect. 2.3) Use Rayleigh's theorem to calculate the percentage of the total energy of an exponential pulse (Example 2.5) that is contained in $|f| \leq 1/2T$ and $|f| \leq 1/T$.

2.18   (Sect. 2.3) Using the superposition and time-delay theorems, find the transforms of the signals shown in Fig. P2.1. Sketch the amplitude spectra taking $\tau \ll T$.

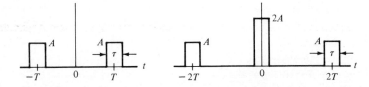

FIGURE P2.1

2.19   (Sect. 2.3) Find $Z(f)$ in terms of $V(f)$ when $z(t) = v(at - t_d)$. *Ans.*: $|a|^{-1}V(f/a)$ $\times e^{-j\omega t_d/a}$.

2.20   (Sect. 2.3) Use the duality theorem to find the transform of $A/[1 + (at)^2]$. (*Hint*: See Table A.)

2.21   (Sect. 2.3) Generate a new transform pair by applying duality to Example 2.8.

2.22   (Sect. 2.3) Prove the frequency-translation theorem, Eq. (21).

2.23   (Sect. 2.3) Use the modulation theorem to find the transform of $Ae^{-t/T}u(t) \sin \omega_c t$.

2.24   (Sect. 2.3) Use the differentiation theorem and Prob. 2.14 to find the transform of $Ate^{-\pi(t/\tau)^2}$.

2.25   (Sect. 2.4) Find $v * w(t)$ when $v(t) = e^{-t}u(t)$ and $w(t) = \Pi(t/2T)$. *Ans.*: 0 for $t < -T$, $1 - e^{-(t+T)}$ for $-T < t < T$, $e^{-(t-T)} - e^{-(t+T)}$ for $t > T$.

2.26 (Sect. 2.4) Find $v * v * v$ when $v(t) = \Pi(t/\tau)$.

2.27 (Sect. 2.4) If $v_1(t) \leftrightarrow V_1(f)$, etc., find $V(f)$ for:

(a) $v(t) = [v_1(t) + v_2(t)] * v_3(t)$

(b) $v(t) = [v_1(t)v_2(t)] * v_3(t)$

(c) $v(t) = [v_1 * v_2(t)]v_3(t)$

2.28 (Sect. 2.4) Use the convolution theorem to find the transform of the trapezoidal pulse in Fig. 2.22b. Sketch the amplitude spectrum taking $\tau_1 = 2\tau_2$.

2.29 (Sect. 2.4) Prove Eq. (5).

2.30 (Sect. 2.4) Evaluate or simplify each of the following:

(a) $\int_{-\infty}^{\infty} t^2 \delta(t - 3) \, dt$

(b) $[t^2] * [\delta(t - 3)]$

(c) $t^2 \delta(t - 3)$

(d) $[t^2] * [\delta(3t)]$

2.31 (Sect. 2.4) Use Eq. (21) and the time-delay theorem to find $c_w(nf_0)$ in terms of $c_v(nf_0)$ when $w(t) = v(t - t_d)$.

2.32 (Sect. 2.4) The signal in Fig. 2.16 can be written as the convolution of $A\Pi(t/\tau)$ with $\delta(t + \tau/2) - \delta(t - \tau/2)$. Use this approach to obtain $Z(f)$.

2.33 (Sect. 2.4) Use the approach suggested in Prob. 2.32 to do Prob. 2.18.

2.34 (Sect. 2.4) The differentiation theorem can be written in the form

$$V(f) = (j2\pi f)^{-n} \mathscr{F}\left[\frac{d^n v(t)}{dt^n}\right]$$

which sometimes simplifies transform calculations. Specifically, if the nth derivative of $v(t)$ consists entirely of simple functions (impulses, rectangular pulses, etc.), then $\mathscr{F}[d^n v/dt^n]$ is easily found and $V(f)$ found from it. The best value of n is the lowest derivative in which impulses first appear, and it is helpful to sketch $v(t)$, dv/dt, etc., so that discontinuities — which become impulses when differentiated — are detected. Use this method to find the transform of $v(t) = 2At\,\Pi(t/\tau)$. *Ans.*: $(jA\tau/\pi f)(\cos \pi f\tau - \operatorname{sinc} f\tau)$.

2.35 (Sect. 2.4) Use the method of Prob. 2.34 to find the transform of $A[1 - (2t/\tau)^2]\Pi(t/\tau)$.

2.36 (Sect. 2.5) A given system has impulse response $h(t)$ and transfer function $H(f)$. Obtain expressions for $y(t)$ and $Y(f)$ when:

(a) $x(t) = A\delta(t - t_d)$

(b) $x(t) = A[\delta(t + t_d) - \delta(t - t_d)]$

2.37 (Sect. 2.5) Do Prob. 2.36 for the case of $x(t) = Ah(t - t_d)$.

2.38 (Sect. 2.5) The input to an RC lowpass filter is $x(t) = \operatorname{sinc} 2Wt$. Plot the energy ratio E_y/E_x as a function of B/W.

2.39 (Sect. 2.5) A rectangular pulse of duration τ is the input to a zero-order hold, Example 2.13. Use the approach of Example 2.12 to find $y(t)$ when $\tau \ll T$, $\tau = T$, and $\tau \gg T$.

2.40 (Sect. 2.5) The signal $x(t) = \Pi(t/\tau) + \Pi(t/\tau) \cos \omega_c t$ with $\tau = 1,000/f_c$ is applied to an RC lowpass filter with $B = 200$ Hz. Use the approach of Example 2.12 to find $y(t)$ when $f_c = 1$ kHz, $f_c = 10$ kHz, and $f_c = 1$ MHz.

2.41 (Sect. 2.5) Find $H(f)$ and $h(t)$ for the system diagramed in Fig. P2.2. *Ans.*: $h(t) =$ $T\Lambda[(t-T)/T]$.

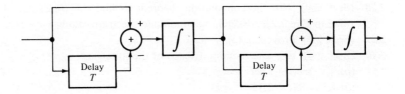

FIGURE P2.2

2.42 (Sect. 2.5) Each of the blocks marked ZOH in Fig. P2.3 are zero-order holds. Find $H(f)$ for the entire system.

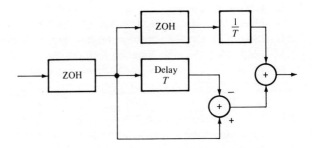

FIGURE P2.3

2.43 (Sect. 2.5) Let the *transition region* of an LPF be defined as the positive-frequency range between the 3-dB and 10-dB bandwidths. Find this region for an RC LPF and express it as a percentage of the 3-dB bandwidth. *Ans.*: 200 percent.

2.44 (Sect. 2.5) Repeat Prob. 2.43 for a *gaussian LPF* with $H(f) = K \exp[-(\ln 2/2)(f/B)^2]$, first showing that B is the 3-dB bandwidth. Is this a better filter than an RC LPF?

2.45 (Sect. 2.5) The transfer function of an *ideal HPF* can be written as $H(f) = K e^{-j\omega t_d}$ $[1 - \Pi(f/2f_{co})]$ where f_{co} is the cutoff frequency. Find the impulse response and identify the precursor.

2.46 (Sect. 2.5) How many reactive elements must a Butterworth filter (Example 2.14) have such that the 1-dB bandwidth is at least $0.9\ B$?

2.47 (Sect. 2.5) Find the sketch $|H(f)|$ for the LPF in Fig. P2.4. Compare with a second-order Butterworth.

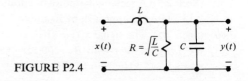

FIGURE P2.4

2.48   (Sect. 2.6) Given the energy signals $v(t) = A\Pi(t/\tau)$ and $w(t) = Bt^2\Pi(t/\tau)$, find $\|v\|^2$, $\|w\|^2$, $\langle v(t), w(t)\rangle$, and confirm Schwarz's inequality. *Ans.*: $\|v\|^2 = A^2\tau$, $\|w\|^2 = B^2\tau^5/80$, $\langle v(t), w(t)\rangle = AB\tau^3/12$.

2.49   (Sect. 2.6) By inspection, state the conditions on α such that each of the following pairs of signals are orthogonal:

    (a) $\Pi(t/\tau)$, $\Pi[(t - \alpha)/\tau]$

    (b) sinc $2Wt$, sinc $2Wt \cos 2\pi\alpha t$

    (c) $e^{-|t|}$, t^α

2.50   (Sect. 2.6) If $v(t)$ and $w(t)$ are complex energy signals, show that $R_{wv}(\tau) = R_{vw}^*(-\tau)$.

2.51   (Sect. 2.6) Confirm the assertion in Example 2.15 that $v(t)$ and $w(t - \tau)$ are orthogonal for all τ.

2.52   (Sect. 2.6) Find the autocorrelation of $A \cos(\omega_0 t + \theta) + B$. (*Hint*: First show that the two terms are orthogonal.)

2.53   (Sect. 2.6) Use Eq. (21) to find $G_v(f)$ and $R_v(\tau)$ for the following energy signals:

    (a) A sinc $2Wt$

    (b) $Ae^{-t/T}u(t)$

2.54   (Sect. 2.6) The gaussian pulse $x(t) = 3e^{-\pi(10t)^2}$ (Prob. 2.14) is applied to a gaussian filter with $H(f) = e^{-\pi(f/5)^2}$. Find and sketch $R_x(\tau)$, $G_x(f)$, $G_y(f)$, and $R_y(\tau)$, and evaluate $\|y\|^2/\|x\|^2$.

2.55   (Sect. 2.6) The energy signal $x(t) = A$ sinc $2Wt$ is applied to an RC LPF with bandwidth B. Find $G_y(f)$ and obtain approximate expressions for $R_y(\tau)$ when $W \ll B$ and $W \gg B$.

2.56   (Sect. 2.6) Derive Eq. (23) by taking the Fourier transform of $R_y(\tau)$, Eq. (24).

3

RANDOM SIGNALS AND NOISE

The signals dealt with in the last chapter were *deterministic signals*; i.e., writing an explicit time function $v(t)$ presumes that the behavior of a signal is known or determined for all time. On the other hand, one characteristic of a *random signal* is that its behavior cannot be predicted in advance. In this sense, and particularly from the receiving-end viewpoint, all meaningful communication signals are random; for if the signal were known beforehand, there would be no point in transmitting it. Stated another way, a known signal conveys no information, an observation which is the keystone of information theory and which will be returned to in Chap. 9. In this chapter, however, the primary emphasis is on *unwanted* random signals or *noise*. Because noise is present in every communication system, it must be included in any realistic description of the system performance.

Our purpose here is to develop mathematical representations or models of random signals for later use. And because such signals cannot be expressed as explicit functions of time, additional analytic techniques are required. In particular, when examined over a long period, a random signal may exhibit certain regularities that are best described in terms of probabilities and statistical averages. Thus, lacking an exact description, we speak instead of average values and the probability that a random signal will be in a given range at some specific time.

This chapter therefore begins with the elementary concepts of probability theory. Random variables and their statistical description are then introduced, with emphasis on the random signal interpretation. Having obtained a statistical description, we relate it to the frequency domain by means of autocorrelation functions and the Wiener-Kinchine theorem. Finally, the properties of white noise and filtered noise are examined in some detail.

Keeping within the objectives of this text, the coverage of probability and statistics is directed specifically toward those aspects that will be used in later chapters. Furthermore, we shall rely heavily on intuitive reasoning rather than mathematical rigor. Those wishing to pursue the subject in more detail will find a wealth of material in the literature.†

3.1 INTRODUCTION TO PROBABILITIES

Probability theory is a mathematical approach to random phenomena. Because random means unpredictable, learning something about such a phenomenon requires experimental observation of its manifestations. Indeed, the language of probability theory is couched in terms of experiments and their outcomes; and this is the approach we shall take to define the concept of probability.

Consider an experiment whose outcome varies from trial to trial and is unknown in advance, called a *random experiment*. Let the event A be one of the possible outcomes. Tossing a coin is such an experiment, the possible outcomes being heads and tails. The experiment is repeated n times and n_A, the number of times A occurred, is recorded. The ratio n_A/n is the *relative frequency of occurrence* of the event A for that particular set of experiments or trials. Now if the experiment has statistical regularity, then n_A/n may approach some definite value as n becomes very large; i.e., further increase in n causes no significant change in n_A/n. Assuming that a unique limiting value exists, we define $P(A)$, the probability of the event A, as the relative frequency in the limit as $n \to \infty$,

$$P(A) \triangleq \lim_{n \to \infty} \frac{n_A}{n} \qquad (1)$$

Thus the assumption of statistical regularity leads intuitively to our definition of probability. From the definition, it is clear that a probability P is a positive number bounded by

$$0 \leq P \leq 1 \qquad (2)$$

† E.g., Papoulis (1965), Beckmann (1967), Drake (1967), Thomas (1969).

The experimentally confirmed fact that n_A/n may approach a constant as the number of trials increases is called the *empirical law of large numbers*. The crucial phrase here is "large numbers," for it is only in the context of a large number of repetitions that probability becomes meaningful. For example, if a coin is tossed 10 times, heads may come up 7 times, $n_H/n = 0.7$. But we feel certain that as n is increased, $n_H/n \to 0.5$ if the coin is honest. This feeling is expressed in the familiar statement that "the chance of heads is 50 percent."

In many cases, such as tossing an honest coin, it is possible to calculate probabilities on the basis of symmetry conditions, etc., without actually performing an experiment. In a sense, the experiments are done mentally. But if the coin is biased, by virtue of uneven wear or intentional weighting, the probabilities would require actual empirical determination. A third case arises when the coin's honesty is unknown and one is forced to estimate a probability, say of heads, without the aid of experimentation. Lacking further information, the only logical guess would be $P(H) = \frac{1}{2}$ since there is no evidence that heads is more or less likely than tails. (This rather simple-minded approach is sometimes useful, and has been given the refined name *the principle of insufficient reason*.)

EXERCISE 3.1   Toss an honest coin N times (until you get tired) and plot n_H/n versus n.

Mutually Exclusive Events

Now consider an experiment which has m *mutually exclusive* outcomes, $A_1, A_2, \ldots, A_m$, where by mutually exclusive we mean that the occurrence of any one outcome A_j prohibits the simultaneous occurrence of any other outcome. We then ask: What is the probability of A_1 or A_2 on a given trial? The probability is written as $P(A_1 + A_2)$. If $n_1 + n_2$ is the number of occurrences of A_1 or A_2 in n trials, then

$$P(A_1 + A_2) = \lim_{n \to \infty} \frac{n_1 + n_2}{n} = P(A_1) + P(A_2)$$

where $P(A_1) = \lim_{n \to \infty} (n_1/n)$, etc. By direct extension to two or more outcomes

$$P(A_i + A_j + A_k + \cdots) = P(A_i) + P(A_j) + P(A_k) + \cdots \tag{3}$$

and if all the possible outcomes are included,

$$P(A_1 + A_2 + \cdots + A_m) = \sum_{j=1}^{m} P(A_j) = 1 \tag{4}$$

Equation (4) merely reflects the fact that, on a given trial, one of the possible outcomes must occur. If all the outcomes have equal probabilities, in which case they are said to be *equally likely*, then

$$P(A_j) = \frac{1}{m} \qquad (5)$$

It must be emphasized that Eqs. (3) to (5) apply only to mutually exclusive events.

On occasion we shall be interested not in the occurrence of the event A but in its *nonoccurrence*. For convenience we designate A^c, read "A complement," as the event *not A*, similar to the corresponding terms of Boolean algebra. Obviously A and A^c are mutually exclusive, and, on a given trial, one or the other must occur. Applying Eq. (4), $P(A) + P(A^c) = 1$, or

$$P(A^c) = 1 - P(A) \qquad (6)$$

which is true in general.

Example 3.1

To illustrate some of these ideas, suppose two honest coins are tossed together. There are four mutually exclusive and equally likely outcomes, HH, HT, TH, TT (note that TH and HT are considered to be different outcomes). Since the number of equally likely outcomes is $m = 4$, the probability of any one is $\frac{1}{4}$. Thus $P(HH) = \frac{1}{4}$, and, using complements, $P(\text{not } HH) = 1 - \frac{1}{4} = \frac{3}{4}$. Two of the outcomes give a *match*, so $P(\text{match}) = P(HH) + P(TT) = \frac{1}{2}$.   ////

Joint and Conditional Probabilities

In the above example, we spoke of some events that were not identical to the basic outcomes of the experiment, e.g., "match" and "not HH." This is often a useful practice but does have a danger in that the derived events may not be mutually exclusive. For instance, the derived events "not HH" and "match" can occur simultaneously if the outcome is TT. To deal with events that are not mutually exclusive, we must speak in terms of *joint probability*, the probability of the joint occurrence of two (or more) events.

Consider the events A and B, which may or may not occur together, and let their joint probability be $P(AB)$. We repeat the experiment n times, where n is very large, and record n_{AB}, the number of times A and B occur together. The joint probability is thus

$$P(AB) = \frac{n_{AB}}{n}$$

In this process A has occurred n_A times, with or without B, so n_A includes n_{AB} and $n_A \geq n_{AB}$.

It is quite possible that the occurrence of B depends in some way on the occurrence of A. To include such additional information we define the *conditional probability* $P(B|A)$, the probability of B given that A has occurred. Again applying the relative-frequency definition to the n_A trials in which A occurs,

$$P(B|A) = \frac{n_{AB}}{n_A} = \frac{n_{AB}/n}{n_A/n} = \frac{P(AB)}{P(A)} \tag{7a}$$

Since n_{BA} is the same as n_{AB}, reversing the argument yields

$$P(A|B) = \frac{P(AB)}{P(B)} \tag{7b}$$

Combining Eqs. (7a) and (7b) gives two relations for the joint probability

$$P(AB) = P(B|A)P(A) = P(A|B)P(B) \tag{8}$$

When Eq. (8) is written in the form

$$P(B|A) = \frac{P(B)P(A|B)}{P(A)}$$

it is known as *Bayes' theorem*, and plays an important role in statistical decision theory.

Statistically Independent Events

Suppose the event B is independent of A, so the occurrence of A does not influence the occurrence of B, and vice versa. Symbolically, $P(B|A) = P(B)$ and $P(A|B) = P(A)$. Thus, using Eq. (8), two events are said to be *statistically independent* if

$$P(AB) = P(A)P(B) \tag{9}$$

Note carefully that statistical independence is quite different from mutual exclusiveness. In fact, if A and B are mutually exclusive, then $P(AB) = 0$ by definition.

It is a simple matter to extend Eq. (9) to more than two events. Thus, if A, B, C, ... are all statistically independent, the probability of their joint occurrence is

$$P(ABC\cdots) = P(A)P(B)P(C)\cdots \tag{10}$$

which the reader should contrast with Eq. (3).

Example 3.2

Continuing Example 3.1, let A designate the event "not HH" and B designate "match"; $P(A) = \frac{3}{4}$ and $P(B) = \frac{1}{2}$. The joint event AB is "match and not HH," which must be TT. Therefore $P(AB) = \frac{1}{4}$ and

$$P(B|A) = \frac{\frac{1}{4}}{\frac{3}{4}} = \frac{1}{3} \qquad P(A|B) = \frac{\frac{1}{4}}{\frac{1}{2}} = \frac{1}{2}$$

(Do these results agree with intuitive calculations?) The reader should also note that in this example $P(B|A) < P(B)$ while $P(B|A^c) = 1 > P(B)$.

Obviously A and B are not statistically independent, since

$$P(A)P(B) = \tfrac{3}{8} \neq P(AB)$$

But the coins themselves are statistically independent, if tossed in a fair manner, and Eq. (9) can be applied to the calculations of Example 3.1.   ////

EXERCISE 3.2 An honest coin is tossed three times. Evaluate the following probabilities: $P(HTH)$, $P(2$ heads and 1 tail$)$, $P($more heads than tails$)$, $P($more heads than tails$|$at least one tail$)$. *Ans.*: $(\tfrac{1}{2})^3$, $3 \times (\tfrac{1}{2})^3$, $4 \times (\tfrac{1}{2})^3$, $3 \times (\tfrac{1}{2})^3/7 \times (\tfrac{1}{2})^3$.

3.2 RANDOM VARIABLES AND PROBABILITY FUNCTIONS

The various games of chance — matching coins, playing cards, etc. — are natural and fascinating subjects for probability calculations. But in the study of communications, we are more concerned with random experiments or processes that have *numerical* outcomes, e.g., the value of a noise voltage at some instant of time or the number of errors in a digital data message. The description and analysis of such *numerical-valued random phenomena* are greatly facilitated by speaking of random variables and probability functions.

Consider a random process or experiment where the result of any one observation is expressed as a single numerical quantity. The totality of *all* possible outcomes forms a set of real numbers $x_1, x_2, \ldots, x_j, \ldots$, and the x_j's can be thought of as points on the real line $-\infty < x < +\infty$. The possible results of this process are thus encompassed by a one-dimensional space (i.e., a line) called the *sample space*. The various points in the sample space represent mutually exclusive events since $x_i \neq x_j$.

A variable is then assigned to the process representing the outcome of a given observation and is called a *random variable* or *variate*. The random variable X therefore may assume any of the possible values of the process with which it is associated. In other words, X is the general symbol for *observed* values, whereas x_j represents the *possible* values.

In this sense, the random-variable concept leads to a useful shorthand notation, for if the process has statistical regularity, we can describe it by *probability functions* succinctly defined in terms of X. To illustrate, the probability that an observed value is greater than x_k but less than or equal to x_l is written $P(x_k < X \leq x_l)$, which is a function of x_k and x_l — but not X. Curiously, probability functions defined using the random-variable approach are *not* functions of the random variable.

Depending on the nature of the process, a random variable may assume discrete or continuous values. If, in any finite interval of the real line, X can assume only a finite number of distinct values, it is called a *discrete* random variable. (This definition does not preclude an infinite number of discrete values, but in a *finite* range the number must be *finite*.) On the other hand, if X can take on *any* value in a given range of the real line, it is said to be a *continuous* random variable. A random process is often classified according to the type of variate associated with it. We shall give separate attention to both types, emphasizing the continuous, after a brief discussion of probability distribution functions.

Distribution Functions

The cumulative distribution function (CDF) of a random process is defined as

$$F(x) \triangleq P(X \leq x) \tag{1}$$

$F(x)$ is simply the probability that an observed value will be less than or equal to the quantity x and applies to either continuous or discrete processes. Since it is a probability, the CDF is bounded by

$$0 \leq F(x) \leq 1 \tag{2}$$

Other properties of $F(x)$ are obtained from the following consideration.

For $x_1 < x_2$, the *events* $X \leq x_1$ and $x_1 < X \leq x_2$ are mutually exclusive, and the event $X \leq x_2$ is the combination of the two, that is, $X \leq x_2$ implies $X \leq x_1$ or $x_1 < X \leq x_2$. (Note the importance of *open* and *closed* inequalities for specifying events.) From Eq. (3), Sect. 3.1, we have

$$P(X \leq x_2) = P(X \leq x_1) + P(x_1 < X \leq x_2)$$

or

$$P(x_1 < X \leq x_2) = F(x_2) - F(x_1) \tag{3}$$

Thus, if the distribution function is known for all values of x, the various probabilities associated with the random variable are completely known.

Since probabilities are nonnegative and Eq. (3) is a probability for any $x_1 < x_2$, we conclude that the CDF is always a *nondecreasing function of x*. Analytically, $dF(x)/dx \geq 0$. Combining this observation with Eq. (2) gives $F(-\infty) = 0$ and $F(+\infty) = 1$.

If we were concerned just with probabilities, the cumulative distribution function of a random process would be a complete and convenient description. However, when it comes to statistical averages, $F(x)$ is less useful than other probability functions that take account of whether the process is of the discrete or continuous type.

Discrete Random Variables — Frequency Functions

A discrete random variable can be described by the *frequency function*

$$P(x_j) \triangleq P(X = x_j)$$

where x_j is one of the discrete values that X may assume and $P(X = x_j)$ is its probability. The frequency function is therefore a function of the possible values x_j; the name stems from the relative-frequency interpretation of probability.

Relating frequency function and distribution function, we note that the x_j's are mutually exclusive, so

$$F(x) = \sum_{x_j \leq x} P(x_j) \qquad (4)$$

If there are m possible outcomes all told, then

$$\sum_{j=1}^{m} P(x_j) = 1$$

i.e., one of the possible outcomes must occur on a given observation.

Further inspection of Eq. (4) reveals several interesting points with respect to distribution functions. Let x_{k-1} and x_k be two *adjacent* possible outcomes. Then

$$F(x_k) - F(x_{k-1}) = \sum_{j=1}^{k} P(x_j) - \sum_{j=1}^{k-1} P(x_j) = P(x_k)$$

which should be obvious from Eq. (3). It then follows that the CDF of a discrete random variable has *stepwise discontinuities* at every $x = x_j$, the "height" of the step being $P(x_j)$. Between steps $F(x)$ is constant. At a discontinuity point the value of $F(x = x_j)$ is taken as the value to the right of $x = x_j$, the larger value.

Example 3.3

Suppose a digital data message consisting of four digits is transmitted over a system whose error probability per digit is known to equal 0.3. We let X be the *total* number of errors observed in the received message, so the possible outcomes are $x_j = 0, 1, \ldots,$ 4 errors. The frequency function $P(x_j)$ and the values of $F(x)$ at $x = x_j$ are tabulated below. A technique for obtaining these probabilities is given in the next section; for

x_j	$P(x_j)$	$F(x_j)$
0	0.2401	0.2401
1	0.4116	0.6517
2	0.2646	0.9163
3	0.0756	0.9919
4	0.0081	1.0000

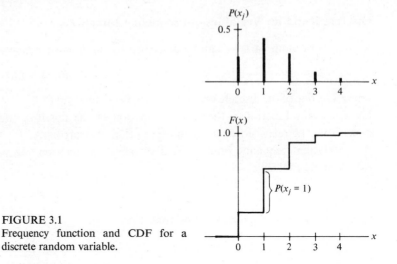

FIGURE 3.1
Frequency function and CDF for a discrete random variable.

the moment we are interested in $F(x)$ as shown in Fig. 3.1 along with $P(x_j)$. The figure nicely demonstrates the properties of CDFs, both the general properties and the discontinuous characteristic when the variate is discrete. A careful examination of the figure is recommended.   ////

EXERCISE 3.3 Suppose three honest coins are tossed and X is designated as the total number of heads that turn up. Calculate and plot $P(x_j)$ and $F(x)$.

Continuous Random Variables — Density Functions

To have something definite to talk about, suppose coins are tossed at a line drawn on the floor, a popular pastime among schoolboys known as penny pitching. The distance from coin to line is a random number that may be any value, positive or negative, within reasonable limits, and we can assign to the process a *continuous* random variable whose range is essentially $[-\infty, +\infty]$.

Whether or not the variate's range is bounded, in the continuum of the range there is an uncountably infinite number of possible values, and distinction between "adjacent" values clearly is impossible. (In contrast, adjacent values of a *discrete* variate are uniquely identifiable, a property implied in the definition of frequency function.) Therefore, the description of continuous variates in terms of frequency function is unsatisfactory. Indeed, even if x_1 is a possible outcome of a continuous random process, $P(X = x_1)$ is usually zero except in certain special cases. The reader who questions this assertion should consider the probability of a tossed coin's landing *exactly* 1 centimeter from the line.

Although $P(X = x_1) = 0$ for any x_1, the coin must land somewhere, and we can speak of such events as $X \leq x_1$ or $x_1 < X \leq x_2$ if $x_1 < x_2$. In short, the CDF description is still valid for continuous variates. And so is its derivative, which turns out to be a better description. Specifically, we define the *probability density function* (PDF)

$$p(x) \triangleq \frac{dF(x)}{dx} \qquad (5a)$$

Then, recalling that $F(-\infty) = 0$,

$$F(x) = \int_{-\infty}^{x} p(\lambda)\, d\lambda = P(X \leq x) \qquad (5b)$$

In words, the *area* under the PDF from $-\infty$ to x is the probability that an observed value will be less than or equal to x.

From Eq. (5) and the known properties of $F(x)$, PDFs are seen to have the following properties:†

$$p(x) = \frac{dF(x)}{dx} \geq 0$$

$$\int_{-\infty}^{\infty} p(x)\, dx = 1 \qquad (6)$$

$$P(x_1 < X \leq x_2) = F(x_2) - F(x_1) = \int_{x_1}^{x_2} p(x)\, dx \qquad (7)$$

Thus, $p(x)$ is a *nonnegative* function whose area from x_1 to x_2 is simply the probability of X being observed in this range. Since X must be found somewhere in $[-\infty, \infty]$, the total area under $p(x)$ is unity.

As a special case of Eq. (7), let $x_1 = x - dx$ and $x_2 = x$; the integral then reduces to $p(x)\, dx$ so

$$p(x)\, dx = P(x - dx < X \leq x) \qquad (8)$$

This equation provides another and very useful interpretation of $p(x)$ and emphasizes its nature as a probability *density*.

---

† Note that a dummy variable λ must be used in Eq. (5b) — since the integral is a function of x — but not in Eqs. (6) and (7).

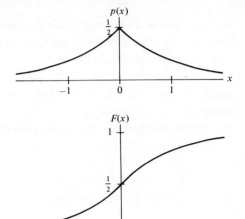

FIGURE 3.2
PDF and CDF for a continuous random
variable.

Example 3.4

Suppose the PDF of a continuous variate is known to be of the form $p(x) = Ke^{-|x|}$, where K is an unknown constant. To evaluate K, we invoke the unit-area property, Eq. (6); thus, observing that $p(x)$ has even symmetry,

$$\int_{-\infty}^{\infty} p(x)\, dx = 2 \int_{0}^{\infty} Ke^{-x}\, dx = 2K = 1$$

Therefore $K = \frac{1}{2}$ and

$$p(x) = \tfrac{1}{2} e^{-|x|} \qquad (9a)$$

The corresponding CDF is

$$F(x) = \begin{cases} \tfrac{1}{2} e^{x} & x \le 0 \\ 1 - \tfrac{1}{2} e^{-x} & x > 0 \end{cases} \qquad (9b)$$

as found using Eq. (5b). Figure 3.2 shows $p(x)$ and $F(x)$. Both of these functions are smooth and continuous, as they must be when the variate is continuous rather than discrete. ////

Impulses in PDFs

Sometimes a continuous variate X has a discrete component in the sense that there is a particular discrete-valued outcome, say x_0, for which $P(X = x_0) \ne 0$. In this case $p(x)$ must include an *impulse*, namely, $P(x_0)\delta(x - x_0)$ and $F(x)$ will have a stepwise discontinuity of height $P(x_0)$ at $x = x_0$.

By the same reasoning, we can construct a PDF from the frequency function $P(x_j)$ of a discrete random variable by replacing the lines with impulses, i.e.,

$$p(x) = \sum_j P(x_j)\delta(x - x_j) \qquad (10)$$

The reader can easily confirm that applying Eqs. (5b) to (10) yields a stepwise CDF, as expected in the discrete case.

One word of caution regarding PDFs with impulses: Particular care must be taken when specifying events (outcomes) using inequalities. In Eq. (10), for instance, $P(X < x_1)$ does not include the impulse at $x = x_1$ whereas $P(X \leq x_1)$ does, so $P(X \leq x_1)$ $= P(X < x_1) + P(x_1)$. On the other hand, if $p(x)$ contains no impulses — meaning that X is strictly continuous — then there is no difference between $P(X < x_1)$ and $P(X \leq x_1)$.

EXERCISE 3.4   Let the random variable Z be defined by

$$Z = \begin{cases} 0 & X \leq 0 \\ X & X > 0 \end{cases}$$

where X has the PDF given by Eq. (9a) in Example 3.4. Show that

$$p(z) = \tfrac{1}{2}\delta(z) + \tfrac{1}{2}e^{-z}u(z)$$

(*Hint*: First sketch $F(z)$ noting that $P(Z < 0) = 0$.)

Transformations of Random Variables

The previous exercise touched lightly on the transformation of random variables, where one random variable is defined as a function of another and it is desired to find the resulting PDF. Such transformations may be relatively simple or quite difficult, and here we will consider only a simple but important class.†

Let the continuous variate Z be a single-valued function of X — whose PDF $p_x(x)$ is known — and let the inverse function exist, i.e.,

$$Z = g(X) \qquad X = g^{-1}(Z)$$

Since each value of Z corresponds to a *unique* value of X, the probability of finding Z in some differential range dz equals the probability that X is in the corresponding range dx. Thus

$$p_z(z)|dz| = p_x(x)|dx| \qquad (11)$$

---

† For a general treatment, see Davenport and Root (1958, chap. 3).

where absolute values are used to ensure that $p_z(z)$ will be nonnegative. Solving for $p_z(z)$ and inserting $x = g^{-1}(z)$ then yields

$$p_z(z) = p_x(x)\left|\frac{dx}{dz}\right| = p_x[g^{-1}(z)]\left|\frac{dg^{-1}(z)}{dz}\right| \qquad (12)$$

To illustrate, given the linear transformation

$$Z = \alpha X + \beta \qquad (13a)$$

we have $x = g^{-1}(z) = (z - \beta)/\alpha$ and

$$p_z(z) = \frac{1}{|\alpha|} p_x\left(\frac{z - \beta}{\alpha}\right) \qquad (13b)$$

Joint and Conditional Density Functions

Some random processes are characterized by two or more random variables, which may or may not be independent, and a process with n random variables has an n-dimensional sample space. The density-function description is readily extended in terms of joint and conditional density functions. For simplicity, we consider only the two-dimensional case.

Let X and Y be continuous variates that can be observed simultaneously. Their joint density function $p(x,y)$ is developed along the lines of Eq. (8), namely,

$$p(x,y)\, dx\, dy = P(x - dx < X \le x, y - dy < Y \le y) \qquad (14)$$

(Note that a comma in the argument is interpreted as "and.") Hence, the probability of finding X in the range $x_1 < X \le x_2$ while at the same time $y_1 < Y \le y_2$ is

$$P(x_1 < X \le x_2, y_1 < Y \le y_2) = \int_{y_1}^{y_2} \int_{x_1}^{x_2} p(x,y)\, dx\, dy$$

which is the two-dimensional equivalent of Eq. (7).

If the two variates are *statistically independent*, then it can be shown that

$$p(x,y) = p_x(x)p_y(y) \qquad (15)$$

If they are not independent, the conditional density functions are needed in the form

$$p(x,y) = p_x(x)p(y|x) = p_y(y)p(x|y) \qquad (16)$$

Finally, given a joint density function $p(x,y)$, the PDF for X alone is obtained by the following procedure. If we are interested only in X, the value of Y does not matter, so $P(X \le x)$ is equivalent to $P(X \le x, -\infty < Y \le +\infty)$. Thus

$$p_x(x) = \int_{-\infty}^{\infty} p(x,y)\, dy \qquad (17)$$

EXERCISE 3.5   Prove Eq. (15) by starting with Eq. (14) and applying Eq. (8), this section, and Eq. (9), Sect. 3.1.

3.3   STATISTICAL AVERAGES

For many of our purposes the probability-function representation of a random variable provides more information than is really necessary. In fact, such a complete description can prove to be an embarrassment of riches, more confusing than illuminating. Thus, we shall often find it simpler and more convenient to describe a random variable by a few characteristic *numbers* that briefly summarize the probability function. These numbers are the various statistical averages or mean values.

Means and Moments

The statistical average or mean value $\bar{x}$ of a random variable X is the numerical average of the values X can assume weighted by their probabilities. Essentially, $\bar{x}$ is the conventional arithmetic average of the observations in the sense that for a very large number of trials N, the *sum* of the observed values is expected to be approximately $N\bar{x}$. (Again, the large-number condition is crucial.) For this reason, mean values are also called *expected values* or *expectations*, and denoted as $\bar{x} = E[x]$.

Consider a *discrete* random process upon which n observations have been made. If $X = x_1$ is observed n_1 times, etc., the sum of the observed values is just

$$n_1 x_1 + n_2 x_2 + \cdots + n_m x_m = \sum_j n_j x_j$$

Dividing by the number of trials and letting $n \to \infty$ yields

$$\bar{x} = \lim_{n \to \infty} \sum_j x_j \frac{n_j}{n} = \sum_j x_j P(x_j) \qquad (1)$$

which we shall take as the definition of $\bar{x}$ for discrete variates. Applying similar reasoning to continuous variates, the summation approaches integration over all x; thus

$$\bar{x} \triangleq \int_{-\infty}^{\infty} x p(x) \, dx \qquad (2)$$

is the mean of a *continuous* random variable. Hereafter, all statistical averages will be written in terms of density functions, recognizing that discrete variates are included by writing $p(x) = \sum P(x_j)\delta(x - x_j)$.

If X is a random variable and $g(\ )$ is any analytic function, then $g(X)$ is a random variable whose mean value is given directly by

$$\mathbf{E}[g(x)] = \int_{-\infty}^{\infty} g(x)p(x)\, dx \qquad (3)$$

When $g(X) = X^n$, its mean value $\overline{x^n}$ is designated as the nth *moment* of X. The *first moment* is, of course, just the mean value $\bar{x}$. The *second moment* $\overline{x^2}$ is commonly called the *mean-square* value. Observe the difference between mean-square value and the mean value squared. The order of operations — averaging and squaring — is not interchangeable and $\overline{x^2} \neq \bar{x}^2$.

Time and statistical averaging have certain similarities; in particular, both are *linear* operations. Thus, if α and β are constants, then

$$\mathbf{E}[\alpha x + \beta] = \alpha \bar{x} + \beta \qquad (4)$$

as is easily proved using Eq. (3) with $g(x) = \alpha x + \beta$. While this result seems rather trivial, it leads to the not-so-obvious relation

$$\mathbf{E}[\bar{x}x] = \bar{x}^2$$

since $\bar{x}$ is a constant.

Variance, Standard Deviation, and Chebyshev's Inequality

A slightly modified form of the second moment is called the *variance*, defined as

$$\sigma_x^2 \triangleq \mathbf{E}[(x - \bar{x})^2] \qquad (5a)$$

where the order of operations must be carefully noted. The square root of the variance, called the *standard deviation*, is a measure of the *spread* of observed values. Before demonstrating this assertion, let us obtain a more convenient expression for σ_x^2 by invoking the linearity of statistical averaging:

$$\sigma_x^2 = \mathbf{E}[x^2 - 2x\bar{x} + \bar{x}^2] = \overline{x^2} - 2\bar{x}^2 + \bar{x}^2$$

or

$$\sigma_x^2 = \overline{x^2} - \bar{x}^2 \qquad (5b)$$

Hence the variance is simply the mean square minus the mean squared.

For the interpretation of variance and standard deviation, we shall use *Chebyshev's inequality*†

$$P(|X - \bar{x}| > \kappa\sigma_x) < \frac{1}{\kappa^2} \qquad \kappa > 0 \qquad (6a)$$

---

† Also spelled Tchebycheff.

which states that the probability of finding X outside $\pm \kappa$ standard deviations of the mean is less than $1/\kappa^2$, *regardless of p(x)*. For example, with $\kappa = 2$, $P < 0.25$; with $\kappa = 10$, $P < 0.01$. Chebyshev's inequality is also written in terms of the event $|X - \bar{x}| \leq \kappa \sigma_x$, which is the complement of the above case so

$$P(|X - \bar{x}| \leq \kappa \sigma_x) \geq 1 - \frac{1}{\kappa^2} \qquad (6b)$$

Thus one can specify an interval, say $\bar{x} \pm 2\sigma_x$ within which observed values are expected with high probability, $P \geq 0.75$. Moreover, a *large standard deviation* implies a *large spread* of likely values for any given observation, and vice versa. When we get to random electric signals, a more physical interpretation of σ is possible. Proof of Eq. (6) can be found in any text on probability and statistics.

Example 3.5

By way of illustration, we apply the above equations to Example 3.4, Sect. 3.2, where $p(x) = \frac{1}{2}e^{-|x|}$. Since $p(x)$ has even symmetry

$$\bar{x} = \int_{-\infty}^{\infty} x p(x)\, dx = 0$$

$$\overline{x^2} = \int_{-\infty}^{\infty} x^2 p(x)\, dx = 2 \int_{0}^{\infty} x^2 \tfrac{1}{2} e^{-x}\, dx = 2$$

and therefore

$$\sigma_x^2 = 2 - 0 = 2 \qquad \sigma_x = \sqrt{2}$$

The probability that an observed value will fall within $\pm 2\sigma_x$ of the mean value $\bar{x} = 0$ is

$$P(|X| \leq 2\sqrt{2}) = \int_{-2\sqrt{2}}^{2\sqrt{2}} p(x)\, dx = 2 \int_{0}^{2\sqrt{2}} \tfrac{1}{2} e^{-x}\, dx = 0.94$$

compared with $P \geq 0.75$ from Chebyshev's inequality. ////

EXERCISE 3.6   Let $Z = 3X + 5$ where X is as in Example 3.5. Without integrating, show that $\bar{z} = 5$ and $\overline{z^2} = 43$. Then find $p_z(z)$ using Eq. (13b), Sect. 3.2, and check these values by integration.

Multiple Random Variables

In the case of two or more random variables, mean values are found using multiple integration and joint density functions in the general form

$$E[g(x,y)] = \iint_{-\infty}^{\infty} g(x,y) p(x,y)\, dx\, dy \qquad (7)$$

Thus, for example,

$$\mathbf{E}[x + y] = \iint\limits_{-\infty}^{\infty} (x + y)p(x,y)\, dx\, dy$$

$$= \int_{-\infty}^{\infty} x \underbrace{\left[\int_{-\infty}^{\infty} p(x,y)\, dy \right]}_{p_x(x)} dx + \int_{-\infty}^{\infty} y \underbrace{\left[\int_{-\infty}^{\infty} p(x,y)\, dx \right]}_{p_y(y)} dy$$

Hence,

$$\overline{x + y} = \int_{-\infty}^{\infty} x p_x(x)\, dx + \int_{-\infty}^{\infty} y p_y(y)\, dy = \bar{x} + \bar{y} \qquad (8)$$

a most simple and satisfying result. Generalizing, it can be said that the *mean of a sum is the sum of the means*, regardless of statistical dependence.

A parallel conclusion applies to the *product* of two or more variates, providing they are *statistically independent*. Thus if X and Y are independent random variables, then

$$\overline{xy} = \bar{x}\bar{y} \qquad (9)$$

Generalizing this rule, if X and Y are independent, then

$$\mathbf{E}[g_1(x)g_2(y)] = \mathbf{E}[g_1(x)]\mathbf{E}[g_2(y)] \qquad (10)$$

where g_1 and g_2 are functions of x and y, respectively.

Now consider $Z = X + Y$, where X and Y are independent. Clearly $\bar{z} = \bar{x} + \bar{y}$, but what is the variance σ_z^2? To answer this, we first calculate $\overline{z^2}$ via

$$\overline{z^2} = \mathbf{E}[x^2 + 2xy + y^2] = \overline{x^2} + 2\bar{x}\bar{y} + \overline{y^2}$$

where the use of Eqs. (4), (8), and (9) has greatly simplified this step. Finally, since $\sigma_z^2 = \overline{z^2} - \bar{z}^2$ and $\bar{z}^2 = (\bar{x} + \bar{y})^2$, we get

$$\sigma_z^2 = (\overline{x^2} - \bar{x}^2) + (\overline{y^2} - \bar{y}^2) = \sigma_x^2 + \sigma_y^2 \qquad (11)$$

In general, the variance of a sum is the sum of the variances providing the components are *independent*.

EXERCISE 3.7   Prove Eq. (10) by inserting Eq. (15), Sect. 3.2, into Eq. (7).

3.4   USEFUL PROBABILITY MODELS

There are numerous probability models, both discrete and continuous, just a few of which are given below. Fortunately, the few we shall discuss cover most of the cases encountered in our later work.

Binomial Distribution

Consider an experiment having only two possible outcomes A and $B = A^c$, tossing a single coin for instance. Let the probabilities be $P(A) = \epsilon$ and $P(B) = 1 - \epsilon$. If the experiment is repeated m times and we total the number of times A occurred, we have generated a numerical-valued discrete random process. Assigning the random variable N as the number of occurrences of A, then N may assume the $m + 1$ discrete values $0, 1, \ldots, m$.

The corresponding frequency function $P(N = n)$ is called the *binomial distribution*, written

$$P_m(n) = \binom{m}{n} \epsilon^n (1 - \epsilon)^{m-n} \qquad (1)$$

where

$$\binom{m}{n} \triangleq \frac{m!}{n!\,(m-n)!} \qquad (2)$$

which is called the *binomial coefficient* since it equals the $(n + 1)$st coefficient in the expansion of $(x + y)^m$. It is readily seen that

$$\binom{m}{m-n} = \binom{m}{n} \qquad \text{and} \qquad \binom{m}{1} = m$$

Some trouble arises when $n = 0$, but that is resolved by defining $0! \triangleq 1$ so

$$\binom{m}{0} = \binom{m}{m} = 1$$

Other values are given in tables or may be found from Pascal's triangle. The derivation of Eq. (1) is omitted here for the sake of brevity.

While tossing coins is not of particular interest to us, error occurrence in digital data transmission definitely is. And if the error probability per digit is the same for all digits, say ϵ, then $P_m(n)$ gives the probability of n errors in a message of m digits, etc. Likewise

$$F_m(k) = \sum_{n=0}^{k} P_m(n)$$

is the probability of k or fewer errors in m digits. As an exercise, the reader may wish to check the values of the frequency function and distribution function given in Example 3.3, Sect. 3.2, where $m = 4$ and $\epsilon = 0.3$.

Turning to the statistical averages of N, the mean and variance of the binomial distribution are found by inserting $P_m(n)$ into Eq. (1), Sect. 3.3, etc. One obtains after some labor

$$\bar{n} = m\epsilon \qquad \sigma_n^2 = m\epsilon(1 - \epsilon) = \bar{n}(1 - \epsilon) \qquad (3)$$

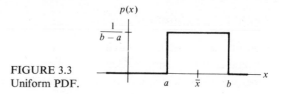

FIGURE 3.3
Uniform PDF.

and since $\sigma_n/\bar{n}$ is proportional to $1/\sqrt{m}$, the *relative spread* of likely values decreases with increasing m.

Equation (3) is particularly important for quick calculations of the expected number of errors in a digital message. For instance, if 10,000 digits are sent with $\epsilon = 0.01$, then $\bar{n} = 100$ and $\sigma_n^2 = 99$; taking $\bar{n} \pm 2\sigma_n$ as the expected range, there would be roughly 80 to 100 errors in a typical message. Incidentally, this is not a very good error rate.

Uniform Distribution

When a continuous variate is equally likely to take on any value in the range $[a,b]$, it is said to be *uniformly distributed*. The PDF is

$$p(x) = \begin{cases} \dfrac{1}{b-a} & a \le x \le b \\ 0 & \text{otherwise} \end{cases} \tag{4}$$

as shown in Fig. 3.3. The mean, mean square, and variance are

$$\bar{x} = \int_{-\infty}^{\infty} \frac{x}{b-a}\, dx = \frac{b+a}{2}$$

$$\overline{x^2} = \int_{-\infty}^{\infty} \frac{x^2}{b-a}\, dx = \frac{b^2 + ab + a^2}{3} \tag{5}$$

$$\sigma_x^2 = \frac{(b-a)^2}{12}$$

The mean falls just where one would expect it, right in the middle of the range. On the other hand, the variance depends only on the *size* of the range, $b - a$, and not on its absolute position.

Gaussian Distribution

The most widely known probability model is the *gaussian* or *normal distribution*. This function occurs in so many applications of statistical analysis because of a

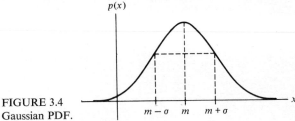

FIGURE 3.4
Gaussian PDF.

remarkable phenomenon called the *central-limit theorem* which, for our purposes, can be stated as follows:

> If X_1, X_2, ..., X_M are independent random variables and the random variable Y is assigned as their sum, then as M becomes very large, the distribution of Y approaches a gaussian distribution. The result is independent of the distributions of the individual components as long as the contribution of each is small compared to the sum.

We shall not attempt to prove the theorem, nor shall we use it explicitly in later work, for great care must be exercised in its application. (It has been said that the central-limit theorem is a dangerous tool in the hands of amateurs.) However, we can observe that electrical noise is often the summation of effects of a large number of randomly moving electrons and therefore will have a gaussian distribution. Similarly, random errors in experimental measurements are due to many irregular and fluctuating causes; such errors will cause measured values to be random with a gaussian distribution about the true value.

The PDF of a gaussian-distributed variate is the familiar bell-shaped curve

$$p(x) = \frac{1}{\sqrt{2\pi}\,\sigma} e^{-(x-m)^2/2\sigma^2} \tag{6}$$

As seen from Fig. 3.4, $p(x)$ describes a continuous random variable that may take on any value in $[-\infty, +\infty]$ but is most likely to be found near $x = m$. In fact, as the reader can verify, m is the mean value $\bar{x}$. And, as the notation implies, the standard deviation is σ. One should also note the even symmetry of $p(x)$ about $x = m$. An immediate consequence is

$$P(X \le m) = P(X > m) = \tfrac{1}{2} \tag{7}$$

Suppose then that a random-noise voltage has a gaussian distribution and we wish to find the probability that an observed value will fall outside the range $m \pm \kappa\sigma$. To simplify a bit, the symmetry of $p(x)$ implies $P(|X - m| > \kappa\sigma) = 2P(X > m + \kappa\sigma)$. Setting up the latter as an integral,

$$P(X > m + \kappa\sigma) = \frac{1}{\sqrt{2\pi}\,\sigma} \int_{m+\kappa\sigma}^{\infty} e^{-(x-m)^2/2\sigma^2} \, dx$$

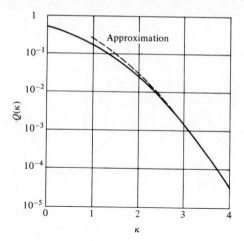

FIGURE 3.5

but, unfortunately, it cannot be solved in closed form and requires numerical evaluation. Accordingly, we introduce the function

$$Q(\kappa) \triangleq \frac{1}{\sqrt{2\pi}} \int_{\kappa}^{\infty} e^{-\lambda^2/2} \, d\lambda \qquad (8)$$

which has been extensively tabulated.† Setting $\lambda = (x - m)/\sigma$, it is seen that

$$P(X > m + \kappa\sigma) = P(X \le m - \kappa\sigma) = Q(\kappa) \qquad (9a)$$

and

$$P(|X - m| > \kappa\sigma) = 2Q(\kappa) \qquad (9b)$$

From Eq. (9a), $Q(\kappa)$ may be referred to as the *area under the gaussian tail*.

When $\kappa \gg 1$, the above probability is very small, so small as to make most tables of $Q(\kappa)$ useless for the calculation. In this case, there is an analytic approximation obtained from Eq. (8) by integration by parts, namely,

$$Q(\kappa) \approx \frac{1}{\sqrt{2\pi}\,\kappa} e^{-\kappa^2/2} \qquad \kappa \gg 1 \qquad (10)$$

Figure 3.5 is a plot of $Q(\kappa)$ showing the exact value and the approximation. The latter is seen to be quite accurate for $\kappa \ge 3$.

Now consider the probability $P(m < X \le m + \kappa\sigma)$. Again symmetry and the area interpretation of the density function are helpful, for we can divide $p(x)$ into

† Table D gives a detailed plot of $Q(\kappa)$ as well as its relation to other functions defined by various authors.

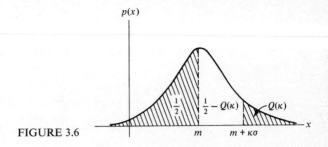

FIGURE 3.6

three areas, as shown in Fig. 3.6. The probability in question is the area between m and $m + \kappa\sigma$ and, recalling that the total area is unity,

$$P(m < X \le m + \kappa\sigma) = 1 - \tfrac{1}{2} - Q(\kappa)$$

so

$$P(m < X \le m + \kappa\sigma) = P(m - \kappa\sigma < X \le m) = \tfrac{1}{2} - Q(\kappa) \qquad (11a)$$

and

$$P(|X - m| \le \kappa\sigma) = 1 - 2Q(\kappa) \qquad (11b)$$

The latter also follows directly from Eq. (9b).

Finally, using Table 3.1, we compare some exact values of $P(|X - m| \le \kappa\sigma)$ with Chebyshev's inequality, $P(|X - \bar{x}| \le \kappa\sigma) \ge 1 - 1/\kappa^2$. Clearly, the lower bound $1 - 1/\kappa^2$ is conservative. Moreover, the expected range of observed values is somewhat less than $m \pm 2\sigma$; a more realistic and frequently used range is $m \pm \sigma$, for which the probability is 0.68.

EXERCISE 3.8 If X is gaussian with $\bar{x} = 5$ and $\overline{x^2} = 89$, show that $P(9 < X \le 25)$ $= Q(0.5) - Q(2.5) \approx 0.30$. (*Hint*: Sketch the PDF and mark the boundaries of the area in question in terms of $m + \kappa\sigma$.)

Table 3.1

κ	$1 - 2Q(\kappa)$	$1 - \dfrac{1}{\kappa^2}$
0.5	0.38	
1.0	0.68	0.00
1.5	0.87	0.56
2.0	0.95	0.75
2.5	0.99	0.84

Bivariate Gaussian Distribution   ★

Two random variables X_1 and X_2 are said to be jointly gaussian if their joint density function is

$$p(x_1,x_2) = \frac{1}{2\pi\sqrt{C_{12}}} \exp\left\{-[\sigma_2{}^2(x_1 - m_1)^2 + \sigma_1{}^2(x_2 - m_2)^2\right.$$
$$\left. - 2\sigma_{12}(x_1 - m_1)(x_2 - m_2)]/2C_{12}\right\} \tag{12}$$

where $m_1 = \overline{x_1}$, $\sigma_1{}^2 = \overline{x_1{}^2} - m_1{}^2$, etc., and

$$\sigma_{12} \triangleq E[(x_1 - m_1)(x_2 - m_2)] = \overline{x_1 x_2} - m_1 m_2 \tag{13a}$$
$$C_{12} \triangleq \sigma_1{}^2 \sigma_2{}^2 - \sigma_{12}{}^2 \tag{13b}$$

The parameter σ_{12} is called the *covariance*; a related parameter is the *correlation coefficient*

$$\rho_{12} \triangleq \frac{\sigma_{12}}{\sigma_1 \sigma_2} \tag{13c}$$

Note that $C_{12} = \sigma_1{}^2 \sigma_2{}^2 (1 - \rho_{12}{}^2)$.

Although Eq. (12) appears to be a rather formidable expression, it simply represents a bell-shaped surface over the $x_1 x_2$ plane whose maximum is at $x_1 = m_1, x_2 = m_2$. This observation, coupled with some routine calculations, reveals that all individual and conditional density functions are also gaussian. Thus

$$p_{x_1}(x_1) = \int_{-\infty}^{\infty} p(x_1,x_2)\,dx_2$$

$$= \frac{1}{\sqrt{2\pi}\,\sigma_1} e^{-(x_1 - m_1)^2/2\sigma_1{}^2} \tag{14a}$$

$$p(x_1|x_2) = \frac{p(x_1,x_2)}{p_{x_2}(x_2)}$$

$$= \frac{1}{\sqrt{2\pi(1 - \rho_{12}{}^2)}\,\sigma_1} e^{-[(x_1 - m_1) - \rho_{12}(\sigma_1/\sigma_2)(x_2 - m_2)]^2/2(1 - \rho_{12}{}^2)\sigma_1{}^2} \tag{14b}$$

and interchanging the subscripts gives $p_{x_2}(x_2)$, etc. If the variates are *statistically independent*, then $\sigma_{12} = 0$ and Eq. (12) reduces to

$$p(x_1,x_2) = p_{x_1}(x_1)p_{x_2}(x_2)$$

as expected. It likewise follows that $\rho_{12} = 0$ and $p(x_1|x_2) = p_{x_1}(x_1)$. Incidentally, *uncorrelated* gaussian variates are always *independent*, but this does not necessarily hold for other probability models; Prob. 3.28 gives a counterexample.

Now consider a new random variable Z formed by linear combination of X_1 and X_2, i.e.,

$$Z = \alpha_1 X_1 + \alpha_2 X_2$$

where α_1 and α_2 are constants. It can be shown that

$$p_z(z) = \frac{1}{\sqrt{2\pi}\,\sigma_z} e^{-(z-m_z)^2/2\sigma_z^2} \tag{15}$$

with

$$m_z = \alpha_1 m_1 + \alpha_2 m_2$$
$$\sigma_z^2 = \alpha_1^2 \sigma_1^2 + \alpha_2^2 \sigma_2^2 + 2\alpha_1 \alpha_2 \rho_{12} \sigma_1 \sigma_2$$

Therefore, a *linear combination of jointly gaussian variates is also a gaussian variate.* Again, this is a unique characteristic of gaussian random variables.

The above analyses can be extended to more than two gaussian variates. However, the notation becomes intractable unless one uses matrix symbols.

3.5   RANDOM SIGNALS

Up to this point we have been speaking in rather general terms about random variables and their statistical averages. Now we concentrate on *random signals*, the manifestations of *random electrical processes* that take place in *time* — also termed *stochastic processes*. Thus, if $v(t)$ is a random signal, the random variable V may be assigned to represent values of $v(t)$ at the observation times.

Under certain conditions, termed *ergodicity*, an intuitively meaningful relationship between statistical averages and time averages will be obtained. This in turn leads to the spectral description of random signals via autocorrelation functions and the Wiener-Kinchine theorem.

We begin by considering ergodic processes and the implications of ergodicity.

Ergodic Processes — Ensemble Averages

Let $v(t)$ be the voltage waveform produced by some noise generator, so that $v(t)$ is a random signal of finite average power. If the waveform is examined for a long period of time, its various *time* averages can be measured or calculated following the definitions of Chap. 2. Furthermore, the meaning of these averages is apparent: $\langle v(t) \rangle$ is the DC component of the noise, $\langle v^2(t) \rangle$ is its average power, and so forth.

Alternately, suppose there were available a very large number of identical generators, called an *ensemble*. The members of the ensemble are identical in the sense

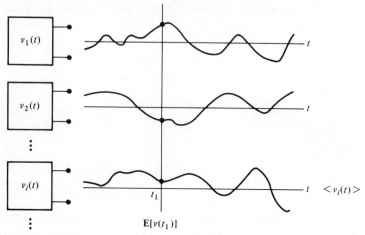

FIGURE 3.7
Time averaging and ensemble averaging.

of having the same statistical description; nonetheless their individual signals—called *sample functions*—will be different. A particular signal, now designated $v_i(t)$ for clarity, is one of the infinitely many sample functions that a given noise generator can produce. The entire family of sample functions will be symbolized by $v(t)$.

Figure 3.7 illustrates this notion and indicates that *two* different kinds of averages are involved: we could take successive measurements of one sample function $v_i(t)$ and find its *time averages* $\langle v_i(t) \rangle$, etc.; or we could examine all the sample functions at one particular time, say t_1, and find the *ensemble averages* $\mathbf{E}[v(t_1)]$, etc. Clearly, the ensemble averages are the same as the statistical averages at $t = t_1$. But how do they relate to the time averages of one sample function?

In general, ensemble averages may differ from such time averages. They surely would be different if the statistical properties of the generators were changing with time, for the time variation would be averaged out in the time averages but not in the ensemble averages. Moreover, ensemble averages at different times also would be different.

However, many of the random signals found in communication systems come from *ergodic processes*, meaning that *time and ensemble averages are identical*, e.g., $\mathbf{E}[v(t)] = \langle v(t) \rangle$, etc. An ergodic process is also *stationary*, since ensemble averages are independent of the time of observation.

In the remainder of this text we shall deal almost exclusively with random signals that are sample functions of ergodic processes. Therefore, these signals are *power* signals, since $\mathbf{E}[v^2(t)]$ does not depend on t, and the following statements can be made:

1 The *mean* $\bar{v}$ is the *DC component* of the signal.

2 The *mean squared* $\bar{v}^2$ is the power in the DC component, i.e., the *DC power*.

3 The *mean square* $\overline{v^2}$ is the total *average power*.

4 The *variance* $\sigma_v^2 = \overline{v^2} - \bar{v}^2$ is the power in the time-varying component, i.e., the *AC power*.

5 The *standard deviation* σ_v is the root mean square of the time-varying component, i.e., the *rms value*.

Although the above relations serve to make an electrical engineer feel more at home in the world of statistics, it must be emphasized that they apply only to the very special case of ergodic sources.†

Correlation

We have two reasons for considering the autocorrelation function of a random signal. First, $R_v(\tau)$ in its own right provides useful information about $v(t)$. Second, by the Wiener-Kinchine theorem, the frequency-domain description of a random signal is its power spectral density $G_v(f) = \mathscr{F}[R_v(\tau)]$. Before tackling the latter, let us see how $R_v(\tau)$ can be interpreted when $v(t)$ is random.

First we define the *scalar product* of two ergodic random signals as

$$\langle v(t), w(t) \rangle \triangleq \mathbf{E}[v(t)w^*(t)] \qquad (1)$$

so the norm squared is $\|v\|^2 = \mathbf{E}[|v(t)|^2]$. Similarly,

$$R_{vw}(\tau) \triangleq \mathbf{E}[v(t)w^*(t - \tau)] \qquad (2)$$

which parallels our definition of the crosscorrelation in Sect. 2.6. But ergodicity means that time and ensemble averages are interchangeable. Therefore, taking $v(t)$ to be *real*, its autocorrelation is

$$R_v(\tau) = \mathbf{E}[v(t)v(t - \tau)] = \langle v(t)v(t - \tau) \rangle \qquad (3)$$

where the second expression is a time average, not a scalar product. Hereafter, we will deal primarily with random signals that are real and ergodic, so either expression in Eq. (3) gives the autocorrelation function. It should be carefully noted that $R_v(\tau)$ is a *deterministic* function even though $v(t)$ is random.

Clearly, all the mathematical properties previously ascribed to $R_v(\tau)$ also apply to the autocorrelation of random signals. In particular

$$R_v(-\tau) = R_v(\tau) \qquad (4a)$$

$$R_v(0) = \overline{v^2} = \sigma^2 + \bar{v}^2 \geq |R_v(\tau)| \qquad (4b)$$

---

† See Lathi (1968, chap. 3) for a discussion of the nonergodic case.

so $R_v(\tau)$ is an even function having a maximum at $\tau = 0$. Additionally, it is true that

$$\lim_{\tau \to \infty} R_v(|\tau|) = \bar{v}^2 \tag{5}$$

providing that the process is nonperiodic. (If the process is periodic, its autocorrelation is also periodic with the same period.)

In a sense, autocorrelation is a measure of both *time variation* and *statistical dependence*. Suppose, for example, we take a value of τ that is very small compared to the time intervals in which $v(t)$ has significant change; then $v(t - \tau) \approx v(t)$, and $R_v(\tau) \approx \overline{v^2(t)} = \sigma^2 + \bar{v}^2$. As $|\tau|$ increases, $R_v(\tau)$ will generally decrease at first (it cannot increase), and the range of τ around $\tau = 0$ for which $R_v(\tau) - \bar{v}^2 \approx \sigma^2$ is a measure of the time variation of $v(t)$. The smaller this range, the more rapid the time variations. On the other hand, if $|\tau|$ is very large, we might find that $v(t)$ and $v(t - \tau)$ have so little in common that they are *statistically independent*; then $R_v(\tau) = \overline{v(t)v(t - \tau)} = \bar{v}^2$. When $|R_v(\tau)| - \bar{v}^2 = 0$, $v(t - \tau)$ and $v(t)$ are *uncorrelated* but not necessarily statistically independent—unless the process is *gaussian*.

EXERCISE 3.9 Show that, for any constants t_1 and t_2,

$$E[v(t - t_1)v(t - t_2)] = R_v(t_1 - t_2) \tag{6}$$

when $v(t)$ is real and ergodic. (*Hint*: Replace the ensemble average by an average over all time and note that t is a dummy variable.)

Power Spectral Density

Turning to the frequency domain, the sole reasonable description of a random signal is its *power spectral density* $G_v(f)$. This is because the only advance knowledge we have about a random signal is its probability function and ensemble averages, the latter being directly related to average power if the source is ergodic.

Invoking the Wiener-Kinchine theorem, the power spectral density of the random signal $v(t)$ is

$$G_v(f) = \mathscr{F}[R_v(\tau)] = \int_{-\infty}^{\infty} E[v(t)v(t - \tau)]e^{-j2\pi f\tau}\, d\tau \tag{7}$$

In view of the properties of $R_v(\tau)$ it immediately follows from Eq. (7) that

$$G_v(-f) = G_v(f) \tag{8a}$$

$$\int_{-\infty}^{\infty} G_v(f)\, df = R_v(0) = \overline{v^2} \tag{8b}$$

so $G_v(f)$ is real and even and its total area equals $\overline{v^2}$.

Usually, $G_v(f)$ is a smooth and continuous function of frequency. However, if $\bar{v} \neq 0$, the spectral density has an *impulse* at $f = 0$ whose weight equals the DC power $\bar{v}^2$. To show this, let $w(t) = v(t) - \bar{v}$ so $\bar{w} = 0$. Then, since $v(t) = w(t) + \bar{v}$,

$$R_v(\tau) = \mathbf{E}[w(t)w(t - \tau) + w(t)\bar{v} + \bar{v}w(t - \tau) + \bar{v}^2]$$
$$= R_w(\tau) + 2\bar{w}\bar{v} + \bar{v}^2 = R_w(\tau) + \bar{v}^2 \tag{9a}$$

and Fourier transformation yields

$$G_v(f) = G_w(f) + \bar{v}^2 \, \delta(f) \tag{9b}$$

The following example, chosen to bolster the reader's confidence in the Wiener-Kinchine theorem for random signals, also leads to an impulsive power spectral density.

Example 3.6   Randomly Phased Sinusoid

Consider the random process

$$v(t) = A \cos (\omega_0 t + \Theta)$$

where A and $\omega_0 = 2\pi f_0$ are constants while Θ is a random variable over the ensemble with a uniform PDF

$$p(\theta) = \frac{1}{2\pi} \qquad -\pi \leq \theta \leq \pi$$

Using trigonometric identities to expand $v(t)v(t - \tau)$, the autocorrelation function is

$$R_v(\tau) = \mathbf{E}\left[\frac{A^2}{2} \cos \omega_0 \tau + \frac{A^2}{2} \cos (2\omega_0 t - \omega_0 \tau + 2\Theta)\right]$$
$$= \frac{A^2}{2} \mathbf{E}[\cos \omega_0 \tau] + \frac{A^2}{2} \mathbf{E}[\cos (2\omega_0 t - \omega_0 \tau + 2\Theta)]$$

But $\mathbf{E}[\cos \omega_0 \tau] = \cos \omega_0 \tau$ since this is not a random quantity, while

$$\mathbf{E}[\cos (2\omega_0 t - \omega_0 \tau + 2\Theta)] = \int_{-\infty}^{\infty} \cos (2\omega_0 t - \omega_0 \tau + 2\theta)p(\theta) \, d\theta$$
$$= \frac{1}{2\pi} \int_{-\pi}^{\pi} \cos (2\omega_0 t - \omega_0 \tau + 2\theta) \, d\theta = 0$$

Therefore

$$R_v(\tau) = \frac{A^2}{2} \cos \omega_0 \tau \tag{10a}$$

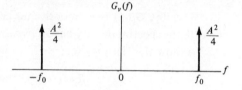

FIGURE 3.8
Power spectral density of a randomly phased sinusoid.

which is identical to the autocorrelation of a *deterministic* sinusoid — see Example 2.15, Sect. 2.6.

Fourier transformation then gives an impulsive power spectral density

$$G_v(f) = \frac{A^2}{4} \delta(f - f_0) + \frac{A^2}{4} \delta(f + f_0) \qquad (10b)$$

as sketched in Fig. 3.8. We see that this random signal has specific amounts of average power concentrated at $f = \pm f_0$ and no spectral density elsewhere, in agreement with intuitive reasoning. Moreover, $\int_{-\infty}^{\infty} G_v(f)\, df = A^2/2$ which clearly equals $\overline{v^2}$, and the fact that there is no impulse at $f = 0$ agrees with $\bar{v} = 0$.   ////

Example 3.7   Random Binary Wave ★

The previous example is rather deceptive owing to its simplicity. More often than not, determining an autocorrelation function from scratch is a sticky analytic problem — as this example will demonstrate.

Figure 3.9 is a sample function of the random binary wave $v(t)$. During any time interval $(n-1)T < t - T_d < nT$, $v(t)$ takes on either the value $+A$ or $-A$. These two amplitudes are equally likely, and the amplitude in any one interval is independent of all other intervals. The delay term T_d is a random variable over the ensemble, uniformly distributed over $[0,T]$.

To find the autocorrelation, we first consider $|\tau| > T$; so, for any sample function, $v(t)$ and $v(t - \tau)$ are in different intervals and hence are *independent*. Thus

$$E[v(t)v(t - \tau)] = \bar{v}^2 = \langle v(t) \rangle^2 = 0$$

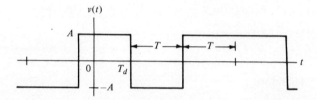

FIGURE 3.9
Sample function of a random binary wave.

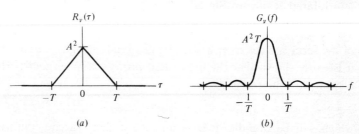

FIGURE 3.10
Random binary wave. (a) Autocorrelation; (b) power spectral density.

where the time average $\langle v(t) \rangle = 0$ follows by inspection of $v(t)$.

Now take $|\tau| < T$ and let $t = 0$; then $v(0)$ and $v(-\tau)$ are in the same interval only if $T_d - T < -|\tau|$. Thus

$$\mathbf{E}[v(0)v(-\tau)] = \begin{cases} A^2 & T_d < T - |\tau| \\ 0 & \text{otherwise} \end{cases}$$

The probability that $T_d < T - |\tau|$ is

$$P(T_d < T - |\tau|) = \int_0^{T-|\tau|} \frac{dt_d}{T} = \frac{T - |\tau|}{T}$$

so

$$\mathbf{E}[v(0)v(-\tau)] = A^2 P(T_d < T - |\tau|) = A^2 \left(1 - \frac{|\tau|}{T}\right)$$

By like reasoning for any value of t

$$R_v(\tau) = \mathbf{E}[v(t)v(t-\tau)] = \begin{cases} A^2 \left(1 - \dfrac{|\tau|}{T}\right) & |\tau| < T \\ 0 & |\tau| > T \end{cases}$$

$$= A^2 \Lambda\left(\frac{\tau}{T}\right)$$

where $\Lambda(\tau/T)$ is the triangle function. Finally, drawing upon the known transform pair,

$$G_v(f) = A^2 T \operatorname{sinc}^2 fT$$

Figure 3.10 shows the autocorrelation function and power spectrum of the random binary wave. ////

Modulated Random Signals

When analyzing communication systems, one often encounters modulated processes of the form $v(t) \cos \omega_0 t$, where $v(t)$ is a random signal. Even though $v(t)$ is ergodic, it is easily shown that the modulated process is nonergodic. However, we can deal instead with the ensemble

$$z(t) = v(t) \cos (\omega_0 t + \Theta) \qquad (11a)$$

which will be orgodic if Θ is an independent variate uniformly distributed over $[-\pi, \pi]$. Adding Θ in this fashion merely recognizes the arbitrary choice of the time origin when $v(t)$ and $\cos \omega_0 t$ come from physically independent sources, as is usually the case.

To find $R_z(\tau)$ in terms of $R_v(\tau)$, we follow essentially the same lines as in Example 3.6, except that ensemble averages must be performed with respect to both $v(t)$ and Θ. Hence, expanding $z(t)z(t - \tau)$,

$$R_z(\tau) = \tfrac{1}{2}E[v(t)v(t - \tau) \cos \omega_0 \tau + v(t)v(t - \tau) \cos (2\omega_0 t - \omega_0 \tau + 2\Theta)]$$
$$= \tfrac{1}{2}E[v(t)v(t - \tau)]\{E[\cos \omega_0 \tau] + E[\cos (2\omega_0 t - \omega_0 \tau + 2\Theta)]\}$$
$$= \tfrac{1}{2}R_v(\tau) \cos \omega_0 \tau \qquad (11b)$$

since $E[\cos \omega_0 \tau] = \cos \omega_0 \tau$ while $E[\cos (2\omega_0 t - \omega_0 \tau + 2\Theta)] = 0$, as previously determined. Setting $\tau = 0$ yields $R_z(0) = \tfrac{1}{2}R_v(0)$, consistent with the fact that $E[z^2(t)] = \tfrac{1}{2}E[v^2(t)]$.

Applying the Wiener-Kinchine theorem, $G_z(f) = \mathscr{F}[R_v(\tau)]$, we have

$$G_z(f) = \tfrac{1}{4}[G_v(f - f_0) + G_v(f + f_0)] \qquad (11c)$$

so modulation has translated the spectral density $G_v(f)$ up and down by f_0 units, similar to the modulation theorem in Sect. 2.3. Also note the similarities and differences between this case and the randomly phased sinusoid.

Incoherent Random Signals

The concepts of orthogonality and incoherence were defined in Sect. 2.6 for deterministic signals. Here we say that two random signals are *incoherent* if they are *orthogonal for all* τ, i.e.,

$$R_{vw}(\tau) = R_{wv}(\tau) = 0 \qquad (12)$$

Referring back to Eq. (1), a sufficient condition for incoherence is that $v(t)$ and $w(t)$ be *statistically independent* and one or the other has *zero mean*, so $\overline{wv} = 0$. When Eq. (12) holds, the signal $z(t) = v(t) + w(t)$ has

$$R_z(\tau) = R_v(\tau) + R_w(\tau) \qquad (13a)$$

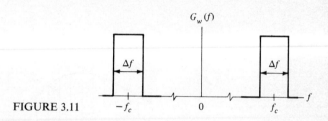

FIGURE 3.11

and, setting $\tau = 0$,

$$\overline{z^2} = \overline{v^2} + \overline{w^2} \qquad (13b)$$

Moreover, from the linearity of Fourier transformation,

$$G_z(f) = G_v(f) + G_w(f) \qquad (13c)$$

so we have superposition of power spectral density as well as superposition of average power.

These results will be especially valuable to us when we study noise and signals contaminated by noise.

Fourier Series Representation of a Random Signal

The autocorrelation and spectral density functions are deterministic representations of a random signal in the τ domain and f domain, respectively. There are also various time-domain series representations, the most important being in the form of a Fourier series. However, such representations are approximate and involve nondeterministic (i.e., random) coefficients.

Consider, to begin with, the random signal $w(t)$ having $G_w(f)$ as shown in Fig. 3.11, where $\Delta f \ll f_c$. Its autocorrelation function is

$$\begin{aligned} R_w(\tau) &= \mathcal{F}^{-1}[G_w(f)] \\ &= 2G_w(f_c)\Delta f \operatorname{sinc} \tau \Delta f \cos \omega_c \tau \end{aligned}$$

since $G_w(f)$ consists of two rectangular functions of the same height, $G_w(f_c) = G_w(-f_c)$. Now if we restrict our attention to relatively small values of τ, so $|\tau| \ll 1/\Delta f$, then sinc $\tau \Delta f \approx 1$ and

$$R_w(\tau) \approx [2G_w(f_c)\Delta f] \cos \omega_c \tau \qquad |\tau| \ll \frac{1}{\Delta f} \qquad (14a)$$

Comparing this with Eq. (10a) in Example 3.6 suggests the approximation

$$w(t) \approx A \cos (\omega_c t + \theta) \qquad (14b)$$

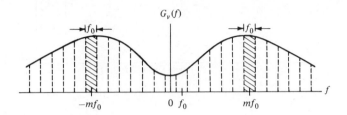

FIGURE 3.12
Partitioned power spectrum.

where A and θ are random variables. Setting $\tau = 0$ in Eq. (14a) shows that $\overline{w^2} = 2G_w(f_c)\Delta f$ so

$$\overline{A^2} = 4G_w(f_c)\Delta f \qquad (14c)$$

We further assume that θ is uniformly distributed since $G_w(f)$ gives no phase information. By this means we have approximated $w(t)$ as a *sinusoid* at frequency f_c with random amplitude and phase; the smaller the value of Δf, the better the approximation. Indeed, if $\Delta f \to 0$, $w(t)$ must be a sinusoid but with vanishingly small amplitude.

The above approximation can be extended to an arbitrary $G_v(f)$ by partitioning it into very narrow bands of width $\Delta f = f_0$ centered at $f = mf_0$, $m = 0, \pm 1, \pm 2, \ldots$, as shown in Fig. 3.12. Each *pair* of bands at $f = \pm mf_0$ corresponds to

$$v_m(t) \approx A_m \cos (m\omega_0 t + \theta_m) \qquad (15a)$$

where θ_m is uniformly distributed and, from Eq. (14c),

$$\overline{A_m^2} = 4f_0 G_v(mf_0) \qquad (15b)$$

Then, because any two different pairs of bands are nonoverlapping, we can write

$$v(t) \approx \sum_{m=0}^{\infty} v_m(t) = \sum_{m=0}^{\infty} A_m \cos (m\omega_0 t + \theta_m) \qquad (16)$$

and all the terms in the sum are mutually incoherent.

In retrospect, Eq. (16) is seen to be a Fourier series expansion with period $T_0 = 1/f_0$ since all components are harmonics of f_0. Thus, our approximation holds over a time interval T_0 seconds long, an interval that can be made arbitrarily large by taking f_0 arbitrarily small—which also improves the approximation.

Converting Eq. (16) to exponential form yields

$$v(t) \approx \sum_{m=-\infty}^{\infty} c_m e^{jm\omega_0 t} \qquad (17a)$$

where the random coefficients c_m can be found from any sample function via the usual rule

$$c_m = \frac{1}{T_0} \int_{T_0} v(t)e^{-jm\omega_0 t}\, dt \qquad (17b)$$

It is readily shown from Eq. (17b) that

$$\overline{c_m} = \begin{cases} \bar{v} & m = 0 \\ 0 & m \neq 0 \end{cases} \qquad (18a)$$

but the other properties of c_m are more easily found by noting that

$$A_m = 2|c_m| \qquad \theta_m = \arg[c_m]$$

Hence†

$$E[|c_m|^2] = f_0\, G_v(mf_0) \qquad (18b)$$

$$E[c_m c_n] = 0 \qquad m \neq n \qquad (18c)$$

To summarize, we have developed an approximate series representation for $v(t)$ over a time interval $T_0 = 1/f_0$. The series coefficients are uncorrelated random variables whose statistical averages are related to the spectral density.

3.6 NOISE AND NOISE FILTERING

Unwanted electric signals come from a variety of sources, generally classified as man-made interference or naturally occurring noise. Man-made interference comes from other communication systems, ignition and commutator sparking, 60 cycle hum, and so forth; natural noise-producing phenomena include atmospheric disturbances, extraterrestrial radiation, and circuit noise. By careful engineering, the effects of many unwanted signals can be reduced or eliminated completely. But there always remain certain inescapable random signals, which present a fundamental limit to systems performance.

One unavoidable cause of electrical noise is the thermal motion of electrons in conducting media — wires, resistors, etc. As long as communication systems are constructed from such material, this *thermal noise* will be with us. Accordingly, this section begins with a brief discussion of thermal noise which, in turn, leads to the abstraction of white noise. We then consider filtered white noise and input-output relations. Other aspects of noise analysis are developed in subsequent chapters and Appendix B.

† Actually, Eqs. (18b) and (18c) are exact only in the limit as $T_0 \to \infty$. See Thomas (1969, chap. 4).

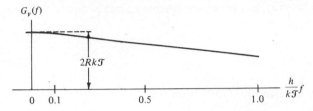

FIGURE 3.13
Thermal noise spectral density, V^2/Hz.

Thermal Noise

Thermal noise, for our purposes, is the noise voltage due to the random motion of charged particles (usually electrons) in conducting media. From kinetic theory, the average energy of a particle at absolute temperature $\mathscr{T}$ is proportional to $k\mathscr{T}$, k being the Boltzmann constant. We thus expect thermal-noise values to involve the product $k\mathscr{T}$; in fact, we shall develop a measure of noise power in terms of temperature.

Historically, Johnson (1928) and Nyquist (1928) first studied thermal noise in metallic resistors, hence the designation *Johnson noise* or *resistance noise*. However, the same basic phenomenon is found in any linear passive media. A general derivation of the properties of thermal noise is omitted here, but, thanks to extensive theoretical and experimental studies, there is a sizable body of knowledge pertaining to the subject, from which we shall freely draw.

When a metallic resistor R is at temperature $\mathscr{T}$, there is a random voltage $v(t)$ produced at the open-circuited terminals by the random electron motion. Consistent with the central-limit theorem, $v(t)$ has a *gaussian distribution* with $\bar{v} = 0$ and

$$\overline{v^2} = \sigma_v{}^2 = \frac{2(\pi k \mathscr{T})^2}{3h} R \qquad \text{volts squared (V}^2) \qquad (1)$$

where

k = Boltzmann constant = 1.37×10^{-23} joules per degree (j/deg)

h = Planck constant = 6.62×10^{-34} joule second (J·s)

and $\mathscr{T}$ is measured in degrees Kelvin. The presence of the Planck constant in Eq. (1) indicates a result from quantum mechanics. It is further shown in quantum mechanics that the spectral density of thermal noise is

$$G_v(f) = \frac{2Rh|f|}{e^{h|f|/k\mathscr{T}} - 1} \qquad \text{volts squared per hertz (V}^2/\text{Hz}) \qquad (2)$$

as plotted in Fig. 3.13 for $f \geq 0$.

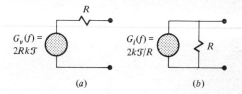

FIGURE 3.14
Thermal resistance noise. (a) Thévenin equivalent circuit; (b) Norton equivalent circuit.

Actually, communication engineers almost never have need for these two expressions. To see why this is so, room temperature or the *standard temperature* is taken to be

$$\mathscr{T}_0 \triangleq 290°K \ (63°F) \qquad (3a)$$

which is rather on the chilly side but does simplify numerical work since

$$k\mathscr{T}_0 \approx 4 \times 10^{-21} \qquad \text{watt second (W·s)} \qquad (3b)$$

Then if the resistance is at $\mathscr{T}_0$, $G_v(f)$ is essentially *constant* for $|f| < 0.1 \, k\mathscr{T}_0/h \approx 10^{12}$ Hz. But this upper limit falls in the infrared portion of the electromagnetic spectrum, far above the point where conventional electrical components have ceased to respond. Even at cryogenic temperatures ($\mathscr{T} \approx 0.01\mathscr{T}_0$) this conclusion holds.

Therefore, to all intents and purposes, we can say that the spectral density of thermal noise is constant, namely,

$$G_v(f) = 2Rk\mathscr{T} \qquad \text{V}^2/\text{Hz} \qquad (4)$$

as obtained from Eq. (2) with $h|f|/k\mathscr{T} \ll 1$. The one trouble with Eq. (4) is that it erroneously predicts $\overline{v^2} = \infty$ when $G_v(f)$ is integrated over all f; bear in mind, however, that one will never have to deal directly with $\overline{v^2}$ since $v(t)$ always is subject to the filtering effects of other circuitry. That topic will be examined shortly. First, however, we will use Eq. (4) to construct the Thévenin equivalent model of a thermal resistor, Fig. 3.14a. Here the resistance is replaced by a fictitious *noiseless* resistance of the same value and the noise is represented by a mean-square voltage generator. Similarly, Fig. 3.14b is the Norton equivalent with a mean-square current generator having $G_i(f) = G_v(f)/R^2 = 2k\mathscr{T}/R$. Both generators are shaded to indicate their special nature.

Instead of dealing with mean-square voltage or current, describing thermal noise by its *available power* cleans up the notation and speeds calculations. Available power is the *maximum* power that can be delivered to a load from a source having fixed nonzero source resistance. The familiar maximum-power-transfer theorem states that this power is delivered only when the load impedance is the complex conjugate of the source impedance. The load is then said to be *matched* to the source, a condition usually desired in a communication system.

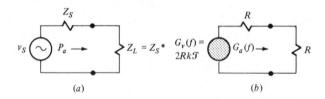

FIGURE 3.15
Available power. (a) Signal source with matched load; (b) thermal resistance with matched load.

Let a conventional signal source have impedance $Z_S = R_S + jX_S$, and let the open-circuit voltage be v_S, Fig. 3.15a. If the load is matched so that $Z_L = Z_S^* = R_S - jX_S$, then the terminal voltage is $v_S/2$, and the available power is

$$P_a = \frac{\langle [v_S(t)/2]^2 \rangle}{R_S} = \frac{\langle v_S^2(t) \rangle}{4R_S}$$

Using the Thévenin model, we can extend this concept to a thermal resistor viewed as a noise source, Fig. 3.15b. By comparison, the *available spectral density* at the load resistance is

$$G_a(f) = \frac{G_v(f)}{4R} = \tfrac{1}{2}k\mathcal{T} \qquad \text{watts per hertz (W/Hz)} \qquad (5)$$

which depends only on the temperature. A thermal resistor therefore delivers a maximum of $k\mathcal{T}/2$ W/Hz to a matched load, regardless of the value of R!

White Noise and Noise Temperature

Besides thermal resistors, many other types of noise sources are gaussian and have a spectral density that is flat over a wide range of frequencies. Such a spectrum has all frequency components in equal proportion and is aptly designated *white* noise, by analogy to white light.

We write the spectral density of white noise in general as

$$G(f) = \frac{\eta}{2} \qquad (6a)$$

where the seemingly extraneous factor of $\frac{1}{2}$ is included to indicate that half the power is associated with positive frequency and half with negative frequency (Fig. 3.16a).

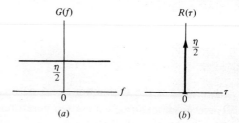

FIGURE 3.16
White noise. (a) Power spectral density;
(b) autocorrelation.

Alternately, η is the *positive-frequency* power density. Since $G(f)$ is known, the auto-correlation function follows immediately by Fourier transformation

$$R(\tau) = \int_{-\infty}^{\infty} \frac{\eta}{2} e^{j\omega\tau} \, df = \frac{\eta}{2} \delta(\tau) \qquad (6b)$$

as in Fig. 3.16b.

From Eq. (6b) or Fig. 3.16b, we see that $R\ (\tau \neq 0) = 0$, so any two different samples of a gaussian white noise signal are *uncorrelated* and hence *statistically independent*. This observation, coupled with the constant power spectrum, leads to an interesting conclusion: if white noise is displayed on an oscilloscope, successive sweeps are always different from each other; yet the waveform always "looks" the same, no matter what sweep speed is used, since all rates of time variation (frequency components) are contained in equal proportion. Similarly, if white noise drives a loudspeaker, it always sounds the same, somewhat like a waterfall. As Pierce† puts it:

> Mathematically, white gaussian noise . . . is the epitome of the various and unexpected. It is the least predictable, the most original of sounds. To a human being, however, all gaussian white noise sounds alike. Its subtleties are hidden from him, and he says that it is dull and monotonous.

The value of η in Eqs. (6a) and (6b) depends on two factors: the type of noise source and the type of spectral density, i.e., mean-square voltage, mean-square current, or available power. If the source is a *thermal resistor*, then

$$\eta_v = 4Rk\mathscr{T} \qquad \eta_i = \frac{4k\mathscr{T}}{R} \qquad \eta_a = k\mathscr{T} \qquad (7)$$

where the type of spectral density is indicated by the subscripts. Moreover, any *thermal* noise source has $\eta_a = k\mathscr{T}$, by definition. Other white noise sources are *nonthermal* in the sense that the available power is unrelated to a physical temperature.

† J. R. Pierce, "Symbols, Signals, and Noise," Harper & Row, Publishers, Incorporated, New York, 1961.

Nonetheless, we can speak of the *noise temperature* $\mathcal{T}_N$ of any white noise source, thermal or nonthermal, by defining

$$\mathcal{T}_N \triangleq \frac{2G_a(f)}{k} = \frac{\eta_a}{k} \qquad (8a)$$

where $\eta_a/2$ is the maximum noise power the source can deliver per unit frequency. Then, given a source's noise temperature,

$$\eta_a = k\mathcal{T}_N \qquad (8b)$$

It must be emphasized that $\mathcal{T}_N$ is not necessarily a physical temperature. For instance, certain electronic noise generators have $\mathcal{T}_N \approx 10\mathcal{T}_0 \approx 3000°\text{K (5000°F)}$ but obviously the devices are not that hot.

Filtered White Noise

The white noise model is reasonable whenever we are concerned with the output of a filter and the input spectral density is more or less constant over the pass band, a very common situation in communication systems. For the study of filtered white noise — or filtering of random signals in general — a basic tool is the input-output power-spectra relationship

$$G_y(f) = |H(f)|^2 G_x(f) \qquad (9a)$$

$H(f)$ being the filter's transfer function. Thus, if the input to a linear time-invariant system is the random signal $x(t)$, the output will be a random signal $y(t)$ with $G_y(f)$ as above, and

$$R_y(\tau) = \int_{-\infty}^{\infty} |H(f)|^2 G_x(f) e^{j\omega\tau} \, df \qquad (9b)$$

$$\overline{y^2} = R_y(0) = \int_{-\infty}^{\infty} |H(f)|^2 G_x(f) \, df \qquad (9c)$$

It is assumed, of course, that $x(t)$ is from an ergodic process, in which case $y(t)$ will also be ergodic.

To illustrate, if white noise is the input to an ideal lowpass filter of unit gain and bandwidth B, then

$$G_y(f) = \frac{\eta}{2} \Pi\left(\frac{f}{2B}\right) \qquad (10a)$$

The output power spectrum is thus a rectangular function (Fig. 3.17a). Likewise, the output autocorrelation is a sinc function (Fig. 3.17b); specifically

$$R_y(\tau) = \eta B \text{ sinc } 2B\tau \qquad (10b)$$

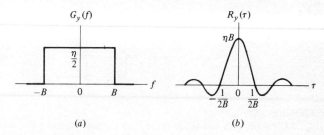

FIGURE 3.17
White noise passed by an ideal LPF. (*a*) Power spectrum; (*b*) autocorrelation.

As evident in the figures, the filtering process has done three things:

1 The power spectrum is no longer white, though it is constant over a finite frequency range.
2 The output power is finite. In fact, $\overline{y^2} = \eta B$.
3 The output signal is correlated over time intervals of about $1/2B$.

Though the above conclusions were based on ideal lowpass filtering, similar results are obtained with any real filter. One should particularly note that the spectrum of filtered white noise takes on the *shape* of $|H(f)|^2$. Since the resulting spectrum is no longer white, filtered white noise is often called *colored noise*.

We would also like to know the probabilistic description of the filtered signal, say its PDF, and in that regard we have both bad news and good news. The bad news is this: there are no general rules relating input and output PDFs, save for one special case. That special case is the good news, namely:

If the input to a linear time-invariant system is a *gaussian* random signal, then the output is also *gaussian*.

This follows from the fact that any linear transformation of a gaussian variate yields another gaussian variate; the statistical averages may be changed, but not the probability model. We consider this special case to be good news simply because the gaussian model is valid for so many (but not all) of the random signals encountered in communication engineering.

Example 3.8 Thermal Noise in an RC Circuit

To pull together several of the topics covered so far, consider the RC circuit in Fig. 3.18*a* where the resistor is at temperature $\mathscr{T}$. Replacing this thermal resistor with its Thévenin model leads to Fig. 3.18*b*, a white noise source with $G_x(f) = 2Rk\mathscr{T}$ V^2/Hz

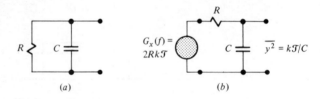

FIGURE 3.18
An RC circuit with resistance noise. (*a*) Circuit diagram; (*b*) noise equivalent circuit.

applied to a *noiseless* RC LPF. Since $|H(f)|^2 = [1 + (f/B)^2]^{-1}$, the output spectral density is

$$G_y(f) = |H(f)|^2 G_x(f) = \frac{2Rk\mathscr{T}}{1 + (f/B)^2} \qquad B = \frac{1}{2\pi RC} \qquad (11a)$$

and the autocorrelation of $y(t)$ is

$$R_y(\tau) = 2Rk\mathscr{T}\pi B e^{-2\pi B|\tau|} = \frac{k\mathscr{T}}{C} e^{-|\tau|/RC} \qquad (11b)$$

as obtained from a transform pair in Table A. $G_y(f)$ and $R_y(\tau)$ are plotted in Fig. 3.19, and the latter shows that the interval over which the filtered noise has appreciable correlation approximately equals the circuit's time constant RC, as might have been suspected.

We can further say that $y(t)$ is a gaussian random signal with $\bar{y} = 0$ (i.e., no DC component)—since $x(t)$ is a zero-mean gaussian—and

$$\overline{y^2} = R_y(0) = \frac{k\mathscr{T}}{C} \qquad (12)$$

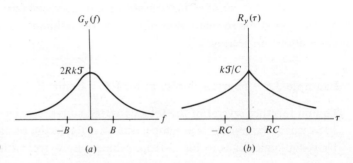

FIGURE 3.19

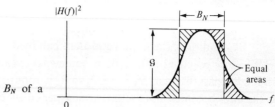

FIGURE 3.20
Noise equivalent bandwidth B_N of a bandpass filter.

Surprisingly, $\overline{y^2}$ depends on C but not on R, even though the noise source is the thermal resistor! This seemingly strange result will be explained later on; here we conclude this example with a numerical calculation.

Suppose the resistor is at room temperature $\mathcal{T}_0$ and $C = 0.1\ \mu\text{F}$; then

$$\overline{y^2} = \frac{4 \times 10^{-21}}{10^{-7}} = 4 \times 10^{-14} \quad \text{V}^2$$

and the rms output voltage is $\sigma_y = 2 \times 10^{-7} = 0.2$ microvolts (μV). Such exceedingly small values are characteristic of thermal noise, which is why thermal noise goes unnoticed in ordinary situations. However, the received signal in a long-distance communication system may be of this same order of magnitude or even smaller, which is why thermal noise is a fundamental limitation in electrical communication.

////

Noise Equivalent Bandwidth

Filtered white noise usually has finite power. To emphasize this, we designate *average noise power* by $N = \overline{y^2}$ and write Eq. (9c) in the form

$$N = \int_{-\infty}^{\infty} |H(f)|^2 \frac{\eta}{2}\, df = \eta \int_{0}^{\infty} |H(f)|^2\, df$$

Noting that the integral depends only on the filter transfer function, we can simplify discussion of noise power by defining a *noise equivalent bandwidth* B_N as

$$B_N \triangleq \frac{1}{\mathcal{G}} \int_{0}^{\infty} |H(f)|^2\, df \qquad (13)$$

where $\mathcal{G}^{1/2} = |H(f)|_{\max}$ is the center-frequency amplitude ratio, i.e., the voltage gain. (This definition assumes the filter has a meaningful center frequency.) Hence the filtered noise power is

$$N = \mathcal{G}\eta B_N \qquad (14)$$

Examining Eq. (14) shows that the effect of the filter has been separated into two parts: the *relative frequency selectivity*, as described by B_N, and the *power gain* (or attenuation), represented by $\mathcal{G}$. Thus, as illustrated in Fig. 3.20 for a bandpass filter, B_N equals the bandwidth of an ideal rectangular filter that would pass as much white noise power as the filter in question, their maximum gains being equal.

By definition, the noise equivalent bandwidth of an ideal filter is its actual bandwidth. For practical filters, B_N is somewhat greater than the 3-dB bandwidth; e.g., an RC lowpass filter has $B_N = \pi B/2$, so B_N is about 50 percent greater than B. However, as the filter becomes more selective (sharper cutoff characteristics), its noise bandwidth approaches the 3-dB bandwidth, and for most applications one is not too far off in taking them to be equal.

Summarizing, if $y(t)$ is filtered white noise of zero mean, then

$$\bar{y} = 0$$
$$\overline{y^2} = \sigma_y^2 = N = \mathscr{G}\eta B_N \qquad (15)$$
$$\sigma_y = \sqrt{N} = \sqrt{\mathscr{G}\eta B_N}$$

This means that given a source of white noise, an average-power meter (or mean-square voltage meter) will read $\overline{y^2} = N = \eta B_N$, where B_N is the noise equivalent bandwidth of the meter itself. Working backward, the source power density can be inferred via $\eta = N/B_N$, providing one is sure that the noise is indeed white over the frequency-response range of the meter.

Example 3.9 Noise Equivalent Bandwidth of an RC LPF

Returning to the RC LPF in the previous example, the filter's center frequency is $f = 0$ so

$$\mathscr{G} = |H(0)|^2 = 1$$

and

$$B_N = \int_0^\infty \frac{df}{1 + (f/B)^2} = \frac{\pi}{2} B = \frac{1}{4RC} \qquad (16)$$

The reason why $\overline{y^2}$ in Eq. (12) is independent of R now becomes apparent if we write $\overline{y^2} = \eta B_N = (4Rk\mathscr{T}) \times (1/4RC)$. Thus, increasing R increases the noise density η (as it should) but decreases the noise bandwidth B_N. These two effects precisely cancel each other and $\overline{y^2} = k\mathscr{T}/C$.   ////

EXERCISE 3.10   Using Eq. (21), Sect. 2.5, show that an Mth-order Butterworth LPF has

$$B_N = \frac{\pi B}{2M \sin(\pi/2M)} \qquad (17)$$

and therefore $B_N \to B$ as $M \to \infty$.

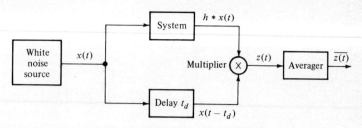

FIGURE 3.21
Impulse response measurement using white noise.

White Noise and Filter Measurements   ★

Because white noise contains all frequencies in equal proportion, it is a convenient signal for filter measurements and experimental design work. Consequently, white noise sources with calibrated power density have become standard laboratory instruments. A few of the measurements that can be made with these sources are discussed below.

Noise equivalent bandwidth   Suppose the gain of an amplifier is known and we wish to find its noise equivalent bandwidth. To do so, we can apply white noise to the input and measure the average output power with a meter whose frequency response is essentially constant over the amplifier's passband. The noise bandwidth in question is then, from Eq. (14), $B_N = N/\mathscr{G}\eta$.

Amplitude response   To find the amplitude response of a given filter, we apply white noise to the input so the output power spectrum is proportional to $|H(f)^2|$. Then we scan the output spectrum with a tunable bandpass filter whose bandwidth is constant and small compared to the variations of $|H(f)|^2$. Thus, if the scanning filter is centered at f_c, the rms noise voltage at its output is proportional to $|H(f_c)|$. By varying f_c, a point-by-point plot of $|H(f)|$ is obtained.

Impulse response   Figure 3.21 shows a method for measuring the impulse response $h(t)$ of a given system. The instrumentation required is a white noise source, a variable time delay, a multiplier, and an averaging device.

Denoting the input noise as $x(t)$, the system output is $h * x(t)$, and the delayed signal is $x(t - t_d)$. Thus, the output of the multiplier is

$$z(t) = x(t - t_d)[h * x(t)]$$

$$= x(t - t_d) \int_{-\infty}^{\infty} h(\lambda)x(t - \lambda) \, d\lambda$$

Now suppose that $z(t)$ is averaged over a long enough time to obtain $\langle z(t) \rangle$. If the noise source is ergodic and the system is linear and time-invariant, the averaged output is the ensemble average

$$\overline{z(t)} = \int_{-\infty}^{\infty} h(\lambda) \mathbf{E}[x(t - t_d) x(t - \lambda)] \, d\lambda$$

where we have interchanged the order of integration and averaging. Inspecting the integral, it can be seen that

$$\mathbf{E}[x(t - t_d) x (t - \lambda)] = R_x(\lambda - t_d)$$

But, with $x(t)$ being white noise, Eq. (6b) says that $R_x(\lambda - t_d) = (n/2)\delta(\lambda - t_d)$. Hence

$$\overline{z(t)} = \frac{\eta}{2} \int_{-\infty}^{\infty} h(\lambda) \, \delta(\lambda - t_d) \, d\lambda = \frac{\eta}{2} h(t_d)$$

Therefore, $h(t)$ is measured by varying the time delay t_d.

The reader may question the practicality of this method, particularly since $h(t)$ can be obtained immediately by applying an impulse (or a brief and intensive pulse) to the system. While this is a valid conclusion for most *filter* measurements, there are many systems, such as industrial processing and control systems, for which an impulsive input cannot be readily achieved or, if achieved, might damage or destroy the system.

3.7   PROBLEMS

3.1   (Sect. 3.1) A thick but otherwise honest coin has probability $P(E) = 0.2$ of landing on its edge. Evaluate the following when the coin is tossed twice: $P(EE)$, $P(\text{no } E)$, $P(\text{not } HH)$, $P(\text{match})$. *Ans.*: 0.04, 0.64, 0.84, 0.32.

3.2   (Sect. 3.1) Three balls are drawn at random from an urn containing 500 white balls, 300 red balls, and 200 black balls. Assuming each ball is replaced before the next is drawn, find the probabilities of the following outcomes: each ball is a different color; two or more balls are the same color; no white balls; two or more black balls given that one ball is black.

3.3   (Sect. 3.1) A binary data system uses two symbols **0** and **1**, transmitted with probabilites P_0 and P_1. Owing to transmission errors a **0** may be changed to a **1** at the receiver with probability p_0, and similarly for p_1. Obtain expressions for the following: the approximate number of errors in a sequence of $n \gg 1$ digits; the probability that a received digit is a **0**; the probability that an error has occurred given that a **0** is received.

3.4   (Sect. 3.2) Three biased coins are tossed and X is assigned as the total number of heads. Find $P(x_j)$ and plot the CDF when $P(H) = 0.4$.

3.5   (Sect. 3.2) A pair of honest dice is rolled. Totaling the number of spots that turn up, the possible outcomes are $x_j = 2, 3, \ldots, 12$. Find $P(x_j)$ and plot the CDF.

3.6 (Sect. 3.2) A certain random variable has

$$F(x) = \begin{cases} 0 & x < 0 \\ Kx^2 & 0 \le x \le 10 \\ 100K & x > 10 \end{cases}$$

Find K, evaluate $P(X \le 5)$ and $P(5 < X \le 7)$, and plot the PDF.

3.7 (Sect. 3.2) Given $p(x) = a^2 x e^{-ax} u(x)$, where a is a constant, find $F(x)$ and evaluate $P(X \le 1/a)$ and $P(1/a < X \le 2/a)$.

3.8 (Sect. 3.2) Find $P(X \le 0)$, $P(0 < X \le 1)$, and $P(X > 1)$ in Example 3.4.

3.9 (Sect. 3.2) Find $P(0 < Z \le 1)$, $P(Z \le 1)$, and $P(Z \ne 0)$ in Exercise 3.4.

3.10 (Sect. 3.2) Let $Z = 3X - 5$ where $p_x(x)$ is given by Eq. (9a). Find $F(z)$.

3.11 (Sect. 3.2) Use Eq. (16) to prove that $\int_{-\infty}^{\infty} p(x|y)\, dx = 1$. Explain why this must be true.

3.12 (Sect. 3.3) Calculate the mean and variance of X when $p(x) = e^{-x} u(x)$. *Ans.:* $\bar{x} = \sigma_x^2 = 1$.

3.13 (Sect. 3.3) Calculate the mean and variance of X given $p(x)$ in Prob. 3.7.

3.14 (Sect. 3.3) Expand $E[(x - \bar{x})^3]$ in terms of the moments of X.

3.15 (Sect. 3.3) Prove that $E[(x - c)^2]$ is minimum when $c = \bar{x}$.

3.16 (Sect. 3.3) Referring to Example 3.5, find the plot $P(|X| \le \kappa\sqrt{2})$ versus κ, and compare with Chebyshev's inequality.

3.17 (Sect. 3.3) Given that X and Y are statistically independent, find σ_z^2 in terms of the statistical parameters of X and Y when: $Z = X - Y + c$, where c is a constant; $Z = XY$ and $\bar{x} = \bar{y} = 0$.

3.18 (Sect. 3.3) Starting with $E[(x - y)^2]$, obtain an upper bound on $\bar{x}\bar{y}$ when X and Y are not statistically independent.

3.19 (Sect. 3.3) N independent observations of a random variable are made and averaged to give

$$Y = \frac{1}{N} \sum_{j=1}^{N} X_j$$

where X_j is the jth observed value. Show that $\bar{y} = \bar{x}$ and $\sigma_y = \sigma_x/\sqrt{N}$.

3.20 (Sect. 3.4) By applying the binomial distribution, find the probability that there will be fewer than three heads when 10 honest coins are tossed. What is the expected range of the number of heads?

3.21 (Sect. 3.4) When $m \gg 1$ and $\epsilon \ll 1$, the binomial distribution may be approximated by the *Poisson distribution* $P(n) = e^{-\bar{n}} \bar{n}^n / n!$, where $\bar{n} = m\epsilon$. Use this to find the probability of no errors in 100 digits when $\epsilon = 10^{-3}$.

3.22 (Sect. 3.4) You have designed a digital transmission system with an error probability of 10^{-6} per digit. The customer will test the system by sending a known message of 10^6 digits and checking the received message. If there are more than two errors, you will be fired. Calculate the probability of losing your job. (*Hint:* See Prob. 3.21.)

3.23 (Sect. 3.4) Let $Y = \cos \pi X$ where X has a uniform PDF over $[-\frac{1}{2}, \frac{1}{2}]$. Find $\bar{y}$ and σ_y.

3.24   (Sect. 3.4) A gaussian variate has $\bar{x} = 10$ and $\sigma_x = 20$. Find $P(X > 20), P(10 < X \leq 20)$, $P(0 < X \leq 20)$, and $P(X > 0)$. *Ans.*: 0.31, 0.19, 0.38, 0.69.

3.25   (Sect. 3.4) A random voltage is known to be gaussian with $\bar{x} = 0$ and $\overline{x^2} = 9$. Find the value of c such that $|X| \leq c$ for:
   (a) 90 percent of the time
   (b) 99 percent of the time

3.26   (Sect. 3.4) Derive the approximation, Eq. (10).

3.27★(Sect. 3.4) Let $Z = X_1 + 2X_2$ where X_1 and X_2 are gaussian variates with $\overline{x_1^2} = \overline{x_2^2} = 25$, $m_1 = 0$, $m_2 = 3$, and $\overline{x_1 x_2} = 6$. Find $p_z(z)$.

3.28★(Sect. 3.4) Let $X_2 = X_1^2$ so, clearly, X_1 and X_2 are not independent. Nevertheless, show that they are uncorrelated ($\rho_{12} = 0$) if $p(x_1)$ has even symmetry.

3.29   (Sect. 3.5) Consider the process $v(t) = A \cos(\omega_0 t + \Theta)$, where A and Θ are independent random variables over the ensemble and Θ has a uniform PDF over $[-\pi, \pi]$. Show that $E[v(t)] = 0$ and $E[v^2(t)] = \overline{A^2}/2$. (*Hint*: Recall that the ensemble average must be taken with respect to both random variables.)

3.30   (Sect. 3.5) Demonstrate that the process in Prob. 3.29 is not ergodic.

3.31   (Sect. 3.5) If $v(t)$ is a random ergodic process that is periodic with period T_0, show that $R_v(\tau)$ also has period T_0.

3.32   (Sect. 3.5) A certain random signal has a DC component of 2 volts (V) and an rms value of 4 V. Further measurements indicate that $v(t)$ and $v(t - \tau)$ are independent for $|\tau| > 5$ μs (microseconds), while $R_v(\tau)$ decreases linearly with $|\tau|$ for $|\tau| \leq 5$ μs.
   (a) Plot $R_v(\tau)$ and fully dimension.
   (b) Find and plot $G_v(f)$.

3.33   (Sect. 3.5) Let $z(t) = v(t) + v(t - T)$, where $v(t)$ is a random signal and T is a constant. Find $R_z(\tau)$ and $G_z(f)$ in terms of $R_v(\tau)$ and $G_v(f)$.

3.34   (Sect. 3.5) Suppose $v(t)$ in Eq. (11a) is a random binary wave (Example 3.7). Sketch $R_z(\tau)$ and $G_z(f)$ taking $f_0 \gg 1/T$. Also show that $E[z^2(t)] = \langle z^2(t) \rangle = A^2/2$.

3.35   (Sect. 3.5) Let $z(t) = v(t)w(t)$, where $v(t)$ and $w(t)$ are independent random signals.
   (a) Show that $R_z(\tau) = R_v(\tau)R_w(\tau)$ and hence $G_z(f) = G_v * G_w(f)$.
   (b) Use these results and Example 3.6 to derive Eqs. (11b) and (11c).

3.36   (Sect. 3.5) By inserting Eq. (17a) into Eq. (2), show that

$$R_v(\tau) \approx f_0 G_v(0) + 2f_0 \sum_{m=1}^{\infty} G_v(mf_0) \cos m\omega_0 \tau$$

3.37   (Sect. 3.6) A 1-kilohm (kΩ) metallic resistor is at 29°K. Calculate the open-circuit rms noise voltage; estimate the frequency range over which $G_v(f)$ is essentially constant; evaluate $G_v(f)$, $G_i(f)$, and $G_a(f)$ in this range, and specify their units.

3.38   (Sect. 3.6) Two thermal resistors R_1 and R_2 at temperatures $\mathcal{T}_1$ and $\mathcal{T}_2$ are connected in series. Find the noise temperature $\mathcal{T}_N$ of the combination. (*Hint*: Use the Thévenin model and recall that spectral densities add when sources are independent.) *Ans.*: $(R_1 \mathcal{T}_1 + R_2 \mathcal{T}_2)/(R_1 + R_2)$.

3.39   (Sect. 3.6) Do Prob. 3.38 for a parallel connection.

3.40 (Sect. 3.6) A temperature-limited vacuum diode noise generator has $G_v(f) = 2Rk\mathcal{T}_0 + eI_b R^2$, where R is the source resistance, e is the electronic charge, and I_b the DC diode current. Obtain an expression for the noise temperature and evaluate it when $R = 50 \ \Omega$ and $I_b = 20$ milliamperes (mA).

3.41 (Sect. 3.6) White noise is the input to a zero-order hold, Example 2.13, Sect. 2.5. Find $G_y(f)$, $R_y(\tau)$, and $\overline{y^2}$.

3.42 (Sect. 3.6) Noise from a 10-kΩ resistor at room temperature is passed through an ideal LPF with $B = 2.5$ MHz and unit gain. Obtain an expression for the PDF of the output voltage $y(t)$. *Ans.*: Gaussian with $\bar{y} = 0$, $\sigma_y = 2 \times 10^{-5}$.

3.43 (Sect. 3.6) The filtered noise in Prob. 3.42 is passed through a full-wave rectifier, giving $z(t) = |y(t)|$. Find $p_z(z)$ and evaluate $\bar{z}$ and σ_z.

3.44★(Sect. 3.6) The filtered noise in Prob. 3.42 is sampled every 0.1 microsecond (μs). Denoting two adjacent sample values as y_1 and y_2, obtain an expression for their joint PDF $p(y_1, y_2)$. (*Hint*: The covariance σ_{12} can be found from $R_y(\tau)$.)

3.45 (Sect. 3.6) Find the noise equivalent bandwidth B_N for the gaussian LPF in Prob. 2.44, and compare it with the 3-dB bandwidth.

4

BASEBAND COMMUNICATION

Baseband communication refers to signal transmission *without modulation*; the name stems from the fact that baseband transmission does not involve frequency translation of the message spectrum that characterizes modulation. And although the majority of communication systems are modulation systems, baseband transmission deserves our study. For one reason, baseband connecting links are part of most modulation systems; for another, many of the concepts and parameters of baseband communication carry over directly to modulation. But perhaps most important, the performance characteristics of baseband transmission serve as useful standards when comparing the various types of modulation.

This chapter, therefore, is devoted to baseband communication. It begins with an investigation of the two fundamental limitations of electrical signaling mentioned in Chap. 1, namely, noise and bandwidth. The results are then applied to three distinct classes of baseband transmission: analog, pulse, and digital. The coverage ranges from elementary but significant design calculations to optional discussion of sophisticated optimization techniques.

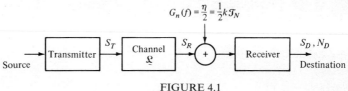

FIGURE 4.1
Parameters of a communication system.

4.1 SIGNALS AND NOISE

We observed in Chap. 3 that noise becomes a significant factor in electrical communication when the received signal is very feeble and therefore of the same order of magnitude as the ever-present thermal noise. In turn, the very small received signal level is due primarily to the large amount of power loss that characterizes long-haul transmission. Hence, our discussion of signals and noise starts with a consideration of transmission loss. Figure 4.1 puts this topic in context and locates the various system parameters with which we shall deal. These parameters are defined as follows:

$$S_T = \text{signal power at the transmitter output}$$
$$\mathscr{L} = \text{transmission power loss of the channel}$$
$$S_R = \text{signal power at the receiver input}$$
$$\mathscr{T}_N = \text{noise temperature referred to the receiver input}$$
$$\eta = \text{noise density (assumed constant) at the receiver input}$$
$$S_D = \text{signal power at the destination}$$
$$N_D = \text{noise power at the destination}$$

This set of notation is used throughout the rest of the text and the reader should carefully study the definitions.

Transmission Loss

When we say that an amplifier has *power gain* $\mathscr{G}$, we mean that the input and output powers are related by $P_{\text{out}} = \mathscr{G} P_{\text{in}}$, so

$$\mathscr{G} \triangleq \frac{P_{\text{out}}}{P_{\text{in}}} \qquad (1a)$$

Frequently gain is expressed in decibels† as

$$\mathscr{G}_{\text{dB}} \triangleq 10 \log_{10} \mathscr{G} = 10 \log_{10} \frac{P_{\text{out}}}{P_{\text{in}}} \qquad (1b)$$

† See Table E for decibel conversions and manipulations.

Hence, if $P_{out} = 100P_{in}$, $\mathcal{G} = 100$ and $\mathcal{G}_{dB} = 20$ dB; if the power gain is unity, then $\mathcal{G}_{dB} = 0$ dB. But almost all transmission channels have $P_{out} < P_{in}$ and $\mathcal{G} < 1$. Thus we define the *power loss*

$$\mathcal{L} \triangleq \frac{1}{\mathcal{G}} = \frac{P_{in}}{P_{out}} \qquad (2a)$$

$$\mathcal{L}_{dB} = -\mathcal{G}_{dB} = 10 \log_{10} \frac{P_{in}}{P_{out}} \qquad (2b)$$

also called the *attenuation*.

Although we have defined $\mathcal{G}$ and $\mathcal{L}$ as power ratios, they can be expressed as ratios of mean-square voltage or current, e.g.,

$$\mathcal{G} = \frac{\overline{v_{out}^2}}{\overline{v_{in}^2}} \qquad (3)$$

where the bar stands for either time average or ensemble average, as appropriate. Equation (3) is consistent with our use of normalized power, and we will not get involved in the distinctions between available power gain, transducer power gain, etc.

Illustrating Eq. (2), the input-output relations for transmission lines, coaxial cables, and waveguides are all of the form

$$P_{out} = e^{-2\alpha l}P_{in} = 10^{-8.68\alpha l}P_{in} \qquad (4)$$

where α is the attenuation coefficient and l is the path length. Therefore the loss in decibels is

$$\mathcal{L}_{dB} = 8.68\alpha l \qquad (5)$$

Table 4.1 lists some representative values. Actually, Eqs. (4) and (5) strictly hold only for sinusoidal signals and α depends on the frequency, as the table implies. For the time being we ignore the frequency dependence since the point here is the potentially

Table 4.1 TYPICAL VALUES OF TRANSMISSION LOSS

Transmission medium	Frequency	Loss, dB/km
Open-wire pair (0.3 cm diameter)	1 kHz	0.05
Twisted-wire pair (16 gauge)	10 kHz	2
	100 kHz	3
	300 kHz	6
Coaxial cable (1 cm diameter)	100 kHz	1
	1 MHz	2
	3 MHz	4
Coaxial cable (15 cm diameter)	100 MHz	1.5
Rectangular waveguide (5 × 2.5 cm)	10 GHz	5
Helical waveguide (5 cm diameter)	100 GHz	1.5

large values of loss. Underscoring that point, a 20-km run of 16-gauge twisted pair at 100 kHz has $\mathscr{L}_{dB} = 3 \times 20 = 60$ dB or $\mathscr{L} = 10^6$, which means that $P_{out} = P_{in}/\mathscr{L} = 10^{-6} P_{in}$! Also observe that the decibel loss is directly proportional to l; so, continuing our example, a 40-km run has $\mathscr{L}_{dB} = 2 \times 60 = 120$ dB and $P_{out} = 10^{-12} P_{in}$!!

In view of the above numbers, it is not surprising that transmission by radio propagation is often preferred for large distances. Although radio systems involve modulation, to be covered in later chapters, it seems appropriate here to mention the difference between cable and radio transmission insofar as path loss is concerned.

Specifically, the power ratio on a line-of-sight radio path is

$$\frac{P_{out}}{P_{in}} = \mathscr{G}_{TA} \mathscr{G}_{RA} \left(\frac{\lambda}{4\pi l}\right)^2 \qquad (6)$$

where $\mathscr{G}_{TA}$ and $\mathscr{G}_{RA}$ are the power gains of the transmitting and receiving antennas and λ is the wavelength of the carrier. Thus

$$\mathscr{L}_{dB} = 22 + 10 \log_{10} \left(\frac{l}{\lambda}\right)^2 - (\mathscr{G}_{TA_{dB}} + \mathscr{G}_{RA_{dB}}) \qquad (7)$$

so a 20-km path with $\lambda = 1$ meter and $\mathscr{G}_{TA} = \mathscr{G}_{RA} = 16$ dB has $\mathscr{L}_{dB} = 22 + 86 - 32 = 76$ dB. But note that Eq. (7) is *not* proportional to l; in fact, doubling l increases the loss by only 6 dB (an assertion the reader should confirm for himself). Therefore, a 40-km path with the above parameters has $\mathscr{L}_{dB} = 76 + 6 = 82$ dB. Incidentally, 40 km is just about the upper limit for line-of-sight paths over flat terrain unless rather high antenna towers are used.

Returning to Fig. 4.1, we can now express S_R in terms of S_T and $\mathscr{L}$ simply as

$$S_R = \frac{S_T}{\mathscr{L}} \qquad (8)$$

Then, if the power gain of the receiver is $\mathscr{G}_R$,

$$S_D = \mathscr{G}_R S_R = \frac{\mathscr{G}_R}{\mathscr{L}} S_T \qquad (9a)$$

Equations such as Eq. (9a) may be written in the form

$$S_{D_{dBW}} = \mathscr{G}_{R_{dB}} - \mathscr{L}_{dB} + S_{T_{dBW}} \qquad (9b)$$

where dBW stands for decibels above 1 watt, e.g., 20 dBW = 100 W. Hence, multiplication and division are replaced by addition and subtraction of decibel values, which is why they are so much used by communication engineers. But the extra subscripts in Eq. (9b), etc., are a nuisance and will be omitted hereafter; it should be clear from the context when dB values are implied.

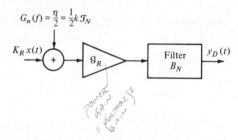

FIGURE 4.2
Model of receiver with additive white noise.

Additive Noise

Having gotten the signal to the receiver, let us look at the effects of contaminating noise. Figure 4.2 extracts the pertinent portion of Fig. 4.1. The waveform at the receiver input is $K_R x(t)$, where $x(t)$ is the information-bearing signal, to which is added white noise having $G_n(f) = \eta/2 = k\mathcal{T}_N/2$. The noise temperature $\mathcal{T}_N$ represents *all* the noise in the system, referred to the receiver input.† Numerical values may range from around 60°K in a carefully engineered low-noise system to several thousand degrees.

For analysis purposes, the receiver has been separated into two parts: an amplifier with power gain $\mathcal{G}_R$ (and voltage gain $\sqrt{\mathcal{G}_R}$) followed by a filter with noise equivalent bandwidth B_N and $\mathcal{G} = 1$. The function of the filter is to pass $x(t)$ but reject as much noise as possible, namely, those noise components outside the signal's frequency range — the *out-of-band* noise, in other words.

Assuming no nonlinearities in the receiver, the total output is

$$y_D(t) = \sqrt{\mathcal{G}_R}\, K_R\, x(t) + n_D(t) \tag{10}$$

where $n_D(t)$ is the output noise. It is not unreasonable to further assume that $x(t)$ and $n_D(t)$ are *statistically independent* and that $\bar{n}_D = 0$; under these conditions, $x(t)$ and $n_D(t)$ are *incoherent* and their crosscorrelation is zero, i.e., $R_{xn_D}(\tau) = R_{n_Dx}(\tau) = 0$. Therefore, using Eq. (10), Sect. 3.5,

$$R_{y_D}(\tau) = \mathcal{G}_R K_R{}^2 R_x(\tau) + R_{n_D}(\tau) \tag{11}$$

and

$$\overline{y_D{}^2} = \underbrace{\mathcal{G}_R K_R{}^2 \overline{x^2}}_{S_D} + \underbrace{\overline{n_D{}^2}}_{N_D} \tag{12}$$

where we have identified the two components of $\overline{y_D{}^2}$ as the output signal and noise powers, respectively. Specifically, since $S_R = K_R{}^2\overline{x^2}$,

$$S_D = \mathcal{G}_R K_R{}^2 \overline{x^2} = \mathcal{G}_R S_R \tag{13}$$

† See Appendix B for the method.

and, from Eq. (14), Sect. 3.6,

$$N_D = \overline{n_D{}^2} = \mathscr{G}_R \eta B_N \qquad (14)$$

in which one can insert $\eta = k\mathscr{T}_N$ if desired. If the noise is not white, then

$$N_D = \mathscr{G}_R \int_{-\infty}^{\infty} |H_R(f)|^2 G_n(f)\, df$$

where $H_R(f)$ describes the filter.

Signal-to-Noise Ratios

Whenever we have an expression like Eq. (12), it is meaningful to speak of the ratio of signal power to noise power—or *signal-to-noise ratio*, for short. In the case at hand, we define the signal-to-noise ratio at the destination

$$\left(\frac{S}{N}\right)_D \triangleq \frac{S_D}{N_D}$$

$$= \frac{K_R \overline{x^2}}{\eta B_N} = \frac{S_R}{\eta B_N} \qquad (15)$$

Note that the receiver gain $\mathscr{G}_R$ has canceled out, being common to both terms. Such cancellation will always occur, and the only function of $\mathscr{G}_R$ is to produce the desired signal level at the output.

On the other hand, any gains or losses that enter the picture *before* the noise has been added will definitely affect $(S/N)_D$. As an important case in point, recall that $S_R = S_T/\mathscr{L}$, so

$$\left(\frac{S}{N}\right)_D = \frac{S_T}{\mathscr{L}\eta B_N} \qquad (16)$$

and we see that the signal-to-noise ratio is inversely proportional to the transmission loss.

One final comment here regarding the assumptions behind these results: if the noise is not additive, or if the receiver has nonlinearities, or if $x(t)$ and $n_D(t)$ are not incoherent, then $R_{y_D}(\tau)$ will include *crosscorrelations* $R_{xn_D}(\tau)$, etc. Therefore, $\overline{y_D{}^2}$ will have crossproduct or signal-times-noise terms so the definition of the signal-to-noise ratio is ambiguous and not particularly meaningful.

Repeater Systems

If the path loss on a given system yields an unsatisfactorily low value for $(S/N)_D$ and the parameters S_T, η, and B_N are fixed, there still remains an alternative, namely, the introduction of one or more amplifier-filter units between source and destination. These units are called *repeaters*.

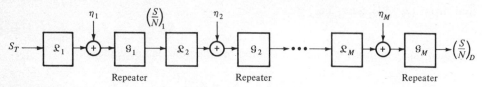

FIGURE 4.3
Repeater system.

A repeater system is block-diagramed in Fig. 4.3, where the filters are combined with the amplifiers. The last repeater and the receiver are one and the same. Typical repeater spacings are as small as 2 km for certain cable systems, and run up to 40 km for microwave radio relay systems. Hence, with the notable exception of communication satellite links, it takes from 100 to 2,000 repeaters to span the North American continent.

Inspecting Fig. 4.3 shows that the S/N at the output of the first repeater is

$$\left(\frac{S}{N}\right)_1 = \frac{S_T}{\mathscr{L}_1 \eta_1 B_N}$$

Usually repeater systems are designed with identical units and just enough gain to overcome the loss, i.e., $\mathscr{G}_1/\mathscr{L}_1 = \mathscr{G}_2/\mathscr{L}_2 = \cdots = 1$. Furthermore, $\eta_1 = \eta_2 = \cdots = \eta_M$ when the units are identical and the amplifier noise dominates other noise sources. Under these conditions† $S_D = S_T$, $N_D = M\mathscr{G}_1\eta_1 B_N = M\mathscr{L}_1\eta_1 B_N$, and

$$\left(\frac{S}{N}\right)_D = \frac{S_T}{M\mathscr{L}_1\eta_1 B_N} = \frac{1}{M}\left(\frac{S}{N}\right)_1 \qquad (17)$$

Therefore, the destination S/N equals $1/M$ times the S/N for one link or hop.

It might appear from Eq. (17) that little has been gained by using repeaters. Bear in mind, however, that $\mathscr{L}_1$ is the loss on just *one* hop; if repeaters are not used, the total loss is $\mathscr{L} = \mathscr{L}_1\mathscr{L}_2 \cdots \mathscr{L}_M = \mathscr{L}_1{}^M$. Hence, $\mathscr{L}_1 = \mathscr{L}^{1/M}$, which represents a substantial loss reduction, as the following exercise will reveal.

EXERCISE 4.1 A signal is to be transmitted 40 km using a transmission line whose loss is 3 dB/km; the receiver has $\mathscr{T}_N = 10\mathscr{T}_0$ and $B_N = 5$ kHz. Calculate ηB_N in decibels above one watt (dBW) and find the value of S_T (in watts) required to get $(S/N)_D = 50$ dB. Repeat the second calculation when there is a repeater at the halfway point. *Ans.*: -157 dBW, 20 W, 40 μW.

<hr>

† Appendix B gives the analysis of the general case.

4.2 SIGNAL DISTORTION IN TRANSMISSION

Besides noise, the other fundamental limitation of electrical communication is bandwidth, the finite bandwidth of any real systems that leads to signal distortion. But *distortionless transmission* does not necessarily imply that the output is identical to the input. Certain differences can be tolerated and not classified as distortion. Our purpose here is to formalize the meaning of distortionless transmission and the requirements for it. With this background, the various types of distortion can be defined and their effects investigated. The emphasis will be on those aspects pertinent to communication systems.

Stated crudely, for distortionless transmission the output should "look like" the input. More precisely, given an input signal $x(t)$, we say that the output is undistorted if it differs from the input only by a multiplying constant and a finite time delay. Analytically, we have distortionless transmission if

$$y(t) = Kx(t - t_d) \tag{1}$$

where K and t_d are constants.

The properties of a distortionless network are easily found by examining the output spectrum

$$Y(f) = \mathscr{F}[y(t)] = Ke^{-j\omega t_d}X(f)$$

Now by definition of transfer function, $Y(f) = H(f)X(f)$, so

$$H(f) = Ke^{-j\omega t_d} \tag{2a}$$

In words, a network giving distortionless transmission must have *constant amplitude response* and negative *linear phase shift*, that is,

$$|H(f)| = K \qquad \arg[H(f)] = -2\pi t_d f \pm m180° \tag{2b}$$

We have added the $\pm m180°$ term to account for the constant being positive or negative. Zero phase is allowable since it implies zero time delay. One more qualification can be added to Eq. (2): these conditions are required only over those frequencies for which the input signal has nonzero spectrum. Thus, if $x(t)$ is bandlimited in W, Eq. (2) need be satisfied only for $|f| < W$.

In practice distortionless transmission is a stringent condition which, at best, can be only approximately satisfied. Thus, an inescapable fact of signal transmission is that distortion will occur, though it can be minimized by proper design. We should therefore be concerned with the *degree* of distortion, measured in some quantitative fashion. Unfortunately, quantitative measures prove to be rather unwieldy and impractical for engineering purposes. As an alternate approach, distortion has been classified as to type, and each type considered separately. But before discussing the various types, it must be emphasized that *distortion is distortion*; a severely distorted output will differ significantly from the input, regardless of the specific cause.

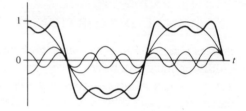

FIGURE 4.4
Test signal $x(t) = \cos \omega_0 t - \frac{1}{3} \cos 3\omega_0 t + \frac{1}{5} \cos 5\omega_0 t$.

The three major classifications of distortion are:

1 Amplitude distortion: $|H(f)| \neq K$
2 Phase (delay) distortion: $\arg [H(f)] \neq -2\pi t_d f \pm m180°$
3 Nonlinear distortion

The first two cases are categorized as *linear* distortion. In the third case the system includes nonlinear elements, and its transfer function is not defined. We now examine these individually.

Amplitude Distortion

Amplitude distortion is easily described in the frequency domain; it means simply that the output frequency components are not in correct proportion. Since this is caused by $|H(f)|$ not being constant with frequency, amplitude distortion is sometimes called *frequency distortion.*

The most common forms of amplitude distortion are excess attenuation or enhancement of extreme high or low frequencies in the signal spectrum. Less common, but equally bothersome, is disproportionate response to a band of frequencies within the spectrum. While the frequency-domain description is easy, the effects in the time domain are far less obvious, save for very simple signals. For illustration, a suitably simple test signal is $x(t) = \cos \omega_0 t - \frac{1}{3} \cos 3\omega_0 t + \frac{1}{5} \cos 5\omega_0 t$, Fig. 4.4, a rough approximation to a square wave. If the low-frequency or high-frequency component is attenuated by one-half, the resulting outputs are as shown in Fig. 4.5. As expected, loss of the high-frequency term reduces the "sharpness" of the waveform.

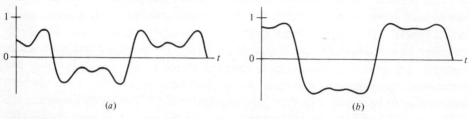

(*a*)   (*b*)

FIGURE 4.5
Test signal with amplitude distortion. (*a*) Low frequency attenuated; (*b*) high frequency attenuated.

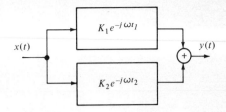

FIGURE 4.6
Block diagram of radio system with two propagation paths.

Beyond qualitative observations, there is little more that can be said about amplitude distortion without experimental study of specific signal types. Results of such studies are usually couched in terms of required *frequency response*, i.e., the range of frequencies over which $|H(f)|$ must be constant to within a certain tolerance (say ± 1 dB) so that the amplitude distortion is sufficiently small.

EXERCISE 4.2 Sometimes radio systems suffer from *multipath distortion* caused by two (or more) propagation paths between transmitter and receiver. As a simple example, suppose that the received signal is

$$y(t) = K_1 x(t - t_1) + K_2 x(t - t_2) \qquad (3a)$$

Show that Fig. 4.6 is the equivalent block diagram and that, if $(K_2/K_1)^2 \ll 1$,

$$|H(f)| \approx K_1 \left[1 + \frac{K_2}{K_1} \cos 2\pi f(t_2 - t_1) \right] \qquad (3b)$$

Hence, a "weak" reflection yields *ripples* in the amplitude ratio.

Phase Shift and Delay Distortion

A linear phase shift yields a constant time delay for all frequency components in the signal. This, coupled with constant amplitude response, yields an undistorted output. If the phase shift is not linear, the various frequency components suffer different amounts of time delay, and the resulting distortion is termed *phase* or *delay distortion*.

For an arbitrary phase shift, the time delay is a function of frequency, call it $t_d(f)$, and can be found by writing arg $[H(f)] = -2\pi f t_d(f)$, so

$$t_d(f) = -\frac{\text{arg } [H(f)]}{2\pi f} \qquad (4)$$

which is independent of frequency only if arg $[H(f)]$ is linear with frequency.

A common area of confusion is *constant time delay* versus *constant phase shift*. The former is desirable and is required for distortionless transmission. The latter, in general, causes distortion. Suppose a system has the constant phase shift θ. Then

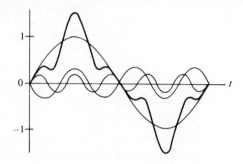

FIGURE 4.7
Test signal with constant phase shift
of $-90°$.

each signal frequency component will be delayed by $\theta/2\pi$ *cycles* of its own frequency; this is the meaning of constant phase shift. But the time delays will be different, the frequency components will be scrambled in time, and distortion will result. However, the constant phase shifts $\theta = 0$ and $\pm m180°$ are acceptable.

That constant phase shift does give distortion is simply illustrated by returning to the test signal of Fig. 4.4 and shifting each component by one-fourth cycle, $\theta = -90°$. Whereas the input was roughly a square wave, the output will look like a triangular wave, Fig. 4.7. With an arbitrary nonlinear phase shift, the deterioration of wave-shape can be even more severe.

One should also note from Fig. 4.7 that the *peak* excursions of the phase-shifted signal are substantially greater (by about 50 percent) than those of the input test signal. This is not due to amplitude response, since the output amplitudes of the three frequency components are, in fact, unchanged; rather, it is because the components of the distorted signal all attain maximum or minimum values at the same time, which was not true of the input. Conversely, had we started with Fig. 4.7 as the test signal, a constant phase shift of $+90°$ would yield Fig. 4.4 for the output waveform. Thus we see that *delay distortion alone* can result in an increase or decrease of peak values as well as other waveshape alterations.

Clearly, delay distortion can be critical in pulse transmission, and much labor is spent *equalizing* transmission delay for digital data systems and the like. On the other hand, the human ear is curiously insensitive to delay distortion; the waveforms of Figs. 4.4 and 4.7 would sound just about the same when driving a loudspeaker. Thus, delay distortion is seldom of concern in voice and music transmission.

Equalization

Linear distortion—i.e., amplitude and delay distortion—is theoretically curable through the use of *equalization* networks. Figure 4.8 shows an equalizer $H_{eq}(f)$ in cascade with a distorting channel $H_C(f)$. Since the overall transfer function is $H(f) =$

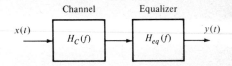

FIGURE 4.8
Channel with equalizer for linear
distortion.

$H_C(f)H_{eq}(f)$ the final output will be distortionless if $H_C(f)H_{eq}(f) = Ke^{-j\omega t_d}$, where K and t_d are more or less arbitrary constants. Therefore, we require that

$$H_{eq}(f) = \frac{Ke^{-j\omega t_d}}{H_C(f)} \qquad (5)$$

wherever $X(f) \neq 0$.

Rare is the case when an equalizer can be designed to satisfy Eq. (5) exactly — which is why we say that equalization is a *theoretical* cure. But excellent approximations often are possible so that linear distortion can be reduced to a tolerable level. Probably the oldest equalization technique is the use of *loading coils* on twisted-pair telephone lines.† These coils are lumped inductors placed in shunt across the line every kilometer or so, giving the improved amplitude ratio typically illustrated in Fig. 4.9. Other lumped-element circuits have been designed for specific equalization tasks.

More recently, the *tapped-delay-line equalizer* or *transversal filter* has emerged as a convenient and flexible device. To illustrate the principle, Fig. 4.10 shows a delay line with total time delay 2Δ having taps at each end and the middle. The tap outputs are passed through adjustable gains, c_{-1}, c_0, and c_1, and summed to form the final output. Thus

$$y(t) = c_{-1}x(t) + c_0 x(t - \Delta) + c_1 x(t - 2\Delta) \qquad (6a)$$

and

$$H_{eq}(f) = c_{-1} + c_0 e^{-j\omega\Delta} + c_1 e^{-j\omega 2\Delta}$$
$$= (c_{-1}e^{+j\omega\Delta} + c_0 + c_1 e^{-j\omega\Delta})e^{-j\omega\Delta} \qquad (6b)$$

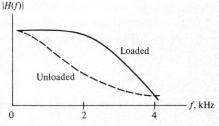

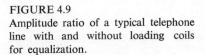

FIGURE 4.9
Amplitude ratio of a typical telephone
line with and without loading coils
for equalization.

† Everitt and Anner (1956, chap. 8) gives the theory of loading.

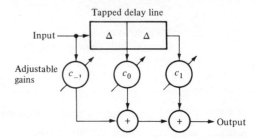

FIGURE 4.10
Tapped-delay-line equalizer (transversal filter) with three taps.

Clearly, this is a convenient arrangement since the tap gains are more readily changed than lumped elements. To demonstrate the flexibility, suppose $c_{-1} = c_1 < c_0/2$; then

$$|H_{eq}(f)| = c_0 + 2c_1 \cos \omega\Delta \qquad \arg [H_{eq}(f)] = -\omega\Delta$$

On the other hand, if $c_{-1} = -c_1$ and $|c_1| \ll c_0$, then

$$|H_{eq}(f)| \approx c_0 \qquad \arg [H_{eq}(f)] \approx -\omega\Delta - \frac{2c_1}{c_0} \sin \omega\Delta$$

Therefore, depending on the tap gains, we can equalize amplitude ripples or phase ripples or both.

Generalizing Eq. (6b) to the case of a $2M\Delta$ delay line with $2M + 1$ taps,

$$H_{eq}(f) = \left(\sum_{m=-M}^{M} c_m e^{-j\omega m\Delta} \right) e^{-j\omega M\Delta} \qquad (7)$$

which has the form of an *exponential Fourier series* with frequency periodicity $1/\Delta$. Therefore, given a channel $H_C(f)$ to be equalized over $|f| < W$, one can approximate the right-hand side of Eq. (5) by a Fourier series with frequency periodicity $1/\Delta \geq W$ (thereby determining Δ), estimate the number of significant terms (which determines M), and match the tap gains to the series coefficients. However, this high-powered theoretical method may not be needed in simple cases such as the following example.

Example 4.1

Suppose we wish to equalize the multipath distortion described in Exercise 4.2, where

$$H_C(f) = K_1 \left[1 + \frac{K_2}{K_1} e^{-j\omega(t_2 - t_1)} \right] e^{-j\omega t_1}$$

with $(K_2/K_1)^2 \ll 1$ and $t_2 > t_1$. Applying Eq. (5), the equalizer should have

$$H_{eq}(f) = \frac{K}{K_1} \frac{e^{-j\omega(t_d - t_1)}}{1 + (K_2/K_1)e^{-j\omega(t_2 - t_1)}}$$

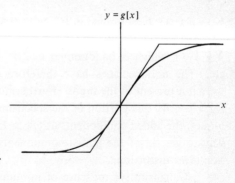

FIGURE 4.11
Transfer characteristic of a nonlinear device.

Taking $K = K_1$ and $t_d = t_1$ and expanding the denominator as a three-term binomial series yields

$$H_{eq}(f) \approx 1 - \frac{K_2}{K_1}e^{-j\omega(t_2-t_1)} + \left(\frac{K_2}{K_1}\right)^2 e^{-j\omega(t_2-t_1)}e^{-j\omega(t_2-t_1)}$$

$$\approx \left[e^{+j\omega(t_2-t_1)} - \frac{K_2}{K_1} + \left(\frac{K_2}{K_1}\right)^2 e^{-j\omega(t_2-t_1)}\right]e^{-j\omega(t_2-t_1)}$$

Comparing this with Eq. (6b) reveals that a three-tap transversal filter will do the job if $c_{-1} = 1$, $c_0 = -(K_2/K_1)$, $c_1 = (K_2/K_1)^2$, and $\Delta = t_2 - t_1$. ////

Nonlinear Distortion

A system having nonlinear elements cannot be described by a transfer function. Instead, the instantaneous values of input and output are related by a curve or function $y(t) = g[x(t)]$, commonly called the *transfer characteristic*. Figure 4.11 is a representative transfer characteristic; the flattening out of the output for large input excursions is the familiar saturation-and-cutoff effect of transistor amplifiers. We shall consider only *memoryless* devices, for which the transfer characteristic is a complete description.

Under small-signal input conditions, it may be possible to linearize the transfer characteristic in a piecewise fashion, as shown by the thin lines in the figure. The more general approach is a polynomial approximation to the curve, of the form

$$y(t) = a_1x(t) + a_2 x^2(t) + a_3 x^3(t) + \cdots \tag{8a}$$

It is the higher powers of $x(t)$ in this equation that give rise to the nonlinear distortion.

Even though we have no transfer function, the output spectrum can be found, at least in a formal way, by transforming Eq. (8a). Specifically, invoking the convolution theorem,

$$Y(f) = a_1 X(f) + a_2 X * X(f) + a_3 X * X * X(f) + \cdots \tag{8b}$$

Now if $x(t)$ is bandlimited in W, the output of a linear network will contain no frequencies beyond $|f| < W$. But in the nonlinear case, we see that the output includes $X * X(f)$, which is bandlimited in $2W$, $X * X * X(f)$, which is bandlimited in $3W$, etc. The nonlinearities have therefore created output frequency components that were not present in the input. Furthermore, since $X * X(f)$ may contain components for $|f| < W$, this portion of the spectrum overlaps that of $X(f)$. Using filtering techniques, the added components at $|f| > W$ can be removed, but there is no convenient way to get rid of the added components at $|f| < W$. These, in fact, constitute the nonlinear distortion.

A quantitative measure of nonlinear distortion is provided by taking a simple cosine wave, $x(t) = \cos \omega_0 t$, as the input. Inserting in Eq. (8a) and expanding yields

$$y(t) = \left(\frac{a_2}{2} + \frac{3a_4}{8} + \cdots\right) + \left(a_1 + \frac{3a_3}{4} + \cdots\right)\cos \omega_0 t + \left(\frac{a_2}{2} + \frac{a_4}{4} + \cdots\right)\cos 2\omega_0 t + \cdots$$

Therefore, the nonlinear distortion appears as *harmonics* of the input wave. The amount of second-harmonic distortion is the ratio of the amplitude of this term to that of the fundamental, or in percent:

$$\text{Second-harmonic distortion} = \frac{a_2/2 + a_4/4 + \cdots}{a_1 + 3a_3/4 + \cdots} \times 100\%$$

Higher-order harmonics are treated similarly. However, their effect is usually much less, and many can be removed entirely by filtering.

If the input is a sum of two cosine waves, say $\cos \omega_1 t + \cos \omega_2 t$, the output will include all the harmonics of f_1 and f_2, plus crossproduct terms which yield $f_2 - f_1, f_2 + f_1, f_2 - 2f_1$, etc. These sum and difference frequencies are designated as *intermodulation distortion*. Generalizing the intermodulation effect, if $x(t) = x_1(t) + x_2(t)$, then $y(t)$ contains the *cross product* $x_1(t)x_2(t)$ (and higher-order products, which we ignore here). In the frequency domain $x_1(t)x_2(t)$ becomes $X_1 * X_2(f)$; and even though $X_1(f)$ and $X_2(f)$ may be separated in frequency, $X_1 * X_2(f)$ can overlap both of them, producing one form of *cross talk*. This aspect of nonlinear distortion is of particular concern in telephone transmission systems. On the other hand the crossproduct term is the desired result when nonlinear devices are used for modulation purposes.

Companding

Although nonlinear distortion has no perfect cure, it too can be minimized by careful design. The basic idea is to make sure that the signal does not exceed the linear operating range of the channel's transfer characteristic. Ironically, one strategy along this

FIGURE 4.12
Companding system.

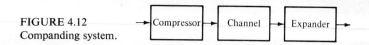

line involves *two nonlinear* devices, a *compressor* and an *expander*, arranged per Fig. 4.12.

A compressor is a device having greater amplification at low signal levels than at high signal levels. Since amplification is the derivative of the transfer characteristic with respect to the input, a typical compressor characteristic $g_{comp}[x(t)]$ would be as shown in Fig. 4.13. Note that a compressor compresses the range of the output signal. Therefore, if the compressed range falls within the linear range of the channel, the signal at the channel output is proportional to $g_{comp}[x(t)]$ which is distorted by the compressor but not the channel. Ideally, then, the expander should have a characteristic that perfectly complements the compressor — i.e., less amplification at low signal levels, etc. Thus, the final output is proportional to $g_{exp}\{g_{comp}[x(t)]\} = x(t)$, as desired.

The joint use of compressing and expanding is called *companding* (surprise?) and is of particular value in telephone systems. Besides combating nonlinear distortion, companding tends to compensate for the signal-level difference between loud and soft talkers. Indeed, the latter is the key advantage of companding compared to the simpler technique of linearly attenuating the signal at the input (to keep it in the linear range of the channel) and linearly amplifying it at the output.

4.3   ANALOG TRANSMISSION

Getting it all together, as it were, this section applies the results of the previous two sections to the case of analog transmission. By *analog transmission* we mean those systems in which information-bearing waveforms are to be reproduced at the destination without employing digital coding techniques.

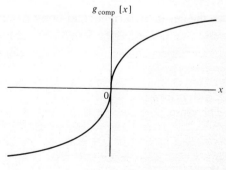

FIGURE 4.13
Typical transfer characteristic of a compressor.

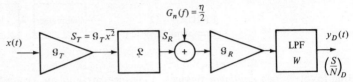

FIGURE 4.14
Analog transmission system.

Our analyses will be in terms of an arbitrary waveform or *message* designated by $x(t)$. Better yet, $x(t)$ represents the ensemble of probable messages from a given source. Though such messages are not strictly bandlimited, it is safe to assume that there exists some upper frequency — call it W — above which the spectral content is negligible and unnecessary for conveying the information in question. Thus, we define

$$W = \text{analog message bandwidth}$$

in the sense that

$$G_x(f) \approx 0 \qquad \text{for } |f| > W \qquad (1)$$

We further assume ergodicity so that $\langle x^2(t)\rangle$ and $\overline{x^2}$ are interchangeable.

Signal-to-Noise Ratio

Figure 4.14 amplifies Fig. 4.1 for the situation in question. Specifically, the transmitter becomes simply an amplifier with power gain $\mathcal{G}_T$, so $S_T = \mathcal{G}_T \overline{x^2}$, and the receiver filter is a nearly ideal LPF with bandwidth W, so $B_N \approx W$. The other parameters are the same as defined in Sect. 4.1.

If the total transmission delay is t_d and there is no distortion over $|f| \leq W$, the output signal is

$$y_D(t) = \left(\frac{\mathcal{G}_T \mathcal{G}_R}{\mathcal{L}}\right)^{1/2} x(t - t_d) + n_D(t) \qquad (2)$$

so the destination signal and noise powers are

$$S_D = \frac{\mathcal{G}_T \mathcal{G}_R}{\mathcal{L}} \, \mathrm{E}[x^2(t - t_d)] = \frac{\mathcal{G}_T \mathcal{G}_R}{\mathcal{L}} \, \overline{x^2}$$

$$N_D = \overline{n_D^2} = \mathcal{G}_R \eta W$$

Therefore

$$\left(\frac{S}{N}\right)_D = \frac{\mathcal{G}_T \overline{x^2}}{\mathcal{L}\eta W} = \frac{S_T}{\mathcal{L}\eta W} \qquad (3)$$

or, since $S_T/\mathscr{L} = S_R$,

$$\left(\frac{S}{N}\right)_D = \frac{S_R}{\eta W} \qquad (4)$$

Table 4.2 lists representative values of $(S/N)_D$ for selected analog signals, along with the frequency range. The upper limit of the frequency range is the nominal value of W. The lower limit also has design significance since, because of transformers and coupling capacitors, most analog transmission systems do not respond all the way down to DC.

Equation (4) expresses $(S/N)_D$ in terms of some very basic system parameters, namely, the signal power and noise density at the receiver input and the message bandwidth. This combination of terms will occur over and over again, particularly when we compare various system types, so we give it a symbol of its own by defining

$$\gamma \triangleq \frac{S_R}{\eta W} \qquad (5)$$

In the present context γ equals $(S/N)_D$ for analog baseband transmission. We can also interpret the denominator ηW as the *noise power in the message bandwidth*, even though N_D differs from ηW by $\mathscr{G}_R$. (Recall that this gain factor cancels out in signal-to-noise ratios.)

Because Eq. (4) presupposes distortionless transmission conditions, additive white noise, and a nearly ideal filter, it is more accurate to say that

$$\left(\frac{S}{N}\right)_D \leq \gamma \qquad (6)$$

In other words, γ generally is an *upper bound* for analog baseband performance that may or may not be achieved in an actual system. For instance, the noise bandwidth of a practical LPF will be somewhat greater than the message bandwidth, giving $(S/N)_D = S_R/\eta B_N < \gamma$. Similarly, nonlinearities that cause the output to include signal-

Table 4.2 TYPICAL TRANSMISSION REQUIREMENTS FOR SELECTED ANALOG SIGNALS

Signal type	Frequency range	Signal-to-noise ratio, dB
Barely intelligible voice	500 Hz–2 kHz	5–10
Telephone-quality voice	200 Hz–3.2 kHz	25–35
AM broadcast-quality audio	100 Hz–5 kHz	40–50
High-fidelity audio	20 Hz–20 kHz	55–65
Television video	60 Hz–4.2 MHz	45–55

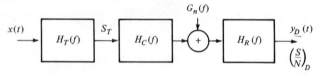

FIGURE 4.15

times-noise terms also reduce the effective S/N. Companding, on the other hand, may yield a net improvement.† The effects of linear distortion and nonwhite noise are examined jointly below.

Optimum Terminal Filters ★

When the noise is nonwhite and/or the channel requires considerable equalization, the rather simple-minded approach taken above should be replaced by a more sophisticated technique in which specially designed filters are incorporated at both terminals, the transmitter and receiver. Figure 4.15 is the system diagram, with the power gains $\mathscr{G}_T$, $1/\mathscr{L}$, and $\mathscr{G}_R$ this time absorbed in the frequency-response functions $H_T(f)$, $H_C(f)$, and $H_R(f)$.

As far as distortionless transmission is concerned, any pair of terminal filters will do, providing

$$H_T(f)H_R(f) = \frac{Ke^{-j\omega t_d}}{H_C(f)} \qquad |f| < W \qquad (7)$$

Hence, if $H_R(f)$ is chosen to minimize the output noise and $H_T(f)H_R(f)$ satisfies Eq. (7), we have *optimized* the terminal filters in the sense that $(S/N)_D$ is maximum and the output signal is undistorted. But the optimization has a subtle constraint; namely, the transmitted power S_T must be kept within reasonable bounds. Accordingly, we seek to minimize $S_T N_D/S_D$ rather than N_D alone.

Assuming Eq. (7) holds, the total output signal is

$$y_D(t) = Kx(t - t_d) + n_D(t)$$

and

$$S_D = K^2 \overline{x^2} \qquad (8)$$

$$N_D = \int_{-\infty}^{\infty} |H_R(f)|^2 G_n(f)\, df \qquad (9)$$

† See Bennett (1970, chap. 3).

At the transmitting end we take $G_x(f)$ as the message spectral density so

$$S_T = \int_{-\infty}^{\infty} |H_T(f)|^2 G_x(f)\, df$$

$$= \int_{-\infty}^{\infty} \frac{K^2 G_x(f)}{|H_C(f)H_R(f)|^2}\, df \qquad (10)$$

where Eq. (7) has been used to eliminate $|H_T(f)|^2$. Therefore, the quantity to minimize is

$$\frac{S_T N_D}{S_D} = \frac{1}{x^2} \left[\int_{-\infty}^{\infty} \frac{G_x}{|H_C H_R|^2}\, df \int_{-\infty}^{\infty} |H_R|^2 G_n\, df \right] \qquad (11)$$

it being understood that all terms are functions of f except $\overline{x^2}$, which is a constant. Note that the only function in Eq. (11) under the designer's control is the receiving filter $H_R(f)$.

Normally, optimization problems require the methods of variational calculus. But this particular problem (and a few others that follow) can be solved by adroit application of *Schwarz's inequality*, Eq. (6), Sect. 2.6, one form of which is

$$\left| \int_{-\infty}^{\infty} V W^*\, df \right|^2 \leq \int_{-\infty}^{\infty} |V|^2\, df \int_{-\infty}^{\infty} |W|^2\, df \qquad (12a)$$

where V and W are arbitrary functions of f and the equality holds when

$$V(f) = \text{constant} \times W(f) \qquad (12b)$$

Now, except for the constant $\overline{x^2}$, Eq. (11) has the same form as the right-hand side of Eq. (12a) with

$$V = \frac{G_x^{1/2}}{|H_C H_R|} \qquad W = |H_R| G_n^{1/2}$$

both of which are real and nonnegative. Thus $S_T N_D / S_D$ is minimized when

$$|H_R(f)|_{\text{opt}}^2 = \frac{G_x^{1/2}(f)}{|H_C(f)| G_n^{1/2}(f)} \qquad (13a)$$

as follows by taking $V(f) = W(f)$, the proportionality constant being immaterial (why?). Equation (13a) is the optimum receiving filter, and the corresponding optimum transmitting filter is, from Eq. (7),

$$|H_T(f)|_{\text{opt}}^2 = \frac{K^2 G_n^{1/2}(f)}{|H_C(f)| G_x^{1/2}(f)} \qquad (13b)$$

with K^2 being determined from the desired value for S_T.

Interpreting these equations, we see that $H_R(f)$ deemphasizes those frequencies where the noise density is large and the signal density is small — a very sensible thing to do — while $|H_T(f)|$ does just the reverse. The phase shift of $H_T(f)$ and $H_R(f)$ does not appear here since we are dealing with spectral densities, but the overall phase must satisfy Eq. (7) for distortionless transmission.

Finally, with optimum filtering the destination S/N is

$$\left(\frac{S}{N}\right)_{D_{max}} = \frac{S_T}{(S_T N_D/S_D)_{min}} = \frac{S_T \overline{x^2}}{\left|\int_{-\infty}^{\infty} \frac{G_x^{1/2}(f)G_n^{1/2}(f)}{|H_C(f)|} df\right|^2} \tag{14}$$

as follows from Eqs. (11) and (12a).

Aside from the question of synthesizing the filters, the major obstacle preventing complete optimization in practice is the assumption implied by Eq. (13) that $G_x(f)$ is known in detail. Usually, the communication engineer does know the general characteristics of the message — or, rather, the class or ensemble of possible messages — but not the complete details. For instance, if the messages are known to be band-limited in W, one might then assume that the spectral density is flat over $|f| < W$, i.e.,

$$G_x(f) = \frac{\overline{x^2}}{2W} \Pi\left(\frac{f}{2W}\right) \tag{15}$$

there being no reason to believe that $G_x(f)$ is larger or smaller at any particular frequency. Proceeding on this assumption would yield a good design but not necessarily optimum.

Actually, Eq. (15) is the underlying assumption of our previous approach where we took the noise to be white and said that the receiving filter serves only to eliminate the out-of-band noise. Clarifying this point, let $G_n(f) = \eta/2$ and let the channel be distortionless so $|H_C(f)|^2 = 1/\mathscr{L}$. Then, inserting in Eq. (13) shows that the terminal filters become ideal LPFs while the denominator of Eq. (14) is

$$\left|\int_{-W}^{W} (\mathscr{L}\overline{x^2}\eta/4W)^{1/2} df\right|^2 = \mathscr{L}\overline{x^2}\eta W$$

so $(S/N)_{D_{max}} = S_T/\mathscr{L}\eta W = S_R/\eta W = \gamma$.

EXERCISE 4.3   Consider a system having $|H_c(f)|^2 = 1/\mathscr{L}$ and $G_n(f) = (\eta/2)$ $(1 + a^2 f^2)^2$. Taking $G_x(f)$ per Eq. (15), find $(S/N)_{D_{max}}$ in terms of S_R and compare with $(S/N)_D$ when the receiving filter is an ideal LPF with $B = W$. *Ans.*: $(S/N)_{D_{max}} = S_R/\eta W[1 + (a^2 W^2/3)]^2$, $(S/N)_D = S_R/\eta W[1 + (2a^2 W^2/3) + (a^4 W^4/5)]$.

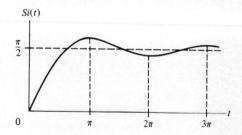

FIGURE 4.16
The sine integral, Si $(t) = \int_0^t (\sin \lambda)/\lambda \, d\lambda$.

4.4 PULSE TRANSMISSION

Pulse transmission differs from analog transmission in that one is not concerned with the faithful reproduction of a message waveform but rather with detecting the presence of a pulse, resolving two or more closely spaced pulses, and measuring the amplitude or time position. Telegraph and radar systems are examples. This section examines the effects of limited bandwidth and additive noise on pulse transmission at baseband.

Bandwidth Requirements

Short pulses have large spectral widths, as we have seen time and again. Reversing this observation, it can be said that given a system of fixed bandwidth, there is a lower limit on the duration of pulses at the output, i.e., a *minimum output pulse duration*. Consequently, the maximum number of distinct output pulses that can be resolved per unit time is limited by the system bandwidth.

To put the matter on a quantitative footing, let a rectangular pulse $x(t) = A\Pi(t/\tau)$ be the input to an ideal or nearly ideal LPF with bandwidth B, unit gain, and zero time delay, so $H(f) = \Pi(f/2B)$. Since the input spectrum $X(f) = A\tau$ sinc $f\tau$ has even symmetry, the inverse Fourier transform for the output $y(t) = \mathscr{F}^{-1}[H(f)X(f)]$ simplifies to

$$y(t) = 2 \int_0^B A\tau \, \frac{\sin \pi f\tau}{\pi f\tau} \cos 2\pi ft \, df$$

$$= \frac{A}{\pi} \left[\int_0^B \frac{\sin \pi f(2t + \tau)}{f} \, df - \int_0^B \frac{\sin \pi f(2t - \tau)}{f} \, df \right]$$

which is still a nonelementary integral requiring series evaluation. Fortunately, the result can be expressed in terms of the tabulated *sine integral*

$$\text{Si} \, (t) \triangleq \int_0^t \frac{\sin \lambda}{\lambda} \, d\lambda \qquad (1)$$

plotted in Fig. 4.16. Changing integration variables finally leads to

$$y(t) = \frac{A}{\pi} \{ \text{Si} \, [\pi B(2t + \tau)] - \text{Si} \, [\pi B(2t - \tau)] \} \qquad (2)$$

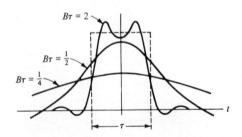

FIGURE 4.17
Pulse response of an ideal LPF.

which is shown in Fig. 4.17 for three values of the product $B\tau$. Notice the precursors caused by the ideal filter.

Despite the rather involved mathematics, the conclusions drawn from Fig. 4.17 are quite simple. We have said that the spectral width of a rectangular pulse is about $1/\tau$. For $B \ll 1/\tau$, the output signal is essentially undistorted; whereas for $B \gg 1/\tau$, the output pulse is stretched and has a duration that depends more on the filter bandwidth than on the input signal. As a rough but highly useful rule of thumb one can say that the minimum output pulse duration and bandwidth are related by

$$\tau_{min} \geq \frac{1}{2B} \qquad (3)$$

providing the input pulse has $\tau \leq \tau_{min}$. Going somewhat further, we can also say that the maximum number of resolved output pulses per unit time is about $1/\tau_{min} = 2B$. This is achieved using input pulses of duration less than $1/2B$ and spaced in time by $1/2B$. Figure 4.18, showing the input and output signals for two pulses spaced by τ, supports this assertion.

Beside pulse detection and resolution, one may be concerned with the question of pulse location or position measured with respect to some reference time. Usually, position measurements are based on the leading edge of the pulse and for that purpose rectangular pulses would be desired since the edge has a unique position. But realizable pulse shapes rise more gradually toward their peak value, causing the position of the leading edge to be ambiguous and its measurement less certain. The conventional

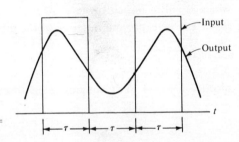

FIGURE 4.18
Pulse resolution of an ideal LPF, $B = 1/2\tau$.

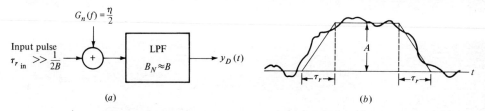

FIGURE 4.19
Pulse measurements in additive noise. (a) Block diagram; (b) filtered pulse with noise.

rule about uncertainty is stated in terms of the *rise time*, defined as the interval required for the pulse to go from zero to full amplitude or from 10 to 90 percent of full amplitude. We then say that the uncertainty of the pulse position measurement approximately equals the rise time τ_r. Referring back to Fig. 4.17 it is seen that the rise time of a filtered pulse is proportional to the bandwidth. Therefore, as another rule of thumb we have

$$\tau_{r_{\min}} \geq \frac{1}{2B} \qquad (4)$$

When the input pulses have $\tau_r \leq \tau_{r_{\min}}$, the output pulses will have rise times no less than $1/2B$ and the minimum location uncertainty is about $1/2B$. Alternately, if the input rise time is greater than $1/2B$, the output rise time will be approximately the same as the input.

Granted that Eqs. (3) and (4) are rough guidelines based on the case of a rectangular input to an ideal LPF, they are nonetheless useful in general. Studies of other pulse shapes and other lowpass filters show that these inequalities are appropriate, taking B as the 3-dB bandwidth.

Pulse Measurements in Additive Noise

Let a pulse (not necessarily rectangular) be contaminated by additive white noise and passed through an LPF whose noise equivalent bandwidth and 3-dB bandwidth are approximately equal, Fig. 4.19a. If the rise time of the input pulse is small compared to $1/2B$, the output pulse shape can be approximated as a *trapezoid* plus noise $n_D(t)$, Fig. 4.19b. Thus, measurements of both the pulse amplitude and position will be in error owing to the noise.

At the peak of the output pulse, $y_D(t) = A + n_D(t)$, so we can define the normalized mean-square amplitude error as

$$\epsilon_A^2 \triangleq \frac{\overline{n_D^2}}{A^2} = \frac{\eta B}{A^2} \qquad (5a)$$

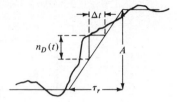

FIGURE 4.20
Expanded view of noise perturbation.

But the energy of the output pulse is $E \approx A^2\tau$ and $\tau \geq 1/2B$; hence

$$\epsilon_A{}^2 \geq \frac{\eta}{2E} \qquad (5b)$$

which gives a lower bound on the error. This lower bound holds when $\tau = 1/2B$.

Position measurements usually are accomplished by noting the time at which the output pulse exceeds some fixed level, say $A/2$. Then, as seen in the expanded view of Fig. 4.20, the time position error is $\Delta t = (\tau_r/A)n_D(t)$—from the similar triangles —and the mean-square error normalized by τ^2 is

$$\epsilon_t{}^2 \triangleq \frac{\overline{\Delta t^2}}{\tau^2} = \overline{n_D{}^2}\,\frac{\tau_r{}^2}{A^2\tau^2} = \eta B\,\frac{\tau_r{}^2}{A^2\tau^2} \qquad (6a)$$

Finally, inserting $\tau_r \geq 1/2B$ and $E = A^2\tau$ yields the lower bound

$$\epsilon_t{}^2 \geq \frac{\eta}{4BE\tau} \qquad (6b)$$

In contrast to Eq. (5b), this lower bound is achieved when $\tau_r = 1/2B$ and $\tau \gg \tau_r$. Thus, unlike amplitude measurement, the largest possible bandwidth should be used to minimize position measurement errors.

By now, the reader may have recognized that our analysis of pulse transmission is largely intuitive and heuristic. More refined investigations of specific cases are possible, notably the case of optimum pulse detection discussed below. However, the admittedly crude results above still are valuable guidelines for the design of pulse transmission systems, and the reciprocals of Eqs. (5) and (6) parallel the concept of signal-to-noise ratio in analog transmission.

Optimum Pulse Detection—Matched Filters ★

Similar to the optimum terminal filters for analog transmission, there exists an optimum receiving filter for detecting a pulse of known shape $x(t)$ contaminated by additive noise with known spectral density $G_n(f)$. Such filters are termed *matched filters*, used extensively in radar and data transmission systems.

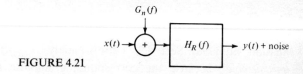

FIGURE 4.21

Consider the situation in Fig. 4.21, where the output pulse shape is unimportant but one desires to maximize its amplitude at some arbitrary time, say t_0, and minimize the output noise. In absence of noise the peak output signal at $t = t_0$ is

$$y(t_0) = \mathscr{F}^{-1}[H(f)X(f)]|_{t=t_0}$$

$$= \int_{-\infty}^{\infty} H(f)X(f)e^{+j\omega t_0}\, df \qquad (7)$$

where $X(f) = \mathscr{F}[x(t)]$. (We use the Fourier transforms rather than the spectral density since the pulse is a known energy signal.) The output noise power is

$$N = \int_{-\infty}^{\infty} |H(f)|^2 G_n(f)\, df \qquad (8)$$

and the quantity to be maximized is

$$\frac{|y(t_0)|^2}{N} = \frac{|\int_{-\infty}^{\infty} HXe^{j\omega t_0}\, df|^2}{\int_{-\infty}^{\infty} |H|^2 G_n\, df} \qquad (9)$$

where $H(f)$ is the only function at our disposal.

To determine $H_{\mathrm{opt}}(f)$, we again draw upon Schwarz's inequality, Eq. (12), Sect. 4.3, this time in the form

$$\frac{|\int_{-\infty}^{\infty} VW^*\, df|^2}{\int_{-\infty}^{\infty} |V|^2\, df} \le \int_{-\infty}^{\infty} |W|^2\, df$$

whose left-hand side is the same as Eq. (9) with

$$V = HG_n^{1/2} \qquad W^* = \frac{HXe^{j\omega t_0}}{V} = \frac{Xe^{j\omega t_0}}{G_n^{1/2}}$$

Since the inequality becomes an equality when $V(f) = KW(f)$, the ratio in Eq. (9) will be maximized if

$$H_{\mathrm{opt}}(f) = K\frac{X^*(f)e^{-j\omega t_0}}{G_n(f)} \qquad (10)$$

where K is an arbitrary constant, as is t_0. Therefore,

$$\left[\frac{|y(t_0)|^2}{N}\right]_{\max} = \int_{-\infty}^{\infty} \frac{|X(f)|^2}{G_n(f)}\, df \qquad (11)$$

if the filter is optimized.

Observe from Eq. (10) that $H_{opt}(f)$ emphasizes those frequencies where $|X(f)|/G_n(f)$ is large, and vice versa, similar to the optimum receiving filter for analog transmission, Eq. (13a), Sect. 4.3. Unfortunately, $H_{opt}(f)$ often turns out to be physically *unrealizable*† because the corresponding impulse response is nonzero for $t < 0$. The following exercise relates Eq. (11) to our previous studies and shows why $H_{opt}(f)$ is called a matched filter.

EXERCISE 4.4   For the case of white noise $G_n(f) = \eta/2$, show that

$$\left[\frac{|y(t_0)|^2}{N}\right]_{max} = \frac{2E_x}{\eta} \qquad (12a)$$

where E_x is the energy in $x(t)$. Also show that

$$h_{opt}(t) = \mathscr{F}^{-1}[H_{opt}(f)] = Kx(t_0 - t) \qquad (12b)$$

so the impulse response has the same shape as the input pulse reversed in time and shifted by t_0. (*Hint*: Use the fact that $v(-t) \leftrightarrow V^*(f)$ when $v(t)$ is real.)

4.5   DIGITAL TRANSMISSION

We conclude this chapter with a brief examination of digital transmission at baseband. Fundamentally, a digital message is nothing more than an ordered sequence of *symbols* drawn from an *alphabet* of finite size μ. (For instance, a binary source has $\mu = 2$ and the alphabet symbols are the digits **0** and **1**.) The objective of a digital communication system is to transmit the message in a prescribed amount of time with a minimum number of errors. Thus, *signaling rate* and *error probability* play the same role in digital transmission that bandwidth and signal-to-noise ratio play in analog transmission. Moverover, there is a close relationship between signaling rate and bandwidth, and between error probability and signal-to-noise ratio.

Waveforms and Signaling Rate

One normally thinks of a digital signal as being a string of discrete-amplitude rectangular pulses. And, in fact, that is often the way it comes from the data source. By way of illustration, Fig. 4.22a shows the binary message **10110100** as it might appear at the output of a digital computer. This waveform, a simple on-off sequence, is said to be *unipolar*, because it has only one polarity, and *synchronous*, because all

---

† Thomas (1969, chap. 5) investigates the optimization problem with a realizability constraint.

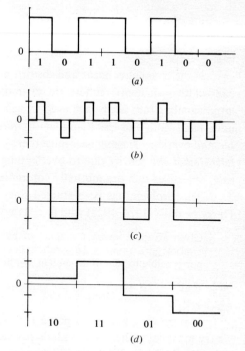

FIGURE 4.22
Digital waveforms. (*a*) Unipolar synchronous; (*b*) polar return-to-zero; (*c*) polar synchronous; (*d*) polar synchronous quaternary.

pulses have equal duration and there is no separation between them. Unipolar signals contain a nonzero DC component that is difficult to transmit, carries no information, and is a waste of power. Similarly, synchronous signals require timing coordination at transmitter and receiver, which means design complications. The *polar* (two-polarity) *return-to-zero* signal of Fig. 4.22*b* gets around both of these problems, but the "spaces" making the signal self-clocking are a waste of transmission time. If efficiency is a dominant consideration, the *polar synchronous* signal of Fig. 4.22*c* would be preferable. Illustrating a multilevel case, Fig. 4.22*d* is a quaternary ($\mu = 4$) signal derived by grouping the binary digits in blocks of two.

Regardless of the specific details, the channel input signal is an analog representation of the digital message that can generally be described as a pulse train of the form†

$$x(t) = \sum_k a_k p\left(t - \frac{k}{r}\right) \qquad (1)$$

where a_k is the amplitude level representing the kth message digit, $p(t)$ is the basic pulse shape with peak value $p(0) = 1$, the pulse-to-pulse spacing is $1/r$, and r is the

---

† The index k indicates time sequence, and its limits, omitted in Eq. (1), depend on when the message starts and stops.

signaling rate. For example, the polar synchronous signal of Fig. 4.22c has $a_k = \pm a$ and $p(t) = \Pi(t/\tau)$, where the pulse duration is $\tau = 1/r$. A return-to-zero signal would have $\tau < 1/r$.

If the channel is linear and distortionless over all frequencies—i.e., has infinite bandwidth—then $p(t)$ suffers no degradation in transmission, and an arbitrarily large signaling rate can be achieved by using very short pulses. But a real channel has finite bandwidth and less than ideal frequency response, causing the pulses to spread out and overlap. The engineer must therefore shape the output signal so as to *minimize intersymbol interference* due to overlapping and, at the same time, *maximize signaling rate*, objectives that are mutually contradictory.

This problem has been studied since the earliest days of telegraphy, but it was Harry Nyquist (1924, 1928) who first stated the bandwidth–signaling rate relationship:

> Given an ideal lowpass channel of bandwidth B, it is possible to send independent symbols at a rate $r \leq 2B$ symbols per second without intersymbol interference. It is not possible to send independent symbols at $r > 2B$.

Note that $r \leq 2B$ agrees with the pulse-resolution rule $\tau_{\min} \geq 1/2B$ of Sect. 4.4 since $\tau \leq 1/r$.

It is an easy matter to prove the second part of the relationship, for suppose we try to signal at $2(B + \epsilon)$ symbols per second, ϵ being positive but arbitrarily small. One possible message sequence consists of two symbols alternating indefinitely, **01010101** ..., for example. The resulting channel waveform is *periodic* with period $1/(B + \epsilon)$ and contains only the fundamental frequency $f_0 = B + \epsilon$ plus its harmonics. Since no frequency greater than B is passed by the channel, the channel output will be zero—aside from a possible but useless DC component.

Signaling at the maximum rate $r = 2B$ requires a very special pulse shape, namely, the *sinc pulse*

$$p(t) = \text{sinc } rt \qquad (2)$$

which is *bandlimited* in $B = r/2$ and therefore suffers no distortion when transmitted over the channel. Of course $p(t)$ is not timelimited, but it does have *periodic zero crossings*, i.e.,

$$p\left(\frac{m}{r}\right) = \text{sinc } m = \begin{cases} 1 & m = 0 \\ 0 & m \neq 0 \end{cases}$$

Thus, if we form the signal

$$x(t) = \sum_k a_k \text{ sinc } r\left(t - \frac{k}{r}\right) = \sum_k a_k \text{ sinc } (rt - k) \qquad (3a)$$

then at any time $t = m/r$,

$$x\left(\frac{m}{r}\right) = \sum_k a_k \text{ sinc } (m - k) = a_m \qquad (3b)$$

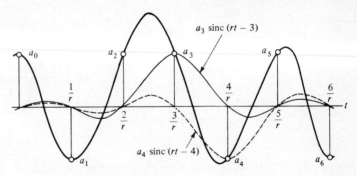

FIGURE 4.23
The digital waveform $x(t) = \sum_k a_k \operatorname{sinc}(rt - k)$.

as illustrated in Fig. 4.23. In other words, because of the zero crossings, the overlapping pulses do not result in intersymbol interference if we periodically sample $x(t)$ at the rate $r = 2B$.

As the reader may have inferred, timing information between transmitter and receiver is required here — i.e., the signaling must be synchronized at exactly $r = 2B$. Furthermore, this approach only works with an ideal lowpass channel. The general question of pulse shaping is deferred to Chap. 10; for the time being we will take $x(t)$ as in Eq. (3), which happens to be the most efficient choice if the bandwidth is limited. On the other hand, if the available bandwidth is large compared to r, then rectangular pulses would be the most expedient choice.

EXERCISE 4.5 Show that synchronous signaling at $r = B$ is possible if $p(t) = \operatorname{sinc}^2 rt$.

Noise and Errors

Figure 4.24 shows the basic elements of a digital baseband receiver. The received signal $K_R x(t)$ is contaminated by additive noise, and a nearly ideal LPF removes the out-of-band noise to yield

$$y(t) = K_R x(t) + n(t)$$

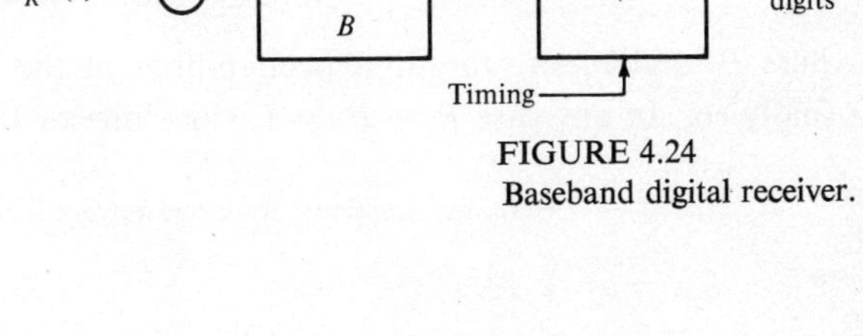

FIGURE 4.24
Baseband digital receiver.

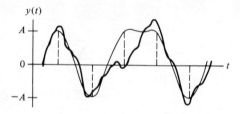

FIGURE 4.25
Polar binary waveform plus noise.

where the D subscripts have been dropped for convenience. The analog signal $y(t)$ is then operated on by an analog-to-digital (A/D) converter whose function is to recover or *regenerate* the digital message. Synchronization is supplied to the A/D converter so it can sample $y(t)$ at the optimum times $t = m/r$ when there is no inter-symbol interference, i.e., $y(m/r) = K_R a_m + n(m/r)$.

To begin with a simple case, consider a received polar binary signal having $K_R a_k = \pm A$ representing the binary digits **1** and **0**. A typical signal-plus-noise wave-form $y(t)$ as it might appear at the input to the A/D converter is illustrated in Fig. 4.25, assuming $\bar{n} = 0$. A direct conversion technique is to decide, at the appropriate times, whether $y(m/r)$ is closer to $+A$ (a **1** presumably intended) or closer to $-A$ (a **0** presumably intended). Intuitively, the logical *decision rule* becomes: choose **1** if $y(m/r) > 0$, choose **0** if $y(m/r) < 0$, and flip a coin if $y(m/r) = 0$. (This last event, being rare, will receive no further attention.) The converter can therefore take the form of a synchronized decision circuit whose crossover or *threshold level* is set at zero, and conversion errors occur whenever the noise causes $y(m/r)$ to be on the wrong side of the threshold at the decision time.

Thus, insofar as error probabilities are concerned, we have *two* random variables†

$$y_1 = A + n \qquad y_0 = -A + n \qquad (4)$$

corresponding to the intended digits **1** and **0**. Then, if a **1** was intended, the *conditional probability* of conversion error is

$$P_{e_1} \triangleq P(\text{error}|\mathbf{1} \text{ sent}) = P(y_1 < 0) = P(A + n < 0) \qquad (5a)$$

and similarly

$$P_{e_0} \triangleq P(\text{error}|\mathbf{0} \text{ sent}) = P(y_0 > 0) = P(-A + n > 0) \qquad (5b)$$

Hence, the *net error probability* becomes

$$P_e = P_1 P_{e_1} + P_0 P_{e_0} \qquad (6)$$

where P_1 and P_0 are the digit probabilities at the source, not necessarily equal but usually so. In any case $P_1 + P_0 = 1$, since one or the other must be transmitted.

---

† Here, for simplicity, we use lowercase letters to symbolize random variables.

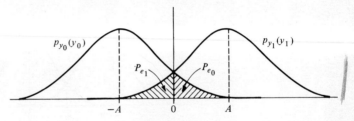

FIGURE 4.26
Signal-plus-noise PDFs for polar binary signaling.

At this point we assume that $n(t)$ is a zero-mean *gaussian* process with variance σ^2, so its probability density function is

$$p_n(n) = \frac{1}{\sqrt{2\pi}\,\sigma} e^{-n^2/2\sigma^2} \qquad (7)$$

This assumption is not unreasonable for linear baseband systems since most electrical noise is gaussian and gaussian functions are invariate under linear operations. It follows from Eq. (4) that y_1 and y_0 are also gaussian with the same variance σ^2 but with mean values

$$\bar{y}_1 = +A \qquad \bar{y}_0 = -A$$

Figure 4.26 conveniently summarizes the situation by showing the two PDFs, $p_{y_1}(y_1) = p_n(y_1 - A)$ and $p_{y_0}(y_0) = p_n(y_0 + A)$, from which we will calculate P_{e_1} and P_{e_0}.

Recalling the area interpretation of probability density functions,

$$P_{e_0} = P(y_0 > 0) = \int_0^\infty p_{y_0}(y_0)\,dy_0$$

$$= \frac{1}{\sqrt{2\pi}\,\sigma} \int_0^\infty e^{-(y_0 + A)^2/2\sigma^2}\,dy_0$$

$$= \frac{1}{\sqrt{2\pi}\,\sigma} \int_{A/\sigma}^\infty e^{-\lambda^2/2}\,d\lambda$$

where the change of variable $\lambda = (y_0 + A)/\sigma$ has been made. This puts P_{e_0} in the same form as the function $Q(\kappa)$, Eq. (8), Sect. 3.4, with $\kappa = A/\sigma$. Furthermore, noting the symmetry of Fig. 4.26, $P(y_1 < 0) = P(y_0 > 0)$ so

$$P_{e_1} = P_{e_0} = Q\!\left(\frac{A}{\sigma}\right) \qquad (8a)$$

Therefore, from Eq. (6), the net error probability is

$$P_e = (P_1 + P_0)Q\!\left(\frac{A}{\sigma}\right) = Q\!\left(\frac{A}{\sigma}\right) \qquad (8b)$$

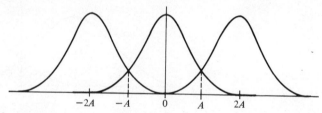

FIGURE 4.27
Signal-plus-noise PDFs for polar trinary signaling.

which is independent of the digit probabilities because $P_{e_1} = P_{e_0}$. Several points in this analysis deserve further comment:

1 Taking the threshold level at zero yields *equal error probabilities* for each digit, $P_{e_1} = P_{e_0}$.

2 This is the *optimum* threshold level if the digits are equiprobable ($P_1 = P_0$) since any other choice would increase P_{e_1} more than it decreases P_{e_0}, or vice versa.

3 Binary signals in gaussian noise have a unique property apparent in Fig. 4.26. If the intended amplitude is $+A$, superimposed positive noise excursions have no detrimental effect; and similarly for $-A$ with negative noise excursions. Hence, because $n(t)$ is equally likely to be positive or negative, the converter will be correct at least half the time, regardless of the noise. However, one should bear in mind that a binary message with 50 percent errors is 100 percent worthless.

4 In view of Eq. (8b), Fig. 3.5 or Table D may be used directly as a plot of P_e versus A/σ and it is evident that P_e decreases dramatically with increasing A/σ. If $A/\sigma = 2.0$, for instance, $P_e \approx 2 \times 10^{-2}$ while if $A/\sigma = 4.0$, $P_e \approx 3 \times 10^{-5}$. Incidentally, most applications require error probabilities of order 10^{-4} or less.

Because we have taken due care in our examination of errors for binary signals, the extension to multilevel or μ-ary signals is quite straightforward, providing the noise is gaussian. Consider, for instance, a polar trinary signal ($\mu = 3$) with output pulse amplitudes $K_R a_k = +2A$, 0, or $-2A$, representing the trinary digits **2**, **1**, and **0**, respectively. The equivalent to Fig. 4.26 has three gaussian density functions (Fig. 4.27), and we see that two threshold levels are required. Under the usual condition of equiprobable digits, the optimum threshold levels are easily shown to be $\pm A$, for which

$$P_{e_2} = P_{e_0} = Q\left(\frac{A}{\sigma}\right)$$

whereas

$$P_{e_1} = 2Q\left(\frac{A}{\sigma}\right)$$

because both positive and negative noise excursions cause errors when $K_R a_k = 0$. (By another choice of thresholds it is possible to equalize the per-digit error probabilities, but the cost is increased net probability P_e.) Hence

$$P_e = P_2 P_{e_2} + P_1 P_{e_1} + P_0 P_{e_0} = \frac{4}{3} Q\left(\frac{A}{\sigma}\right)$$

where we have inserted $P_2 = P_1 = P_0 = \frac{1}{3}$.

Generalizing to arbitrary μ with equal digit probabilities, similar reasoning gives

$$P_e = 2\left(1 - \frac{1}{\mu}\right)Q\left(\frac{A}{\sigma}\right) \qquad (9)$$

where the *spacing* between adjacent output pulse amplitudes is $2A$ — so $2(\mu - 1)A$ is the peak-to-peak range — and the $\mu - 1$ threshold levels are centered between the pulse amplitudes. Equation (9) clearly reduces to Eq. (8b) when $\mu = 2$. Nonetheless it fails to tell the full story, for three reasons: first, a μ-ary digit in general represents more information than a binary digit; second, there are differing severities of error in μ-ary systems, depending on whether the noise shifts the apparent amplitude by one or more steps; third, the relationship between error probability and signal-to-noise ratio is not explicit. An analytic assessment of the first two is quite difficult, but the third can be treated as follows.

Signal-to-Noise Ratios

If the contaminating noise is white, then the filtered noise power is

$$N = \eta B \qquad (10a)$$

and

$$\sigma = \sqrt{N} = \sqrt{\eta B} \qquad (10b)$$

since we have assumed $\bar{n} = 0$. If the noise is not white, the best receiving filter is not an ideal LPF. The question of *optimum* filtering for digital transmission with arbitrary noise spectrum is covered in Chap. 10.

To calculate the signal power, a short digression on the properties of $p(t) = \text{sinc } rt$ is needed. It is readily shown (Prob. 4.32) that

$$\int_{-\infty}^{\infty} A_k p\left(t - \frac{k}{r}\right) A_m p\left(t - \frac{m}{r}\right) dt = \begin{cases} \dfrac{A_k^2}{r} & m = k \\ 0 & m \neq k \end{cases} \qquad (11)$$

which means that the pulses that make up $K_R x(t)$ are *mutually orthogonal* with energy A_k^2/r per pulse. But orthogonality is a sufficient condition for *superposition of energy*, and a message M digits long, say

$$K_R x(t) = \sum_{k=1}^{M} A_k p\left(t - \frac{k}{r}\right)$$

has energy

$$E_M = \frac{1}{r} \sum_{k=1}^{M} A_k^2$$

which would also be true for *rectangular* pulses with $\tau = 1/r$. Then, since average power equals energy per unit time and an M-digit message is M/r seconds long, the received signal power is

$$S_R = \frac{E_M}{(M/r)} = \frac{1}{M} \sum_{k=1}^{M} A_k^2$$

or simply the *average* of A_k^2. Generalizing, we have that if

$$K_R x(t) = \sum_{k=-\infty}^{\infty} A_k \operatorname{sinc}(rt - k) \qquad (12a)$$

and if the A_k are statistically independent, then

$$S_R = K_R^2 \overline{x^2} = \overline{A^2} \qquad (12b)$$

where $\overline{A^2}$ is the statistical or *ensemble average* of A_k^2. As it happens, this result will also be of use several times in future chapters.

In the case of a polar binary wave with $A_k = \pm A$, equally likely,

$$\overline{A^2} = (+A)^2 P(+A) + (-A)^2 P(-A) = \frac{A^2}{2} + \frac{A^2}{2} = A^2$$

In the polar μ-ary case with μ even,

$$A_k = \pm A, \pm 3A, \ldots, \pm(\mu - 1)A$$

and assuming equiprobable symbols so $P(A_k) = 1/\mu$, applying Eq. (1), Sect. 3.3, gives

$$\overline{A^2} = \sum_{k=1}^{\mu} A_k^2 P(A_k) = \frac{2}{\mu} \sum_{k=1}^{\mu/2} (2k-1)^2 A^2$$

Thus, with the help of the summations in Table B, we have

$$S_{posisd} \quad \overline{A^2} = \frac{\mu^2 - 1}{3} A^2 \qquad (13)$$

μ even or odd

*∂ uniform
Amplitude space]*

2A

μ = #poss.b.

Equation (13) also holds for any polar wave, μ even or odd, with uniform amplitude spacing $2A$.

Finally, combining Eqs. (10), (12), and (13), the signal-to-noise ratio at the input to the A/D converter is

$$\frac{S}{N} = \frac{S_R}{\eta B} = \frac{\mu^2 - 1}{3} \left(\frac{A}{\sigma}\right)^2 \qquad (14)$$

and Eq. (9) can be written as

$$P_e = 2\left(1 - \frac{1}{\mu}\right)Q\left(\sqrt{\frac{3}{\mu^2 - 1}\frac{S}{N}}\right) \qquad (15)$$

Alternatively, it is useful to define the system parameter

$$\rho \triangleq \frac{S_R}{\eta r} \qquad (16)$$

where r is the signaling rate and, hence, S_R/r equals the average received energy per digit. The parameter ρ plays essentially the same role in digital transmission that γ plays in analog transmission. For the pulse shape in question, $r = 2B$ so $S_R/\eta B = 2S_R/\eta r = 2\rho$ and Eq. (15) becomes

$$P_e = 2\left(1 - \frac{1}{\mu}\right)Q\left(\sqrt{\frac{6\rho}{\mu^2 - 1}}\right) \qquad (17a)$$

$$= Q(\sqrt{2\rho}) \qquad \mu = 2 \qquad (17b)$$

Again, like analog transmission, Eq. (15) or (17) is an upper bound on system performance — that is, a *lower bound* on P_e — and various imperfections will cause the error probability to be higher than predicted. In particular, the wasted DC power in a *unipolar* waveform changes the picture appreciably.

EXERCISE 4.6 Consider a unipolar binary system with $A_k = 2A$, or 0, and the decision threshold at A. Show that $S_R = 2A^2$ if $P_1 = P_0$, and

$$P_e = Q\left(\frac{A}{\sigma}\right) = Q\left(\sqrt{\frac{S}{2N}}\right) = Q(\sqrt{\rho}) \qquad (18)$$

Then calculate P_e for a polar and unipolar system, both having $\rho = 8.0$. *Ans.*: 3×10^{-5}, 2×10^{-3}.

Example 4.2

It is desired to transmit quarternary ($\mu = 4$) digits at a rate of 5,000 per second on a system having $S_R/\eta = 80,000$. Assuming sinc pulses are used, the bandwidth required is $B = r/2 = 2,500$, and applying Eqs. (16) and (17) gives

$$\rho = \frac{S_R}{\eta r} = 16.0$$

$$P_e = \frac{3}{2} Q\left(\sqrt{\frac{2\rho}{5}}\right) \approx 10^{-2}$$

so the system is not very reliable.

Suppose, however, that each quaternary digit is replaced by *two* binary digits. The required rate is then $r' = 2 \times 5,000 = 10,000$ and

$$\rho' = \frac{S_R}{\eta r'} = 8.0$$

$$P_e' = Q(\sqrt{2\rho'}) \approx 3 \times 10^{-5}$$

which is a substantial performance improvement. The price of that improvement is a *larger bandwidth*, $B' = 2B$, plus *encoding* and *decoding* units.

Later chapters will generalize these observations under the headings of *wideband noise reduction* and *information theory*. ////

Regenerative Repeaters

Long-haul transmission requires repeaters, be it for analog or digital communication. But unlike analog-message repeaters, digital repeaters can be *regenerative* in the sense that each repeater has an A/D converter as well as an amplifier. If the error probability per repeater is reasonably low and the number of hops M is large, the regeneration advantage turns out to be rather spectacular. This will be demonstrated for the case of polar binary transmission.

When analog repeaters are used and Eq. (17), Sect. 4.1, applies, the final signal-to-noise ratio is $S/N = (1/M)(S/N)_1$ and

$$P_e = Q\left[\sqrt{\frac{1}{M}\left(\frac{S}{N}\right)_1}\right] \qquad (19)$$

where $(S/N)_1$ is the signal-to-noise ratio after one hop. Therefore, the transmitted power *per repeater* must be increased linearly with M just to stay even, a factor not to be sneezed at since, for example, it takes 100 or more repeaters to cross the continent. The $1/M$ term in Eq. (19) stems from the fact that the contaminating noise progressively builds up from repeater to repeater.

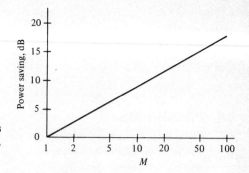

FIGURE 4.28
Power saving gained by regeneration as a function of the number of repeaters, $P_e = 10^{-5}$

In contrast, a regenerative repeater station consists of a complete receiver and transmitter back to back in one package. The receiving portion converts incoming signals to message digits, making a few errors in the process; the digits are then delivered to the transmitting portion, which in turn generates a new signal for transmission to the next station. The regenerated signal is thereby completely stripped of random noise but does contain some errors.

To analyze the performance, let ϵ be the error probability at each repeater, namely,

$$\epsilon = Q\left[\sqrt{\left(\frac{S}{N}\right)_1}\right] \qquad (20)$$

assuming identical units. As a given digit passes from station to station, it may suffer cumulative conversion errors. If the number of erroneous conversions is *even*, they cancel out, and a correct digit is delivered to the destination. (Note that this is true only for *binary* data.) The probability of n errors in M successive conversions is given by the *binomial distribution* of Eq. (1), Sect. 3.4:

$$P_M(n) = \binom{M}{n}\epsilon^n(1 - \epsilon)^{M-n}$$

The net error probability is then the probability that n is *odd*; specifically,

$$P_e = \sum_{n \text{ odd}} P_M(n) = \binom{M}{1}\epsilon(1 - \epsilon)^{M-1} + \binom{M}{3}\epsilon^3(1 - \epsilon)^{M-3} + \cdots \approx M\epsilon$$

where the approximation applies for $\epsilon \ll 1$ and M not too large. Hence, inserting Eq. (20),

$$P_e \approx MQ\left[\sqrt{\left(\frac{S}{N}\right)_1}\right] \qquad (21)$$

so P_e increases linearly with M, which generally requires a much smaller power increase to counteract than Eq. (19).

Figure 4.28 illustrates the power saving provided by regeneration as a function of M, the error probability being fixed at $P_e = 10^{-5}$. Thus, for example, a 10-station nonregenerative baseband system requires about 8.5 dB more transmitted power (per repeater) than a regenerative system.

4.6 PROBLEMS

4.1 (Sect. 4.1) A 20-km cable system has $S_T = 10$ dBW, $\alpha = 0.64$, and $B_N = 500$ kHz. The noise is additive and white with $\mathcal{T}_N = 25\mathcal{T}_0$. Find $(S/N)_D$ and $\mathcal{G}_R$ in decibels such that $S_D = 0$ dBW. *Ans.*: 33, 100.

4.2 (Sect. 4.1) Repeat Prob. 4.1 with $\alpha = 0.32$ and $B_N = 5$ MHz.

4.3 (Sect. 4.1) A 400-km repeater system employs a cable with 8.68 $\alpha = 0.5$. If $S_T/\eta_1 B_N = 70$ dB, what is the minimum number of repeaters such that $(S/N)_D \geq 20$ dB? Assume equal repeater spacing so $\mathcal{L}_1 = \mathcal{L}^{1/M}$.

4.4★ (Sect. 4.1) All other parameters being fixed, show that the number of equally spaced repeaters that maximizes $(S/N)_D$ is $M = \ln \mathcal{L} = 0.23\mathcal{L}_{dB}$.

4.5★ (Sect. 4.1) Owing to nonlinearities, the output of a baseband system is $y_D(t) = x(t) + n(t) + \frac{1}{2}[x(t) + n(t)]^2$. Find $\overline{y_D{}^2}$ assuming that $x(t)$ and $n(t)$ are independent and all of their odd moments are zero. Is it possible to define $(S/N)_D$ in this case?

4.6★ (Sect. 4.1) The open-circuit signal output of an oscillator is $A \cos 2\pi f_0 t$. The source resistance is R_S and there is internally generated thermal noise with temperature $\mathcal{T}_N$. A capacitor C is placed across the output terminals to improve S/N.
(*a*) Obtain an expression for S/N.
(*b*) What value of C maximizes S/N?

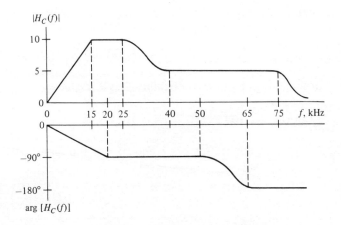

FIGURE P4.1.

4.7 (Sect. 4.2) Figure P4.1 shows the amplitude ratio and phase shift of a certain transmission channel. What frequency range or ranges has: amplitude distortion, phase distortion, distortionless transmission?

4.8 (Sect. 4.2) Show that an RC LPF gives essentially distortionless transmission if $x(t)$ is bandlimited in $W \ll B = 1/2\pi RC$.

4.9 (Sect. 4.2) The input to an RC LPF is the test signal in Fig. 4.4. Plot the output waveform when $f_0 = B/3$.

4.10 (Sect. 4.2) Find $t_d(f)$ for an RC LPF and evaluate it at $f = B/4$, B, and $4B$ when $B = 1$ kHz.

4.11 (Sect. 4.2) Consider a transfer function with *ripples in the amplitude ratio*, $H(f) = (1 + 2\alpha \cos \omega t_0)e^{-j\omega t_d}$, $|\alpha| \le \frac{1}{2}$.

(a) Show that $y(t) = x(t - t_d) + \alpha x(t - t_d + t_0) + \alpha x(t - t_d - t_0)$, so there is a pair of "echoes".

(b) Taking $\alpha = \frac{1}{2}$ and $x(t) = \Pi(t/\tau)$, sketch $y(t)$ for $t_0 = 2\tau$, $\tau/2$, and $\tau/4$.

4.12★(Sect. 4.2) Find $y(t)$ in terms of $x(t)$ when there are *small ripples in the phase shift*, i.e., $H(f) = \exp[-j(\omega t_d - \alpha \sin \omega t_0)]$, $|\alpha| \ll \pi$. Compare with Prob. 4.11. (*Hint:* Use a series expansion for $\exp(j\alpha \sin \omega t_0)$.)

4.13 (Sect. 4.2) Sketch $|H_{eq}(f)|$ and $\arg[H_{eq}(f)]$ needed to equalize $H_C(f)$ in Fig. P4.1 over $5 < |f| < 25$ kHz.

4.14 (Sect. 4.2) Suppose $x(t) = v(t) + \cos 2\pi f_1 t$ is applied to a nonlinear system with $y(t) = x(t) + 0.4x^2(t) + 0.1x^3(t)$.

(a) Find $y(t)$ and sketch a typical $Y(f)$ when $v(t)$ is bandlimited in $W \ll f_1$.

(b) If $v(t) = \cos 2\pi f_2 t$, $f_2 > f_1$, list all the frequency components in $y(t)$.

4.15 (Sect. 4.3) A system designed for telephone-quality voice transmission has $(S/N)_D = 30$ dB when $S_T = -3$ dBW. If the bandwidth is appropriately increased, what value of S_T is required to upgrade the system for high-fidelity audio transmission, all other factors being unchanged? *Ans.:* 30 to 40 dBW.

4.16 (Sect. 4.3) A system designed for an analog signal with $W = 10$ kHz uses an RC LPF with 3-dB bandwidth $B = 15$ kHz at the receiver.

(a) Find $(S/N)_D$ in terms of γ.

(b) Repeat for a second-order Butterworth filter (Exercise 3.10, Sect. 3.6) with $B = 12$ kHz.

4.17 (Sect. 4.3) A distorting channel with $H_C(f) = [1 + j(2f/W)]^{-1}$ and white noise is used for a signal with $G_x = (1/2W)\Pi(f/2W)$. To compensate for the distortion, the receiving filter is $H_R(f) = [1 + j(2f/W)]\Pi(f/2W)$. The transmitting filter is simply an amplifier with unit gain. Show that $(S/N)_D \approx 0.78\gamma$.

4.18★(Sect. 4.3) Referring to Fig. 4.15, obtain expressions for $\mathcal{G}_T$, $\mathcal{L}$, and $\mathcal{G}_R$ in terms of $H_T(f)$, $H_C(f)$, $H_R(f)$, and $G_x(f)$. (*Hint:* By definition, $\mathcal{G}_T = S_T/x^2$, etc.)

4.19★(Sect. 4.3) Given $H_C(f)$ and $G_x(f)$ in Prob. 4.17, find the optimum terminal filters and evaluate $(S/N)_{D_{max}}$ in terms of γ.

4.20 (Sect. 4.4) Redraw Fig. 4.18 for the case of an RC LPF with $B = 1/2\tau$ and $B = 1/4\tau$.

4.21 (Sect. 4.4) A sinc pulse $x(t) = A$ sinc $2Wt$ is applied to an ideal LPF having bandwidth B. Taking the duration of sinc at to be $\tau \triangleq 2/a$, plot the ratio of output duration to input duration as a function of B/W.

4.22 (Sect. 4.4) A rectangular pulse with $\tau \gg 1/B$ is applied to an RC LPF. Find the 10 to 90 percent rise time in terms of the 3-dB bandwidth B.

4.23★(Sect. 4.4) It is sometimes convenient for analytic purposes to define the *effective bandwidth* of an LPF and the *effective duration* of its impulse response as follows:

$$B_{\text{eff}} \triangleq \frac{\int_{-\infty}^{\infty} |H(f)| df}{2|H(f)|_{\max}} \qquad \tau_{\text{eff}} \triangleq \frac{\int_{-\infty}^{\infty} h(t) dt}{|h(t)|_{\max}}$$

Show that $B_{\text{eff}} \tau_{\text{eff}} \geq \frac{1}{2}$. (*Hint*: First prove that

$$\left| \int_{-\infty}^{\infty} H(f) \exp(j\omega t) df \right| \leq \int_{-\infty}^{\infty} |H(f)| df$$

4.24 (Sect. 4.4) A rectangular pulse plus white noise is the input to an RC LPF.
(a) Show that $\epsilon_A{}^2 = \pi B\tau (1 - e^{-2\pi B\tau})^{-2} (\eta/2E)$, where E is the energy of the *input* pulse.
(b) Plot $\epsilon_A{}^2$ versus $B\tau$ and find the best value of $B\tau$ for amplitude measurements.

4.25 (Sect. 4.4) A pulse transmission system is to be designed so that $\epsilon_A{}^2 \leq 10^{-2}$ and $\overline{\Delta t^2} \leq 10^{-12}$ when $\eta = 10^{-4}$. Assuming rectangular pulses at the input to the receiving filter, find the minimum values for B, τ, and E.

4.26★(Sect. 4.4) A matched filter is to be designed for the case of $x(t) = \Pi[(t - \tau/2)/\tau]$ and $G_n(f) = \eta/2$. Sketch $h_{\text{opt}}(t)$ and determine the condition on t_0 such that the filter is physically realizable, at least in principle. Then sketch $y(t)$ in absence of noise.

4.27★(Sect. 4.4) Suppose the system in Prob. 4.26 uses an RC LPF with $B = 1/2\tau$ instead of a matched filter. Find $|y(t_0)|^2/N$ in terms of the theoretical maximum possible value.

4.28 (Sect. 4.5) Consider digital signaling with a gaussian pulse shape $p(t) = e^{-\pi(t/\tau)^2}$, which is neither timelimited nor bandlimited and does not have periodic zero crossings. Let it be required that $p(m/r) \leq 0.01$ to minimize intersymbol interference and let the bandwidth B be defined such that $|P(f)| \leq 0.01 |P(0)|$ for $|f| \geq B$. Find r in terms of B under these conditions. *Ans.*: $r = (\pi/2 \ln 10)B \approx 0.7B$.

4.29 (Sect. 4.5) Using a sketch like Fig. 4.26, show graphically that any threshold level $b \neq 0$ yields $P_e > Q(A/\sigma)$. Can you prove this analytically?

4.30 (Sect. 4.5) Digital systems sometimes suffer from *impulse noise* whose PDF can be approximated as $p(n) = (1/\sqrt{2}\sigma) \exp(-\sqrt{2} |n|/\sigma)$. Find P_e for a polar binary system with impulse noise, and compare with $Q(A/\sigma)$.

4.31 (Sect. 4.5) Prove Eq. (11) using Eq. (13), Sect. 2.3.

4.32★(Sect. 4.5) Show that Eq. (13) also holds when μ is odd so the possible values of A_k are $0, \pm 2A, \pm 4A, \ldots, \pm(\mu - 1)A$.

4.33 (Sect. 4.5) A certain polar digital system has $\rho = 220$. What is the largest permitted value of μ such that $P_e \leq 10^{-5}$?

4.34 (Sect. 4.5) A polar binary system with 20 nonregenerative repeaters has $P_e = 10^{-4}$.
(a) Find $(S/N)_1$.
(b) By what factor can r be increased without increasing P_e if the repeaters are made regenerative and the bandwidth is appropriately modified?

LINEAR MODULATION

The several purposes of modulation were itemized in Chap. 1 along with a qualitative description of the process. To briefly recapitulate: *modulation* is the systematic alteration of one waveform, called the *carrier*, according to the characteristics of another waveform, the modulating signal or message. The fundamental goal is producing an information-bearing modulated wave whose properties are best suited to the given communication task.

We now launch upon a quantitative discussion and analysis of modulation systems, the *how* and the *why*. This subject forms the core of our study of communication and will be divided into four parts: *linear modulation* (Chap. 5), *exponential modulation* (Chap. 6), *noise in CW modulation* (Chap. 7), and *pulse modulation* (Chap. 8). The division of material, while convenient, is by no means clear-cut and some overlapping will be encountered. In particular, both linear and exponential modulation are types of *continuous-wave* (CW) *modulation*; i.e., the carrier is a sinusoid. Consequently, there are inevitable similarities of techniques and instrumentation. Pulse modulation, for which the carrier is a periodic pulse train, may resemble linear modulation, exponential modulation, or neither, depending on the type. But more to the point, modern pulse technology has been applied with great success to the generation and detection of CW modulation; conversely, many pulse-modulation systems involve CW modulation for the final step in transmission.

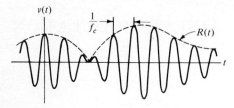

FIGURE 5.1
A bandpass signal.

As to the specific topic at hand, linear modulation is essentially direct frequency translation of the message spectrum. Double-sideband modulation (DSB) is precisely that. Minor modifications of the translated spectrum yield conventional amplitude modulation (AM), single-sideband modulation (SSB), or vestigial-sideband modulation (VSB). Each of these variations has its own distinct advantages and significant practical applications. Each will be given due consideration in this chapter, including such matters as waveforms and spectra, detection methods, transmitters, and receivers. The chapter begins with a general discussion of bandpass signals and systems, pertinent to all forms of CW modulation.

5.1   BANDPASS SIGNALS AND SYSTEMS

A bandpass signal is one whose spectrum is concentrated in the vicinity of some frequency $f_c \neq 0$, called the carrier frequency. Therefore, as Fig. 5.1 shows, the waveform looks like a sinusoid at frequency f_c with slowly changing envelope and phase. Formally we write

$$v(t) = R(t) \cos [\omega_c t + \phi(t)] \qquad R(t) \geq 0 \qquad (1)$$

where $R(t)$ is the *envelope* and $\phi(t)$ the *phase*, both being functions of time. By definition, the envelope is *nonnegative*; i.e., negative "amplitudes" are absorbed in the phase by adding $\pm 180°$, so the dashed line in Fig. 5.1 is $R(t)$.

Figure 5.2a is a phasor representation of $v(t)$ as a vector in the complex plane whose length equals $R(t)$ and whose angle equals $\omega_c t + \phi(t)$. But the angular term $\omega_c t$ represents a steady counterclockwise rotation at f_c revolutions per second and can just as well be suppressed, leading to Fig. 5.2b. This phasor representation, used regularly hereafter, relates to Fig. 5.2a in the following manner: If the origin of Fig. 5.2b is pinned and the entire figure is rotated counterclockwise at the rate f_c, it becomes Fig. 5.2a.

Further inspection of Fig. 5.2b suggests another way of writing $v(t)$. If we define

$$v_i(t) \triangleq R(t) \cos \phi(t) \qquad v_q(t) \triangleq R(t) \sin \phi(t) \qquad (2)$$

then

$$v(t) = v_i(t) \cos \omega_c t - v_q(t) \sin \omega_c t \qquad (3)$$

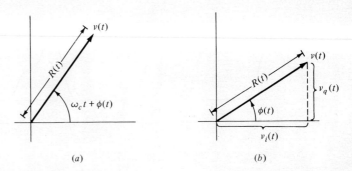

(a)   (b)

FIGURE 5.2

called the *quadrature-carrier* description of a bandpass signal as distinguished from the *envelope-and-phase description*, Eq. (1); $v_i(t)$ and $v_q(t)$ are named the *in-phase* and *quadrature components*, respectively. The quadrature-carrier designation comes about from the fact that the two terms in Eq. (3) may be represented by phasors with the second at an angle of $+90°$ compared to the first — see Fig. 5.2*b*. The minus sign in Eq. (3) may seem puzzling, but the reader can justify it from Eq. (1) by expanding $\cos [\omega_c t + \phi(t)]$.

While both descriptions of a bandpass signal are useful, the latter has advantages for the frequency-domain interpretation. Specifically, if $V_i(f) = \mathscr{F}[v_i(t)]$, etc., then application of the frequency-translation theorem, Eq. (22), Sect. 2.3, to Eq. (3) yields

$$V(f) = \frac{1}{2}[V_i(f-f_c) + V_i(f+f_c)] + \frac{j}{2}[V_q(f-f_c) - V_q(f+f_c)] \qquad (4)$$

since $-\sin \omega_c t = \cos(\omega_c t + 90°)$ and $e^{\pm j90°} = \pm j$. An immediate implication of Eq. (4) is that if $v(t)$ is in fact a bandpass signal, then $v_i(t)$ and $v_q(t)$ are *lowpass* signals bandlimited in $W < f_c$ (why?). The envelope-and-phase description does not readily convert to the frequency domain since, from Eq. (2) or Fig. 5.2*b*,

$$R(t) = \sqrt{v_i^2(t) + v_q^2(t)} \qquad \phi(t) = \arctan \frac{v_q(t)}{v_i(t)} \qquad (5)$$

which are not Fourier-transformable.

Lowpass Equivalent Signals and Systems ★

Consider the bandpass frequency function $V(f)$ in Fig. 5.3*a*. Its *lowpass equivalent* is defined to be

$$V_{\mathrm{LP}}(f) \triangleq V(f+f_c)u(f+f_c) = \begin{cases} V(f+f_c) & f > -f_c \\ 0 & f < -f_c \end{cases} \qquad (6a)$$

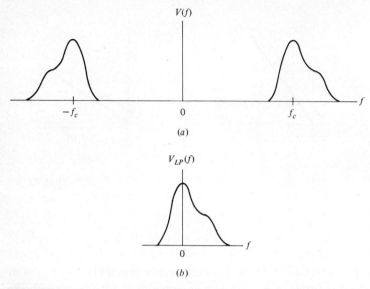

FIGURE 5.3
(a) Bandpass frequency function $V(f)$; (b) lowpass equivalent frequency function $V_{\mathrm{LP}}(f)$.

which is nothing more than the positive-frequency portion of $V(f)$ translated downward f_c units, Fig. 5.3b. Equation (6a) is a bandpass-to-lowpass transformation and generally results in a nonhermitian function. Underscoring that observation, the lowpass equivalent time function is

$$v_{\mathrm{LP}}(t) = \frac{1}{2} R(t)e^{j\phi(t)} = \frac{1}{2} v_i(t) + \frac{j}{2} v_q(t) \qquad (6b)$$

a *complex* function of time. To derive this expression, we start with Eq. (4) and replace f by $f + f_c$, giving $V(f + f_c) = (\frac{1}{2})[V_i(f) + V_i(f + 2f_c)] + (j/2)[V_q(f) - V_q(f + f2_c)]$. Then since $V_i(f)$ and $V_q(f)$ are lowpass functions, $V(f + f_c)u(f + f_c) = (\frac{1}{2})V_i(f) + (j/2)V_q(f)$ and inverse transformation yields Eq. (6b).

Given $v_{\mathrm{LP}}(t)$, the bandpass time function $v(t)$ is easily written in either envelope-and-phase or quadrature-carrier form using

$$v(t) = 2 \operatorname{Re}\left[v_{\mathrm{LP}}(t)e^{j\omega_c t}\right] \qquad (7a)$$

which follows by comparing Eq. (6b) with Eqs. (1) and (3). Similarly, the bandpass frequency function is related to its lowpass equivalent by

$$V(f) = V_{\mathrm{LP}}(f - f_c) + V_{\mathrm{LP}}^*(-f - f_c) \qquad (7b)$$

the derivation being left as an exercise.

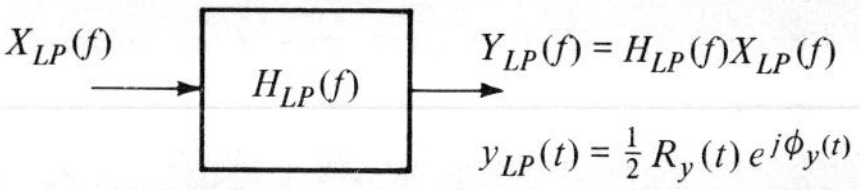

FIGURE 5.4
Bandpass analysis using lowpass equivalents.

$$X_{LP}(f) \rightarrow \boxed{H_{LP}(f)} \rightarrow Y_{LP}(f) = H_{LP}(f)X_{LP}(f)$$
$$y_{LP}(t) = \tfrac{1}{2}R_y(t)\,e^{j\phi_y(t)}$$

The value of Eqs. (6) and (7) rests on the fact that they apply to bandpass *systems* as well as bandpass signals. Thus, if $H(f)$ is a bandpass transfer function, the equivalent lowpass transfer function is simply

$$H_{\text{LP}}(f) = H(f + f_c)u(f + f_c) \qquad (8)$$

Similarly, we can speak of the equivalent lowpass impulse response $h_{\text{LP}}(t) = \mathscr{F}^{-1}[H_{\text{LP}}(f)]$.

Putting these definitions to work, suppose $x(t)$ is a bandpass signal at the input to a bandpass system. If $X(f) = \mathscr{F}[x(t)]$, then the output spectrum is $Y(f) = H(f)X(f)$, as usual. Alternatively, it can be shown that†

$$Y_{\text{LP}}(f) = H_{\text{LP}}(f)X_{\text{LP}}(f) \qquad (9a)$$

$$y_{\text{LP}}(t) = h_{\text{LP}} * x_{\text{LP}}(t) \qquad (9b)$$

so a bandpass analysis problem may be carried out in terms of the lowpass equivalents, often an easier task. Thus, for instance, the envelope and phase of the bandpass output signal $y(t)$ are

$$R_y(t) = 2|y_{\text{LP}}(t)| \qquad \phi_y(t) = \arg[y_{\text{LP}}(t)] \qquad (10)$$

Figure 5.4 summarizes this method.

EXERCISE 5.1 Derive Eq. (7b) from Eq. (7a). (Hint: For any complex quantity Z, $2\,\text{Re}\,[Z] = Z + Z^*$.)

Example 5.1   Carrier and Envelope Delay ★

Let $x(t) = R_x(t)\cos \omega_c t$ be a bandpass signal applied to a bandpass system having constant amplitude ratio $|H(f)| = K$ but *nonlinear* phase $\arg[H(f)] = \theta(f)$ over the frequency range of $x(t)$. Since $H(f) = Ke^{j\theta}(f)$,

$$H_{\text{LP}}(f) = Ke^{j\theta(f+f_c)}u(f + f_c) \qquad (11)$$

If the phase nonlinearities are not too severe, we can expand $\theta(f + f_c)$ in a Taylor series, keeping only the first two terms, thus:

$$\theta(f + f_c) = \theta(f_c) + f\left.\frac{d\theta(f)}{df}\right|_{f=f_c} + \cdots \approx -\omega_c t_c - \omega t_R \qquad (12)$$

† See Frederick and Carlson (1971, chap. 7).

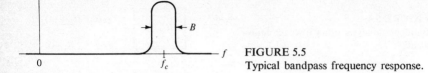

FIGURE 5.5
Typical bandpass frequency response.

in which we have introduced

$$t_c \triangleq -\frac{\theta(f_c)}{2\pi f_c} \qquad t_R \triangleq -\frac{1}{2\pi}\frac{d\theta(f)}{df}\bigg|_{f=f_c} \tag{13}$$

These parameters are called the *carrier delay* and *envelope delay*, respectively, for reasons soon to emerge.

Inserting Eqs. (12) and (11) in Eq. (9) gives

$$Y_{\text{LP}}(f) = Ke^{-j\omega_c t_c}X_{\text{LP}}(f)e^{-j\omega t_R}u(f+f_c)$$

so

$$y_{\text{LP}}(t) = Ke^{-j\omega_c t_c}x_{\text{LP}}(t-t_R) = Ke^{-j\omega_c t_c}(\tfrac{1}{2})R_x(t-t_R)$$

where we have used the time-delay theorem and noted that $x_{\text{LP}}(t) = (\tfrac{1}{2})R_x(t)$ since $\phi_x(t) = 0$ by assumption. Finally, from Eqs. (10) and (7a),

$$y(t) = 2 \text{ Re } [Ke^{-j\omega_c t_c}(\tfrac{1}{2})R_x(t-t_R)e^{j\omega_c t}]$$
$$= KR_x(t-t_R) \cos \omega_c(t-t_c) \tag{14}$$

Therefore, as implied above, the output envelope has been delayed by t_R while the carrier delay is t_c. And since t_R is independent of frequency, at least to the extent of the approximations involved, the envelope has not suffered delay distortion.

In certain applications—called frequency-division multiplexing systems—several bandpass signals at different carriers are transmitted over a single channel. Plots of $d\theta/df$ versus f are then used as an aid in evaluating the channel's envelope-delay characteristics. If this curve is not reasonably flat over a proposed frequency range, excessive envelope distortion will result.   ////

Carrier Frequencies and Bandwidths

An analog bandpass system has the same general form as a baseband system (Fig. 4.14) except that the transmitter, channel, and receiver are bandpass units. Thus, per Fig. 5.5, the bandwidth B is nominally centered at the carrier frequency f_c. Although the parameters B and f_c would seem to be unrelated, practical factors cause them to be connected, albeit rather loosely.

Table 5.1 SELECTED CARRIER FREQUENCIES
AND NOMINAL BANDWIDTH

Frequency band	Carrier frequency	Bandwidth
Longwave radio	100 kHz	2 kHz
Shortwave radio	5 MHz	100 kHz
VHF	100 MHz	2 MHz
Microwave	5 GHz	100 MHz
Millimeterwave	100 GHz	2 GHz
Optical	5×10^{14} Hz	10^{13} Hz

For instance, the antennas in a radio system produce considerable distortion unless the frequency range is small compared to the carrier frequency. And, more generally, designing a bandpass amplifier with distortionless frequency response turns out to be nearly impossible if B is either very large or very small compared to f_c. As a rough rule of thumb, the *fractional bandwidth* B/f_c must be bounded by

$$0.01 < \frac{B}{f_c} < 0.1 \qquad (15)$$

otherwise there will be signal distortion beyond the scope of practical equalizers. Incidentally, as applied to the quality factor Q of simple resonant circuits, Eq. (15) becomes $10 < Q < 100$ since $B = f_r/Q$ — see Fig. 2.12a.

As an immediate consequence of Eq. (15) we can say that *large bandwidths require high carrier frequencies*. This effect was discussed briefly in Chap. 1. It is further underscored by Table 5.1, which lists selected carrier frequencies and their nominal bandwidths $B \approx 0.02f_c$. To be sure, larger bandwidths can be achieved, but at substantially greater costs. As a further consequence of Eq. (15), the terms *bandpass* and *narrowband* are virtually synonymous.

Bandpass Pulse Transmission

Finally, consider the case of a bandpass or modulated pulse signal of the form

$$v(t) = p(t) \cos (\omega_c t + \theta) \qquad (16)$$

where $p(t)$ is a baseband pulse shape and θ is a constant. We immediately know from the modulation theorem that the spectrum of $v(t)$ is centered at $f = f_c$ and has *twice* the spectral width of $p(t)$, as illustrated in Example 2.7, Sect. 2.3. We also know that if $p(t)$ has duration τ, then successful pulse resolution at baseband requires a lowpass system of bandwidth $B_{LP} \geq 1/2\tau$, per Eq. (3), Sect. 4.4.

Putting two and two together, it follows that successful resolution of $v(t)$ requires a bandpass system with bandwidth $B = 2B_{LP} \geq 1/\tau$. Hence, our rule of thumb for the relation between output duration and system bandwidth for bandpass pulses is

$$\tau_{\min} \geq \frac{1}{B} \qquad (17a)$$

and, by similar reasoning for the output rise time,

$$\tau_{r_{\min}} \geq \frac{1}{B} \qquad (17b)$$

These equations have long served as rough but useful guidelines in radar work and related fields.

5.2 DOUBLE-SIDEBAND MODULATION: AM AND DSB

Historically, the first type of modulation to evolve was conventional amplitude modulation, the familiar AM of standard radio broadcasting. We shall reserve the term *amplitude modulation* for this specific type, and use *linear modulation* for the general class. DSB differs from AM by *carrier suppression*, a minor alteration that has major repercussions. But before plunging into the details, a few conventions and matters of nomenclature must be disposed of.

Message Conventions

Our analysis of analog baseband transmission was couched in terms of an *arbitrary message* or ensemble of messages designated by $x(t)$. Wherever possible, that practice will be continued here and in subsequent chapters. We will also continue to assume that $x(t)$ is approximately bandlimited in W, called the *message bandwidth*. Thus

$$\left. \begin{array}{c} G_x(f) \approx 0 \\ X(f) \approx 0 \end{array} \right\} \quad |f| > W \qquad (1)$$

The Fourier transform $X(f) = \mathscr{F}[x(t)]$ will be appropriate in many cases (implying that the message is an energy signal), and Fig. 5.6a is a representative message spectrum. Figure 5.6b shows a typical energy spectral density for a voice signal and indicates that W may be taken to be in the vicinity of 3 to 4 kHz.

Furthermore, for mathematical convenience, let the messages be scaled or normalized to have a magnitude not exceeding unity, i.e.,

$$|x(t)| \leq 1 \qquad (2)$$

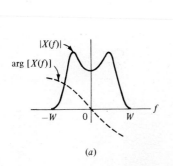

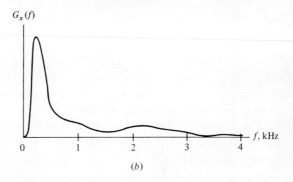

FIGURE 5.6
(a) Representative message spectrum; (b) typical energy spectral density for voice signals.

Consequently, when average power is considered,

$$\langle x^2(t) \rangle = \overline{x^2} \leq 1 \qquad (3)$$

assuming the source is ergodic. Note, by the way, that we will freely move back and forth between deterministic energy-signal models and random power-signal models, whatever best suits the problem at hand.

Occasionally an analysis with arbitrary $x(t)$ proves difficult, if not impossible. For such situations it is necessary to resort to a specific modulating signal, usually the simple sinusoid

$$x(t) = A_m \cos 2\pi f_m t \qquad A_m \leq 1 \qquad f_m < W \qquad (4)$$

which is called *tone modulation*. With tone modulation, a positive-frequency line spectrum will suffice for frequency-domain studies. Although tone modulation may seem unduly simplified, the approach has definite advantages. For one thing, tones are often the only tractable signals in complex problems; they facilitate the calculation of spectra, average powers, etc., that otherwise would be prohibitive. Moreover, if we can find the response of the modulation system to a specific frequency in the message band, we can infer the response for all frequencies in W.

Amplitude Modulation (AM)

The unique feature of AM is that the *envelope* of the modulated carrier has the same *shape* as the message waveform. This is achieved by adding the translated message, appropriately proportioned, to the unmodulated carrier. Specifically, the modulated signal is

$$x_c(t) \triangleq A_c \cos \omega_c t + mx(t)A_c \cos \omega_c t$$
$$= A_c[1 + mx(t)] \cos \omega_c t \qquad (5)$$

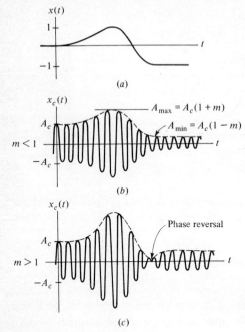

FIGURE 5.7
AM waveforms. (a) $x(t)$; (b) $x_c(t)$ with $m < 1$; (c) $x_c(t)$ with $m > 1$.

where $A_c \cos \omega_c t$ is the unmodulated carrier, $f_c = \omega_c / 2\pi$ is the carrier frequency, and the constant m is called the *modulation index*. Since A_c is the unmodulated carrier amplitude, we can think of the modulated amplitude as being a linear function of the message, namely,

$$A_c(t) = A_c[1 + mx(t)]$$

underscoring the meaning of *amplitude* modulation.

Figure 5.7 shows a portion of a typical message and the resulting AM wave for two values of m. The envelope has the shape of $x(t)$ providing that: the carrier frequency is much greater than the rate of variation of $x(t)$, otherwise an envelope cannot be visualized; and there are no *phase reversals* in the modulated wave, i.e., the amplitude $A_c[1 + mx(t)]$ does not go negative. Preserving the desired relationship between envelope and message thus requires

$$f_c \gg W \quad \text{and} \quad m \leq 1 \tag{6}$$

The latter follows since $|x(t)| \leq 1$ by our convention.

The carrier-frequency condition is, of course, in agreement with the frequency-translation aspect of modulation, though it sometimes proves to be detrimental. The condition $m \leq 1$ sets an upper limit on how heavily the carrier can be modulated. With $m = 1$, known as 100 percent modulation, the modulated amplitude varies

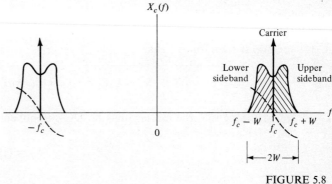

FIGURE 5.8
AM spectrum.

between 0 and $2A_c$. *Overmodulation*, $m > 1$, results in carrier phase reversals and *envelope distortion*, as illustrated in Fig. 5.7c,

Turning to the frequency domain, the Fourier transform of an AM wave is easily found to be

$$X_c(f) = \frac{A_c}{2}\left[\delta(f+f_c) + \delta(f-f_c)\right] + \frac{mA_c}{2}\left[X(f-f_c) + X(f+f_c)\right] \qquad (7)$$

While Eq. (7) may look imposing, the spectrum consists of nothing more than the translated message spectrum, plus a pair of impulses at $\pm f_c$ representing the carrier itself, Fig. 5.8. Two properties of the AM spectrum should be carefully noted.

1 There is *symmetry* about the carrier frequency, the amplitude being even and the phase being odd. That portion of the spectrum above f_c is called the *upper sideband*, while that below f_c is the *lower sideband*; hence the designation *double-sideband* amplitude modulation.

2 The *transmission bandwidth* B_T required for an AM signal is exactly *twice* that of the message bandwidth, so

$$B_T = 2W \qquad (8)$$

This result points out that AM is not attractive when one must conserve band-width—after all, the message could be sent at baseband with one-half the AM bandwidth.

We shall find that transmission bandwidth is one of the characteristic parameters of modulation types; another important parameter is the *average transmitted power* in the modulated wave, defined as

$$S_T = \mathbf{E}[x_c^2(t)]$$

To compute this ensemble average, we add a random angle Θ to the carrier so that $x_c(t)$ has the form of a modulated random process, Eq. (11a), Sect. 3.5, with $v(t) = A_c[1 + mx(t)]$. It then follows that

$$S_T = \tfrac{1}{2}\mathbf{E}[v^2(t)] = (1 + 2m\bar{x} + m^2\overline{x^2})\,\frac{A_c{}^2}{2}$$

Therefore, assuming that the message has no DC component,†

$$S_T = (1 + m^2\overline{x^2})\,\frac{A_c{}^2}{2} \tag{9}$$

Equation (9) has an interesting interpretation relative to the AM spectrum. From Fig. 5.8, S_T includes the power in the carrier-frequency component plus two symmetric sidebands. Hence

$$S_T = \frac{A_c{}^2}{2} + m^2\overline{x^2}\,\frac{A_c{}^2}{2} = P_c + 2P_{SB}$$

where the *carrier power* is

$$P_c = \tfrac{1}{2}A_c{}^2$$

and the *power per sideband* is

$$P_{SB} = \frac{m^2\overline{x^2}P_c}{2} \le \tfrac{1}{2}P_c$$

The upper limit on P_{SB} follows from $m^2\overline{x^2} \le 1$. Thus

$$P_c = S_T - 2P_{SB} \ge \tfrac{1}{2}S_T \tag{10}$$

which says that at least 50 percent of the total transmitted power resides in the carrier. But, referring back to Eq. (5), the carrier term alone is seen to be independent of the message and does not contain any of the information. We therefore conclude that a substantial portion of the transmitted power S_T is "wasted" in the carrier itself. It will later be shown that true envelope modulation, and the simplicity of *envelope detection*, depends on this wasted power.

AM with Tone Modulation

Setting $x(t) = A_m \cos 2\pi f_m t$ gives the tone-modulated AM waveform

$$x_c(t) = A_c(1 + mA_m \cos \omega_m t) \cos \omega_c t$$

$$= A_c \cos \omega_c t + \frac{mA_m A_c}{2}[\cos(\omega_c - \omega_m)t + \cos(\omega_c + \omega_m)t] \tag{11}$$

---

† For reasons discussed in Sect. 5.5, messages having $\bar{x} \neq 0$ are seldom transmitted via AM.

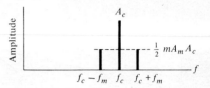

FIGURE 5.9
AM line spectrum, tone modulation.

where we have used the trigonometric expansion for the product of two cosines. The corresponding positive-frequency line spectrum is shown in Fig. 5.9.

With tone modulation, an AM wave can be treated as a *sum of phasors*, one for each spectral line. An especially informative way of constructing the diagram is shown in Fig. 5.10, where the sideband phasors have been added to the tip of the carrier phasor. Since the carrier phasor rotates at f_c Hz, the sideband phasors rotate at speeds of $\pm f_m$ *relative* to the carrier. Note that as long as the sideband lines are equal and of correct phase, the resultant of the sideband phasors is *collinear* with the carrier phasor. Moreover, the magnitude of the resultant is the envelope $R(t)$.

This observation leads to a simple way of qualitatively studying the effects of transmission imperfections, interference, etc. For example, if the lower sideband line is severely attenuated (Fig. 5.11), the resultant envelope is

$$R(t) = \left[\left(A_c + \frac{mA_m A_c}{2} \cos \omega_m t \right)^2 + \left(\frac{mA_m A_c}{2} \sin \omega_m t \right)^2 \right]^{1/2}$$

$$= A_c \left[1 + \left(\frac{mA_m}{2} \right)^2 + mA_m \cos \omega_m t \right]^{1/2} \tag{12}$$

from which the *envelope distortion* can be determined.

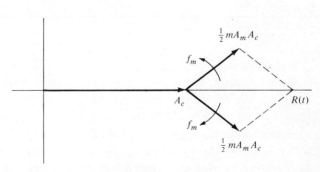

FIGURE 5.10
Phasor diagram for AM with tone modulation.

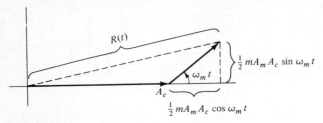

FIGURE 5.11

Double-Sideband Suppressed-Carrier Modulation (DSB)

Because the carrier-frequency component of AM is independent of the message and represents wasted power, it can just as well be eliminated from the modulated wave. This results in double-sideband suppressed-carrier amplitude modulation — *double-sideband modulation*, or DSB† for short.

Dropping the carrier term and the now meaningless modulation index from Eq. (5) gives

$$x_c(t) \triangleq x(t)A_c \cos \omega_c t \qquad (13)$$

for the definition of DSB. Unlike AM, the modulated wave is zero in absence of modulation: $x_c(t) = 0$ when $x(t) = 0$. Since the carrier has been suppressed, the average transmitted power is

$$S_T = 2P_{SB} = \tfrac{1}{2}\overline{x^2}A_c^2 \qquad (14)$$

The DSB spectrum is simply the translated message spectrum

$$X_c(f) = \frac{A_c}{2}[X(f - f_c) + X(f + f_c)] \qquad (15)$$

Of course, the transmission bandwidth is unchanged from the AM case, so

$$B_T = 2W$$

Comparing Eqs. (15) and (7) shows that AM and DSB are quite similar in the frequency domain, but the time-domain picture is another story. As illustrated by Fig. 5.12, the DSB envelope is not the same shape as the message since negative values of $x(t)$ are reflected in the carrier *phase*. So whenever $x(t)$ crosses zero, the modulated wave has a *phase reversal*. Full recovery of the message therefore entails an awareness of these phase reversals, and an envelope detector would not be sufficient. Stated another way, DSB involves more than just "amplitude" modulation.

† The abbreviations DSB-SC and DSSC are also used.

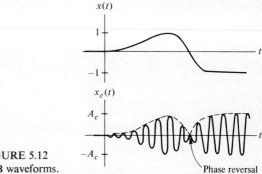

FIGURE 5.12
DSB waveforms.

This consideration suggests, and later analysis confirms, that there is a trade-off between power efficiency and demodulation methods. DSB conserves power but requires complex detection circuitry; conversely, AM demodulation is simply envelope detection but at the cost of greater transmitted power.

EXERCISE 5.2   Show that the envelope-and-phase and quadrature-carrier representations of AM (with $m \leq 1$) and DSB are as follows.

$$R_{AM}(t) = A_c[1 + mx(t)] \qquad R_{DSB}(t) = A_c|x(t)| \tag{16a}$$

$$\phi_{AM}(t) = 0 \qquad \phi_{DSB}(t) = \begin{cases} 0 & x(t) > 0 \\ 180° & x(t) < 0 \end{cases} \tag{16b}$$

$$v_{i_{AM}}(t) = R_{AM}(t) \qquad v_{i_{DSB}}(t) = A_c x(t) \tag{16c}$$

$$v_{q_{AM}}(t) = 0 \qquad v_{q_{DSB}}(t) = 0 \tag{16d}$$

EXERCISE 5.3   Let $x(t)$ be the random binary wave of Fig. 3.9 with $A = 1$. Sketch the resulting modulated waveforms if the modulation is AM with $m = 0.5$, AM with $m = 1.0$, and DSB. Use these sketches to explain why DSB is sometimes referred to as AM with 200 percent modulation.

5.3   MODULATORS AND TRANSMITTERS

We have seen that new frequencies are created in the modulation process. The device that generates an AM wave, a *modulator*, must therefore be either *time-varying* or *nonlinear*, since linear time-invariant systems cannot produce new frequency com-

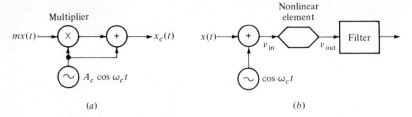

FIGURE 5.13
AM modulators using: (a) multiplier; (b) nonlinear element.

ponents. Figure 5.13a illustrates a possible modulator directly derived from the definition of AM. Because a multiplier is required, the system can be termed a *product modulator*. Indeed, recalling that multiplying by cos $\omega_c t$ yields frequency translation, the product operation is basic to linear modulation systems. In practice, multiplication is achieved with the aid of a nonlinear element and filtering, arranged as in Fig. 5.13b, where the nonlinearity may be of the *power-law* or *piecewise-linear* (switching) variety.

Power-Law Modulators

Taking the power-law case, let the nonlinear device have as its transfer characteristic

$$v_{out} = a_1 v_{in} + a_2 v_{in}^2$$

By omitting higher-order terms, we are assuming a *square-law* device. Then, if $v_{in}(t) = x(t) + \cos \omega_c t$,

$$v_{out}(t) = a_1 x(t) + a_2 x^2(t) + a_2 \cos^2 \omega_c t + a_1 \left[1 + \frac{2a_2}{a_1} x(t) \right] \cos \omega_c t \qquad (1)$$

The last term is the desired AM wave, with $A_c = a_1$ and $m = 2a_2/a_1$, providing it can be separated from the rest.

As to the feasibility of separation, Fig. 5.14 shows the spectrum $V_{out}(f) = \mathcal{F}[v_{out}(t)]$ taking $X(f)$ as in Fig. 5.6a. Note that the $x^2(t)$ term in Eq. (1) becomes $X * X(f)$, which is bandlimited in $2W$. Therefore, if $f_c > 3W$, there is no spectral overlapping and the required separation can be accomplished by a bandpass filter of bandwidth $B_T = 2W$ centered at f_c.

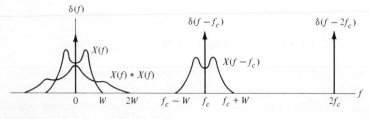

FIGURE 5.14

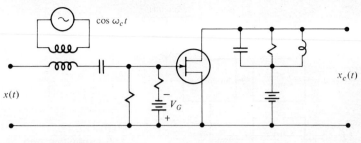

FIGURE 5.15
AM modulator circuit using an FET as a square-law device.

A circuit realization of the complete modulator employing a field-effect transistor (FET) is shown in Fig. 5.15. The battery V_G serves to bias the FET in its saturation region where it has a square-law characteristic, and the parallel RLC circuit is the bandpass filter.†

Because of the heavy filtering required, power-law modulators are used primarily for *low-level* modulation, i.e., at power levels lower than the transmitted value. Substantial linear amplification is then necessary to bring the power up to S_T. But RF power amplifiers of the required linearity are not without problems of their own, and it often is better to employ *high-level* modulation if S_T is to be large.

Switching Modulators

Efficient high-level modulators are arranged so that undesired modulation products never fully develop and need not be filtered out. This is usually accomplished with the aid of a *switching* device, whose detailed analysis is postponed to Chap. 8. However, the basic operation of the supply-voltage modulated class C amplifier is readily understood from its idealized equivalent circuit and waveforms, Fig. 5.16.

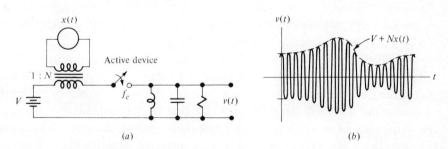

FIGURE 5.16
Supply-voltage-modulated class C amplifier. (*a*) Equivalent circuit; (*b*) output waveform.

† Clarke and Hess (1971, chap. 8) gives the complete analysis.

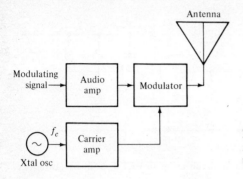

FIGURE 5.17
AM transmitter with high-level modulation.

The active device, a vacuum tube or transistor, serves as a switch driven at the carrier frequency, closing briefly every $1/f_c$ seconds. The load, called a *tank* circuit, is tuned to resonate at f_c, so the switching action causes the tank circuit to "ring" sinusoidally. The steady-state load voltage in absence of modulation is then $v(t) = V \cos \omega_c t$. Adding the message to the supply voltage, say via transformer, gives $v(t) = [V + Nx(t)] \cos \omega_c t$, where N is the transformer turns ratio. If V and N are correctly proportioned, the desired modulation has been accomplished without appreciable generation of undesired components.

A complete AM transmitter is diagramed schematically in Fig. 5.17 for the case of high-level modulation. The carrier wave is generated by a crystal-controlled oscillator to ensure stability of the carrier frequency. Because high-level modulation demands husky input signals, both the carrier and message are amplified before modulation. The modulated signal is then delivered directly to the antenna.

Balanced Modulators

DSB modulators differ from AM modulators only by the suppression of the carrier component; in theory, this requires nothing more or less than a *multiplier*. As the reader can verify, the system of Fig. 5.13b will generate DSB if the nonlinear element is a *perfect* square-law device such that $v_{\text{out}} = av_{\text{in}}^2$.

Unfortunately, perfect square-law devices are rare, so in practice DSB is obtained using *two* AM modulators arranged in a balanced configuration to cancel out the carrier. Figure 5.18 shows such a *balanced modulator* in block-diagram form. Assuming the AM modulators are identical, save for the reversed sign of one input, the outputs are $A_c[1 + \frac{1}{2}x(t)] \cos \omega_c t$ and $A_c[1 - \frac{1}{2}x(t)] \cos \omega_c t$. Subtracting one from the other yields $x_c(t) = x(t) A_c \cos \omega_c t$, as required. Hence, a balanced modulator is a multiplier. It should be noted that if the message has a *DC term*, that component is *not* canceled out in the modulator, even though it appears at the carrier frequency in the modulated wave.

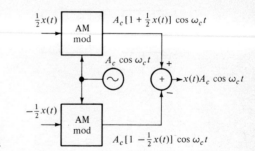

FIGURE 5.18
Balanced modulator.

A balanced modulator using switching is discussed in Chap. 8 under the heading of *chopper modulation*. Other circuit realizations can be found in the literature.

EXERCISE 5.4   Suppose the AM modulators in Fig. 5.18 are constructed with identical nonlinear elements having $v_{out} = a_1 v_{in} + a_2 v_{in}^2 + a_3 v_{in}^3$. Taking an arbitrary input $x(t)$, show that the AM signals have second-harmonic distortion but, nonetheless, the final output is undistorted DSB.

5.4   SUPPRESSED-SIDEBAND MODULATION: SSB AND VSB

Conventional AM is wasteful of both transmitted power and transmission bandwidth. Suppressing the carrier overcomes the former shortcoming; suppressing one sideband, in whole or part, reduces the latter and leads to single-sideband modulation (SSB) or vestigial-sideband modulation (VSB).

Single-Sideband Modulation (SSB)

The upper and lower sidebands of AM and DSB are uniquely related by symmetry about the carrier frequency; given the amplitude and phase of one, we can always construct the other. Hence, transmission bandwidth can be cut in half if one sideband is suppressed along with the carrier. Total elimination of carrier and one sideband from the AM spectrum in Fig. 5.8 produces SSB, for which it is obvious that

$$B_T = W \qquad S_T = P_{SB} = \tfrac{1}{4}\overline{x^2} A_c^2 \qquad (1)$$

SSB is readily visualized in the frequency domain: it is the output of a balanced modulator processed by a *sideband filter*, Fig. 5.19a. The filter is a bandpass circuit

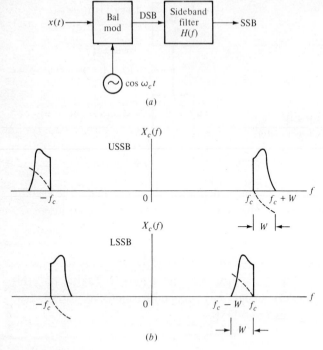

FIGURE 5.19
Single-sideband modulation. (*a*) Modulator; (*b*) spectra.

passing the upper sideband (USSB) or the lower si deband (LSSB), so the resulting spectra are as given in Fig. 5.19*b*.

On the other hand, a time-domain description of the waveform is somewhat more difficult, save for the case of *tone modulation*. With tone modulation $x_c(t)$ is simplicity itself: suppressing the carrier and one sideband line in Fig. 5.9 leaves only the other sideband line, i.e.,

$$x_c(t) = \tfrac{1}{2}A_m A_c \cos (\omega_c \pm \omega_m)t \qquad (2)$$

The frequency of the modulated wave is therefore offset from f_c by $\pm f_m$, while the amplitude is constant but proportional to the tone amplitude.

For arbitrary $x(t)$, an analysis given later shows that

$$x_c(t) \triangleq \tfrac{1}{2}A_c[x(t) \cos \omega_c t \mp \hat{x}(t) \sin \omega_c t] \qquad (3)$$

where the upper sign is taken for USSB and vice versa, and where $\hat{x}(t)$ is the *Hilbert transform* of $x(t)$. Physically, $\hat{x}(t)$ is simply $x(t)$ with its frequency components phase-shifted by $-90°$. Checking Eq. (3) with tone modulation, $\hat{x}(t) = A_m \cos (\omega_m t - 90°) = A_m \sin \omega_m t$, so $x_c(t) = \tfrac{1}{2}A_c(A_m \cos \omega_m t \cos \omega_c t \mp A_m \sin \omega_m t \sin \omega_c t)$, which reduces to Eq. (2).

Upon examination, Eq. (3) is seen to be a *quadrature-carrier* expression with $v_i(t) = A_c x(t)/2$ and $v_q(t) = \pm A_c \hat{x}(t)/2$. Therefore, unlike AM and DSB, the quadrature component of SSB is not zero. The SSB envelope is then

$$R_{SSB}(t) = \frac{A_c}{2} \sqrt{x^2(t) + \hat{x}^2(t)} \qquad (4)$$

while $\phi_{SSB}(t) = \pm \arctan[\hat{x}(t)/x(t)]$. The presence of the SSB quadrature component turns out to be essential for sideband suppression. To see this, note that Eq. (3) also may be interpreted as *two DSB waves* in phase quadrature, one modulated by $x(t)$ and the other by $\hat{x}(t)$. Since $x_c(t)$ is *single* sideband, the two DSB waves must be such that their sidebands cancel on one side of f_c and add on the other side. That observation leads to an alternate method of SSB generation to be described shortly. First, however, the implications of Eq. (4) will be illustrated.

Example 5.2 SSB with Square-Wave Modulation

Whenever the SSB modulating signal $x(t)$ has stepwise transitions, the quadrature term $\hat{x}(t)$ exhibits sharp peaks; hence, per Eq. (4) the envelope will also have sharp peaks, sometimes called *horns*. To demonstrate this effect in a simple fashion, let the modulating signal be approximated by

$$x(t) \approx \cos \omega_m t - \tfrac{1}{3} \cos 3\omega_m t + \tfrac{1}{5} \cos 5\omega_m t \qquad (5a)$$

which is the test signal used in Sect. 4.2, Fig. 4.4. We could then write $x_c(t)$ as a sum of three terms, each in the form of Eq. (2). But $\hat{x}(t)$ is easily found in this case by phase shifting $x(t)$, i.e.,

$$\hat{x}(t) \approx \sin \omega_m t - \tfrac{1}{3} \sin 3\omega_m t + \tfrac{1}{5} \sin 5\omega_m t \qquad (5b)$$

which approximates a *triangular* wave, as previously plotted in Fig. 4.7.

Inserting Eqs. (5a) and (5b) into Eq. (4) and carrying out some routine manipulations gives the result

$$R(t) = \frac{A_c}{2} \left[\left(1 + \frac{1}{9} + \frac{1}{25} \right) - \frac{4}{5} \cos 2\omega_m t + \frac{2}{5} \cos 4\omega_m t \right]^{1/2} \qquad (6)$$

which is sketched in Fig. 5.20 along with $x(t)$. The envelope horns are clearly visible and, had we taken an ideal square wave, those horns would have been infinite spikes. Clearly, this does not bode well for pulse transmission via SSB.   ////

EXERCISE 5.5 Draw the one-sided line spectrum and find P_{SB} and S_T for AM ($m = 1$), DSB, and USSB when $x(t) = \tfrac{1}{3} \cos \omega_m t + \tfrac{2}{3} \cos 4\omega_m t$.

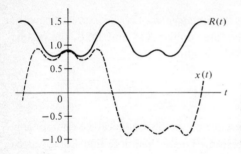

FIGURE 5.20
The envelope of an SSB waveform (with $A_c = 2$) when $x(t)$ approximates a square wave.

Hilbert Transforms and Analytic Signals ★

A complete analysis of SSB requires study of the Hilbert transform and the related concept of the analytic signal. These, in turn, are related to *quadrature phase shifting*, which will be our starting point.

Consider a network or filter that does nothing more than shift the phase of all positive frequency components by $-90°$ and all negative frequency components by $+90°$. Since a $\pm 90°$ phase shift is equivalent to multiplying by $e^{\pm j90°} = \pm j$, the transfer function is as drawn in Fig. 5.21 and can be written as

$$H_Q(f) = -j \operatorname{sgn} f \qquad (7)$$

where sgn f, read "signum f," is the *sign function*

$$\operatorname{sgn} \lambda \triangleq \begin{cases} 1 & \lambda > 0 \\ -1 & \lambda < 0 \end{cases} \qquad (8)$$

If $X(f)$ is the input spectrum to the network, the output spectrum is $-j \operatorname{sgn} f X(f)$.

But quadrature phase shift is not so easily interpreted in the time domain, and, for this purpose, we turn to the impulse response of the quadrature phase shifter. Taking the inverse transform of Eq. (8) requires either contour integration or a limiting operation. A simpler approach to the impulse response is through the use of transform theorems and a little ingenuity. Recall the differentiation theorem, $dv(t)/dt \leftrightarrow j2\pi f V(f)$. Its dual is $-j2\pi t v(t) \leftrightarrow dV(f)/df$, and so $v(t) = (j/2\pi t)\mathcal{F}^{-1}[dV(f)/df]$. With the aid

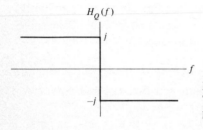

FIGURE 5.21
The transfer function of a quadrature phase shifter.

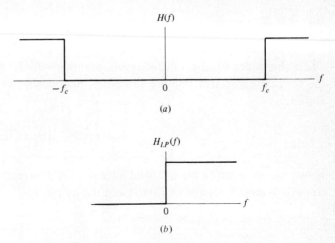

FIGURE 5.22
(a) Ideal USSB sideband filter; (b) lowpass equivalent filter.

of Fig. 5.21, $H_Q(f) = -j \,\text{sgn} f$ can be differentiated, yielding $dH_Q(f)/df = -j2\,\delta(f)$. Therefore the corresponding inpulse response is

$$h_Q(t) = \frac{j}{2\pi t}\,\mathscr{F}^{-1}[-j2\,\delta(f)] = \frac{1}{\pi t}$$

Generalizing and applying duality, we have derived the transform pairs

$$\frac{1}{\pi t} \leftrightarrow -j\,\text{sgn} f \qquad (9a)$$

$$\text{sgn}\, t \leftrightarrow \frac{-j}{\pi f} \qquad (9b)$$

We can now say that if $x(t)$ is the input to a quadrature phase shifter, the output time function is

$$\hat{x}(t) = [x(t)] * \left[\frac{1}{\pi t}\right] = \frac{1}{\pi}\int_{-\infty}^{\infty} \frac{x(\lambda)}{t - \lambda}\,d\lambda \qquad (10)$$

We shall define $\hat{x}(t)$ as the Hilbert transform of $x(t)$, though some authors use the negative of Eq. (10) corresponding to a $+90°$ phase shift. $\hat{x}(t)$ is also called the *harmonic conjugate* of $x(t)$. Note that Hilbert transformation is basically convolution and does not produce a change of *domain*; if x is a function of time, then $\hat{x}$ is also a function of time.

Applying these results to SSB generation per Fig. 5.19a, take the case of USSB so the sideband filter is a highpass filter, Fig. 5.22a. The equivalent lowpass filter, Fig. 5.22b, is found from Eq. (8), Sect. 5.1, as

$$H_{LP}(f) = u(f) = \frac{1}{2}(1 + \text{sgn}\, f) = \frac{1}{2} + \frac{j}{2}(-j\,\text{sgn}\, f) \qquad (11a)$$

where the rather strange third expression anticipates the next step, namely, finding the lowpass equivalent impulse response. Specifically, as follows from Eqs. (11a) and (9a),

$$h_{LP}(t) = \mathcal{F}^{-1}[H_{LP}(f)] = \frac{1}{2}\delta(t) + \frac{j}{2}\frac{1}{\pi t} \qquad (11b)$$

Now since the input to the sideband filter is a DSB wave, $A_c x(t) \cos \omega_c t$, the lowpass equivalent input is simply $(A_c/2)x(t)$ and the output is

$$y_{LP}(t) = [h_{LP}(t)] * \left[\frac{A_c}{2}x(t)\right]$$

$$= \frac{A_c}{4}[x(t) + j\hat{x}(t)] \qquad (12)$$

since $[\delta(t)] * [x(t)] = x(t)$ while $[1/\pi t] * [x(t)] = \hat{x}(t)$. Finally, the lowpass-to-bandpass transformation, Eq. (7a), Sect. 5.1, gives the USSB output

$$x_c(t) = 2 \,\text{Re}\,[y_{LP}(t)e^{j\omega_c t}] = \tfrac{1}{2}A_c[x(t)\cos \omega_c t - \hat{x}(t)\sin \omega_c t]$$

By similar analysis, the LSSB case differs only in the sign of the second term.

Somewhat parenthetically, we mention that Eq. (12) is proportional to the *analytic signal*, defined by

$$x_{an}(t) \triangleq \tfrac{1}{2}[x(t) + j\hat{x}(t)] \qquad (13a)$$

Thus, assuming $x(t)$ is real, the real and imaginary parts of $x_{an}(t)$ are a Hilbert transform pair. Interesting though that may be, the real significance lies in the spectrum for, as the reader can prove,

$$X_{an}(f) = \begin{cases} X(f) & f > 0 \\ 0 & f < 0 \end{cases} \qquad (13b)$$

so $X_{an}(f)$ is just the positive-frequency portion of $X(f)$. Moreover, the Fourier transform of $x_{an}^*(t)$ is the negative-frequency portion of $X(f)$. The SSB spectrum consists of these two portions translated in frequency.

EXERCISE 5.6   Confirm the sideband cancellation and addition implied in Eq. (3) by taking its Fourier transform and using the fact that $\mathcal{F}[\hat{x}(t)] = -j\,\text{sgn}\, f X(f)$.

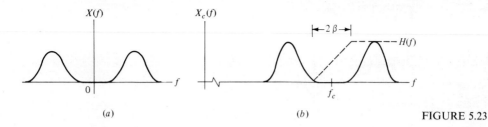

FIGURE 5.23

SSB Modulators

The inherent efficiencies of SSB make it quite attractive, particularly when *bandwidth conservation* is an important factor. However, certain instrumentation problems in SSB are distinct drawbacks, one being the sideband filter included in Fig. 5.19a.

The required sharp cutoff characteristic for $H(f)$ cannot be synthesized exactly, so one must either attenuate a portion of the desired sideband or pass a portion of the undesired sideband. (Doing both is tantamount to vestigial-sideband modulation.) Fortunately, many modulating signals of practical interest have little or no low-frequency content, their spectra having "holes" at zero frequency, Fig. 5.23a. Such spectra are typical of audio signals (voice and music), for example. After translation by the balanced modulator, the zero-frequency hole appears as a vacant space centered about the carrier frequency into which the *transition region* of a practical sideband filter can be fitted, Fig. 5.23b.

As a rule of thumb, the width 2β of the transition region cannot be much smaller than 1 percent of the nominal cutoff frequency, that is, $f_{co} < 200\beta$. Since 2β is constrained by the width of the spectral hole and f_{co} should equal f_c, it may not be possible to obtain a sufficiently high carrier frequency with a given message spectrum. For these cases the modulation process can be carried out in two or more steps to overcome the limitation (see Prob. 5.18).

An alternate means of SSB generation is suggested by Eq. (3) and its interpretation as two DSB waves having quadrature carriers modulated by $x(t)$ and $\hat{x}(t)$. Starting with $x(t)$ and the carrier $\cos \omega_c t$, two balanced modulators and a pair of phase shifters arranged as in Fig. 5.24 will produce USSB or LSSB, depending on whether we add or subtract the outputs. This technique, known as the *phase-shift method*, bypasses the need for sideband filters. However, design of the phase-shift circuitry is not trivial, and imperfections generally result in distortion of the low-frequency components. Thus, the system works best with message spectra of the type previously discussed. (Another phase-shift system is described in Prob. 5.19.)

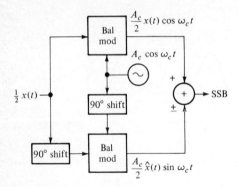

FIGURE 5.24
Phase-shift SSB modulator.

Vestigial-Sideband Modulation (VSB)

Consider a modulating signal of very large bandwidth having significant low-frequency content. Principal examples are television video, facsimile, and high-speed data signals. Bandwidth conservation argues for the use of SSB, but practical SSB systems have poor low-frequency response. On the other hand, DSB works quite well for low message frequencies but the transmission bandwidth is twice that of SSB. Clearly, a compromise modulation scheme is desired; that compromise is VSB.

VSB is derived by filtering DSB (or AM) in such a fashion that one sideband is passed almost completely while just a trace, or *vestige*, of the other sideband is included. The key to VSB is the sideband filter, a typical transfer function being that of Fig. 5.25a. While the exact shape of the response is not crucial, it must have odd symmetry about the carrier frequency and a relative response of ½ at that point. Therefore, taking the upper sideband case,

$$H(f) = u(f - f_c) - H_\beta(f - f_c) + u(-f + f_c) - H_\beta(-f + f_c) \qquad (14a)$$

where

$$H_\beta(-f) = -H_\beta(f) \qquad \text{and} \qquad H_\beta(f) = 0 \qquad |f| > \beta \qquad (14b)$$

as shown in Fig. 5.25b.

The VSB sideband filter is thus a *practical* sideband filter with transition width 2β, and a VSB modulator† takes the form of Fig. 5.19a. (If carrier suppression is not wanted, the balanced modulator is replaced by an AM modulator.) Because the width of the partial sideband is one-half the filter transition width, the transmission bandwidth is

$$B_T = W + \beta \approx W \qquad (15)$$

VSB and SSB spectra are quite similar, particularly when $\beta \ll W$, which is often true. The similarities exist in the time domain as well, and one can write $x_c(t)$ in a

---

† In practice, the required filter symmetry is achieved primarily at the receiver.

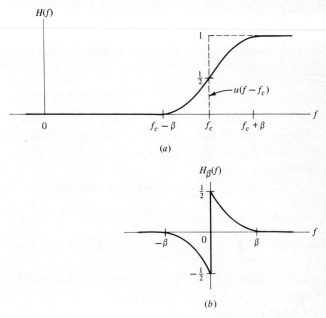

FIGURE 5.25
VSB filter characteristics.

form paralleling Eq. (3), namely,

$$x_c(t) = \tfrac{1}{2}A_c\{x(t)\cos\omega_c t - [\hat{x}(t) + x_\beta(t)]\sin\omega_c t\} \tag{16}$$

where the quadrature component consists of $\hat{x}(t)$ plus

$$x_\beta(t) \triangleq j2\int_{-\beta}^{\beta} H_\beta(f)X(f)e^{j\omega t}\,df$$

If $\beta \ll W$, VSB approximates SSB and $x_\beta(t) \approx 0$; conversely, for large β, VSB approximates DSB and $\hat{x}(t) + x_\beta(t) \approx 0$. The transmitted power S_T is not easy to determine exactly, but is bounded by

$$\tfrac{1}{4}\overline{x^2}A_c{}^2 \le S_T \le \tfrac{1}{2}\overline{x^2}A_c{}^2 \tag{17}$$

depending on the vestige width β.

Compatible Single Sideband ★

On occasion it is desired to combine the envelope modulation of AM with the bandwidth conservation of suppressed sideband. The purpose is to allow envelope detection without the price of excessive transmission bandwidth; hence the name *compatible single sideband*.

Although perfect envelope modulation requires symmetric sidebands, it can be approximated by suppressed-sideband modulation with unsuppressed or reinserted carrier. Adding a carrier term and modulation index to Eq. (16), the resultant modulated wave is

$$x_c(t) = A_c\{[1 + mx(t)] \cos \omega_c t - m\zeta(t) \sin \omega_c t\} \tag{18}$$

where $\zeta(t) = \hat{x}(t) + x_\beta(t)$ is the quadrature term that cancels out one sideband in whole or part. If $\zeta(t) = 0$, Eq. (18) reduces to conventional *amplitude modulation*; if $\zeta(t) = \mp \hat{x}(t)$, we have SSB plus carrier (SSB + C); for VSB + C, $\zeta(t)$ takes on an intermediate value.

The envelope of $x_c(t)$ is found in the usual fashion to be

$$R(t) = A_c\{[1 + mx(t)]^2 + [m\zeta(t)]^2\}^{1/2}$$

$$= A_c[1 + mx(t)] \left\{ 1 + \left[\frac{m\zeta(t)}{1 + mx(t)} \right]^2 \right\}^{1/2} \tag{19}$$

which is a distorted AM envelope. However, for $|m\zeta(t)| \ll 1$, the envelope is approximately

$$R(t) \approx A_c[1 + mx(t)]$$

as desired. The key to compatible single sideband is therefore keeping the quadrature component small.

If one sideband is *totally* suppressed, i.e., SSB + C, $\zeta(t)$ itself cannot be ignored; effective envelope modulation then requires $m \ll 1$. Under this condition a substantial amount of power is wasted in the carrier, far more than that of AM. Consequently, there is active interest in other schemes for generating compatible single sideband.†

Alternately, if a *vestigial* sideband can be tolerated and its width is not too small, $|\zeta(t)|$ is small compared to $|x(t)|$ most of the time. One can then use a larger modulation index without excessive envelope distortion and thereby reduce the relative carrier power. In fact, it is readily shown from Eq. (18) that

$$S_T = [1 + m^2(\overline{x^2} + \overline{\zeta^2})](A_c^2/2) \approx (1 + m^2\overline{x^2})P_c \tag{20}$$

essentially the same as AM.

The necessary width of the vestigial sideband must be determined by empirical studies of the envelope with typical program material. In the case of television video signals, which are in fact transmitted as VSB + C, the distortion can be quite sizable without detracting from picture quality, permitting a transmission bandwidth only 30 percent greater than the message bandwidth. See Appendix C for more information about TV systems.

† Schwartz, Bennett, and Stein (1966, chap. 4) gives a summary and references.

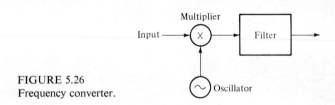

FIGURE 5.26
Frequency converter.

5.5 FREQUENCY CONVERSION, DETECTION, AND RECEIVERS

Linear modulation is primarily direct frequency translation of the message spectrum. *Demodulation*, or *detection*, is the process by which the message is recovered from the modulated wave at the receiver. Therefore, for linear modulation in general, the detection process is basically one of *downward frequency translation*.

Referring to Figs. 5.8 and 5.19*b*, for instance, it is seen that if the spectra are shifted down in frequency by f_c units (up by f_c for the negative-frequency components), the original message spectrum is reproduced, plus a possible DC component corresponding to the translated carrier. The reader is urged to try this translation graphically for himself. It is particularly instructive in the case of LSSB.

Frequency translation, or *conversion*, is also used to shift a modulated signal to a new carrier frequency (up or down) for amplification or other processing. Thus, translation is a fundamental operation of linear modulation systems and includes modulation and detection as special cases. Before examining detectors, we should look briefly at the general process of frequency conversion.

Frequency Conversion

Conversion is accomplished, at least analytically, by multiplication by a sinusoid. Consider, for example, the DSB wave $x(t) \cos \omega_1 t$. Multiplying by $\cos \omega_2 t$, we get

$$x(t) \cos \omega_1 t \cos \omega_2 t = \tfrac{1}{2}x(t) \cos (\omega_1 + \omega_2)t + \tfrac{1}{2}x(t) \cos (\omega_1 - \omega_2)t \qquad (1)$$

The product consists of the *sum* and *difference frequencies*, $f_1 + f_2$ and $|f_1 - f_2|$, each modulated by $x(t)$. [We can write $|f_1 - f_2|$ for clarity, since $\cos(\omega_2 - \omega_1)t = \cos(\omega_1 - \omega_2)t$.] Assuming $f_2 \neq f_1$, multiplication has translated the signal spectra to *two* new carrier frequencies. With appropriate filtering, the signal is up-converted or down-converted. Devices that carry out this operation are called *frequency converters* or *mixers*. The operation itself is termed *heterodyning* or *mixing*.

A generalized frequency converter is diagramed in Fig. 5.26. Its analysis follows directly from the modulation theorem. The multiplier is usually constructed using nonlinear or switching devices, similar to modulators. Other converter applications

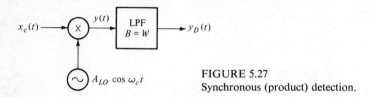

FIGURE 5.27
Synchronous (product) detection.

include beat-frequency oscillators, regenerative frequency dividers, speech scramblers, and spectrum analyzers.

EXERCISE 5.7 Sketch the spectrum of Eq. (1) for $f_2 < f_1$, $f_2 = f_1$, and $f_2 > f_1$, taking $X(f)$ as in Fig. 5.6.

Synchronous Detection

All types of linear modulation can be detected by the *product* demodulator of Fig. 5.27. The incoming signal is first multiplied with a locally generated sinusoid and then lowpass-filtered, the filter bandwidth being the same as the message bandwidth W or somewhat larger. It is assumed that the local oscillator (LO) is *exactly synchronized* with the carrier, in both phase and frequency, accounting for the name *synchronous detection.*†

For purposes of analysis, let us write the input signal in the generalized form

$$x_c(t) = [K_c + K_m x(t)] \cos \omega_c t - K_m \zeta(t) \sin \omega_c t \tag{2}$$

which can represent any type of linear modulation with proper identification of K_c, K_m, and $\zeta(t)$—for example, $K_c = 0$ for suppressed carrier, $\zeta(t) = 0$ for double sideband, etc. The filter input is thus the product

$$x_c(t) A_{\mathrm{LO}} \cos \omega_c t = \frac{A_{\mathrm{LO}}}{2} \{[K_c + K_m x(t)] + [K_c + K_m x(t)] \cos 2\omega_c t - K_m \zeta(t) \sin 2\omega_c t\}$$

Since $f_c > W$, the double-frequency terms are rejected by the lowpass filter, leaving only the leading term

$$y_D(t) = K_D[K_c + K_m x(t)] \tag{3}$$

where K_D is the detection constant. The DC component $K_D K_c$ corresponds to the translated carrier if it is not suppressed in the modulated wave. This can be removed

† Also called *coherent detection* because the carrier wave and LO output must be coherent.

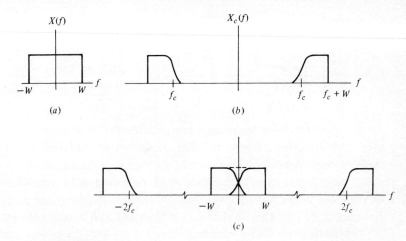

FIGURE 5.28
VSB spectra. (*a*) Message; (*b*) modulated signal; (*c*) frequency-translated signal
before lowpass filtering.

from the output by a blocking capacitor or transformer; however, any DC term in $x(t)$ will be removed as well. With this minor qualification we can say that the message has been fully recovered from $x_c(t)$.

Although perfectly correct, the above manipulations fail to bring out what goes on in the demodulation of VSB. This is best seen in the frequency domain with the message spectrum taken to be constant over W, Fig. 5.28*a*, so the modulated spectrum takes the form of Fig. 5.28*b*. The downward-translated spectrum at the filter input will then be as shown in Fig. 5.28*c*. Again, high-frequency terms are eliminated by filtering, while the down-converted sidebands overlap around zero frequency. Recalling the symmetry property of the vestigial filter, we find that the portion removed from the upper sideband is exactly restored by the corresponding vestige of the lower sideband, so $X(f)$ has been reconstructed at the output and the detected signal is proportional to $x(t)$.

Theoretically, product demodulation borders on the trivial; in practice, it can be rather tricky. The crux of the problem is *synchronization*—synchronizing an oscillator to a sinusoid that is not even present in the incoming signal if carrier is suppressed. To facilitate the matter, suppressed-carrier systems may have a small amount of carrier reinserted in $x_c(t)$ at the transmitter. This *pilot carrier* is picked off at the receiver by a narrow bandpass filter, amplified, and used in place of an LO. The system, shown in Fig. 5.29, is called *homodyne detection*. (Actually, the amplified pilot more often serves to synchronize a separate oscillator rather than being used directly.)

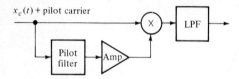

$x_c(t)$ + pilot carrier

Pilot filter — Amp

X — LPF

FIGURE 5.29
Homodyne detection.

A variety of other techniques are possible for synchronization, including the use of highly stable, crystal-controlled oscillators at transmitter and receiver, the oscillators being synchronized periodically rather than on a continuous basis. Nonetheless, some degree of asynchronism must be expected in synchronous detectors. It is therefore important to investigate the effects of phase and frequency drift in various applications. This we shall do for DSB and SSB in terms of tone modulation.

Let the local oscillator wave be $\cos(\omega_c t + \omega' t + \phi')$, where ω' and ϕ' represent slowly drifting frequency and phase errors compared to the carrier. For double sideband with tone modulation, the detected signal becomes

$$y_D(t) = K_D \cos \omega_m t \cos(\omega' t + \phi') \tag{4}$$

$$= \begin{cases} \dfrac{K_D}{2} [\cos(\omega_m + \omega')t + \cos(\omega_m - \omega')t] & \phi' = 0 \\[2mm] K_D \cos \omega_m t \cos \phi' & \omega' = 0 \end{cases}$$

Similarly, for single sideband, where $x_c(t) = \cos(\omega_c \pm \omega_m)t$,

$$y_D(t) = K_D \cos[\omega_m t \pm (\omega' t + \phi')] \tag{5}$$

$$= \begin{cases} K_D \cos(\omega_m \pm \omega')t & \phi' = 0 \\ K_D \cos(\omega_m t \pm \phi') & \omega' = 0 \end{cases}$$

Clearly, in both DSB and SSB, a frequency drift that is not small compared to W will substantially alter the detected tone. The effect is more severe in DSB since a *pair* of tones, $f_m + f'$ and $f_m - f'$, is produced. If $f' \ll f_m$, this sounds like warbling or the beat note heard when two musical instruments, slightly out of tune, play in unison. While only one tone is produced with SSB, this too can be disturbing, particularly for music transmission. To illustrate, the major triad chord consists of three notes whose frequencies are related as the integers 4, 5, and 6. Frequency error in detection shifts each note by the same absolute amount, destroying the harmonic relationship and giving the music an oriental flavor. (Note that the effect is *not* like playing recorded music at the wrong speed, which preserves the frequency ratios.) For voice transmission, subjective listener tests have shown that frequency drifts of less than ± 10 Hz are tolerable, otherwise, everyone sounds rather like Donald Duck.

As to phase drift, again DSB is more sensitive, for if $\phi' = \pm 90°$ (LO and carrier in quadrature), the detected signal vanishes entirely. With slowly varying ϕ',

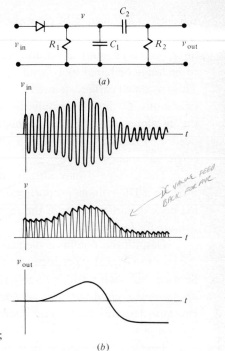

FIGURE 5.30
Envelope detection. (*a*) Circuit;
(*b*) waveforms.

we get an apparent *fading* effect. Phase drift in SSB appears as *delay distortion*, the extreme case being $\phi' = \pm 90°$, for which the demodulated signal is $\hat{x}(t)$. However, as was remarked before, the human ear can tolerate sizable delay distortion, so phase drift is not so serious in voice-signal SSB systems.

To summarize, phase and frequency synchronization requirements are rather modest for voice transmission via SSB. But in data, facsimile, and video systems with suppressed carrier, careful synchronization is a necessity. It is primarily for this reason that carrier is not suppressed in television transmission.

Envelope Detection

Very little was said above about synchronous demodulation of AM for the simple reason that it is almost never used. True, synchronous detectors work for AM, but so does an *envelope detector*, which is much simpler. Because the envelope of an AM wave has the same shape as the message, independent of carrier frequency and phase, demodulation can be accomplished by extracting the envelope with no worries about synchronization.

A simplified envelope detector and its waveforms are shown in Fig. 5.30, where the diode is assumed to be piecewise-linear. In absence of further circuitry, the voltage v would be just the half-rectified version of the input v_{in}. But $R_1 C_1$ acts as a lowpass filter, responding only to variations in the peaks of v_{in}. This assumes the time constant to be long compared to $1/f_c$ but short compared to the message variation time $1/W$. Thus, as noted earlier, we need $f_c \gg W$ so the envelope is clearly defined. Under these conditions, C_1 discharges only slightly between carrier peaks, and v is approximately the envelope of v_{in}. More sophisticated filtering produces further improvement if needed. Finally, $R_2 C_2$ acts as a DC block to remove the bias of the unmodulated carrier component.

The voltage v may also be filtered to remove the envelope variations and produce a DC voltage proportional to the carrier amplitude. This voltage in turn is fed back to earlier stages of the receiver for *automatic volume control* (AVC) to compensate for fading.

Despite the nonlinear element, Fig. 5.30 is termed a *linear envelope detector*; the output is linearly proportional to the input envelope. Power-law diodes can also be used, but then v will include terms of the form v_{in}^2, v_{in}^3, etc., and there may be appreciable second-harmonic distortion unless $m \ll 1$. In fact, the design of linear envelope detectors has several interesting problems not immediately apparent in our discussion.†

Envelope detection is appropriate whenever the wave in question has suitable envelope modulation, e.g., television video transmitted via VSB plus carrier. Furthermore, some suppressed-carrier systems use envelope detectors rather than product demodulators, a large carrier term being inserted ahead of the detector to *reconstruct* the envelope. (This works for SSB as well as for DSB if the local carrier is large enough.) But the procedure does not bypass the need for synchronism, since envelope reconstruction requires the added carrier to be well synchronized.

One final point. The DC blocking capacitor in Fig. 5.30 causes the detector to have poor response to low-frequency message components. Therefore envelope detection may prove unsatisfactory for signals with important DC and slowly varying terms unless additional steps are taken.

EXERCISE 5.8 Figure 5.31 is an *envelope reconstruction* system for the demodulation of suppressed-carrier modulation; note that the LO ouput is *added* to $x_c(t)$ so a multiplier is not required. Taking $x_c(t) = A_c[x(t) \cos \omega_c t - \zeta(t) \sin \omega_c t]$ to represent DSB, SSB, or VSB, and taking the LO signal as $A_{LO} \cos [\omega_c t + \theta(t)]$ where $\theta(t) = \omega' t + \phi'$ accounts for possible asynchronism, show that the envelope at the input to the envelope detector is

$$R(t) = A_{LO} \left\{ 1 + \frac{2A_c}{A_{LO}} [x(t) \cos \theta(t) + \zeta(t) \sin \theta(t)] + \left(\frac{A_c}{A_{LO}}\right)^2 [x^2(t) + \zeta^2(t)] \right\}^{1/2} \tag{6}$$

† See, for instance, Clarke and Hess (1971, chap. 10).

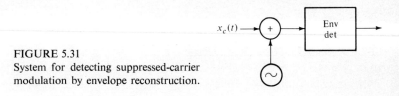

FIGURE 5.31
System for detecting suppressed-carrier
modulation by envelope reconstruction.

Then show that $x(t)$ can be recovered without quadrature distortion providing
$A_{LO} \gg A_c$ and $\theta(t) \approx 0$.

Receivers

All that is really required of a receiver is some tuning mechanism, a demodulator,
and amplifiers. With sufficiently strong transmitted signal, even the amplifiers may
be omitted — witness the historic crystal set. Most radio receivers, however, are the
more sophisticated *superheterodyne* type, whose block diagram is given in Fig. 5.32
complete with AVC.

There are three types of amplifiers in a superheterodyne: the *radio-frequency*
(RF) amplifier, which is tuned to the desired carrier frequency; the *intermediate-frequency* (IF) amplifier, which is fixed-tuned and provides most of the gain and
selectivity; and the *audio-frequency* (AF) amplifier, which follows the detector and
brings the power level up to that required for the loudspeaker. The mixer is a frequency
converter that translates the RF output to the IF band by converting f_c to f_{IF}. The
LO provides the mixing frequency and is adjusted in parallel with the RF stage.

The operations in a superheterodyne are best understood by considering the
relative amplitude of the IF output as a function of input frequency at various points
in the receiver. If a constant-amplitude variable-frequency sinusoid is applied to the

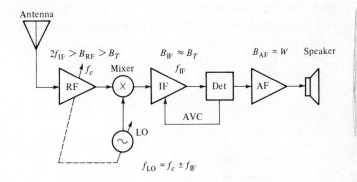

FIGURE 5.32
Superheterodyne receiver.

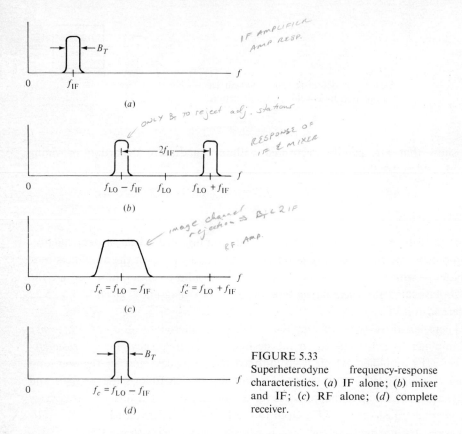

FIGURE 5.33
Superheterodyne   frequency-response characteristics. (a) IF alone; (b) mixer and IF; (c) RF alone; (d) complete receiver.

IF input, the response is just the amplitude ratio of the IF amplifier itself, Fig. 5.33a. Since the IF must pass the modulated signal at the translated carrier frequency, its bandwidth equals or exceeds B_T. Considering the mixer plus LO alone, there are *two* input frequencies that will result in f_{IF} at the output, namely, $|f_{LO} \pm f_{IF}|$. Thus, the response of the IF and mixer is as shown in Fig. 5.33b for the usual case where $f_{IF} < f_{LO}$. Note that if we are trying to receive a station at $f_c = f_{LO} - f_{IF}$, we will also pick up $f'_c = f_{LO} + f_{IF}$, which is called the *image frequency*. For a given LO setting, the carrier and image frequencies are related by

$$|f_c - f'_c| = 2f_{IF} \qquad f_{IF} < f_{LO} \qquad (7a)$$

or

$$|f_c - f'_c| = 2f_{LO} \qquad f_{IF} > f_{LO} \qquad (7b)$$

The latter case is quite rare in practice.

The purpose of the RF stage, whose response is shown in Fig. 5.33c, is to reject the image frequency before it gets to the mixer. It can be seen that the RF amplifier need have a bandwidth no narrower than about $2f_{\rm IF}$. On the other hand, the IF bandwidth should be no larger than B_T, for it is up to the IF stage to reject carriers in the immediate vicinity of the desired signal; i.e., the IF provides *adjacent-channel selectivity* while the RF provides *image-channel rejection*. In conventional operation, the RF center frequency is tuned to the desired carrier while the LO is simultaneously adjusted to $f_{\rm LO} = f_c + f_{\rm IF}$ so the correct difference frequency $f_c - f_{\rm LO} = f_{\rm IF}$ is obtained at the mixer output. Figure 5.33d shows the overall receiver response obtained by multiplying Figs. 5.33b and c.

So far we have considered only an ideal superhet. Actual receivers will exhibit *spurious responses* at various other frequencies due to feed-through and nonlinearities. For example, when a strong signal of frequency near $\frac{1}{2}f_{\rm IF}$ gets to the IF input, its second harmonic may be produced if the first stage of the IF amplifier is nonlinear. This second harmonic, being approximately $f_{\rm IF}$, will then be amplified by later stages and appear at the detector output as interference, usually a high-frequency audio tone, or whistle.

Other types of receivers used for various purposes include: the *heterodyne* receiver, in which the RF stage is omitted, and hence images are a potential problem; the *tuned-RF* (TRF) receiver, in which detection immediately follows the RF stage; and the *double-conversion* receiver, commonly employed for high-quality shortwave AM and single-sideband systems. As the name implies, double-conversion receivers have two mixers and two IF amplifiers. The first IF is fixed-tuned above or just below the desired carrier-frequency band. The large value of $f_{\rm IF_1}$ maximizes the spacing $2f_{\rm IF_1}$ between a carrier and its image, improving the image rejection of the RF stage. The second IF has a relatively low center frequency to permit much sharper discrimination against adjacent channels than is otherwise possible.

Example 5.3 AM Superheterodyne Receiver

The carrier-frequency allocations in commercial AM range from 540 to 1,600 kHz with 10-kHz spacing, and the message bandwidth is about 5 kHz. Most AM radios are superhets with $f_{\rm IF} = 455$ kHz and $f_{\rm LO} = f_c + f_{\rm IF}$. Using these values, the receiver bandwidths are

$$10 \text{ kHz} < B_{\rm RF} < 910 \text{ kHz} \qquad B_{\rm IF} \approx 10 \text{ kHz} \qquad B_{\rm AF} \approx 5 \text{ kHz}$$

The RF tuning range is, of course, 540 to 1,600 kHz, while the LO must tune over 955 to 2,055 kHz. The tuning ratio of the LO is therefore roughly $2:1$. On the other hand, if $f_{\rm LO}$ is taken as $f_c - f_{\rm IF}$, then the tuning range would be 85 to 1,145 kHz; this corresponds to a ratio of $13:1$ and would be much harder to implement with variable capacitors, etc.

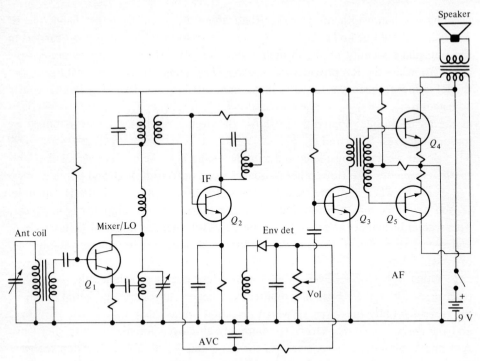

FIGURE 5.34
Schematic diagram of an AM superheterodyne radio.

Figure 5.34 is the schematic diagram of a typical inexpensive battery-powered AM radio. Transistor Q_1 serves as both local oscillator and mixer; the tuned circuit connected to its emitter is magnetically coupled to the coil in the collector circuit, causing oscillation at a frequency determined by the adjustable capacitor which, in turn, is mechanically linked to the tuning capacitor in the antenna coil so that f_c and f_{LO} track together. There is no RF amplification, but the antenna-coil circuit provides image rejection and delivers the desired carrier frequency to the base of Q_1. Nonlinearity then produces the frequencies $f_c + f_{LO}$ and $f_c - f_{LO}$ in the collector current, and $f_{IF} = f_c - f_{LO}$ is selected by the tuned collector circuit and coupled to the IF amplifier Q_2. The IF output drives the diode D, via magnetic coupling, and the envelope signal is applied to the first stage of the audio amplifier Q_3 through the volume control. Additionally, the average envelope voltage is fed back to Q_2 to modify its base bias for automatic volume control. Transistors Q_4 and Q_5 constitute a class B audio amplifier that drives the loudspeaker. ////

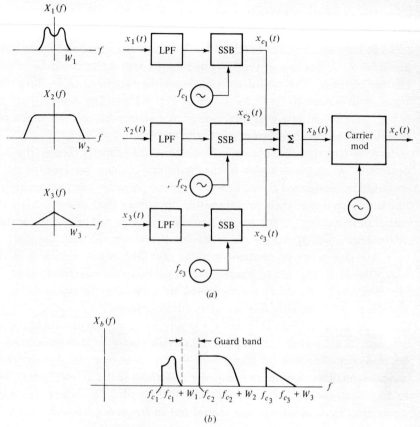

(a)

(b)

FIGURE 5.35
Typical FDM transmitter. (a) Block diagram; (b) baseband spectrum.

EXERCISE 5.9 A superheterodyne receiver is desired to cover $f_c = 1$ to 3 MHz with $f_c' \geq 5$ MHz and $f_{IF} < f_{LO}$. Find appropriate values for f_{IF} and f_{LO}. *Ans.:* 2 MHz, 3 to 5 MHz.

5.6 FREQUENCY-DIVISION MULTIPLEXING

It is often desirable to transmit several messages on one transmission facility, a process called *multiplexing*. Applications of multiplexing range from the vital, if prosaic, telephone network to the glamour of FM stereo and space-probe telemetry systems. There are two basic multiplexing techniques: *frequency-division multiplexing* (FDM) treated here, and *time-division multiplexing* (TDM) discussed in Chap. 8.

The principle of FDM is illustrated by Fig. 5.35a, where several input messages (three are shown) individually modulate the *subcarriers* f_{c_1}, f_{c_2}, etc., after passing through LPFs to limit the message bandwidths. We show the subcarrier modulation as SSB, and it often is; but any of the CW modulation techniques could be employed, or a mixture of them. The modulated signals are then summed to produce the *baseband signal*, with spectrum $X_b(f)$, as shown in Fig. 5.35b. (The designation "baseband" is used here to indicate that final carrier modulation has not yet taken place.) The baseband time function $x_b(t)$ is left to the reader's imagination.

Assuming that the subcarrier frequencies are properly chosen, the multiplexing operation has assigned a slot in the frequency domain for each of the individual messages in modulated form, hence the name *frequency-division* multiplexing. The baseband signal may then be transmitted directly or used to modulate a transmitted carrier of frequency f_c. We are not particularly concerned here with the nature of the final carrier modulation, since it is baseband spectrum that tells the story.

Message recovery or demodulation of FDM is accomplished in three steps, Fig. 5.36. First, the carrier demodulator reproduces the baseband signal $x_b(t)$. Then the modulated subcarriers are separated by a bank of bandpass filters in parallel, following which the messages are individually detected.

The major practical problem of FDM is *cross talk*, the unwanted coupling of one message into another. Intelligible cross talk (cross modulation) arises primarily because of nonlinearities in the system, which cause one message signal to partially modulate another subcarrier.† Equally disturbing is the unintelligible cross talk due to imperfect spectral separation by the filter bank. To reduce this coupling, the modulated message spectra are spaced out in frequency by *guard bands* into which

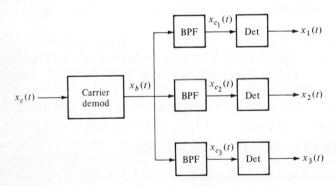

FIGURE 5.36
Typical FDM receiver.

† Thus, negative feedback to reduce amplifier nonlinearity is usually a necessity in FDM systems.

Table 5.2   BELL SYSTEM FDM HIERARCHY

Designation	Frequency range	Bandwidth	Number of voice channels
Group	60–108 kHz	48 kHz	12
Supergroup	312–552 kHz	240 kHz	60
Mastergroup	564–3,084 kHz	2.52 MHz	600
Jumbogroup	0.5–17.5 MHz	17 MHz	3,600

the filter transition regions can be fitted. For example, the guard band between $X_{c_1}(f)$ and $X_{c_2}(f)$ in Fig. 5.35b is of width $f_{c_2} - (f_{c_1} + W_1)$. The net *baseband bandwidth* is therefore the sum of the modulated message bandwidths plus the guard bands.

While the concept of FDM is quite simple, typical systems may be very elaborate. A case in point is the Bell Telephone type L4 carrier system, in which 3,600 voice channels (each with $W = 4$ kHz nominally) are multiplexed together for transmission via coaxial cable. All modulation is single sideband, both USSB and LSSB, and the final baseband spectrum runs from 0.5 to 17.5 MHz, including pilot carrier and guard bands. All subcarriers are multiples of 4 kHz derived from a common oscillator, and the 512-kHz pilot provides synchronization. To avoid excessive guard-band width at the upper end of the baseband spectrum, the multiplexing is done by *groups* in four stages, an arrangement which also facilitates switching and routing of the various channels. (The reader who perchance is not fully convinced of the power of frequency-domain analysis should consider the design of such a system without the aid of spectral concepts.) For reference purposes, Table 5.2 lists the Bell System FDM hierarchy.†

Example 5.4   FM Stereo Multiplexing

To conclude this chapter, we briefly describe the FDM system used in commercial FM stereophonic broadcasting. Referring to Fig. 5.37a, the left-speaker and right-speaker signals are first *matrixed* to produce $x_L(t) + x_R(t)$ and $x_L(t) - x_R(t)$. (The sum signal is heard with a monophonic receiver; matrixing is required so the monaural listener will not be subjected to sound gaps in program material having stereophonic Ping-Pong effects.) The $x_L(t) + x_R(t)$ signal is then inserted directly into the baseband, while $x_L(t) - x_R(t)$ DSB modulates a 38-kHz subcarrier derived from a 19-kHz supply. Double-sideband modulation is employed to preserve fidelity at low frequencies. The 19-kHz pilot tone is added for receiver synchronization, resulting in the baseband spectrum of Fig. 5.37b. Figure 5.38 block-diagrams the receiver and shows how the pilot tone is used for synchronous demodulation.

† Bell Telephone Laboratories (1971, chap. 6).

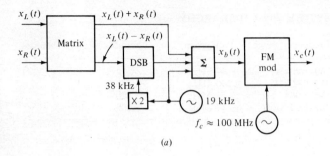

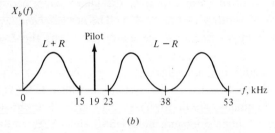

(a)

(b)

FIGURE 5.37
FM stereo multiplexing. (a) Transmitter; (b) baseband spectrum.

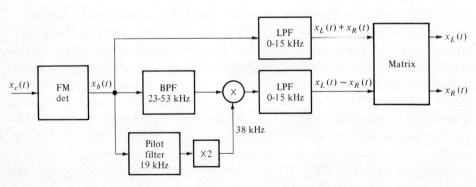

FIGURE 5.38
FM stereo multiplex receiver.

Incidentally, discrete four-channel (quadraphonic) disk recording uses a logical extension of the above strategy to multiplex four independent signals on the two channels of a stereophonic record. Denoting the four signals as L_F, L_R, R_F, and R_R (for left-front, left-rear, etc.), $L_F + L_R$ is recorded directly on one channel along with $L_F - L_R$ multiplexed via frequency modulation of a 30-kHz subcarrier. $R_F + R_R$ and $R_F - R_R$ are likewise multiplexed on the other channel. Because the resulting base-band spectrum goes up to 45 kHz, discrete quadraphonic signals cannot be transmitted in full on stereo FM. Other quadraphonic systems† have only two independent channels and are compatible with FM stereo.

We will have more to say about FM stereophonic broadcasting after examining the properties of the carrier modulation, which is *exponential*. ////

5.7 PROBLEMS

5.1 (Sect. 5.1) Using a phasor diagram, find expressions for $v_i(t)$, $v_q(t)$, $R(t)$, and $\phi(t)$ when $v(t) = v_1(t) \cos [\omega_c t + \theta_1(t)] + v_2(t) \cos [\omega_c t + \theta_2(t)]$. *Ans.*: $v_i(t) = v_1(t) \cos \theta_1(t) + v_2(t) \cos \theta_2(t)$, $v_q(t) = v_1(t) \sin \theta_1(t) + v_2(t) \sin \theta_2(t)$.

5.2 (Sect. 5.1) Repeat Prob. 5.1 for $v(t) = \cos \omega_c t + \alpha \cos (\omega_c + \omega_0)t$. Approximate $R(t)$ and $\phi(t)$ for the case where $\alpha^2 \ll 1$.

5.3 (Sect. 5.1) When $z(t)$ is a lowpass signal bandlimited in $W < f_0$, use Eq. (13), Sect. 2.3, to prove that $\int_{-\infty}^{\infty} z(t) \cos (\omega_0 t + \theta) \, dt = 0$.

5.4 (Sect. 5.1) If $v_i(t)$ and $v_q(t)$ are energy signals bandlimited in $W < f_c$, show from Eq. (3) that $E_v = (E_{v_i} + E_{v_q})/2$. (*Hint*: See Prob. 5.3.)

5.5★ (Sect. 5.1) Given $V(f)$ in Fig. P5.1, find $v_{LP}(t)$ and the quadrature-carrier expression for $v(t)$.

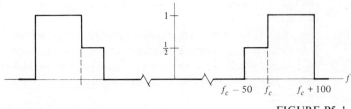

FIGURE P5 1.

5.6★ (Sect. 5.1) When $Q \gg 1$, the transfer function of the tuned circuit in Example 2.3, Sect. 2.2, may be approximated by $H(f) \approx R/[1 + j(2Q/f_c)(f - f_c)]$ for $f > 0$, where $f_c = f_r$.

(*a*) Show that $H_{LP}(f)$ has the form of an RC LPF and find $h(t)$ from $h_{LP}(t)$.

(*b*) Use Eq. (9*b*) to find the bandpass response $y(t)$ when $x(t) = A \cos \omega_c t \, u(t)$.

† Jurgen (1972) describes the various approaches to quadraphonics.

5.7 (Sect. 5.1) The channel having $H_C(f)$ in Fig. P4.1 is to be used for bandpass pulse transmission without equalization. Select an appropriate value for f_c and find τ_{min}.

5.8 (Sect. 5.1) A radar system is to be designed for 1-μs bandpass pulses. What is the lowest practical value for f_c?

5.9 (Sect. 5.2) If $x(t) = 0.5\,u(t) - 1.5\,u(t - \tau), \tau \gg 1/f_c$, sketch $x_c(t)$ and indicate the envelope when the modulation is: AM with $m < 1$, AM with $m > 1$, DSB.

5.10 (Sect. 5.2) The multitone modulating signal $x(t) = K(2\cos\omega_m t + \cos 2\omega_m t + 3\cos 5\omega_m t)$ is the input to an AM system with $m = 1$.
   (*a*) Find K so that $x(t)$ is properly normalized, and plot the positive-frequency line spectrum of $x_c(t)$.
   (*b*) Calculate P_{SB}/P_c and P_c/S_T.

5.11 (Sect. 5.2) Construct the phasor diagram and find $v_i(t)$, $v_q(t)$, and $R(t)$ for AM with full-load tone modulation when:
   (*a*) The upper sideband is attenuated by a factor of $\frac{1}{2}$.
   (*b*) The upper sideband is phase-shifted by 180°.

5.12 (Sect. 5.2) Derive Eq. (9) by taking the time average of $x_c{}^2(t)$. (*Hint*: See Prob. 5.3.)

5.13 (Sect. 5.2) Suppose $x(t)$ is a zero-mean gaussian random signal so the normalization Eq. (2) cannot be applied. Taking $m = 1$, find the maximum value of $\overline{x^2}$ such that overmodulation occurs no more than 10 percent of the time. Compute $2P_{SB}/S_T$ under this condition.

5.14★(Sect. 5.3) Design in block-diagram form an AM modulator using a nonlinear device having $v_{out} = av_{in}{}^3$. (*Hint*: A frequency multiplier or divider will be needed.)

5.15 (Sect. 5.3) Suppose the AM modulators in Fig. 5.18 are *unbalanced*; i.e., one nonlinear device has $v_{out} = a_1 v_{in} + a_2 v_{in}{}^2 + a_3 v_{in}{}^3$ while the other has $v_{out} = b_1 v_{in} + b_2 v_{in}{}^2 + b_3 v_{in}{}^3$. Find the final output signal.

5.16 (Sect. 5.3) Practical modulators often have a *peak power limitation* as well as an average power limit. Find $x_c{}^2(t)|_{max}$ in terms of $2P_{SB}$ for AM and DSB, and compare.

5.17 (Sect. 5.4) Taking tone modulation, show that the output in Fig. 5.24 has the form of Eq. (2).

5.18 (Sect. 5.4) Let $x(t)$ be a typical voice signal so $X(f) \approx 0$ for $|f| < 200$ and $|f| > 3,200$ Hz. By sketching spectra at appropriate points, demonstrate that the system in Fig. P5.2 produces USSB, and find the maximum permitted values of f_{c_1} and f_{c_2} if the transition regions of the HPFs must satisfy $2\beta \geq 0.1\,f_{co}$.

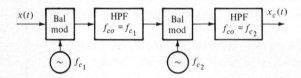

FIGURE P5-2.

5.19 (Sect. 5.4) Figure P5.3 is *Weaver's SSB modulator.* Analyze its operation by taking $x(t) = \cos 2\pi f_m t$, $f_m < W$.

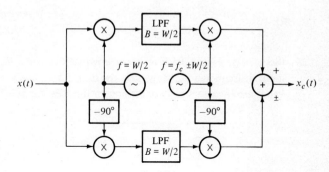

FIGURE P5–3.

5.20★(Sect. 5.4) If $w(t) = \hat{v}(t)$, show that $\hat{w}(t) = -v(t)$ and thereby derive the inverse Hilbert transform $v(t) = -[\hat{v}(t)] * [1/\pi t]$.

5.21★(Sect. 5.4) Prove Eq. (13b).

5.22★(Sect. 5.4) When $x(t) = A\Pi(t/\tau)$, its Hilbert transform may be written as

$$\hat{x}(t) = \frac{A}{\pi} \ln \left| \frac{t + \tau/2}{t - \tau/2} \right|$$

(a) Use the graphical interpretation of convolution to sketch $\hat{x}(t) = [x(t)] * [1/\pi t]$ and show that your sketch agrees with the above expression.

(b) Sketch the SSB envelope for this case.

5.23 (Sect. 5.4) Obtain an expression for VSB with tone modulation taking $H(f_c + f_m) = 0.5 + a$ and $H(f_c - f_m) = 0.5 - a$. Write your answer in both quadrature-carrier and envelope-and-phase form, and show that $x_c(t)$ reduces to DSB or SSB when $a = 0$ or ± 0.5, respectively.

5.24★(Sect. 5.4) Show that Eq. (16) results when a DSB signal is applied to the VSB filter of Eq. (14). (*Hint:* Use the lowpass equivalents for $H(f)$ and $x_c(t)$.)

5.25 (Sect. 5.4) With tone modulation SSB + C can be written as $x_c(t) = A_c[\cos \omega_c t + a \cos (\omega_c \pm \omega_m)t]$.

(a) Construct the corresponding phasor diagram and find $R(t)$.

(b) Assuming $a \ll 1$, find the condition on P_{SB}/P_c such that the second-harmonic envelope distortion is less than 5 percent.

5.26 (Sect. 5.4) Derive Eq. (20) by adding a random phase Θ to both carrier terms in Eq. (18) and finding $E[x_c^2(t)]$.

5.27 (Sect. 5.5) The system in Fig. P5.4 is a simplified *speech scrambler* used to ensure communication privacy and foil wiretapping. Analyze its operation by sketching the spectrum at each stage, taking $X(f)$ as shown. Also demonstrate that an identical unit will suffice as an unscrambler.

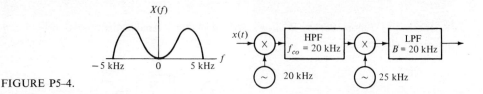

FIGURE P5–4.

5.28 (Sect. 5.5) Figure P5.5 is a *regenerative frequency divider*. Assuming a sinusoidal input at frequency f_0, show that the output frequency is f_0/M, where M is an integer. What are the necessary conditions on the BPF for this?

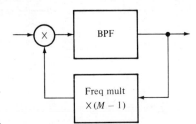

FIGURE P5–5.

5.29 (Sect. 5.5) Taking $x_c(t)$ as in Eq. (2), find $y_D(t)$ for synchronous detection when the LO output is $\cos(\omega_c t + \phi)$, where ϕ is a constant phase error. Then write separate answers for AM, DSB, SSB, and VSB by appropriate substitution for K_c, K_m, and $\zeta(t)$.

5.30 (Sect. 5.5) Suppose the diode in Fig. 5.30 has a *square-law characteristic*. Find and discuss the resulting demodulated signal.

5.31★(Sect. 5.5) Referring to the envelope detector of Fig. 5.30, determine suitable upper and lower limits on the time constant R_1C_1 as dictated by the carrier frequency f_c and maximum modulating frequency W. From these limits find the minimum practical value of f_c/W. (*Hint*: First sketch the rectified wave for the case of tone modulation with $mA_m = 1$ and $f_m = W$.)

5.32 (Sect. 5.5) Is it possible to design an AM superheterodyne radio such that the image frequency always falls outside of the AM broadcast band? If so, what is the necessary value of f_{IF} and the range of f_{LO}?

5.33 (Sect. 5.5) Draw and fully label the block diagram of a superheterodyne receiver with the following specifications: DSB modulation with pilot carrier, $W = 15$ kHz, $f_c = 8$ to 10 MHz, $f_c' \leq 4$ MHz, homodyne detection.

5.34 (Sect. 5.6) Ten voice signals, each bandlimited to 3 kHz, are to be FDMed with 1-kHz guard bands between channels. The subcarrier modulation is SSB and $f_{c_1} = 0$.
(*a*) Calculate the baseband bandwidth.
(*b*) Sketch the spectrum of the transmitted signal if the carrier modulation is AM.

5.35 (Sect. 5.6) Taking $f_{c_1} = 0$, sketch a typical spectrum for an FDM system using AM subcarrier and carrier modulation. What are the advantages and disadvantages of this scheme?

5.36 (Sect. 5.6) Referring to Table 5.2, draw the block diagram of the FDM system needed to generate a supergroup from five groups. Take USSB modulation throughout. Assuming one bank of subcarrier oscillators can be used for all twelve groups, count the total number of oscillators and modulators and compare with the number required when all the voice channels are FDMed directly in one step.

5.37 (Sect. 5.6) The BPFs in a certain FDM receiver have $H(f) = 10^{-(f-f_0)^2/2B^2}$ for $f > 0$, where f_0 is the center frequency and B is essentially the 3-dB bandwidth. Find the necessary guard-band width in terms of B if it is specified that $|H(f)| \leq 10^{-1/2}$ in the rejection regions to minimize cross talk.

5.38 (Sect. 5.6) Two signals $x_1(t)$ and $x_2(t)$, each bandlimited in W, are FDMed on sub-carriers $f_1 \gg W$ and $f_2 = f_1 + 2W$, respectively, and transmitted over a nonlinear channel whose output includes $a_2 x_b^2(t) + a_3 x_b^3(t)$.

   (a) If the subcarrier modulation is DSB, show that all the *cross talk* at the output is *nonintelligible* and vanishes after filtering if $a_3 = 0$.

   (b) Repeat for AM subcarrier modulation, which will also have *intelligible* cross talk due to terms of the form $x_1(t) \cos \omega_2 t$.

6

EXPONENTIAL MODULATION

Two properties of *linear* modulation bear repetition at the outset of this chapter: the modulated spectrum is basically the translated message spectrum, and the transmission bandwidth never exceeds twice the message bandwidth. A third property, derived in Chap. 7, is that the destination signal-to-noise ratio $(S/N)_D$ is no better than baseband transmission and can be improved only by increasing the transmitted power. *Exponential* modulation differs on all three counts.

In contrast to linear modulation, exponential modulation is a *nonlinear* process; therefore, it should come as no surprise that the modulated spectrum is not related in a simple fashion to the message spectrum. Moreover, it turns out that the transmission bandwidth is usually much greater than twice the message bandwidth. Compensating for the bandwidth liability is the fact that exponential modulation can provide increased signal-to-noise ratios without increased transmitted power.

To gain a qualitative appreciation of this property, consider a form of exponential modulation wherein the instantaneous frequency of the modulated wave is varied in accordance with the message waveform, i.e., frequency modulation. The demodulated signal therefore is proportional to the range of frequency variation, called the deviation, and one can increase output signal power by increasing the deviation. Since only the frequency is modulated in this process, the carrier amplitude remains constant, and the improved output is realized without increasing transmitted power. However, larger frequency deviation does require a greater transmission bandwidth. Thus, with exponential modulation, one can trade bandwidth for signal-to-noise ratio, an intriguing possibility.

Ironically, frequency modulation was first conceived as a means of bandwidth reduction, the argument going somewhat as follows: If, instead of modulating the carrier amplitude, we modulate the frequency by swinging it over a range of, say, ± 50 Hz, then the transmission bandwidth will be 100 Hz regardless of the message bandwidth. As we shall soon see, this argument has a serious flaw; specifically, it ignores the distinction between *instantaneous frequency* and *spectral frequency*. Carson (1922) recognized the fallacy of the bandwidth-reduction notion and cleared the air on that score. Unfortunately, he and many others also felt that exponential modulation had no advantages over linear modulation with respect to noise. It took some time to overcome this belief, but, thanks to Armstrong (1936), the merits of exponential modulation were finally appreciated. Before we can understand them fully, more careful consideration must be given to the fundamental concepts.

6.1 FUNDAMENTAL CONCEPTS

In exponential modulation, the modulated wave in phasor form is an exponential function of the message, that is,

$$x_c(t) = \text{Re}\,[A_c e^{j\theta_c(t)}] = A_c \cos \theta_c(t)$$

where $\theta_c(t)$ is a linear function of $x(t)$ and A_c is constant. Since θ_c is the angular position of the phasor, an equally appropriate name for the process is *angle* modulation.

While there are many possible forms of exponential modulation, only two have proved to be practical, namely *frequency modulation* (FM) and *phase modulation* (PM). These designations suggest time-varying frequency or phase, concepts that require special interpretation. This is particularly true of time-varying frequency since frequency implies periodicity and time-varying periodicity is meaningless.

To clarify the matter, we begin by writing θ_c as

$$\theta_c(t) \triangleq 2\pi f_c t + \phi(t) \tag{1}$$

so that the carrier frequency f_c is uniquely specified. The second term of Eq. (1) can then be interpreted as a *relative phase angle*, in the sense that the phasor $e^{j\theta_c}$ differs in angular position from $e^{j\omega_c t}$ by $\phi(t)$. Pressing these notions further, it should be recalled that angular frequency (in radians per second) is the time derivative of angular position. Therefore we are led to define *instantaneous frequency deviation* $f(t)$ (in revolutions or cycles per second) by

$$f(t) \triangleq \frac{1}{2\pi} \frac{d\phi(t)}{dt} \tag{2}$$

which can be interpreted as the velocity of $e^{j\theta_c}$ compared to $e^{j\omega_c t}$. Thus, $\theta_c(t)$ is related to $f(t)$ by integration in the form

$$\theta_c(t) = 2\pi f_c t + 2\pi \int_{-\infty}^{t} f(\lambda) \, d\lambda \tag{3}$$

The lower limit of integration represents a constant phase term that can be dropped without loss of generality if desired. With these preliminaries kept in mind, phase modulation is defined as the process whereby the phase $\phi(t)$ is proportional to the message, while in frequency modulation the instantaneous frequency deviation $f(t)$ is proportional to the message.

Specifically, the relative phase of a PM wave is

$$\phi(t) \triangleq \phi_\Delta x(t) \tag{4}$$

where ϕ_Δ is the phase-deviation constant, i.e., the maximum phase shift produced by $x(t)$ since we are still using the message convention $|x(t)| \leq 1$. The modulated wave is then

$$x_c(t) = A_c \cos [\omega_c t + \phi_\Delta x(t)] \tag{5}$$

Similarly, the instantaneous frequency deviation of an FM wave is

$$f(t) \triangleq f_\Delta x(t) \tag{6}$$

where f_Δ is the frequency-deviation constant. Substituting Eq. (6) into Eq. (3) yields

$$\theta_c(t) = 2\pi f_c t + 2\pi f_\Delta \int_{-\infty}^{t} x(\lambda) \, d\lambda \tag{7a}$$

and hence

$$x_c(t) = A_c \cos \left[\omega_c t + 2\pi f_\Delta \int_{-\infty}^{t} x(\lambda) \, d\lambda \right] \tag{7b}$$

is the modulated waveform.

It is assumed above that the message has no DC component; that is, $\bar{x} = 0$. Otherwise the integral in Eq. (7) would diverge as $t \to \infty$. Physically, a DC term in $x(t)$ produces a constant phase shift $\phi_\Delta \bar{x}$ in phase modulation or a carrier-frequency shift $f_\Delta \bar{x}$ in frequency modulation. Practically, any DC message component is usually blocked in the modulator circuits.

Table 6.1

	$\phi(t)$	$f(t)$
PM	$\phi_\Delta x(t)$	$\dfrac{\phi_\Delta}{2\pi}\dfrac{dx(t)}{dt}$
FM	$2\pi f_\Delta \displaystyle\int_{-\infty}^{t} x(\lambda)\,d\lambda$	$f_\Delta x(t)$

Comparing Eq. (5) with Eq. (7), there appears to be little difference between PM and FM, the essential distinction being the integration of the message in FM. Moreover, nomenclature notwithstanding, both FM and PM have both time-varying phase and frequency, as underscored by Table 6.1. These relations clearly indicate that, with the help of integrating and differentiating networks, a phase modulator can produce frequency modulation and vice versa. In fact, in the case of tone modulation it is virtually impossible to visually distinguish FM and PM waves.

On the other hand, a comparison of exponential modulation with linear modulation reveals some pronounced differences. For one thing, the amplitude of an FM or PM wave is always constant; therefore, regardless of the message $x(t)$, the average transmitted power is†

$$S_T = \tfrac{1}{2}A_c^2 \qquad (8)$$

For another, the zero crossings of an exponentially modulated wave are not periodic, whereas they are always periodic in linear modulation. Indeed, because of the constant-amplitude property of FM and PM, it can be said that the message resides in the *zero crossings alone*, providing the carrier frequency is large.‡ Finally, since exponential modulation is a nonlinear process, the modulated wave does not look at all like the message waveform.

Figure 6.1 illustrates some of these points by showing typical AM, FM, and PM waves. As a mental exercise the reader may wish to check these waveforms against the corresponding modulating signals. For FM and PM this is most easily done by considering the instantaneous frequency rather than by substituting $x(t)$ in Eqs. (5) and (7).

Despite the many similarities of PM and FM, frequency modulation turns out to have superior noise-reduction properties and thus will receive most of our attention. Fortunately, results and conclusions based on a study of FM are applicable with but minor modifications to all forms of exponential modulation.

---

† There are theoretical exceptions to this condition when $f(t) \leq - f_c$, but they seldom occur in practice.

‡ Schwartz (1970, chap. 4) demonstrates this.

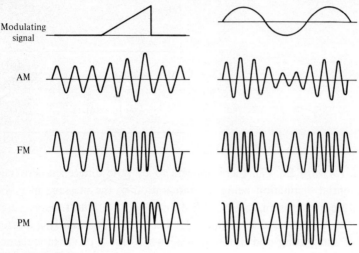

FIGURE 6.1
Illustrative AM, FM, and PM waveforms.

EXERCISE 6.1 Suppose that FM were defined in direct analogy with AM as $x_c(t) = A_c \cos \omega_c[1 + mx(t)]t$. Demonstrate the physical impossibility of this definition by finding $f(t)$ when $x(t) = \cos \omega_m t$. *Ans.:* $mf_c[\cos \omega_m t - \omega_m t \sin \omega_m t]$.

6.2 FM SPECTRAL ANALYSIS

The time-domain description of an FM wave with arbitrary message $x(t)$ is provided by Eq. (7), Sect. 6.1. Hence, we begin our study with the frequency-domain description, or spectral analysis, of FM. Before doing so, it is necessary to observe that $f(t)$ is not the same thing as *spectral frequency f*. The former is a time-dependent quantity describing $x_c(t)$ in the time domain; the latter is the independent variable of spectral analysis wherein $X_c(f)$ describes $x_c(t)$ in the frequency domain in terms of fixed-frequency sinusoidal components. Therefore we cannot expect a simple one-to-one correspondence between $f(t)$ and the FM spectrum.

As implied by these considerations, an exact description of FM spectra is difficult save for certain simple modulating signals. (This of course merely reflects the fact that exponential modulation is a *nonlinear* process.) Therefore, instead of attempting the analysis with arbitrary $x(t)$, we shall as an alternate tactic examine several specific cases, beginning with tone modulation, and formulate general conclusions based on them. This approach is admittedly roundabout but necessary.

Tone Modulation

With tone modulation, the instantaneous frequency of an FM signal varies in a sinusoidal fashion about the carrier frequency, a typical waveform being illustrated in Fig. 6.1. Specifically, if $x(t) = A_m \cos \omega_m t$, then, omitting the lower limit of integration,

$$\theta_c(t) = 2\pi f_c t + 2\pi f_\Delta \int^t A_m \cos \omega_m \lambda \, d\lambda$$

and

$$x_c(t) = A_c \cos \left(\omega_c t + \frac{2\pi f_d A_m}{\omega_m} \sin \omega_m t \right)$$

To simplify the notation let

$$\beta \triangleq \frac{2\pi f_\Delta A_m}{\omega_m} = \frac{A_m f_\Delta}{f_m} \tag{1}$$

so that

$$x_c(t) = A_c \cos (\omega_c t + \beta \sin \omega_m t) \tag{2}$$

This result should be contrasted with Eq. (11), Sect. 5.2, the equivalent expression for AM with tone modulation.

The parameter β introduced above is called the FM *modulation index*, and has two rather unusual properties: it is defined only for tone modulation, and it depends on both the amplitude and frequency of the modulating tone. Physically, β is the *maximum phase deviation* (in radians) produced by the tone in question. This conclusion follows from inspection of Eq. (2), which shows that the relative phase of $x_c(t)$ is

$$\phi(t) = \beta \sin \omega_m t = \frac{A_m f_\Delta}{f_m} \sin \omega_m t \tag{3}$$

Thus, different tones having the same amplitude-to-frequency ratio yield the same phase deviation but at different rates. However, since $f(t) = f_\Delta A_m \cos \omega_m t$, the frequency deviation depends only on the tone amplitude and f_Δ, the latter being a property of the modulator.

As to the spectral analysis of $x_c(t)$, we shall not attempt a direct Fourier transformation of Eq. (2), for rather obvious reasons. But it is possible to express $x_c(t)$ as a sum of sinusoids, which then gives us the positive-frequency line spectrum. For this purpose we first write Eq. (2) in the form

$$x_c(t) = A_c[\cos \omega_c t \cos (\beta \sin \omega_m t) - \sin \omega_c t \sin (\beta \sin \omega_m t)] \tag{4}$$

and observe that, even though $x_c(t)$ itself is not necessarily periodic, $\cos(\beta \sin \omega_m t)$ and $\sin(\beta \sin \omega_m t)$ are periodic in $1/f_m$ and thus can be expanded via Fourier series. In particular, it is well known in applied mathematics that

$$\cos(\beta \sin \omega_m t) = J_0(\beta) + \sum_{n \text{ even}}^{\infty} 2J_n(\beta) \cos n\omega_m t$$

$$\sin(\beta \sin \omega_m t) = \sum_{n \text{ odd}}^{\infty} 2J_n(\beta) \sin n\omega_m t \tag{5}$$

where n is positive and

$$J_n(\beta) \triangleq \frac{1}{2\pi} \int_{-\pi}^{\pi} e^{j(\beta \sin \lambda - n\lambda)} \, d\lambda \tag{6}$$

The coefficients $J_n(\beta)$ are *Bessel functions* of the first kind, of order n and argument β. With the aid of Eq. (6), the reader should encounter little difficulty in deriving the trigonometric expansions given in Eq. (5).

Substituting Eq. (5) into Eq. (4) and expanding products of sines and cosines finally results in

$$x_c(t) = A_c J_0(\beta) \cos \omega_c t$$

$$+ \sum_{n \text{ odd}}^{\infty} A_c J_n(\beta)[\cos(\omega_c + n\omega_m)t - \cos(\omega_c - n\omega_m)t]$$

$$+ \sum_{n \text{ even}}^{\infty} A_c J_n(\beta)[\cos(\omega_c + n\omega_m)t + \cos(\omega_c - n\omega_m)t] \tag{7a}$$

Alternately, taking advantage of the property that $J_{-n}(\beta) = (-1)^n J_n(\beta)$, we get the more compact but less informative expression

$$x_c(t) = A_c \sum_{n=-\infty}^{\infty} J_n(\beta) \cos(\omega_c + n\omega_m)t \tag{7b}$$

In either form, Eq. (7) is the mathematical representation for a constant-amplitude wave whose instantaneous frequency is varying sinusoidally. A phasor interpretation, to be given shortly, will shed more light on the matter.

Examining Eq. (7), we see that the FM spectrum consists of a carrier-frequency line plus an *infinite* number of sideband lines at frequencies† $f_c \pm nf_m$. As illustrated in the typical spectrum of Fig. 6.2, all lines are equally spaced by the modulating frequency and the odd-order lower sideband lines are reversed in phase (i.e., have "negative" amplitudes) compared to the unmodulated carrier. In general, the relative

---

† We are dealing with a positive-frequency line spectrum, so apparent negative frequencies due to $nf_m > f_c$ are folded back to the positive values $|f_c - nf_m|$. Such components are usually negligible in practice when the carrier frequency is many orders greater than the modulating frequency.

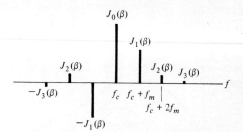

FIGURE 6.2
FM line spectrum, tone modulation.

amplitude of a line at $f_c + nf_m$ is given by $J_n(\beta)$, so before we can say more about the spectrum, we must examine the behavior of Bessel functions.

Figure 6.3 shows a few Bessel functions of various order plotted versus the argument β. Several important properties can be noted from this plot.

1 The relative amplitude of the carrier line $J_0(\beta)$ varies with the modulation index and hence depends on the modulating signal. Thus, in contrast to linear modulation, the carrier-frequency component of an FM wave "contains" part of the message information. Nonetheless, there will be spectra in which the carrier line has zero amplitude since $J_0(\beta) = 0$ when $\beta = 2.4, 5.5$, etc.

2 The number of sideband lines having appreciable relative amplitude also is a function of β. With $\beta \ll 1$ only J_0 and J_1 are significant, so the spectrum will consist of carrier and two sideband lines, much like AM save for the phase reversal of the lower sideband line. On the other hand, if $\beta \gg 1$, there will be many sideband lines, giving a spectrum quite unlike linear modulation.

3 Large β implies a large bandwidth to accommodate the extensive sideband structure — this in agreement with our physical interpretation of large frequency deviation.

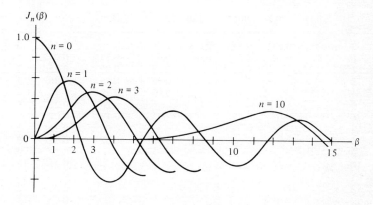

FIGURE 6.3
Bessel functions of fixed order plotted versus the argument β.

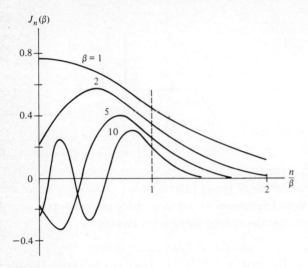

FIGURE 6.4
Bessel functions of fixed argument plotted versus n/β.

Some of the above points are better illustrated by Fig. 6.4, which gives $J_n(\beta)$ as a function of n/β for various *fixed* values of β. Since FM with tone modulation has constant β, these curves represent the "envelope" of the sideband lines if we multiply the horizontal axis by βf_m to obtain the line position $n f_m$ relative to f_c. Observe in particular that all $J_n(\beta)$ decay monotonically for $n/\beta > 1$ and that $|J_n(\beta)| \ll 1$ if $|n/\beta| \gg 1$. Similar to Fig. 6.4, Table 6.2 lists selected values of $J_n(\beta)$, rounded off at the second decimal place.† Blanks in the table correspond to $|J_n(\beta)| < 0.01$.

Table 6.2   SELECTED VALUES OF $J_n(\beta)$

n	$J_n(0.1)$	$J_n(0.2)$	$J_n(0.5)$	$J_n(1.0)$	$J_n(2.0)$	$J_n(5.0)$	$J_n(10)$	n
0	1.00	0.99	0.94	0.77	0.22	−0.18	−0.25	0
1	0.05	0.10	0.24	0.44	0.58	−0.33	0.04	1
2			0.03	0.11	0.35	0.05	0.25	2
3				0.02	0.13	0.36	0.06	3
4					0.03	0.39	−0.22	4
5						0.26	−0.23	5
6						0.13	−0.01	6
7						0.05	0.22	7
8						0.02	0.32	8
9							0.29	9
10							0.21	10
11							0.12	11
12							0.06	12
13							0.03	13
14							0.01	14

† More extensive tabulations are given in Jahnke and Emde (1945).

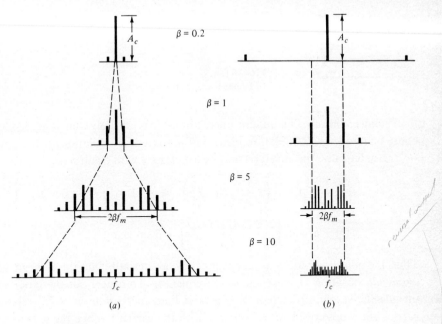

FIGURE 6.5
Tone-modulated FM line spectra. (a) f_m fixed, $A_m f_\Delta$ increasing; (b) $A_m f_\Delta$ fixed, f_m decreasing.

Typical line spectra are shown in Fig. 6.5, where reversals of the odd-order lower sideband lines have been omitted for clarity. These spectra should be carefully scrutinized by the reader for the relative influence of modulating amplitude and frequency. Note also the concentration of the spectrum within $f_c \pm \beta f_m$ when β is large.

EXERCISE 6.2   Draw the line spectrum when $f_c = 12$ kHz, $f_m = 2$ kHz, and $A_m f_\Delta = 4$ kHz. If $A_m f_\Delta = 10$ kHz, show that $x_c(t)$ has a DC component and hence $S_T \neq A_c{}^2/2$.

Phasor Interpretation

Because $x_c(t)$ as written in Eq. (7) is so cumbersome, let us construct the FM phasor diagram to aid physical interpretation. As a starting point suppose that $\beta \ll 1$, so that $J_0(\beta) \approx 1$, $J_1(\beta) \approx \beta/2$, and all higher-order lines are negligible. This yields the phasor diagram of Fig. 6.6, a diagram that differs from the AM case (Fig. 5.9) only in the phase reversal of the lower sideband line. But because of the phase reversal, the contribution of the sideband pair is perpendicular or *quadrature* to the carrier rather

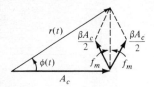

FIGURE 6.6
FM phasor diagram for $\beta \ll 1$.

than being collinear. This quadrature relationship is precisely what is needed to produce phase or frequency modulation instead of amplitude modulation.

Analytically, the envelope and phase of $x_c(t)$ with small β are

$$R(t) \approx \sqrt{A_c^2 + \left(2\frac{\beta}{2}A_c \sin \omega_m t\right)^2} \approx A_c\left[1 + \frac{\beta^2}{4} - \frac{\beta^2}{4}\cos 2\omega_m t\right]$$

$$\phi(t) \approx \arctan\left[\frac{2(\beta/2)A_c \sin \omega_m t}{A_c}\right] \approx \beta \sin \omega_m t$$

(8)

Thus the phase variation is approximately as desired, but there is an additional *amplitude* variation at twice the tone frequency. To cancel out the latter we should include the second-order pair of sideband lines that rotate at $\pm 2f_m$ relative to the carrier and whose resultant is collinear with the carrier. While the second-order pair virtually wipes out the undesired amplitude modulation, it also distorts $\phi(t)$. The phase distortion is then corrected by adding the third-order pair, which again introduces amplitude modulation, and so on ad infinitum.

When all spectral lines are included, the odd-order pairs have a resultant in quadrature with the carrier that provides the desired frequency modulation plus unwanted amplitude modulation. The resultant of the even-order pairs, being collinear with the carrier, corrects for the amplitude variations. The net effect is then as illustrated in Fig. 6.7. The tip of the resultant sweeps through a circular arc, reflecting the constant amplitude A_c.

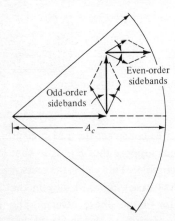

FIGURE 6.7
FM phasor diagram for arbitrary β.

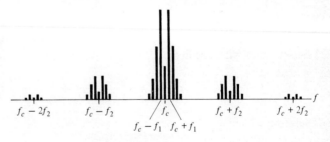

FIGURE 6.8

Double-tone FM line spectrum, $f_1 \ll f_2$, $\beta_1 > \beta_2$.

Multitone Modulation

The Fourier series technique used to arrive at Eq. (7) also can be applied to the case of multitone modulation. For instance, suppose that $x(t) = A_1 \cos \omega_1 t + A_2 \cos \omega_2 t$, where f_1 and f_2 are not harmonically related. The modulated wave is first written as

$$x_c(t) = A_c[\cos \omega_c t(\cos \alpha_1 \cos \alpha_2 - \sin \alpha_1 \sin \alpha_2)$$
$$- \sin \omega_c t(\sin \alpha_1 \cos \alpha_2 + \cos \alpha_1 \sin \alpha_2)]$$

where $\alpha_1 = \beta_1 \sin \omega_1 t$, $\beta_1 = A_1 f_\Delta/f_1$, etc. Terms of the form $\cos \alpha_1$, $\sin \alpha_1$, etc., are then expanded according to Eq. (5), and, after some routine manipulations, one arrives at the compact result

$$x_c(t) = A_c \sum_{n=-\infty}^{\infty} \sum_{m=-\infty}^{\infty} J_n(\beta_1)J_m(\beta_2) \cos (\omega_c + n\omega_1 + m\omega_2)t \qquad (9)$$

Interpreting this expression in the frequency domain, the spectral lines can be divided into four categories: (1) the carrier line of amplitude $A_cJ_0(\beta_1)J_0(\beta_2)$; (2) sideband lines at $f_c \pm nf_1$ due to one tone alone; (3) sideband lines at $f_c \pm mf_2$ due to the other tone alone; and (4) sideband lines at $f_c \pm nf_1 \pm mf_2$ which appear to be beat-frequency modulation at the sum and difference frequencies of the modulating tones and their harmonics. This last category may come as a surprise, for it is un-paralleled in linear modulation where simple superposition of sideband lines is the rule. But then we must recall that FM is *nonlinear* modulation, so superposition is not to be expected. A double-tone FM spectrum showing the various types of spectral lines is given in Fig. 6.8 for $f_1 \ll f_2$ and $\beta_1 > \beta_2$. Under these conditions there exists the curious property that each sideband line at $f_c \pm mf_2$ looks like another FM carrier with tone modulation of frequency f_1.

If absolutely necessary, the above technique can be extended to modulation by more than two nonharmonic tones; the procedure is straightforward but messy.

When the tone frequencies are harmonically related—i.e., $x(t)$ is a *periodic* waveform—then $\phi(t)$ is periodic and so is $e^{j\phi(t)}$. The latter can be expanded in an exponential Fourier series with coefficients

$$c_n = \frac{1}{T_0} \int_{T_0} \exp j[\phi(t) - n\omega_0 t] \, dt \qquad (10a)$$

Therefore

$$x_c(t) = \operatorname{Re}\left[A_c \sum_{n=-\infty}^{\infty} c_n e^{j(\omega_c + n\omega_0)t} \right] \qquad (10b)$$

Further discussion is omitted here since it adds nothing of particular importance.†

Pulse Modulation

Despite the complexities of FM spectra, there are a few modulating signals for which $x_c(t)$ is amenable to direct Fourier transformation. One such signal is the rectangular pulse $x(t) = \Pi(t/\tau)$, an important and informative example.

The key to transformation is the instantaneous frequency since, for pulse modulation, it is simply $f(t) = f_\Delta \Pi(t/\tau)$. By inspection or integration of $f(t)$ we have

$$x_c(t) = \begin{cases} A_c \cos (\omega_c + \omega_\Delta)t & |t| < \dfrac{\tau}{2} \\[2mm] A_c \cos \omega_c t & |t| > \dfrac{\tau}{2} \end{cases}$$

But better suited to our purposes is the form

$$x_c(t) = A_c\left[\cos \omega_c t - \Pi\!\left(\frac{t}{\tau}\right) \cos \omega_c t + \Pi\!\left(\frac{t}{\tau}\right) \cos (\omega_c + \omega_\Delta)t \right] \qquad (11)$$

which says that the modulated signal is a sinusoidal wave of frequency f_c minus an RF pulse of frequency f_c plus an RF pulse of frequency $f_c + f_\Delta$.

Although Eq. (11) may seem unduly formal, it does lend itself readily to Fourier analysis; indeed, with the result of Example 2.7, Sect. 2.3, $x_c(t)$ can be transformed term by term to give

$$X_c(f) = \frac{A_c}{2} [\delta(f - f_c) + \delta(f + f_c)] - \frac{A_c\tau}{2} [\operatorname{sinc} (f - f_c)\tau + \operatorname{sinc} (f + f_c)\tau]$$

$$+ \frac{A_c\tau}{2} [\operatorname{sinc} (f - f_c - f_\Delta)\tau + \operatorname{sinc} (f + f_c + f_\Delta)\tau] \qquad (12)$$

† Panter (1965, chap. 7) gives further details and several interesting examples.

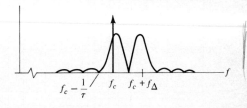

FIGURE 6.9
Pulse-modulated FM spectrum,
$f_\Delta = 2/\tau$.

The positive-frequency portion of $|X_c(f)|$ is sketched in Fig. 6.9 for $f_\Delta = 2/\tau$. We see that the spectrum is *not symmetric* about the carrier frequency and has more content above f_c than below, a state of affairs that might have been anticipated in view of the fact that $f_c + \not{f}(t)$ is never less than f_c. Moreover, even though other frequencies are present, the spectrum is concentrated at the two discrete values f_c and $f_c + f_\Delta$.

6.3 FM BANDWIDTHS

We have seen that, in general, an FM spectrum has infinite extent. Consequently, the generation and transmission of *pure* FM requires systems of *infinite bandwidth*, whether or not the message is bandlimited. But practical FM systems having finite bandwidth do exist and perform quite well. Their success depends upon the fact that, sufficiently far away from the carrier frequency, the spectral components are quite small and may be discarded. True, omitting any portion of the spectrum will cause *distortion* in the demodulated signal; but the distortion can be minimized by keeping all *significant* spectral components.

Determination of FM transmission bandwidth thus boils down to the question: How much of the modulated signal spectrum is significant? Of course, significance standards are not absolute, being contingent upon the amount of distortion that can be tolerated in a specific application. However, rule-of-thumb criteria based on studies of tone modulation have met with considerable success and lead to useful approximate relations. Our discussion of FM bandwidth requirements therefore begins with the significant sideband lines for tone modulation.

Significant Sideband Lines

Figure 6.4 indicated that $J_n(\beta)$ falls off rapidly for $|n/\beta| > 1$, particularly if $\beta \gg 1$. Assuming that the modulation index β is large, we can say that $|J_n(\beta)|$ is significant only for $|n| \leq \beta = A_m f_\Delta/f_m$. Therefore, all significant sideband lines are contained in the frequency range $f_c \pm \beta f_m = f_c \pm A_m f_\Delta$, a conclusion agreeing with intuitive reasoning. On the other hand, suppose the modulation index is small; then *all*

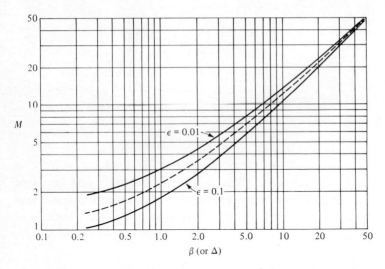

FIGURE 6.10
The number of significant sideband pairs as a function of β (or Δ).

sideband lines are small compared to the carrier, since $J_0(\beta) \gg J_{n \neq 0}(\beta)$ when $\beta \ll 1$. But we must retain at least the first-order sideband pair, else there would be no frequency modulation at all. Hence, for small β, the significant sideband lines are contained in $f_c \pm f_m$.

To put the above observations on a quantitative footing, all sideband lines having relative amplitude $|J_n(\beta)| > \epsilon$ are *defined* as being significant, where ϵ ranges from 0.01 to 0.1 according to the application. Then, if $|J_M(\beta)| > \epsilon$ and $|J_{M+1}(\beta)| < \epsilon$, there are M significant sideband *pairs* and $2M + 1$ significant lines all told. The bandwidth is thus

$$B = 2M(\beta)f_m \qquad M \geq 1 \qquad (1)$$

since the lines are spaced by f_m and M depends on the modulation index β. The condition $M \geq 1$ has been included in Eq. (1) to account for the fact that B cannot be less than $2f_m$.

Figure 6.10 shows M as a continuous function of β for $\epsilon = 0.01$ and 0.1. Experimental studies indicate that the former is often overly conservative, while the latter may result in small but noticeable distortion. Values of M between these two bounds, as indicated by the dashed line, are acceptable for most purposes and will be used hereafter.

But the bandwidth B is not the transmission bandwidth B_T; rather it is the minimum bandwidth necessary for modulation by a tone of specified amplitude and frequency. To illustrate, the maximum frequency deviation f_Δ of commercial FM is limited by the FCC to 75 kHz, and modulating frequencies typically cover 30 Hz to 15 kHz. If a 15-kHz tone has unit amplitude ($A_m = 1$), then $\beta = {}^{75}\!/_{15} = 5$, $M = 7$, and $B = 2 \times 7 \times 15 = 210$ kHz. Had the amplitude been less, the maximum frequency deviation would not be developed, and the bandwidth would be smaller.† Moreover, a lower-frequency tone, say 7.5 kHz, with full amplitude would result in a larger modulation index ($\beta = 10$), a greater number of significant sideband pairs ($M = 12$), but a smaller bandwidth, namely, $B = 2 \times 12 \times 7.5 = 180$ kHz. In short, bandwidth is determined in a rather complex fashion by both $A_m f_\Delta$ and f_m (or β and f_m), not just β alone.

Pursuing this last point, let us calculate the *maximum* bandwidth required when the tone parameters are constrained by $A_m \leq 1$ and $f_m \leq W$. For this purpose, the dashed line in Fig. 6.10 can be approximated by

$$M(\beta) \approx \beta + \alpha \qquad (2)$$

where α is essentially constant with a value between 1 and 2 (the exact value is immaterial at the moment). Inserting Eq. (2) into Eq. (1) gives

$$B \approx 2(\beta + \alpha)f_m = 2\left(\frac{A_m f_\Delta}{f_m} + \alpha\right)f_m = 2(A_m f_\Delta + \alpha f_m)$$

Now, bearing in mind that f_Δ is a property of the modulator, what tone produces the maximum bandwidth? Clearly, it is the *maximum-amplitude maximum-frequency* tone having $A_m = 1$ and $f_m = W$. The worst-case tone-modulation bandwidth is then

$$B_{\max} = 2(f_\Delta + \alpha W) \qquad (3)$$

Note carefully that the corresponding modulation index $\beta = f_\Delta/W$ is not the maximum value of β but rather the value which, combined with the maximum modulating frequency, yields the maximum bandwidth. Any other tone having $A_m < 1$ or $f_m < W$ will require less bandwidth even though β may be larger.

Transmission Bandwidth

We now focus attention on the transmission bandwidth B_T required when $x(t)$ is an *arbitrary modulating signal* having the message bandwidth W and satisfying the normalization convention $|x(t)| \leq 1$. But we do not turn our backs on the previous conclusions; in fact, we shall estimate B_T directly from the worst-case tone-modulation analysis, assuming that any component in $x(t)$ of smaller amplitude or frequency will require a smaller bandwidth than $B_{\max}$. Admittedly, this procedure ignores the fact

---

† It is paradoxical that in *frequency* modulation (with fixed f_Δ) the bandwidth depends on the tone *amplitude*, whereas in *amplitude* modulation the bandwidth depends on the tone *frequency*.

that superposition is not applicable to exponential modulation. However, our investigation of multitone spectra has shown that the beat-frequency sideband pairs are contained primarily within the bandwidth of the dominating tone alone, as illustrated by Fig. 6.8.

Therefore, extrapolating tone modulation to an arbitrary modulating signal, we define the *deviation ratio*†

$$\Delta \triangleq \frac{f_\Delta}{W} \qquad (4)$$

as the maximum deviation divided by the maximum modulating frequency, analogous to the modulation index of worst-case tone modulation. The transmission bandwidth required for $x(t)$ is then

$$B_T = 2M(\Delta)W \qquad M \geq 1 \qquad (5)$$

where Δ is treated just like β to find $M(\Delta)$, say from Fig. 6.10.

Lacking appropriate curves or tables for $M(\Delta)$, there are several approximations to B_T that can be invoked. With extreme values of the deviation ratio we find that

$$B_T = \begin{cases} 2\Delta W = 2f_\Delta & \Delta \gg 1 \\ 2W & \Delta \ll 1 \end{cases}$$

paralleling our results for tone modulation with β very large or very small. Both of these approximations are combined in the convenient relation

$$B_T \approx 2(f_\Delta + W) = 2(\Delta + 1)W \qquad \begin{matrix} \Delta \gg 1 \\ \Delta \ll 1 \end{matrix} \qquad (6)$$

known as *Carson's rule*. Perversely, the majority of actual FM systems have $2 < \Delta < 10$, for which Carson's rule somewhat underestimates the transmission bandwidth. A better approximation for equipment design is then

$$B_T \approx 2(f_\Delta + 2W) = 2(\Delta + 2)W \qquad \Delta > 2 \qquad (7)$$

which would be used, for example, to determine the 3-dB bandwidths of RF and IF amplifiers.

Applying these relations to commercial FM, $f_\Delta = 75$ kHz and $W = 15$ kHz, so $\Delta = 5$. We have already found that $M = 7$ for $\beta = 5$, hence Eq. (5) gives $B_T = 210$ kHz. (High-quality FM radios have IF bandwidths of at least 200 kHz.) Carson's rule underestimates B_T by about 10 percent, giving $2(5 + 1) \times 15 = 180$ kHz, whereas Eq. (7) is right on the mark with $2(5 + 2) \times 15 = 210$ kHz.

The reader is encouraged to review these several approximations and their regions of validity. In deference to most of the literature we shall frequently take B_T

---

† Some authors use this term for f_Δ/f_c, which does not have the same meaning.

as given by Carson's rule, Eq. (6), bearing in mind its limitations. However, when $x(t)$ is far from bandlimited, e.g., a rectangular pulse, it is necessary and prudent to carry out the spectral analysis (if possible) and determine the bandwidth therefrom.

EXERCISE 6.3 Calculate B_T/W for $\Delta = 0.3$, 3, and 30 using the approximations of Eqs. (6) and (7) where applicable. Repeat using Eq. (5) and Fig. 6.10, and compare your results.

Narrowband FM (NBFM)

Our bandwidth investigations point to the conclusion that there are two special FM cases, corresponding to very small or very large values of the deviation ratio. These cases have such distinctly different properties that they have been given the characteristic names of *narrowband* FM and *wideband* FM, respectively.

NBFM is in many ways similar to double-sideband linear modulation. To underscore that point, let $\phi(t) = 2\pi f_\Delta \int_{-\infty}^{t} x(\lambda) \, d\lambda$ and assume that

$$|\phi(t)|_{max} = \Delta \ll 1 \qquad (8)$$

which we take as the defining condition for NBFM. Then the modulated wave is

$$
\begin{aligned}
x_c(t) &= A_c \cos\left[\omega_c t + \phi(t)\right] \\
&= A_c[\cos \phi(t) \cos \omega_c t - \sin \phi(t) \sin \omega_c t] \\
&\approx A_c \cos \omega_c t - A_c \phi(t) \sin \omega_c t \qquad (9a)
\end{aligned}
$$

where the approximations $\cos \phi \approx 1$ and $\sin \phi \approx \phi$ have been used. Since Eq. (9a) is in quadrature-carrier form and since

$$V_q(f) = \mathscr{F}[A_c \phi(t)] = A_c 2\pi f_\Delta \left[\frac{X(f)}{j2\pi f}\right]$$

application of Eq. (4), Sect. 5.1, gives the spectrum as

$$X_c(f) \approx \frac{A_c}{2} [\delta(f-f_c) + \delta(f+f_c)] + \frac{A_c f_\Delta}{2} \left[\frac{X(f-f_c)}{f-f_c} - \frac{X(f+f_c)}{f+f_c}\right] \qquad (9b)$$

which has the same general form as an AM spectrum. Therefore, if $x(t)$ is bandlimited in W,

$$B_T \approx 2W \qquad (10)$$

as expected.

Not surprisingly, it also turns out that NBFM has no inherent advantage over linear modulation insofar as noise performance is concerned. Consequently, NBFM is seldom used for transmission purposes although it often is encountered as an intermediate step in the generation of wideband FM.

Wideband FM (WBFM)

The distinguishing feature of WBFM is that $\Delta \gg 1$ and hence B_T is large compared to the message bandwidth. In fact, B_T is *independent* of the message bandwidth, i.e.,

$$B_T \approx 2\Delta W = 2f_\Delta \qquad (11)$$

since $\Delta = f_\Delta / W$.

There is no simple approximation for the WBFM waveform $x_c(t)$, but there is an approximation for the *power spectral density* $G_{x_c}(f)$ in terms of the *probability density function* $p_x(x)$ of the modulating signal. The approximation stems from the fact that, when $f_\Delta \gg W$, the instantaneous frequency deviation $f'(t)$ varies so slowly that $x_c(t)$ looks more or less like an ordinary sinusoid of frequency $f_c + f'(t)$ over time intervals of order $1/W$ which is large compared to $1/f_\Delta$. Of course $f'(t)$ does change since $f'(t) = f_\Delta x(t)$ and, invoking Eq. (13), Sect. 3.2,

$$p_{f'}(f) = \frac{1}{f_\Delta} p_x\!\left(\frac{f}{f_\Delta}\right) \qquad (12)$$

Therefore, the fractional time that $x_c(t)$ is in the frequency range $f - df$ to f is

$$\text{Prob}\,[f - df < f_c + f' \leq f] = \text{Prob}\,[f - f_c - df < f' \leq f - f_c] = p_{f'}(f - f_c)\, df$$

so $p_{f'}(f - f_c)$ is proportional to the positive-frequency power density at f. The two-sided power density is then

$$G_{x_c}(f) = \tfrac{1}{2}S_T p_{f'}(f - f_c) + \tfrac{1}{2}S_T p_{f'}(f + f_c)$$

$$= \frac{S_T}{2f_\Delta}\left[p_x\!\left(\frac{f - f_c}{f_\Delta}\right) + p_x\!\left(\frac{f + f_c}{f_\Delta}\right) \right] \qquad (13)$$

where $S_T = A_c{}^2/2$ is the total power.

Subject to the condition $\Delta \gg 1$, Eq. (13) may be used whenever the PDF of $x(t)$ exists, at least in the sense of relative frequency of occurrence. The example and exercise below illustrate two applications involving a random and a nonrandom modulating signal, respectively.

Example 6.1   WBFM with Gaussian Modulation   ★

Let $x(t)$ be a gaussian random signal bandlimited in $W \ll f$ with $\bar{x} = 0$. Our usual convention $|x(t)| \leq 1$ cannot be applied but — recalling Chebyshev's inequality — we require that

$$\sigma_x = 1/\kappa$$

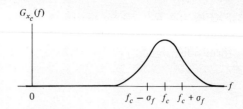

FIGURE 6.11
Power spectrum of WBFM with gaussian modulating signal, $f \geq 0$.

so Prob $[|x(t)| > 1] \leq 1/\kappa^2$ which can be made arbitrarily small by choice of κ. From Eq. (13), the power spectral density is

$$G_{x_c}(f) = \frac{S_T}{2\sqrt{2\pi}\,\sigma_f} [e^{-(f-f_c)^2/2\sigma_f^2} + e^{-(f+f_c)^2/2\sigma_f^2}] \qquad (14)$$

where

$$\sigma_f = f_\Delta \sigma_x = \frac{f_\Delta}{\kappa}$$

as sketched in Fig. 6.11 for $f > 0$.

Clearly, the bandwidth is not well-defined so, in a procedure similar to the above, we determine B_T by requiring that the power in the frequency range $f_c - B_T/2 \leq |f| \leq f_c + B_T/2$ equals $(1 - 1/\kappa^2)S_T$. This is equivalent to $B_T/2\sigma_f = \kappa$, and hence

$$B_T = 2\kappa\sigma_f = 2f_\Delta$$

An alternate bandwidth definition is explored in Prob. 6.15. ////

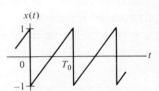

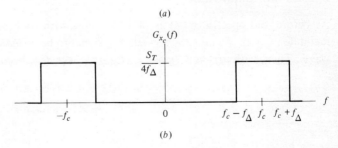

(a)

(b)

FIGURE 6.12

EXERCISE 6.4 Show that both of the deterministic periodic signals in Fig. 6.12a yield $G_{x_c}(f)$ in Fig. 6.12b providing $f_\Delta \gg 1/T_0$. (*Hint*: First justify that $p_x(x)$ is uniformly distributed.)

6.4 PHASE MODULATION (PM)

Phase and frequency modulation have many similarities. Consequently, our analysis of PM will be quite abbreviated, drawing heavily upon the FM results. Nonetheless, a subtle but significant difference might perhaps be noted at the start.

Recall that PM was defined as having the relative phase $\phi(t) = \phi_\Delta x(t)$, where ϕ_Δ is the phase deviation constant such that

$$-\phi_\Delta \leq \phi(t) \leq \phi_\Delta$$

since $|x(t)| \leq 1$. Consider now the demodulation of a PM wave: if ambiguities are to be avoided in demodulation, $\phi(t)$ must not exceed the range $\pm 180°$; after all, there is no physical distinction between phase angles of $+270°$ and $-90°$, for instance. Hence the deviation constant is constrained by

$$\phi_\Delta \leq \pi \qquad \text{radians} \qquad (1)$$

This restriction is directly analogous to the restriction $m \leq 1$ in AM, and ϕ_Δ can justly be called the phase modulation index.

A like constraint on the FM deviation constant f_Δ is not necessary because one can always distinguish $f_c + f_\Delta$ from $f_c - f_\Delta$ providing only that f_Δ is less than f_c. Therefore the FM deviation can be made as large as desired, going to higher carrier frequencies if necessary. Later it will be shown that the absolute limit on ϕ_Δ, as contrasted with the relative limit on f_Δ, accounts in part for the superiority of FM performance in the presence of noise.

Spectra and Bandwidth

As before, our spectral analysis of PM begins with tone modulation. However, to facilitate matters, we take the modulating signal to be a *sine* wave rather than a cosine wave. Then, with $x(t) = A_m \sin \omega_m t$, Eq. (5), Sect. 6.1, becomes

$$\begin{aligned} x_c(t) &= A_c \cos(\omega_c t + \phi_\Delta A_m \sin \omega_m t) \\ &= A_c \cos(\omega_c t + \beta_p \sin \omega_m t) \end{aligned} \qquad (2)$$

where

$$\beta_p \triangleq A_m \phi_\Delta \qquad (3)$$

The reason for using sine-wave modulation is now obvious if one compares Eq. (2) with the FM expression, Eq. (2), Sect. 6.2; they are identical save that β_p is independent of the tone frequency whereas β depends on both tone amplitude and frequency. Therefore, PM line spectra have the same general characteristics as FM, with the following exception: If the modulating frequency f_m is changed while holding the amplitude A_m fixed, β_p remains constant, and only the line *spacing* is altered. (Both line spacing and relative line amplitude would be affected in the FM case.) Thus, the left-hand side of Fig. 6.5 applies to PM as well as FM, while the right-hand side does not.

In connection with bandwidths, we could repeat the arguments of Sect. 6.3 with appropriate modifications. However, it is only necessary to note that $\Delta = f_\Delta / W$ is the *maximum phase deviation* of an FM wave under worst-case bandwidth conditions. This reveals that Δ and ϕ_Δ are equivalent parameters, since ϕ_Δ is the maximum phase deviation of a PM wave. Therefore, the transmission bandwidth for PM with arbitrary $x(t)$ is given by

$$B_T = 2M(\phi_\Delta)W \qquad M \geq 1 \qquad (4a)$$

or

$$B_T \approx 2(\phi_\Delta + 1)W \qquad (4b)$$

which is the approximation equivalent to Carson's rule. These expressions differ from the FM case in that ϕ_Δ is independent of W.

Narrowband Phase Modulation (NBPM)

Because of the constraint $\phi_\Delta \leq 180°$, there is no "wideband" PM in the same sense as WBFM. But NBPM, having $\phi_\Delta \ll 180°$, is both interesting and easy to handle analytically. With small phase deviation the PM wave becomes

$$x_c(t) \approx A_c \cos \omega_c t - A_c \phi_\Delta x(t) \sin \omega_c t \qquad (5a)$$

as follows from Eq. (9a), Sect. 6.3, with $\phi(t) = \phi_\Delta x(t)$. The spectrum is then

$$X_c(f) = \frac{A_c}{2} [\delta(f - f_c) + \delta(f + f_c)] + \frac{jA_c \phi_\Delta}{2} [X(f - f_c) - X(f + f_c)] \qquad (5b)$$

and $B_T = 2W$, as expected.

Comparing the NBPM spectrum with that of AM shows that the similarities are even more pronounced than those of NBFM. Moreover, it appears from Eq. (5) that NBPM is a *linear* modulation process, at least approximately, and can be generated using linear modulation devices. Specifically, a balanced modulator together with a quadrature phase shifter can produce NBPM when arranged as diagramed in Fig. 6.13.

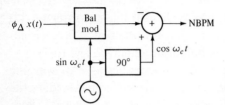

FIGURE 6.13
Narrowband phase modulator constructed using a balanced modulator.

Because NBPM is generated with relative ease, it forms the core of many FM modulation systems, an integrator being tacked on the input to produce frequency rather than phase modulation. This and other modulators are described in the next section.

EXERCISE 6.5   Show that the phase at the output of Fig. 6.13 is more precisely given by

$$\phi(t) = \phi_\Delta x(t) - \frac{\phi_\Delta^3}{3} x^3(t) + \frac{\phi_\Delta^5}{5} x^5(t) - \cdots \qquad (6)$$

so there is distortion at all odd harmonics unless ϕ_Δ is very small.

6.5   TRANSMITTERS AND RECEIVERS

When discussing the equipment used for exponential modulation systems, one should keep in mind that the instantaneous phase or frequency varies linearly with the message waveform. Devices are thus required that produce or are sensitive to phase or frequency variation in a linear fashion. Such characteristics can be approximated in a variety of ways, but it is sometimes difficult to obtain a suitably linear relationship over a wide operating range.

On the other hand, the constant-amplitude property of exponential modulation is a definite advantage from the hardware viewpoint. For one thing, the designer need not worry about excessive power dissipation or high-voltage breakdown due to extreme peaks in the waveform. But more important, nonlinear amplitude distortion has virtually no effect on message transmission since the information resides in the zero crossings of the wave and not in the amplitude. (Phase-shift or delay distortion is of course intolerable.) It likewise follows that any spurious amplitude variations can be eliminated by peak-clipping devices, called *limiters*, without removing the message. Consequently, considerable latitude is possible in the design and selection of equipment. As a case in point, the microwave repeater links of long-distance telephone communications use FM primarily because the wideband linear amplifiers required for amplitude modulation are unavailable at microwave frequencies.

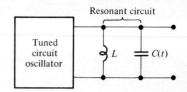

FIGURE 6.14
Direct FM using variable reactance.

Turning specifically to FM, there are two basic generation methods, known as the *direct* and *indirect* systems. We shall examine these one at a time and then take up the subject of FM demodulation. The presentations are largely in block-diagram form; the interested student is referred to the literature† for specific circuit realizations and further detailed analyses.

Direct Frequency Modulation

Conceptually, direct FM is straightforward and requires nothing more than a *voltage-controlled oscillator* (VCO) whose oscillation frequency has a linear dependence on applied voltage. This is readily implemented in the microwave band ($f_c \geq 1$ GHz), where devices such as the klystron tube have linear VCO characteristics over a substantial frequency range, typically several megahertz. If a lower carrier frequency is desired, the modulated signal can be down-converted by heterodyning with the output of a fixed-frequency oscillator. Some laboratory test generators use precisely this technique.

Alternately, for lower carrier frequencies, it is possible to modulate a conventional tuned-circuit oscillator by introducing a *variable-reactance* element as part of the LC parallel resonant circuit, Fig. 6.14. If the capacitance has a time dependence of the form

$$C(t) = C_0 - Cx(t)$$

and if $Cx(t)$ is "small enough" and "slow enough," then the oscillator's output is $A_c \cos \theta_c(t)$ where

$$\frac{d\theta_c(t)}{dt} = \frac{1}{\sqrt{LC(t)}} = \frac{1}{\sqrt{LC_0}} \left[1 - \frac{C}{C_0} x(t) \right]^{-1/2} \tag{1}$$

Letting $\omega_c = 1/\sqrt{LC_0}$ and assuming $|(C/C_0)x(t)| \ll 1$, the binomial series expansion gives $d\theta_c(t)/dt \approx \omega_c[1 + (C/2C_0)x(t)]$, or

$$\theta_c(t) \approx 2\pi f_c t + 2\pi \frac{C}{2C_0} f_c \int_{-\infty}^{t} x(\lambda)\, d\lambda \tag{2}$$

† Clarke and Hess (1971, chaps. 11 and 12), etc.

which is frequency modulation with $f_\Delta = (C/2C_0)f_c$—see Eq. (7), Sect. 6.1. Since $|x(t)| \leq 1$, the approximation is good to within 1 percent when $C/C_0 < 0.013$ so the attainable frequency deviation is limited by

$$f_\Delta = \frac{C}{2C_0} f_c \leq 0.006 f_c \qquad (3)$$

This limitation quantifies our meaning of $Cx(t)$ being "small" and it seldom imposes a design hardship. Similarly, the usual condition $W \ll f_c$ ensures that $Cx(t)$ is "slow enough."

The variable reactance can be obtained in numerous ways. The workhorse of early direct FM modulators was the reactance tube, a pentode biased such that its output impedance contains a capacitive term proportional to grid voltage. Other modulators use Miller effect capacitance, saturable-reactor elements, or the diode reactance of varactors.

The principal advantage of direct FM is that large frequency deviations are possible without additional operations. The major disadvantage is that the carrier frequency tends to drift and must be stabilized by rather elaborate feedback frequency control. Because satisfactory stabilization techniques have emerged only recently, many older FM transmitters are of the indirect type.

Indirect Frequency Modulation

The heart of indirect FM is a *narrowband phase modulator* whose carrier frequency is supplied by a stable source, usually a crystal-controlled oscillator, to ensure stability. Figure 6.15 shows the parts of a complete indirect system as conceived by Armstrong (1936). The functions are as follows.

Prior to modulation the message is integrated so as to yield frequency rather than phase modulation. The phase modulator itself may be as shown in Fig. 6.13 or a variety of other types. In any case the resulting NBFM often contains inherent *distortion* (as demonstrated in Exercise 6.5) unless the deviation ratio $\Delta_1 = f_{\Delta_1}/W$ is very small. It is therefore necessary to increase the deviation ratio after modulation, this being accomplished by a chain of frequency doublers and triplers forming a *frequency multiplier*.

An ideal frequency multiplier operates on instantaneous frequency such that if $f_{c_1} + f_{\Delta_1} x(t)$ is the input, n-fold multiplication produces $f_{c_2} + f_{\Delta_2} x(t) = n f_{c_1} + n f_{\Delta_1} x(t)$. Note that this is a subtle process, affecting the *range* of frequency variation but not the *rate*. Multiplication of a tone-modulated signal, for example, increases the carrier frequency and the modulation index but not the modulating frequency; thus the relative amplitudes of the sideband lines are altered, but the line spacing remains the same.

Returning to Fig. 6.15, n is chosen to give the desired final deviation, namely,

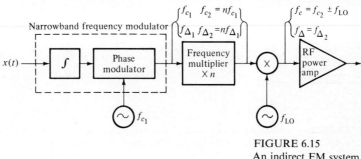

FIGURE 6.15
An indirect FM system.

$n = f_\Delta/f_{\Delta_1} = \Delta/\Delta_1$. But this multiplication factor usually results in f_{c_2} being much higher than the desired carrier frequency. Heterodyning the multiplier output with a second crystal-controlled oscillator translates the spectrum *intact* to the proper location. (Usually, the heterodyning is done in the middle of the multiplier chain to keep the center frequencies from getting too high.) All these steps are done at low power levels, so the final system component is an RF power amplifier of sufficient bandwidth but whose linearity is not crucial.

By way of illustration with representative values, an early indirect transmitter for commercial FM has $f_{c_1} = 200$ kHz and $f_{\Delta_1} = 25$ Hz. With $W = 15$ kHz, the initial deviation ratio is $\Delta_1 = 25/(15 \times 10^3) \approx 2 \times 10^{-3}$, this minute value being required to minimize distortion and guarantee good fidelity. Since the final deviation is to be $f_\Delta = 75$ kHz, the multiplication factor needed is $n = 75 \times 10^3/25 = 3,000$, which entails six triplers and two doublers. After multiplication, the spectrum is located at $f_{c_2} = 3,000 \times 200 \text{ kHz} = 600$ MHz, so the second oscillator must have $f_{LO} \approx 600 \pm 100$ MHz to bring the carrier down to the FM band of 88 to 108 MHz.

These calculations indicate that although indirect FM gets around the frequency-stability problem, it is not without difficulties, principally that of the multiplication factor. Indeed, broadband multipliers of the requisite phase characteristics are just as complex as the frequency-control circuits of direct FM, and the latter have been greatly improved by the development of digital counters. Consequently, there is a trend back to direct FM with modest amounts of frequency multiplication for high-quality large-deviation transmitters.

Limiters

A limiter is a nonlinear device that removes spurious amplitude variations from an exponentially modulated wave without destroying the modulation. As such, it finds a place in both FM transmitters and receivers.

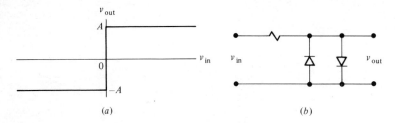

FIGURE 6.16
Limiter. (*a*) Ideal transfer characteristic; (*b*) circuit realization.

Figure 6.16*a* gives the transfer characteristic of an ideal *hard limiter*, while Fig. 6.16*b* is a simple circuit realization thereof. Since the voltage across a semiconductor diode in the forward direction flattens off at about 1 V as soon as the diode begins to conduct strongly, the output voltage is clipped rectangularly when the input amplitude exceeds that level. Clearly, if the input is an unmodulated sinusoid whose amplitude is several volts, the output will be essentially a square wave. More generally,

$$v_{out}(t) = A \operatorname{sgn} v_{in}(t) = \begin{cases} +A & v_{in}(t) > 0 \\ -A & v_{out}(t) < 0 \end{cases} \tag{4}$$

assuming an ideal hard limiter.

Suppose then that $v_{in}(t)$ is an FM or PM wave with amplitude variations, say $v_{in}(t) = A_c(t) \cos \theta_c(t)$ where we assume that $A_c(t) > 1$. Although $v_{in}(t)$ is not necessarily periodic, v_{out} may be viewed as a *periodic function of* θ_c—namely, a square wave with amplitude A and period 2π. Thus, from Eq. (17), Sect. 2.2, we can write the trigonometric Fourier series expansion

$$v_{out} = \frac{4A}{\pi} \left[\cos \theta_c - \frac{1}{3} \cos 3\theta_c + \frac{1}{5} \cos 5\theta_c - \cdots \right] \tag{5}$$

Substituting $\theta_c(t) = \omega_c t + \phi(t)$ yields

$$v_{out}(t) = \frac{4A}{\pi} \left\{ \cos \left[\omega_c t + \phi(t) \right] - \frac{1}{3} \cos \left[3\omega_c t + 3\phi(t) \right] + \cdots \right\} \tag{6}$$

which is a phase- or frequency-modulated square wave.

Inspecting Eq. (6) shows that a bandpass filter of suitable bandwidth centered at f_c will extract the first term, a *constant-amplitude* modulated signal. Limiters built for use in receivers normally have such a filter as an integral part. On the other hand, if the BPF is centered at $3f_c$ or $5f_c$, we have achieved frequency multiplication as well

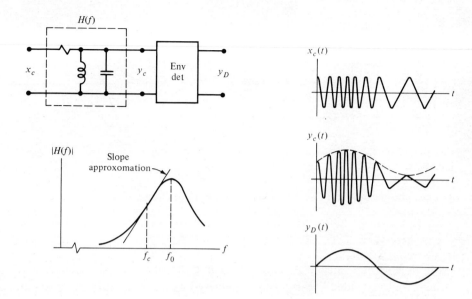

FIGURE 6.17
FM slope detection, circuit and waveforms.

as amplitude limiting, which would be useful for transmitters. Observe that the multiplication factor affects both the carrier frequency and the relative phase, as discussed previously.

FM Detection—Frequency Discriminators

An FM demodulator, or *frequency discriminator*, must produce an output voltage linearly dependent on input frequency. Slightly above or below resonance, a simple tuned circuit plus envelope detector has this property over a limited range. This is called *slope detection* and is illustrated in Fig. 6.17. For a qualitative analysis† of slope detection, suppose $x_c(t)$ is tone-modulated and f_c is less than f_0. Then, as $f(t)$ swings above or below f_c, the amplitude ratio of the tuned circuit converts the frequency variation to an amplitude variation on top of the FM signal, yielding the waveform $y_c(t)$. Extracting only the amplitude variation with an envelope detector (plus DC block) produces $y_D(t)$ and completes the demodulation.

There are two problems with slope detection as described above: the detector also responds to spurious amplitude variations of the input FM, and the range of

---

† Quantitative analysis of circuit response to time-varying frequency is a difficult matter. Baghdady (1960, chap. 19) presents a concise discussion of the problem and methods of solution.

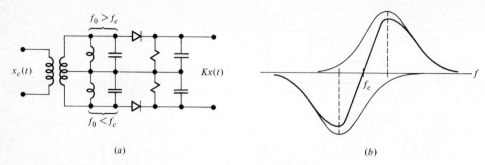

FIGURE 6.18
Balanced discriminator. (*a*) Circuit; (*b*) frequency-to-voltage characteristic.

linear slope is quite small. A limiter preceding the tuned circuit takes care of the former, while extended linearity can be achieved by using the *balanced* configuration of Fig. 6.18*a*. A balanced discriminator has two resonant circuits, one tuned above f_c and the other below. Thus, as $f(t)$ changes, the amplitude variations are in opposite directions, and taking the difference of these variations gives the frequency-to-voltage characteristic of Fig. 6.18*b*, the well-known S curve. The DC component is automatically canceled, bypassing the need for a DC block and thereby improving response to low modulating frequencies. However, an input limiter is still necessary.

Balanced discriminators are often employed as the frequency-sensing element in automatic frequency control, which has many applications aside from exponential modulation systems. They are readily adapted to the microwave band, with resonant cavities serving as tuned circuits and crystal diodes for envelope detectors. Other common FM demodulators are the *Foster-Seeley phase-shift discriminator* and the *ratio detector*, whose descriptions can be found in texts on radio electronics. The ratio detector is particularly ingenious and economical, for it combines the operations of limiting and demodulating into one unit. For specialized applications, the *phase-lock* or *frequency-lock loop* may be used; a relative of these, the FMFB receiver is discussed in Sect. 7.5.

Before leaving the subject of demodulation, it must be pointed out that any device whose output is the *time derivative* of the input will perform an FM-to-AM conversion and therefore can be used to detect FM. That this should be the case follows from the differentiation theorem $dv/dt \leftrightarrow j2\pi f V(f)$, so a differentiator has a linear frequency-to-amplitude characteristic. Specifically, if $x_c(t) = A_c \cos \theta_c(t)$, then

$$\frac{dx_c(t)}{dt} = -A_c \frac{d\theta_c(t)}{dt} \sin \theta_c(t)$$

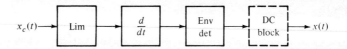

FIGURE 6.19
Frequency discriminator using FM-to-AM conversion by differentiation.

But from Eq. (7), Sect. 6.1, $d\theta_c/dt = 2\pi[f_c + f_\Delta x(t)]$, so

$$\frac{dx_c(t)}{dt} = -2\pi A_c[f_c + f_\Delta x(t)] \sin \theta_c(t) \qquad (7)$$

a waveform having both amplitude and frequency modulation. Figure 6.19 diagrams a frequency discriminator (with limiter) based on Eq. (7). Unlike the balanced discriminator, this system would have a poor low-frequency response.

Example 6.2   FM Detection Using a Delay Line

Equation (7) suggests yet another way of detecting frequency modulation drawing upon the fundamental definition of differentiation,

$$\frac{dv(t)}{dt} = \lim_{\epsilon \to 0} \frac{1}{\epsilon} [v(t) - v(t - \epsilon)]$$

Thus,

$$\frac{dx_c(t)}{dt} \approx \frac{1}{\tau} [x_c(t) - x_c(t - \tau)] \qquad (8)$$

so differentiation can be approximated using a delay line arranged per Fig. 6.20. Implementation is not particularly difficult since the approximation requires that τ be small compared to the time variations of $x_c(t)$, i.e., $\tau \ll 1/f_c$. The Foster-Seeley and ratio detectors are based on this idea but use the nearly linear phase shift of a resonant circuit to achieve the time delay.   ////

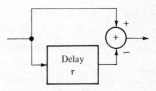

FIGURE 6.20
Delay line approximation for a differentiator.

FM Receivers

Most FM receivers are of the superheterodyne variety. They differ from Fig. 5.32 in two respects: a limiter-discriminator (or ratio detector) replaces the envelope detector, and automatic frequency control (AFC) is provided to correct for frequency drift of the LO. Commercial FM radios have a tuning range of 88 to 108 MHz, $f_{IF} = 10.7$ MHz, and an IF bandwidth of 200 to 300 kHz. Thus the fractional bandwidth of the IF amplifier is about 2×10^{-2}, the same as for AM superheterodynes.

There is a third difference between FM and AM receivers, in that an FM receiver may have a *deemphasis filter* at the output. The purpose of this filter will be explained in our treatment of interference and noise in exponential modulation systems.

6.6 PROBLEMS

6.1   (Sect. 6.1) Sketch and fully label $\phi(t)$ and $f(t)$ for a PM and FM wave when the modulating signal is a triangular pulse, $x(t) = A\Lambda(t/\tau)$.

6.2   (Sect. 6.1) A frequency-sweep generator produces a sinusoidal output whose frequency is f_1 at $t = 0$ and increases linearly to f_2 at $t = T$. Obtain an expression for the output in the form $\cos \theta(t)$. *Ans.*: $\theta(t) = 2\pi[f_1 t + (f_2 - f_1)t^2/2T]$.

6.3   (Sect. 6.1) Two other possible forms of exponential modulation are phase-integral modulation, where $\phi(t) = K\, dx(t)/dt$, and phase-acceleration modulation, where $f(t) = K \int^t x(\lambda)\, d\lambda$. Add these to Table 6.1 and find the maximum values of $\phi(t)$ and $f(t)$ for all four types when $x(t) = \cos 2\pi f_m t$.

6.4   (Sect. 6.2) Using Eqs. (5) and (6), carry out all the details between Eqs. (4) and (7a).

6.5   (Sect. 6.2) Construct phasor diagrams for tone-modulated FM with $\beta = 1.0$ when $\omega_m t = 0$, $\pi/4$, and $\pi/2$. Include at least three sideband pairs, and verify that the resultant phase shift is correct and that the amplitude is constant.

6.6   (Sect. 6.2) A tone-modulated FM signal with $\beta = 1.0$ and $f_m = 200$ is passed through an ideal BPF with $B = 500$ centered on f_c. Draw the line spectrum and phasor diagram of the output signal and describe what would be observed if the waveform is displayed on an oscilloscope.

6.7   (Sect. 6.2) The carrier-frequency component of a tone-modulated FM signal is zero whenever $J_0(\beta) = 0$. Using this property, devise an experimental procedure for calibrating the deviation characteristics of an FM modulator.

6.8★ (Sect. 6.2) Apply Eq. (10) to the case where $x(t)$ is a unit-amplitude square wave. Write $x_c(t)$ as a sum of sinusoids, and sketch the amplitude spectrum taking $f_\Delta \gg 1/T_0$.

6.9   (Sect. 6.3) A message has $W = 10$ kHz. Find the FM transmission bandwidth when $f_\Delta = 0.1$, 1.0, 10, 100, and 1,000 kHz. In each case select the appropriate relationship from Eqs. (5), (6), and (7).

6.10 (Sect. 6.3) An FM system has $f_\Delta = 10$ kHz. Calculate B_T for:

(*a*) Barely intelligible voice transmission.

(*b*) Telephone-quality voice transmission.

(*c*) High-fidelity audio transmission.

(*Hint*: Use Table 4.2 and choose the appropriate curve in Fig. 6.10 for each case.)

6.11 (Sect. 6.3) An analog data signal with $W = 2$ kHz is to be sent via FM on a system with $B_T = 12$ kHz. If high-fidelity reproduction is desired, what is the maximum permitted value of f_Δ? *Ans.*: 1.9 kHz.

6.12★(Sect. 6.3) Certain FDM telemetry systems use *proportional-bandwidth* FM subcarrier modulation in which the parameters of the ith channel are related by $f_{\Delta_i} = af_{c_i} = W_i/b$, where a and b are constants.

(*a*) Show that B_{T_i}, the bandwidth of the ith subcarrier signal, is proportional to f_{c_i}, assuming Carson's rule is applicable.

(*b*) Obtain a lower bound on f_{c_i} in terms of f_{c_1}, a, and b.

(*Hint*: To avoid sideband overlapping, it is necessary that $f_{c_i} - B_{T_i}/2 \geq f_{c_{i-1}} + B_{T_{i-1}}/2$.)

6.13 (Sect. 6.3) Derive Eq. (9*b*) starting from (9*a*).

6.14 (Sect. 6.3) If Θ is a random angle uniformly distributed over 2π radians and $X = A \cos \Theta$, it can be shown that $p_x(x) = [\pi\sqrt{A^2 - x^2}]^{-1}\Pi(x/2A)$. Use this fact and Eq. (13) to find $G_{x_c}(f)$ when $x(t) = \cos 2\pi f_m t$, $f_m \ll f_\Delta$. Sketch $G_{x_c}(f)$ for $f > 0$ and compare with Fig. 6.5.

6.15★(Sect. 6.3) The *rms bandwidth* of a bandpass signal centered on f_c is defined by $B_{rms}^2 = (8/S_T)\int_0^\infty (f - f_c)^2 G_{x_c}(f)\, df$.

(*a*) Assuming Eq. (13) applies, show that this reduces to $B_{rms} = 2f_\Delta \sigma_x$ when $f_c \gg f_\Delta$ and $\bar{x} = 0$.

(*b*) Find B_{rms} for a gaussian modulating signal normalized such that Prob $[|x(t)| > 1] = 0.2$.

6.16 (Sect. 6.4) Tone modulation is applied simultaneously to an FM and PM modulator and the output line spectra are identical. How will these spectra change, in general, if: the tone frequency is increased or decreased; the tone amplitude is increased or decreased?

6.17 (Sect. 6.4) If $W = 10$ kHz, approximately what percentage of B_T is occupied when the modulating signal is a unit-amplitude tone at $f_m = 0.1$, 1.0, or 5.0 kHz and the modulation is FM with $f_\Delta = 30$ kHz? Repeat for PM with $\phi_\Delta = 3$ and compare.

6.18 (Sect. 6.4) Analyze the properties of phase-integral modulation and phase-acceleration modulation defined in Prob. 6.3, giving particular attention to their line spectra and bandwidth requirements.

6.19 (Sect. 6.5) When a sinusoid at frequency f_c is applied to a linear system with a time-varying component whose variations are "slow" compared to f_c, one can use a *quasi-steady-state* AC analysis to approximate the output by writing the transfer function as $H(f_c,t)$, where the time dependence reflects the time-varying component. Use this approach to analyze the RC phase modulator in Fig. P6.1 where $R(t) = R_0 - Rx(t)$ with $R \ll R_0$ and $\omega_c R_0 C \gg 1$. Estimate the maximum phase deviation that can be achieved without significant distortion in $x_c(t)$.

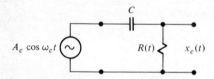

FIGURE P6.1.

6.20 (Sect. 6.5) Figure P6.2 is a direct FM generator using a *voltage-controlled oscillator* (VCO). The VCO output has $d\theta(t)/dt = 2\pi[f_0 + K_1 v(t) + \epsilon(t)]$, where $v(t)$ is the input (control) voltage and $\epsilon(t)$ is a random frequency drift. To combat the drift, the output is mixed with a stable oscillator and fed back through a discriminator whose output voltage is $K_2[\cancel{f}_{in}(t) - f_{IF}]$. Assuming $x(t)$ has $\bar{x} = 0$ and is bandlimited in W, while $\epsilon(t)$ is bandlimited in $W_\epsilon \ll W$, show that this arrangement reduces the drift by a factor of $1/(1 + K_1 K_2)$. Why is it necessary that $\bar{x} = 0$?

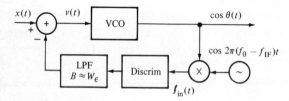

FIGURE P6.2.

6.21 (Sect. 6.5) An integrator is added to Fig. 6.13 so the input to the balanced modulator becomes $\phi_\Delta \int^t x(\lambda)\, d\lambda$, $\phi_\Delta \ll \pi$.
   (a) Show that the output has $\cancel{f}(t) \approx f_\Delta x(t)\{1 - [\phi_\Delta \int^t x(\lambda)\, d\lambda]^2\}$, where $f_\Delta = \phi_\Delta / 2\pi$.
   (b) Taking $x(t) = \cos 2\pi f_m t$, show that $\cancel{f}(t)$ has third-harmonic distortion with a relative amplitude of approximately $(f_\Delta / 2f_m)^2$.
   (c) Give a brief physical explanation why the *lowest* modulating frequency suffers the most distortion.

6.22 (Sect. 6.5) A multiplexed baseband signal whose spectrum covers 100 to 2,500 kHz is to be transmitted with FM carrier modulation. Using the information in Prob. 6.21, design an indirect FM transmitter with the following specifications: $f_c = 10$ GHz, $\Delta = 2$, third-harmonic distortion less than 10 percent.

6.23★(Sect. 6.5) An indirect FM transmitter is to be designed for $f_c = 10$ MHz and $f_\Delta = 12$ kHz. The message has $W = 4$ kHz. The multiplier chain will consist of six triplers, each being a hard limiter followed by a BPF. Each BPF must satisfy the fractional-bandwidth constraint of Eq. (15), Sect. 5.1, but their bandwidths may be greater than the signal bandwidth at any point as long as unwanted signals are rejected. Draw a complete diagram of the transmitter, specifying values for f_{Δ_1}, f_{c_1}, and f_{LO}, and bandwidths and center frequencies of the BPFs. Locate the mixer/LO such that no frequency exceeds 12 MHz.

6.24 (Sect. 6.5) The quasi-steady-state AC approximation mentioned in Prob. 6.19 can be modified to find the response of a filter to an FM input signal having $|\dot{f}(t)| \ll f_c$. One simply views the input as a sinusoid at frequency $f_c + \dot{f}(t)$ so the transfer function becomes $H[f_c + \dot{f}(t)]$. Taking this approach, show that an RC LPF with $B = f_c$ can replace the tuned circuit in Fig. 6.17 providing that sign inversion of the modulating signal is acceptable.

6.25★(Sect. 6.5) The tuned circuit in Fig. 6.17 has $H(f) \approx [1 + j(2Q/f_0)(f - f_0)]^{-1}$ for $f > 0$, where $Q = R\sqrt{C/L} \gg 1$ and $f_0 = 1/2\pi\sqrt{LC}$.

(a) Show that the slope of $|H(f)|$ is maximum at $f_0 - f_0/2\sqrt{2}Q$.

(b) Use the method of Prob. 6.24 to approximate $y_c(t)$, assuming f_c is at the maximum-slope point.

6.26★(Sect. 6.5) Devise and analyze an automatic frequency control (AFC) system for an FM superheterodyne receiver using a VCO (Prob. 6.20) having $f_0 = f_c - f_{IF}$ in place of the LO.

7

NOISE IN CW MODULATION

Following the discussion of the two classes of CW modulation, this chapter covers the performance of CW communication systems in the presence of additive noise. Thus, we focus here on *bandpass* transmission as contrasted with baseband transmission. However, many of the baseband concepts introduced in Chap. 4 will be applied to the bandpass case.

Specific topics at hand include system models and parameters, interference, bandpass noise, and signal-to-noise ratios. The chapter culminates in a comparison of the several types of linear and exponential modulation with each other and with baseband transmission.

7.1 SYSTEM MODELS AND PARAMETERS

Figure 7.1 diagrams the general form of a CW communication system. As before, the message $x(t)$ is taken to be an analog signal of bandwidth W with $|x(t)| \le 1$ and $\overline{x^2} \le 1$. We assume the transmitter is ideal and the channel gives nearly distortionless

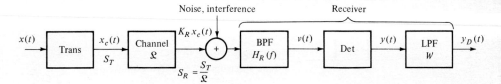

FIGURE 7.1
CW communication system.

transmission† over the transmission bandwidth B_T, with power loss $\mathscr{L}$ and negligible time delay. We further assume that the predetection portion of the receiver may be modeled as a bandpass filter $H_R(f)$ having unit gain over $B_R \geq B_T$. In a superheterodyne receiver, $H_R(f)$ is the frequency response of the IF amplifier referred (translated) to the carrier frequency — see Fig. 5.33d.

Under these conditions, and momentarily ignoring any interference or additive noise, the signal at the detector input is

$$v(t) = K_R x_c(t) \qquad (1)$$

where

$$K_R \triangleq \frac{1}{\sqrt{\mathscr{L}}} \qquad (2)$$

Similarly, $A_R \triangleq K_R A_c$ is the carrier amplitude at the input to the detector. Then, in terms of the transmitted power S_T,

$$\langle v^2(t) \rangle = K_R{}^2 \langle x_c{}^2(t) \rangle = \frac{S_T}{\mathscr{L}} = S_R \qquad (3)$$

S_R being the received power. Expressions for $x_c(t)$, S_T, and B_T have been developed in Chaps. 5 and 6 for the various types of modulation.

Although a clean, virtually noise-free wave may be transmitted, the signal delivered to the demodulator is always accompanied by noise, including that generated in preceding stages of the receiver itself. Furthermore, there may be *interfering* signals in the desired band that are not rejected by $H_R(f)$. Both noise and interference give rise to undesired components at the detector output. When interference or noise is included, we will write the contaminated signal $v(t)$ in envelope-and-phase or quadrature-carrier form, namely,

$$v(t) = R_v(t) \cos\left[\omega_c t + \phi_v(t)\right] \qquad (4a)$$

$$= v_i(t) \cos \omega_c t - v_q(t) \sin \omega_c t \qquad (4b)$$

† Otherwise, equalization would be required. Generally, such equalizers must be bandpass units located before the detector since detection is a nonlinear operation. One exception is the case of synchronous detection where baseband equalization may be used.

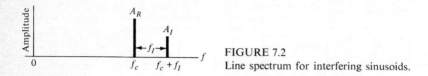

FIGURE 7.2
Line spectrum for interfering sinusoids.

which facilitates analysis of the demodulated signal $y(t)$. Specifically, the demodulation operation is represented by the following idealized mathematical models:†

$$
y(t) = \begin{cases} v_i(t) & \text{Synchronous detector} & (5a) \\ R_v(t) - \bar{R}_v & \text{Envelope detector} & (5b) \\ \phi_v(t) & \text{Phase detector} & (5c) \\ \dfrac{1}{2\pi} \dfrac{d\phi_v(t)}{dt} & \text{Frequency detector} & (5d) \end{cases}
$$

output of detector

The term $\bar{R}_v = \langle R_v(t) \rangle$ in Eq. (5b) reflects the DC block normally found in an envelope detector; the other detectors may or may not have this feature. A detection constant could be included in Eq. (5) but adds nothing in the way of generality.

Note, however, that $y(t)$ does not necessarily equal the final output signal $y_D(t)$ at the destination since Fig. 7.1 has a lowpass filter following the detector. Therefore, assuming the LPF merely removes any out-of-band frequency components,

Final output e destination

$$
y_D(t) = \int_{-W}^{W} Y(f) e^{j\omega t} \, df \qquad (6)
$$

where $Y(f) = \mathscr{F}[y(t)]$. This operation is termed *postdetection* filtering, as distinguished from the bandpass *predetection* filtering performed by $H_R(f)$.

Finally, when we come to additive noise, we will assume it to be zero-mean white noise with spectral density $G(f) = \eta/2$ at the input to $H_R(f)$. Thus, there is additive *bandpass* noise at the detector input. Section 7.3 develops the representation of bandpass noise subsequently employed in Sects. 7.4 and 7.5 to find $(S/N)_D$, the destination signal-to-noise ratio. Paving the way for those topics is our discussion of interference.

7.2 INTERFERENCE

We begin by considering a very simple case, an unmodulated carrier with an interfering cosine wave (Fig. 7.2). Let the interference have amplitude A_I and frequency $f_c + f_I$. The total signal entering the demodulator is the sum of two sinusoids

$$
v(t) = A_R \cos \omega_c t + A_I \cos (\omega_c + \omega_I) t
$$

† Idealized in the sense of perfect synchronization, perfect amplitude limiting, etc.

FIGURE 7.3
Phasor diagram for interfering sinusoids.

so

$$R_v(t) = \sqrt{(A_R + A_I \cos \omega_I t)^2 + (A_I \sin \omega_I t)^2}$$

$$\phi_v(t) = \arctan \frac{A_I \sin \omega_I t}{A_R + A_I \cos \omega_I t} \tag{1}$$

as follows from the phasor construction of Fig. 7.3.

For arbitrary values of A_R and A_I, these expressions cannot be further simplified. However, if the interference is small compared to the carrier, the phasor diagram shows that the resultant envelope is essentially the sum of the in-phase components, while the quadrature component determines the phase angle. That is, if $A_I \ll A_R$, then

$$R_v(t) \approx A_R + A_I \cos \omega_I t \tag{2a}$$

$$\phi_v(t) \approx \frac{A_I}{A_R} \sin \omega_I t \tag{2b}$$

and hence

$$v(t) = A_R(1 + m_I \cos \omega_I t) \cos (\omega_c t + m_I \sin \omega_I t) \tag{3}$$

where

$$m_I \triangleq \frac{A_I}{A_R} \ll 1$$

The same result is obtained from first-order expansions of Eq. (1).

At the other extreme, if $A_I \gg A_R$, the analysis is performed by taking the interference as the reference and decomposing the carrier phasor, which gives $v(t) = A_I(1 + m_I^{-1} \cos \omega_I t) \cos [(\omega_c + \omega_I)t - m_I^{-1} \sin \omega_I t]$, as might be expected.

We see from Eq. (3) that the interfering wave *amplitude-modulates and phase-modulates* a carrier just like a modulating tone of frequency f_I with modulation index m_I. On the other hand, with strong interference, we can consider the carrier to be modulating the interfering wave. In either case, the apparent modulation frequency is the difference frequency f_I.

EXERCISE 7.1   Consider the case of interference caused by reflections from a low-altitude aircraft such that $A_I \approx A_R$ and $f_I = v f_c / c$ where v is the relative velocity and c the speed of light. Show that $R_v(t) = 2 A_R |\cos(\pi v f_c t/c)|$.

Interference in Linear Modulation

Suppose there is small amplitude interference in an AM system with envelope detection. Using Eq. (2a), this section, plus Eqs. (5b) and (6), Sect. 7.1, the output signal becomes

$$y_D(t) = \begin{cases} A_I \cos \omega_I t & |f_I| < W \\ 0 & |f_I| > W \end{cases} \tag{4}$$

since $\bar{R}_v = A_R$. Similarly, for synchronous detection,

$$y_D(t) = A_R + A_I \cos \omega_I t \qquad |f_I| < W \tag{5}$$

since $v_i(t) = A_R + A_I \cos \omega_I t$ — see Fig. 7.3. The DC component in Eq. (5) may or may not be blocked. In either case, any interference in the band $f_c \pm W$ produces a detected signal whose amplitude depends only on A_I, the interference amplitude, providing $A_I \ll A_R$.

The reader may well wonder why we bother with this simple problem whose results are almost obvious by inspection. The reason is twofold: first, as might be inferred from Eq. (1), the complications rapidly multiply when the interference is large or the carrier is modulated; second, some interesting and significant differences occur in exponential modulation.

Interference in Exponential Modulation

With a phase or frequency detector, the detected interference is found by inserting Eq. (2b), this section, into Eqs. (5c) and (5d), Sect. 7.1. Thus, for $|f_I| < W$,

$$y_D(t) = \frac{A_I}{A_R} \sin \omega_I t \qquad \text{PM} \tag{6}$$

$$y_D(t) = \frac{A_I f_I}{A_R} \cos \omega_I t \qquad \text{FM} \tag{7}$$

where f_I appears as a multiplying factor in Eq. (7) but not Eq. (6) because of the differentiation of $\phi_y(t)$.

Comparing Eqs. (6) and (7) with Eqs. (4) and (5), together with the fact that $A_I / A_R \ll 1$, one finds that exponential modulation is less vulnerable to small-amplitude interference than linear modulation, all other factors being equal. Moreover, from

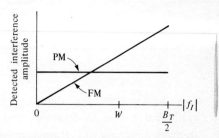

FIGURE 7.4
Detected interference amplitude as a function of $|f_I|$ for an interfering wave of frequency $f_c + f_I$.

Eqs. (6) and (7), FM is less vulnerable than PM when $|f_I|$ is small since the detected interference is proportional to both the amplitude and frequency of the interfering wave. In PM systems, like linear modulation, only the amplitude enters the picture.

This latter difference can be understood with the aid of simple physical considerations. The strength of a detected signal in FM depends on the maximum *frequency deviation*. Interfering waves close to the carrier frequency cannot cause significant change in the frequency of the resultant and therefore produce little effect. The greater the difference between f_c and $f_c + f_I$, the greater the frequency deviation, so we can expect the demodulated output to be proportional to $|f_I|$. But for PM the maximum *phase deviation* depends only on relative amplitudes, as shown by the phasor diagram of Fig. 7.3.

The performance of FM and PM with respect to interference is best displayed by plotting the amplitude of the *unfiltered* signal $y(t)$ as a function of $|f_I|$, Fig. 7.4. Of course $y_D(t) = y(t)$ for $|f_I| < W$, but $y(t)$ includes frequencies at least up to $B_T/2$ since $H_R(f)$ passes $f_c \pm B_T/2$ (assuming $B_R \approx B_T$) and $B_T/2$ generally exceeds W with exponential modulation. Figure 7.4 illustrates that when the interference is due to a *cochannel*† station, then $f_c + f_I \approx f_c$, $|f_I|$ is small, and FM clearly is less vulnerable. Conversely, PM has better performance with respect to *adjacent-channel* interference, where $|f_I|$ is relatively large. In either case, a lowpass filter of bandwidth W should follow the demodulator to eliminate detected interference components that are outside of the message band but not rejected by the predetection filter, i.e., interference at $W < |f_I| < B_T/2$. Such postdetection filtering is desirable but not a necessity in linear modulation systems because the transmission bandwidth is no greater than $2W$.

Deemphasis and Preemphasis Filtering

The fact that detected FM interference is most severe at large values of $|f_I|$ suggests a method for improving system performance with selective postdetection filtering, called *deemphasis filtering*.

---

† *Cochannel* and *adjacent-channel* refer to stations having the same or adjacent carrier-frequency assignments. Cochannel interference also comes from image frequencies.

FIGURE 7.5
Complete FM demodulator.

Suppose the demodulator is followed by a lowpass filter having an amplitude ratio that begins to decrease gradually *below* W; this will *deemphasize* the high-frequency portion of the message band and thereby reduce the more serious interference. A sharp-cutoff (ideal) lowpass filter is still required to remove any residual components above W, so the complete demodulator consists of a frequency detector, deemphasis filter, and lowpass filter, Fig. 7.5.

Obviously deemphasis filtering also attenuates the high-frequency components of the message itself, causing distortion of the output signal unless corrective measures are taken. But it is a simple matter to compensate for deemphasis distortion by *predistorting* or *preemphasizing* the modulating signal at the transmitter before modulation. The preemphasis and deemphasis filter characteristics should be related by

$$H_{pe}(f) = \frac{1}{H_{de}(f)} \qquad |f| \leq W \qquad (8)$$

to yield net undistorted transmission.

In essence, we preemphasize the message before modulation (where the interference is absent) so we can deemphasize the interference relative to the message after demodulation. The technique is by no means restricted to FM systems; it can be used to advantage whenever undesired contaminations predominate at certain portions of the message band. For example, high frequencies are commonly preemphasized in sound recording so that high-frequency surface noise can be deemphasized during playback.† On the other hand, phase modulation and linear modulation systems profit little from deemphasis because the interference is independent of frequency and there is no *selective* advantage. To be sure, high-frequency deemphasis does yield some improvement, but hardly enough to justify the added complexity.

Returning to FM per se, the deemphasis filter is usually a simple RC network having

$$H_{de}(f) = \left[1 + j\left(\frac{f}{B_{de}} \right) \right]^{-1} \approx \begin{cases} 1 & |f| \ll B_{de} \\ \dfrac{B_{de}}{jf} & |f| \gg B_{de} \end{cases} \qquad (9)$$

where the 3-dB bandwidth $B_{de} = 1/2\pi RC$ is considerably less than the message bandwidth W. Since the interference amplitude increases linearly with $|f_I|$ in the absence

† The *Dolby* system for tape recording goes even further by dynamically adjusting the amount of preemphasis/deemphasis in inverse proportion to the high-frequency content; see Horowitz (1972).

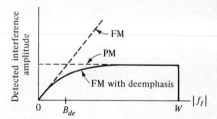

FIGURE 7.6
Detected interference amplitude for FM
with deemphasis filtering.

of filtering, the deemphasized interference response is $|H_{de}(f_I)| \times |f_I|$, as sketched in Fig. 7.6. Note that, like PM, this becomes constant for $|f_I| \gg B_{de}$. Therefore, FM can be superior to PM for both adjacent-channel and cochannel interference.

At the transmitting end, the corresponding preemphasis filter is†

$$H_{pe}(f) = \left[1 + j\left(\frac{f}{B_{de}}\right)\right] \approx \begin{cases} 1 & |f| \ll B_{de} \\ \dfrac{jf}{B_{de}} & |f| \gg B_{de} \end{cases} \tag{10}$$

which has little effect on the lower message frequencies. At higher frequencies, however, the filter acts as a *differentiator*, the output spectrum being proportional to $fX(f)$ for $|f| \gg B_{de}$. But differentiating a signal before frequency modulation is equivalent to *phase modulation*! Hence, preemphasized FM is actually a combination of FM and PM, combining the advantages of both with respect to interference. As might be expected, this turns out to be equally effective for reducing *noise*.

Referring to $H_{pe}(f)$ as given above, we see that the amplitude of the maximum modulating frequency is increased by a factor of W/B_{de}, which means that the frequency deviation is increased by this same factor. Generally speaking, the increased deviation requires a greater transmission bandwidth, so the preemphasis-deemphasis improvement is not without price. Fortunately, many modulating signals of interest, particularly audio signals, have relatively little energy in the high-frequency end of the message band, and therefore the higher frequency components do not develop maximum deviation, the transmission bandwidth being dictated by lower components of larger amplitude. Adding high-frequency preemphasis tends to equalize the message spectrum so that all components require the same bandwidth. Under this condition, the transmission bandwidth need not be increased.

EXERCISE 7.2 Taking $H_{pe}(f)$ per Eq. (10), justify the assertion that preemphasis does not increase B_T providing the spectral density of $x(t)$ satisfies

$$G_x(f) \le \left(\frac{B_{de}}{f}\right)^2 G_{max} \quad \text{for} \quad |f| > B_{de} \tag{11}$$

† Problem 7.5 gives a circuit realization.

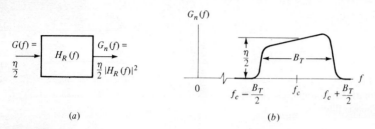

FIGURE 7.7
Bandpass filtered white noise. (a) Block diagram; (b) output spectral density, $f \geq 0$.

where $G_{\max}$ is the maximum value of $G_x(f)$ in $|f| < B_{\mathrm{de}}$. Does the typical voice spectrum of Fig. 5.6b satisfy Eq. (11)?

7.3 BANDPASS NOISE

Figure 7.7a isolates that part of Fig. 7.1 relevant to a discussion of the *bandpass* (or *narrowband*) *noise* $n(t)$ at the output of the predetection filter. Taking $G(f) = \eta/2$ at the input, the spectral density of $n(t)$ is

$$G_n(f) = \frac{\eta}{2} |H_R(f)|^2 \qquad (1)$$

as sketched in Fig. 7.7b assuming $H_R(f_c) = 1$ and $B_R \approx B_T$. Then, if the noise equivalent bandwidth of $H_R(f)$ approximately equals B_T, the total filtered noise power is

$$N_R \triangleq \overline{n^2} = \sigma_n^2 = \eta B_T \qquad (2)$$

referred to hereafter as the *received* noise power. (With the white noise assumption, noise power is undefined prior to the predetection filter.)

Presumably, in view of the bandpass nature of $n(t)$, we can represent it in the usual forms

$$n(t) = R_n(t) \cos [\omega_c t + \phi_n(t)] \qquad (3a)$$

$$= n_i(t) \cos \omega_c t - n_q(t) \sin \omega_c t \qquad (3b)$$

But $n(t)$ is a *random* signal so $R_n(t)$, $\phi_n(t)$, $n_i(t)$, and $n_q(t)$ must also be random. Hence, we are interested here in the statistical averages of these variates and —hopefully— their probability density functions. Although there is no direct route from power spectra to PDFs, advanced techniques do yield answers for this particular case. We will give a qualitative description of the approach and discuss the results.

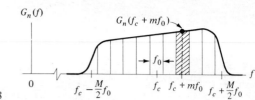

FIGURE 7.8

Section 3.5 included a Fourier series representation of a random signal obtained by partitioning its power spectrum into narrow bands. Accordingly, we partition $G_n(f)$ into $M = B_T/f_0$ bands of width f_0, Fig. 7.8, and invoke Eq. (16), Sect. 3.5, to get

$$n(t) \approx \sum_{m=-M/2}^{M/2} A_m \cos \left[(\omega_c + m\omega_0)t + \theta_m \right] \qquad (4)$$

where

$$\overline{A_m{}^2} = 4f_0\, G_n(f_c + mf_0) = 2\eta f_0\, |H_R(f_c + mf_0)|^2$$

and θ_m is uniformly distributed. But

$$\cos \left[(\omega_c + m\omega_0)t + \theta_m \right] = \cos (m\omega_0 t + \theta_m) \cos \omega_c t - \sin (m\omega_0 t + \theta_m) \sin \omega_c t$$

so Eq. (4) has the same form as Eq. (3b) with

$$n_i(t) \approx \sum_{m=-M/2}^{M/2} A_m \cos (m\omega_0 t + \theta_m) \qquad (5a)$$

$$n_q(t) \approx \sum_{m=-M/2}^{M/2} A_m \sin (m\omega_0 t + \theta_m) \qquad (5b)$$

which are the quadrature components of bandpass noise.

Quadrature Components

Examining Eqs. (5a) and (5b), we find the highest-frequency term in each is at $Mf_0/2 = B_T/2$. Usually, $B_T/2$ is much less than f_c and hence we can say that $n_i(t)$ and $n_q(t)$ are *lowpass* random signals whose time variations are slow compared to the carrier frequency. Furthermore, even though the quadrature components do not exist as physical entities at this point, a power spectral density can be assigned to each.

For that purpose, we first find the autocorrelation function of $n_i(t)$ by applying superposition to Eq. (14), Sect. 3.5, i.e.,

$$R_{n_i}(\tau) \approx \sum_{m=0}^{M/2} 2f_0[G_n(f_c - mf_0) \cos (-m\omega_0 \tau) + G_n(f_c + mf_0) \cos m\omega_0 \tau]$$

$$\approx 2 \sum_{mf_0=0}^{B_T/2} [G_n(f_c - mf_0) + G_n(f_c + mf_0)] \cos (m\omega_0 \tau)\, f_0$$

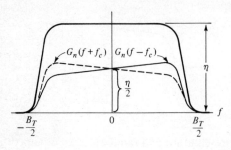

FIGURE 7.9
Spectral density of quadrature components of bandpass noise, $G_{n_i}(f)$ and
$G_{n_q}(f)$.

This approximation then becomes exact in the limit as $f_0 \rightarrow df$, $mf_0 \rightarrow f$, and summation
goes to integration. Thus

$$R_{n_i}(\tau) = 2 \int_0^{B_T/2} [G_n(f_c - f) + G_n(f_c + f)] \cos \omega\tau \, df \tag{6}$$

and $R_{n_q}(\tau)$ will be the same since the phase terms θ_m do not appear here. If we set
$\tau = 0$, noting that $G_n(f_c \pm f) \approx 0$ for $f > B_T/2$, it quickly follows that

$$\overline{n_i^2} = \overline{n_q^2} = N_R \tag{7}$$

a result that is not inconsistent with Eq. (2) because $\overline{n^2} = (\overline{n_i^2} + \overline{n_q^2})/2$.

Recall now the Wiener-Kinchine theorem $R(\tau) \leftrightarrow G(f)$ and the fact that $G(f)$
has even symmetry when the signal in question is real. Consequently, one may write

$$R(\tau) = \mathscr{F}^{-1}[F(f)] = 2 \int_0^\infty G(-f) \cos \omega\tau \, df$$

and comparing this with Eq. (6) yields

$$G_{n_i}(f) = G_{n_q}(f) = G_n(f - f_c) + G_n(f + f_c) \qquad |f| < B_T/2 \tag{8}$$

as sketched in Fig. 7.9. More often than not, $|H_R(f)|^2$ has symmetry about f_c and
Eq. (8) simplifies to $G_{n_i}(f) = 2G_n(f - f_c)$, etc. In any case, Fig. 7.9 supports our earlier
comment that $n_i(t)$ and $n_q(t)$ are low pass signals.

Further inspection of Eqs. (5a) and (5b) suggests that the *central-limit theorem* is
applicable; n_i and n_q are formed by summing a large number of variates, each of which
makes but a small contribution to the sum. The crucial question is the statistical dependence of the individual terms. More sophisticated analysis reveals that they are
statistically independent. Hence n_i and n_q are *gaussian-distributed* with zero mean and
variance N_R. It can also be shown that n_i and n_q are themselves statistically independent, leading to the joint PDF

$$p(n_i, n_q) = p_{n_i}(n_i)p_{n_q}(n_q) = \frac{1}{2\pi N_R} e^{-(n_i + n_q)^2/2N_R} \tag{9}$$

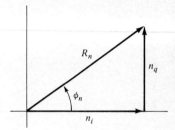

FIGURE 7.10
Phasor diagram for bandpass noise components.

Even though $n_i(t)$ and $n_q(t)$ are statistically independent, they are both related to $n(t)$. Specifically,†

$$n_i(t) = n(t) \cos \omega_c t + \hat{n}(t) \sin \omega_c t$$
$$n_q(t) = \hat{n}(t) \cos \omega_c t - n(t) \sin \omega_c t$$

where $\hat{n}(t)$ is the Hilbert transform of $n(t)$. From a physical viewpoint, the quadrature components (and the envelope and phase components) must depend on $n(t)$ and only on $n(t)$. However, thanks to the statistical independence, we can treat n_i and n_q as distinct entities whenever doing so expedites an analysis.

EXERCISE 7.3   Derive $\overline{n^2} = (\overline{n_i^2} + \overline{n_q^2})/2$ by taking the time average of both sides of Eq. (3b).

Envelope and Phase

Turning to the envelope-and-phase representation, we relate Eqs. (3a) and (3b) via the standard phasor diagram, Fig. 7.10. Clearly,

$$R_n^2 = n_i^2 + n_q^2 \qquad \phi_n = \arctan \frac{n_i}{n_q} \qquad (10a)$$

and conversely

$$n_i = R_n \cos \phi_n \qquad n_q = R_n \sin \phi_n \qquad (10b)$$

We also remember from Sect. 5.1 that spectral descriptions of the envelope and phase are difficult. Nonetheless, it is possible to find the PDFs for R_n and ϕ_n by functional transformation of Eq. (9).

Since the functional transformations at hand are nonlinear, we must start from scratch by writing the two-dimensional equivalent of Eq. (11), Sect. 3.2,

$$p_{n_i}(n_i) p_{n_q}(n_q) |dn_i \, dn_q| = p(R_n, \phi_n) |dR_n \, d\phi_n|$$

† Schwartz, Bennett, and Stein (1966, chap. 1) gives a compact treatment of bandpass noise, with further references.

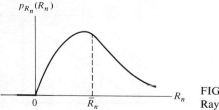

FIGURE 7.11
Rayleigh PDF.

where $p(R_n,\phi_n)$ is the joint PDF of R_n and ϕ_n. Inserting Eq. (9) with $n_i^2 + n_q^2 = R_n^2$ and noting that $dn_i\, dn_q = R_n\, dR_n\, d\phi_n$ yields

$$p(R_n,\phi_n) = \frac{|R_n|}{2\pi N_R}\, e^{-R_n^2/2N_R} \tag{11}$$

a result that requires two qualifications. First, by definition, R_n cannot be negative; second, phase ambiguities must be avoided by limiting the range of ϕ_n, say to $[-\pi,\pi]$. Thus, $p(R_n,\phi_n) = 0$ for $R_n < 0$ or $|\phi_n| > \pi$.

Equation (11) still is a trifle disturbing because ϕ_n does not appear explicitly. However, from Eq. (17), Sect. 3.2, integrating with respect to R_n gives

$$p_{\phi_n}(\phi_n) = \int_0^\infty p(R_n,\phi_n)\, dR_n = \frac{1}{2\pi} \qquad |\phi_n| < \pi \tag{12}$$

so ϕ_n is *uniformly distributed* over $[-\pi,\pi]$, a most logical conclusion in view of Fig. 7.10 and the PDFs of n_i and n_q. Proceeding in like fashion for the PDF of R_n, we integrate with respect to ϕ_n and get

$$p_{R_n}(R_n) = \frac{R_n}{N_R}\, e^{-R_n^2/2N_R} \qquad R_n \geq 0 \tag{13}$$

which is called the *Rayleigh distribution*, sketched in Fig. 7.11. Note carefully that N_R is the variance of n (and n_i and n_q) but not R_n. In fact

$$\overline{R_n^2} = 2N_R \qquad \overline{R_n} = \sqrt{\frac{\pi N_R}{2}} \tag{14}$$

while

$$\overline{\phi_n^2} = \frac{\pi^2}{3} \qquad \overline{\phi_n} = 0 \tag{15}$$

as the reader can check.

Finally, from Eqs. (11), (12), and (13), $p(R_n,\phi_n) = p_{R_n}(R_n)p_{\phi_n}(\phi_n)$, meaning that R_n and ϕ_n are *statistically independent*. Therefore, we have described bandpass noise

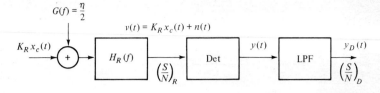

FIGURE 7.12

as a random sinusoid of frequency f_c whose envelope has a Rayleigh distribution and whose phase has a uniform distribution. The envelope and phase variations are statistically independent and, inferring from Eqs. (8) and (10), they change slowly compared to f_c.

EXERCISE 7.4   A happy feature of the Rayleigh distribution is its ease of integration for determining probabilities. Specifically, show that

$$\text{Prob}\,[R_n > r] = e^{-r^2/2N_R} \qquad (16)$$

(*Hint*: Let $\lambda = R_n^2/2N_R$ in $\int_r^\infty p(R_n)\,dR_n$.)

7.4 NOISE IN LINEAR MODULATION

We now analyze the performance of linear modulation systems in the presense of noise. Figure 7.12 is our model for the receiver, the modulated signal plus bandpass noise at the detector input being

$$v(t) = K_R x_c(t) + n(t) \qquad (1)$$

which also holds for exponential modulation with appropriate $x_c(t)$. Since linear modulation has $B_T = 2W$ or W, depending on whether or not a sideband has been suppressed, the three possible noise spectra $G_n(f)$ are as shown in Fig. 7.13 taking $H_R(f)$ to be symmetrical

The average signal power at the detector input is $K_R^2\langle x_c^2(t)\rangle = S_R$, and $\overline{n^2} = N_R = \eta B_T$ is the noise power assuming the noise equivalent bandwidth of the predetection filter equals B_T. The signal and noise are additive in Eq. (1), so it is meaningful to define the *predetection signal-to-noise ratio*

$$\left(\frac{S}{N}\right)_R \triangleq \frac{S_R}{N_R} = \frac{S_R}{\eta B_T} \qquad (2)$$

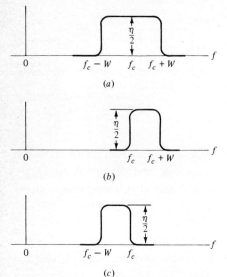

FIGURE 7.13
Predetection noise spectrum $G_n(f)$ in linear modulation. (*a*) Double sideband (*b*) upper sideband; (*c*) lower sideband.

which is suggestive of the parameter $\gamma = S_R/\eta W$ introduced in Sect. 4.3; specifically, for equal values of S_R, η, and W,

$$\left(\frac{S}{N}\right)_R = \frac{W}{B_T}\gamma \qquad (3)$$

Hence, $(S/N)_R = \gamma$ for single sideband ($B_T = W$) while $(S/N)_R = \gamma/2$ for double sideband. However, the interpretation to keep in mind is that γ equals the maximum value of the *destination* signal-to-noise ratio $(S/N)_D$ of analog baseband transmission. By the same token, Eqs. (2) and (3) actually are *upper bounds*, e.g., $(S/N)_R < S_R/\eta B_T$ if $B_R > B_T$, etc. Finally, we also need

$$S_R = \frac{S_T}{\mathscr{L}} = K_R^2 S_T = \left(\frac{A_R}{A_c}\right)^2 S_T \qquad (4)$$

which relates S_R to the previous expressions for S_T.

With the preliminaries disposed of, the question at hand is this: Given $x_c(t)$ and the type of detector, what is the final output signal-plus-noise waveform $y_D(t)$? And if the signal and noise are additive at the output, what is the destination signal-to-noise ratio $(S/N)_D$, say in terms of $(S/N)_R$ or γ? We will attempt to answer these questions by investigating the two cases of synchronous detection and envelope detection.

Synchronous Detection

If the modulation is DSB, then $x_c(t) = A_c x(t) \cos \omega_c t$ and $B_T = 2W$. When we write the noise in quadrature-carrier form, Eq. (1) becomes

$$v(t) = \underbrace{[A_R x(t) + n_i(t)]}_{v_i(t)} \cos \omega_c t - n_q(t) \sin \omega_c t \qquad (5)$$

so, invoking the detector model of Eq. (5a), Sect. 7.1,

$$y(t) = v_i(t) = A_R x(t) + n_i(t)$$

Thus, after lowpass filtering,

$$y_D(t) = A_R x(t) + n_i(t) \qquad (6)$$

since both of these components are bandlimited in $W = B_T/2$.

Three important conclusions can be gained from Eq. (6). First, the message and noise are additive at the output; second, the quadrature noise component $n_q(t)$ is completely rejected; third, the output noise power spectrum is $G_{n_i}(f)$ which has the shape of $G_n(f)$ translated to zero frequency. If $|H_R(f)|$ is relatively flat over B_T, the output noise is essentially white over the message bandwidth W.

Taking mean-square values of the two terms in Eq. (6), the destination S/N is

$$\left(\frac{S}{N}\right)_D = \frac{A_R^2 \overline{x^2}}{\overline{n_i^2}} = \frac{2S_R}{\eta B_T} = 2\left(\frac{S}{N}\right)_R \qquad (7a)$$

since $\overline{n_i^2} = \overline{n^2} = \eta B_T$ and $A_R^2 \overline{x^2} = 2S_R$ for DSB. Alternately, from Eq. (3),

$$\left(\frac{S}{N}\right)_D = \frac{S_R}{\eta W} = \gamma \qquad \text{DSB} \qquad (7b)$$

Therefore, insofar as noise is concerned, DSB with ideal† synchronous detection is equivalent to baseband transmission, even though the transmission bandwidth is twice as great.

From a frequency-translation viewpoint one might have suspected a different result, namely, $(S/N)_D = (S/N)_R = \gamma/2$, since the modulated signal spectrum and the noise spectrum are both shifted down to zero frequency. However, the translated signal sidebands overlap in a *coherent* fashion, whereas the noise sidebands sum *incoherently*. In fact, it is the sideband coherence that counterbalances the doubled predetection noise power $\eta B_T = 2\eta W$ compared to baseband.

The results for synchronously demodulated AM can be readily inferred from

---

† See Prob. 7.13 for the effects of phase errors in synchronism.

Eqs. (6) and (7) by recalling that $x_c(t) = A_c[1 + mx(t)] \cos \omega_c t$ and the information-bearing portion of the transmitted power is $2P_{SB} = S_T - P_c = m^2\overline{x^2}A_c^2/2$. Therefore

$$y_D(t) = A_R mx(t) + n_i(t) \qquad (8)$$

and

$$\left(\frac{S}{N}\right)_D = \frac{A_R^2 m^2\overline{x^2}}{\eta B_T} = \frac{2m^2\overline{x^2}}{1 + m^2\overline{x^2}} \left(\frac{S}{N}\right)_R$$

$$= \frac{m^2\overline{x^2}}{1 + m^2\overline{x^2}} \gamma \qquad \text{AM} \qquad (9)$$

This ratio is bounded by $(S/N)_D \leq \gamma/2$, reflecting our earlier observation that 50 percent or more of the transmitted power is wasted in the AM carrier. Other factors being equal, an AM system must transmit at least twice as much power as a suppressed-carrier system to achieve the same output. Thus, on an average power basis, AM is inferior to DSB by 3 dB or more.

Under the best conditions $(S/N)_D = \gamma/2$, corresponding to $m^2\overline{x^2} = 1$; with full-load tone modulation $m^2\overline{x^2} = \frac{1}{2}$ and $(S/N)_D = \gamma/3$. More typically, however, $m^2\overline{x^2} \approx 0.1$, for which $(S/N)_D$ is some 7 dB below the maximum value and 10 dB below DSB. The consequent reduction of signal-to-noise ratio is a serious problem in AM broadcasting. Hence, special techniques such as volume compression and peak limiting are frequently employed at the transmitter to ensure that the carrier is fully modulated most of the time. These techniques actually distort the recovered message and would be unacceptable for analog data transmission; for audio program material the distortion is more tolerable.

For the case of SSB (or VSB), the DSB analysis must be modified by a quadrature component in $x_c(t)$ and the offset carrier frequency compared to the center frequency f_0 of $H_R(f)$. With these changes

$$v(t) = \frac{A_R}{2}[x(t) \cos \omega_c t \mp \hat{x}(t) \sin \omega_c t] + [n_i(t) \cos \omega_0 t - n_q(t) \sin \omega_0 t] \qquad (10)$$

where $\omega_0 = 2\pi(f_c \pm W/2)$. Leaving the details to the reader, the demodulated output is

$$y_D(t) = \frac{A_R}{2} x(t) + n_i(t) \cos \pi Wt \pm n_q(t) \sin \pi Wt \qquad (11)$$

and

$$\left(\frac{S}{N}\right)_D = \frac{A_R^2 \overline{x^2}}{4\eta B_T} = \left(\frac{S}{N}\right)_R = \gamma \qquad \text{SSB} \qquad (12)$$

since $B_T = W$ and $S_R = A_R{}^2\overline{x^2}/4$. Note that the quadrature signal component $\hat{x}(t)$ is absent from $y_D(t)$, as it should be, but the quadrature noise term now appears at the output. This is because the center frequency of the noise spectrum $G_n(f)$ differs from the carrier frequency by $\pm W/2$. Frequency-translation arguments then suggest that the demodulated noise should be "bandpass" noise centered at $W/2$. The last two terms of $y_D(t)$ have precisely this interpretation, so the output noise spectrum is essentially constant over W except for a possible hole at DC.

Equation (12) is equally valid for suppressed-carrier VSB, providing the width of the vestigial band is small compared to the message bandwidth. For the case of VSB plus carrier it is easily shown that

$$\left(\frac{S}{N}\right)_D \approx \frac{m^2\overline{x^2}}{1 + m^2\overline{x^2}}\,\gamma \qquad \text{VSB} + \text{C} \qquad (13)$$

which follows from the approximations $B_T \approx W$ and $S_T \approx (1 + m^2\overline{x^2})A_c{}^2/2$. The reader may wish to consider why this result is the same as for AM, as given by Eq. (9). Reviewing Eqs. (6) to (13), we can state the following general characteristics of synchronously detected linear modulation.

1   The message and noise are additive at the output if they are additive at the detector input.

2   If the predetection noise spectrum is reasonably flat over the transmission bandwidth, the destination noise spectrum is essentially constant over the message bandwidth.

3   Insofar as output signal-to-noise ratios are concerned, suppressed-sideband modulation (SSB and VSB) has no particular advantage over double-sideband modulation (AM and DSM). This is because of the coherence property of double sideband, which compensates for the reduced predetection noise power of single sideband.

4   Making due allowance for the "wasted" power in unsuppressed-carrier systems, all types of linear modulation have the same performance as baseband transmission on the basis of average transmitted power and fixed noise density.

Up to this point we have compared systems assuming equal values of S_R, the *average* power. However, it is perhaps more realistic to hold *peak* powers equal, reflecting the peak-power constraint of practical transmitters. Under this condition the destination S/N or DSB is four times that of AM (6 dB better) since the peak powers are proportional to $A_c{}^2$ and $4A_c{}^2$, respectively. Peak-power calculations for single sideband with representative modulating signals indicate† that SSB is 2 to 3

† Downing (1964, chap. 4).

dB better than DSB and 8 to 9 dB better than AM. But SSB is *inferior* to DSB if the message has pronounced discontinuities causing envelope "horns."

EXERCISE 7.5   Carry out all the details between Eqs. (10), (11), and (12). (*Hint*: The noise part of Eq. (11) is bandpass noise at $W/2$, so its mean-square value equals $(\overline{n_i^2} + \overline{n_q^2})/2$.)

Envelope Detection and Threshold Effect

Inasmuch as AM is normally demodulated by an envelope detector, it is necessary to see how this differs from synchronous detection when noise is present. At the detector input we have, as before,

$$v(t) = A_R[1 + mx(t)] \cos \omega_c t + [n_i(t) \cos \omega_c t - n_q(t) \sin \omega_c t] \qquad (14)$$

The phasor construction of Fig. 7.14a shows that the resultant envelope and phase are

$$R_v(t) = (\{A_R[1 + mx(t)] + n_i(t)\}^2 + [n_q(t)]^2)^{1/2}$$

$$\phi_v(t) = \arctan \frac{n_q(t)}{A_R[1 + mx(t)] + n_i(t)} \qquad (15)$$

Clearly, further analysis calls for some simplifications, so let us assume the signal is either very large or very small.

Taking the signal to dominate, say $A_R^2 \gg \overline{n^2}$, then $A_R[1 + mx(t)]$ will be large compared to $n_i(t)$ and $n_q(t)$, at least most of the time. The envelope can then be approximated by

$$R_v(t) \approx A_R[1 + mx(t)] + n_i(t) \qquad (16)$$

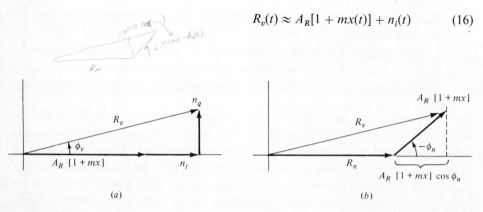

(a)   (b)

FIGURE 7.14
Phasor diagrams for AM plus noise. (a) $(S/N)_R \gg 1$; (b) $(S/N)_R \ll 1$.

which shows the modulation due to noise, similar to interference modulation. The approximation follows from Fig. 7.14a or expansion of Eq. (15). Hence

$$y_D(t) = R_v(t) - \overline{R}_v = A_R m x(t) + n_i(t)$$

identical to that of synchronous detection, Eq. (8). The postdetection signal-to-noise ratio is then as previously given in Eq. (9). A similar analysis can be made for compatible signal-sideband modulation, SSB + C or VSB + C, with similar results.

But one must bear in mind the condition for these results, namely, $A_R{}^2 \gg \overline{n^2}$. Since $A_R{}^2/\overline{n^2}$ is proportional to $S_R/\eta B_T$, an equivalent requirement is $(S/N)_D \gg 1$. (There is no such condition with synchronous detection.) Thus, providing the predetection signal-to-noise ratio is large, envelope demodulation in the presence of noise has the same performance quality as synchronous demodulation.

At the other extreme, $(S/N)_R \ll 1$, the situation is quite different. For if $A_R{}^2 \ll \overline{n^2}$, the noise dominates in a fashion similar to strong interference, and we can think of $x_c(t)$ as modulating $n(t)$ rather than the reverse. To expedite the analysis, $n(t)$ is represented in envelope-and-phase form

$$n(t) = R_n(t) \cos [\omega_c t + \phi_n(t)]$$

leading to the phasor diagram of Fig. 7.14b. In this figure the noise phasor is the reference because we are taking $n(t)$ to be dominant. By inspection, the envelope is approximately

$$R_v(t) \approx R_n(t) + A_R[1 + mx(t)] \cos \phi_n(t) \qquad (17)$$

from which

$$y(t) = R_n(t) + A_R m x(t) \cos \phi_n(t) - \overline{R}_n \qquad (18)$$

The principal output component is obviously the noise envelope $R_n(t)$, as expected. Furthermore, there is no term in Eq. (18) strictly proportional to the message; though signal and noise were *additive* at the input, the detected message term is *multiplied* by noise in the form of $\cos \phi_n(t)$, which is random. The message is therefore hopelessly *mutilated*, and its information has been lost. In fact, it can be said that the message *does not exist* at the output since it cannot be recovered. Under these circumstances, an output signal-to-noise ratio is difficult to define, if not meaningless.

The mutilation or loss of message at low predetection signal-to-noise ratios is called *threshold effect*. The name comes about because there is some value of $(S/N)_R$ above which mutilation is negligible and below which system performance rapidly deteriorates Thus, if the transmitted signal fades or the receiver noise increases, the message disappears rather suddenly. Note carefully that the threshold effect occurs only with envelope detection. With synchronous detection, the output signal and noise are always additive; true, the message is buried in noise if $(S/N)_R \ll 1$, but its identity is preserved.

Actually, the threshold is not a unique point unless some convention is established for its definition. Generally speaking, threshold effects are minimal if $A_R \gg R_n$ most of the time. To be more specific we shall define the *threshold level* as that value of $(S/N)_R$ for which $A_R \geq R_n$ with probability 0.99, i.e., $\text{Prob}\,[R_n > A_R] = 0.01$. From Eq. (16), Sect. 7.3,

$$\text{Prob}\,[R_n > A_R] = e^{-A_R{}^2/2N_R} \approx e^{-S_R/2N_R}$$

where we have assumed $m^2\overline{x^2} \approx 1$, so $A_R{}^2 \approx S_R$. Solving $e^{-S_R/2N_R} = 0.01$ for the threshold level gives

$$\left(\frac{S}{N}\right)_{R_{\text{th}}} = 4 \ln 10 \approx 10 \qquad (19a)$$

or, since $(S/N)_R = \gamma/2$,

$$\gamma_{\text{th}} = 8 \ln 10 \approx 20 \qquad (19b)$$

If $(S/N)_R < (S/N)_{R_{\text{th}}}$ (or $\gamma < \gamma_{\text{th}}$), message mutilation must be expected, along with the consequent loss of information.

Looking at the value of $(S/N)_{R_{\text{th}}}$ and recalling that $(S/N)_D < (S/N)_R$ leads to a significant conclusion: threshold effect is usually not a serious limitation of AM systems. To clarify this assertion, reasonable intelligibility in voice transmission demands a postdetection signal-to-noise ratio of about 30 dB or more, $(S/N)_D \geq 1,000$, for which $(S/N)_R$ is well above the threshold level. In other words, additive noise obscures the signal long before multiplicative noise mutilates it. On the other hand, sophisticated processing techniques exist for recovering *digital* signals buried in additive noise. Hence, if AM is used for digital transmission, synchronous detection may be necessary to avoid threshold effects.

Finally, it is informative to consider how an envelope detector can act in synchronous fashion and why this requires large $(S/N)_R$. Referring back to Fig. 5.30 and assuming the input noise is negligible, we see that the diode functions as a switch, closing briefly on the positive carrier peaks; therefore the switching is perfectly synchronized with the carrier. But when noise dominates, the switching is controlled primarily by the noise peaks, so synchronism is lost. The latter effect never occurs in true synchronous detectors, where the locally generated carrier can always be much greater than the noise.

EXERCISE 7.6 A voice signal with $\overline{x^2} = 0.2$ and $W = 3$ kHz is to be transmitted via linear modulation on a system having $S_T = 600$ W, $\mathscr{L} = 30$ dB, and $\eta = 10^{-8}$ W/Hz. Assuming no bandwidth constraints, select an appropriate modulation type and find $(S/N)_D$ in decibels. Repeat for $\mathscr{L} = 40$ dB.

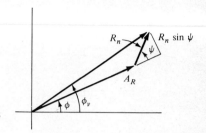

FIGURE 7.15
Phasor diagram for FM or PM plus
noise, $(S/N)_R \gg 1$.

7.5 NOISE IN EXPONENTIAL MODULATION

Turning to the demodulation of FM or PM contaminated by noise, the situation is
the same as Fig. 7.12 with $x_c(t) = A_c \cos [\omega_c t + \phi(t)]$ where

$$\phi(t) = \phi_\Delta x(t) \qquad \text{PM}$$

$$\frac{1}{2\pi} \frac{d\phi(t)}{dt} = f_\Delta x(t) \qquad \text{FM} \tag{1}$$

In either case, the bandpass noise is symmetric about f_c with $N_R = \eta B_T$ while $S_R = A_R^2/2$ so

$$\left(\frac{S}{N}\right)_R = \frac{A_R^2}{2\eta B_T} \tag{2}$$

With $n(t)$ written in envelope-and-phase form, the detector input is

$$v(t) = A_R \cos [\omega_c t + \phi(t)] + R_n(t) \cos [\omega_c t + \phi_n(t)] \tag{3}$$

and immediately we see analytic difficulties in finding the resultant phase $\phi_v(t)$ to
insert in the mathematical model of the detector. Let us therefore do as we did with
envelope detection, namely, assume the signal component dominates the noise.

Figure 7.15 shows the phasor diagram with the phase difference

$$\psi(t) = \phi_n(t) - \phi(t)$$

Taking the usual small-angle approximation,

$$\phi_v(t) \approx \phi(t) + \frac{R_n(t)}{A_R} \sin \psi(t) \tag{4}$$

providing $(S/N)_R \gg 1$. Not surprisingly, the leading term of Eq. (4) is the message
modulation, but the second term contains both message and noise and is another

source of difficulty dealt with momentarily. Meanwhile, applying Eqs. (5c) and (5d),
Sect. 7.1, to $\phi_v(t)$ yields the demodulated signal

$$y(t) = \begin{cases} \phi_\Delta x(t) + \xi_{PM}(t) & PM \\ f_\Delta x(t) + \xi_{FM}(t) & FM \end{cases} \tag{5}$$

where we have defined

$$\xi_{PM}(t) = \frac{R_n(t)}{A_R} \sin \psi(t) \tag{6a}$$

$$\xi_{FM}(t) = \frac{1}{2\pi} \frac{d\xi_{PM}(t)}{dt} \tag{6b}$$

Interpreting these as the *postdetection noise* terms, even though they depend in part
on the modulating signal, Eq. (5) has the form of signal plus noise, i.e., *additive* noise
at the output. Moreover,

$$S_D = \begin{cases} \phi_\Delta^2 \overline{x^2} & PM \\ f_\Delta^2 \overline{x^2} & FM \end{cases} \tag{7}$$

is the output signal power.

Despite these conclusions we cannot immediately write down the signal-to-noise
ratios $(S/N)_D$. For one reason, the evaluation of $\overline{\xi^2}$ is a more than trivial task; for
another, we have not as yet included the effects of postdetection filtering on the noise.
For both reasons one must go to the frequency domain and examine the postdetection
noise power spectra.

Postdetection Noise Characteristics

A qualitative description of the postdetection noise spectra is obtained by recalling
that bandpass noise can be thought of as a summation of random sinusoids distributed
equally over $f_c \pm B_T/2$. Since it was assumed that $(S/N)_R \gg 1$, the amplitudes of these
sinusoids are very small and each will act as a small interfering signal. Drawing upon
our interference studies and Fig. 7.4, we infer that the postdetection noise power
spectrum of PM will be constant over $|f| < B_T/2$. But for FM, where interference
amplitude increases linearly with frequency, the power spectrum will go as frequency
squared. This *parabolic power spectrum* reflects the notion that input noise components
close to the carrier frequency cannot cause as much frequency deviation as those
farther away from f_c.

Going from the qualitative to the quantitative, we shall calculate $G_\xi(f)$ from
Eq. (6) by ignoring the carrier modulation and replacing $\psi(t) = \phi_n(t) - \phi(t)$ by $\phi_n(t)$
alone. The approach is justified because ϕ_n is uniformly distributed; hence, in the

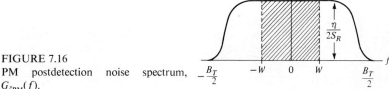

FIGURE 7.16
PM postdetection noise spectrum, $G_{\xi_{PM}}(f)$.

sense of ensemble averages, $\phi_n - \phi$ differs from ϕ_n only by a shift of the mean value.†
With this simplification, $R_n(t) \sin \psi(t)$ reduces to the quadrature noise component
$n_q(t) = R_n(t) \sin \phi_n(t)$, and the detected noise becomes

$$\xi_{PM}(t) = \frac{1}{A_R} n_q(t) \tag{8a}$$

$$\xi_{FM}(t) = \frac{1}{2\pi A_R} \frac{dn_q(t)}{dt} = \frac{1}{2\pi} \frac{d\xi_{PM}(t)}{dt} \tag{8b}$$

That these do not depend on the in-phase noise component $n_i(t)$ agrees with our phasor interpretation of exponential modulation, Fig. 6.7, wherein we saw that only those components in quadrature with the carrier produce phase or frequency modulation.

Focusing first on the PM case, we find from Eq. (8a) that the noise spectral density is $G_{\xi_{PM}}(f) = G_{nq}(f)/A_R^2$. But $A_R^2 = 2S_R$ and, from Eqs. (1) and (8), Sect. 7.3, $G_{nq}(f) = (\eta/2)[|H_R(f - f_c)|^2 + |H_R(f + f_c)|^2]$. Putting these together, we have that

$$G_{\xi_{PM}}(f) = \frac{\eta}{4S_R} [|H_R(f - f_c)|^2 + |H_R(f + f_c)|^2] \tag{9a}$$

$$\approx \frac{\eta}{2S_R} \Pi\left(\frac{f}{B_T}\right) \tag{9b}$$

where Eq. (9b) assumes that $|H_R(f)| \approx 1$ over $f_c \pm B_T/2$, as would usually be true — ignoring the gain factor that will cancel out in signal-to-noise ratios. Under this condition, $G_{\xi_{PM}}(f)$ is essentially flat over $|f| < B_T/2$, Fig. 7.16. But $B_T/2$ normally exceeds the message bandwidth, meaning that out-of-band noise components — like

† Downing (1964, chap. 5) shows that when $\phi(t)$ is accounted for, there are additional components in $G_\xi(f)$ but at frequencies above the message band. Such components are chopped off by the output filter and do not concern us.

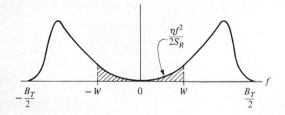

FIGURE 7.17
FM postdetection noise spectrum, $G_{\xi FM}(f)$.

out-of-band interference — should be removed by postdetection filtering. Accordingly, with an ideal LPF at the output of the detector, the noise power at the destination is

$$N_D = \int_{-W}^{W} G_{\xi PM}(f)\, df$$

$$= \int_{-W}^{W} \frac{\eta}{2S_R}\, df = \frac{\eta W}{S_R} \qquad \text{PM} \qquad (10)$$

using Eq. (9b) for $G_{\xi PM}(f)$.

Having found $G_{\xi PM}(f)$, the FM case now becomes routine in view of Eq. (8b). Specifically, applying the differentiation relation for power spectra, Eq. (27), Sect. 2.6, yields

$$G_{\xi FM}(f) = \left(\frac{1}{2\pi}\right)^2 (2\pi f)^2 G_{\xi PM}(f) \qquad (11a)$$

$$\approx \frac{\eta f^2}{2S_R}\, \Pi\!\left(\frac{f}{B_T}\right) \qquad (11b)$$

which, as sketched in Fig. 7.17, goes as f^2 over the message band. This figure, together with Fig. 5.37b, shows why FM stereo suffers from more noise than monaural FM since, before subcarrier modulation, the translated difference signal $x_L(t) - x_R(t)$ resides between 23 and 53 kHz, where the noise spectral density is much higher than in the 0- to 15-kHz range of the monaural signal. Similarly, when designing any FDM system with FM carrier modulation, the *parabolic postdetection noise* characteristic must be taken into account.

As for the total postdetection noise power, we again assume $|H_R(f)|$ is reasonably flat so Eq. (11b) holds. Therefore, with an ideal LPF removing out-of-band noise at the output,

$$N_D = \int_{-W}^{W} G_{\xi FM}(f)\, df = \frac{\eta W^3}{3S_R} \qquad \text{FM} \qquad (12)$$

without deemphasis filtering.

Adding a deemphasis filter modifies the output noise spectrum and, in general,

$$N_D = \int_{-W}^{W} |H_{de}(f)|^2 G_{\xi FM}(f)\, df \qquad (13)$$

For the RC filter of Eq. (9), Sect. 7.2,

$$N_D = \int_{-W}^{W} \left[1 + \left(\frac{f}{B_{de}}\right)^2 \right]^{-1} \left(\frac{\eta f^2}{2S_R}\right) df$$

$$= \left(\frac{\eta B_{de}^3}{S_R}\right)\left[\left(\frac{W}{B_{de}}\right) - \arctan\left(\frac{W}{B_{de}}\right)\right] \qquad (14a)$$

$$\approx \frac{\eta B_{de}^2 W}{S_R} \qquad \frac{W}{B_{de}} \gg 1 \qquad (14b)$$

where the approximation comes from arctan $(W/B_{de}) \approx \pi/2 \ll W/B_{de}$. Comparing Eq. (14b) with Eq. (12) shows that deemphasis has substantially reduced the output noise, i.e.,

$$\frac{N_D \text{ (with deemphasis)}}{N_D \text{ (without deemphasis)}} \approx 3\left(\frac{B_{de}}{W}\right)^2 \qquad \frac{B_{de}}{W} \ll 1 \qquad (15)$$

A similar analysis for PM with high-frequency deemphasis gives a less impressive reduction factor of approximately $\pi B_{de}/2W$.

EXERCISE 7.7 Find the noise reduction factor for PM with an RC deemphasis filter. *Ans.*: $(B_{de}/W) \arctan (W/B_{de})$.

Destination Signal-to-Noise Ratios

Having found the output signal power and noise power, we come at last to the signal-to-noise ratios at the destination and an assessment of *wideband noise reduction* in exponential modulation systems. We assume $(S/N)_R \gg 1$ throughout and that any deemphasis filtering is compensated by prior preemphasis filtering. Regarding the latter, it is presumed that the message spectrum is such that preemphasis does not significantly increase the transmission bandwidth.

Beginning with phase modulation, S_D and N_D are given by Eqs. (7) and (10), respectively, so

$$\left(\frac{S}{N}\right)_D = \frac{\phi_\Delta^2 \overline{x^2}}{(\eta W/S_R)} = \phi_\Delta^2 \overline{x^2}\, \frac{S_R}{\eta W} = \phi_\Delta^2 \overline{x^2} \gamma \qquad \text{PM} \qquad (16)$$

Since γ is the output S/N for baseband transmission (or suppressed-carrier linear modulation) with power S_R, bandwidth W, and noise density η, it follows that PM gives an improvement over baseband of exactly $\phi_\Delta^2 \overline{x^2}$. But because of the ambiguity constraint $\phi_\Delta \leq \pi$, the PM improvement is no greater than $\phi_\Delta^2 \overline{x^2}\big|_{max} = \pi^2$, or about 10 dB at best. Of course if $\phi_\Delta^2 \overline{x^2} < 1$, the PM performance is inferior to baseband, while the transmission bandwidth is still $B_T \geq 2W$.

For FM without deemphasis filtering Eqs. (7) and (12) yield

$$\left(\frac{S}{N}\right)_D = \frac{f_\Delta^2 \overline{x^2}}{(\eta W^3/3S_R)} = 3\left(\frac{f_\Delta}{W}\right)^2 \overline{x^2} \frac{S_R}{\eta W}$$

Hence, inserting the deviation ratio $\Delta = f_\Delta/W$,

$$\left(\frac{S}{N}\right)_D = 3\Delta^2 \overline{x^2}\gamma \qquad \text{FM} \qquad (17)$$

Adding an RC deemphasis filter with $B_{de} \ll W$ further reduces the output noise by about $3(B_{de}/W)^2$, so

$$\left(\frac{S}{N}\right)_D = \frac{3\Delta^2 \overline{x^2}\gamma}{3(B_{de}/W)^2} = \left(\frac{W}{B_{de}}\right)^2 \Delta^2 \overline{x^2}\gamma$$

$$= \left(\frac{f_\Delta}{B_{de}}\right)^2 \overline{x^2}\gamma \qquad B_{de} \ll W \qquad (18)$$

But with or without deemphasis, FM exhibits substantial wideband noise reduction in that $(S/N)_D$ increases with the deviation ratio and the concomitant large transmission bandwidth. In fact, it appears that $(S/N)_D$ can be made *arbitrarily large* by increasing only the deviation, a conclusion that requires further qualification and is reexamined later.

To emphasize the transmission-bandwidth dependence, we recall that wideband FM ($\Delta \gg 1$) has $B_T = 2f_\Delta = 2\Delta W$, so $\Delta^2 = B_T^2/4W^2$, and Eq. (17) becomes

$$\left(\frac{S}{N}\right)_D = \frac{3}{4}\left(\frac{B_T}{W}\right)^2 \overline{x^2}\gamma \qquad \text{WBFM} \qquad (19)$$

Under this condition the system performance improves as the *square* of the bandwidth ratio B_T/W. With smaller deviations the break-even point compared to baseband occurs at $3\Delta^2 \overline{x^2} = 1$; hence

$$\Delta = (3\overline{x^2})^{-1/2} \approx 0.6$$

is sometimes designated as the dividing line between NBFM and WBFM.

Just how much can be gained with wideband FM is well illustrated by commercial broadcast FM, for which $f_\Delta = 75$ kHz, $W = 15$ kHz, $\Delta = 5$, and the standard deemphasis filter has $B_{de} = 2.1$ kHz, corresponding to the time constant $RC = 75$

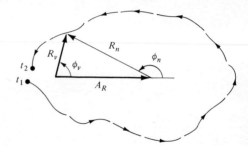

FIGURE 7.18
Phasor diagram and locus for
$A_R{}^2 \approx R_n{}^2$.

μs. Taking $\overline{x^2} = \frac{1}{2}$ as a representative value and excluding deemphasis, $(S/N)_D = (3 \times 5^2 \times \frac{1}{2})\gamma = 37.5\gamma$, or about 16 dB better than baseband. Including the deemphasis improvement we have $(S/N)_D = 640\gamma$ and, other factors being equal, a 1-W FM system could replace a 640-W baseband system with no reduction in output signal-to-noise ratio. But bear in mind that the FM transmission bandwidth is 14 times as large as the message bandwidth, underscoring the trade-off of bandwidth for power or signal-to-noise ratio made possible by exponential modulation.

Regarding this FM bandwidth-power exchange, in practice several factors work against full realization of reduced transmitted power at the expense of increased transmission bandwidth. And indeed the goal of commercial FM is not to minimize transmitter power but rather to provide the best possible output signal-to-noise ratio. However, there are numerous other situations where minimum power is essential; for such applications the condition $(S/N)_R \gg 1$ is a definite hardship, and the FM threshold effect becomes a matter of grave concern.

FM Threshold Effect

All the above results were based on the approximation of Eq. (4), assuming a large predetection signal-to-noise ratio. When, on the other hand, $(S/N)_R \ll 1$, the resultant phase at the detector input is

$$\phi_v(t) \approx \phi_n(t) + \frac{A_R}{R_n(t)} \sin\left[\phi(t) - \phi_n(t)\right] \qquad (20)$$

and clearly the message—contained in $\phi(t)$—has been mutilated by noise beyond all hope of recovery.

Actually, significant mutilation begins to occur when $(S/N)_R \approx 1$ for then $A_R{}^2 \approx \overline{R_n{}^2}$ so the signal and noise phasors are of nearly equal length and variations of the noise phase cause comparable variations of $\phi_v(t)$. A particularly interesting case is illustrated by the phasor diagram of Fig. 7.18, omitting the modulation $\phi(t)$, where $\phi_v(t_1) \approx \phi_n(t_1) \approx -\pi$ while $\phi_v(t_2) \approx +\pi$. If the phase variation between t_1 and

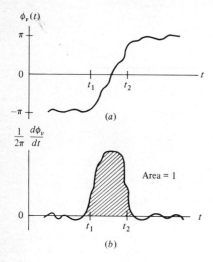

FIGURE 7.19
Typical noise variations near threshold. (a) Phase deviation with step; (b) frequency deviation with spike.

t_2 follows the dashed locus, then $\phi_v(t)$ looks like Fig. 7.19a and the corresponding frequency deviation $f_v(t) = (1/2\pi)\, d\phi_v(t)/dt$ is Fig. 7.19b, a *spike* of unit area and minimum duration $(t_2 - t_1)_{\min} \approx 2/B_T$ (why?). Aurally, these spikes give rise to a crackling or clicking sound masking the desired signal.

One infers from this qualitative picture that the output noise spectrum is no longer parabolic but tends to fill in at DC, the output spikes having appreciable low-frequency content. This conclusion has been verified through detailed analysis using the "click" approach as refined by Rice.† The analysis is complicated (and placed beyond our scope) by the fact that the spike characteristics change when the carrier is modulated, the so-called modulation-suppression effect. Thus, quantitative results are obtained only for specific modulating signals. In the case of tone modulation, the total output noise becomes

$$N_D = \frac{\eta W^3}{3S_R} \left[1 + \frac{12\Delta}{\pi} \gamma e^{-(W/B_T)\gamma} \right] \qquad (21)$$

where the second term is the contribution of the spikes.

Figure 7.20 shows $(S/N)_D$ in decibels plotted versus γ (also in decibels) for two values of the deviation ratio Δ, taking tone modulation and N_D given by Eq. (21). The rather sudden drop-off of these curves, traced to the exponential factor in Eq. (12), is the FM threshold effect. When the system is operating near the "knee" of a curve, small variations of signal power cause sizable changes in the output signal; one moment

---

† See Rice (1948) and Stumpers (1948) for the original work, or the tutorial treatment of Taub and Schilling (1971, chap. 10).

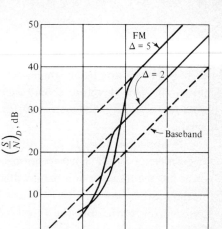

FIGURE 7.20
FM noise performance as a function of $\gamma = S_R/\eta W$, deemphasis not included.

it is there, the next moment it has gone. This sudden loss of output is not uncommon in fringe-area FM reception.†

But Fig. 7.20 is, in some ways, deceptive, for it implies a usable output signal below the knee whereas an arbitrary modulating signal would be suffering from mutilation. Experimental studies indicate that mutilation is negligible in most cases of interest if $(W/B_T)\gamma = (S/N)_R \geq 10$ or thereabouts. Hence, we define the threshold point to be at

$$(S/N)_{R_{th}} = 10 \qquad (22)$$

so

$$\gamma_{th} = 10\,\frac{B_T}{W} = 20M(\Delta) \qquad (23a)$$

$$\approx 20(\Delta + 2) \qquad \Delta > 2 \qquad (23b)$$

where use has been made of the FM bandwidth equation $B_T = 2M(\Delta)W \approx 2(\Delta + 2)W$. Equations (22) and (23) also apply to PM with Δ replaced by ϕ_Δ.

Figure 7.20 correctly demonstrates that FM performance above threshold is quite impressive—after all, baseband transmission at best gives $(S/N)_D = \gamma$. And Fig. 7.20 does not include the additional improvement afforded by deemphasis filtering. But observe what happens if one attempts to make $(S/N)_D$ arbitrarily large

---

† A similar phenomenon occurs with cochannel interference of two signals having nearly equal amplitudes at the receiver. Small variations of relative amplitude then cause the stronger of the two to suddenly dominate the situation, displacing the other completely at the output. This has been given the apt name *capture effect*.

by increasing only the deviation ratio while holding γ fixed, say at 20 dB. With $\Delta = 2$ ($B_T \approx 7W$) we are just above threshold, and $(S/N)_D \approx 28$ dB; but with $\Delta = 5$ ($B_T \approx 14W$) we are below threshold, and the output signal is useless because of mutilation. One therefore cannot achieve an unlimited exchange of bandwidth for signal-to-noise ratio, and system performance may actually deteriorate with increased deviation.

Swapping bandwidth in favor of reduced power is likewise restricted. Suppose, for example, a 30-dB signal-to-noise ratio is desired with a minimum of transmitted power but the transmission bandwidth can be as large as $B_T = 14W$. Were it not for threshold, we could use FM with $\Delta = 5$ and $\gamma = 14$ dB, a power saving compared to baseband of 16 dB. But the threshold point for $\Delta = 5$ is $\gamma_{\text{th}} = 21.5$ dB, for which $(S/N)_D = 37.5$ dB. Thus, the design is dictated by the threshold point rather than the desired signal-to-noise ratio, and the potential power reduction cannot be fully realized.

In view of these considerations, it is useful to calculate $(S/N)_D$ at the threshold point. Thus, again omitting deemphasis, we substitute Eq. (23) into Eq. (17) to get

$$\left(\frac{S}{N}\right)_{D_{\text{th}}} = 3\Delta^2 \overline{x^2} \gamma_{\text{th}} \tag{24a}$$

$$\approx 60\Delta^2(\Delta + 2)\overline{x^2} \qquad \Delta > 2 \tag{24b}$$

which is the minimum value of $(S/N)_D$ as a function of Δ. Given a specified value for $(S/N)_D$ and no bandwidth constraint, one can solve Eq. (24) for the deviation ratio Δ that yields the *most efficient performance* in terms of signal power. Of course, some allowance must be made for possible signal fading since it is unadvisable to operate with no margin relative to the threshold point.

EXERCISE 7.8   Design a minimum-power FM system with no bandwidth constraint such that $(S/N)_D = 50$ dB, given $\overline{x^2} = \frac{1}{2}$, $W = 10$ kHz, and $\eta = 10^{-8}$ W/Hz. *Ans.:* $\Delta \approx 14$, $B_T \approx 320$ kHz, $S_R \geq 32$ mW.

FM Threshold Extension (FMFB) ★

Because the threshold limitation is a serious constraint on the design of minimum-power FM systems, there has been considerable interest in *threshold-extension* techniques — especially for space communication. But long before the space applications arose, Chaffee (1939) proposed a means for extending the FM threshold point using a frequency-following or frequency-compressive feedback loop in the receiver, i.e., FM feedback (FMFB). Here, we outline the basic idea of FMFB. Other threshold-

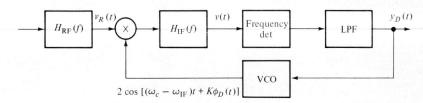

FIGURE 7.21
FMFB receiver.

extension techniques—notably, the phase-lock loop receiver (PLL)—can be found in the literature† along with detailed analysis of FMFB.

An FMFB receiver is a superheterodyne in which the local oscillator is replaced by a VCO whose instantaneous output frequency is controlled by the demodulated signal, giving the feedback configuration of Fig. 7.21. Qualitatively, the VCO follows or tracks the instantaneous frequency of the modulated signal so that, as we shall see, the effective frequency deviation at the IF input is reduced and the IF bandwidth can be much smaller than B_T (but, of course, no less than $2W$). If $B_{IF} \ll B_T$, the noise power at the detector input is much less than N_R and hence the threshold level has been lowered.

Specifically, $N_{IF} = (B_{IF}/B_T)N_R$ and mutilation is avoided if $S_R/N_{IF} = (B_T/B_{IF})(S/N)_R \geq 10$. Therefore, the new threshold level is

$$\left(\frac{S}{N}\right)_{R_{th}} = 10\,\frac{B_{IF}}{B_T}$$

or

$$\gamma_{th} = 10\,\frac{B_{IF}}{B_T}\frac{B_T}{W} = 10\,\frac{B_{IF}}{W} \geq 20 \tag{25}$$

as compared with $\gamma_{th} = 20M(\Delta)$ for a conventional receiver. It remains to be shown that B_{IF} can be smaller than B_T and that the performance above threshold has not been degraded. This we shall do by first taking the case of a modulated signal without noise and then looking at an unmodulated carrier with noise.

With reference to Fig. 7.21, the VCO output equals $2 \cos [(\omega_c - \omega_{IF})t + K\phi_D(t)]$ where $\omega_{IF} = 2\pi f_{IF}$, K is a constant, and

$$\phi_D(t) = 2\pi \int_{-\infty}^{t} y_D(\lambda)\, d\lambda$$

† Taub and Schilling (1971, chap. 10); Schwartz, Bennett, and Stein (1966, chap. 3).

In absence of noise, the received signal $v_R(t)$ is

$$v_R(t) = A_R \cos \left[\omega_c t + \phi(t) \right] \quad \text{with} \quad \phi(t) = 2\pi f_\Delta \int_{-\infty}^{t} x(\lambda)\, d\lambda$$

Therefore, assuming $H_{IF}(f)$ removes the sum-frequency term from the mixer output, the input to the detector will be the difference-frequency signal

$$v(t) = A_R \cos \left[\omega_{IF} t + \underbrace{\phi(t) - K\phi_D(t)}_{\phi_v(t)} \right]$$

Thus

$$y_D(t) = \frac{1}{2\pi} \frac{d\phi_v(t)}{dt} = f_\Delta x(t) - Ky_D(t)$$

and solving for $y_D(t)$ yields

$$y_D(t) = \frac{f_\Delta}{1 + K} x(t) \qquad (26)$$

so the frequency deviation has been reduced by $1/(1 + K)$ owing to the frequency-following effect of the feedback. And this deviation reduction also holds at the mixer output since $\phi_v(t) = 2\pi[f_\Delta/(1 + K)]\phi(t)$; accordingly, the IF bandwidth can be

$$B_{IF} = 2M(\Delta_{IF}) \qquad \Delta_{IF} = \frac{f_\Delta}{(1 + K)W}$$

and $B_{IF} \approx 2W$ if K is chosen such that $B_{IF} \ll 1$.

Now consider an unmodulated carrier plus noise with $S_R/N_{IF} \gg 1$. Letting $n_{qIF}(t)$ be the quadrature noise at the IF output, it follows that the noise spectral density is constant over B_{IF} if $B_{IF} \ll B_T$ so

$$G_{n_{qIF}}(f) = \eta \, |H_{IF}(f - f_{IF})|^2$$

Then we infer from Eqs. (25), (8b), and (12) that the demodulated noise is

$$\xi(t) = \frac{1}{(1 + K)2\pi A_R} \frac{dn_{qIF}(t)}{dt}$$

and

$$N_D = \frac{\eta W^3}{(1 + K)^2 3 S_R}$$

Finally, from Eq. (26), $S_D = f_\Delta^2 \overline{x^2}/(1 + K)^2$ so $(S/N)_D$ is the same as for a conventional receiver, Eq. (17), since $(1 + K)^2$ cancels out in the ratio.

Not to mislead the student, several factors have been glossed over in this rough analysis. We have not really looked at the performance near threshold, and the whole subject of tracking error and transient behavior has been omitted. Our conclusion about $(S/N)_D$ above threshold is correct and so is the bandwidth reduction. However, it turns out that the threshold point has a dependence on the deviation ratio Δ not included in Eq. (25). As a result, FMFB threshold extension is limited to about 5 to 7 dB—a nonetheless significant factor in minimum-power designs.

7.6 COMPARISON OF CW MODULATION SYSTEMS

At last we are in position to make a meaningful comparison of the various types of CW modulation. Table 7.1 summarizes the points to be compared: normalized transmission bandwidth, $\mathscr{B} \triangleq B_T/W$; destination signal-to-noise ratio $(S/N)_D$ normalized by γ; threshold point, if any; DC or low-frequency response; and instrumentation complexity. The table also includes baseband transmission for reference purposes. As before, $\gamma \triangleq S_R/\eta W$ where W is the message bandwidth, S_R is the received signal power, and $\eta = k \mathscr{T}_N$ is the noise density referred to the receiver input. Nearly ideal systems are assumed, so the values of $(S/N)_D$ are upper bounds.

Of the several types of linear modulation, suppressed carrier methods are superior to conventional AM on several counts; signal-to-noise ratios are better, and there is no threshold effect. When *bandwidth conservation* is important, single sideband and vestigial sideband are particularly attractive. But one seldom gets something for nothing in this world, and the price of efficient linear modulation is the increased complexity of instrumentation, especially at the receiver. Synchronous detection, no matter how it is accomplished, requires highly sophisticated circuitry compared to the envelope detector. For *point-to-point* communication (one transmitter, one receiver) the price may be worthwhile. But for *broadcast* systems (one transmitter, *many* receivers) economic considerations tip the balance toward the simplest possible receiver, and hence envelope detection.

From an instrumentation viewpoint AM is the least complex linear modulation, while suppressed-carrier VSB, with its special sideband filter and synchronization requirements, is the most complex. Of DSB and SSB (in their proper applications) the latter is less difficult to instrument because synchronization is not so critical. In addition, improved filter technology has made the required sideband filters more readily available. Similarly, VSB + C is classed as of "moderate" complexity, despite the vestigial filter, since envelope detection is sufficient.

Compared to baseband or linear modulation, exponential modulation can provide substantially increased values of $(S/N)_D$—especially FM with deemphasis—with only

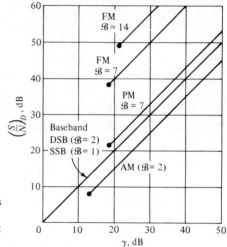

FIGURE 7.22

Performance of CW modulation systems as a function of $\gamma = S_R/\eta W$ and $\mathscr{B} = B_T/W$; 12-dB deemphasis improvement included for FM.

moderately complex instrumentation. Figure 7.22 illustrates this in a form similar to Fig. 7.20 (again taking $\overline{x^2} = \frac{1}{2}$) except that a representative 12-dB deemphasis improvement has been added to the FM curves and performance below threshold is omitted. All curves are labeled with the bandwidth ratio $\mathscr{B}$.

Clearly, for equal values of $\mathscr{B}$, FM is markedly superior to PM insofar as noise performance is concerned. (Phase modulation does have advantages over FM for *digital* signal transmission, to be discussed in Chap. 10.) And as long as the system is above threshold, the improvement can be made arbitrarily large by increasing $\mathscr{B}$, whereas PM is limited to $\mathscr{B} \leq 10$ since $\phi_\Delta \leq \pi$.

The penalty for this improvement is excessive transmission bandwidth. Therefore, wideband exponential modulation is most appropriate when extremely clean output signals are desired and bandwidth conservation is a secondary factor. Typical applications include commercial FM and television audio. At microwave frequencies, both the noise-reduction and constant-amplitude properties are advantageous, so that most microwave systems have exponential carrier modulation.

As to power conservation, FM with moderate values of $\mathscr{B}$ does offer a saving over linear modulation, threshold limitations notwithstanding. In this capacity it is used for point-to-point radio, especially mobile systems, where synchronous detection would be a nuisance. Moreover, thanks to threshold-extension techniques, wideband FM is employed in certain satellite and space-probe communication systems, where transmitter power is at a premium.

Regarding transmission of modulating signals having significant low-frequency components, we have already argued the superiority of DSB and VSB; this explains their use in data transmission, both analog and digital. For facsimile and TV video,

Table 7.1 COMPARISON OF CW MODULATION SYSTEMS

Type	$\mathscr{B} = B_T/W$	$(S/N)_D/\gamma$	γ_{th}	DC	Complexity	Comments	Typical applications
Baseband	1	1	...	No[a]	Minor	No modulation	Short-haul links
AM	2	$\dfrac{m^2\overline{x^2}}{1+m^2\overline{x^2}}$	20	No	Minor	Envelope detection $m \le 1$	Broadcast radio
DSB	2	1	...	Yes	Major	Synchronous detection	Analog data, multiplexing
SSB	1	1	...	No	Moderate	Synchronous detection	Point-to-point voice, multiplexing
VSB	1+	1	...	Yes	Major	Synchronous detection	Digital data
VSB+C	1+	$\dfrac{m^2\overline{x^2}}{1+m^2\overline{x^2}}$	20	Yes[b]	Moderate	Envelope detection $m < 1$	Television video
PM[c]	$2M(\phi_\Delta)$	$\phi_\Delta^2\overline{x^2}$	$10\mathscr{B}$	Yes	Moderate	Phase detection $\phi_\Delta \le \pi$	Digital data
FM[c,d]	$2M(\Delta)$	$3\Delta^2\overline{x^2}$	$10\mathscr{B}$	Yes	Moderate	Frequency detection	Broadcast radio, microwave relay

[a] Unless direct-coupled.
[b] With electronic DC restoration.
[c] $\mathscr{B} \ge 2$.
[d] Deemphasis not included.

electronic DC restoration makes envelope-detected VSB possible and desirable. (AM could also be used in this way, but the bandwidth is prohibitive. Suppressed-carrier single sideband is virtually out of the question.) Also it was briefly noted in Sect. 6.5 that a balanced discriminator has excellent low-frequency response; hence the low-frequency performance of FM can equal that of DSB or VSB, and without troublesome synchronization. Consequently, small-deviation FM or PM subcarrier modulation is often used in telemetry systems for the less active input signals. For similar reasons, high-quality magnetic-tape recorders are equipped with an FM mode in which the input is recorded as a frequency-modulated wave.

Not shown in the table is relative system performance in the face of time-varying transmission characteristics, frequency-selective fading, multiple-path propagation, etc. An unstable transmission medium has a *multiplicative* effect which is particularly disastrous for envelope detection. (Late-night listeners to distant AM stations are familiar with the garbled result.) Similarly, transmission instabilities often preclude wideband modulation.

To summarize briefly is impossible. There is no universal solution to all communication problems. The communication engineer must therefore approach each new task with an open mind and a careful review of all available information.

7.7 PROBLEMS

7.1 (Sect. 7.1) Show that Eqs. (5a) to (5d) are appropriate models by taking $v(t) = K_R x_c(t)$ where $x_c(t)$ has the corresponding type of modulation, i.e., DSB or SSB, AM, PM, and FM, respectively.

7.2 (Sect. 7.2) Find an approximate expression for the envelope of a tone-modulated AM wave plus an interfering sinusoid $A_I \cos[(\omega_c + \omega_I)t + \theta]$ with $A_I \ll A_R$.

7.3 (Sect. 7.2) Investigate the performance of AM envelope detection versus AM synchronous detection in the presence of *multipath propagation* such that $v(t) = x_c(t) + \alpha x_c(t - t_d)$, where $\alpha^2 < 1$ and $x_c(t) = [1 + mx(t)] \cos \omega_c t$. Note especially the differences when $\omega_c t_d \approx n\pi$ and $\omega_c t_d \approx (n + \frac{1}{2})\pi$.

7.4 (Sect. 7.2) Starting with Eq. (1), show that the instantaneous frequency deviation of $v(t)$ is $f_v(t) = m_I f_I(m_I + \cos \omega_I t)/(1 + m_I^2 + 2m_I \cos \omega_I t)$ where $m_I = A_I/A_R$. Taking $m_I = 0.5$, sketch $f_v(t)$ for $0 \le \omega_I t \le 180°$.

7.5 (Sect. 7.2) Figure P7.1 is the standard *preemphasis circuit* when an RC LPF is used for deemphasis. Find $H_{pe}(f)$ and show that it approximates Eq. (10) to within a proportionality constant when $2\pi RC = 1/B_{de}$ and $R_0 \ll R$.

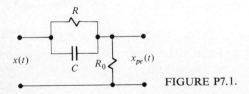

FIGURE P7.1.

7.6★ (Sect. 7.2) When Eq. (11) is not satisfied, preemphasis filtering will increase the bandwidth of the FM signal. One can estimate the increase using the *rms frequency deviation* $f_{\Delta_{pe}} = f_\Delta \overline{(x_{pe}^2)}^{1/2}$, where $x_{pe}(t)$ is the output of $H_{pe}(f)$ and it is assumed that $x(t)$ and $x_{pe}(t)$ are both bandlimited in W with $\bar{x} = \bar{x}_{pe} = 0$ and $\overline{x^2} = 1$. The bandwidth with preemphasis is then calculated using $f_{\Delta_{pe}}$ in place of f_Δ.

(a) Taking $H_{pe}(f) = K/H_{de}(f)$ and $H_{de}(f)$ per Eq. (9), show that $(f_{\Delta_{pe}}/f_\Delta)^2 = K^2[1 + \int_{-\infty}^{\infty} (f/B_{de})^2 G_x(f) \, df]$.

(b) Evaluate $B_{T_{pe}}/B_T$ when $K = 1$, $G_x(f) = (1/2W)\Pi(f/2W)$, $B_{de} = W/3$, and $f_\Delta = 5W$.

7.7 (Sect. 7.3) Sketch $G_{n_i}(f)$ when $\eta = 40$ and $|H_R(f)|$ is as plotted in Fig. P5.1.

7.8 (Sect. 7.3) Suppose $|H_R(f)|$ has symmetry about $\pm f_c$ and $B_N \approx B_T \ll f_c$, so one can write $|H_R(f)|^2 = |H_{LP}(f - f_c)|^2 + |H_{LP}(f + f_c)|^2$ where $H_{LP}(f) = H_R(f + f_c)u(f + f_c)$. Show that the autocorrelation of $n(t)$ is $R_n(\tau) = \eta B_T \rho(\tau) \cos 2\pi f_c \tau$ where $\rho(\tau) = (1/B_T)\mathscr{F}^{-1}[|H_{LP}(f)|^2]$, and justify the approximation $\rho(\tau) \approx 1$ for $|\tau| \ll 1/B_T$.

7.9 (Sect. 7.3) Carry out all the details between Eqs. (9) and (11).

7.10 (Sect. 7.3) Consider the random signal $y(t) = 2n(t) \cos(\omega_c t + \theta)$ where $n(t)$ is bandpass noise centered on f_c. Analyze and discuss the properties of $y(t)$, giving attention to its dependence on θ.

7.11 (Sect. 7.3) Bandpass noise is processed by a device whose output $y(t)$ is the square of the input envelope. Find $p_y(y)$, $\bar{y}$, and $\overline{y^2}$. Ans.: $p_y(y) = (2\sigma_n^2)^{-1}e^{-y/2\sigma_n^2}u(y)$.

7.12 (Sect. 7.3) Bandpass noise with $B_T \ll f_c$ is passed through a hard limiter. Sketch a typical sample of the output $y(t)$ and write an expression for $p_y(y)$.

7.13 (Sect. 7.4) The product demodulator of Fig. 5.27 has DSB plus noise at the input and there is a *phase error* ϕ' in the oscillator so its output is $A_{LO} \cos(\omega_c t + \phi')$. Find $y_D(t)$ and show that $(S/N)_D$ is reduced by the factor $\cos^2 \phi'$.

7.14 (Sect. 7.4) A USSB receiver has $|H_R(f)|^2$ shown in Fig. P7.2. Sketch the output noise spectrum and find $(S/N)_D$ in terms of γ.

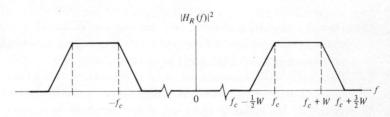

$|H_R(f)|^2$

$-f_c$ 0 $f_c - \frac{1}{2}W$ f_c $f_c + W$ $f_c + \frac{3}{2}W$ f

FIGURE P7.2.

7.15★(Sect. 7.4) Analyze the performance of a DSB *homodyne detector*, Fig. 5.29, when the input has additive bandpass noise. Take $x_c(t) = [x(t) + a] \cos \omega_c t$, where $a \cos \omega_c t$ is is the pilot carrier, and let the pilot filter be a BPF centered on f_c with bandwidth $B_p \ll 2W$.

7.16 (Sect. 7.4) An AM system with envelope detection has $(S/N)_D = 30$ dB under full-load tone-modulation conditions with $W = 8$ kHz. If all bandwidths are increased accordingly while other parameters are fixed, what is the largest value of W for which the system is above threshold?

7.17   (Sect. 7.4) A *heterodyne* receiver is a superhet without RF filtering. With the aid of Fig. 5.33, explain why $(S/N)_D$ may be 3 dB less than that of a comparable superheterodyne receiver. Discuss the differences when most of the noise is generated within the receiver rather than coming in with the signal.

7.18   (Sect. 7.4) Use noise considerations to explain the following statements.

   (a) In an SSB receiver it is desirable to have $|H_R(f)|$ nearly rectangular with $B_R = B_T$, whereas this is not critical for DSB.

   (b) In an AM receiver with envelope detection it is desirable to have $|H_R(f)|$ nearly rectangular with $B_R = B_T$, whereas this is not critical for synchronous detection of AM.

7.19   (Sect. 7.4) Let $v(t) = 4 \cos \omega_c t + n(t)$, where $n(t)$ is bandpass noise centered on $f_c + 20$ with $B_T = 8$ and $\eta = 0.02$. Obtain an approximate expression for $R_v(t)$ and evaluate $\overline{R_v^2}$.

7.20   (Sect. 7.5) Sketch $G_{\hat{z}_{FM}}(f)$ when $|H_R(f)|$ is as in Prob. 6.25 with $f_0 = f_c$ and $Q = f_c/B_T$.

7.21   (Sect. 7.5) Equations (10) and (12) are for an ideal LPF. Find N_D for FM and PM when the postdetection filter is an Mth-order Butterworth LPF with $|H(f)| = [1 + (f/W)^{2M}]^{-1/2}$. Assume $|H_R(f - f_c)|^2 \approx 1$ for $|f| \leq B_T/2$ and $B_T \gg 2W$.

7.22   (Sect. 7.5) Estimate the noise reduction factor for FM with a gaussian deemphasis filter $|H_{de}(f)|^2 = \exp[-(\ln 2)(f/B_{de})^2]$ where $B_{de} \ll W \ll B_T/2$. Compare with Eq. (15).

7.23   (Sect. 7.5) A certain PM system has $(S/N)_D = 30$ dB. If the modulation is changed to FM with the same B_T and an RC deemphasis filter with $B_{de} = W/10$ is added, what is the new value of $(S/N)_D$? *Ans.*: 50 dB.

7.24   (Sect. 7.5) The signal $x(t) = \cos 2\pi 200t$ is sent via FM without deemphasis. There is an ideal BPF passing $100 \leq |f| \leq 300$ at the discriminator output. Calculate $(S/N)_D$ if $f_\Delta = 1$ kHz and $S_R/\eta = 500$.

7.25   (Sect. 7.5) Modify Eq. (24) to include RC deemphasis filtering and repeat Exercise 7.8 taking $B_{de} = 2$ kHz.

7.26 ★ (Sect. 7.5) Referring to Prob. 7.6a, suppose K is chosen such that $f_{\Delta_{pe}} = f_\Delta$ so pre-emphasis does not significantly increase the transmission bandwidth.

   (a) Show that $S_D = (Kf_\Delta)^2 \overline{x^2}$ and hence $(S/N)_D = f_\Delta^2 \overline{x^2} \gamma / [B_{de}^2 + \int_{-\infty}^{\infty} f^2 G_x(f) \, df]$.

   (b) Simplify this expression assuming $G_x(f) = [f_0/\pi(f^2 + f_0^2)]\Pi(f/2W)$ where $f_0 = B_{de} \ll W$. Compare with Eqs. (17) and (18).

7.27   (Sect. 7.5) The spikes or clicks in FM near threshold occur also when there is interference with $A_I \approx A_R$. Demonstrate this by roughly sketching $\not{f}_v(t)$ in Prob. 7.4 with $m_I = 1 + \epsilon$, $\epsilon^2 \ll 1$. (Be careful near $\cos \omega_I t = -1$.) What happens when $\epsilon \to 0$?

7.28   (Sect. 7.6) A communication system has $\mathscr{L} = 100$ dB, $\eta = 10^{-14}$ W/Hz, $\overline{x^2} = 1$, and $W = 10$ kHz. Calculate the value of S_T in kilowatts required for $(S/N)_D \geq 40$ dB when the modulation is:

   (a) SSB

   (b) AM with $m = 1$ and $m = 0.1$

   (c) PM with $\phi_\Delta = \pi$

(d) FM with $f_\Delta = 10$, 50, and 100 kHz

Omit deemphasis in the FM case, but check for threshold limitations. *Ans.*: (a) 10; (b) 20, 1,010; (c) 1; (d) 3.3, 0.14, 0.24.

7.29 (Sect. 7.6) Repeat Prob. 7.28 with $W = 20$ kHz.

7.30 (Sect. 7.6) A signal with $\overline{x^2} = \frac{1}{2}$ is transmitted via AM with $m = 1$ and $(S/N)_D = 13$ dB. If the modulation is changed to FM (without deemphasis) and the bandwidths are increased while other parameters are fixed, find the largest usable value of Δ and the resulting $(S/N)_D$.

7.31★(Sect. 7.6) An FDM system uses USSB subcarrier modulation and FM carrier modulation. There are K independent input signals, each bandlimited in W_0, and the subcarrier frequencies are $f_{c_k} = (k - 1)W_0$, $k = 1, 2, \ldots, K$. The baseband signal applied to the FM modulator is $x_b(t) = \sum \alpha_k x_k(t)$ where $x_k(t)$ is the kth subcarrier signal, each having $\overline{x_k^2} = 1$, and α_k are constants. At the receiver the discriminator is followed by a bank of BPFs and synchronous detectors. Show that the S/N at the output of the kth channel is $(S/N)_k = f_\Delta^2 \alpha_k^2 / N_k$ where $N_k = (3k^2 - 3k + 1)\eta W_0^3 / 3S_R$. (*Hint*: Recall that the input and output S/N are equal for SSB synchronous detection.)

7.32★(Sect. 7.6) In the system described in Prob. 7.31 the α_k are to be chosen such that $\overline{x_b^2} = 1$ and all channels have the same value of $(S/N)_k$. Obtain expressions for α_k and $(S/N)_k$ under these conditions.

7.33★(Sect. 7.6) FM *stereo multiplexing* uses preemphasis/deemphasis filtering not shown in Figs. 5.37 and 5.38. Specifically, the matrixed signals $x_1(t) = x_L(t) + x_R(t)$ and $x_2(t) = x_L(t) - x_R(t)$ are each preemphasized before they are multiplexed at the transmitter; similarly, they are each deemphasized after demultiplexing but prior to the matrix at the receiver. RC filters with $B_{de} = 2.1$ kHz are used throughout. The signal-plus-noise inputs to the receiver matrix are $y_1(t) = f_\Delta x_1(t) + n_1(t)$ and $y_2(t) = f_\Delta x_2(t) + n_2(t)$, and the final outputs are $y_1(t) \pm y_2(t)$.

(a) Show that $n_2(t)$ has $G_{n_2}(f) = |H_{de}(f)|^2 (\eta/S_R)(f^2 + f_{sc}^2)\Pi(f/2W)$, where $f_{sc} = 38$ kHz, assuming the BPF and the synchronous detection are ideal. Then show that $\overline{n_2^2} \gg \overline{n_1^2}$. (*Hint*: Sketch the noise spectrum at the BPF output and apply frequency translation.)

(b) Taking $\overline{x_L x_R} = 0$ and $\overline{x_L^2} = \overline{x_R^2} \approx \frac{1}{3}$—so that $\overline{x_b^2} \approx 1$ if the pilot amplitude is small—show that the per-channel $(S/N)_D$ for stereo transmission is about 20 dB less than monaural transmission.

8

SAMPLING AND PULSE MODULATION

Experimental data and mathematical functions are frequently displayed as *continuous* curves even though a finite number of *discrete points* may have been used to construct the graph. If these discrete points, or *samples*, have sufficiently close spacing, a smooth curve is drawn through them, and intermediate values can be interpolated to any reasonable degree of accuracy. It can therefore be said that the continuous display is adequately described by the sample points alone.

In similar fashion, an electric signal satisfying certain requirements can be reproduced entirely from an appropriate set of instantaneous samples. If this is so, and sampling theory will tell us the necessary conditions, we need transmit only the sample values as they occur instead of sending the signal continuously. This is *pulse modulation*.

The key distinction between pulse modulation and CW modulation is as follows: in CW modulation, some parameter of the modulated wave varies continuously with the message; in pulse modulation, some parameter of each pulse is modulated by a particular sample value of the message. Usually the pulses are quite short compared to the time between them, so a pulse-modulated wave is "off" most of the time.

Because of this property, pulse modulation offers two potential advantages over CW. First, the transmitted power can be concentrated into short bursts rather than being delivered continuously. This gives the system engineer added latitude in equipment selection, since certain devices, such as high-power microwave tubes and lasers, are operable only on a pulsed basis. Second, the time intervals between pulses can be filled with sample values from other messages, thereby permitting the transmission of many messages on one communication system. Such multiplexing in the time domain is known as *time-division multiplexing* (TDM).

Another distinction between pulse and CW modulation is that the pulsed wave may contain appreciable DC and low-frequency content. Efficient transmission therefore entails a second operation, namely, CW modulation, to provide complete frequency translation. In this light, pulse modulation is a *message-processing* technique rather than modulation in the usual sense. As a matter of fact, the most common use of pulse modulation is message processing for TDM.

There are two basic types of pulse modulation: *analog*, such as pulse-amplitude or pulse-position modulation, which is in many ways similar to linear or exponential modulation; and *digital* or *coded* pulse modulation, which has no CW equivalent. Both types are examined in this chapter, the latter being emphasized because of its unique and desirable properties.

Regardless of type, the key operation for pulsed communication is extracting sample values from the message waveform. Moreover, the sampling concept plays an equally important role in *information theory*, the subject of Chap. 9, and in the theory of sampled-data control systems. We therefore begin this chapter with a study of sampling, both theoretical and practical.

8.1 SAMPLING THEORY AND PRACTICE

A simple but highly informative approach to sampling theory is via the switching operation of Fig. 8.1a. The switch periodically shifts between two contacts at a rate of $f_s = 1/T_s$ Hz, dwelling on the input-signal contact for τ seconds and on the grounded contact for the remainder of each period. The output $x_s(t)$ then consists of short

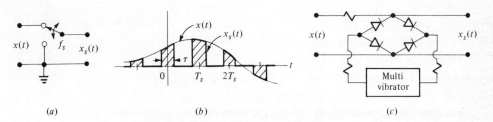

(a) (b) (c)

FIGURE 8.1
A switching sampler. (a) Diagram; (b) waveforms; (c) electronic circuit.

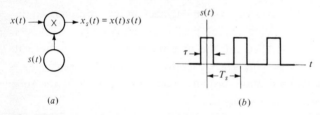

FIGURE 8.2
Sampling interpreted as multiplication. (*a*) Diagram; (*b*) switching function $s(t)$.

segments of the input $x(t)$, as shown in Fig. 8.1*b*. Figure 8.1*c* is an electronic version of Fig. 8.1*a*; the output voltage equals the input voltage except when the multivibrator forward-biases the diodes and thereby clamps the output to zero. This operation, variously called *single-ended* or *unipolar chopping*, is not instantaneous sampling in the strict sense. Nonetheless, $x_s(t)$ will be designated the sampled wave and f_s the sampling frequency.

We now ask: Are the sampled segments sufficient to describe the original input signal, and, if so, how can $x(t)$ be retrieved from $x_s(t)$? The answer to this question lies in the frequency domain, namely, in the spectrum of the sampled wave.

As a first step toward finding the spectrum, we introduce a *switching function* $s(t)$ such that

$$x_s(t) = x(t)s(t) \tag{1}$$

Thus the sampling operation becomes multiplication by $s(t)$, as indicated schematically in Fig. 8.2*a*, where $s(t)$ is nothing more than the periodic pulse train of Fig. 8.2*b*. Since $s(t)$ is periodic, it can be written as a Fourier series. Using the results of Example 2.2, Sect. 2.2, we have

$$s(t) = \sum_{n=-\infty}^{\infty} f_s \tau \operatorname{sinc} n f_s \tau \, e^{j2\pi n f_s t}$$

$$= c_0 + \sum_{n=1}^{\infty} 2c_n \cos n\omega_s t \tag{2}$$

where

$$c_n = f_s \tau \operatorname{sinc} n f_s \tau \qquad \omega_s = 2\pi f_s$$

Combining Eq. (2) with Eq. (1) yields the term-by-term expansion

$$x_s(t) = c_0 x(t) + 2c_1 x(t) \cos \omega_s t + 2c_2 x(t) \cos 2\omega_c t + \cdots \tag{3}$$

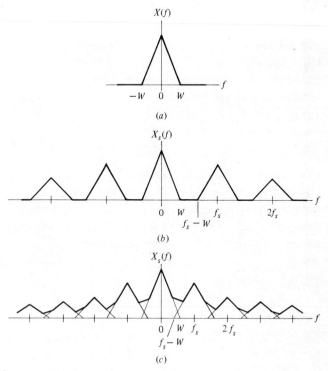

FIGURE 8.3
Spectra for switching sampling. (*a*) Message; (*b*) sampled message, $f_s > 2W$; (*c*) sampled message, $f_s < 2W$.

Thus, if the input spectrum is $X(f) = \mathscr{F}[x(t)]$, the output spectrum is

$$
\begin{aligned}
X_s(f) = c_0\, X(f) &+ c_1[X(f - f_s) + X(f + f_s)] \\
&+ c_2[X(f - 2f_s) + X(f + 2f_s)] \\
&+ \cdots
\end{aligned}
\tag{4}
$$

which follows directly from the modulation theorem.

    While Eq. (4) appears rather messy, the spectrum of the sampled wave is readily sketched if the input signal is assumed to be *bandlimited*, say in W. Figure 8.3 shows a convenient $X(f)$ and the corresponding $X_s(f)$ for two cases, $f_s > 2W$ and $f_s < 2W$. Examining this figure reveals something quite surprising: the sampling operation has left the message spectrum *intact*, merely repeating it periodically in the frequency domain with a spacing of f_s. We also note that the first term of Eq. (4) is precisely the message spectrum, attenuated by the *duty cycle* $c_0 = f_s \tau = \tau / T_s$.

    If sampling preserves the message spectrum, it should be possible to recover or *reconstruct* $x(t)$ from the sampled wave $x_s(t)$. The reconstruction technique is not at all obvious from the time-domain relations, Eqs. (1) and (3), but referring again to Fig. 8.3, we see that $X(f)$ can be separated from $X_s(f)$ by *lowpass filtering*, providing the "sidebands" do not overlap. And if $X(f)$ alone is filtered from $X_s(f)$, we have recovered $x(t)$. Two conditions obviously are necessary to prevent overlapping sidebands: the message must be bandlimited, and the sampling frequency must be sufficiently great that $f_s - W \geq W$, that is,

$$f_s \geq 2W \qquad \text{or} \qquad T_s \leq \frac{1}{2W} \qquad (5)$$

The minimum sampling frequency $f_{s_{\min}} = 2W$ is called the *Nyquist rate*. When Eq. (5) is satisfied and $x_s(t)$ is filtered by an ideal LPF, the output signal will be proportional to $x(t)$; message reconstruction from the sampled signal therefore has been achieved. The exact value of the filter bandwidth is unimportant as long as the filter passes $X(f)$ and rejects all other components, i.e.,

$$W \leq B \leq f_s - W \qquad (6)$$

as follows from Fig. 8.3*b*.

This analysis has shown that if a bandlimited signal is sampled at a frequency greater than the Nyquist rate, it can be *completely reconstructed* from the sampled wave. Reconstruction is accomplished by lowpass filtering. These conclusions may be difficult for the reader to believe at first exposure; they certainly test our faith in spectral analysis. Nonetheless, they are quite correct.

Finally, it should be pointed out that our results are independent of the sample-pulse duration, save as it appears in the duty cycle. If τ is made very small, $x_s(t)$ approaches a string of *instantaneous sample points*, which corresponds to *ideal sampling*. And while the above analysis is representative of practical sampling and is sufficient for many purposes, we shall now devote our attention to ideal sampling, the study of which provides further insight to the how and why of sampling and reconstruction, along with proof of the uniform-sampling theorem.

EXERCISE 8.1   Consider the case of an imperfect chopper wherein the pulses that make up $s(t)$ are not rectangular, so

$$s(t) = \sum_{k=-\infty}^{\infty} p(t - kT_s) \qquad (7a)$$

where the pulse shape $p(t)$ equals zero for $|t| > T_s/2$ but is otherwise arbitrary. Letting $P(f) = \mathscr{F}[p(t)]$ and $c_n = P(nf_s)/T_s$, show that

$$x_s(t) = c_0 x(t) + \sum_{n=1}^{\infty} |2c_n| x(t) \cos(n\omega_s t + \arg[c_n]) \qquad (7b)$$

and hence our previous conclusions about recovering $x(t)$ still apply.

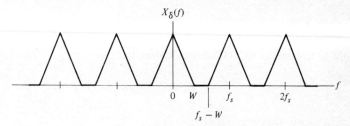

$X_\delta(f)$

0 W f_s $2f_s$ f

$f_s - W$

FIGURE 8.4
Spectrum of an ideally sampled message.

Ideal Sampling and Reconstruction

By definition, ideal sampling is *instantaneous* sampling. The switching device of Fig. 8.1a yields instantaneous values only if $\tau \to 0$; but then $f_s\tau \to 0$, and so does $x_s(t)$ — see Eq. (3). Conceptually, this difficulty is overcome by multiplying $x_s(t)$ by $1/\tau$ so that, as $\tau \to 0$ and $1/\tau \to \infty$, the sampled wave becomes a train of *impulses* whose *areas* equal the instantaneous sample values of the input signal. Formally we define

$$s_\delta(t) \triangleq \sum_{k=-\infty}^{\infty} \delta(t - kT_s) \qquad (8)$$

called the ideal sampling function. Then, in the notation of Exercise 8.1, $p(t) = \delta(t)$, $P(f) = \mathscr{F}[\delta(t)] = 1$, and $c_n = 1/T_s = f_s$ for all n. Therefore, from Eq. (7b),

$$x_\delta(t) \triangleq x(t)s_\delta(t) \qquad (9a)$$

$$= f_s\left[x(t) + \sum_{n=1}^{\infty} 2x(t) \cos n\omega_s t\right] \qquad (9b)$$

and

$$X_\delta(f) = \mathscr{F}[x_\delta(t)]$$

$$= f_s \sum_{n=-\infty}^{\infty} X(f - nf_s) \qquad (10)$$

which is illustrated in Fig. 8.4 for the message spectrum of Fig. 8.3a, taking $f_s > 2W$. Note that $X_\delta(f)$ is *periodic in frequency* with period f_s, a crucial observation in the study of sampled-data systems.

We call $x_\delta(t)$ the *ideal sampled wave*; it consists of a train of impulses with spacing T_s whose areas equal the instantaneous sample values $x(kT_s)$. This is shown by combining Eqs. (8) and (9a) thus:

$$x_\delta(t) = x(t) \sum_{k=-\infty}^{\infty} \delta(t - kT_s) \qquad (11a)$$

$$= \sum_{k=-\infty}^{\infty} x(kT_s)\, \delta(t - kT_s) \qquad (11b)$$

since $x(t)\, \delta(t - t_d) = x(t_d)$.

Somewhat parenthetically, we can also develop an expression for $S_\delta(f) = \mathscr{F}[s_\delta(t)]$ as follows. From Eq. (9a) and the convolution theorem, $X_\delta(f) = [X(f)] * [S_\delta(f)]$ whereas Eq. (10) is equivalent to

$$X_\delta(f) = [X(f)] * \left[\sum_{n=-\infty}^{\infty} f_s \, \delta(f - nf_s) \right]$$

Therefore, we conclude that

$$S_\delta(f) = f_s \sum_{n=-\infty}^{\infty} \delta(f - nf_s) \qquad (12)$$

so the spectrum of a periodic string of unit-weight impulses in the time domain is a periodic string of impulses in the frequency domain with spacing $f_s = 1/T_s$; in both domains we have a function that looks like a picket fence.

Returning to the main subject and Fig. 8.4, it is immediately apparent that if we invoke the same conditions as before — $x(t)$ bandlimited in W and $f_s \geq 2W$ — then a filter of suitable bandwidth will reconstruct $x(t)$ from the ideal sampled wave. Specifically, for an ideal LPF of voltage gain K, time delay t_d, and bandwidth B, the transfer function is

$$H(f) = K\Pi\left(\frac{f}{2B}\right) e^{-j\omega t_d}$$

so filtering $x_s(t)$ produces the output spectrum

$$Y(f) = H(f)X_\delta(f) = Kf_s X(f) e^{-j\omega t_d}$$

assuming B satisfies Eq. (6). The output time function is then

$$y(t) = \mathscr{F}^{-1}[Y(f)] = Kf_s x(t - t_d) \qquad (13)$$

which is the original signal amplified by Kf_s and delayed by t_d.

Further confidence in the sampling process can be gained by examining reconstruction in the time domain. The impulse response of the above filter is

$$h(t) = 2BK \text{ sinc } 2B(t - t_d)$$

And since the input $x_\delta(t)$ is a train of weighted impulses, the output is a train of weighted *impulse responses*, namely,

$$y(t) = [h(t)] * [x_\delta(t)] = \sum_k x(kT_s)h(t - kT_s)$$

$$= 2BK \sum_{k=-\infty}^{\infty} x(kT_s) \text{ sinc } 2B(t - t_d - kT_s) \qquad (14)$$

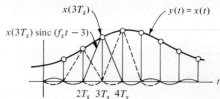

FIGURE 8.5
Ideal reconstruction.

Now suppose for simplicity that $B = f_s/2$, $K = 1/f_s$, and $t_d = 0$, so

$$y(t) = \sum_k x(kT_s) \text{ sinc } (f_s t - k)$$

We can then carry out the reconstruction process graphically, as shown in Fig. 8.5. Clearly the correct values are reconstructed at the sampling instants $t = kT_s$, for all sinc functions are zero at these times save one, and that one yields $x(kT_s)$. Between sampling instants $x(t)$ is *interpolated* by summing the precursors and postcursors from *all* the sinc functions. For this reason the LPF is often called an *interpolation filter*, and its impulse response is called the *interpolation function*.

The Uniform Sampling Theorem

The above results are well summarized by stating the important theorem of uniform (periodic) sampling. While there are many variations of this theorem,† the following form is best suited to our purposes.

If a signal contains no frequency components for $|f| \geq W$, it is completely described by instantaneous sample values uniformly spaced in time with period $T_s \leq 1/2W$. If a signal has been sampled at the Nyquist rate or greater ($f_s \geq 2W$) and the sample values are represented as weighted impulses, the signal can be exactly reconstructed from its samples by an ideal LPF of bandwidth B, where $W \leq B \leq f_s - W$.

EXERCISE 8.2 Using Eqs. (13) and (14), show that any bandlimited signal may be expanded in a series of sinc functions

$$x(t) = 2BT_s \sum_{k=-\infty}^{\infty} x(kT_s) \text{ sinc } 2B(t - kT_s) \qquad (15)$$

providing $T_s \leq 1/2W$ and B satisfies Eq. (6). Therefore, just as a periodic signal is completely described by its Fourier series coefficients, a bandlimited signal is completely

† Black (1953, chap. 4) lists several theorems pertaining to periodic sampling.

described by its instantaneous sample values *whether or not the signal actually is sampled.*

Practical Sampling

Having stated and proved the theorem for ideal sampling, we must now examine electric-waveform sampling as it occurs in practice. Practical sampling differs from ideal sampling in three obvious respects:

1 The sampled wave consists of pulses having finite amplitude and duration, rather than impulses.

2 Practical reconstruction filters are not ideal filters.

3 The messages to be sampled are *timelimited* signals and therefore cannot be bandlimited.

We shall treat these differences one at a time and show that only the last one is troublesome.

Regarding pulse-shape effects, our investigation of the unipolar chopper plus Exercise 8.1 has shown that virtually any pulse shape $p(t)$ will do when the sampling operation can be modeled mathematically as multiplication, $x_s(t) = x(t)s(t)$. Certain other sampling devices, especially the sample-and-hold variety, produce a sampled wave of the form

$$x_s(t) = \sum_k x(kT_s)p(t - kT_s)$$

$$= [p(t)] * \left[\sum_k x(kT_s)\delta(t - kT_s)\right] \quad (16a)$$

so that

$$X_s(f) = P(f)\left[f_s \sum_n X(f - nf_s)\right] = P(f)X_\delta(f) \quad (16b)$$

where $P(f) = \mathscr{F}[p(t)]$ and $X_\delta(f)$ is the spectrum of the ideal sampled wave.

Interpreting Eq. (16b), one can think of $P(f)$ as a filter operating on $X_\delta(f)$ and attenuating all frequency components above about $1/\tau$, τ being the nominal duration of $p(t)$. Generally, the reconstructed signal will be distorted because $P(f)$ attenuates the upper portion of the message spectrum. This loss of high-frequency message components is sometimes called the *aperture effect*—the sampling aperture (pulse duration) is too large—and can be corrected by an *equalizing filter* having $H_{eq}(f)$ $= 1/P(f)$. However, usually $1/\tau \gg W$, so $P(f)$ is essentially constant over the message band and equalization may not be required. We can thus say that pulse-shape effects are relatively inconsequential, and the sampling theorem is valid for nonimpulsive sampled waves.

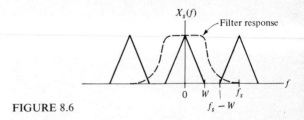

FIGURE 8.6

The effect of nonideal reconstruction filters is also readily treated in the frequency domain. Consider, for example, a typical filter response superimposed on a sampled-wave spectrum, as in Fig. 8.6. If the filter is reasonably flat over the message band, its output will consist of $x(t)$ plus spurious frequency components at $|f| > f_s - W$, which is outside the message band. Note that these components are considerably attenuated compared to $x(t)$. In audio systems such components would sound like high-frequency garble or hissing. However, their strength is proportional to the message, disappearing when $x(t) = 0$, and the message tends to mask their presence, making them easier to tolerate.

Good filter design is obviously the best way to minimize the spurious frequencies. Alternately, for a given filter response, they can be further suppressed by increasing the sampling frequency which increases $f_s - W$ and produces *guard bands* in the spectrum of the sampled wave. There is an interesting parallel here with FDM: in FDM, guard bands are used to allow message separation by practical bandpass filters with a minimum of *cross talk*; in sampling systems, guard bands are used to allow message reconstruction by practical lowpass filters with a minimum of high-frequency garble.

Example 8.1   Reconstruction Using a Zero-Order Hold

When the sampled wave consists of flat-topped rectangular pulses, simply stretching the pulses gives a staircase approximation to $x(t)$ shown in Fig. 8.7a. Analytically, letting $h(t) = \Pi[(t - \frac{1}{2}T_s)/T_s]$, the output is

$$y(t) = \sum_k x(kT_s)h(t - kT_s) = [h(t)] * [x_\delta(t)]$$

and

$$Y(f) = H(f)X_\delta(f) \qquad H(f) = \mathscr{F}[h(t)]$$

similar to Eqs. (16a) and (16b). But $h(t)$ has the same form as the impulse response of the *zero-order hold*† described in Example 2.13, Sect. 2.5. Therefore, $|H(f)| =$

---

† The name comes from the property that an mth-order hold can perfectly reconstruct signals of the form $x(t) = a_0 + a_1t + \cdots + a_m t^m$.

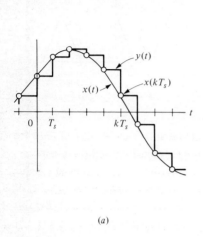

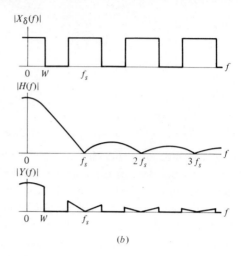

(a)   (b)

FIGURE 8.7
Reconstruction using zero-order hold. (*a*) Staircase waveform; (*b*) spectra.

$T_s|\mathrm{sinc}\, fT_s|$ and $|Y(f)|$ is as sketched in Fig. 8.7*b*, taking $X(f)$ to be constant over $|f| \leq W$.

Clearly, this reconstruction method suffers from both the aperture effect and out-of-band "noise" — both of which would be mitigated by additional filtering. If, however, $f_s \gg 2W$, both effects are small and $y(t)$ is a good approximation to $x(t)$. The condition $f_s \gg 2W$ is not very practical for signal transmission, but it is for sampled-data control systems and digital simulation where staircase reconstruction is commonly employed.   ////

Nonbandlimited Signals — Aliasing

Thus far we have ignored the fact that real signals are not strictly bandlimited. But a message spectrum like Fig. 8.8*a* is considered to be virtually bandlimited if the frequency content above W is small and presumably unimportant for conveying the information. When such a message is sampled, there will be unavoidable overlapping of spectral components, Fig. 8.8*b*. In reconstruction, frequencies originally outside the nominal message band will appear at the filter output in the form of much *lower* frequencies. Thus, for example, $f_1 > W$ becomes $f_s - f_1 < W$, as indicated in the figure.

This phenomenon of downward frequency translation occurs whenever a frequency component is *undersampled*, that is, $f_s < 2f_1$, and is given the descriptive name of *aliasing*. The aliasing effect is far more serious than spurious frequencies passed by

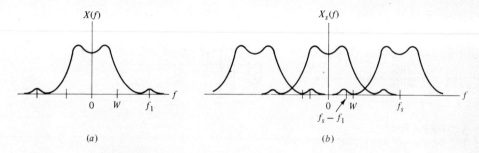

FIGURE 8.8
Aliasing effect: (*a*) Nonbandlimited message spectrum; (*b*) sampled message spectrum with overlaps.

nonideal reconstruction filters, for the latter fall *outside* the message band, whereas aliased components can fall *within* the message band. Aliasing is combated by filtering the message as much as possible *before* sampling and, if necessary, sampling at much greater than the nominal Nyquist rate.

As illustration, the average voice spectrum (Fig. 5.6*b*) extends well beyond 10 kHz, though most of the energy is concentrated in the range 100 to 600 Hz and a bandwidth of 3 kHz is sufficient for intelligibility. When a voice wave is first processed by a 3-kHz LPF and then sampled at $f_s = 8$ kHz, the standard for telephone systems, aliased components are typically 30 dB below the desired signal and are virtually unnoticed.

EXERCISE 8.3   Demonstrate the aliasing effect for yourself by making a careful sketch of $\cos 2\pi 10t$ and $\cos 2\pi 70t$ for $0 \le t \le \frac{1}{10}$. Put both sketches on the same set of axes and find the sample values at $t = 0, \frac{1}{80}, \frac{2}{80}, \ldots, \frac{8}{80}$, which corresponds to $f_s = 80$. Also, convince yourself that no other waveform bandlimited in $10 < W < 40$ can be interpolated from the sample values of $\cos 2\pi 10t$.

The Sampling Theorem Restated

To summarize our investigation of *practical* sampling as distinguished from *ideal* sampling, we can restate the sampling theorem in the following manner:

If a signal has been lowpass-filtered to yield negligible spectral content for $|f| > W$, it is adequately described for most purposes by sample values, either instantaneous or of finite duration, uniformly spaced in time with period $T_s \le 1/2W$. If a signal has been sampled at the nominal Nyquist rate or greater

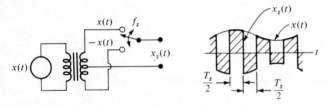

FIGURE 8.9
Bipolar chopper and typical waveforms.

$(f_s \geq 2W)$ and the samples are represented by periodic pulses whose amplitudes are proportional to the sample values, the signal can be approximately reconstructed from its samples by lowpass filtering.

Admittedly, *perfect* reconstruction, like distortionless transmission, is impossible; but with careful planning, good filter design, and suitable sampling frequency, the recovered wave can be made as close as desired to the original signal for all but the most extreme cases.

Chopper Modulation

Before applying sampling theory to pulse-modulation systems, it should be pointed out that practical samplers can be used as *balanced modulators* for linear modulation systems. In particular, returning to the output spectrum of the unipolar chopper (Fig. 8.3*b*), we see that each harmonic of the sampling frequency is *double-sideband-modulated* by the input signal $x(t)$. Bandpass-filtering the sampled wave will thus produce DSB, a technique known as *chopper modulation*. The modulation is relatively unaffected by imperfect switching, as shown by our study of pulse-shape effects.

For purposes of suppressed-carrier modulation, switching or chopping methods are often superior to the conventional balanced modulator, which requires more components and carefully matched nonlinear elements. However, the unipolar chopper is not so efficient a modulator as the *bipolar* chopper of Fig. 8.9. This device produces DSB at only the odd harmonics of f_s, and its output contains no DC component. The analysis follows that of unipolar chopping but with a square-wave switching function.

Aside from modulation for signal transmission, bipolar choppers find application in control systems, where a suppressed-carrier wave is used to drive two-phase servomotors, and for the amplification of slowly varying signals (DC amplifiers). Additionally, Prob. 8.12 indicates how a bipolar chopper can be modified to achieve the baseband multiplexing for FM stereophonic transmitters.

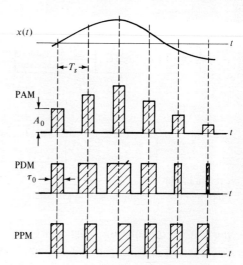

FIGURE 8.10
Types of analog pulse modulation.

8.2 ANALOG PULSE MODULATION: PAM, PDM, AND PPM

If a message is adequately described by its sample values, it can be transmitted via analog pulse modulation, wherein the sample values directly modulate a periodic pulse train with one pulse for each sample. There are numerous varieties of analog pulse modulation. and the terminology has not been standardized. However, the three types we shall be concerned with are usually designated as *pulse-amplitude modulation* (PAM), *pulse-duration modulation* (PDM), and *pulse-position modulation* (PPM). PDM and PPM are also lumped together under the general heading of *pulse-time modulation*.

Figure 8.10 shows a typical message and corresponding pulse-modulated waveforms. For clarity, the pulses are shown as rectangular, and the pulse duration has been grossly exaggerated. Moreover, actual modulated waves are slightly delayed in time compared to the message, since the pulses cannot be generated before the sampling instants.

As shown in the figure, the modulated pulse parameter—amplitude, duration, or relative position—is varied in direct proportion to the sample values. However, in PAM and PDM sample values equal to zero are usually represented by nonzero amplitude or duration. This practice is followed to prevent "missing" pulses and to preserve a constant pulse rate. The latter is particularly important for synchronization purposes in time-division multiplexing.

With the aid of Fig. 8.10, certain parallels can be drawn between analog pulse modulation and CW modulation. Thus, the message information (in the form of sample values) is conveyed by the *amplitude* of a PAM wave, so PAM is analogous to

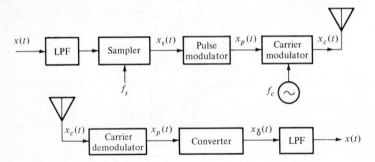

FIGURE 8.11
Pulse-modulation communication system.

linear CW modulation, particularly AM. In PDM and PPM the information is conveyed by a *time* parameter, namely, the location of the pulse edges. Recalling that instantaneous frequency and phase are also time parameters, we can say that pulse-time modulation is analogous to *exponential* CW modulation.

Pulse-Modulation Systems

Before proceeding to more detailed analysis, three general observations about analog pulse-modulation systems can be stated.

1 Pulse-modulated waves have appreciable DC and low-frequency content, especially near the first few harmonics of $f_s = 1/T_s$. Direct transmission may therefore be difficult, if not impossible.

2 When pulse-modulated waves are transmitted, care must be taken to prevent the pulses from overlapping, for overlapping would destroy the modulation. From the pulse resolution requirements of Sect. 4.4, a baseband bandwidth of at least $1/2\tau$ is necessary, τ being the nominal pulse duration.

3 Pulse-modulated waves can be demodulated via *reconstruction*. Conceptually, the sample values are extracted from the modulated wave, converted into weighted impulses, and lowpass-filtered.

With respect to the first point, short-distance pulse transmission may be feasible over wire circuits or coaxial cable, but efficient radio transmission requires additional frequency translation. Hence, most pulse systems have a carrier-modulation step in which the pulses are converted to RF pulses. Analytically, if $x_p(t)$ is the pulse-modulated wave, the actual transmitted signal is $x_c(t) = x_p(t)A_c \cos \omega_c t$, where $f_c \gg f_s$. Though the carrier modulation is properly classified as DSB, envelope detection can be employed at the receiver if $x_p(t) \geq 0$ and carrier phase reversals do not occur.

A complete pulse transmission system is diagramed in Fig. 8.11. The transmitter consists of a lowpass filter, sampler, pulse modulator, and carrier modulator. The receiver includes carrier demodulation followed by a converter which changes the pulse-modulated wave to a train of weighted impulses $x_\delta(t)$ or the realizable equivalent. Message recovery is then by lowpass filtering.

As to transmission bandwidth, the practical advantages of analog pulse modulation depend on the pulse duration being small compared to the time between pulses, that is,

$$\tau \ll T_s \leq \frac{1}{2W} \qquad (1)$$

so the baseband transmission bandwidth is

$$B_{T_{BB}} \geq \frac{1}{2\tau} \gg W \qquad (2)$$

and carrier modulation doubles this, giving

$$B_{T_{RF}} = 2B_{T_{BB}} \gg 2W \qquad (3)$$

But, with or without carrier modulation, the required bandwidth is large compared to the message bandwidth W.

By analogy with exponential modulation, one suspects that the large bandwidth of analog pulse modulation results in *wideband noise reduction*. And *pulse-time modulation* does indeed have this useful property; moreover, the bandwidth is essentially determined by the desired amount of noise reduction rather than by the message bandwidth per se.

On the other hand, as might be inferred from its similarity to AM, PAM is no better than baseband transmission as far as noise is concerned, and the excessive bandwidth is a definite liability. Because of this shortcoming, PAM is seldom used for single-channel message transmission. (In fact, single-channel pulse communication systems of any type are rare.) However, PAM plays an important role in TDM, in message reconstruction, and in the study of more sophisticated pulse-modulation techniques. A few more words about PAM are thus in order.

Pulse-Amplitude Modulation (PAM)

The usual PAM waveform consists of nonrectangular unipolar pulses whose peak amplitudes are proportional to instantaneous sample values of the message. Specifically,

$$x_p(t) = \sum_k A_0[1 + mx(kT_s)]p(t - mT_s) \qquad (4)$$

where A_0 is the unmodulated pulse amplitude, $p(t)$ is the pulse shape, and m is the modulation index directly comparable to the AM modulation index. The condition $[1 + mx(kT_s)] > 0$ is normally imposed to preserve single polarity and prevent missing pulses, as mentioned earlier. Therefore, invoking our normalization convention $|x(t)| \leq 1$, the modulation index is bounded by $m < 1$.

Since Eq. (4) has the same form as Eq. (16a), Sect. 8.1, with $x(kT_s)$ replaced by $A_0 + A_0 mx(kT_s)$, it follows that the spectrum is given by Eq. (16b) plus impulses at DC, f_s, $2f_s$, etc. Therefore, a PAM demodulator consists simply of equalization and lowpass filtering with removal of the DC term — which also removes $\bar{x}$ if the message has a DC component.

To calculate the average transmitted power $S_T = \langle x_p{}^2(t) \rangle$, we follow the approach used for digital signals in Sect. 4.5. Taking $p(t)$ as a rectangular pulse of duration τ, for simplicity, the energy in the kth pulse is $A_0{}^2[1 + mx(kT_s)]^2\tau$ so

$$S_T = \frac{1}{T_s} A_0{}^2 \langle [1 + mx(kT_s)]^2 \rangle \tau$$

$$= \frac{A_0{}^2\tau}{T_s}(1 + m^2\overline{x^2}) \tag{5}$$

assuming $\bar{x} = 0$.

Pulse-Duration Modulation (PDM)

In PDM, the duration of the kth pulse conveys the sample value. Mathematically,

$$\tau(k) = \tau_0[1 + mx(kT_s)] \tag{6a}$$

where τ_0 is the unmodulated duration and m plays the same role as above. Thus

$$x_p(t) = \sum_k A_0 p\left[\frac{t - kT_s}{\tau(k)/\tau_0}\right] \tag{6b}$$

and

$$S_T = \frac{A_0{}^2}{T_s}\langle \tau(k) \rangle = \frac{A_0{}^2\tau_0}{T_s} \tag{7}$$

again taking $\bar{x} = 0$ and $p(t)$ to be rectangular.

Equation (6) represents a PDM wave in which both pulse edges are modulated and the pulse-to-pulse spacing is constant. In practice, the leading edge is usually fixed at $t = kT_s$ and only the trailing edge is modulated so the pulse spacing is variable. But regardless of which edge or edges are modulated, spectral analysis of PDM is

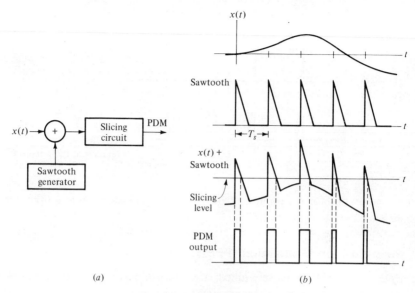

FIGURE 8.12
PDM generation. (*a*) Block diagram; (*b*) waveforms.

quite complicated. Using an approximation based on $\tau_0 \ll T_s$, it can be shown that†

$$x_p(t) \approx \frac{A_0 \tau_0}{T_s} [1 + mx(t)] + \text{frequency-translated terms} \qquad (8)$$

and therefore PDM, like PAM, is directly demodulated via lowpass filtering, etc.

A very simple technique for the generation of PDM is illustrated in Fig. 8.12, where the message and a sawtooth waveform are summed, forming the input to a *slicing circuit*. The slicing circuit, essentially a clipping and squaring device, produces A_0 volts whenever the input exceeds the slicing level and has zero output otherwise. The resulting wave is PDM with trailing-edge modulation, and the operations of sampling and modulation have been combined into one step. Reversing the sawtooth produces leading-edge modulation; replacing the sawtooth by a triangular wave produces modulation on both edges. However, as the attentive reader may have noticed, the final pulse duration corresponds to message samples at the time location of the modulated edge, not the apparent sampling time $t = kT_s$. Thus, the sample values are *nonuniformly* spaced, and uniform sampling theory is not strictly applicable. Of course the difference between uniform and nonuniform sampling is insignificant if the pulse duration is small compared to T_s. From the hardware viewpoint, non-uniform sampling is preferred because of its simplified instrumentation. And as a

† The method is outlined in Prob. 8.17; see Black (1953, chap. 17) for details.

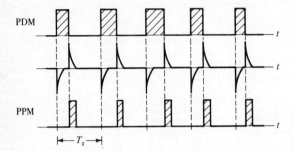

FIGURE 8.13
Generating PPM from PDM.

bonus, nonuniform sampling yields less inherent distortion in the filtered output message than uniform sampling.

Pulse-Position Modulation (PPM)

PDM and PPM are closely allied, a relationship underscored by Fig. 8.13, showing how PPM can be generated from PDM with trailing-edge modulation. The duration-modulated pulses are inverted and differentiated, changing the modulated edges into position-modulated positive spikes. With a little reshaping these spikes become the desired PPM wave.

As a matter of fact, the principal use of duration modulation is for the generation (and detection) of position modulation because PPM is markedly superior to PDM for message transmission. To appreciate why this is so, recall that the information resides in the time location of the pulse *edges*, not in the pulses themselves. Thus, somewhat like the carrier-frequency power of AM, the pulse power of pulse-time modulation is "wasted" power, and it would be more efficient to suppress the pulses and just transmit the edges! Of course we cannot transmit edges without transmitting pulses to define them. But we can send very short pulses indicating the position of the edges, a process equivalent to PPM. The reduced power required for PPM is a fundamental advantage over PDM, an advantage that will be more apparent when we examine the signal-to-noise ratios.

Since PPM with nonuniform sampling is the most efficient type of pulse-time modulation for transmission purposes, we shall take the time to analyze its spectrum. The analysis method is, itself, worthy of examination.

PPM Spectral Analysis ★

To begin, let t_k be the time location (center) of the kth pulse. If the sampling is uniform, the kth pulse carries the sample value at $t = kT_s$, and

$$t_k = kT_s + t_0 x(kT_s)$$

where t_0 is the modulation constant, i.e., the *maximum displacement* relative to $t = kT_s$. But with nonuniform sampling the sample value is actually extracted at t_k, not kT_s, so

$$t_k = kT_s + t_0 x(t_k) \qquad (9)$$

By definition, the PPM wave is a summation of constant-amplitude position-modulated pulses, and can be written as

$$x_p(t) = \sum_k A_0 p(t - t_k) = A_0[p(t)] * \left[\sum_k \delta(t - t_k) \right]$$

where A_0 is the pulse amplitude and $p(t)$ the pulse shape. A simplification at this point is made possible by noting that $p(t)$ will (or should) have a very small duration compared to T_s. Hence, for our purposes, the pulse shape can be taken as impulsive, that is, $p(t) \approx \delta(t)$, so

$$x_p(t) \approx A_0 \sum_k \delta(t - t_k) \qquad (10)$$

If desired, Eq. (10) can later be convolved with $p(t)$ to account for the nonimpulsive shape.

In their present form, Eqs. (9) and (10) are unsuited to further manipulation; the trouble is the position term t_k, which cannot be solved for explicitly. Fortunately, Rowe (1965, chap. 5) has devised a technique whereby t can be eliminated entirely, as follows. Consider any function $g(t)$ having a single first-order zero at $t = \lambda$; that is, $g(\lambda) = 0$, $g(t \neq \lambda) \neq 0$, and $g'(\lambda) = dg/dt|_{t=\lambda} \neq 0$. Using the properties of impulses, one can show that[†]

$$\delta[g(t)] = \frac{\delta(t - \lambda)}{|g'(t)|}$$

hence

$$\delta(t - \lambda) = |g'(t)| \delta[g(t)] \qquad (11)$$

whose right-hand side is independent of λ. Equation (11) can therefore be used to remove t_k from $\delta(t - t_k)$ if we can find a function $g(t)$ that satisfies $g(t_k) = 0$ and the other conditions but does not contain t_k.

Suppose we take $g(t) = t - kT_s - t_0 x(t)$, which is zero at $t = kT_s + t_0 x(t)$. Now, for a given value of k, there is only one PPM pulse, and it occurs at $t_k = kT_s + t_0 x(t_k)$. Thus $g(t_k) = t_k - kT_s - t_0 x(t_k) = 0$, as desired. Inserting $\lambda = t_k$, $g'(t) = 1 - t_0 x'(t)$, etc., into Eq. (11) gives

$$\delta(t - t_k) = |1 - t_0 x'(t)| \delta[t - kT_s - t_0 x(t)]$$

[†] See Friedman (1956).

and the PPM wave of Eq. (10) becomes

$$x_p(t) = A_0[1 - t_0 x'(t)] \sum_k \delta[t - t_0 x(t) - kT_s]$$

The absolute value is dropped since $|t_0 x'(t)| < 1$ for most signals of interest if $t_0 \ll T_s$. We then convert the sum of impulses to a sum of exponentials via†

$$\sum_{k=-\infty}^{\infty} \delta(t - kT_s) = f_s \sum_{n=-\infty}^{\infty} e^{jn\omega_s t} \qquad (12)$$

to finally obtain

$$x_p(t) = A_0 f_s[1 - t_0 x'(t)] \sum_{n=-\infty}^{\infty} e^{jn\omega_s[t - t_0 x(t)]}$$

$$= A_0 f_s[1 - t_0 x'(t)]\left\{1 + \sum_{n=1}^{\infty} 2 \cos\left[n\omega_s t - n\omega_s t_0 x(t)\right]\right\} \qquad (13)$$

Interpreting Eq. (13), we see that PPM with nonuniform sampling is a combination of linear and exponential carrier modulation, for each harmonic of f_s is phase-modulated‡ by the message $x(t)$ and amplitude-modulated by the derivative $x'(t)$. The spectrum therefore consists of AM and PM sidebands centered at all multiples of f_s, plus a DC component and the spectrum of $x'(t)$. Needless to say, sketching such a spectrum is a tedious exercise even for tone modulation. The leading term of Eq. (13) suggests that the message can be retrieved by lowpass filtering and *integrating*. However, the integration method does not take full advantage of the noise-reduction properties of PPM, so the usual procedure is conversion to PAM or PDM followed by lowpass filtering.

Signal-to-Noise Ratios

Regardless of the particular technique employed, the demodulation of a pulse-modulated wave is inherently message reconstruction from sample values. This viewpoint allows us to treat added noise in a relatively simple fashion. Specifically, if the received signal plus noise is

$$v(t) = K_R x_p(t) + n(t)$$

then reconstruction must be based on contaminated samples; i.e., the output of the converter in Fig. 8.10 is

$$y_\delta(t) = \sum_k [M_p x(kT_s) + \epsilon_k]\delta(t - kT_s) \qquad (14)$$

---

† Equation (12) is simply the exponential Fourier series expansion of $s_\delta(t)$ since we have already shown that $c_n = 1/T_s = f_s$. Alternately, consider the inverse Fourier transform of $S_\delta(f)$, Eq. (12), Sect. 8.1.

‡ Thus, the *serrasoid system* for generating narrowband phase modulation starts with a PPM wave; see Prob. 8.18.

where M_p is the modulation constant relating $x(kT_s)$ to $x_p(t)$ and ϵ_k is the error introduced by the presence of $n(t)$. Then, assuming an ideal LPF with $B \approx f_s/2$, the filtered output is

$$y_D(t) = M_p x(t) + \underbrace{\sum_k \epsilon_k \operatorname{sinc}(f_s t - k)}_{\xi(t)} \qquad (15)$$

as follows from Eqs. (14) and (15), Sect. 8.1, with $K = 1$ and $t_d = 0$ for simplicity. Since the noise $\xi(t)$ in Eq. (15) is additive, we can form the destination signal-to-noise ratio S_D/N_D where $S_D = M_p{}^2 \overline{x^2}$ and $N_D = \overline{\xi^2}$. In general, $\xi(t)$ does not equal $\varepsilon(t)$ because the latter waveform, if it physically exists, is not necessarily bandlimited. However, it follows immediately from Eq. (12), Sect. 4.5, that $\overline{\xi^2} = \overline{\epsilon^2}$ and therefore

$$\left(\frac{S}{N}\right)_D = \frac{M_p{}^2 \overline{x^2}}{\overline{\epsilon^2}} \qquad (16)$$

$\overline{\epsilon^2}$ being the mean-square value of the error term.

We shall assume the pulses are transmitted without carrier modulation over a system having bandwidth B_T. Then $n(t)$ is bandlimited white noise of power density η, and $N_R = \overline{n^2} = \eta B_T$. The average signal power is $S_R = K_R{}^2 S_T$, as usual, and $A_R = K_R A_0$ denotes the received amplitude.

PAM plus noise is readily analyzed since the sample values are contained in the modulated amplitude $A_R m x(kT_s)$, and the noise adds directly to the amplitude. Hence, $M_p = A_R m$, $\epsilon_k = n(kT_s)$, $\overline{\epsilon^2} = \overline{n^2} = \eta B_T$, and

$$\left(\frac{S}{N}\right)_D = \frac{A_R{}^2 m^2 \overline{x^2}}{\eta B_T} = \frac{m^2 \overline{x^2}}{1 + m^2 \overline{x^2}} \frac{T_s}{\tau} \left(\frac{S}{N}\right)_R$$

or

$$\left(\frac{S}{N}\right)_D = \frac{m^2 \overline{x^2}}{1 + m^2 \overline{x^2}} \frac{T_s W}{\tau B_T} \gamma \qquad \text{PAM} \qquad (17)$$

where $\gamma = S_R/\eta W$. It was stated earlier that PAM is no better than direct baseband transmission insofar as noise is concerned. Equation (17) shows this to be true, for $T_s \leq 1/2W$ and $B_T \geq 1/2\tau$, so $T_s W/\tau B_T \leq 1$ and $(S/N)_D \leq \gamma/2$. The equality is realized only by sampling at the Nyquist rate with $m^2 \overline{x^2} = 1$. These conditions are seldom achieved in practice; nor are they sought after, for the merit of PAM is its simplicity in multiplexing, not its noise performance.

Turning to pulse-time modulation, we recall that the message samples are contained in the relative position of the pulse edges. If the received pulses were perfectly rectangular, additive noise would have no effect on the edges since the noise is a *vertical* perturbation. But rectangular pulses require *infinite* transmission bandwidth; with finite bandwidth the pulses have nonzero rise time $\tau_r \approx 1/2B_T$ and the noise will alter the edge position as we studied in Sect. 4.4, Fig. 4.20. Applying the results of that study,

$$\overline{\epsilon^2} = \overline{\Delta t^2} = \frac{\eta B_T \tau_r^2}{A_R^2} = \frac{\eta}{4B_T A_R^2}$$

Note that the mean-square error *decreases* as the bandwidth *increases*; hence we have the promised *wideband noise reduction*.

As to the signal parameters, the variation in pulse duration or pulse position is $t_0 x(kT_s)$, letting $t_0 = m\tau_0$ in PDM, so $M_p = t_0$. The average power is $S_R = (\tau/T_s)A_R^2 = \tau f_s A_R^2$ since the pulse amplitude is constant. Therefore

$$\left(\frac{S}{N}\right)_D = \frac{t_0^2 \overline{x^2} 4 B_T S_R}{\tau \eta f_s} = \frac{4 t_0^2 B_T W}{\tau f_s} \overline{x^2} \gamma \qquad (18)$$

which applies to both PDM and PPM without carrier modulation. In the case of PDM, τ must be interpreted as the *average* pulse duration τ_0.

The only difference between PPM and PDM, as reflected in Eq. (18), is the smaller pulse duration of PPM. This difference can be made more apparent by considering the best one can do for a given bandwidth B_T. Clearly, maximizing $(S/N)_D$ requires the minimum sampling frequency ($f_s = 2W$) with maximum t_0 and minimum average pulse duration. In PPM, t_0 and τ are independent and can be treated separately. The minimum possible pulse duration is $\tau \approx 2\tau_r \approx 1/B_T$, for which the pulse degenerates into a triangular shape. The maximum pulse displacement must be limited so that the *range* of possible pulse positions, $kT_s \pm 2t_0$, does not exceed the time between samples, that is, $t_0 \leq T_s/2 = 1/4W$. Taking all values to be optimum gives

$$\left(\frac{S}{N}\right)_{D_{\max}} = \frac{1}{8}\left(\frac{B_T}{W}\right)^2 \overline{x^2} \gamma \qquad \text{PPM} \qquad (19)$$

which more clearly exhibits the exchange of bandwidth for signal-to-noise ratio. However, practical systems may fall short of this maximum by an order of magnitude or more.

A similar optimization applied to PDM results in $m\tau_0 \approx 1/4W$, so

$$\left(\frac{S}{N}\right)_{D_{\max}} = \frac{1}{2}\frac{B_T}{W} \overline{x^2} \gamma \qquad \text{PDM} \qquad (20)$$

Note that the signal-to-noise ratio increases linearly with the bandwidth ratio B_T/W rather than as $(B_T/W)^2$. Moreover, to achieve Eq. (20) the average pulse duration must be one-half the time between samples. Under this condition, the duty cycle is $\tau_0/T_s = \frac{1}{2}$, and the practical advantages of pulse modulation with small duty cycle are lost.

It is particularly interesting to compare these results with those of exponential modulation. Recall, for example, that WBFM without deemphasis produced

$$\left(\frac{S}{N}\right)_D = \frac{3}{4}\left(\frac{B_T}{W}\right)^2 \overline{x^2}\gamma$$

Contrasting this with Eq. (20) shows that PDM falls far short of the noise reduction of FM having the same bandwidth, assuming $B_T/W \gg 1$. PPM is considerably better, giving a signal-to-noise ratio about 8 dB below that of FM. It thus appears that, while pulse-time modulation does give wideband noise reduction, the reduction is far less effective than exponential carrier modulation. But one should remember that the average power S_T is delivered as short-duration high-power pulses, whereas S_T must be generated continuously in FM. Practical limitations of the carrier supply may favor pulsed operation.

EXERCISE 8.4 Suppose a pulse-modulated signal is transmitted as RF pulses with average power S_{RF} and bandwidth B_{RF}. Show that Eqs. (17) to (20) must be modified by the replacements

$$B_T \to \frac{B_{RF}}{2} \qquad S_R \to 2S_{RF} \qquad (21)$$

Then show that PPM with carrier modulation falls at least 11 dB below WBFM.

Threshold Level

In concluding this discussion, it must be mentioned that the bandwidth ratio cannot be increased without limit, for pulse-time modulation suffers a *threshold effect* similar to that of FM. It is true that $\overline{\epsilon^2} \to 0$ as $B_T \to \infty$. But as $N_R = \eta B_T$ increases, the rms noise voltage increases, and occasional noise peaks will be mistaken for signal pulses. If such *false pulses* occur often enough, the desired message will be lost completely, for the reconstructed signal will have no relationship to $x(t)$.

We will say that false pulses are sufficiently infrequent if $P(n > A_R) \leq 0.01$. Assuming gaussian noise, the corresponding threshold condition is approximately

$$A_R \geq 2\sqrt{N_R}$$

i.e., the pulse amplitude must be strong enough to "lift" the noise by at least twice its rms value. (This is the same condition as the *tangential sensitivity* of pulsed radar systems.) Thus, since $A_R^2 = S_R/\tau f_s$ in PDM and PPM,

$$\left(\frac{S}{N}\right)_{R_{th}} = 4\tau f_s \qquad (22a)$$

and

$$\gamma_{th} = \frac{B_T}{W} 4\tau f_s \geq 8 \qquad (22b)$$

so the threshold level is appreciably lower than that of exponential modulation.

8.3 PULSE-CODE MODULATION: PCM, DM, AND DPCM

All the modulation types covered so far, whether pulse or CW, have been analog representations of the message. Pulse-code modulation (PCM) is distinctly different in concept; it is digital modulation in which the message is represented by a coded group of digital (discrete-amplitude) pulses. Delta modulation (DM) and differential pulse-code modulation (DPCM) are variations of PCM. The reasoning behind the digitizing procedure is as follows.

In analog modulation, the modulated parameter varies continuously and can take on *any* value corresponding to the range of the message. When the modulated wave is adulterated by noise, there is no way for the receiver to discern the exact transmitted value. Suppose, however, that only a few *discrete* values are allowed for the modulated parameter; if the separation between these values is large compared to the noise perturbations, it will be a simple matter to decide at the receiver precisely which specific value was intended. Thus the effects of random noise can be virtually eliminated, which is the whole idea of PCM. Collateral with the discrete-amplitude property, long-haul PCM systems can employ *regenerative* repeaters described in Sect. 4.5, thereby gaining a further advantage over any form of analog transmission.

But the question now arises: How do we represent an analog message in digital form? The answer lies in sampling, quantizing, and coding.

Quantizing and Coding

The elements of PCM generation are diagramed in Fig. 8.14. The continuous signal $x(t)$ is first lowpass-filtered (why?) and sampled to give $x_s(t)$. The sample values are then rounded off or quantized to the nearest predetermined discrete value or *quantum level*. The resulting sampled and quantized signal $x_{sq}(t)$ is discrete in time (by virtue

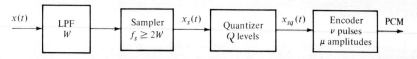

FIGURE 8.14
PCM generation system.

of sampling) and amplitude (by virtue of quantizing). Finally, $x_{sq}(t)$ is operated on by an encoder that converts quantized samples to appropriate *digital code words*, one code word for each sample, and generates the corresponding baseband PCM signal as a digital waveform. Note that, viewed in another light, Fig. 8.14 is an analog-to-digital (A/D) converter.

Obviously the parameters of the encoded signal depend upon the number of quantum levels Q, for each code word must uniquely represent one of the possible quantized samples. To ascertain the relationship, let v be the number of digits in the code word, each having one of μ discrete values. Since there are μ^v different possible code words, we require $\mu^v \geq Q$ for unique encoding. Therefore, when the parameters are chosen so the equality is realized,

$$\mu^v = Q \qquad v = \log_\mu Q \qquad (1)$$

Examining Eq. (1), we see that if $\mu = Q$, then $v = 1$, and the quantized signal requires no code translation. In general, however, $\mu < Q$ and $v > 1$. The most common form of PCM is *binary* PCM, for which $\mu = 2$; the number of quantum levels then is taken as some power of 2, namely $Q = 2^v$.

Figure 8.15 illustrates these operations for binary PCM. Eight quantum levels are shown, corresponding to $\pm\frac{1}{8}, \pm\frac{3}{8}, \ldots, \pm\frac{7}{8}$, so the levels are uniformly spaced by $2 \times \frac{1}{8} = 2/Q$ and, including rounding off, they span the range -1.0 to $+1.0$ consistent with our normalization convention $|x(t)| \leq 1$. A code number $0, 1, \ldots, 7$ is assigned to each quantum level and the binary code word is simply the binary equivalent of the code number, e.g., $5 \rightarrow$ **101**, etc. Three binary digits per code word are needed since $v = \log_2 8 = \log_2 2^3 = 3$.

Because several digits are required for each message sample, it appears that the PCM bandwidth will be much greater than the message bandwidth. An estimate of the bandwidth is obtained as follows. Quantized samples occur at a rate of $f_s \geq 2W$ samples per second, so there must be $r = vf_s$ digits per second. Recalling the bandwidth-signaling rate relationship of Sect. 4.5, we have that

$$B_{T_{BB}} \geq \frac{r}{2} = \frac{vf_s}{2} \geq vW \qquad (2)$$

The baseband PCM bandwidth is thus a minimum of $v = \log_\mu Q$ times the message bandwidth.

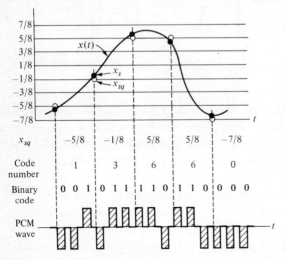

x_{sq}	-5/8	-1/8	5/8	5/8	-7/8
Code number	1	3	6	6	0
Binary code	0 0 1	0 1 1	1 1 0	1 1 0	0 0 0

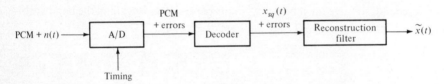

FIGURE 8.15

As the final step of PCM generation, the baseband signal may modulate an RF carrier for transmission purposes. The carrier modulation can be ASK (*amplitude-shift keying*), *phase-shift keying* (PSK), or *frequency-shift keying* (FSK). (These are forms of CW modulation for digital signals discussed in Chap. 10.) Of course the carrier modulation results in an even greater transmission bandwidth than that of Eq. (2), but we shall restrict our attention to the baseband case.

Quantization Noise

Figure 8.16 shows that portion of a PCM receiver following carrier demodulation, if any. The analog PCM waveform contaminated by random noise $n(t)$ is operated on by an A/D converter that regenerates the digital code words (plus errors) as described in Sect. 4.5. From these code words, the decoder determines the quantized sample values (again with errors) and generates $x_{sq}(t)$ which is processed by an LPF to yield the output analog signal $\tilde{x}(t)$.

FIGURE 8.16
PCM receiver.

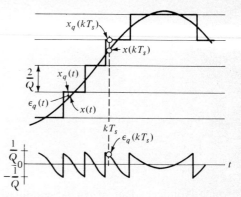

FIGURE 8.17
PCM quantization error.

If the signal-to-noise ratio at the A/D converter is only modestly large, the error probability is sufficiently small that one can ignore the effects of the random noise. Despite this condition, $\tilde{x}(t)$ will not be identical to the message $x(t)$ since the LPF input is $x_{sq}(t)$, not $x_s(t)$; i.e., reconstruction is based on the quantized samples rather than exact sample values. Furthermore, there is no way of obtaining exact values at the receiver; that information was discarded at the transmitter in the quantizing process. Therefore, perfect message reconstruction is impossible in pulse-code systems, even when random noise has negligible influence.

As a result, the quantization effect is a basic limitation of coded systems, just as random noise is a limitation of conventional analog systems. It is this quantization effect we wish to examine in more detail.

For analysis we decompose $x(t)$ into a stepwise-quantized signal $x_q(t)$ and a *quantizing-error term $\epsilon_q(t)$*, such that

$$x_q(t) = x(t) + \epsilon_q(t) \qquad (3a)$$

as illustrated in Fig. 8.17. Because the order of sampling and quantizing is interchangeable, the quantized sample values as decoded at the receiver can be written in the form

$$x_q(kT_s) = x(kT_s) + \epsilon_q(kT_s) \qquad (3b)$$

and reconstruction filtering gives

$$\tilde{x}(t) = x(t) + \sum_k \epsilon_q(kT_s) \operatorname{sinc}(f_s t - k) \qquad (4)$$

Hence, the quantizing error appears in a form identical to random noise errors in analog pulse modulation, Eq. (15), Sect. 8.2. Accordingly, we call $\overline{\epsilon_q^2}$ the quantization noise.

This noise is readily evaluated when the quantum levels have *uniform* spacing

$2/Q$ so $|\epsilon_q(t)| \le 1/Q$—see Fig. 8.17. Lacking information to the contrary, we assume that ϵ_q is uniformly distributed over $[-1/Q, 1/Q]$; i.e., its PDF is $p(\epsilon_q) = Q/2$, $|\epsilon_q| \le 1/Q$. Thus

$$\overline{\epsilon_q^{\,2}} = \int_{-1/Q}^{1/Q} \epsilon_q^{\,2} \frac{Q}{2}\, d\epsilon_q = \frac{1}{3Q^2} \tag{5}$$

and

$$\left(\frac{S}{N}\right)_D = \overline{x^2}/\overline{\epsilon_q^{\,2}} = 3Q^2\overline{x^2} \tag{6}$$

which is independent of carrier modulation, transmitted power, and random noise since we are ignoring decoding errors here.

Clearly, the performance quality increases with Q, the number of quantum levels. This merely reiterates that if many quantum levels of small spacing are employed, the quantized samples closely approximate the exact sample values and the output can be made as near as desired to $x(t)$. Surprisingly few levels often yield satisfactory performance; for instance, $Q = 2^7$ or 2^8 is standard in voice telephony. However, it should be pointed out that the rms error is fixed at $1/\sqrt{3}Q$ regardless of the instantaneous value of $x(t)$. Hence, if $|x(t)|$ is small for extended periods of time, the apparent signal-to-noise ratio will be much less than the design value. The effect is particularly acute if the message waveform has a large *crest factor* (the ratio of peak amplitude to rms value), for then $|x(t)| \ll 1$ most of the time, and $\overline{x^2} \ll 1$.

For the transmission of audio signals, typically characterized by large crest factors, it is advantageous to taper the spacing between quantum levels, with small spacing near zero and large spacing at the extremes. A suitable *nonuniform* quantization can result in $\epsilon_q(t)$ substantially proportional to $|x(t)|$, thereby masking the noise with the signal insofar as a listener is concerned. In practice, tapered quantization is accomplished with uniformly spaced levels, the message being nonlinearly *compressed* prior to sampling; a complementary expander restores the waveshape at the receiver.

EXERCISE 8.5 The quantizing error for a PCM system with $\mu = 2$ is specified to be no greater than ± 5 percent of the peak-to-peak range of $x(t)$. Find the minimum number of digits per code word. *Ans.:* $v = 4 > \log_2 10$, since it must be an integer.

Error Threshold

Now consider the situation when the decoding errors due to random noise cannot be ignored, so we have *decoding noise* as well as quantization noise. Calculating the mean-square decoding noise $\overline{\epsilon_d^{\,2}}$ is complicated by the fact that the number of errors per

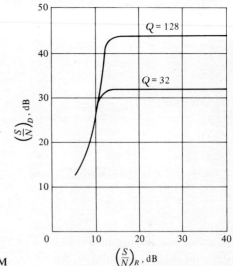

FIGURE 8.18
Noise performance of PCM

code word is random and the severity of an error depends on where it occurs, an error in the leading (most significant) digit being more serious than other errors in the same word. Assuming the error probability per digit P_e is not too large, one can show for binary PCM that[†]

$$\overline{\epsilon_d^2} = \frac{4(Q^2 - 1)P_e}{3Q^2} \qquad (7a)$$

and

$$\left(\frac{S}{N}\right)_D = \frac{\overline{x^2}}{\overline{\epsilon_q^2} + \overline{\epsilon_d^2}} = \frac{3Q^2\overline{x^2}}{1 + 4(Q^2 - 1)P_e} \qquad (7b)$$

where P_e depends on $(S/N)_R$, the signal-to-noise ratio at the receiver.

Figure 8.18 plots $(S/N)_D$ versus $(S/N)_R$ (both in decibels) for binary PCM with $Q = 32$ and 128, assuming gaussian noise and $\overline{x^2} = \frac{1}{2}$. The precipitous decline at low $(S/N)_R$ strongly suggests the FM threshold effect where, below threshold, we found that the message was mutilated beyond use. PCM also suffers from mutilation since it is readily appreciated that the reconstructed waveform bears little resemblance to the original message when decoding errors are frequent. In other words, the message is mutilated by decoding noise.

† Downing (1964, chap. 7).

To establish the PCM threshold level, we will say that decoding errors are negligible if $P_e \leq 10^{-4}$. Then taking P_e as given by Eq. (15), Sect. 4.5, i.e.,

$$P_e = 2\left(1 - \frac{1}{\mu}\right)Q\left[\sqrt{\frac{3}{\mu^2 - 1}\left(\frac{S}{N}\right)_R}\right] \leq 10^{-4} \qquad (8)$$

we solve for $(S/N)_{R_{\min}}$ to get

$$\left(\frac{S}{N}\right)_{R_{th}} \approx 5(\mu^2 - 1) \qquad (9)$$

Finally, since $\gamma = (B_T/W)(S/N)_R$ and $B_T \geq vW$,

$$\gamma_{th} = 5\frac{B_T}{W}(\mu^2 - 1) \geq 5v(\mu^2 - 1) \qquad (10)$$

A subtle but important implication of Eq. (9) is its limitation on μ, the number of different digits. Specifically, for any value of $(S/N)_R$ the system is above threshold only if $5(\mu^2 - 1) \leq (S/N)_R$, or

$$\mu^2 \leq \frac{1}{5}\left(\frac{S}{N}\right)_R + 1 \qquad (11)$$

which further implies a limitation on Q since $\mu^2 = Q^{2/v}$.

PCM versus Analog Modulation

Above threshold, the destination S/N of PCM is constant and fixed at the transmitter by the number of quantum levels. It remains to be demonstrated that PCM has the desirable characteristic of wideband noise reduction along with the undesirable characteristic of mutilation below threshold. For this purpose, we assume that the sampling frequency is close to the Nyquist rate so the baseband bandwidth is $B_T \approx vW$, per Eq. (2). Then $Q = \mu^v \approx \mu^{\mathscr{B}}$ where $\mathscr{B} = B_T/W$ is the bandwidth ratio, and Eq. (6) becomes

$$\left(\frac{S}{N}\right)_D \approx 3\mu^{2\mathscr{B}}\overline{x^2} \qquad (12)$$

which shows the noise reduction as being an *exponential* exchange of bandwidth for signal-to-noise ratio. This exchange is far more dramatic than that of wideband analog modulation, where $(S/N)_D$ increases linearly or as the square of the bandwidth ratio.

Figure 8.19 illustrates the performance of binary PCM ($\mu = 2$), as described by Eqs. (10) and (12), for three values of bandwidth ratio. For comparison the corresponding performance of several analog systems is also shown. The PCM and PPM

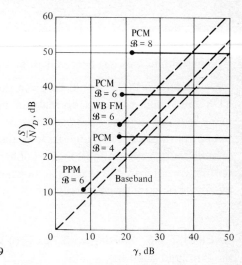

FIGURE 8.19

curves are for direct transmission without carrier modulation, and in all cases $\overline{x^2} = \frac{1}{2}$ is assumed. As usual, threshold points are indicated by heavy dots.

Examining the figure reveals that, in the name of efficiency, PCM systems should be operated just above threshold, for increasing the transmitted power beyond γ_{th} causes no improvement in $(S/N)_D$; the latter is dictated only by the number of quantum levels or, equivalently, the bandwidth ratio. But even at threshold, PCM does not show up so well as might have been hoped. Moreover, the instrumentation is considerably more complex and costly than that of uncoded systems. (For precisely this reason, PCM was deemed totally impractical prior to the emergence of high-speed solid-state digital electronics in the late 1950s, some 20 years after PCM's invention.) Why then is PCM so highly touted? This is an involved and controversial question with several answers.

1 For a given bandwidth ratio, PCM near threshold is superior to all other forms of *pulse* modulation, a significant factor if time-division multiplexing is desired.

2 PCM has a small but definite margin over FM at the lower signal-to-noise ratios. And even a 3-dB power reduction, being a factor of 2, may spell the difference between success or failure in minimum-power applications.

3 A PCM system designed for analog message transmission is readily adapted to other input signals, particularly digital data, thereby promoting flexibility and increasing system utilization.†

---

† In an interesting survey article, Franklin and Law (1966) discuss the problems of PCM interconnection and compatibility.

4 By virtue of the *regeneration* capability, PCM is distinctly advantageous for systems having many repeater stations. Indeed, with respect to long-distance telephone, this has been called the real payoff of PCM.

Therefore, PCM should be given due consideration for applications involving TDM, minimum power, a diversity of message types (i.e., analog and digital), or many repeater stations. Because most of these factors are present in long-haul telephone transmission, PCM appears to be the way of the future in telephony.† However in more routine applications, the cost of hardware for coded modulation usually proves prohibitive compared to that for analog modulation—a conclusion subject to reversal by advances in integrated circuits.

EXERCISE 8.6 Starting with Eqs. (10) and (12), prove that a PCM system just at the threshold point has

$$\left(\frac{S}{N}\right)_{D_{th}} = 3\left[1 + \left(\frac{\gamma_{th}}{5\mathscr{B}}\right)\right]^{\mathscr{B}} \overline{x^2} \qquad (13)$$

Compare this with WBFM by letting $\Delta = \mathscr{B}/2 \gg 1$ in Eq. (24), Sect. 7.5.

Delta Modulation (DM) ★

Delta modulation is an offspring of PCM that has the advantage of greatly simplified hardware; indeed, DM is the simplest known method for converting an analog signal to digital form. In exchange for these equipment savings, DM generally requires a larger transmission bandwidth than PCM. For voice signals, however, recent refinements have brought the bandwidth requirement down to the point where DM is a strong competitor with PCM. Here we will outline the operational principles of delta modulation, leaving the details for the perusal of the interested reader.‡

Figure 8.20a is the functional block diagram of a delta modulator. The message $x(t)$ is compared with a stepwise approximation $\tilde{x}(t)$ by subtraction, the difference being passed through a hard limiter whose output equals $\pm\Delta$ depending on the sign of $x(t) - \tilde{x}(t)$. This, in turn, modulates the ideal sampling wave $s_\delta(t)$ to produce

$$x_p(t) = \sum_k \Delta \operatorname{sgn}\left[x(kT_s) - \tilde{x}(kT_s)\right] \delta(t - kT_s) \qquad (14)$$

an impulse waveform from which $\tilde{x}(t)$ is generated by integration. Since there are only two possible impulse weights in $x_p(t)$, the signal actually transmitted is a binary waveform. The demodulator (Fig. 8.20b) consists of an integrator and lowpass filter, yielding $x(t)$ plus quantization noise.

† See Reeves (1965) for additional speculation along these lines by the pioneer of PCM.
‡ A good starting point is Schindler (1970).

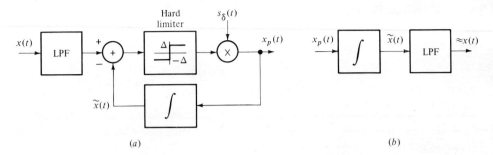

(a)   (b)

FIGURE 8.20
Delta modulation. (*a*) Modulator; (*b*) demodulator.

To clarify these operations, Fig. 8.21 shows typical waveforms $x(t)$, $\tilde{x}(t)$, and $x_p(t)$. Initially, let $\tilde{x}(t) < x(t)$ so the first impulse has weight $+\Delta$. When fed back and integrated, that impulse produces a stepwise change in $\tilde{x}(t)$ of height $+\Delta$. This process continues through the start-up interval until $\tilde{x}(t)$ exceeds $x(t)$ and causes a negative impulse. If $x(t)$ then remains constant, $\tilde{x}(t)$ exhibits a hunting behavior known as *idling noise*. When $x(t)$ is changing, $\tilde{x}(t)$ follows it in a stepwise fashion unless the rate of change is too great, illustrated at the right of the figure. This *slope-overload* phenomenon is a basic limitation of DM.

Barring slope overload, $\tilde{x}(t)$ reasonably approximates $x(t)$—especially if Δ and T_s are small—and lowpass filtering at the demodulator further improves the approximation. But observe that $x(t)$ is not the transmitted signal. Rather, the transmitted signal is a binary representation of $x_p(t)$ and the binary digits merely indicate the *polarity of the difference* between $x(t)$ and $\tilde{x}(t)$ at $t = kT_s$; hence the name delta modulation.

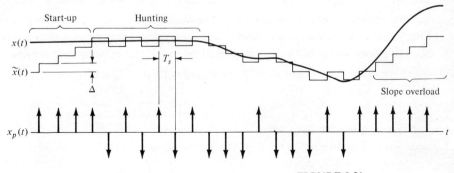

FIGURE 8.21
Delta modulation waveforms.

To analyze the performance of DM, we first derive a condition for preventing slope overload with tone modulation, $x(t) = A_m \cos 2\pi f_m t$. The maximum message slope then is

$$\left[\frac{dx(t)}{dt}\right]_{\max} = 2\pi f_m A_m \leq 2\pi W$$

where the upper bound comes from our message conventions $A_m \leq 1$ and $f_m \leq W$. Now the maximum slope of $\tilde{x}(t)$ is $\Delta/T_s = \Delta f_s$ so a sufficient condition for no slope overload is

$$f_s \geq \frac{2\pi W}{\Delta} \qquad (15)$$

and therefore $f_s \gg 2W$ if $\Delta \ll 1$, the latter being required to make $\tilde{x}(t)$ a good approximation to $x(t)$. Equation (15) is overly conservative unless the message spectrum is flat over W. More typically, message spectra fall off well below $f = W$ and the condition can be relaxed. Thus, if there is some frequency $f_0 < W$ such that

$$G_x(f) \leq \left(\frac{f_0}{f}\right)^2 G_x(f_0) \qquad f_0 \leq |f| \leq W \qquad (16)$$

then $|dx(t)/dt| \leq 2\pi f_0$ and, instead of Eq. (15),

$$f_s \geq \frac{2\pi f_0}{\Delta} \qquad (17)$$

Voice signals generally satisfy Eq. (16) with $f_0 \approx 800$ Hz as compared to $W \approx 4$ kHz, so Eq. (17) represents a significant reduction of the sampling frequency and the transmission bandwidth $B_T \geq f_s/2$.

Turning to the quantization noise, we write $\tilde{x}(t) = x(t) + \epsilon(t)$ where, from Fig. 8.21, $|\epsilon(t)| = |\tilde{x}(t) - x(t)| \leq \Delta$ in absence of slope overload. Assuming as before that $\epsilon(t)$ has a uniform distribution, the mean-square error equals $\overline{\epsilon^2} = \Delta^2/3$. We cannot, however, take $\overline{\epsilon^2}$ as the output quantization noise N_D because the LPF in Fig. 8.20b operates on the stepwise signal $\tilde{x}(t)$, rather than reconstructing quantized sample values as in PCM. To find N_D, we make the reasonable assumption that $G_\epsilon(f)$ is essentially constant over $|f| \leq W$ and $G_\epsilon(0) \approx \overline{\epsilon^2} T_s = \overline{\epsilon^2}/f_s$ (why?). Therefore,

$$N_D = \int_{-W}^{W} G_\epsilon(f)\, df \approx \frac{W\overline{\epsilon^2}}{f_s} = \Delta^2 \frac{W}{3f_s}$$

and

$$\left(\frac{S}{N}\right)_D = \left(\frac{3f_s}{\Delta^2 W}\right)\overline{x^2}$$

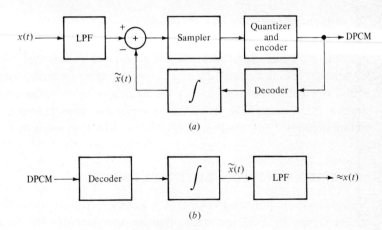

(a)

(b)

FIGURE 8.22
Differential PCM. (a) Modulator; (b) demodulator.

Finally, using Eq. (17) to eliminate Δ and inserting the bandwidth ratio $\mathscr{B} = B_T/W \geq f_s/2W$, we have

$$\left(\frac{S}{N}\right)_{D\text{max}} = \frac{6}{\pi^2} \left(\frac{W}{f_0}\right)^2 \mathscr{B}^3 \overline{x^2} \qquad (18)$$

which also includes the case of Eq. (15) by letting $f_0 = W$.

On the basis of Eq. (18) it can be said that the performance of DM falls somewhere between PCM and PPM since the wideband noise reduction goes as $\mathscr{B}^3$. Like PCM, the transmitted signal is digital so regenerative repeaters are allowed, while the terminal equipment is much less complex than PCM. Various DM modifications promise to reduce the problems of slope overload and idle noise.

Differential PCM ★

Concluding this treatment of digital transmission methods for analog signals, we briefly describe a technique that combines the feedback comparison strategy of DM with the multilevel quantization of PCM. Known as differential PCM (DPCM), this technique has particular promise for video signals.

Functionally, the DPCM signal is a PCM representation of the difference signal $x(t) - \tilde{x}(t)$ generated as shown in Fig. 8.22a. But $\tilde{x}(t)$ now has a variable step size ranging from $\pm\Delta$ to $\pm Q\Delta/2$, Q being the number of quantum levels, so it more accurately follows $x(t)$. (If $Q = 2$, DPCM reduces to DM.) Thus, especially if companding is used, there will be much lower idle noise, faster start-up, and less chance of slope overload. Figure 8.22b is the demodulator.

Clearly, DPCM with $Q > 2$ requires equipment just as complex as conventional PCM. In return, it offers potential transmission bandwidth reduction. This follows since the difference signal $x(t) - \tilde{x}(t)$ is adequately represented with fewer quantum levels if $x(t)$ does not change drastically from sample to sample. For instance, DPCM with $Q = 8 = 2^3$ (a three-bit code) gives acceptable video-signal reproduction whereas straight PCM must have $Q = 2^8$ for comparable monochrome† (black-and-white) picture quality. Thus, the transmission bandwidth is reduced by $\frac{3}{8}$.

8.4   TIME-DIVISION MULTIPLEXING

Time-division multiplexing (TDM) is a technique for transmitting several messages on one facility by dividing the time domain into slots, one slot for each message.

The essentials of TDM are quite simple, as illustrated by Fig. 8.23. The several

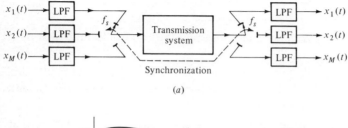

(a)

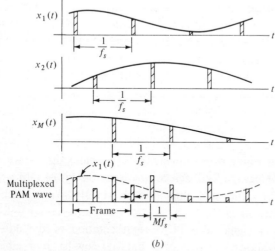

(b)

FIGURE 8.23
TDM system. (a) Block diagram; (b) waveforms.

† $Q = 2^9$ is used for color TV transmission via PCM.

input signals, all bandlimited in W by the input LPFs, are sequentially sampled at the transmitter by a rotary switch or *commutator*. The switch makes one complete revolution in $T_s \leq 1/2W$, extracting one sample from each input. Hence, the commutator output is a PAM waveform containing the individual message samples periodically interlaced in time. If there are M inputs, the pulse-to-pulse spacing is $T_s/M = 1/Mf_s$, while the spacing between successive samples from any one input is of course T_s. A set of pulses consisting of one sample from each input is called a *frame*.

At the receiver a similar rotary switch, the *decommutator* or *distributor*, separates the samples and distributes them to a bank of lowpass filters, which in turn reconstruct the original messages. The switching action is usually electronic, and synchronizing signals are provided to keep the distributor in step with the commutator. In fact, synchronization is perhaps the most critical aspect of TDM.†

Within this basic framework are numerous varieties of time-division systems, involving both pulsed and CW modulation, just as there are many combinations of subcarrier and carrier modulation in frequency-division systems. The interlaced sample values can be directly converted to PDM, PPM, or PCM and transmitted with or without carrier modulation. In fact, it is time-division-multiplexed PCM that holds the most promise for telephony. For noise-reduction purposes, PPM-AM, PCM-FM, etc., are particularly attractive. But before getting into the details, let us pause to contrast the two mutiplexing methods.‡

Clearly TDM and FDM accomplish the same goals, though the means are different. Indeed, they can be visualized as *dual* techniques; for in TDM the signals are separate in the time domain but jumbled together in frequency, whereas in FDM the signals are separate in the frequency domain but jumbled together in time. It is therefore reasonable to ask what advantages, if any, TDM offers compared to FDM. From a theoretical viewpoint there are none. From a practical viewpoint TDM can be superior in two respects.

First, TDM instrumentation is somewhat simpler. Recall that FDM requires subcarrier modulators, bandpass filters, and demodulators for *each* message channel; these are all replaced by the commutator and distributor of TDM. And TDM synchronization is but slightly more demanding than that of FDM with suppressed-carrier modulation.

Second, and equally important, TDM is invulnerable to the usual sources of FDM interchannel cross talk, i.e., imperfect channel filtering and cross modulation due to nonlinearities. In fact, there is no cross talk in TDM if the pulses are completely isolated and nonoverlapping, since message separation is achieved by decommutation

---

† Bell Telephone Laboratories (1971, chaps. 25 and 26) covers the exotica of digital multiplexing using statistical framing, pulse stuffing, and elastic stores.
‡ See Bennett (1970, chap. 9) for a more detailed comparison.

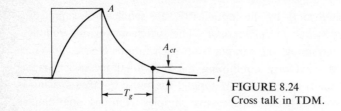

FIGURE 8.24
Cross talk in TDM.

or gating in time, rather than by filtering. TDM cross-talk immunity is therefore contingent upon a wideband response and the absence of phase-shift (delay) distortion, keeping the pulses short and confined. (Note that phase distortion does not cause cross talk in FDM.)

TDM Cross Talk

Actual pulse shapes, having decaying tails, do tend to overlap. However, the resulting cross talk can be effectively reduced by providing *guard times* between pulses, analogous to the guard bands of FDM. Thus, a practical time-division system will have both guard times and guard bands, the former to suppress cross talk, the latter to facilitate message reconstruction with practical filters.

For a quantitative estimate of cross talk, we know that the pulses decay more or less exponentially with a time constant of order $1/2\pi B$ where B is the 3-dB bandwidth of the channel, taken to be a baseband channel. If T_g is the guard time in the sense of minimum pulse spacing, then the worst-case overlap is as illustrated in Fig. 8.24, highly exaggerated. Since $A_{ct} = Ae^{-2\pi BT_g}$, we define the *cross-talk factor*

$$\kappa \triangleq \left(\frac{A_{ct}}{A}\right)^2 = e^{-4\pi BT_g} \qquad (1a)$$

or

$$\kappa \approx -54.5\, BT_g \qquad \text{dB} \qquad (1b)$$

Thus, for example, keeping the cross talk below -30 dB requires $T_g \geq 1/2B$.

Guard times are especially important when the multiplexed pulses are PDM or PPM rather than PAM because time-modulated pulses "move around" in their portion of the frame.

EXERCISE 8.7   Ten voice signals are to be transmitted over a baseband channel of bandwidth 400 kHz using TDM-PPM. Taking $\tau = 5$ μs and $f_s = 8$ kHz, calculate T_g such that $\kappa = -60$ dB and find the maximum permitted displacement t_0 per pulse. *Ans.*: $T_g = 2.75$ μs, $t_0 = [(1/Mf_s) - \tau - T_g]/2 = 2.37$ μs.

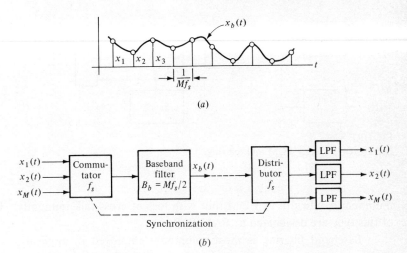

(a)

(b)

FIGURE 8.25
TDM baseband filtering. (a) Filtered waveform; (b) system diagram.

Baseband Filtering

One more point remains to complete our FDM-TDM comparison, namely, the matter of bandwidth conservation. Consider an FDM system with M inputs bandlimited in W. If the guard bands are small compared to W and SSB modulation is used throughout, the transmission bandwidth will be MW, which is obviously the absolute minimum. But what about TDM? It would appear from Fig. 8.23b and our earlier discussion of PAM that the bandwidth of the multiplexed waveform far exceeds the minimum; i.e., the pulse duration is $\tau \ll 1/Mf_s$, so transmission as RF pulses requires a bandwidth of $1/\tau \gg MW$.

But note that the multiplexed wave is nothing more than a series of periodic sample points, albeit from different messages. Reversing the sampling theorem, these points can be completely described by a *continuous* waveform $x_b(t)$ having no relation to the original messages save that it passes through the correct sample values at the corresponding sample times, Fig. 8.25a. Then, since the points are spaced in time by $1/Mf_s$, $x_b(t)$ can be bandlimited in $B_b = Mf_s/2$. In fact, $x_b(t)$ is obtained by lowpass (baseband) filtering the multiplexed wave as indicated in Fig. 8.25b. At the receiver, the distributor picks out the original sample points from $x_b(t)$ for reconstruction in the usual fashion.

If baseband filtering is employed, if the sampling frequency is close to the Nyquist rate ($f_s = 2W$), and if the carrier modulation is SSB, the TDM transmission bandwidth becomes $Mf_s/2 = MW$. Under these conditions TDM can achieve the same

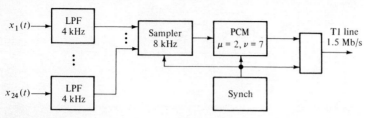

FIGURE 8.26
Bell System T1 voice PCM multiplexing.

minimum bandwidth as FDM, but with loss of cross-talk immunity. TDM systems of this type are designated as PAM-SSB.

Baseband filtering is most commonly employed in applications having both TDM and FDM, notably for telemetry systems.† The usual arrangement is to combine several slowly varying signals via TDM with baseband filtering, forming a composite wave, which is then FDMed with other signals of comparable bandwidth.

Example 8.2 TDM-PCM Telephony

Analogous to its FDM hierarchy, the Bell System has a *digital* TDM hierarchy in which the binary pulse rate or *bit rate* plays the role that bandwidth did in FDM. Currently, the building blocks are the T1 through T4 "lines" (twisted pairs or coaxial cables) having bit rates of approximately 1.5, 6.3, 45, and 274 megabits per second (Mb/s), respectively — subject to change with technological advances. These lines are capable of transmitting digital data signals or PCM analog signals of various bit rates.

The T1 voice-signal multiplexing arrangement is diagramed in Fig. 8.26. Twenty-four voice signals are sampled at $f_s = 8$ kHz and the resulting TDM-PAM signal is converted to PCM with $\mu = 2$ and $v = 7$. Additional binary pulses ("housekeeping bits") for synchronization and framing are inserted, bringing the output rate up to 1.544 Mb/s. Four T1 signals can then be combined using the M12 multiplexer to produce a T2 signal, and so forth up the hierarchy.

Indicative of the flexibility, Fig. 8.27 shows how voice, digital data, Picturephone®, and color TV signals may be combined for transmission on a T4 line. The T1 signals include PCM voice as described above, and TDMed digital data. T2 signals are multiplexed T1 signals or differential PCM Picturephone® signals ($f_s \approx 2$ MHz, $\mu = 2$, $v = 3$). An M23 multiplexer combines seven T2 signals to form a T3 signal. Alternately, since binary PCM color TV requires 90 Mb/s ($f_s \approx 10$ MHz,

---

† See, for example, Nichols and Rauch (1956).

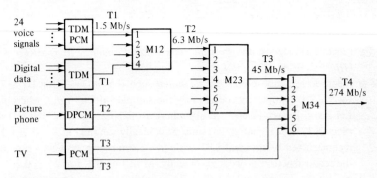

FIGURE 8.27
Illustrative configuration of the Bell System digital TDM hierarchy.

$v = 9$), two T3 lines may be used for this purpose. Finally, the T4 signal is generated from six T3 signals.

A fifth building block for the hierarchy is presently under development in the form of a helical waveguide operating in the 100-GHz band. Should it prove feasible, this waveguide will have an anticipated capacity of $60 \times 274 = 16,440$ Mb/s, equivalent to a quarter-million two-way voice channels!

8.5 PROBLEMS

8.1   (Sect. 8.1) If $x(t) = \cos 2\pi 100t + \cos 2\pi 220t$ is ideally sampled at $f_s = 300$ and $x_\delta(t)$ is passed through an ideal LPF with $B = 150$, what frequency components are present at the output? (*Hint*: Sketch the two-sided line spectrum of $x_\delta(t)$.) *Ans.*: 80 and 100 Hz.

8.2   (Sect. 8.1) The signal whose spectrum is shown in Fig. P8.1 is ideally sampled at $f_s = 20$ Hz. Sketch the spectrum of $x_\delta(t)$ for $|f| \le 40$ Hz. Can $x(t)$ be recovered? If so, how? Repeat with $f_s = 30$ Hz.

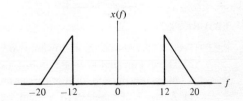

FIGURE P8.1.

8.3   (Sect. 8.1) Let $x(t)$ be a *bandpass* signal with bandwidth B centered on $f_0 \gg B$. By sketching typical spectra, show that $x(t)$ can be recovered from $x_\delta(t)$ when $f_s > 2B$, even though the highest frequency in $x(t)$ is $f_0 + B/2 > f_s/2$.

8.4 (Sect. 8.1) Derive Eq. (12) by expanding $s_\delta(t)$ in an exponential Fourier series and applying Eq. (21), Sect. 2.4.

8.5★ (Sect. 8.1) Derive the *Poisson summation formula* $\sum_{k=-\infty}^{\infty} x(kT_s) = f_s \sum_{n=-\infty}^{\infty} X(nf_s)$. (*Hint*: Consider $\int_{-\infty}^{\infty} x(t)s_\delta(t)\, dt$.)

8.6★ (Sect. 8.1) Suppose $v(t)$ is *timelimited* such that $v(t) = 0$ for $|t| \geq T$. Show that its *spectrum* is completely specified by the sample values $V(nf_0)$, where $f_0 \leq 1/2T$. (*Hint*: Let $z(t) = [v(t)] * [\sum \delta(t - kT_0)]$, where $T_0 = 1/f_0$, and note that $v(t) = z(t)\Pi(t/2T)$.)

8.7 (Sect. 8.1) The signal $x(t) = \operatorname{sinc}^2 5t$ is ideally sampled at $t = 0, \pm 0.1, \pm 0.2, \ldots,$ and reconstructed by an ideal LPF with $B = 5$, unit gain, and zero time delay. Carry out the reconstruction process graphically, as in Fig. 8.5, for $|t| \leq 0.2$.

8.8 (Sect. 8.1) A rectangular pulse with $\tau = 2$ is sampled and reconstructed using an ideal LPF with $B = f_s/2$. Sketch the resulting output waveforms when $T_s = 0.8$ and 0.4. Assume one sample time is at the center of the pulse.

8.9★ (Sect.. 8.1) Figure P2.3 is a *first-order hold* and has $H(f) = T(1 + j2\pi fT)$ $\operatorname{sinc}^2 fTe^{-j2\pi fT}$. Taking $T = T_s$, analyze its performance using sketches like Fig. 8.7. (*Hint*: Find $h(t)$ from the block diagram, not from $H(f)$.)

8.10 (Sect. 8.1) **Sketch** the switching function for the bipolar chopper in Fig. 8.9 and show that $s(t) = (4/\pi) \cos \omega_s t - (4/3\pi) \cos 3\omega_s t + (4/5\pi) \cos 5\omega_s t + \cdots$.

8.11 (Sect. 8.1) The usable frequency range of a certain amplifier is f_{co} to $f_{co} + B$. Devise a method employing bipolar choppers so the amplifier can be used for a signal having significant DC content and $W \ll B$, assuming $B \gg f_{co}$. (*Hint*: See Prob. 8.10.)

8.12 (Sect. 8.1) Show that the chopper system in Fig. P8.2 combines the operations of matrixing and subcarrier modulation and thereby produces the baseband signal required for FM stereo (Fig. 5.37). (*Hint*: There are effectively two switching functions having $\tau = T_s/2$ and differing by a time delay of $T_s/2$.)

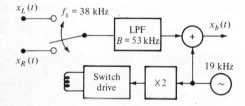

FIGURE P8.2.

8.13 (Sect. 8.2) Explain the following two statements.

(a) Direct conversion to RF pulses, rather than conventional AM, FM, or PM, is the most appropriate form of carrier modulation in analog pulse modulation systems.

(b) A single-channel PPM system requires a synchronizing signal, whereas PAM and PDM do not.

8.14 (Sect. 8.2) Find $H_{eq}(f)$ for a PAM system with $p(t) = \cos \pi t/\tau$, $|t| \leq \tau/2$. Sketch the amplitude ratio over $0 \leq f \leq W$ when $\tau = 1/5W$.

8.15★(Sect. 8.2) In some PAM systems the sampling device extracts an *average* value, so $x(kT_s)$ is replaced by $\bar{x}(kT_s) \triangleq (1/\tau) \int_{kT_s-\tau}^{kT_s} x(\lambda)\, d\lambda$. Find an appropriate equalization filter when $p(t) = \Pi(t/\tau)$. (*Hint*: What filter produces $\bar{x}(t)$ when $x(t)$ is the input?)

8.16 (Sect. 8.2) A PDM signal has $\tau \ll T_s$ and fixed leading edges at $t = kT_s$. By sketching typical waveforms, show that the device of Fig. P8.3 will approximately reconstruct $x(t)$ if $RC \gg T_s$ and the switch is closed momentarily every $t = kT_s$.

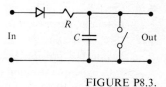

FIGURE P8.3.

8.17 (Sect. 8.2) Derive Eq. (8) by first ignoring the modulation and writing $x_p(t)$ as a trigonometric Fourier series similar to Eq. (2), Sect. 8.1. Then replace τ by $\tau_0[1 + mx(t)]$ and show that the frequency-translated terms have the form

$$(2A_0/n\pi) \sin \{n\pi\tau_0 f_s[1 + mx(t)]\} \cos n\omega_s t.$$

8.18★(Sect. 8.2) *Day's serrasoid system* for narrowband PM is diagramed in Fig. P8.4. (The PPM signal is developed using a sawtooth generator per Figs. 8.12 and 8.13, which explains the system's name, *serra* being Latin for "saw.") Using Eq. (13) show that the output is of the form $A_c \cos [\omega_c t + \phi_\Delta x(t)]$ when the BPF is centered on $f_c = Mf_s$.

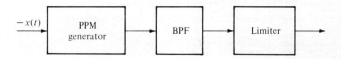

FIGURE P8.4.

8.19 (Sect. 8.2) Calculate $(S/N)_D$ in terms of γ for a typical PAM system having $f_s = 2.5W$, $\tau = 0.2T_s$, $B_T = 3/4\tau$, and $m^2\overline{x^2} = \frac{1}{2}$.

8.20 (Sect. 8.2) Calculate γ_{th} and $(S/N)_D$ in terms of γ for a PPM system with $f_s = 2.5W$, $\tau = 0.1T_s$, $t_0 = 0.25T_s$, and $B_T/W = 50$. Compare with $(S/N)_{D_{max}}$. *Ans.:* $(S/N)_D = 20\overline{x^2}\gamma$.

8.21 (Sect. 8.3) A signal having negligible content above 3.6 kHz is to be transmitted via binary PCM on a channel whose maximum pulse rate is 40,000 pulses per second. Draw a block diagram of the transmitter, specifying values for all design parameters. *Ans.:* $f_s = 8$ kHz, $\nu = 5$, $Q = 32$.

8.22 (Sect. 8.3) A signal having negligible content above 20 kHz is to be transmitted via PCM on a channel having $B_T = 70$ kHz. It is required that $Q \geq 60$. Draw a block diagram of the transmitter, specifying values for all design parameters.

8.23 (Sect. 8.3) Generalizing on Exercise 8.5, show that $\nu \geq \log_\mu 50/P$ when the maximum quantizing error is not to exceed P percent of the peak-to-peak signal swing.

8.24 (Sect. 8.3) Consider a binary PCM signal transmitted as on-off RF pulses. If $f_s = 2.5W$ and $\overline{x^2} = \frac{1}{2}$, plot $(S/N)_D$ in decibels versus $B_{T_{RF}}/W$ for $Q = 4, 16, 64$, and 256. Explain why this plot is a straight line.

8.25   (Sect. 8.3)   A voice signal with a nominal bandwidth of 3 kHz is to be transmitted over a 20-kHz baseband channel such that $(S/N)_D \geq 18,000\overline{x^2}$. Design a PCM system to accomplish this, giving values for μ, ν, $\mathcal{Q}$, and f_s. *Ans.*: $\mu = 3$, $\nu = 4$, $\mathcal{Q} = 81$, $f_s = 10$ kHz.

8.26   (Sect. 8.3)   A PCM system has fixed values of γ and $\mathcal{B}$. Taking threshold into account, obtain an expression for the maximum value of $\mathcal{Q}$.

8.27   (Sect. 8.3)   Any M successive quantized samples can be represented by *one* number having $\mathcal{Q}^M$ possible values, a process called *hyperquantization*. Discuss how PCM with hyperquantization can achieve *bandwidth compression*, $B_T/W < 1$.

8.28★(Sect. 8.3)   PCM quantization noise was computed in Eq. (5) assuming $\epsilon_q(t)$ to have a uniform PDF, which implies that $x(t)$ has a uniform PDF and that the quantum levels are equally spaced. More generally, if b_k is the kth quantum level and a_k and a_{k+1} are the adjacent round-off boundaries, then

$$\overline{\epsilon_q^2} = \sum_{k=1}^{\mathcal{Q}} \int_{a_k}^{a_{k+1}} (x - b_k)^2 p_x(x)\, dx$$

where $a_k \leq b_k \leq a_{k+1}$. Show that $\overline{\epsilon_q^2} \approx 1/3\mathcal{Q}^2$ when there are $\mathcal{Q} \gg 1$ levels equally spaced by $2/\mathcal{Q}$, so $a_k = b_k - 1/\mathcal{Q}$ and $a_{k+1} = b_k + 1/\mathcal{Q}$, and $p_x(x)$ is reasonably smooth but not necessarily uniform over $[-1,1]$. (*Hint*: Note that $(2/\mathcal{Q})p_x(b_k) \approx \text{Prob } [a_k \leq x \leq a_{k+1}]$.)

8.29★(Sect. 8.3)   Referring to Prob. 8.28, suppose $\mathcal{Q} = 2$ and $p_x(x) = (\tfrac{3}{2})(1 - |x|)^2$, $|x| \leq 1$, which is a signal with a large crest factor.

   (*a*)   Calculate $\overline{\epsilon_q^2}$ for equally spaced levels, i.e., $b_k = -\tfrac{1}{2}$ and $\tfrac{1}{2}$, $a_k = -1$, 0, and 1.

   (*b*)   Taking $b_k = \pm b$ and a_k as before, find the value of b that minimizes $\overline{\epsilon_q^2}$ and compare the resulting value with $\tfrac{1}{3}\mathcal{Q}^2 = 1/12$.

8.30★(Sect. 8.3)   A signal with $W/f_0 = 4$ is to be transmitted via binary PCM or DM. Over what range of $\mathcal{B}$ will DM give the larger value of $(S/N)_D$, assuming both systems are above threshold?

8.31   (Sect. 8.4)   Twenty-five voice signals having $W = 3$ kHz are to be TDMed and transmitted via PAM-AM, i.e., AM carrier modulation. Allowing for a 2-kHz reconstruction guard band, determine the minimum transmission bandwidth required and draw block diagrams of the transmitter and receiver. *Ans.*: $f_s = 8$ kHz, $B_T = 200$ kHz.

8.32   (Sect. 8.4)   Four signals bandlimited in W, W, $2W$, and $4W$, respectively, are to be TDMed. Devise a commutator configuration such that each signal is periodically sampled at its own Nyquist rate and the sample values are properly interlaced.

8.33   (Sect. 8.4)   Ten signals, each with $W = 4$ kHz, are to be transmitted via TDM-PPM without carrier modulation. Taking $\tau = 1$ μs and allowing a guard time of 2 μs and reconstruction guard bands of 2 kHz, calculate the maximum possible displacement per pulse. Estimate the resulting reduction in output S/N per channel, compared to a single-channel PPM system having the same pulse duration, same guard band, one-tenth the average power, and one-tenth the transmission bandwidth.

8.34★(Sect. 8.4)   Five analog data signals are to be transmitted via baseband TDM-PCM with $\mu = 2$ and $\mathcal{Q} = 256$. The signals are not strictly bandlimited, but experimentation has shown that passing any one through a third-order Butterworth LPF (Fig. 2.37) with $B = 800$ Hz does not cause significant distortion. The channel has $\mathscr{L} = 60$ dB and $\eta = 10^{-10}$ W/Hz. Assuming the interlaced binary signal has sinc-pulse shaping as discussed in Sect. 4.5, draw and fully label a complete block diagram of the system, including the minimum value of S_T.

8.35★(Sect. 8.4) The cross talk illustrated in Fig. 8.24 is negligible beyond the adjacent time slot for reasonable values of κ. But there is also cross talk due to imperfect *low-frequency* transmission, and this may affect several time slots. Demonstrate this effect by considering the rectangular-pulse response when $H(f) = 1 - \Pi(f/2f_{co})$ where $f_{co} \ll 1/\tau$. (*Hint*: Approximate the output waveform rather than attempting to find an exact expression.)

8.36   (Sect. 8.4) Discuss the relative merits of TDM versus FDM when the channel is subject to *selective fading*; i.e., a narrow band of frequencies suffers severe attenuation compared to the rest of the band. Consider two extreme cases:

(*a*) When the fading is slow and prolonged compared to message duration

(*b*) When the fading is of brief duration compared to the message.

9

INFORMATION THEORY AND
COMMUNICATION SYSTEMS

The past several chapters have dealt with electrical communication primarily in terms of signals, both desired and undesired. We have devised signal models, examined the effects of networks on signals, and analyzed modulation as a means of signal transmission. Although many rewards and much insight have been gained by this approach, signal theory alone is not sufficient for a complete understanding of our subject matter, particularly when it comes to the design of new and improved systems. What is needed is a more encompassing view of the communication process, a broader perspective leading to basic principles for system design and comparison—in short, a general theory of communication.

Prior to the 1940s a few steps were taken toward such a theory in the telegraphy investigations of Nyquist and Hartley. But then, shortly after World War II, Claude Shannon (1948) and Norbert Wiener (1949) set forth new concepts that had and continue to have major impact. Taken together, the ideas of Wiener and Shannon established the foundation of modern (statistical) *communication theory*. Both men were concerned with extracting information from a background of noise, and both applied statistical concepts to the problem.† There were, however, differences in emphasis.

---

† Both men are also famous for other accomplishments. Wiener founded the subject known as cybernetics, and Shannon first pointed out the relationship of Boolean algebra to switching-circuit design — in his master's thesis!

Wiener treated the case where the information-bearing signals are beyond the designer's control, in whole or part, all the processing being at the receiving end. The problem then can be stated in this fashion: Given the set of possible signals, not of our choosing, plus the inevitable noise, how do we make the best estimate of the present and future values of the signal being received? Optimum solutions to this and similar problems are sought in the discipline known as *detection theory*.

Shannon's work is more nearly akin to what we think of as communication, where signal processing can take place at both transmitter and receiver. Shannon posed this problem: given the set of possible messages a source may produce, not of our choosing, how shall the messages be represented so as best to convey the information over a given system with its inherent physical limitations? To handle this problem in quite general terms it is necessary to concentrate more on the *information* per se than on the signals, and Shannon's approach was soon rechristened *information theory*.

Information theory is a mathematical subject dealing with three basic concepts: the measure of information, the capacity of a communication channel to transfer information, and coding as a means of utilizing channels at full capacity. These concepts are tied together in what can be called the fundamental theorem of information theory, as follows.

Given an information source and a communication channel, there exists a coding technique such that the information can be transmitted over the channel at any rate less than the channel capacity and with arbitrarily small frequency of errors despite the presence of noise.

The surprising, almost astonishing aspect of this theorem is *error-free* transmission on a *noisy* channel, a condition achieved through the use of coding. In essence, coding is used to match the source and channel for maximum reliable information transfer, roughly analogous to impedance matching for maximum power transfer.

But the study of coding is, by and large, tangential to our immediate aims. Thus, with some reluctance, we limit this chapter primarily to the concepts of information measure and channel capacity, with emphasis on the latter. By so doing we shall eventually arrive at answers to these significant questions:

1 Precisely how do the fundamental physical limitations (i.e., bandwidth and noise) restrict information transmission?
2 Is there such a thing as an *ideal* communication system, and, if so, what are its characteristics?
3 How well do existing communication systems measure up to the ideal, and how can their performance be improved?

Answers to these questions are certainly germane to electrical communication.

They will be explored in some detail at the close of the chapter. But we must begin with information theory.

9.1 INFORMATION MEASURE: ENTROPY

The crux of information theory is the measure of information. Here we are using *information* as a technical term, not to be confused with its more conventional interpretations. In particular, the information of information theory has little to do with knowledge or meaning, concepts which defy precise definition, to say nothing of quantitative measurement. In the context of communication, information is simply that which is produced by the source for transfer to the user. This implies that before transmission, the information was not available at the destination; otherwise the transfer would be zero. Pursuing this line of reasoning, consider the following somewhat contrived situation.

A man is planning a trip to Chicago. To determine what clothes he should pack, he telephones the Chicago weather bureau and receives one of the following forecasts:

The sun will rise.
It will rain.
There will be a tornado.

Clearly, the amount of information gained from these messages is quite different. The first contains virtually no information, since we are reasonably sure in advance that the sun will rise; there is no uncertainty about this, and the call has been wasted. But the forecast of rain does provide information not previously available to the traveler, for rain is not an everyday occurrence. The third forecast contains even more information, tornadoes being relatively rare and unexpected events.

Note that the messages have been listed in order of decreasing likelihood and increasing information. The less likely the message, the more information it conveys to the user. We are thus inclined to say that information measure is related to *uncertainty*, the uncertainty of the user as to what the message will be. Moreover, the amount of information depends only on the message uncertainty, rather than its actual content or possible interpretations. Had the Chicago weather forecast been "The sun will rain tornadoes," it would convey information, being quite unlikely, but not much meaning.

Alternately, going to the transmitting end of a communication system, information measure is an indication of the *freedom of choice* exercised by the source in selecting a message. If the source can freely choose from many different messages, the user is highly uncertain as to which message will be selected. But if there is no choice at all, only one possible message, there is no uncertainty and hence no information.

Whether one prefers the uncertainty viewpoint or the freedom-of-choice interpretation, it is evident that the measure of information involves *probabilities*. Messages of high probability, indicating little uncertainty on the part of the user or little choice on the part of the source, convey a small amount of information, and vice versa. This notion is formalized by defining self-information in terms of probability.

Self-Information

Consider a source that produces various messages. Let one of the messages be designated A, and let P_A be the probability that A is selected for transmission. Consistent with our discussion above, we write the self-information associated with A as

$$\mathscr{I}_A = f(P_A)$$

where the function $f(\ )$ is to be determined. As a step toward finding $f(\ )$, intuitive reasoning suggests that the following requirements be imposed:

$$f(P_A) \geq 0 \quad \text{where } 0 \leq P_A \leq 1 \tag{1}$$

$$\lim_{P_A \to 1} f(P_A) = 0 \tag{2}$$

$$f(P_A) > f(P_B) \quad \text{for } P_A < P_B \tag{3}$$

The student should have little trouble interpreting these requirements.

Many functions satisfy Eqs. (1) to (3). The final and deciding factor comes from considering the transmission of *independent* messages. When message A is delivered, the user receives $\mathscr{I}_A$ units of information. If a second message B is also delivered, the total information received should be the sum of the self-informations, $\mathscr{I}_A + \mathscr{I}_B$. This summation rule is readily appreciated if we think of A and B as coming from different sources. But suppose both messages come from the same source; we can then speak of the compound message $C = AB$. If A and B are statistically independent, $P_C = P_A P_B$ and $\mathscr{I}_C = f(P_A P_B)$. But the received information is still $\mathscr{I}_C = \mathscr{I}_A + \mathscr{I}_B = f(P_A) + f(P_B)$ and therefore

$$f(P_A P_B) = f(P_A) + f(P_B) \tag{4}$$

which is our final requirement for $f(\ )$.

There is one and only one function† satisfying the conditions (1) to (4), namely, the *logarithmic function* $f(\ ) = -\log_b(\ )$, where b is the logarithmic base. Thus self-information is defined as

$$\mathscr{I}_A \triangleq -\log_b P_A = \log_b \frac{1}{P_A} \tag{5}$$

† See Ash (1965, chap. 1) for proof.

where b is unspecified for the moment. The minus sign in $-\log_b P_A$ is perhaps disturbing at first glance. But, since probabilities are bounded by $0 \le P_A \le 1$, the negative of the logarithm is positive, as desired. The alternate form $\log_b (1/P_A)$ helps avoid confusion on this score, and will be used throughout.

Specifying the logarithmic base b is equivalent to selecting the *unit* of information. While common or natural logarithms ($b = 10$ or $b = e$) seem obvious candidates, the standard convention of information theory is to take $b = 2$. The corresponding unit of information is termed the *bit*, a contraction for *binary digit* suggested by J. W. Tukey. Thus

$$\mathscr{I}_A = \log_2 \frac{1}{P_A} \qquad \text{bits}$$

The reasoning behind this rather strange convention goes like this. Information is a measure of choice exercised by the source; the simplest possible choice is that between two equiprobable messages, i.e., an unbiased binary choice. The information unit is therefore normalized to this lowest-order situation, and 1 bit of information is the amount required or conveyed by the choice between two equally likely possibilities, i.e., if $P_A = P_B = \frac{1}{2}$, then $\mathscr{I}_A = \mathscr{I}_B = \log_2 2 = 1$ bit.

Binary *digits* enter the picture simply because any two things can be represented by the two binary digits **0** and **1**. Note, however, that one binary digit may convey more or less than 1 bit of information, depending on the probabilities. To prevent misinterpretation, binary digits as message elements are called *binits* in this chapter.

Since tables of base 2 logarithms are relatively uncommon, the following conversion relationship is needed:

$$\log_2 v = \log_2 10 \, \log_{10} v \approx 3.32 \log_{10} v \qquad (6)$$

Thus, if $P_A = \frac{1}{10}$, $\mathscr{I}_A = 3.32 \log_{10} 10 = 3.32$ bits. In the remainder of this chapter, all logarithms will be base 2 unless otherwise indicated.

Example 9.1 The Information in a Picture

It has often been said that one picture is worth a thousand words. With a little stretching, information measure supports this old saying.

For analysis we decompose the picture into a number of discrete dots, or elements, each element having a brightness level ranging in steps from black to white. The standard television image, for instance, has about $500 \times 600 = 3 \times 10^5$ elements and eight easily distinguishable levels. Hence, there are $8 \times 8 \times \ldots = 8^{3 \times 10^5}$ possible pictures, each with probability $P = 8^{-(3 \times 10^5)}$ if selected at random. Therefore

$$\mathscr{I} = \log_2 8^{3 \times 10^5} = 3 \times 10^5 \log_2 8 \approx 10^6 \text{ bits}$$

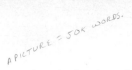

Alternately, assuming the levels to be equally likely, the information per element is $\log 8 = 3$ bits, for a total of $3 \times 10^5 \times 3 \approx 10^6$ bits, as before.

But what about the thousand words? Suppose, for the sake of argument, that a vocabulary consists of 100,000 equally likely words. The probability of any one word is then $P = 10^{-5}$, so the information contained in 1,000 words is

$$\mathscr{I} = 1,000 \log_2 10^5 = 10^3 \times 3.32 \log_{10} 10^5 \approx 2 \times 10^4 \text{ bits}$$

or substantially less than the information in one picture.

The validity of the above assumptions is of course open to question; the point of this example is the method, not the results. ////

Entropy and Information Rate

Self-information is defined in terms of the individual messages or symbols a source may produce. It is not, however, a useful description of the source relative to communication. A communication system is not designed around a particular message but rather all possible messages, i.e., what the source could produce as distinguished from what it does produce on a given occasion. Thus, although the instantaneous information flow from a source may be erratic, one must describe the source in terms of the *average information* produced. This average information is called the source *entropy*.

For a discrete source whose symbols are *statistically independent*, the entropy expression is easily formulated. Let m be the number of different symbols, i.e., an alphabet of size m. When the jth symbol is transmitted, it conveys $\mathscr{I}_j = \log(1/P_j)$ bits of information. In a long message of $N \gg 1$ symbols, the jth symbol occurs about NP_j times, and the total information in the message is approximately

$$NP_1\mathscr{I}_1 + NP_2\mathscr{I}_2 + \cdots + NP_m\mathscr{I}_m = \sum_{j=1}^{m} NP_j\mathscr{I}_j \quad \text{bits}$$

which, when divided by N, yields the average information per symbol. We therefore define the entropy of a discrete source as

$$\mathscr{H} \triangleq \sum_{j=1}^{m} P_j\mathscr{I}_j = \sum_{j=1}^{m} P_j \log\frac{1}{P_j} \quad \text{bits/symbol} \tag{7}$$

It should be observed that Eq. (7) is an ensemble average. If the source is nonstationary, the symbol probabilities may change with time and the entropy is not very meaningful. We shall henceforth assume that information sources are *ergodic*, so that time and ensemble averages are identical.

The name *entropy* and its symbol $\mathscr{H}$ are borrowed from a similar equation in statistical mechanics. Because of the mathematical similarity, various attempts have been made to relate communication entropy with thermodynamic entropy.† However, the attempted relationships seem to cause more confusion than illumination, and it is perhaps wiser to treat the two entropies as different things with the same name. For this reason the alternate designation *comentropy* has been suggested for communication entropy.

But what is the meaning of communication entropy as written in Eq. (7)? Simply this: although one cannot say which symbol the source will produce next, on the average we expect to get $\mathscr{H}$ bits of information per symbol or $N\mathscr{H}$ bits in a message of N symbols, if N is large.

For a fixed alphabet size (fixed m) the entropy of a discrete source depends on the symbol probabilities but is bounded by

$$0 \leq \mathscr{H} \leq \log_2 m \tag{8}$$

These extreme limits are readily interpreted and warrant further discussion. The lower limit, $\mathscr{H} = 0$, implies that the source delivers no information (on the average), and hence there is no uncertainty about the message. We would expect this to correspond to a source that continually produces the same symbol; i.e., all symbol probabilities are zero, save for one symbol having $P = 1$. It is easily shown that $\mathscr{H} = 0$ in this case. At the other extreme, the maximum entropy must correspond to maximum uncertainty or maximum freedom of choice. This implies that all symbols are equally likely; there is no bias, no preferred symbol. A little further thought reveals that the symbol probabilities must be the same; i.e., $\mathscr{H} = \mathscr{H}_{max} = \log m$ when all $P_j = 1/m$, which has particular significance for our later work.

The variation of $\mathscr{H}$ between the limits of Eq. (8) is best illustrated by considering a binary source ($m = 2$). The symbol probabilities are then related and can be written as P and $1 - P$. Thus

$$\mathscr{H} = P \log_2 \frac{1}{P} + (1 - P) \log_2 \frac{1}{1 - P} \tag{9}$$

which is plotted versus P in Fig. 9.1. Note the rather broad maximum centered at $P = 0.5$, the equally likely case, where $\mathscr{H} = \log 2 = 1$ bit.

Bringing the time element into the picture, suppose two sources have equal entropies but one is "faster" than the other, producing more symbols per unit time. In a given period, more information must be transferred from the faster source than from the slower, which obviously places greater demands on the communication system. Thus, for our purposes, the description of a source is not its entropy alone but its *entropy rate*, or information rate, in bits per second. The entropy rate of a discrete source is simply defined as

† See Brillouin (1956).

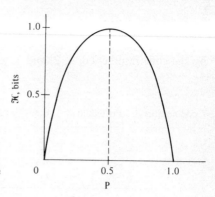

FIGURE 9.1
Entropy of a binary source versus the
probability of one symbol.

$$\mathscr{R} \triangleq \frac{\mathscr{H}}{\bar{\tau}} \quad \text{bits/s} \quad (10)$$

where $\bar{\tau}$ is the average symbol duration, namely,

$$\bar{\tau} = \sum_{j=1}^{m} P_j \tau_j \quad (11)$$

so $1/\bar{\tau}$ equals the average number of symbols per unit time.

EXERCISE 9.1 Calculate the entropy rate of a telegraph source having $P_{\text{dot}} = \frac{2}{3}$, $\tau_{\text{dot}} = 0.2$ s, $P_{\text{dash}} = \frac{1}{3}$, $\tau_{\text{dash}} = 0.4$ s. *Ans.*: $\mathscr{R} = 3.44$ bits/s.

Example 9.2 Entropy and PCM

As an example of entropy applied to our earlier studies, consider a PCM system whose input is the continuous signal $x(t)$ bandlimited in $W = 50$ Hz. Suppose $x(t)$ is sampled at the Nyquist rate $f_s = 2W$, and let there be four quantum levels such that the quantized values have probabilities $\frac{1}{2}$, $\frac{1}{4}$, $\frac{1}{8}$, and $\frac{1}{8}$. Identifying each possible quantized value as a "symbol," the output of the quantizer then looks like a discrete source with $m = 4$ and

$$\mathscr{H} = \frac{1}{2}\log_2 2 + \frac{1}{4}\log_2 4 + \frac{1}{8}\log_2 8 + \frac{1}{8}\log_2 8$$
$$= 1.75 \text{ bits/symbol}$$

Since the symbol rate is $1/\bar{\tau} = f_s = 100$,

$$\mathscr{R} = 100 \times 1.75 = 175 \quad \text{bits/s}$$

Thus, it should be possible to represent this same information by equiprobable binary digits (binits) generated at a rate of 175 binits/s.

To check this idea, suppose that the system is in fact *binary* PCM with the quantized samples transmitted as coded binary pulses. Labeling the quantum levels by the code numbers 0, 1, 2, and 3, let us assume the following coding:

Code number	Probability	Binary code
0	$\frac{1}{2}$	00
1	$\frac{1}{4}$	01
2	$\frac{1}{8}$	10
3	$\frac{1}{8}$	11

Since there are two binary digits for each sample, the PCM signal has 200 pulses per second. Now we argued that 175 binary digits per second should be sufficient; yet 200 per second is required with this code.

The anomaly is quickly resolved by noting that the binary digits are not equally likely; in fact, $P_0 = \frac{11}{16}$ and $P_1 = \frac{5}{16}$, as the reader can verify. Clearly, the suggested code is not optimum. On the other hand, it is simple and reasonably efficient.

Pressing onward, the binit rate and probabilities given above suggest that the information rate at the encoder output is

$$\mathcal{R} = 200(\tfrac{11}{16} \log \tfrac{16}{11} + \tfrac{5}{16} \log \tfrac{16}{5})$$
$$= 200 \times 0.897 = 179 \text{ bits/s}$$

Again something is wrong, for the information rate into the encoder is only 175 bits/s. Surely direct encoding does not *add* information!

To explain the discrepancy we must recall that the entropy equation (7) is based on statistically *independent* symbols. And, while it may be true that successive quantized samples are independent, the successive binary pulses are not, because we have encoded in groups of two. For the case of dependent symbols, we must modify the measure of information and introduce conditional entropy.   ////

Conditional Entropy and Redundancy

Discrete sources are often constrained by certain rules which limit the choice in selecting successive symbols. The resulting *intersymbol influence* reduces uncertainty and thereby reduces the amount of information produced. We account for this effect by using conditional probabilties and conditional entropy.

Written text, being governed by rules of spelling and grammar, is a good example of intersymbol influence. On a relative-frequency basis, the probability of U in printed English is $P_U = 0.02$; but if the previous letter is Q, the conditional probability of U given Q is $P(U|Q) \approx 1$, whereas in contrast $P(U|W) < 0.001$. The influence may well extend over several symbols, phrases, or even complete sentences, as illustrated by the fact that in most textbooks, including this one, $P(\text{THAT}|\text{IT CAN BE SHOWN}) \approx 1$.

The expression for conditional entropy therefore is formulated by considering the entire past history of the source—more precisely, all possible past histories. Thus, if j represents the next symbol (or group of symbols) and i represents the preceding sequence, the information conveyed by j given i is $\log_2 [1/P(j|i)]$. Averaging over all j's and i's gives the conditional entropy

$$\mathcal{H}_c = \sum_i \sum_j P_i P(j|i) \log_2 \frac{1}{P(j|i)} \qquad (12)$$

In general $\mathcal{H}_c \leq \mathcal{H}$; the equality applies only when the symbols are independent and $P(j|i) = P_j$.

A source producing dependent symbols is said to be *redundant*, meaning that symbols are generated which are not absolutely essential to convey the information. (Is it really necessary to explicitly write the U following every Q in English?) The redundancy of English text is estimated to be roughly 50 percent. This implies that in the long run, half the symbols are unnecessary: yu shld babl t rcad ths evntho sevrl ltrs r msng. The reader may wish to ponder the observation that without redundancy, abbreviation would be impossible, and any two-dimensional array of letters would form a valid crossword puzzle.

For very long passages of printed English, the conditional entropy may be as low as 0.5 to 1.0 bits/symbol because of contextual inferences. Thus, with suitable coding, printed English theoretically could be transmitted in binary form with an average of one binary digit per symbol. Contrast this with existing teletype systems that use five binary digits per character.

From the viewpoint of efficient communication, redundancy in a message is undesirable; the same information could be sent with fewer nonredundant (independent) symbols. Thus, coding to reduce intersymbol influence is a method of improving efficiency. On the other hand, redundancy is a definite aid in resolving ambiguities if the message is received with *errors*, a not uncommon phenomenon in telegraphy, for example. Indeed, coding for error protection is based on the insertion of redundant symbols.

Optimum transmission therefore entails coding to reduce the inefficient redundancy of the message, plus coding to add "efficient" redundancy for error control. Much has been done in the area of error-detecting and error-correcting codes, but coding to reduce message redundancy is far more difficult, and relatively little has been accomplished in this direction. (In retrospect, the bandwidth-reduction feature of differential PCM relies on the redundancy of the input signal.)

Continuous Information Sources

Having discussed discrete sources at some length, the next logical step would be the definition of entropy for *continuous* sources, sources whose messages are continuously varying functions of time. Such a definition is possible but will not be presented here. For one reason, the mathematics gets rather complicated and tends to obscure physical interpretation; for another, the entropy of a continuous source turns out to be a relative measure instead of an absolute measure of information.

Fortunately, the goals of this chapter can be achieved by sticking to the discrete formulation, and most of our conclusions will apply to continuous sources with minor modification. But more important, we shall find that because of the fundamental physical limitations, communication is inherently a *discrete process* regardless of the source. This striking conclusion is one of Shannon's principal contributions to the theory of communication, but it was noted by Hartley as far back as 1928.

9.2   CHANNEL CAPACITY AND DISCRETE CHANNELS

We have seen that it is often convenient to treat the terminal equipment of a communication system as being perfect (noise-free, distortionless, etc.) and think of all undesired effects as taking place in the channel. The communication channel is therefore an abstraction, a model representing the vehicle of transmission plus all phenomena that tend to restrict transmission. The fact that there are fundamental physical limitations to information transfer by electrical means leads to the notion of *channel capacity*.

Just as entropy rate measures the amount of information produced by a source in a given time, capacity is a measure of the amount of information a channel can transfer per unit time. Channel capacity is symbolized by $\mathscr{C}$, and its units are bits per second. Restating the fundamental theorem in terms of $\mathscr{R}$ and $\mathscr{C}$, we have:

> Given a channel of capacity $\mathscr{C}$ and a source having entropy rate $\mathscr{R}$, then if $\mathscr{R} \leq \mathscr{C}$, there exists a coding technique such that the output of the source can be transmitted over the channel with an arbitrarily small frequency of errors, despite the presence of noise. If $\mathscr{R} > \mathscr{C}$, it is not possible to transmit without errors.

Although we shall attempt to make the theorem plausible, complete proof involves a great deal of coding theory and is omitted here. Instead we shall concentrate on aspects more pertinent to electrical communication.

Channel Capacity

The fundamental theorem implicitly defines channel capacity as the maximum rate at which the channel supplies reliable information to the destination. With this interpretation in mind we can formulate a general expression for capacity by means of the following argument.

Consider all the different messages of length T a source might produce. If the channel is noisy, it will be difficult to decide at the receiver which particular message was intended and the goal of information transfer is partially defeated. But suppose we restrict the messages to only those that are "very different" from each other, such that the received message can be correctly identified with sufficiently small probability of error. Let $M(T)$ be the number of these very different messages of length T.

Now, insofar as the destination or user is concerned, the source-plus-channel combination may be regarded as a new source generating messages at the receiving end. With the above message restriction, this equivalent source is discrete and has an alphabet of size $M(T)$. Correspondingly, the maximum entropy produced by the equivalent source is $\log M(T)$, and the maximum entropy rate at the destination is $(1/T) \log M(T)$. Hence, letting $T \to \infty$ to ensure generality,

$$\mathscr{C} = \lim_{T \to \infty} \frac{1}{T} \log M(T) \qquad \text{bits/s} \qquad (1)$$

an alternate definition for channel capacity. The following discussion of discrete channels shows that Eq. (1) is an intuitively meaningful definition.

Discrete Noiseless Channels

A discrete channel is one that transmits information by successively assuming various disjoint electrical states — voltage levels, instantaneous frequency, etc. Let μ be the number of possible states and r the signaling rate in states per unit time. If the signal-to-noise ratio is sufficiently large, the error probability at the receiver can be extremely small, so small that to all intents and purposes the channel is deemed to be noiseless. Under this assumption, any sequence of symbols will be correctly identified and the capacity calculation is straightforward.

A received message of length T will consist of rT symbols, each symbol being one of the μ possible states. The number of different messages is thus $M(T) = \mu^{rT}$ and hence

$$\mathscr{C} = \lim_{T \to \infty} \frac{1}{T} \log \mu^{rT} = \lim_{T \to \infty} \frac{rT}{T} \log \mu$$

$$= r \log \mu \qquad \text{bits/s} \qquad (2)$$

The capacity of a noiseless discrete channel is therefore proportional to the signaling rate and the logarithm of the number of states. For a binary channel ($\mu = 2$) the capacity is numerically equal to the signaling rate, that is, $\mathscr{C} = r$.

According to Eq. (2), one can double channel capacity by doubling the signaling speed (which is certainly reasonable) or by *squaring* the number of states (somewhat more subtle to appreciate). In regard to the latter, suppose two identical but independent channels are operated in parallel so their combined capacity is clearly $2(r \log \mu) = 2r \log \mu = r \log \mu^2$. At the output we can say that we are receiving $2r$ symbols per second, each symbol being drawn from an alphabet of size μ; or the output can be viewed as r *compound* symbols per second, each being drawn from an alphabet of size $\mu \times \mu = \mu^2$.

The following example illustrates a coding technique that achieves $\mathscr{R} = \mathscr{C}$ on a noiseless discrete channel.

Example 9.3

Consider the PCM source in Example 9.2. In theory a noiseless binary channel will suffice to convey the information if $r \geq 175$ binits/s. To minimize $\mathscr{R}$ we cannot use the previous code because it requires two binary digits per source symbol and $r = 200$. A more efficient code is as follows.

Code number	Probability	Binary code
0	½	0
1	¼	10
2	⅛	110
3	⅛	111

With this code, a message containing $N \gg 1$ source symbols requires the transmission of $N/2 + 2(N/4) + 3(N/8) + 3(N/8) = 1.75N$ channel symbols, that is, 1.75 binary digits per source symbol. The required signaling rate is then $r = 1.75/\bar{t} = 175$, and we have achieved transmission at $\mathscr{R} = \mathscr{C}$; the encoding has produced a perfect match between source and channel.

Although this example is admittedly a special case, there are two general hints about efficient encoding to be gained from it. First, the code is such that the channel symbols **0** and **1** are equally likely and statistically independent. (The skeptical reader should verify this.) Second, the source symbol with the highest probability is assigned the shortest word code, and so forth down the line to the least probable symbol, which gets the longest code. Systematic procedures for devising such codes are described in the literature.†

Somewhat parenthetically we might note that assigning shorter code words to the more probable symbols is just common sense. Over a century ago, long before Shannon, Samuel Morse constructed his telegraph code using this very principle,

† E.g., Gallager (1968, chap. 3) or Thomas (1969, chap. 8).

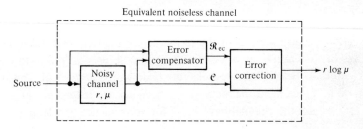

Equivalent noiseless channel

FIGURE 9.2

representing the letter E by a single dot, etc. Lacking the necessary data, Morse estimated letter frequencies by counting the distribution of type in a printer's font.

////

Discrete Channels with Noise

When channel noise cannot be ignored, the capacity is less than $r \log \mu$ because of the errors. We calculate the capacity reduction by thinking of a fictitious *error compensator*, Fig. 9.2, which examines the channel input and output and tells us what corrections should be made. Let the channel be operating at its maximum of $\mathscr{C}$ bits/s, and let the information rate supplied by the compensator be $\mathscr{R}_{ec}$ bits/s. Then, since the noisy channel plus compensator is equivalent to the same channel without noise, the net information rate over the noisy channel is $r \log \mu$ minus the information rate from the compensator, that is,

$$\mathscr{C} = r \log \mu - \mathscr{R}_{ec} \qquad (3)$$

If $\mathscr{R}_{ec} < r \log \mu$, the fundamental theorem asserts that it is possible to get a nonzero rate of virtually errorless information at the channel output.

EXERCISE 9.2 The so-called *binary symmetric channel* (BSC) is one in which both states have the same error probability, say p. Show that $\mathscr{R}_{ec} = r\{p \log (1/p) + (1 - p) \log [1/(1 - p)]\}$ and hence

$$\mathscr{C} = r[1 + p \log p + (1 - p) \log (1 - p)] \qquad (4)$$

Note that $\mathscr{C} = 0$ if $p = \frac{1}{2}$. Why? (*Hint*: The error compensator produces two possible messages, "Error" and "No error.")

Coding for the Binary Symmetric Channel ★

As part of his proof of the fundamental theorem, Shannon demonstrated the possibility of nearly errorless transmission at $\mathscr{R} \leq \mathscr{C}$ on a BSC. His demonstration, outlined below, involves selecting code words at *random*, and it met with criticism at first. Since then, the method has been acknowledged as one of great insight.

Let the channel have $r = 1$ for convenience and let $q = 1 - p$, so, from Eq. (4),

$$\mathscr{C} = 1 + p \log p + q \log q \tag{5}$$

Let the source have m equiprobable messages each of which is represented by a code word having N binary digits. This requires that $\bar{\tau} = N$ and hence

$$\mathscr{R} = \frac{\log m}{N} \tag{6}$$

since $\mathscr{H} = \mathscr{H}_{max}$.

Owing to noise, the received code words will have errors and, from our study of the binomial distribution, the expected number of errors per word is $\bar{n} = Np$. But this does not necessarily mean that the decoded message will be wrong for, if $m \ll 2^N$, we can select the m code words so that they are "very different" from each other and correctly recognized despite errors. By way of illustration, suppose $m = 2$ and $N = 3$; there are $2^3 = 8$ possible three-digit binary code words but we only need $m = 2$ of them. If the selected words are **000** and **111**, a single error is easily corrected automatically using majority rule, e.g., decode **001** as **000** and **101** as **111**. Generalizing, if one selects the code words in such a way that they differ from each other by at least $\bar{n} + 1$ digits, then the probability of decoding errors becomes negligibly small providing $N \gg m$.

Shannon, however, said that the code words could be randomly selected when $N \gg 1$ and $p < \frac{1}{2}$. (If $p > \frac{1}{2}$, we simply interchange the **1**s and **0**s at the receiver!) Under these conditions he showed that the probability of a decoding error is†

$$P_e \approx \frac{m}{2^N} p^{-pN} q^{-qN} \sqrt{\frac{pN}{2\pi q}} \tag{7}$$

which approximates the probability that any two or more words differ by Np digits or less. Then, multiplying Eq. (5) by $-N$ yields $2^{-N\mathscr{C}} = 2^{-N} p^{-pN} q^{-qN}$ (a very clever manipulation) so

$$P_e \approx m 2^{-N\mathscr{C}} \sqrt{\frac{pN}{2\pi q}} \tag{8}$$

† See Thomas (1969, chap. 8).

Therefore, imposing the condition

$$m \leq \frac{2^{N\mathscr{C}}}{N^{\alpha}} \qquad \alpha > \tfrac{1}{2} \qquad (9)$$

and letting $N \to \infty$, we have

$$P_e \leq \lim_{N \to \infty} \frac{1}{N^{\alpha - \frac{1}{2}}} \sqrt{\frac{p}{2\pi q}} = 0 \qquad (10)$$

Finally, inserting Eq. (9) in Eq. (6),

$$\mathscr{R} \leq \lim_{N \to \infty} \frac{1}{N} \left[N\mathscr{C} - \left(\frac{\alpha}{N}\right) \log N \right] = \mathscr{C} \qquad (11)$$

which proves error-free transmission at $\mathscr{R} \leq \mathscr{C}$, at least in the limit as $N \to \infty$.

   More practically speaking, it seems reasonable to infer that one can come arbitrarily close to this situation with carefully chosen code words and large but finite N. The techniques of practical error-control coding are examined in Chap. 10. For now, we turn our attention to the case of continuous channels.

9.3   CONTINUOUS CHANNELS

A continuous channel is one in which messages are represented as waveforms, i.e., continuous functions of time, and the relevant parameters are bandwidth B and signal-to-noise ratio S/N. For simplicity, we will deal only with a baseband channel whose frequency response has been equalized to be flat over $|f| \leq B$. Although the channel is continuous and has noise, it is informative to develop an intuitive relationship to r and μ, the parameters of a discrete noiseless channel.

   Relative to the signaling rate r, it has already been shown in Sect. 4.5 that $r \leq 2B$ where the equality entails using sinc pulses. As to the equivalent number of channel "states" (i.e., voltage levels, etc.), there is no inherent limitation on μ in absence of noise; voltage levels having arbitrarily small spacing still could be distinguished at the output. The value of μ on a noisy channel is estimated in terms of the signal-to-noise ratio in the following manner.

   Let the average signal power and noise power at the channel output be S and N, respectively, so the total received power is $S + N$, and the rms output voltage is $\sqrt{S + N}$. Because of noise corruption one can never exactly identify the intended signal voltage. But it can be identified with reasonably low probability of error if the voltage levels are separated by an amount equal to or exceeding the rms noise voltage σ. Thus, at the receiving end we have voltage levels *spaced* by $\sigma = \sqrt{N}$ and an rms voltage *range* of $\sqrt{S+N}$. The maximum number of channel states is therefore approximately

$$\mu = \frac{\sqrt{S+N}}{\sqrt{N}} = \left(1 + \frac{S}{N}\right)^{1/2}$$

For example, a binary channel would require $(1 + S/N)^{1/2} = 2$, or $S/N = 3$; with gaussian noise, the corresponding error probability is about 0.05.

Combining these values for r and μ yields

$$\mathscr{C} = r \log_2 \mu = 2B \log_2 \left(1 + \frac{S}{N}\right)^{1/2}$$

Hence,

$$\mathscr{C} = B \log_2 \left(1 + \frac{S}{N}\right) \qquad \text{bits/s} \qquad (1)$$

This famous equation is called the *Hartley-Shannon law*. (Hartley did the preliminary spadework and Shannon derived it with rigor.) It is written in terms of parameters that apply equally well to discrete or continuous channels, suggesting that the capacity of a continuous channel is $B \log (1 + S/N)$. In fact, Shannon's derivation was based on the continuous case and will be discussed shortly.

The Hartley-Shannon law, coupled with the fundamental theorem, has two important implications for communication engineers. First, it tells us the absolute best that can be done in the way of reliable information transmission, given the channel parameters. Second, for a specified information rate, it says we can reduce signal power providing we increase the bandwidth an appropriate amount, and vice versa.

The exchange of bandwidth for power or signal-to-noise ratio is not new to us, for we have noted the effect in wideband noise reduction systems such as FM and PCM. But the Hartley-Shannon law specifies the *optimum* possible exchange and further implies that bandwidth *compression is possible*. To illustrate, suppose it is desired to transmit digital data at a rate of 30,000 bits/s. According to the theory, we could use a channel having $B = 30$ kHz and $S/N = 1$, since

$$\mathscr{C} = 30 \times 10^3 \log (1 + 1) = 3 \times 10^4 \text{ bits/s}$$

Alternately, the bandwidth can be reduced to $B = 3$ kHz if the power is increased by a factor of 1,000, that is, $S/N = 10^3 = 30$ dB. (Note the handy approximation $10^3 \approx 2^{10}$.) Incidentally, the latter parameters are typical of standard voice telephone circuits; but when used for digital signals, the data rate on such channels is normally 4,800 bits/s or less, indicating considerable room for improvement.

Some of the above matters are further pursued in Sect. 9.4 after we examine the continuous channel more closely. Since practically all communication systems are capable of handling continuous signals and all systems have noise, the noisy continuous channel merits detailed investigation. As a preliminary, we will describe the characteristics of an ideal communication system with a continuous channel.

EXERCISE 9.3   If $(S/N) \gg 1$, show that minimum time required to transmit K binary digits is

$$T_{\min} \approx \frac{3K}{B(S/N)_{\text{dB}}} \tag{2}$$

(*Hint*: See Eq. (6), Sect. 9.1.)

Ideal Communication Systems

A communication system capable of transmitting without errors at a rate of $B \log (1 + S/N)$ bits/s, where B and S/N are the channel parameters, is called an *ideal* system. While no practical system is or can be ideal, it is possible to visualize systems whose performance approaches that of the ideal. As an aid to the design of such systems, let us examine the characteristics of a nearly ideal system.

To begin with, the number of different signals (or messages or symbols) of length T is $M = (1 + S/N)^{BT}$, and the maximum information rate is $\mathcal{R} = (1/T) \log M$. The channel signals are chosen such that they can be identified at the receiver with very small probability of error. Shannon has shown that if the signals themselves are randomly selected sample functions of gaussian white noise and if $2BT \gg 1$, then this condition is closely approximated.

The information produced by a source is conveyed over the system in the following fashion. The source output is observed for T seconds, and the message is represented (encoded) as one of the noiselike channel signals which is then transmitted; thus, the information is encoded in *blocks* of length T. (This implies that the number of possible source messages of length T is not greater than M.) At the output, the received signal plus noise is compared with stored copies of the channel signals.† The one that best matches the signal plus noise is presumed to be the signal actually transmitted, and the corresponding message is decoded. A total time delay of $2T$ is therefore required for the encoding and decoding operations.

Throughout the above description it has been tacitly assumed that $T \to \infty$,

---

† Appendix A covers implementation of this comparison process under the heading Detection Theory.

for only in this limit are all the conditions satisfied so that $\mathscr{R} = B \log (1 + S/N)$. Thus, the characteristics of an ideal system are as follows:

1 The information rate approaches $B \log (1 + S/N)$.
2 The frequency of errors approaches zero.
3 The statistical properties of the transmitted signal approach those of band-limited gaussian white noise.
4 The coding time delay increases indefinitely.

Additionally, as will be shown, the system has a sharp threshold effect.

Of course, if the channel bandwidth is large enough, we can still have $2BT \gg 1$ with reasonable values of T. However, the design of nearly ideal systems is no trivial matter, for one must balance off coding delay and signal selection against reliability. Accurate signal identification argues for large T. But as T is increased, M must increase exponentially to maintain constant information rate. Rice (1950) has shown that to achieve $\mathscr{R} = 0.96\mathscr{C}$ with $S/N = 10$ and an error probability of 10^{-5}, the number of channel signals required is $M = 2^{10,000}$!

Clearly, efficient *block coding* with its extravagant number of channel signals is just as impractical as the infinite coding delay of an ideal system. Alternate schemes using *sequential coding* are nearly as efficient and require relatively simple equipment.

Signal-Space Description of Communication ★

Not so long ago imaginary numbers were playthings of pure mathematics, deemed to have no practical value. But physicists and electrical engineers have since assigned a useful interpretation to $\sqrt{-1}$, and it is now almost unthinkable to discuss signal analysis, electromagnetic waves, or system theory without the aid of this tool. Similarly, the once esoteric geometry of multidimensional spaces (*hyperspace*) was given new meaning by Shannon (1949) for the study of communication on continuous channels, reducing an otherwise intractable problem to more familiar terms. This section outlines his derivation of the Hartley-Shannon law using concepts of signal space.

Consider a continuous baseband channel of bandwidth B so that, of necessity, all signals at the receiving end are bandlimited in B. Borrowing a page from sampling theory—namely Eq. (15), Sect. 8.1—any of the information signals can be written as

$$x(t) = \sum_k x_k \operatorname{sinc} (2Bt - k) \tag{3}$$

where

$$x_k \triangleq x(kT_s) \qquad T_s = \frac{1}{2B}$$

We assume that these signals are drawn from an ergodic ensemble with an average-power constraint so

$$S = \overline{x^2} = \overline{x_k^2} \qquad (4)$$

as follows from Eq. (12), Sect. (4.5).

Now temporarily suppose that $x(t)$ is essentially zero outside a "long" time interval of duration T; then it is completely described by $D = T/T_s = 2BT$ sample values, $x_1, x_2, \ldots, x_D$. (True, a bandlimited signal cannot be simultaneously timelimited, and we will eventually let $T \to \infty$ to compensate for this.) The fact that D numbers uniquely specify $x(t)$ leads to the notion of *signal space*, a D-dimensional space in which $x(t)$ is represented by a *vector* (or D-tuple)

$$x = (x_1, x_2, \ldots, x_D) \qquad D = 2BT \qquad (5)$$

The vector starts at the origin and terminates at a point whose coordinates are x_1, $x_2, \ldots, x_D$.

D-dimensional space is like ordinary space save that it has D mutually perpendicular axes. And though we cannot construct more than three such axes in our three-dimensional world,† we can deal logically and mathematically with spaces of higher dimensionality. In particular, signal space is *euclidean*, i.e., the square of the distance from the origin to any point is the sum of the squares of the coordinates. The magnitude or norm squared of a signal vector is therefore

$$\|x\|^2 = x_1^2 + x_2^2 + \cdots + x_D^2 = \sum_{k=1}^{D} x_k^2 \qquad (6)$$

If $T \gg 1/2B$, which quantifies our meaning of a "long" time interval, then $D \gg 1$ and

$$\frac{1}{D} \sum_{k=1}^{D} x_k^2 \approx \overline{x_k^2} \qquad (7)$$

Therefore, combining Eqs. (4), (6), and (7)

$$\|x\| = \sqrt{DS} = \sqrt{2BTS} \qquad (8)$$

so the length of all signal vectors is proportional to the square root of the average signal power.

If the tip of x is swept through all possible positions, the surface generated thereby is a *hypersphere* of radius $\|x\|$ and all possible signal vectors terminate at the surface of this hypersphere. The "volume" enclosed by such a sphere is‡

$$\mathscr{V}_D = K_D \|x\|^D \qquad (9)$$

---

† Abbott (1950) is an amusing discourse on the mysteries of three-dimensional space as viewed by a native of Flatland, a two-dimensional space.
‡ Sommerville (1929).

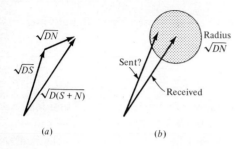

FIGURE 9.3
Signal-space representations. (*a*) Signal and noise vectors; (*b*) uncertainty sphere due to noise.

where the constant K_D does not particularly concern us here. A curious consequence of Eq. (9) is that most of the volume of a hypersphere of high dimensionality ($D \gg 1$) is concentrated at the surface. To illustrate, the relative volume between $\|x\|/2$ and $\|x\|$ is $1 - 2^{-D}$, so if $D = 3$ (a conventional sphere), 87.5 percent of the volume is in the outer "half"; if $D = 100$, the relative volume of the outer portion is approximately $1 - 10^{-30}$. This *volume-concentration* effect proves to be useful in our development, for the dimensionality of typical signal spaces is indeed large. For example, a 3-minute telephone call with $B = 4$ kHz has $D \approx 10^6$.

Our vector description of the channel signals also applies to the *noise* providing it is gaussian white noise from an ergodic source, bandlimited in B. With this condition, sample values spaced by $1/2B$ are uncorrelated and statistically independent. The noise energy in time T is then very nearly NT, N being the average noise power. Hence, the noise is represented in signal space by a vector of length $\sqrt{DN}$, and all possible noise signals are contained within a sphere of that radius. Because the noise is *random*, it might seem that the noise sphere should be "fuzzy"; i.e., a particular sample function of length T may have an energy quite different from NT. But if the dimensionality is high, volume concentration indicates that the noise sphere is quite sharply defined, like a Ping-Pong ball rather than a cloud of gas.

Consider now the state of affairs at the channel output, where we have the desired signal contaminated by noise. Under the usual assumption that signal and noise are independent, their average powers add, and the received signal plus noise vector has length $\sqrt{D(S + N)}$. Figure 9.3a shows the geometric interpretation of the transmitted signal, added noise, and signal plus noise. The transmitted signal is seen to lie within a sphere of radius $\sqrt{DN}$ at the tip of the signal-plus-noise vector (Fig. 9.3b), and this noise sphere indicates the uncertainty of the receiver as to which signal was intended.

If the possible transmitted signals are known in advance at the receiver, and if the sphere of uncertainty contains the tip of one and only one of the possible signal vectors, then the intended signal can be *exactly determined* despite the noise. Thus, suppose we put into the hypersphere of radius $\sqrt{D(S + N)}$ a large number of non-

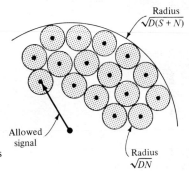

FIGURE 9.4
Signal vectors for virtually errorless transmission.

overlapping noise spheres of radius $\sqrt{DN}$ and then send only those signals corresponding to the center points of the noise spheres, Fig. 9.4. When transmitted signals are selected in this fashion, it is possible to convey information over a noisy continuous channel with vanishingly small error probability.

How many little noise spheres can be packed into the big signal-plus-noise sphere without overlapping? The calculation is important, for it tells us $M = M(T)$, the number of "very different" signals (messages) of length T that can be correctly identified at the channel output, from which we then can find the channel capacity. Clearly, M does not exceed the volume of the big sphere divided by the volume of one of the little spheres, i.e., using Eq. (9),

$$M \leq \frac{K_D[\sqrt{D(S+N)}]^D}{K_D[\sqrt{DN}]^D} = \left(1 + \frac{S}{N}\right)^{D/2} \tag{10}$$

Note that M is finite for all but truly noiseless channels. Moreover, because a real channel has noise and M is finite, communication over a continuous channel is inherently a *discrete* process. Setting $D = 2BT$ and inserting M into Eq. (1), Sect. 9.2, gives

$$\mathscr{C} \leq \lim_{T \to \infty} \frac{1}{T} \log_2\left(1 + \frac{S}{N}\right)^{BT} = B \log_2\left(1 + \frac{S}{N}\right) \tag{11}$$

which is an upper bound on the capacity of a continuous channel.

To show that information can actually be transmitted at $\mathscr{R} \leq B \log(1 + S/N)$ with negligible errors, Shannon proposed selecting the M waveforms at *random*. If a particular waveform or signal is sent and results in the received signal-plus-noise vector diagramed in Fig. 9.5, there will be no confusion and no "decoding" error providing all other $M - 1$ signal vectors fall outside the lens-shaped volume indicated. Hence, since the signals are randomly chosen, the error probability P_e equals $(M - 1)$ times the ratio of the lens-shaped volume to the volume of the signal sphere.

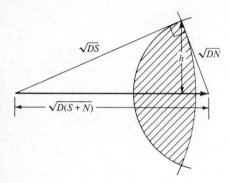

FIGURE 9.5

The volume of a D-dimensional lens is hard to calculate, but it is clearly less than the volume of a sphere with radius h where, from simple geometry, $h = \sqrt{DSN/(S + N)}$. Therefore

$$P_e \le (M - 1) \frac{K_D h^D}{K_D \|x\|^D} = (M - 1) \left(\frac{N}{S + N}\right)^{D/2} \tag{12}$$

so P_e can be made as small as desired if

$$M - 1 \le \left(1 + \frac{S}{N}\right)^{BT} P_e \tag{13}$$

similar to Eq. (9), Sect. 9.2. Finally, taking the logarithm of Eq. (13), we have

$$\frac{1}{T} \log_2(M - 1) \le B \log_2\left(1 + \frac{S}{N}\right) - \frac{1}{T} \log_2 \frac{1}{P_e}$$

Hence, M may be chosen such that $\mathcal{R} = (1/T) \log M$ approaches arbitrarily close to $\mathcal{C} = B \log (1 + S/N)$ in the limit as $T \to \infty$. Furthermore, since Eq. (12) assumes randomly selected signals, there must be some specific sets of M signals that yield an even lower error probability.

Threshold Effect and Wideband Modulation ★

It is important to observe that attaining information transmission at a rate of $B \log (1 + S/N)$ bits/s requires $D = 2BT \gg 1$ and $M(T) = (1 + S/N)^{BT}$; in other words, the noise spheres must be packed as closely as possible without overlapping. Now suppose the signal-to-noise ratio drops slightly below the design value. The noise spheres will then overlap and the receiver will make frequent decoding errors. Hence there is a sharp *threshold effect* in that a small increase of noise power (or a decrease of signal power) produces a large increase in the probability of error. As a result of these errors the information is lost.

Rather surprisingly, this same explanation holds for the threshold effect in analog message transmission using wideband modulation, e.g., FM and PCM. The signal-space description of modulation is a *one-to-one mapping* of the space of message vectors into the space of modulated signal vectors; if the modulation is wideband ($B_T \gg W$), the mapping is between spaces of different dimensionality. But a well-known theorem of topology says that any one-to-one mapping between spaces of different dimensionality must be *discontinuous* in that a continuous path in one space maps into a broken path in the other. Hence, adjacent vectors in the modulated signal space do not necessarily represent adjacent vectors in the message space, and a slight overlapping of the noise spheres may cause the receiver to "demodulate" a message totally unlike the one that was sent. Accordingly, we conclude that *mutilation and threshold effect are inevitable in all types of wideband modulation.*

9.4 SYSTEM COMPARISONS

The Hartley-Shannon law applies to a restricted class of channels, namely, continuous channels having an average power constraint and additive gaussian white noise. But this description fits many practical communication systems to a reasonable degree, so the hypothetical ideal system that delivers information at a rate $\mathscr{C} = B \log_2(1 + S/N)$ is the generally accepted standard for system comparisons. In this section we re-examine various existing systems in the light of information theory and see how they measure up against the ideal.

One aspect of particular interest is wideband noise reduction. Hence, as a preliminary, we investigate the exchange of bandwidth for signal-to-noise ratio (or transmitted power) implied by the Hartley-Shannon law, for this is the optimum bandwidth-power exchange.

Optimum Bandwidth-Power Exchange

Suppose it is desired to transmit a signal, bandlimited in W, such that the output signal-to-noise ratio at the destination is $(S/N)_D$. No matter how the transmission is accomplished, the information rate at the output can be no greater that $\mathscr{R}_{max} = W \log_2[1 + (S/N)_D]$. Further suppose that an ideal system is available for this purpose and that the channel (transmission) bandwidth is B_T, the noise power density is η, and the average signal power at the receiver is S_R. In other words, the channel capacity is $\mathscr{C} = B_T \log[1 + (S/N)_R]$, where $(S/N)_R = S_R/\eta B_T$. These factors are summarized in Fig. 9.6.

If information is neither destroyed not accumulated in the receiver, the output

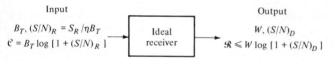

Input

$B_T, (S/N)_R = S_R/\eta B_T$

$\mathscr{C} = B_T \log [1 + (S/N)_R]$

Ideal receiver

Output

$W, (S/N)_D$

$\mathscr{R} \leqslant W \log [1 + (S/N)_D]$

FIGURE 9.6

rate must equal the information rate on the channel. Assuming the system is operating at capacity and the output rate is maximum, then $\mathscr{R}_{\max} = \mathscr{C}$, so

$$B_T \log_2\left[1 + \left(\frac{S}{N}\right)_R\right] = W \log_2\left[1 + \left(\frac{S}{N}\right)_D\right]$$

Solving for $\left(\dfrac{S}{N}\right)_D$ yields

$$\left(\frac{S}{N}\right)_D = \left[1 + \left(\frac{S}{N}\right)_R\right]^{B_T/W} - 1 \qquad (1)$$

which shows that the optimum exchange of bandwidth for power is *exponential*. To emphasize this relation, note that $(S/N)_D \approx (S/N)_R{}^{B_T/W}$ if the signal-to-noise ratios are large. The exponential trade-off is realized by an ideal system operating to its fullest capacity.

However, with fixed channel *noise density*, as distinguished from fixed noise power, Eq. (1) does not tell the exact story. For as channel bandwidth is increased, the noise power $N_R = \eta B_T$ is likewise increased, and $(S/N)_R$ decreases. A more equitable basis for comparison is obtained by rewriting Eq. (1) in terms of the normalized parameters

$$\gamma = \frac{S_R}{\eta W} \qquad \text{and} \qquad \mathscr{B} = \frac{B_T}{W}$$

used in previous chapters.

The signal to-noise ratio at the receiver input is then $(S/N)_R = (S_R/\eta W)(W/B_T) = \gamma/\mathscr{B}$, and Eq. (1) becomes

$$\left(\frac{S}{N}\right)_D = \left(1 + \frac{\gamma}{\mathscr{B}}\right)^{\mathscr{B}} - 1 \qquad (2)$$

$$\approx \left(\frac{\gamma}{\mathscr{B}}\right)^{\mathscr{B}} \qquad \frac{\gamma}{\mathscr{B}} \gg 1$$

Thus, while the exchange is not strictly exponential it is very nearly so for large signal-to-noise ratios. This means that doubling the transmission bandwidth of an ideal system squares (approximately) the output signal-to-noise ratio. Alternately, since γ is proportional to S_T, the transmitted power can be reduced to about the square root of its original value without reducing $(S/N)_D$ if bandwidth is increased by a factor of 2. As demonstrated shortly, this exchange is considerably better than that of most existing systems.

Equation (2) also shows what is involved in bandwidth *compression* — transmitting a signal of bandwidth W over a channel of bandwidth $B_T < W$, so that $\mathscr{B} < 1$. Inserting typical values, one finds that such compression is exceedingly costly in terms of transmitted power. To illustrate, suppose we want $(S/N)_D = 10^4$ and suppose that $\eta W = 10^{-6}$. Transmission at baseband ($\mathscr{B} = 1$) requires $S_R = \eta W (S/N)_D = 10$ mW. But to compress bandwidth by a factor of $\frac{1}{2}$ we need $\gamma = \mathscr{B}[1 + (S/N)_D]^{1/\mathscr{B}} - \mathscr{B} \approx \frac{1}{2}(10^4)^2 = 5 \times 10^7$, or $S_R = 50$ W, which is 5,000 times the baseband power. Similarly, for $\mathscr{B} = \frac{1}{10}$, the power requirement is a colossal 10^{33} W!

As a general conclusion we can say that even the optimum bandwidth-power exchange is practical in one direction only, the direction of increasing bandwidth and decreasing power.

Analog Signal Transmission

It is a difficult matter to assess the information rate of analog signals: voice and music waveforms, television video, etc. Furthermore, communication systems designed for such signals have as their goal reasonably faithful reproduction of the signals themselves, with a minimum of noise and distortion. This goal is not quite the same thing as reliable information transfer in the sense of information theory; i.e., the communication engineer may be more concerned with transmission bandwidth, threshold power requirements, and signal-to-noise ratios than he is with channel capacity and its utilization.

Nonetheless, information theory does have something to say in regard to analog signal transmission. Specifically, it tells us the best signal-to-noise ratio that can be obtained with given channel parameters; it tells us the minimum power required to achieve a specified signal-to-noise ratio, as a function of bandwidth; and it indicates the optimum possible exchange of bandwidth for power. Therefore, let us compare the performance of existing systems with that of an ideal system as described by Eq. (2).

Table 9.1 summarizes many of our earlier results. It is assumed that the signal-to-noise ratios are large, all systems are above threshold, and the message is normalized so that $\overline{x^2} = \frac{1}{2}$. The values for the pulsed systems assume $f_s = 2W$, etc., and would not be achieved in practice. Clearly, none of the practical systems exhibit the output improvement that can be had in an ideal system by increasing *either* γ (power) or $\mathscr{B}$ (bandwidth). PCM does have an exponential bandwidth dependence, but, once above threshold, increasing transmitted power yields no further improvement of

Table 9.1 COMPARISON OF ANALOG
MESSAGE TRANSMISSION
SYSTEMS

System	$(S/N)_D$
AM	$\gamma/3$
SSB	γ
PDM	$\mathscr{B}\gamma/4$
PPM	$\mathscr{B}^2\gamma/16$
WBFM	$3\mathscr{B}^2\gamma/8$
DM†	$3\mathscr{B}^3/\pi^2$
PCM	$3\mu^2\mathscr{B}/2$
Ideal	$(\gamma/\mathscr{B})^{\mathscr{B}}$

† Assuming $f_0 = W$.

$(S/N)_D$; its value is determined by the quantization. It also might be noticed that SSB is just as good as an ideal system having $\mathscr{B} = 1$. Of course the SSB bandwidth ratio is fixed at $\mathscr{B} = 1$, so there is no possibility of wideband noise reduction.

Since, in general, the output signal-to-noise ratio depends on both γ and $\mathscr{B}$, it is difficult to give a complete graphical display of the relations in Table 9.1. As an alternate we can plot $(S/N)_D$ as a function of γ for typical bandwidth ratios (Fig. 9.7) or plot the value of γ required for a specified $(S/N)_D$ as a function of $\mathscr{B}$ (Fig. 9.8).

Figure 9.7 repeats some of the curves from Chaps. 7 and 8, with the addition of a curve for an ideal system having $\mathscr{B} = 6$. Also shown are the threshold points of the practical systems — which is precisely the reason for the figure. It can be seen that

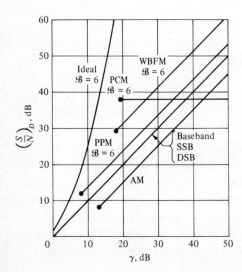

FIGURE 9.7
Postdetection S/N versus $\gamma = S_R/\eta W$.

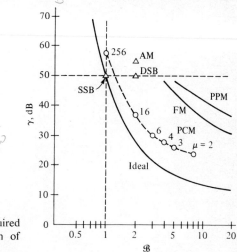

FIGURE 9.8
Normalized power $\gamma = S_R/\eta W$ required for $(S/N)_D = 50$ dB as a function of bandwidth ratio $\mathscr{B} = B_T/W$.

practical wideband noise-reduction systems, e.g., FM, PPM, and PCM, fall short of ideal performance primarily because of threshold limitations. For example, FM and PCM with $\mathscr{B} = 6$ have threshold points offset horizontally by about 8 dB from an ideal system with the same bandwidth ratio. The PPM threshold is much closer but occurs at too low a value of $(S/N)_D$ to be useful for analog signals.

As to the exchange of bandwidth for power, Fig. 9.8 shows the minimum value of γ needed for $(S/N)_D = 50$ dB as a function of bandwidth ratio. For this relatively high output S/N we see that PCM does considerably better than FM or PPM but requires 6 to 8 dB more power than an ideal system. (Just how the PCM curve was obtained is discussed under the next heading.) We might also point out the sharp increase in γ for the ideal system when $\mathscr{B} < 1$, echoing our earlier observation about bandwidth compression.

In summary; at high signal-to-noise ratios FM and PCM give the best wideband performance, PCM being somewhat better. From the power-bandwidth viewpoint, all practical wideband systems are an order of magnitude below the ideal. At low signal-to-noise ratios, only SSB and DSB are useful, having no threshold effect.

The Channel Capacity of PCM

Of the various systems we have discussed, PCM is the most amenable to direct analysis in terms of information theory. This is because the transmitted signal is discrete, even though it represents an analog signal, and the information rate can be readily calculated. Therefore, let us find the channel capacity of PCM and make a direct comparison with the Hartley-Shannon law.

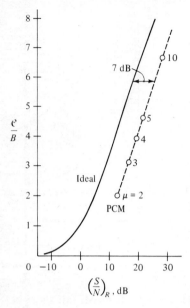

FIGURE 9.9
Channel capacity per unit bandwidth for PCM (with $P_e \approx 10^{-4}$) compared to an ideal system.

Consider a baseband PCM system having transmission bandwidth B, μ equally spaced coded pulse amplitudes, and channel signal-to-noise ratio $(S/N)_R$. Since the entropy of the digital signal is $\mathcal{H} \leq \log \mu$ and the signaling rate is $r \leq 2B$, the information rate on the channel is $\mathcal{R} \leq 2B \log \mu$. Hence,

$$\mathcal{C} = \mathcal{R}_{max} = 2B \log_2 \mu = B \log_2 \mu^2$$

providing decoding errors can be ignored. But we previously determined that decoding errors are ignorable if the system is above threshold, which requires that

$$\mu^2 \leq 1 + \frac{1}{5}\left(\frac{S}{N}\right)_R \tag{3}$$

Therefore, just above threshold,

$$\mathcal{C} = B \log_2\left[1 + \frac{1}{5}\left(\frac{S}{N}\right)_R\right] \tag{4}$$

so, if $(S/N)_R \gg 5$, $\mathcal{C} \approx B \log_2[(S/N)_R/5]$ or

$$\mathcal{C} \approx \mathcal{C}_{ideal} - B \log_2 5 \tag{5}$$

Based on Eq. (4), Fig. 9.9 plots $\mathcal{C}/B$ versus $(S/N)_R$. The corresponding curve for an ideal system is also given by way of comparison. Viewed in this light, PCM is seen to require about 7 dB more power than an ideal system. However, it is well to bear in mind that an ideal system would have vanishingly small error probability, whereas the PCM curve is for $P_e \approx 10^{-4}$. The reason why PCM compares as favorably as it does to an ideal system stems from the earlier conclusion that because of channel noise, electrical communication is inherently a discrete process. PCM design recognizes and accepts this fact; the transmitted PCM signal, being discrete, is better suited to the noisy channel than uncoded continuous signals.

Communication Efficiency ★

Finally, let us examine minimum power requirements in terms of information rate. This viewpoint is particularly relevant to long-range systems not having a bandwidth constraint — e.g., space communication systems — and leads to the so-called communication efficiency. As before, our reference is the ideal system with

$$\mathscr{C} = B_T \log \left(1 + \frac{S_R}{\eta B_T}\right)$$

$$= \frac{S_R}{\eta} \log \left(1 + \frac{S_R}{\eta B_T}\right)^{\eta B_T / S_R} \tag{6}$$

which has been rewritten to show that if S_R and η are fixed, $\mathscr{C}$ is maximized by taking $B_T \to \infty$. Therefore, using the fact that $\lim_{v \to 0} (1 + v)^{1/v} = e$, the maximum information rate on an ideal system is

$$\mathscr{R}_{\max} = \lim_{B_T \to \infty} \mathscr{C} = \frac{S_R}{\eta} \log_2 e = 1.44 \frac{S_R}{\eta} \tag{7a}$$

or, for a specified information rate $\mathscr{R}$,

$$S_{R_{\min}} = 0.693 \, \eta \mathscr{R} \tag{7b}$$

both of which require a coding technique such that the transmission bandwidth approaches infinity. And at the same time $(S/N)_R = S_R/\eta B_T$ goes to zero!

Now consider any system having an information rate $\mathscr{R}$ and received power S_R. Its communication efficiency may be defined as $\mathscr{E} = \mathscr{R}/\mathscr{R}_{\max} = S_{R_{\min}}/S_R$ or, using Eq. (7),

$$\mathscr{E} \triangleq 0.693 \frac{\eta \mathscr{R}}{S_R} \tag{8}$$

so if $\mathscr{E} = 0.2$, for instance, the system requires five times as much power as an ideal system operating with $B_T \to \infty$. To underscore the meaning of $\mathscr{E}$, let $\eta = k\mathscr{T}_N$

where k is the Boltzmann constant and $\mathcal{T}_N$ the system noise temperature; if $\mathcal{L}$ is the transmission loss, then the *transmitted* power required is

$$S_T = \mathcal{L}S_R = 0.693k\frac{\mathcal{L}\mathcal{T}_N\mathcal{R}}{\mathcal{E}}$$

$$\approx 10^{-23}\frac{\mathcal{L}\mathcal{T}_N\mathcal{R}}{\mathcal{E}} \tag{9}$$

Clearly, minimizing S_T entails maximizing $\mathcal{E}$.

Relative to the design of efficient practical systems, we infer from Eq. (7) that $\mathcal{E}$ is maximized if B_T is made as large as possible and $(S/N)_R$ as small as possible. We can get large B_T with *wideband modulation* techniques, but the inevitable threshold effect prohibits very small values of $(S/N)_R$ and thereby precludes operation at highest efficiency. This point is further demonstrated by again examining PCM.

Assuming the PCM information rate to be $\mathcal{R} = \mathcal{C}$, with $\mathcal{C}$ given by Eq. (4), the efficiency is

$$\mathcal{E} = 0.693\frac{\eta}{S_R}B_T\log\left[1 + \frac{1}{5}\left(\frac{S}{N_R}\right)\right]$$

$$= \frac{0.693}{(S/N)_R}\log\left[1 + \frac{1}{5}\left(\frac{S}{N}\right)_R\right]$$

However, from Eq. (3), the threshold condition is $(S/N)_R \geq 5(\mu^2 - 1)$, so we cannot take $(S/N)_R$ arbitrarily small. The best we can do is $\mu = 2$ (*binary* PCM), which gives the largest transmission bandwidth, the smallest channel signal-to-noise ratio, and the highest efficiency. Several times in the past we have suspected that binary PCM is superior to PCM with $\mu > 2$; that suspicion is now confirmed from the power viewpoint. For $\mu = 2$, $(S/N)_R \geq 15$, and

$$\mathcal{E} = \frac{0.693}{15}\log 4 = 0.0924$$

Therefore, the efficiency is in the neighborhood of 9 percent. Such a low efficiency may seem discouraging at first. Putting the matter in proper perspective, it is better to say that binary PCM requires about 10 dB more power than an *ideal* system with *infinite* bandwidth.

Turning to analog modulation, we are faced with the problem of estimating the information rate $\mathcal{R}$ of an analog signal.† A crude but simple expedient is to take the upper bound $\mathcal{R} \leq W\log[1 + (S/N)_D]$, where $(S/N)_D$ and W are the signal parameters after demodulation. This gives an *upper bound* on the efficiency, namely,

$$\mathcal{E} \leq \frac{0.693}{\gamma}\log\left[1 + \left(\frac{S}{N}\right)_D\right] \tag{10}$$

† Sanders (1960) gives a more complete discussion.

For suppressed-carrier linear modulation (SSB and DSB) we have $(S/N)_D = \gamma$, and such systems are normally operated with signal-to-noise ratios of 30 to 40 dB. The corresponding efficiency is substantially less than 1 percent, not unexpected since the transmission bandwidth is relatively small. On the other hand, wideband analog modulation should prove to be better, and in fact it is.

For FM (without deemphasis) it can be shown that there is an optimum deviation ratio, $\Delta_{opt} \approx 2$, giving $\mathscr{E} < 0.1$; with $\Delta < 2$ the loss of wideband noise reduction decreases efficiency, while for $\Delta > 2$ the higher threshold level counterbalances the S/N improvement and again decreases efficiency. Clearly, the threshold-extension techniques mentioned in Sect. 7.5 would be of benefit here since they lower the value of γ_{th}. In theory, FM with frequency-compressive feedback in the receiver (FMFB) is capable of achieving 50 percent maximum efficiency; in practice, efficiencies of 25 to 30 percent are possible. PPM appears to have efficiencies comparable to FMFB thanks to its low threshold level.

Example 9.4

To illustrate the implications of Eq. (9), suppose it is desired to transmit a still picture from Mars to earth with $S_T = 10$ W, $\mathscr{L} = 200$ dB, and $\mathscr{T}_N = 50°$K. If the system has 100 percent efficiency ($\mathscr{E} = 1$), the maximum information rate is

$$\mathscr{R} = 10^{23} \frac{\mathscr{E} S_T}{\mathscr{L} \mathscr{T}_N} = 200 \text{ bits/s}$$

Assuming that the photograph is quantized into $200 \times 200 = 4 \times 10^4$ elements, each element having one of 64 possible brightness levels, the total information to be transferred is $\mathscr{I} = 24 \times 10^4$ bits (see Example 9.1). Therefore, the total transmission time T must be

$$T = \frac{\mathscr{I}}{\mathscr{R}} = \frac{24 \times 10^4}{200} = 1,200 \text{ s} = 20 \text{ min}$$

The Mariner IV mission, using a less efficient but practical system, required 8 hours to transmit each picture. ////

9.5 PROBLEMS

9.1 (Sect. 9.1) State in words and interpret the requirements on $f(\;)$ in Eqs. (1) to (3).

9.2 (Sect. 9.1) A card is selected at random from a deck of 52. You are told it is a heart. How much information (in bits) have you received? How much more information is needed to completely specify the card? *Ans.:* 2 bits, 3.7 bits.

9.3 (Sect. 9.1) Calculate the amount of information needed to open a lock whose combination consists of three numbers, each ranging from 00 to 99.

9.4   (Sect. 9.1) A source produces six symbols with probabilities $\frac{1}{2}$, $\frac{1}{4}$, $\frac{1}{8}$, $\frac{1}{16}$, $\frac{1}{32}$, and $\frac{1}{32}$. Find the entropy $\mathcal{H}$.

9.5   (Sect. 9.1) A source has an alphabet of size m. One symbol has probability ϵ while the other symbols are equally likely. Find $\mathcal{H}$ in terms of m and ϵ.

9.6★ (Sect. 9.1) Show that $\sum_{j=1}^{m} P_j \log_2 (1/mP_j) = \mathcal{H} - \log_2 m$ and use this, together with the fact that $\ln v \leq v - 1$, to prove that $\mathcal{H} \leq \log_2 m$.

9.7★ (Sect. 9.1) Suppose you are given nine pennies, eight of which are good. The remaining coin is counterfeit and weighs more or less than a good one. Given an uncalibrated balancing scale, how many weighings are necessary in theory to locate the bad coin and determine whether it is light or heavy? (Hint: The scale has three possible positions, balanced and unbalanced on one side or the other. The average information per weighing, i.e., the entropy, is maximized if each of these positions is equally likely. Although it is not required, you may wish to devise the actual weighing procedure.)

9.8   (Sect. 9.1) A certain data source has eight symbols that are produced in blocks of three at a rate of 1,000 blocks per second. The first symbol in each block is always the same (presumably for synchronization); the remaining two places are filled by any of the eight symbols with equal probability. What is the entropy rate $\mathcal{R}$? Ans.: 6,000 bits/s.

9.9   (Sect. 9.1) A certain data source has 16 possible and equiprobable symbols, each 1 millisecond (ms) long. The symbols are sent in blocks of 15, separated by a 5-ms synchronization pulse. Calculate $\mathcal{R}$.

9.10 (Sect. 9.1) A binary data source has $P_0 = \frac{3}{8}$, $P_1 = \frac{5}{8}$, and intersymbol influence extending over groups of two successive symbols such that $P(1|0) = \frac{3}{4}$ and $P(0|1) = \frac{1}{16}$. Calculate the conditional entropy $\mathcal{H}_c$ and compare with $\mathcal{H}$.

9.11 (Sect. 9.1) Analogous to Eq. (7) the entropy of a *continuous signal* $x(t)$ can be defined as

$$\mathcal{H}(x) = -\int_{-\infty}^{\infty} p(x) \log p(x)\, dx$$

where $p(x)$ is the probability density function. Show that this is a relative rather than absolute measure of information by considering $\mathcal{H}(x)$ and $\mathcal{H}(y)$ when $y(t) = Kx(t)$ and $x(t)$ is uniformly distributed over $[-1, 1]$.

9.12 (Sect. 9.2) Verify that $P(1) = P(0) = \frac{1}{2}$ in Example 9.3.

9.13 (Sect. 9.2) A noiseless discrete channel is to convey information at a rate of 900 bits/s. Determine the minimum number of channel states required if $r = 200$ or $1,000$. Ans: 23, 2.

9.14 (Sect. 9.2) A discrete source produces the symbols A and B with $P_A = \frac{3}{4}$ and $P_B = \frac{1}{4}$ at a rate of 100 symbols/s. In an attempt to match the source to a noiseless binary channel, the symbols are grouped in blocks of two and encoded as follows:

Grouped symbol	Binary code
AA	1
AB	01
BA	001
BB	000

By calculating the source entropy rate and the channel symbol rate, show that this code is not optimum but is reasonably efficient.

9.15★(Sect. 9.2) Consider a binary channel with noise that affects the channel symbols in blocks of three such that a block is received without errors or there is exactly one error in the first, second, or third digit. These four possibilities are equiprobable.
(a) Show that $\mathscr{C} = r/3$.
(b) Devise a code that yields error-free transmission at $\mathscr{R} = \mathscr{C}$.

9.16 (Sect. 9.2) The per-digit error and no-error probabilities for a *nonsymmetric binary channel* are indicated schematically in Fig. P9.1, i.e., $P(0 \text{ received} | 0 \text{ sent}) = \alpha$, etc. Show that

$$\mathscr{R}_{ec} = r\left(\frac{1 - \alpha + \beta}{2} \log \frac{2}{1 - \alpha + \beta} + \frac{1 + \alpha - \beta}{2} \log \frac{2}{1 + \alpha - \beta}\right)$$

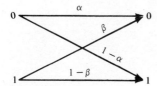

FIGURE P9.1.

9.17 (Sect. 9.2) The channel in Prob. 9.16 is said to be *useless* if $\alpha = \beta$. Justify this mathematically and intuitively.

9.18 (Sect. 9.3) A noiseless discrete channel has $r = 10^5$. Investigate the possibility of replacing it with a continuous channel having $B = 8$ kHz and $S/N = 31$.

9.19 (Sect. 9.3) Find the minimum time required to transmit 600 *decimal* digits on the continuous channel in Prob. 9.18. *Ans.*: 0.05 s.

9.20 (Sect. 9.3) A certain communication system uses RF pulses with four possible amplitude levels. If an information rate of 10^6 bits/s is desired, what is the minimum practical value for the carrier frequency f_c? (*Hint*: Recall the fractional bandwidth constraints.)

9.21 (Sect. 9.3) Estimate $M(T)$ for a typical telephone channel with $B = 3$ kHz, $S/N = 30$ dB, and $T = 3$ min.

9.22★(Sect. 9.3) Consider the set of channel signals $x_i(t) = \text{sinc}(2Bt - i), i = 0, \pm 1, \pm 2, \ldots$. Discuss the signal-space interpretation and determine the upper limit on $|i|$ for a space of D dimensions.

9.23★(Sect. 9.3) A continuous channel has $S/N = 63$ and $B = 1$ kHz. Obtain numerical bounds on M and T such that $\mathscr{R} = 5,000$ with $P_e \le 10^{-3} \approx 2^{-10}$.

9.24 (Sect. 9.4) An engineer claims to have designed a communication system giving $(S/N)_D = 10^6$ when $(S/N)_R = 3$ and $B_T = 10$ W. Do you believe him? Explain.

9.25 (Sect. 9.4) An ideal system has $\mathscr{B} = 4$ and $(S/N)_D = 40$ dB. What is the new value of $(S/N)_D$ if B_T is tripled while all other parameters are fixed? *Ans.*: 72 dB.

9.26 (Sect. 9.4) Repeat Prob. 9.25 with B_T changed to $W/2$ instead of being tripled.

9.27 (Sect. 9.4) A communication system has $B_T = 5$ kHz, $\mathscr{L} = 30$ dB, and $\eta = 10^{-7}$ W/Hz. Find the theoretical minimum value for S_T to yield $(S/N)_D = 50$ dB when $W = 1$ kHz.

9.28★(Sect. 9.4) Consider the efficiency of an ideal system with finite B_T.

   (*a*) Show that $\mathscr{E} = 0.693(\mathscr{R}/B_T)/(2^{\mathscr{R}/B_T} - 1)$.

   (*b*) Sketch $\mathscr{E}$ versus $B_T/\mathscr{R}$ and discuss the implications of this curve.

9.29★(Sect. 9.4) Using Eq. (10) and Carson's rule, obtain an upper bound on $\mathscr{E}$ in terms of Δ for an FM system (without deemphasis) operating just above threshold.

9.30★(Sect. 9.4) Suppose it is desired to have live voice transmission from Mars to earth via binary PCM with $f_s = 8$ kHz and $\mathcal{Q} = 64$. Estimate the power requirement at the Mars transmitter by inserting typical values into Eq. (9).

10
DIGITAL DATA SYSTEMS

Until about 1950, analog signal transmission was the primary stock-in-trade of the communications industry, save, of course, for teletype and telegraph. But that was before the advent of automation and the computer revolution. Today, enormous quantities of digital data are being generated in government, commerce, and science. Furthermore, the need to eliminate manual handling and human error has led to the concept of integrated data processing systems. These developments, coupled with a growing trend toward decentralization, have made the transmission and distribution of digital signals a major task of electrical communication.

While according to information theory, highly efficient and virtually errorless data transmission is possible, the vast majority of applications simply do not warrant the cost and complexity demanded by a near-ideal communication system. This is not to say that information theory has no place in the study of data transmission but rather that it may be better to do the job now, in less than optimum fashion, than wait until technological breakthroughs permit a more sophisticated solution. Consequently the design of a practical data system is usually quite pragmatic, based on two elementary considerations: the gross source rate in digits per second, as distinguished from the entropy rate in bits per second; and the desired transmission reliability, i.e., the tolerated error rate. Before going on, it is perhaps helpful to get a feeling for typical values of these parameters.

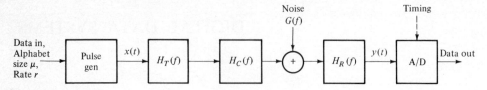

FIGURE 10.1
Baseband data system.

Just as analog signals have a wide range of bandwidths, so digital signals have a wide range of *bit rates*,† depending on the source and application. The output of manual keyboard devices, such as the teletypewriter, is seldom more than 100 bits/s. Telemetry rates may be even lower. At the other extreme, a PCM color TV signal requires roughly 100 megabits/s. Intermediate rates of 1 to 100 kilobits/s are attained by electromechanical and electromagnetic data readers. Currently, the best wideband systems have speed capabilities of several hundred megabits per second. But most digital transmission is via standard telephone voice circuits with top speeds of 1,000 to 5,000 bits/s.

Unlike signaling speed, the question of acceptable error rate is rather nebulous. Obviously, errors are of grave concern in computerized banking systems (especially if *your* bank balance is adversely affected) whereas requirements can be quite relaxed if one is telemetering data from measuring instruments having 10 percent accuracy. For the former an error probability of 10^{-5} is probably intolerable; for the latter a probability of 10^{-3} would be an extravagant waste. Nonetheless, error probabilities of order 10^{-4} are representative and suitable to many applications. We shall take this value as a guideline for comparison purposes, bearing in mind its arbitrary nature.

This chapter surveys digital data systems, their problems, and design principles. It begins where we left off in Sect. 4.5 with baseband design techniques, many of which are then applied to digital modulation systems. An introduction to error-control coding closes the chapter.

10.1 BASEBAND SYSTEM DESIGN

The functional elements of a baseband data system are laid out in Fig. 10.1. A data source having an alphabet of μ possible digits (or symbols) delivers r digits/s to a pulse generator that forms the analog signal

$$x(t) = \sum_k a_k p_S\left(t - \frac{k}{r}\right) \qquad p_S(0) = 1 \qquad (1)$$

---

† Bowing to convention, we use the terms *bit* and *binary digit* interchangeably in this chapter.

where $p_S(t)$ is the normalized pulse shape and the a_k represent the source digits. After passage through a transmitting filter $H_T(f)$ and the channel $H_C(f)$ the signal is corrupted by additive noise, so the signal plus noise at the output of the receiving filter $H_R(f)$ is

$$y(t) = \sum_k A_k p\left(t - t_d - \frac{k}{r}\right) + n(t) \tag{2}$$

where t_d is the total time delay and K_R the amplification, i.e.,

$$A_k = K_R a_k \qquad p(0) = 1$$

The A/D converter operates on $y(t)$ by sampling it at the optimum times

$$t_m = \frac{m}{r} + t_d$$

giving

$$y(t_m) = A_m + \sum_{k \neq m} A_k p\left(\frac{m - k}{r}\right) + n(t_m) \tag{3}$$

of which the first term represents the mth digit while the other two terms are *intersymbol interference* (ISI) and *noise*, respectively. Finally, the digital message (plus errors) is regenerated by comparing $y(t_m)$ with a set of threshold levels.

Equation (3) brings out two aspects of baseband system design for reliable data transmission, namely, minimizing the noise and eliminating or minimizing ISI. Additionally, if there is a bandwidth constraint, it may be desired to maximize the signaling rate r for a given channel bandwidth B or minimize the bandwidth required for a given rate. All these aspects are considered here. Unless otherwise stated, the noise is presumed to be zero-mean gaussian with spectral density $G(f) = \eta/2$. The source is always taken to be ergodic with equiprobable digits.

Ideal Baseband System

In Sect. 4.5 we assumed the channel was distortionless with bandwidth B, i.e., $H_C(f) = K_R e^{-j\omega t_d}$ when time delay is included. Accordingly, we took the bandlimited pulse shape $p_S(t) = \text{sinc } rt$ with $r = B/2$ and let $H_R(f)$ be an ideal LPF. Therefore, the signaling rate is maximum

$$r = 2B \tag{4}$$

and there is no intersymbol interference since

$$p(t) = \text{sinc } rt \qquad p\left(\frac{m - k}{r}\right) = \begin{cases} 1 & m = k \\ 0 & m \neq k \end{cases} \tag{5}$$

We also assumed a polar signal with level spacing $2A$, i.e.,

$$A_k = \begin{cases} 0, \pm 2A, \pm 4A, \dots, \pm(\mu - 1)A & \mu \text{ odd} \\ \pm A, \pm 3A, \dots, \pm(\mu - 1)A & \mu \text{ even} \end{cases} \tag{6}$$

so the received signal power is

$$S_R = \overline{A^2} = \frac{(\mu^2 - 1)A^2}{3} \tag{7}$$

It was then shown that, with zero-mean gaussian noise, the optimum threshold levels are midway between the values of A_k and

$$P_e = 2\left(1 - \frac{1}{\mu}\right)Q\left(\frac{A}{\sigma}\right) \tag{8}$$

where σ is the rms value of n so

$$\sigma^2 = \overline{n^2} = N = \eta B = \frac{\eta r}{2}$$

Thus

$$\left(\frac{A}{\sigma}\right)^2 = \frac{3}{\mu^2 - 1}\frac{S_R}{\eta B} = \frac{3}{\mu^2 - 1}\frac{S}{N} = \frac{6}{\mu^2 - 1}\rho \tag{9}$$

where

$$\rho \triangleq \frac{S_R}{\eta r} \tag{10}$$

This system will be called the *ideal* baseband system, and its performance serves as a benchmark for system comparisons — especially in terms of the normalized parameter ρ.

Rectangular-Pulse System — Integrate-and-Dump Filtering

Thanks to its very special pulse shape, the ideal system achieves maximum signaling rate on a bandlimited channel. But if there is no bandwidth constraint, we might just as well use nonoverlapping rectangular pulses

$$p_S(t) = \Pi\left(\frac{t}{\tau}\right) \qquad \tau \le \frac{1}{r} \tag{11}$$

which are much simpler to generate. Recalling our study of the random binary wave, Example 3.7, Sect. 3.5, it follows that the available bandwidth must be $B \gg 1/\tau \ge r$ to prevent pulse smearing and ISI. However, this does not mean that the receiving

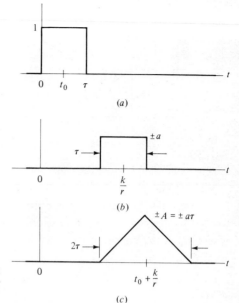

FIGURE 10.2
Matched filtering. (a) Impulse response;
(b) received pulse; (c) matched filter
output.

filter should be wide open, for that would lead to excessive output noise and high error rates. Clearly, the pivotal element of such a system is $H_R(f)$, which must be designed to minimize simultaneously the noise and the ISI due to smearing at the filter output.

As far as noise is concerned, we know that a *matched filter* has the desirable effect of maximizing the peak of an output pulse compared to the rms noise. Hence, drawing upon Eq. (12b), Sect. 4.4, suppose the impulse response of the receiving filter is

$$h_R(t) = \Pi\left(\frac{t_0 - t}{\tau}\right) = \Pi\left(\frac{t - t_0}{\tau}\right) \qquad (12)$$

as sketched in Fig. 10.2a for $t_0 = \tau/2$. To analyze the performance we will assume a binary signal and ignore any transmission distortion or delay, so the kth pulse at the receiver input is of the form $\pm a\Pi[(t - k/r)/\tau]$, Fig. 10.2b. Convolving with $h_R(t)$ yields a *triangular* pulse of height $\pm a\tau$ and width 2τ, Fig. 10.2c, i.e.,

$$A_k p\left(t - \frac{k}{r}\right) = \pm A\Lambda\left(\frac{t - t_0 - k/r}{\tau}\right) \qquad A = a\tau \qquad (13)$$

Clearly, the optimum sampling times are now $t_m = (m/r) + t_0$ (to which any time delay t_d must be added), and there is *no intersymbol interference* since $p(t - k/r) = 0$ for $|t - k/r| \geq 1/r$ if $\tau \leq 1/r$.

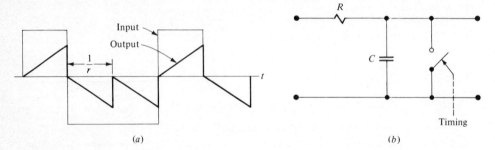

FIGURE 10.3
Integrate-and-dump filtering. (*a*) Waveforms; (*b*) circuit.

Assuming sampling at the optimum times, the error probability is $P_e = Q(A/\sigma)$ for the binary case under discussion. But from Eq. (12*a*), Sect. 4.4, $(A/\sigma)^2 = 2E_R/\eta$ where E_R is the energy in the received pulse. With rectangular polar binary pulses, $E_R = (\pm a)^2\tau = S_R/r$, and

$$\left(\frac{A}{\sigma}\right)^2_{max} = \frac{2E_R}{\eta} = \frac{2S_R}{\eta r} = 2\rho \qquad (14)$$

identical to Eq. (9) with $\mu = 2$. Similar analysis for the μ-ary case shows that Eq. (9) still holds, and we conclude that the error rate of a rectangular pulse system is just as good as an ideal system providing the receiving filter is designed according to Eq. (12).

Unfortunately, that proviso turns out to be a stumbling block, for one cannot synthesize a perfectly rectangular impulse response, and all approximations have decaying tails that cause ISI. But there is usually more than one way to skin a cat, and referring to Fig. 10.2*c* shows that the trailing part of the triangular pulse after $t = t_0 + k/r$ is unnecessary. Therefore, suppose we simply integrate each incoming pulse and then reset or "dump" the integrator immediately after the sampling time. This *integrate-and-dump* filtering takes care of the intersymbol-interference problem, as illustrated in Fig. 10.3*a*, and achieves the same maximum value of A/σ. Figure 10.3*b* is a circuit realization; if $RC \gg 1/r$, the output rises linearly over the input pulse duration until momentary closure of the switch discharges the capacitor and resets the output to zero. Needless to say, the sampling and dumping must be carefully synchronized. Even so, the integrate-and-dump filter represents virtually the only case where matched filtering is closely approximated in practice.

EXERCISE 10.1   Consider a rectangular-pulse system with $\tau = 1/2r$ and a receiving filter that is a simple RC LPF *without* a discharging switch. Assuming RC is sufficiently small that ISI is negligible, show that

$$\left(\frac{A}{\sigma}\right)^2 = \frac{2S_R}{(\eta/4RC)} = 4RCr(2\rho)$$

Evaluate $4RCr$ such that the output pulses decay to 0.001 of their maximum value by the next sample time. *Ans.*: 0.58.

Nyquist Pulse Shaping

Between the extremes of sinc pulses ($B = r/2$) and rectangular pulses ($B \gg r$), there is a compromise made possible using Nyquist-shaped pulses — pulses bandlimited in $B \geq r/2$ having periodic zero crossings to eliminate ISI. We will consider only the case of $r/2 \leq B \leq r$, which has the greatest practical interest and for which Nyquist's *vestigial-symmetry theorem* can be presented as follows:† Let

$$P(f) = [P_\beta(f)] * \left[\left(\frac{1}{r}\right) \Pi\left(\frac{f}{r}\right) \right] \qquad (15a)$$

with

$$P_\beta(f) = 0 \qquad |f| > \beta \leq \frac{r}{2}$$

$$\int_{-\infty}^{\infty} P_\beta(f) \, df = p_\beta(0) = 1 \qquad (15b)$$

Then

$$p(t) = \mathscr{F}^{-1}[P(f)] = p_\beta(t) \operatorname{sinc} rt \qquad (16a)$$

$$p\left(\frac{k}{r}\right) = \begin{cases} 1 & k = 0 \\ 0 & k \neq 0 \end{cases} \qquad (16b)$$

and $P(f)$ is bandlimited in $B = (r/2) + \beta \leq r$, so

$$r = 2B - \beta$$

Proof of these assertions should be self-evident.

Infinitely many functions satisfy the above conditions, and they include the ideal case $p(t) = \operatorname{sinc} rt$ — i.e., if $p_\beta(f) = \delta(f)$, then $p_\beta(t) = 1$, $\beta = 0$, and $r = 2B$. One class of functions has the *sinusoidal roll-off* or *raised cosine* frequency characteristic plotted in Fig. 10.4a. Analytically,

$$P_\beta(f) = \frac{\pi}{4\beta} \cos \frac{\pi f}{2\beta} \, \Pi\left(\frac{f}{2\beta}\right) \qquad 0 < \beta \leq \frac{r}{2} \qquad (17a)$$

---

† See Lucky, Salz, and Weldon (1968, chap. 4) for the general statement and proof of the Nyquist criterion, as well as the specialized pulse shaping known as *duobinary* or *partial response* that accepts controlled amounts of ISI in exchange for faster signaling.

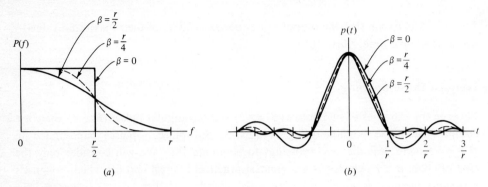

FIGURE 10.4
Nyquist pulse shaping. (a) Spectra; (b) time functions.

so

$$
P(f) = \begin{cases} \dfrac{1}{r} & |f| < \dfrac{r}{2} - \beta \\[2mm] \dfrac{1}{r}\cos^2\dfrac{\pi}{4\beta}\left(|f| - \dfrac{r}{2} + \beta\right) & \dfrac{r}{2} - \beta < |f| < \dfrac{r}{2} + \beta \\[2mm] 0 & |f| > \dfrac{r}{2} + \beta \end{cases} \qquad (17b)
$$

and the required pulse-shaping filters are relatively easy to synthesize approximately. The corresponding time functions are

$$
p(t) = \frac{\cos 2\pi\beta t}{1 - (4\beta t)^2}\,\text{sinc } rt \qquad (18a)
$$

$$
= \frac{\text{sinc } 2rt}{1 - (2rt)^2} \qquad \beta = \frac{r}{2} \qquad (18b)
$$

shown in Fig. 10.4b for $\beta = r/4$ and $r/2$ along with sinc rt. Note that the leading and trailing oscillations of $v(t)$ decay more rapidly than those of sinc rt; this means that synchronization will be less critical than a sinc-pulse system since modest timing errors do not cause large amounts of intersymbol interference.†

Further inspection reveals two other convenient properties of $p(t)$ when $\beta = r/2$: the half-amplitude pulse width exactly equals the pulse-to-pulse spacing $1/r$, and there are additional zero crossings at $t = \pm 3/2r, \pm 5/2r, \ldots$. Consequently, a polar digital signal constructed from such pulses will have zero crossings precisely halfway between

† On the other hand, $\Sigma_{k \neq m}\, A_k\, p[(m - k)/r]$ may actually be *unbounded* if $p(t) =$ sinc $(r + \epsilon)t$ where ϵ is a small error in the signaling rate.

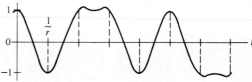

FIGURE 10.5
Baseband waveform for **10110100** using
Nyquist pulses with $\beta = r/2$.

the pulse centers whenever there is a change of polarity. Figure 10.5 illustrates this for the binary message **10110100**. These zero crossings can then be used to generate a *timing signal* for synchronization purposes, bypassing the need for separately transmitted timing information. Nyquist proved that $p(t)$ per Eq. (18b) is the *only* bandlimited pulse shape possessing all these convenient features. But the penalty is a 50 percent reduction of signaling speed, since $r = B$ rather than $2B$.

Optimum Terminal Filters ★

Now consider the overall design of a baseband system using Nyquist-shaped pulses; i.e., the output pulse shape $p(t)$ has the form of Eq. (16). With reference to Fig. 10.6, the input signal $x(t) = \sum_k a_k p_S(t - k/r)$ is filtered by $H_T(f)$ yielding the average transmitted power S_T; at the receiving end the signal plus noise is passed through $H_R(f)$ giving the output $y(t) = \sum_k A_k p(t - t_d - k/r) + n(t)$. If $p_S(t)$, S_T, $H_C(f)$, $G(f)$, and $p(t)$ are specified, we need to find $H_T(f)$ and $H_R(f)$ such that $\overline{n^2}/S_T$ is minimized so $(A/\sigma)^2$ is maximized and P_e is minimized. The matched-filter strategy does not apply here because we have specified the output pulse shape. Instead, our analysis will follow the lines of Sect. 4.3, where we derived optimum terminal filters for analog transmission.

Since $p(t)$ and $p_S(t)$ are given, one design constraint is

$$P_S(f)H_T(f)H_C(f)H_R(f) = K_R e^{-j\omega t_d} P(f) \tag{19}$$

where $P(f) = \mathscr{F}[p(t)]$, etc. The second constraint involves the transmitted power S_T which we compute by finding the average power in one sample function and then take the ensemble average, this roundabout technique being necessary because the pulses

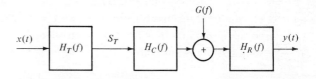

FIGURE 10.6

are not necessarily orthogonal. Proceeding with the calculation, the signal at the output of $H_T(f)$ is $\sum_k a_k p_T(t - k/r)$ where $p_T(t) = \mathscr{F}^{-1}[H_T(f)P_S(f)]$, so

$$S_T = \mathrm{E}\left\{\lim_{M \to \infty} \frac{r}{2M} \int_{-M/r}^{M/r} \left[\sum_{k=-M}^{M} a_k p_T\left(t - \frac{k}{r}\right)\right]^2 dt\right\}$$

$$= \lim_{M \to \infty} \frac{r}{2M} \sum_{k=-M}^{M} \sum_{m=-M}^{M} \mathrm{E}[a_k a_m] \int_{-M/r}^{M/r} p_T\left(t - \frac{k}{r}\right) p_T\left(t - \frac{m}{r}\right) dt$$

If the source digits are statistically independent

$$\mathrm{E}[a_k a_m] = \begin{cases} \overline{a^2} & m = k \\ 0 & m \neq k \end{cases}$$

and

$$S_T = \overline{ra^2} \int_{-\infty}^{\infty} p_T^2(t)\, dt = \overline{ra^2} \int_{-\infty}^{\infty} |H_T(f)P_S(f)|^2 \, df \tag{20a}$$

where, since $A_k = K_R a_k$,

$$\overline{a^2} = \frac{\overline{A^2}}{K_R^2} = \frac{(\mu^2 - 1)A^2}{3K_R^2} \tag{20b}$$

which follows from Eq. (7) even though S_R may not equal $\overline{A^2}$. As for the output noise power,

$$N = \sigma^2 = \overline{n^2} = \int_{-\infty}^{\infty} |H_R(f)|^2 G(f)\, df \tag{21}$$

Combining Eqs. (19), (20), and (21), we eliminate $H_T(f)$ to get

$$\left(\frac{A}{\sigma}\right)^2 = \frac{3S_T}{(\mu^2 - 1)r} \left[\int_{-\infty}^{\infty} |H_R(f)|^2 G(f)\, df \int_{-\infty}^{\infty} \frac{|P(f)|^2}{|H_C(f)H_R(f)|^2}\, df\right]^{-1}$$

and the product of integrals has a form like that of Eq. (11), Sect. 4.3. Using Schwarz's inequality in the same fashion, the product is minimized when

$$|H_R(f)|_{\mathrm{opt}}^2 = \frac{K|P(f)|}{|H_C(f)|G^{1/2}(f)} \tag{22a}$$

$$|H_T(f)|_{\mathrm{opt}}^2 = \frac{K_R^2|P(f)|G^{1/2}(f)}{K|P_S(f)|^2|H_C(f)|} \tag{22b}$$

where K is an arbitrary constant. These may be compared with the optimum terminal filters for analog transmission, Eq. (13), Sect. 4.3. As before, the filters' phase shifts are arbitrary providing that Eq. (19) is satisfied.

With the optimum filters

$$\left(\frac{A}{\sigma}\right)^2_{\max} = \frac{3S_T}{(\mu^2 - 1)r} \left[\int_{-\infty}^{\infty} \frac{|P(f)|G^{1/2}(f)}{|H_C(f)|}\, df\right]^{-2} \tag{23}$$

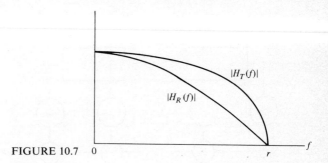

FIGURE 10.7

For the case of white noise and a distortionless channel, substituting $G(f) = \eta/2$ and $|H_C(f)| = K_R$ yields

$$\left(\frac{A}{\sigma}\right)^2_{\max} = \frac{6K_R^2 S_T}{(\mu^2 - 1)\eta r} \left[\int_{-\infty}^{\infty} |P(f)|\, df\right]^{-2} \tag{24}$$

But $K_R^2 S_T = S_R$ when the channel is distortionless, and Nyquist-shaped pulses per Eq. (17) have $\int_{-\infty}^{\infty} |P(f)|\, df = 1$, so

$$\left(\frac{A}{\sigma}\right)^2_{\max} = \frac{6S_R}{(\mu^2 - 1)\eta r} = \frac{6}{\mu^2 - 1}\, p$$

Thus system performance is again identical to an ideal baseband system.

Example 10.1

To illustrate these results, take the case of white noise and a distortionless channel with $p_S(t) = \Pi(t/\tau)$, $\tau = 1/r$, and $p(t)$ given by Eq. (18b). Then

$$P_S(f) = \frac{1}{r} \operatorname{sinc}\left(\frac{f}{r}\right) \qquad P(f) = \frac{1}{r}\cos^2\left(\frac{\pi f}{2r}\right)\Pi\left(\frac{f}{2r}\right)$$

Inserting these in Eq. (22) and dropping the proportionality constants gives

$$|H_R(f)| = \cos\left(\frac{\pi f}{2r}\right)\Pi\left(\frac{f}{2r}\right) \qquad |H_T(f)| = \frac{\cos(\pi f/2r)}{\operatorname{sinc}^{1/2}(f/r)}\Pi\left(\frac{f}{2r}\right) \tag{25}$$

as plotted in Fig. 10.7. Note the slight high-frequency rise in $|H_T(f)|$; if $\tau \ll 1/r$, this rise is negligible and $|H_T(f)| \approx |H_R(f)|$ so one design serves for both filters, a production advantage when many such systems are to be implemented.　　　　////

Equalization

Regardless of which particular pulse shape is chosen for the baseband digital signal, some amount of residual ISI inevitably occurs owing to imperfect filter design, incomplete knowledge of the channel characteristics, etc. Hence, an adjustable

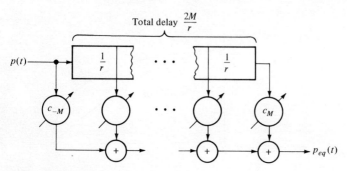

FIGURE 10.8
Transversal equalizer.

equalizing filter is often inserted between the receiving filter and the A/D converter, particularly on switched systems where the specific channel characteristics are not known in advance. Such "mop-up" equalizers usually take the form of a tapped-delay-line or transversal filter discussed before in conjunction with linear distortion, Sect. 4.2. However, the design strategy for mop-up equalization is somewhat different, and deserves consideration here.

Figure 10.8 shows a transversal equalizer with $2M + 1$ taps and total delay $2M/r$. If $p(t)$ is the input pulse shape, then the equalized output is

$$p_{eq}(t) = \sum_{m=-M}^{M} c_m p\left(t - \frac{m + M}{r}\right) \qquad (26)$$

Assuming $p(t)$ has its peak at $t = 0$ and ISI on both sides, the sampling times at the output should be taken as

$$t_k = \frac{k + M}{r}$$

so

$$p_{eq}(t_k) = \sum_{m=-M}^{M} c_m p\left(\frac{k - m}{r}\right) \qquad (27)$$

Equation (27) has the mathematical form known as *discrete convolution*.

Ideally, we would like to have

$$p_{eq}(t_k) = \begin{cases} 1 & k = 0 \\ 0 & k \neq 0 \end{cases}$$

thereby completely eliminating ISI. But this condition cannot be realized because we have only $2M + 1$ variables at our disposal, namely, the tap gains c_m. Moreover, the optimum setting for the tap gains is not immediately obvious. One approach is to set the c_m such that

$$p_{eq}(t_k) = \begin{cases} 1 & k = 0 \\ 0 & k = \pm 1, \pm 2, \ldots, \pm M \end{cases} \qquad (28)$$

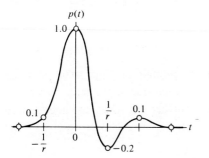

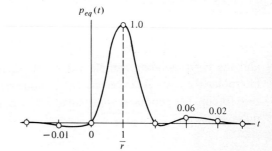

FIGURE 10.9

which together with Eq. (27) yields $2M + 1$ simultaneous linear equations that can be solved for the c_m's. Equation (28) describes a *zero-forcing equalizer* since $p_{eq}(t_k)$ has M zero values on each side. This strategy is optimum in the sense that it minimizes the peak intersymbol interference, and it has the added advantage of simplicity. Other strategies are known to be optimum in a different sense.

When the values of $p[(k - m)/r]$ are not known in advance, the tap gains must be set using an iterative process and an error criterion; i.e., starting from an initial setting, a test pulse is transmitted, the error is measured, the taps are reset, and the operation is repeated one or more times. The obvious cumbersomeness of this procedure has prompted considerable interest in automatic or *adaptive* equalizers that adjust themselves using error measures derived from the actual data signal.†odeleteAdaptive equalization has special value when the channel characteristics change with time.

Mop-up equalization (fixed or adaptive) does have one hidden catch in that the equalizer somewhat increases the noise power at the input to the A/D converter. But that effect generally is more than compensated for by the ISI reduction.

Example 10.2

A three-tap ($M = 1$) zero-forcing equalizer is to be designed for the distorted pulse $p(t)$ of Fig. 10.9a. The tap gains are readily calculated by expressing Eqs. (27) and (28) in the matrix form

$$\begin{bmatrix} 1.0 & 0.1 & 0.0 \\ -0.2 & 1.0 & 0.1 \\ 0.1 & -0.2 & 1.0 \end{bmatrix} \begin{bmatrix} c_{-1} \\ c_0 \\ c_1 \end{bmatrix} = \begin{bmatrix} 0 \\ 1 \\ 0 \end{bmatrix}$$

† Lucky, Salz, and Weldon (1968, chap. 6) discusses equalizer-adjustment algorithms and implementation of adaptive equalization.

Therefore,

$$c_{-1} = -0.096 \qquad c_0 = 0.96 \qquad c_1 = 0.2$$

and the corresponding sample values of $p_{eq}(t)$ are plotted in Fig. 10.9*b* with an interpolated curve. As expected, there is one zero on each side of the peak. However, zero forcing has produced some small ISI at points further out where the unequalized pulse was zero. ////

Binary versus μ-ary Signaling

Up till now we have taken the values of r and μ as dictated by the source. But one need not stick with that limitation as long as the transmission information rate accommodates the source data. A smattering of information theory helps put this in quantitative form. Specifically, if the source parameters are r_S and μ_S, then the source information rate is

$$\mathcal{R}_S = r_S \log_2 \mu_S \qquad \text{bits/s}$$

while, ignoring errors, the system has capacity

$$\mathcal{C} = r \log_2 \mu \qquad \text{bits/s}$$

Hence, the designer may select any convenient values of r and μ providing $\mathcal{C} \geq \mathcal{R}_S$.

If power is at a premium and bandwidth is not, one should use the *smallest* value of μ—i.e., *binary* signaling. Since $\mathcal{C} = r$ when $\mu = 2$, and since $B \geq r/2$, the required bandwidth is

$$B \geq \tfrac{1}{2}\mathcal{R}_S \qquad (29)$$

The extent to which the available bandwidth exceeds $\mathcal{R}_S/2$ indicates how much flexibility the designer has in selecting the pulse shape. Assuming gaussian white noise and optimum filters for the chosen pulse shape, the signal power requirement is computed from the desired error probability P_e via

$$Q\left(\sqrt{\frac{2S_R}{\eta \mathcal{R}_S}}\right) \leq P_e \qquad (30)$$

which follows from Eqs. (8) to (10) with $\mu = 2$ and $r = \mathcal{R}_S$.

On the other hand, bandwidth is minimized if μ is taken as the *largest* possible value since $r = \mathcal{R}_S/\log_2 \mu$. Accordingly, one must find the largest value of μ such that

$$2\left(1 - \frac{1}{\mu}\right)Q\left(\sqrt{\frac{6 \log_2 \mu}{\mu^2 - 1}\frac{S_R}{\eta \mathcal{R}_S}}\right) \leq P_e \qquad (31)$$

Then

$$B \geq \frac{\mathcal{R}_S}{2 \log_2 \mu_{\max}} \qquad (32)$$

where achieving the lower bound entails sinc pulses.

In any case, appropriate code translation must be provided at transmitter and receiver whenever $\mu \neq \mu_S$. This coding merely serves to create a better match between source and channel, and should not be confused with error-control coding or coding that decreases redundancy in the source messages.

EXERCISE 10.2   A certain computer produces octal digits ($\mu_S = 8$) at a rate of 10,000 per second. If the available transmission bandwidth is 20 kHz and $\eta = 5 \times 10^{-8}$ W/Hz, select appropriate system parameters such that $P_e \leq 10^{-4}$. *Ans.*: $\mu = 2$ and $r = 30,000$; pulse shape per Eq. (18a) with $\beta \leq 2B - r = 10$ kHz; $S_R \geq (3.7)^2 \eta \mathcal{R}_S / 2 \approx 21$ mW.

Other Design Considerations

There are numerous other factors that, quite properly, might be deemed important considerations in the design of practical baseband systems. One of these is *impulse noise*, the sporadic pulses caused by electrical storms and switching equipment which can be a particularly vexatious problem for data transmission via telephone circuits. Other factors include synchronization methods, DC removal and restoration for AC-coupled systems, and various line coding techniques.

Each, however, is a special topic in its own right and must be omitted here in deference to subjects of more general interest. The interested student will find ample material in the professional literature, to which the selected supplementary reading list is a guide and a starting point.

10.2 DIGITAL MODULATION: ASK, FSK, AND PSK

Just as there are a multitude of modulation techniques for analog signals, so is it that digital information can be impressed upon a carrier wave in many ways. This section covers the basic types and some of their variations, drawing upon the results of the previous section coupled with the modulation theory from Chaps. 5 to 7. Primary emphasis will be given to system performance in the presence of noise, i.e., error probabilities as a function of ρ. For the most part, we shall confine our attention to binary signals; the extension to μ-ary signals is not conceptually difficult but involves more arduous mathematics.

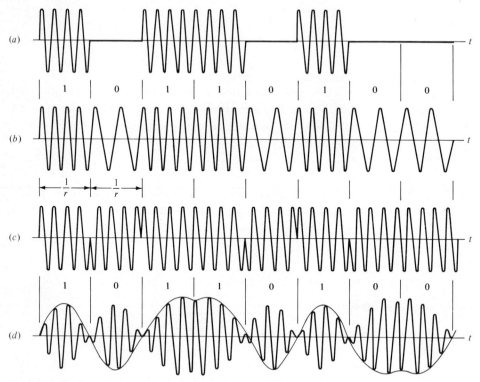

FIGURE 10.10
Digital modulation waveforms for the binary message **10110100**. (a) ASK;
(b) FSK; (c) PSK; (d) DSB with baseband pulse shaping.

Given a digital message, the simplest modulation technique is *amplitude-shift keying* or ASK, wherein the carrier amplitude is switched between two or more values, usually *on* and *off* for binary signals. The resultant modulated wave then consists of RF pulses or *marks*, representing binary **1**, and *spaces*, representing binary **0**, Fig. 10.10a. Similarly, one could key the frequency or phase, Figs. 10.10b and c, giving *frequency-shift keying* (FSK) or *phase-shift keying* (PSK). These modulation types correspond to AM, FM, and PM, respectively, with a rectangluar-pulse modulating signal. Clearly, the price of this simplicity is excessive transmission bandwidth, i.e., $B_T \gg r$. ASK also has wasted power in the carrier, just like analog AM.

Transmission bandwidth can be reduced if the pulses are *shaped* (bandlimited) prior to modulation. For instance, Fig. 10.10d is the DSB-modulated version of the baseband signal in Fig. 10.5 and has $B_T = 2B = 2r$. The minimum possible bandwidth is $B_T \approx r/2$, corresponding to sinc pulses at baseband and VSB modulation. Other

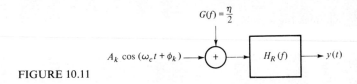

FIGURE 10.11

types of modulation include FM, PM, and VSB + C with baseband shaping.† SSB is not feasible for the reasons covered in Sect. 5.4.

Despite the number of modulation options, performance analysis depends primarily on the type of demodulation or detection — of which there are just two major classes: *coherent* (synchronous) detection and *noncoherent* (envelope) detection. Noncoherent detection is the simpler to implement and, generally speaking, is used in conjunction with ASK and FSK. Such systems usually incorporate matched (integrate-and-dump) filters since the modulated signal consists of rectangular pulses. Coherent detection is used for PSK, DSB, and VSB, with matched or otherwise optimum or near-optimum terminal filters.

We will analyze the more important noncoherent and coherent digital modulation systems. First, however, it is helpful to examine the statistical properties of a sinusoid corrupted by bandpass noise, that situation being common to all cases.

Envelope and Phase of a Sinusoid plus Bandpass Noise

Consider a digital modulation system with carrier frequency f_c. At the receiver, the signal is contaminated by white noise and then passed through a bandpass filter $H_R(f)$ centered at f_c, Fig. 10.11. The output bandpass noise is, from Sect. 7.3,

$$n(t) = n_i(t) \cos (\omega_c t + \theta) - n_q(t) \sin (\omega_c t + \theta) \qquad (1a)$$

$$= R_n(t) \cos [\omega_c t + \theta + \phi_n(t)] \qquad (1b)$$

where an arbitrary constant phase θ has been included. We recall that the in-phase and quadrature components $n_i(t)$ and $n_q(t)$ are independent zero-mean gaussian variates with

$$\overline{n_i^2} = \overline{n_q^2} = \overline{n^2} = N = \frac{\eta}{2} \int_{-\infty}^{\infty} |H_R(f)|^2 \, df \qquad (2)$$

---

† Croisier and Pierret (1970) have devised a promising alternative they call *digital echo modulation*.

whereas the envelope $R_n = \sqrt{n_i^2 + n_q^2}$ has the *Rayleigh* PDF

$$P_{R_n}(R_n) = \frac{R_n}{N} e^{-R_n^2/2N} \qquad R_n \geq 0$$

$$\overline{R_n} = \sqrt{\frac{\pi N}{2}} \qquad \overline{R_n^2} = 2N \tag{3}$$

while the phase $\phi_n = \arctan(n_i/n_q)$ is uniformly distributed over $|\phi_n| \leq \pi$.

In the absence of noise, let the modulated signal at the output of $H_R(f)$ be of the form

$$K_R x_c(t) = A_k \cos(\omega_c t + \phi_k) \qquad t = \frac{k}{r}$$

where A_k and/or ϕ_k represent the kth message digit. Taking $\theta = \phi_k$ in Eq. (1), the signal plus noise is

$$y(t) = [A_k + n_i(t)] \cos(\omega_c t + \phi_k) - n_q(t) \sin(\omega_c t + \phi_k) \tag{4a}$$

$$= R(t) \cos[\omega_c t + \phi_k + \phi(t)] \tag{4b}$$

where

$$R^2 = (A_k + n_i)^2 + n_q^2 \qquad \phi = \arctan \frac{n_q}{A_k + n_i} \tag{5}$$

Equation (5) relates the envelope and phase of a sinusoid plus bandpass noise to the signal and noise components, and we are specifically interested in the PDFs of R and ϕ.

Before plunging into the details, let us speculate on the nature of $p_R(R)$ and $p_\phi(\phi)$ under extreme conditions. When $A_k = 0$, R and ϕ reduce to R_n and ϕ_n, the envelope and phase of the noise alone, which have Rayleigh and uniform PDFs, respectively. At the other extreme, if $A_k \gg \sqrt{N}$, $R \approx A_k + n_i$ and $\phi \approx n_q/A_k$ so both will be approximately gaussian. Since A_k^2 is proportional to the signal power S_R, this case corresponds to $S_R/N \gg 1$.

For intermediate cases we follow the procedure that led to Eq. (11), Sect. 7.3, replacing n_i by $A_k + n_i$. This yields the joint PDF

$$p(R, \phi) = \frac{R}{2\pi N} e^{-(R^2 - 2A_k R \cos\phi + A_k^2)/2N} \tag{6}$$

with $R \geq 0$ and $|\phi| \leq \pi$ by definition. Unlike the case of bandpass noise alone, the product term $R \cos \phi$ in Eq. (6) means that R and ϕ are not statistically independent.

Separation of $p_R(R)$ and $p_\phi(\phi)$ therefore requires integration, i.e.,

$$p_R(R) = \int_{-\pi}^{\pi} p(R,\phi)\, d\phi$$

$$= \frac{R}{N} e^{-(R^2 + A_k{}^2)/2N} \frac{1}{2\pi} \int_{-\pi}^{\pi} e^{(A_k R/N)\cos\phi}\, d\phi$$

$$= \frac{R}{N} e^{-(R^2 + A_k{}^2)/2N} I_0\left(\frac{A_k R}{N}\right) \qquad R \geq 0 \qquad (7)$$

where I_0 is the modified Bessel function of the first kind and zero order. Equation (7) is called the *Rice distribution*; its formidable appearance is perhaps discouraging, and indeed this is not a trivial function. Fortunately, most systems will satisfy the large-signal condition $A_k \gg \sqrt{N}$ for which $I_0(A_k R/N) \approx \sqrt{N/2\pi A_k R}\, e^{A_k R/N}$. Hence, if $S_R/N \gg 1$,

$$p_R(R) \approx \sqrt{\frac{R}{2\pi A_k N}}\, e^{-(R - A_k)^2/2N} \qquad R \geq 0 \qquad (8)$$

which is essentially gaussian with $\bar{R} = A_k$ and $\sigma_R{}^2 = N$. That conclusion stems from the fact that $R/2\pi A_k N \approx 1/2\pi N$ in the vicinity of $R = A_k$ where $p_R(R)$ has the bulk of its area.

Turning to the phase, $p_\phi(\phi)$ can be found exactly by integrating Eq. (6) over $R = 0$ to ∞; the integration is somewhat lengthy and the result is analytically cumbersome — see Prob. 10.14. Consistent with $S_R/N \gg 1$, it simplifies to

$$p_\phi(\phi) \approx \sqrt{\frac{A_k{}^2}{2\pi N}} \cos\phi\, e^{-(A_k \sin\phi)^2/2N} \qquad |\phi| \leq \frac{\pi}{2} \qquad (9)$$

which, for small values of ϕ, approximates a gaussian with $\bar{\phi} = 0$ and $\overline{\phi^2} = N/A_k{}^2$. Equation (9) is invalid for $|\phi| > \pi/2$ (why?), but the probability of that event is vanishingly small under the assumed condition.

Noncoherent ASK

Putting the above results to work, we start with noncoherent binary ASK. We assume the received waveform looks like Fig. 10.10a with $\tau = 1/r$ and $f_c \gg r$. If E_R is the energy in each received marking pulse (representing **1**), then the average signal power is $S_R = \frac{1}{2} r E_R$ since marks and spaces are equally likely.

The detection system consists of a bandpass filter (or integrate-and-dump filter) matched to the RF marking pulses, i.e.,

$$h_R(t) = \cos \omega_c t\, \Pi[r(t - t_0)] \qquad (10)$$

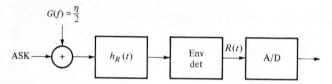

FIGURE 10.12
Noncoherent detection of ASK.

followed by an envelope detector and A/D converter, Fig. 10.12. When a marking pulse is received, the filtered output is a triangular RF pulse with peak value

$$A = \sqrt{\frac{E_R}{2r}} = \sqrt{\frac{S_R}{r^2}} \tag{11}$$

Thus, at the optimum sampling times, the envelope has $A_k = A$ or 0 (the no-pulse or space output). The filtered noise power is

$$N = \frac{\eta}{2} \int_{-\infty}^{\infty} |H_R(f)|^2 \, df = \frac{\eta}{2} \int_{-\infty}^{\infty} h_R^2(t) \, dt = \frac{\eta}{4r} \tag{12}$$

so

$$\left(\frac{A^2}{N}\right)_{\text{max}} = \frac{2E_R}{\eta} = \frac{4S_R}{\eta r} = 4\rho \tag{13}$$

where $\rho = S_R/\eta r$ as before.

Calculating the error probability involves two PDFs: when a **0** or space is sent, the resultant envelope has a Rayleigh PDF, $p(R \,|\, A_k = 0) = pR_n(R_n)$; when a **1** or mark is sent, $p(R \,|\, A_k = A)$ has a Rice PDF. Figure 10.13 shows the two density functions,

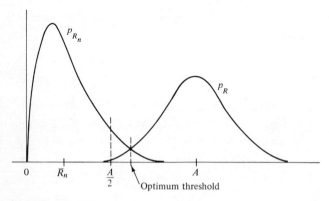

FIGURE 10.13
PDFs for noncoherent detection of ASK.

assuming $\rho \gg 1$ so Eq. (8) can be used for $p(R \mid A_k = A)$. Clearly, the decision threshold level of the A/D converter should be set between 0 and A, but the best value is not necessarily $A/2$. In point of fact, there is no " best " threshold in the sense of equalizing P_{e_1} and P_{e_0} and simultaneously minimizing P_e. Minimum P_e is achieved by taking the threshold where the two curves intersect (explain this assertion!), which turns out to be approximately $(A/2)\sqrt{1 + (2/\rho)}$.

Usually, the threshold is set at $A/2$ which is nearly optimum if $\rho \gg 1$. Then

$$P_{e_0} = \int_{A/2}^{\infty} p_{R_n}(R_n)\, dR_n = e^{-A^2/8N} = e^{-\rho/2} \qquad (14a)$$

while

$$P_{e_1} = \int_{0}^{A/2} p_R(R)\, dR \approx Q\left(\frac{A}{2\sqrt{N}}\right) = Q(\sqrt{\rho})$$

where the approximation is the area from $-\infty$ to $A/2$ of a gaussian with $\bar{R} = A$ and $\sigma_R^2 = N$. Introducing the asymptotic expression for $Q(\sqrt{\rho})$, Eq. (10), Sect. 3.5, gives

$$P_{e_1} \approx \frac{1}{\sqrt{2\pi\rho}}\, e^{-\rho/2} \qquad (14b)$$

thereby bringing out the fact that $P_{e_1} \ll P_{e_0}$ when $\rho \gg 1$. Finally,

$$P_e = P_0 P_{e_0} + P_1 P_{e_1}$$

$$\approx \frac{1}{2}\left(1 + \frac{1}{\sqrt{2\pi\rho}}\right) e^{-\rho/2} \qquad (15)$$

To compare this result with baseband transmission under the same conditions, we have from Eq. (8), Sect. 10.1, with $\rho \gg 1$,

$$P_{e_{BB}} = Q(\sqrt{2\rho}) \approx \frac{1}{2\sqrt{\pi\rho}}\, e^{-\rho} \qquad (16)$$

Therefore,

$$P_{e_{ASK}} \approx \sqrt{\pi\rho}\, e^{+\rho/2} P_{e_{BB}}$$

so if $\rho = 10$, the ASK error probability is about 800 times that of a well-designed baseband system — and almost all of the errors change 0s to 1s. Clearly, ASK does not compare very favorably. Moreover, as in most of our previous studies, Eq. (15) represents virtually the best that can be achieved by this system. Imperfect filter design, poor synchronization, etc., all work in the direction of increasing P_e. In particular, bandpass matched filters are difficult to build, so practical systems usually

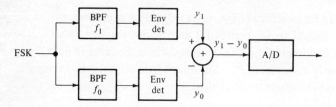

FIGURE 10.14
Noncoherent detection of binary FSK.

have an integrate-and-dump *baseband* filter after the envelope detector, further degrading the performance. But then one should not expect too much from a system having relatively unsophisticated components.

EXERCISE 10.3   Carry out the calculation of Eq. (12) and show that Eq. (11) is correct by substituting the value of N into $A^2/N = 2E_R/\eta$, which always holds for a matched filter.

Noncoherent FSK

It may seem unusual that envelope detection works for FSK as well as ASK. However, careful examination of the binary FSK signal in Fig. 10.10b reveals that it basically consists of two interleaved ASK signals of differeng carrier frequencies, say f_1 and f_0. Accordingly, noncoherent detection can be accomplished using a pair of matched filters and envelope detectors arranged per Fig. 10.14, one branch responding to the pulses at f_1, the other to f_0. To prevent cross talk at the sampling times, it is necessary that

$$|f_1 - f_0| = Mr$$

where M is an integer, usually taken to be unity to minimize bandwidth. (Unfortunately, this condition results in a signal that has discrete-frequency sinusoidal components, which may have an adverse effect in certain applications.)

In absence of noise and cross talk, $y_1 = A$ and $y_0 = 0$ when the received frequency is f_1, and vice versa for f_0. Since the envelope difference $y_1 - y_0$ is the input to the A/D converter, the threshold level should be set at zero, regardless of the value of A. Thus, $P_{e_1} = P(y_1 - y_0 < 0)$ and, from symmetry, $P_{e_0} = P_{e_1} = P_e$, so

$$P_e = P(y_0 > y_1) \qquad (17)$$

where, based on our study of ASK, y_0 has a Rayleigh PDF while y_1 is Rician. But because the FSK wave lacks the "spaces" of ASK, $S_R = rE_R$ and

$$\left(\frac{A^2}{N}\right)_{\text{max}} = \frac{2E_R}{\eta} = \frac{2S_R}{\eta r} = 2\rho \qquad (18)$$

at the output of either filter, depending on the input frequency.

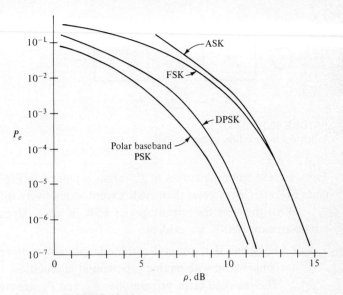

FIGURE 10.15
Error probabilities for binary digital modulation systems.

To compute the probability Eq. (17) we first note that $p_{y_0}(y_0) = p_{R_n}(y_0)$ so, for a given value of y_1,

$$P(y_0 > y_1 | y_1) = \int_{y_1}^{\infty} p_{R_n}(y_0)\, dy_0 = e^{-y_1^2/2N}$$

Then, accounting for all possible values of y_1,

$$P_e = \int_0^{\infty} P(y_0 > y_1 | y_1) p_R(y_1)\, dy_1$$

$$= \int_0^{\infty} e^{-y_1^2/2N} \frac{y_1}{N} e^{-(y_1^2 + A^2)/2N} I_0\left(\frac{Ay_1}{N}\right) dy_1$$

in which $p_{y_1}(y_1) = p_R(y_1)$ per Eq. (7) with $A_k = A$. Rather amazingly, this integral can be evaluated in closed form with no approximations. For that purpose, we let $\lambda = \sqrt{2}\, y_1$ and $a = A/\sqrt{2}$, giving

$$P_e = \frac{1}{2} e^{-A^2/4N} \int_0^{\infty} \frac{\lambda}{N} e^{-(\lambda^2 + a^2)/2N} I_0\left(\frac{a\lambda}{N}\right) d\lambda$$

and comparison with Eq. (7) shows that the integrand now has exactly the same form as a Rician PDF; consequently, the area (integral) equals unity. Finally, since $A^2/4N = \rho/2$, we have the simple result that

$$P_e = \frac{1}{2} e^{-\rho/2} \tag{19}$$

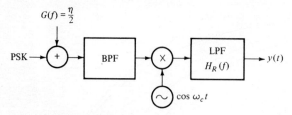

FIGURE 10.16
Synchronous detection of binary PSK.

Thus, as seen from the curves of P_e versus ρ plotted in Fig. 10.15, noncoherent FSK gives no better error rates than ASK except at relatively small values of ρ.

What then are the advantages of FSK, if any? Upon further reflection, three advantages over ASK are evident:

1 FSK has the constant-amplitude property whose merits were covered in conjunction with analog exponential modulation.
2 The per-digit error probabilities P_{e_1} and P_{e_0} are equal.
3 The optimum threshold level is independent of A and ρ, and need not be readjusted if the signal strength varies with time, a not uncommon phenomenon in radio transmission.

It is precisely for this last reason that FSK is preferred to ASK in applications where fading is expected and synchronous detection is not feasible.

One final point remains to be discussed here, namely, why binary FSK does not give the wideband noise reduction usually associated with FM. For the system here described the reason is very simple: it is basically AM rather than FM. If one uses true FM, including detection by a limiter-discriminator,† it turns out that the transmission bandwidth required to control intersymbol interference is so large that the noise-reduction effect is essentially canceled by the increased predetection noise. However, for multilevel signals ($\mu > 2$) some advantage in the form of a bandwidth-power exchange is possible; after all, if $\mu \to \infty$, digital and analog signals are equivalent.

Coherent PSK

Coherent or synchronous detection relies on precise knowledge of the phase of the received carrier wave as well as its frequency, and thus involves more sophisticated hardware. In return, it offers improved performance.

Consider, for instance, the binary PSK signal of Fig. 10.10c — or, for that matter, the DSB signal of Fig. 10.10d, since both signals can be said to have $A_k = \pm A$ or $\phi_k = 0$ or π. An appropriate synchronous detector is shown in Fig. 10.16, where the

† See Bennett and Davey (1965, chap. 9).

FIGURE 10.17
Phasors and thresholds of PSK with $\mu = 4$.

local oscillator is synchronized and $H_R(f)$ is a *lowpass* filter; the bandpass filter before the mixer serves only to prevent overload from excessive noise. From our study of synchronous detection for analog signals, it immediately follows that the filtered output is of the form

$$y(t) = \pm A + n_i(t) \tag{20a}$$

and, with optimum filtering,

$$\left(\frac{A^2}{\overline{n_i^2}}\right)_{max} = \frac{2S_R}{\eta r} = 2\rho \tag{20b}$$

Therefore, since $n_i(t)$ is gaussian,

$$P_e = Q\left(\frac{A}{\sqrt{\overline{n_i^2}}}\right) = Q(\sqrt{2\rho}) \tag{21}$$

the same as optimum baseband transmission and, from Fig. 10.15, 3 to 4 dB better than noncoherent modulation.

Because of its performance quality, combined with the constant-amplitude property, *multilevel* ($\mu > 2$) PSK has considerable practical value. Note, especially, that increasing μ increases the equivalent bit rate without the need for larger transmission bandwidth. It thus behooves us to spend some time on μ-ary PSK where

$$K_R x_c(t) = A \cos(\omega_c t + \phi_k) \qquad \phi_k = 0, \frac{2\pi}{\mu}, \frac{4\pi}{\mu}, \ldots, \frac{2(\mu-1)\pi}{\mu} \tag{22}$$

Conceptually, such a signal is detected by phase discrimination with decision angles $\pi/\mu, 3\pi/\mu, \ldots$ centered between the expected carrier-phase values. Figure 10.17 shows a phasor diagram for quaternary PSK ($\mu = 4$) and the corresponding angular thresholds.

The received signal plus noise, after bandpass filtering, has the form of Eq. (4b), so errors occur whenever the noise-induced phase perturbation $\phi(t)$ crosses the threshold. Therefore, by symmetry, the per-digit error probabilites are equal and

$$P_e = P\left(|\phi| > \frac{\pi}{\mu}\right) = 1 - \int_{-\pi/\mu}^{\pi/\mu} p_\phi(\phi)\, d\phi \tag{23a}$$

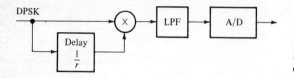

FIGURE 10.18
Phase-comparison detection of differentially coherent binary PSK.

Assuming optimum bandpass filtering, $A^2/N = 2\rho$ so if $\rho \gg 1$,

$$\int_{-\pi/\mu}^{\pi/\mu} P_\phi(\phi)\, d\phi = \frac{2}{\sqrt{2\pi}} \int_0^{\sqrt{2\rho}\,\sin\,\pi/\mu} e^{-\lambda^2/2}\, d\lambda \qquad (23b)$$

where we have used Eq. (9) and let $\lambda = \sqrt{2\rho}\,\sin\,\phi$. Consistent with the large-signal condition one finally obtains

$$P_e \approx \frac{1}{\sqrt{\pi\rho\,\sin\,\pi/\mu}}\, e^{-\rho\,\sin^2\,\pi/\mu} \qquad (24)$$

which holds for $\mu \geq 4$ and $\rho \gg 1$.

Differentially Coherent PSK

A clever technique known as *phase-comparison* or *differentially coherent* PSK (DPSK) has been devised to get around the synchronization problems of coherent detection. The strategy is diagramed in Fig. 10.18 for binary DPSK; somewhat as with homodyne detection, the local oscillator is replaced by the signal itself delayed in time by exactly $1/r$, the bit spacing. If adjacent digits are of like phase, their product results in a positive output (or binary **1**); conversely, opposite phases result in a negative output (binary **0**). Thus, it is the *shift* or *no shift* between transmitted phase values that represents the message information, so appropriate coding, called *differential encoding*, is required at the transmitter.

Differential encoding starts with an arbitrary first digit and thereafter indicates the message digits by successive transition or no transition. A transition stands for message **0**, and no transition for message **1**. The coding process is illustrated below.

Input message		1	0	1	1	0	1	0	0	
Encoded message	1	1	0	0	0	1	1	0	1	
Transmitted phase	0	0	π	π	π	0	0	π	0	
Phase-comparison output		+	−	+	+	−	+	−	−	
Output message		1	0	1	1	0	1	0	0	

Differential encoding is most often used for PSK systems but is not restricted to such applications. In general, it is advantageous for systems having no sense of absolute polarity.

As to the noise performance of DPSK it might appear that differential detection requires twice as much power as coherent detection because the phase reference is itself contaminated by noise. However, the perturbations actually tend to cancel in the comparison process, so the degradation is not so great. We will carry out the analysis for the case where the two adjacent phases are the same, say $\phi_k = \phi_{k-1} = 0$, so an error occurs if the output is negative. Writing the received (and filtered) signal plus noise as $[A + n_i(t)] \cos \omega_c t - n_q(t) \sin \omega_c t$, the output of the delay unit will be $[A + n_i(t')] \cos \omega_c t' - n_q(t') \sin \omega_c t'$ where $t' = t - 1/r$. Thus, providing that f_c is an integer multiple of r (which can be guaranteed by heterodyning if necessary), the A/D input is proportional to

$$y(t) = [A + n_i(t)][A + n_i(t')] + n_q(t)n_q(t') \qquad (25)$$

and $P_e = P(y < 0)$.

Equation (25), involving products of gaussian variates, is called a *quadratic form*. It can be simplified through a diagonalization process by defining four new variates:

$$\alpha_i = A + \frac{n_i(t) + n_i(t')}{2} \qquad \alpha_q = \frac{n_q(t) + n_q(t')}{2}$$

$$\beta_i = \frac{n_i(t) - n_i(t')}{2} \qquad \beta_q = \frac{n_q(t) - n_q(t')}{2} \qquad (26a)$$

Then, letting

$$\alpha = |\alpha_i + j\alpha_q| \qquad \beta = |\beta_i + j\beta_q| \qquad (26b)$$

one can show that $y(t) = \alpha^2 - \beta^2$ and therefore

$$P_e = P(y < 0) = P(\alpha^2 < \beta^2) = P(\beta > \alpha) \qquad (27)$$

the last step following since α and β are nonnegative. Now we have an expression identical to that of noncoherent FSK with α and β replacing y_1 and y_0. Moreover, as the reader can check from the definitions, α is Rician and β is Rayleigh. The only difference here is that the mean-square noise terms are reduced by a factor of 2, e.g., assuming $n_q(t)$ and $n_q(t')$ are independent, $\overline{\alpha_q^2} = (\overline{n_q^2} + \overline{n_q^2})/4 = N/2$. Therefore,

$$P_e = \tfrac{1}{2}e^{-\rho} \qquad (28)$$

as obtained from Eq. (19) with ρ replaced by $\rho/2$ reflecting the noise reduction.

Referring to the curves of Fig. 10.15 we see that DPSK has a 2- to 3-dB power advantage over noncoherent detection and a penalty of less than 1 dB compared to coherent PSK at $P_e \leq 10^{-4}$. And remember that DPSK does not require separate synchronization. Additionally, with slight modification of the transmitted wave, a timing signal is easily derived for the A/D converter. The only significant disadvantage is that because of the fixed delay time $1/r$ in the detector, the system is locked in on a specific signaling speed, thereby precluding variable speed (asynchronous) transmission. A minor annoyance is the fact that errors tend to occur in groups of two (why?).

For μ-ary DPSK, the error probability has the same form as Eq. (24), save that ρ must be increased by a factor of

$$\frac{\sin^2(\pi/\mu)}{2 \sin^2(\pi/2\mu)} \qquad (29)$$

to achieve the same P_e as coherent detection. With $\mu = 4$ the penalty is about 2 dB and increases asymptotically toward 3 dB as $\mu \to \infty$. Thus, only for large μ does differential detection fully suffer from the noisy phase reference.

Example 10.3

High-speed data transmission over voice telephone channels has been a subject of intense practical concern for many years. One of the earliest and most successful designs, used in the Bell System model 201, 205, and 207 data sets, is described here. Incorporating quaternary DPSK modulation, it achieves synchronous transmission at rates up to 2,400 bits/s on telephone lines that have been *conditioned* (equalized) for digital signals.

Figure 10.19a diagrams† the transmitter. Incoming binary digits are grouped into blocks of two, called *dibits*, so $\mu = \mu_S^2 = 4$ and $r = r_S/2 = 1,200$. The dibits differentially phase modulate the carrier and the DPSK wave is then envelope-modulated to yield

$$x_c(t) = \sum_k p\left(t - \frac{k}{r}\right) \cos(2\pi f_c t + \phi_k)$$

where

$$p(t) = \cos^2\left(\frac{\pi r t}{2}\right) \Pi(2rt)$$

This equivalent baseband pulse shape is not bandlimited but, by applying duality to Eqs. (17) and (18), one can show that $P(f)$ has negligible content for $|f| > r$. Hence, $B_T \approx 2r = 2,400$ Hz centered on the carrier frequency $f_c = 1,800$ Hz. The carrier

---

† Baker (1962) details the hardware realizations of transmitter and receiver functions, some of which are particularly ingenious.

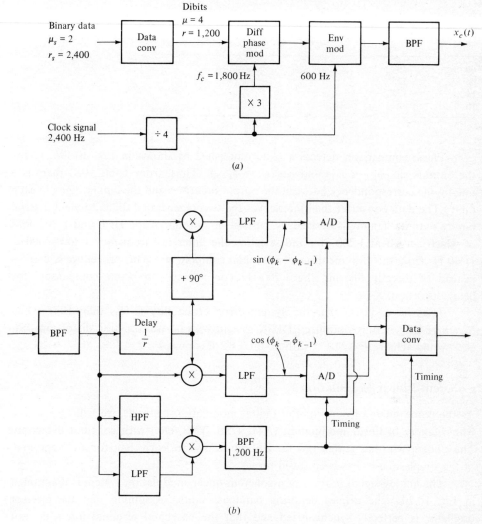

FIGURE 10.19
Quaternary PSK system. (*a*) Transmitter; (*b*) receiver.

and envelope modulation frequencies are both derived from the incoming 2,400-Hz clock frequency.

As Table 10.1 indicates, the differential phase shift has an added term of $+45°$ so that ϕ_k can never equal ϕ_{k-1} and there is a phase shift in the modulated wave every $1/r$ seconds. This feature, combined with the envelope modulation, produces discrete frequency components at $f_c \pm 600$ that are used at the receiver to generate the timing signal.

Table 10.1

Dibit	$\phi_k - \phi_{k-1}$	$\sin(\phi_k - \phi_{k-1})$	$\cos(\phi_k - \phi_{k-1})$
00	$+45°$	$+$	$+$
01	$+135°$	$+$	$-$
11	$-135°$	$-$	$-$
10	$-45°$	$-$	$+$

Phase comparison detection is accomplished as shown in Fig. 10.19b, giving the outputs $\sin(\phi_k - \phi_{k-1})$ and $\cos(\phi_k - \phi_{k-1})$. Thus, from Table 10.1, there is a one-to-one correspondence between the output polarities and the binary digits in each dibit. The data converter then interleaves the two regenerated digits to yield a serial binary output. Timing is derived by mixing the outputs of the HPF and LPF, both of which cut off at 1,200 Hz, and selecting the difference frequency $1,800 - 600 = 1,200$ Hz from the aforementioned sinusoidal components. This procedure is used — instead of directly filtering the 1,200-Hz component — to better compensate for delay distortion.

Tests have shown that the system error probability is less than 10^{-5} when $S/N = 15$ dB. A fully optimized DPSK system with no transmission distortion, ISI, etc., would achieve $P_e = 10^{-5}$ with about 3 dB less power.   ////

Coherent Linear Modulation

As the grand finale of our study of digital modulation methods, we will look at the whole family of linear modulation (AM, DSB, VSB, etc.) with coherent detection. The student who has gotten this far will be pleased to learn that, for a change, one of the simplest cases has been saved till last.

The analog-signal portion of a coherent linear modulation system is diagramed in Fig. 10.20a, the primes denoting bandpass units. Assuming that the receiver oscillator is perfectly synchronized and that the baseband terminal filters do not respond above f_c, frequency-translation analysis shows that, as far as signal transmission is concerned, the entire bandpass section plus modulator and demodulator is equivalent to a *lowpass* filter

$$H_{TCR}(f) = \frac{1}{4}[H'_{TCR}(f - f_c) + H'_{TCR}(f + f_c)] \qquad |f| < f_c \qquad (30a)$$

where

$$H'_{TCR}(f) = H'_T(f)H'_C(f)H'_R(f) \qquad (30b)$$

Likewise, the lowpass equivalent noise is gaussian and has spectral density

$$G(f) = \frac{1}{4}[G'(f - f_c) + G'(f + f_c)] \qquad |f| < f_c \qquad (31a)$$

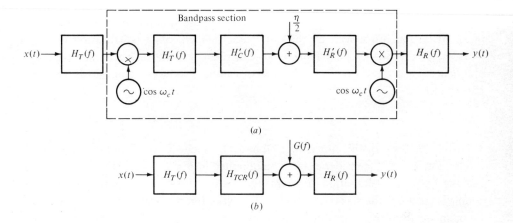

FIGURE 10.20
Coherent linear modulation. (a) Block diagram of analog portion; (b) equivalent baseband system.

where

$$G'(f) = \frac{\eta}{2} |H_R'(f)|^2 \qquad (31b)$$

Therefore, for analysis or design purposes, Fig. 10.20a may be replaced by the *equivalent baseband system* of Fig. 10.20b and, in the classic tradition of mathematics, we have thereby reduced the problem to one that has already been solved, i.e., baseband data transmission.

All of the results from Sect. 10.1 apply here with the substitution of Eqs. (30) and (31). Specifically, if $G(f)$ is flat over the passband of $H_R(f)$ and if the carrier is suppressed at the transmitter (i.e., DSB or VSB), then

$$P_e \geq 2\left(1 - \frac{1}{\mu}\right)Q\left[\sqrt{\frac{6\rho}{\mu^2 - 1}}\right]$$

$$\approx \left(1 - \frac{1}{\mu}\right)\sqrt{\frac{\mu^2 - 1}{3\pi\rho}}\exp\left(-\frac{3\rho}{\mu^2 - 1}\right) \qquad \rho \gg 1 \qquad (32)$$

where the lower bound requires optimum terminal filters and is the same as optimum baseband transmission. Therefore, the polar baseband curve in Fig. 10.15 also holds for binary linear modulation with coherent detection and suppressed carrier. The case of *unsuppressed* carrier hardly deserves mention here since, with coherent detection, the wasted power in the carrier offers no compensating benefits.

Finally, it should be noted from the equivalent baseband system that direct *baseband equalization* is possible with coherent linear modulation and will correct linear distortion introduced by the bandpass channel. Such equalization does not work as well for incoherent systems because incoherent detection is a nonlinear process and hence linear distortion in the bandpass channel produces nonlinear distortion at baseband.

EXERCISE 10.4   Justify either Eq. (30) or (31), whichever you find more interesting. (*Hints*: For Eq. (30), consider a signal bandlimited in $B < f_c$ applied to the modulator; use the frequency-translation theorem and follow through the system with a few simple sketches of the spectra. For Eq. (31), write the bandpass noise at the detector input in quadrature-carrier form, multiply it by $\cos \omega_c t$, and use the results from Sect. 7.3.)

10.3   ERROR-CONTROL CODING

We have seen that error probability in digital transmission is a direct function of ρ or, equivalently, S/N. If, for a given system, the signal power is limited to some maximum value and errors are still unacceptably frequent, then some other means of improving reliability must be sought. Often, error-control coding provides the best solution.

In a nutshell, error-control coding is the calculated use of *redundancy*. Taking a hint from information theory, one systematically adds extra digits to the transmitted message, digits which themselves convey no information but make it possible for the receiver to detect or even correct errors in the information-bearing digits. Theoretically, near-errorless transmission is possible; more practically, there is the inevitable trade-off between transmission reliability, efficiency, and complexity of terminal equipment. Reflecting this factor, a multitude of error-detecting and error-correcting codes have been devised to suit various applications.

This section is an introduction to error-control coding. We will deal only with binary codes since relatively little has been accomplished in the realm of practical multilevel codes. (Remember the unique feature of binary digits: If one merely knows which digits are in error, the correct digits are immediately determined.) Furthermore, our treatment will be primarily qualitative because coding theory has evolved from the black art of its early days to a highly sophisticated mathematical discipline. Hence, we are barely scratching the surface of a fascinating subject; the reader whose interest is thereby aroused, and who has the essential aptitude for modern algebra, will find additional material in the supplementary reading list.

Coding Concepts and Trade-offs

By way of introduction, consider a repeated code in which each binary message digit is repeated three times — roughly analogous to repeating your words when you are trying to talk to someone on the other side of a noisy room. The allowed code words are then **000** and **111**, so any other received work such as **101** clearly indicates the presence of errors. To correct single errors, one might use a majority-rule decision and the following decoding table:

Decoded digit	0	1
	000	**111**
Received	**001**	**110**
words	**010**	**101**
	100	**011**

This yields a *single-error correcting code* and decoding errors occur only when there are two or three erroneous digits in a word; e.g., two errors change **000** to **101**, etc. Therefore, assuming the *per-digit error probability* is ϵ, we find the decoding error probability from the binomial distribution, Eq. (1), Sect. 3.4, as

$$P_e = P(2 \text{ or } 3 \text{ errors in 3 digits}) = P_3(2) + P_3(3)$$

$$= \binom{3}{2} \epsilon^2 (1 - \epsilon) + \binom{3}{3} \epsilon^3 = 3\epsilon^2 - 2\epsilon^3 \qquad (1)$$

Since ϵ is the error probability without coding, and since $\epsilon < \frac{1}{2}$ on any reasonable channel, coding has certainly improved the reliability.

The triple-repetition code also works for *double-error detection* if we give up single-error correction; i.e., any received code word other than **000** or **111** is treated as a detected but uncorrected error. Decoding errors, in the sense of undetected errors, occur with probability

$$P_e = P_3(3) = \epsilon^3 \qquad (2)$$

which is obviously smaller than Eq. (1). Despite the triviality of this example code, it does lead to three important and general conclusions about error-control coding.

1 Through the addition of extra digits, called *check digits*, the code words can be made "very different" from each other. Analytically, the difference between any two binary words is measured in terms of the *Hamming distance d*, defined simply as the number of places in which the words have different digits; thus, it takes *d* errors (in the right places) to change one word into the other. Pursuing this line of thought, a code that detects up to K errors per word or corrects up to K errors per word must consist of code words having

$$d_{\min} = \begin{cases} K+1 & \text{error detection} \\ 2K+1 & \text{error correction} \end{cases} \qquad (3)$$

an assertion left for the student to ponder. The triple-repetition code clearly has $d = 3$ so, as we have seen, it can detect $K = 2$ errors or correct $K = 1$ error per word. For an arbitrary code with

$$k = \text{message digits per word}$$
$$q = \text{check digits per word}$$
$$n = k + q = \text{total digits per word}$$

there are 2^k binary code words (formed with k message digits) out of a possible $2^n = 2^q \times 2^k$ n-digit words. Accordingly, the check digits should be chosen such that the 2^k code words satisfy the distance requirement (3).

2   If the per-digit error probability ϵ is reasonably small, then the probability of $M + 1$ errors in an n-digit word will be much less than the probability of M errors, i.e., $P_n(M + 1) \ll P_n(M)$. To underscore this point, and for reference purposes, Table 10.2 lists approximate expressions for $P_n(M)$ obtained via binomial-series expansion. Therefore, if a code corrects or detects up to K errors, the decoding error probability per word is

$$P_{e,\text{word}} = \sum_{i=K+1}^{n} P_n(i) \approx P_n(K + 1) \qquad (4a)$$

the approximation being quite accurate if $n\epsilon \leq 0.1$. Since the majority of decoding errors are due to $K + 1$ digit errors of which the fraction k/n are erroneous message digits (the rest are check-digit errors), the net error probability per message digit or bit is

$$P_{e,\text{bit}} \approx \frac{k}{n}(K + 1)P_{e,\text{word}} \qquad (4b)$$

Table 10.2   SERIES APPROXIMATIONS FOR
          THE BINOMIAL DISTRIBUTION

M	$P_n(M) = \binom{n}{M} \epsilon^M (1 - \epsilon)^{n-M}$
0	$1 - n\epsilon + \frac{1}{2}n(n-1)\epsilon^2 - \frac{1}{6}n(n-1)(n-2)\epsilon^3$
1	$n\epsilon - \quad n(n-1)\epsilon^2 + \frac{1}{2}n(n-1)(n-2)\epsilon^3$
2	$\frac{1}{2}n(n-1)\epsilon^2 - \frac{1}{2}n(n-1)(n-2)\epsilon^3$
3	$\frac{1}{6}n(n-1)(n-2)\epsilon^3$

3 The insertion of check digits for error control reduces the effective rate at which message digits are transmitted. Quantitatively, we define the *rate efficiency factor* of a code as†

$$\mathscr{E} = \frac{k}{k+q} = \frac{k}{n} \tag{5}$$

so if the gross signaling rate is r, the message digit rate is

$$r_m = \mathscr{E}r \tag{6}$$

Generally speaking, codes that are both easily instrumented and effective in error control require a relatively large percentage of check digits. Thus, practical error control tends to go hand in hand with bit-rate reduction.

But there are other less elegant ways of decreasing errors at the expense of signaling rate, the signal power being fixed. And to properly evaluate the merits of a given code we should at least consider one other option, namely, signaling-rate reduction without coding. Reducing r increases $\rho = S_R/\eta r$ (if the terminal filters are adjusted accordingly) and thereby decreases the error probability.

Suppose, for comparison purposes, that a certain code with rate efficiency $\mathscr{E}$ has been proposed for use on a binary baseband channel having

$$\epsilon = Q(\sqrt{2\rho}) \qquad \rho = \frac{S_R}{\eta r}$$

so that $P_{e,\text{bit}}$ is given by Eq. (4b) with the above value of ϵ. On the other hand, one could simply reduce the signaling rate by a factor of $\mathscr{E}$, giving the same message bit rate with

$$P_{e,\text{uncoded}} = Q\left(\sqrt{\frac{2\rho}{\mathscr{E}}}\right) \tag{7}$$

If Eq. (7) is of the same order of magnitude as $P_{e,\text{bit}}$, the value of the particular code under consideration is questionable.

Example 10.4

The triple-repetition code has $k = 1$, $q = 2$, $n = 3$, and $\mathscr{E} = \frac{1}{3}$. If it is used for single-error correction on a baseband channel with $\rho = 7$ and $r = 1,200$, the message bit rate is $r_m = \frac{1200}{3} = 400$ and $\epsilon = Q(\sqrt{2\rho}) \approx 10^{-4}$ so, from Eq. (1),

$$P_{e,\text{bit}} \approx 3\epsilon^2 \approx 3 \times 10^{-8}$$

† Not to be confused with communication efficiency defined in Eq. (8), Sect. 9.4.

Equation (4b) does not apply in this case since the decoded message digit is always erroneous when there are two or three errors.

If, however, the signaling rate is reduced to $r = 300$ and no coding is used,

$$P_{e,\text{uncoded}} = Q\left(\sqrt{\frac{2\rho}{\mathscr{E}}}\right) = Q(\sqrt{42}) \approx 5 \times 10^{-9}$$

so simple signaling-rate reduction is superior to this rudimentary code.   ////

Error Detection by Parity Check

For many applications, errors can be rendered harmless if they are simply *detected* with no immediate attempt at correction. This is true, for instance, in data telemetry when a large number of values are gathered for statistical analysis; erroneous values, if detected, are simply omitted from further processing, and the loss is negligible. Similarly, given a two-way communication link, the fact that an error has been detected can be sent back to the transmitter for appropriate action, i.e., retransmission. Such decision feedback is especially advantageous if the system is subject to variable transmission conditions. When conditions are good and errors infrequent, a low-redundancy code with its higher data rate is satisfactory; when conditions are unfavorable, as indicated by frequent error detection, the transmitter may switch to a code of higher redundancy or temporarily cease transmission. But with or without feedback, simple error detection suffices only if ϵ is small to begin with and the probability of undetected errors is at a suitably low level.

Most error-detecting codes are based on the notion of *parity*. The parity of a binary word is said to be even when the word includes an even number of **1**s, while odd parity means an odd number of **1**s. For error detection by parity check, we divide the message into groups of k digits and add one check digit to each group such that every $(k + 1)$-digit word has the same parity, say even. Thus, the check digit is related to the message digits by

$$c = m_1 \oplus m_2 \oplus \cdots \oplus m_k \qquad (8a)$$

where $\oplus$ stands for *modulo-2 addition*. Modulo-2 arithmetic, defined on the binary digits **0** and **1**, is the same as ordinary arithmetic except that $\mathbf{1} \oplus \mathbf{1} = \mathbf{0}$ and there is no difference between addition and subtraction.† Hence Eq. (8a) is equivalent to

$$m_1 \oplus m_2 \oplus \cdots \oplus m_k \oplus c = \mathbf{0} \qquad (8b)$$

The efficiency factor is

$$\mathscr{E} = \frac{k}{k + 1} \qquad (9)$$

indicating reasonable efficiency if k is large.

† In hardware terms, $\oplus$ is an EXCLUSIVE-OR gate.

Of the 2^{k+1} possible binary words having $k+1$ digits, parity-check coding excludes precisely half, the half with odd parity, thereby ensuring that the code has Hamming distance $d \geq 2$ as required for single-error detection. Therefore, if the parity of a received word is odd, we know there is an error—or three errors, or, in general, an odd number of errors. Error detection can then be implemented by checking the parity of each word as it arrives. Of course error correction is not possible, since we do not know *where* the errors are located within the word. Furthermore, an even number of errors preserves valid parity and hence goes undetected.

Neglecting all but the double-error case, $P_{e,\text{word}} \approx P_{k+1}(2) \approx \frac{1}{2}(k+1)k\epsilon^2$ and hence, from Eq. (4b),

$$P_{e,\text{bit}} \approx \frac{k}{k+1} 2P_{e,\text{word}} \approx k^2\epsilon^2 \qquad (10)$$

For example, if $k = 9$ and $\epsilon = 10^{-3}$, parity-check coding drops the error probability by more than one order of magnitude with a rate reduction of only $\frac{9}{10}$.

The probability of a detected error is also of interest, for it indicates the amount of data that must be retransmitted or discarded. Since primarily single errors are detected, we have *per word*

$$P_{\text{de}} \approx \binom{k+1}{1}\epsilon(1-\epsilon)^k \approx (k+1)\epsilon \qquad (11a)$$

In a message of $N \gg 1$ total message digits, there are N/k words, of which $(N/k)(k+1)\epsilon$ have detected errors. If detected errors are discarded, the fractional number of message digits thrown away is

$$\frac{1}{N}\left[k\frac{N}{k}(k+1)\epsilon\right] = (k+1)\epsilon = P_{\text{de}} \qquad (11b)$$

If $k = 9$ and $\epsilon = 10^{-3}$, $P_{\text{de}} \approx 0.01$ or 1 percent.

Two final comments with respect to practical matters are in order here. First, it is preferable to use odd-word parity and an odd number of message digits per word; this ensures that every word has at least one transition, thereby aiding synchronization and preventing apparent loss of signal if the message contains an extended string of like digits. Second, as a result of impulse noise on switched circuits or short-duration fading on radio paths, errors may tend to occur in *bursts* of several successive digits; since multiple errors wreak havoc on parity checking, the check digits should be *interlaced* such that the digits checked are widely spaced. An example of interlacing is given in Fig. 10.21, where one parity word is indicated by lines connecting the digits.

EXERCISE 10.5 Write down all the code words for a parity-check code with $k = 3$ and verify that $d \geq 2$.

FIGURE 10.21
Interlaced parity checking; $m=$ message digit, $c=$ check digit.

Error-Correcting Block Codes

The idea of *error-correcting* codes is certainly far more appealing and exciting than mere error detection, suggesting as it does the one-way errorless transmission hypothesized by Shannon. And there are numerous applications, notably one-way links, for which error correction is a necessity. It also turns out that encoding at the transmitter is not very different for detection or correction; the receiving decoder is the problem in error-correcting systems. Consequently, when transmission equipment is constrained, e.g., satellites, it may prove more practical to correct errors at the receiver than to provide for retransmission facilities, even though a two-way path is available.

Parity-check coding is readily extended to error correction by observing that correction requires the detection of an error and its *location* in the word. Thus, if two checks are made on the same word but in two different patterns, errors result in characteristic symptoms of invalid parity.

Most error-correcting block codes have n-digit words in which the first k digits are message digits and the remaining $q = n - k$ are parity check digits. Such a code is called an (n,k) *systematic parity-check code*, and the ith digit of a code word is

$$x_i = \begin{cases} m_i & i = 1, 2, \ldots, k \\ c_{i-k} & i = k + 1, \ldots, n \end{cases} \tag{12}$$

For analytic convenience, a typical code word is represented by an $n \times 1$ matrix (or column vector) $\mathbf{x}$. For instance, a (7,4) code word would be

$$\mathbf{x} = [m_1 \quad m_2 \quad m_3 \quad m_4 \quad c_1 \quad c_2 \quad c_3]^T$$

which has been written as the transpose of a $1 \times n$ matrix to save space.

Given the message digits for a particular word, the check digits are chosen such that

$$\mathbf{Hx} = \mathbf{0} \tag{13}$$

where the *parity-check matrix* $\mathbf{H}$ is a rectangular $q \times n$ matrix of the form

$$\mathbf{H} = \overbrace{\begin{bmatrix} h_{11} & h_{12} & \cdots & h_{1k} & \overbrace{1 & 0 & 0 & \cdots & 0} \\ h_{21} & h_{22} & \cdots & h_{2k} & 0 & 1 & 0 & \cdots & 0 \\ \vdots & \vdots & & \vdots & \vdots & \vdots & \vdots & & \vdots \\ h_{q1} & h_{q2} & \cdots & h_{qk} & 0 & 0 & 0 & \cdots & 1 \end{bmatrix}}^{k} \left.\vphantom{\begin{bmatrix} 1 \\ 1 \\ 1 \\ 1 \end{bmatrix}}\right\}q \tag{14}$$

Note that the right-hand portion of **H** is a $q \times q$ unit matrix; hence, combining Eqs. (12) and (14), each row of Eq. (13) is a parity-check equation involving only one check digit, i.e.,

$$h_{j1} m_1 \oplus h_{j2} m_2 \oplus \ldots \oplus h_{jk} m_k \oplus c_j = 0 \qquad j = 1, 2, \ldots, q$$

The components h_{11}, h_{12}, etc., of **H** are binary digits, but we have not yet specified them since they determine the error-correction properties of the code, about which we need more information.

Suppose a word **x** is transmitted and, owing to errors, results in the received word

$$\mathbf{y} = \mathbf{x} \oplus \mathbf{e} \qquad (15a)$$

which stands for the digit-by-digit sum

$$y_i = x_i \oplus e_i \qquad i = 1, 2, \ldots, n \qquad (15b)$$

with **e** being the *error pattern*, i.e.,

$$e_i = \begin{cases} 1 & y_i \neq x_i \\ 0 & y_i = x_i \end{cases}$$

As an illustration, if

$$\mathbf{x} = [0 \quad 1 \quad 0 \quad 0 \quad 1]^T$$

and

$$\mathbf{y} = [0 \quad 1 \quad 1 \quad 0 \quad 0]^T$$

then

$$\mathbf{e} = [0 \quad 0 \quad 1 \quad 0 \quad 1]^T$$

indicating errors in the third and fifth digits.

If we could determine **e** at the receiver, we could correct all errors; but finding **e** from **y** requires knowing **x**, the transmitted word! We can, however, calculate a q-digit *syndrome*

$$\mathbf{s} = \mathbf{Hy} \qquad (16a)$$

which does provide some useful information. Specifically, from Eqs. (13) and (15),

$$\mathbf{s} = \mathbf{Hx} \oplus \mathbf{He} = \mathbf{He} \qquad (16b)$$

so $\mathbf{s} = \mathbf{0}$ when $\mathbf{e} = \mathbf{0}$, i.e., no errors. Furthermore, if **y** has just one error, say in the jth message digit,

$$\mathbf{s} = [h_{1j} \quad h_{2j} \quad \ldots \quad h_{qj}]^T \qquad j \leq k \qquad (17)$$

and this is identical to the jth column of the parity-check matrix. Therefore, the syndrome unambiguously indicates the no-error condition or the position of a single error providing *all columns of* **H** *are different and nonzero*; and we then have a single-error-correcting code.

When used in this mode, an (n,k) code has $P_{e,\text{word}} \approx P_n(2)$ and

$$P_{e,\text{bit}} \approx \frac{k}{n} 2P_n(2) \approx k(n-1)\epsilon^2 \tag{18}$$

Multiple errors cause complications, however, since we may miss the actual errors and wrongly "correct" another message digit, making matters worse. Consequently, unless ϵ is so small that multiple errors are very rare, a more powerful code is desirable.

Unfortunately, devising an appropriate syndrome and parity-check matrix for multiple-error correction is a far more complicated task — so much so that the first double-error-correcting codes were created by inspired trial-and-error work rather than designed by a specific method. Slepian (1956) finally put coding theory on a solid mathematical foundation when he discovered its relationship to concepts of modern algebra. Soon thereafter, using the theory of Galois fields,† Bose, Chaudhuri, and Hocquenghem developed a class of multiple-error-correcting codes (now named BCH codes) that are efficient and have relatively simple hardware requirements for encoding and decoding. Needless to say, such codes are beyond the intended scope of this text.

EXERCISE 10.6   Verify that a triple-repetition code is a (3,1) systematic parity-check code with

$$\mathbf{H} = \begin{bmatrix} 1 & 1 & 0 \\ 1 & 0 & 1 \end{bmatrix}$$

In particular, show that $\mathbf{Hx} = \mathbf{0}$ and find **s** for each single error position.

Example 10.5   Hamming Codes

Before Slepian's discovery and even before the matrix formulation of block codes, Hamming (1950) devised a rather elegant class of block codes. In our present notation, and dealing only with single-error correction, Hamming's strategy is as follows. If there are q check digits per word, then the syndrome is a q-digit word that can be made to spell out in binary form the exact position of a single error, if any. With $q = 3$, for instance, $\mathbf{s} = \mathbf{000}$ means "no error" (as before), $\mathbf{s} = \mathbf{001}$ means "error in the first digit," and so forth.

---

† Rumor has it that a theoretical mathematician specializing in Galois fields abandoned the subject upon hearing of the practical application.

Since $n + 1$ error indications are required ("no error" or one error in any of the n code-word digits), and since there are 2^q different syndrome words, the numbers of check digits and message digits in a Hamming code are related by

$$2^q = k + q + 1 \qquad \text{where } k + q = n \qquad (19)$$

Accordingly, the efficiency factor is

$$\mathscr{E} = \frac{k}{n} = 1 - \frac{1}{n} \log_2 (n + 1) \qquad (20)$$

so reasonable efficiency is achieved using long code words.

The parity-check matrix is easily constructed drawing upon the above stipulation for $\mathbf{s}$ and the fact that $\mathbf{s}$ equals the jth column of $\mathbf{H}$ when there is a single error in the jth digit. Therefore, reading from left to right, the columns of $\mathbf{H}$ are simply the binary versions of the numbers $1, 2, \ldots, n$, as illustrated below for a (7,4) Hamming code:

$$\mathbf{H} = \begin{bmatrix} 0 & 0 & 0 & 1 & 1 & 1 & 1 \\ 0 & 1 & 1 & 0 & 0 & 1 & 1 \\ 1 & 0 & 1 & 0 & 1 & 0 & 1 \end{bmatrix} \qquad (21a)$$

It then follows by comparison with Eq. (14) that this is not a systematic code; since the check-digit positions must correspond to the columns of $\mathbf{H}$ having just one $\mathbf{1}$, the (7,4) code word has the form

$$\mathbf{x} = [c_1 \quad c_2 \quad m_1 \quad c_3 \quad m_2 \quad m_3 \quad m_4]^T \qquad (21b)$$

and the check-digit equations are

$$c_1 = m_1 \oplus m_2 \oplus m_4$$
$$c_2 = m_1 \oplus m_3 \oplus m_4 \qquad (21c)$$
$$c_3 = m_2 \oplus m_3 \oplus m_4$$

Observe that each message digit is checked by at least two check digits, which is essential for error correction. ////

EXERCISE 10.7 Taking the system parameters from Example 10.4, find $P_{e,\text{bit}}$ for a (7,4) Hamming code, and compare with $P_{e,\text{uncoded}}$ with $\mathscr{E} = 4\!/7$. Ans.: $P_{e,\text{bit}} \approx 2 \times 10^{-7}$, $P_{e,\text{uncoded}} \approx 4 \times 10^{-7}$.

Convolutional Codes

Convolutional codes, also known as sequential or recurrent codes, differ from block codes in that the check digits are continuously interleaved in the coded bit stream rather than being grouped into words. The encoding/decoding procedure therefore

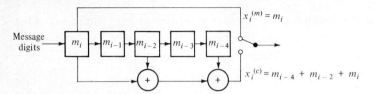

FIGURE 10.22
Convolutional encoder using shift register.

is a continuous process, eliminating the buffering or storage hardware required with block codes. The theory of convolutional codes is quite involved, but the principle can be demonstrated by a simple example.

Figure 10.22 is a convolutional encoder; it consists of a five-cell *shift register*, through which the message digits move from left to right, plus a modulo-2 adder and a switch. The switch alternately picks up the ith message digit $x_i^{(m)} = m_i$ and the ith check digit

$$x_i^{(c)} = m_{i-4} \oplus m_{i-2} \oplus m_i$$
$$= x_{i-4}^{(m)} \oplus x_{i-2}^{(m)} \oplus x_i^{(m)} \qquad (22)$$

The message digits are then shifted over one cell and the process is repeated. Hence, the transmitted sequence $x_1^{(m)}x_1^{(c)}x_2^{(m)}x_2^{(c)}\ldots$ has twice the bit rate of the incoming data, and $\mathscr{E} = \frac{1}{2}$. Such high redundancy is not a necessity, but most convolutional codes do have relatively low rate efficiency factors.

At the decoder we form the ith syndrome digit from the received sequence according to the rule

$$s_i = y_{i-4}^{(m)} \oplus y_{i-2}^{(m)} \oplus y_i^{(m)} \oplus y_i^{(c)} \qquad i \geq 5$$

where, owing to errors, $y_i^{(m)} = x_i^{(m)} \oplus e_i^{(m)}$, etc. Thus, from Eq. (22) it follows that

$$s_i = e_{i-4}^{(m)} \oplus e_{i-2}^{(m)} \oplus e_i^{(m)} \oplus e_i^{(c)} \qquad i \geq 5 \qquad (23a)$$

which checks parity in the sense that $s_i = 1$ if there is an odd number of errors while $s_i = 0$ otherwise. For the start-up transient, $1 \leq i \leq 4$,

$$\begin{array}{ll} s_1 = e_1^{(m)} \oplus e_1^{(c)} & s_3 = e_1^{(m)} \oplus e_3^{(m)} \oplus e_3^{(c)} \\ s_2 = e_2^{(m)} \oplus e_2^{(c)} & s_4 = e_2^{(m)} \oplus e_4^{(m)} \oplus e_4^{(c)} \end{array} \qquad (23b)$$

Figure 10.23 displays Eq. (23) in graphical form; e.g., the $\times$s in the first column indicate that $e_1^{(m)}$ appears in s_1, s_3, and s_5. Studying this figure reveals that if there are two or three 1s in $s_1 s_3 s_5$, then most likely $e_1^{(m)} = 1$, meaning that $y_1^{(m)}$ is erroneous and should be corrected; similarly, one should correct $y_2^{(m)}$ if there are more 1s than

	$e_1^{(m)}$	$e_1^{(c)}$	$e_2^{(m)}$	$e_2^{(c)}$	$e_3^{(m)}$	$e_3^{(c)}$	$e_4^{(m)}$	$e_4^{(c)}$	$e_5^{(m)}$	$e_5^{(c)}$	$e_6^{(m)}$	$e_6^{(c)}$
s_1	X	X										
s_2			X	X								
s_3	X				X	X						
s_4			X				X	X				
s_5	X				X				X	X		
s_6			X				X				X	X

FIGURE 10.23

0s in $s_2 s_4 s_6$, and so on. The student can verify that this algorithm, known as *threshold decoding*, will correct up to four successive errors (check digits included) providing that the following eight digits are error-free.

Threshold decoding is particularly effective for those channels where isolated *error bursts* due to impulse noise are the major problem. Another decoding algorithm for convolutional codes is the probabilistic or *sequential* method invented by Wozencraft. Because the theory of convolutional codes is not as well developed as that of block codes, it is difficult to make an accurate assessment of their relative merits.

10.4 PROBLEMS

10.1 (Sect. 10.1) Consider a system having $p(t) = \text{sinc } r(1 + \epsilon)t$, $0 < \epsilon \ll 1$, so the signaling rate r is slightly less than the synchronous rate $r(1 + \epsilon)$. The data is a sequence of $2M + 1$ alternating **1**s and **0**s, i.e., $A_k = (-1)^k A$, $k = 0, \pm 1, \pm 2, \ldots, \pm M$. Show that the ISI term in Eq. (3) at $m = 0$ is $[2A\epsilon/(1 + \epsilon)] \sum_{k=1}^{M} \text{sinc } k\epsilon \approx 2M\epsilon A$ if $M\epsilon \ll 1$.

10.2 (Sect. 10.1) A binary system suffers from ISI such that, in absence of noise, the values of $y(t_m)$ and their probabilities are as tabulated below when a **1** is sent; the table also applies when a **0** is sent, except that A is replaced by $-A$.

$$y(t_m): \quad A - \alpha \quad A \quad A + \alpha$$
$$P[y(t_m)]: \quad \tfrac{1}{4} \quad \tfrac{1}{2} \quad \tfrac{1}{4}$$

(a) Assuming gaussian noise, obtain an expression for P_e in terms of A, α, and σ.
(b) Evaluate P_e for $A/\sigma = 4.0$ when $\alpha/A = 0.05$ and 0.25. Compare with P_e when $\alpha = 0$.

10.3 (Sect. 10.1) A polar binary signal is sent via two different ideal channels, denoted a and b, to the same destination where the signals are combined as indicated in Fig. P10.1. This arrangement is called a *diversity* system. Channel a has an amplifier with

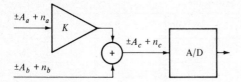

FIGURE P10.1.

adjustable voltage gain K, and n_a and n_b are independent gaussian variates with $\overline{n_a^2} = \sigma_a^2$, $\overline{n_b^2} = \sigma_b^2$.

(a) Find the value of K that maximizes A_c/σ_c and thereby minimizes P_e. Ans.: $K_{opt} = A_a \sigma_b^2 / A_b \sigma_a^2$.

(b) Taking $K = K_{opt}$, $A_b/\sigma_b = 3.0$, and $A_a/\sigma_a = \alpha(A_b/\sigma_b)$, plot P_e for the diversity system and for channel a alone as a function of α, $0 \le \alpha \le 2$.

10.4   (Sect. 10.1) Let $\pm a\Pi[(t - \tau/2)/\tau]$ plus white noise $n(t)$ be the input to an ideal integrate-and-dump filter. Show that the output at $t = \tau$ has $(A/\sigma)^2 = 2E_R/\eta$, so the performance does equal that of matched filtering. (*Hint*: Use $\sigma^2 = E\{[\int_0^\tau n(t)\, dt]^2\}$ and recall that $E[n(t_1)n(t_2)] = = R_n(t_1 - t_2) = (\eta/2)\,\delta(t_1 - t_2)$.)

10.5   (Sect. 10.1) Consider a polar binary system in the form of Fig. 10.1 with $a_k = \pm a$, $H_T(f) = 1$, $G(f) = \eta/2$, and $H_R(f) = P_s^*(f)H_c^*(f)$, where $P_s(f) = \mathscr{F}[p_s(t)]$, so the receiving filter is *matched* to the received pulse shape. Because this arrangement does not shape the output pulse $p(t)$ for ISI considerations, it is used only when $p_s(t)$ is timelimited (but not necessarily rectangular) with duration much less than $1/r$.

(a) By considering the transmission of one isolated pulse, show that $P(f)$ is real so $A = ap(0) = a\int_{-\infty}^{\infty} P(f)\, df$, and hence

$$\left(\frac{A}{\sigma}\right)^2 = \left[\frac{\int_{-\infty}^{\infty}|P_s(f)H_c(f)|^2 df}{\int_{-\infty}^{\infty}|P_s(f)|^2 df}\right]\left(\frac{2S_T}{\eta r}\right)$$

where $S_T = rE_T$ and E_T is the transmitted-pulse energy.

(b) Prove that this is equivalent to Eq. (14).

10.6   (Sect. 10.1) Use Eqs. (15a) and (16a) to find and sketch $P(f)$ and $p(t)$ for:

(a) $P_\beta(f) = (1/2\beta)\Pi(f/2\beta)$, $\beta = r/4$

(b) $P_\beta(f) = (1/\beta)\Lambda(f/\beta)$, $\beta = r/2$

10.7   (Sect. 10.1) Carry out all the details leading to Eqs. (17b) and (18a) starting from Eq. (17a).

10.8★   (Sect. 10.1) Consider a polar binary system with $r = 2 \times 10^4$, $p_s(t) = \Pi(2rt)$, $|H_c(f)| = 10^{-2}$, $G(f) = 10^{-10}(1 + 3 \times 10^{-4}|f|)^2$, and $p(t)$ per Eq. (18b) so $P(f) = (1/r)\cos^2(\pi f/2r)\,\Pi(f/2r)$.

(a) Find and sketch the amplitude ratio for the optimum terminal filters.

(b) Calculate the value of S_T needed so that $P_e = 10^{-6}$. Ans.: $S_T = 3.49$.

10.9★   (Sect. 10.1) Repeat Prob. 10.8 for a quaternary ($\mu = 4$) system with $r = 100$, $p_s(t) = \Pi(10rt)$, $|H_c(f)| = 10^{-3}/(1 + 32 \times 10^{-4}f^2)^{1/2}$, $G(f) = 10^{-10}$, and $p(t) = \text{sinc } rt$.

10.10★(Sect. 10.1) The terminal filters for a system have been optimized assuming white noise and a distortionless channel. However, it turns out that the channel does introduce some linear distortion so an equalizer with $H_{eq}(f) = K/H_C(f)$ is added after $H_R(f)$.

(a) Obtain an expression for the resulting $(A/\sigma)^2$ in terms of $H_C(f)$ and $P(f)$ at the output of the equalizer.

(b) Taking $P(f)$ as in Prob. 10.8, by what factor must S_T be increased to get the same error probability as if $H_C(f) = K_R$ when $H_C(f) = K_R/[1 + j(2f/r)]$ and $H_{eq}(f)$ is used?

10.11 (Sect. 10.1) Find the tap gains c_m for a 3-tap zero-forcing equalizer when $p(-1/r) = 0.4$, $p(0) = 1.0$, $p(1/r) = 0.2$, and $p(k/r) = 0$ for $|k| > 1$. Also compute $p_{eq}(t_k)$, $-4 \leq k \leq 4$.

10.12 (Sect. 10.1) Repeat Exercise 10.2 with an available bandwidth of 10 kHz, choosing parameters to minimize the power requirement.

10.13 (Sect. 10.2) Consider the *bandpass* pulse shape $p(t) = \text{sinc } Bt \cos 2\pi f_c t$, which has bandwidth B.

(a) Show that $p(k/2B) = 0$ for $k \neq 0$ if $f_c = MB/2$ with M being an odd integer. Sketch $p(t) - p(t - 1/2B)$ taking $M = 3$.

(b) Discuss the implications of this for digital modulation, including the advantages and disadvantages.

10.14 (Sect. 10.2) Integrate Eq. (6) over $0 \leq R \leq \infty$ to get

$$p_\phi(\phi) = \frac{A_k \cos \phi}{\sqrt{2\pi N}} e^{-(Ak2 \sin 2\phi)/2N} \left[1 - Q\left(\frac{A_k \cos \phi}{\sqrt{N}} \right) \right] + \frac{1}{2\pi} e^{-Ak2/2N}$$

and obtain Eq. (9) by taking $A_k^2/N \gg 1$. (*Hint*: Start with the change-of-variable $\lambda = (R - A_k \cos \phi)/\sqrt{N}$ and use the fact that $Q(-\kappa) = 1 - Q(\kappa)$.)

10.15 (Sect. 10.2) Consider a *trinary* ASK system with $A_k = 0$, A, and $2A$. Find P_e in terms of ρ assuming $\rho \gg 1$. (*Hint*: Justify the approximation $P_e \approx P_{e0}/3$ and note that $S_R = (5r/3)E$ where E is the energy in the middle-level pulse.)

10.16 (Sect. 10.2) Suppose a binary ASK signal is *coherently* detected, per Fig. 10.16, with the threshold at $A/2$. Find P_e and compare with Eqs. (15) and (21).

10.17 (Sect. 10.2) A binary FSK signal is transmitted over a radio channel having *Rayleigh fading* such that A is a slowly changing Rayleigh-distributed variate with $\overline{A^2} = A_0^2$, so $p(A) = (2A/A_0^2) \exp(- A^2/A_0^2)$, $A \geq 0$.

(a) Show that the average error probability is $E[P_e] = 1/[2 + (A_0^2/2N)]$.

(b) Discuss the value of a diversity arrangement as in Prob. 10.3 for this application.

10.18 (Sect. 10.2) Figure P10.2 is a coherent detection system for quaternary PSK with $\phi_k = 0°$, $90°$, $180°$, and $270°$. Ignoring noise, construct a table similar to Table 10.1 giving the values of v_A and v_B for each value of ϕ_k when the phase shifts are $\psi_A = 45°$ and $\psi_B = -45°$. Repeat for $\psi_A = 0°$ and $\psi_B = -90°$. Discuss these two alternatives, giving special consideration to the case where each value of ϕ_k represents two binary digits.

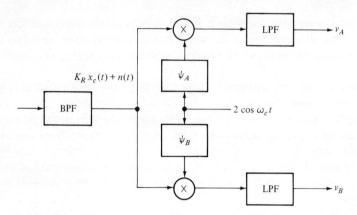

FIGURE P10.2.

10.19★(Sect. 10.2) Referring to the system in Prob. 10.18 with $\psi_A = 45°$ and $\psi_B = -45°$, write the noise $n(t)$ in the form of Eq. (1a) with $\theta = \psi_B$ and obtain v_A and v_B when noise is present. Show that $P(\text{no error}) = P(n_i \geq -A/\sqrt{2}$ and $n_q \geq -A/\sqrt{2})$ and from this derive $P_e = 1 - [1 - Q(\sqrt{\rho})]^2$, $\rho = A^2/2N$.

10.20★(Sect. 10.2) Differential encoding is to be used on a *baseband* polar binary system to protect against possible polarity inversions in transmission. Thus, if the kth message digit is a **1**, then $A_k = A_{k-1}$; if the kth digit is a **0**, then $A_k = -A_{k-1}$. The possible values of A_k are $\pm A$. Assuming gaussian noise, show that $P_e = 2[Q(A/\sigma) - Q^2(A/\sigma)]$ if the polarity of $A_k + n_k$ is determined using a zero-threshold A/D and then compared with the previously determined polarity of $A_{k-1} + n_{k-1}$. (*Hint*: An error occurs if there is one and only one polarity error in each pair.)

10.21★(Sect. 10.2) As an alternative to the detection scheme in Prob. 10.20, suppose the receiver has the form of Fig. P10.3. Show that the A/D must have *two* threshold levels—at $\pm A$—and hence $P_e = \tfrac{3}{2}Q(A/\sqrt{2}\,\sigma)$. Is this scheme better than the other?

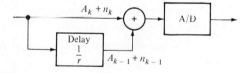

FIGURE P10.3.

10.22★(Sect. 10.2) Digital data with $\mu = 8$ modulates both the amplitude and phase of a carrier, giving $K_R x_c(t) = A_k \cos(\omega_c t + \phi_k)$ where $A_k = A$ and $2A$ and $\phi_k = 0°$, $90°$, $180°$, and $270°$.

(a) Draw a block diagram of the receiver using a coherent local oscillator and integrate-and-dump filters. (*Hint*: See Prob. 10.18.)

(b) Analyze the performance of this system in the presence of noise.

10.23 (Sect. 10.3) A certain code with $n = 7$ and $k = 3$ is simultaneously single-error-correcting and double-error-detecting. Assuming $\epsilon \ll 1$, calculate the following probabilities: a word has a corrected error; a word has detected but uncorrected errors; $P_{e,\text{word}}$; $P_{e,\text{bit}}$.

10.24 (Sect. 10.3) An ideal binary baseband system has $r = 10,000$ and $\sigma = 0.2$. It is desired to send data at a usable rate of 7,000 bits/s with parity-check coding for error detection such that $P_{\text{de}} \leq 0.08$. Find appropriate values for k and A, and calculate $P_{e,\text{bit}}$. *Ans.*: $k = 3$, $A \geq 0.41$, $P_{e,\text{bit}} \leq 0.0036$.

10.25 (Sect. 10.3) Consider a system combining parity-check *error detection* and *decision feedback* so that when a word is received with a detected error, the receiver tells the transmitter to repeat that word. If $\epsilon \ll 1$, the probability of more than one repetition is negligible. Including the effects of retransmission, find $P_{e,\text{bit}}$ and the ratio of total digits transmitted per message digit in terms of k and ϵ.

10.26★(Sect. 10.3) An analog method of error detection, known as *null-zone detection*, uses a no-decision zone centered at each threshold level such that if the signal plus noise falls in this zone, it is deemed a detected but uncorrected error.

    (*a*) Obtain expressions for P_{de} and P_e per bit for a polar binary baseband system with null-zone boundaries at $\pm \alpha A$.

    (*b*) Compare null-zone detection with error detection by parity-check coding when both systems have the same message bit rate.

10.27 (Sect. 10.3) Figure P10.4 illustrates the *square-array parity-check code* wherein $k = k_0^2$ message digits are arranged in a square whose rows and columns are checked by $2\sqrt{k}$ check digits. A transmission error in one message digit causes a row and column parity failure with the error at the intersection point, so the code is single-error correcting and double-error detecting.

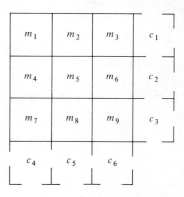

FIGURE P10.4.

    (*a*) Obtain expressions for $\mathscr{E}$ and $P_{e,\text{bit}}$ in terms of k_0.

    (*b*) Discuss what happens when there is one error in a check digit and when there are two or more errors.

10.28 (Sect. 10.3) Construct an **H** matrix for a single-error-correcting (6,3) systematic parity-check code. Write out the parity-check equations, the allowed code words, and the single-error syndromes. What happens when there are double errors?

10.29 (Sect. 10.3) The Hamming code in Example 10.5 provides error indications for the check digits as well as the message digits, even though correcting erroneous check digits is unnecessary. However, use Eq. (14) and the conditions on **H** to prove that any single-error-correcting (n,k) parity-check code must have $2^q \geq k + q + 1$, so the check-digit syndromes come automatically, whether or not they are used.

10.30 (Sect. 10.3) A (7,4) Hamming code is being considered for binary data transmission via FSK. Find the numerical condition on ρ such that the coding yields a lower error probability than signaling-rate reduction.

10.31 (Sect. 10.3) Figure P10.5 is the shift register for a *Hagelbarger code*, one of the first convolutional codes. The switch alternately picks up message digits and check digits, so $\mathscr{E} = \frac{1}{2}$. Neglecting the start-up transient, find the parity-check linkages and verify that six successive errors can be detected if the 19 previous digits are correct.

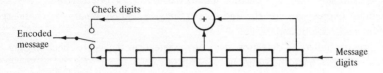

FIGURE P10.5

SIGNAL SPACE AND COMMUNICATION

By describing signals as vectors in a multidimensional space, the familiar relations and insights of geometry can be applied to numerous problems of signal analysis and communication system design. Some of the results have been drawn upon in the body of this text, particularly Schwarz's inequality and the scalar product concept. Here we derive those results and survey additional applications. The presentation is compact and informal, with a minimum of special notation.†

A.1 VECTOR SPACE THEORY

A *vector space* (or linear space) $\mathscr{S}$ is a set of elements called vectors having the property that they may always be combined linearly. Thus, for any vectors v and w in $\mathscr{S}$ and any scalars α and β there is another vector

$$z = \alpha v + \beta w \qquad (1)$$

which is also in $\mathscr{S}$. In other words, the set of all elements in $\mathscr{S}$ is *closed under linear combination*. Similarly, if $\mathscr{P}$ is a subset of elements of $\mathscr{S}$ and is also closed under linear combination, then we say that $\mathscr{P}$ is a *subspace* of $\mathscr{S}$.

---

† See Frederick and Carlson (1971, chaps. 5 and 12) or Wozencraft and Jacobs (1965, chaps. 4 and 5) for more details.

The vectors may be functions of time, including complex functions, while the scalars are numbers, possibly complex. By way of example, the set of all energy signals $v(t)$ having $\int_{-\infty}^{\infty} |v(t)|^2\, dt < \infty$ constitutes a vector space since it is closed under linear combination, and the subset of energy signals restricted by $v(t) = 0$ for $t < 0$ would be a subspace. On the other hand, the set of all signals constrained by $0 \leq v(t) \leq 1$ is not closed under linear combination and does not qualify as a vector space.

Vector addition and scalar multiplication in $\mathscr{S}$ are defined in the usual fashion and, as implied by Eq. (1), there is a null vector θ such that $v + \theta = v$, $0 \cdot v = \theta$, etc. Hence, every subspace of a vector space includes the origin.

Scalar Product and Norm

We will impose two further conditions on vector spaces used in signal analysis, namely, that they by normed and possess a scalar product. The *scalar product* is a complex number associated with any pair of vectors v and w in $\mathscr{S}$, symbolized by $\langle v,w \rangle$, with the following properties:

$$\langle v,\theta \rangle = 0 \tag{2}$$

$$\langle v,w \rangle = \langle w,v \rangle^* \tag{3}$$

$$\langle \alpha v, \beta w \rangle = \alpha \beta^* \langle v,w \rangle \tag{4}$$

$$\langle v + w, x + y \rangle = \langle v,x \rangle + \langle v,y \rangle + \langle w,x \rangle + \langle w,y \rangle \tag{5}$$

The *norm* of any vector v is a real number defined by

$$\|v\| = \langle v,v \rangle^{1/2} \tag{6}$$

with the properties

$$\|v\| \geq 0 \tag{7a}$$

$$\|v\| = 0 \quad \text{only if} \quad v = \theta \tag{7b}$$

$$\|\alpha v\| = |\alpha|\,\|v\| \tag{8}$$

Formally, the above conditions characterize a pre-Hilbert space. Intuitively, they give us measures of vector length (the norm) and relative angle (the scalar product). These interpretations are developed subsequently. We also postpone giving explicit formulas for $\langle v,w \rangle$ and $\|v\|$ since they depend on the particular space in question. Even so, the analytic power of vector space theory resides in the fact that the relationships considered next apply to any vector space.

Inequalities and Orthogonality

Using Eqs. (2) to (8) we can derive several important equations. To begin with, consider $v + \beta w$ where v and w are in $\mathscr{S}$, β is an arbitrary scalar, and $w \neq \theta$. Applying Eqs. (6), (5), (4), and (3) sequentially yields

$$\|v + \beta w\|^2 = \langle v + \beta w, v + \beta w \rangle$$
$$= \|v\|^2 + \beta^* \langle v,w \rangle + \beta \langle v,w \rangle^* + |\beta|^2 \|w\|^2 \tag{9}$$

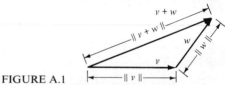

FIGURE A.1

Setting $\beta = -\langle v,w\rangle/\|w\|^2$ and noting from Eq. (7a) that $\|v + \beta w\|^2 \geq 0$ for any β, we have $\|v\|^2 - (|\langle v,w\rangle|/\|w\|)^2 \geq 0$ or

$$|\langle v,w\rangle| \leq \|v\|\|w\| \qquad (10a)$$

which is *Schwarz's inequality*. Equality clearly holds in the trivial case where $v = \theta$ or $w = \theta$; otherwise, it follows from Eq. (7b) that

$$|\langle v,w\rangle| = \|v\|\|w\| \qquad \text{only if} \quad v = \alpha w \qquad (10b)$$

where α is arbitrary. One can also readily show from Eqs. (9) and (10) that

$$\|v + w\| \leq \|v\| + \|w\| \qquad (11)$$

called the *triangle inequality*.

Finally, if $\langle v,w\rangle = 0$—so $\langle v,w\rangle^* = 0$—then

$$\|v + w\|^2 = \|v\|^2 + \|w\|^2 \qquad \text{if} \quad \langle v,w\rangle = 0 \qquad (12)$$

Because Eq. (12) resembles the pythagorean theorem of geometry, we say that v and w are *orthogonal* (perpendicular) when their scalar product equals zero. Therefore, taking the norm as the measure of "length" in vector space, Eqs. (11) and (12) are identical to the common relationships for oblique and right triangles whose sides are v, w, and $v + w$, Fig. A.1. When Schwarz's inequality is viewed in this light, the scalar product is seen to be equivalent to the familiar dot product and thus may be interpreted as a measure of relative "angle." That interpretation is enhanced by considering vector projections.

Vector Projections

Figure A.2 shows two vectors and the *orthogonal projection* v_w of v on w defined by the properties $v_w = \alpha w$ and $\langle v - v_w, w\rangle = 0$, equivalent to dropping a perpendicular from v to w. Combining these properties gives

$$v_w = \frac{\langle v,w\rangle}{\|w\|^2} w \qquad (13)$$

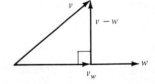

FIGURE A.2
The projection of v on w.

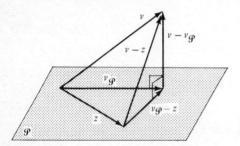

FIGURE A.3
Vector construction for the projection theorem.

so $\langle v,w \rangle$ is proportional to the cosine of the "angle" between v and w; i.e., v_w equals zero when the vectors are orthogonal and it is maximum when they are collinear (proportional). Presumably, $\|v - v_w\|$ is the shortest "distance" between the tip of v and any point along w.

Generalizing, if v is in $\mathscr{S}$ and $v_{\mathscr{P}}$ is its projection on the subspace $\mathscr{P}$, then $v - v_{\mathscr{P}}$ is the shortest "distance" between v and any point in $\mathscr{P}$. This is a rough statement of the important and versatile *projection theorem*. More precisely stated, $v_{\mathscr{P}}$ is a unique vector in $\mathscr{P}$ such that, for any vector $z \neq v_{\mathscr{P}}$ in $\mathscr{P}$,

$$\langle v - v_{\mathscr{P}}, z \rangle = 0 \qquad (14)$$

$$\|v - v_{\mathscr{P}}\| < \|v - z\| \qquad (15)$$

Equation (14) defines $v_{\mathscr{P}}$ while Eq. (15) is the projection theorem. The theorem is easily proved using the construction diagramed in Fig. A.3 where $v - v_{\mathscr{P}}$ and $v_{\mathscr{P}} - z$ are orthogonal (by definition) and $v - z = (v - v_{\mathscr{P}}) + (v_{\mathscr{P}} - z)$. Applying Eq. (12) then yields $\|v - z\|^2 = \|v - v_{\mathscr{P}}\|^2 + \|v_{\mathscr{P}} - z\|^2 > \|v - v_{\mathscr{P}}\|^2$.

Basis Vectors

Closing this section, we introduce the concept of basis vectors. Although not all vector spaces have basis vectors, it further enhances our geometric interpretations when they do.

Suppose a space includes a set of K linearly independent† vectors ϕ_k, $k = 1, 2, \ldots, K$, such that any vector v in the space is expressible in the form

$$v = \sum_{k=1}^{K} \alpha_k \phi_k \qquad (16)$$

We say that the space has K *dimensions*, symbolized by $\mathscr{S}_K$, and that the ϕ_k are *basis vectors spanning* $\mathscr{S}_K$. The scalars α_k in Eq. (16) are the *coordinates* of v in the ϕ basis and are uniquely determined given v and ϕ_k.

However, the basis for $\mathscr{S}_K$ is not unique, and it is advantageous to further require that the ϕ_k be *orthonormal*, i.e.,

$$\langle \phi_k, \phi_m \rangle = \begin{cases} 1 & m = k \\ 0 & m \neq k \end{cases} \qquad (17)$$

† Linear independence means that none of the ϕ_k can be formed by a linear combination of the others.

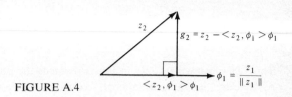

FIGURE A.4

which ensures linear independence. Moreover, with this stipulation the basis vectors are directly analogous to the unit vectors of ordinary two- and three-dimensional spaces in that they have unit norm (length) and are mutually orthogonal (perpendicular). Sets of functions $\phi_k(t)$ that obey Eq. (17) include harmonically related trigonometric functions, Legendre polynomials, and Walsh functions,† to name a few.

Equation (17) imposes no serious limitation since the *Gram-Schmidt procedure* can be used to generate an orthonormal set spanning any set of vectors, as follows. Given the set z_k, $k = 1, 2, \ldots, K$, an equivalent orthonormal basis is

$$\phi_k = \frac{g_k}{\|g_k\|} \qquad (18a)$$

where

$$g_1 = z_1$$

$$g_k = z_k - \sum_{m=1}^{k-1} \langle z_k, \phi_m \rangle \phi_m \qquad 2 \leq k \leq K \qquad (18b)$$

Note from Eq. (13) that $\langle z_k, \phi_m \rangle \phi_m$ is precisely the projection of z_k along ϕ_m since $\|\phi_m\|^2 = 1$. Thus, g_k is orthogonal to $\phi_1, \phi_2, \ldots, \phi_{k-1}$ as illustrated in Fig. A.4 for $k = 2$. If it happens that the z_k are not linearly independent, then one or more of the ϕ_k will equal θ, meaning that the dimensionality is less than K.

If we have an orthonormal basis spanning $\mathscr{S}_K$, we can express the scalar product of any two vectors v and w in terms of their coordinates, say α_k and β_k. Introducing a dummy index m,

$$\langle v, w \rangle = \left\langle \left(\sum_{k=1}^{K} \alpha_k \phi_k \right), \left(\sum_{m=1}^{K} \beta_m \phi_m \right) \right\rangle$$

$$= \sum_{k=1}^{K} \alpha_k \left(\sum_{m=1}^{K} \beta_m^* \langle \phi_k, \phi_m \rangle \right)$$

$$= \sum_{k=1}^{K} \alpha_k \beta_k^* \qquad (19)$$

where we have used Eqs. (5), (4), and (17), the latter reducing the sum on m to one term, β_k^*. Setting $\beta_k = \alpha_k$ shows that $\langle v, v \rangle = \sum \alpha_k \alpha_k^*$ or

$$\|v\| = \left(\sum_{k=1}^{K} |\alpha_k|^2 \right)^{1/2} \qquad (20)$$

which generalizes the euclidean norm to the case of K complex-valued coordinates.

† See Harmuth (1969) for a discussion of Walsh functions in the context of communication.

As to the coordinates per se, they are easily found from v and ϕ_k, namely,

$$\alpha_k = \langle v, \phi_k \rangle \qquad k = 1, 2, \ldots, K \tag{21}$$

Thus, each component of v in Eq. (16) equals the projection of v along the corresponding basis vector, just as conventional vectors can be decomposed into their projections along the axes. Equation (21) follows from Eq. (19) by replacing w with ϕ_m so $\beta_m = 1$ and $\beta_k = 0$, $k \neq m$. Finally, if v is in any space of which $\mathscr{P}_J$ is a J-dimensional subspace spanned by ϕ_k, $1 \leq k \leq J$, then the projection of v on $\mathscr{P}_J$ equals

$$v_{\mathscr{P}} = \sum_{k=1}^{J} \alpha_k \phi_k \tag{22}$$

where Eq. (21) still applies since the α_k must be such that $\langle v - v_{\mathscr{P}}, \phi_k \rangle = 0$ for $k = 1, 2, \ldots, J$.

A.2 SIGNAL SPACE APPLICATIONS

Armed with the foregoing theory we proceed to its applications and interpretations in signal analysis. This is accomplished by defining classes or sets of signals that are closed under linear combination and, for each class, determining an appropriate scalar-product formula. One familiar class will be examined in some detail, while the results for other useful classes are summarized.

Periodic Power Signals

Consider the set of all signals $v(t)$ that have the same period T_0 and well-defined average power. This set constitutes a vector space and the scalar product may be taken to be

$$\langle v, w \rangle = \frac{1}{T_0} \int_{T_0} v(t) w^*(t) \, dt \tag{1}$$

It is readily confirmed that Eq. (1) has the necessary properties, Eqs. (2) to (5), Sect. A.1. The squared norm then equals the average power,

$$\|v\|^2 = \frac{1}{T_0} \int_{T_0} |v(t)|^2 \, dt = P_v \tag{2}$$

Thus, the null signal $\theta(t)$ is a periodic signal with $P_\theta = 0$; for all practical purposes, this implies that $\theta(t) = 0$, $-\infty < t < \infty$. In passing, we also note that

$$\bar{v} = \langle v, 1 \rangle = \frac{1}{T_0} \int_{T_0} v(t) \, dt \tag{3}$$

is the average value of $v(t)$.

Any two signals in this set are collinear if they are proportional, e.g., $w(t) = \alpha v(t)$. At the other extreme, drawing upon the fact that $\|v\|^2 = P_v$ and Eq. (12), Sect. A.1, orthogonal signals have the property of superposition of average power, i.e.,

$$P_{v+w} = P_v + P_w \qquad \text{if} \quad \langle v, w \rangle = 0 \tag{4}$$

Between these extremes, the projection of v along w is

$$v_w(t) = \frac{\langle v, w \rangle}{\|w\|^2} \, w(t) \qquad (5)$$

which tells how much of one signal, $v(t)$, is "contained" in another, $w(t)$.

An important subspace is spanned by the orthonormal basis

$$\phi_k(t) = e^{j2\pi kt/T_0} \qquad k = 0, \pm 1, \pm 2, \ldots, \pm K \qquad (6)$$

the dimensionality being $2K + 1$. If we denote $\tilde{v}(t)$ as the projection of $v(t)$ on this subspace, then

$$\tilde{v}(t) = \sum_{k=-K}^{K} \alpha_k \phi_k(t) = \sum_{k=-K}^{K} \alpha_k e^{j2\pi kt/T_0} \qquad (7a)$$

where, from Eq. (21), Sect. A.1,

$$\alpha_k = \langle v, \phi_k \rangle = \frac{1}{T_0} \int_{T_0} v(t) e^{-j2\pi kt/T_0} \, dt \qquad (7b)$$

Equation (7a) will be recognized as the first $2K + 1$ terms of the *exponential Fourier series* and α_k, the coordinates of $\tilde{v}(t)$, are the usual series coefficients. From the projection theorem it can be said that $\tilde{v}(t)$ is a *least-square-error* approximation to $v(t)$ in that the error signal $v(t) - \tilde{v}(t)$ has minimum norm.

A very sophisticated mathematical theorem (omitted here) shows that in the limit as $K \to \infty$, $\tilde{v}(t) \to v(t)$ in the sense that $\|v - \tilde{v}\|^2 \to 0$, called *convergence in the mean*. Correspondingly, the subspace becomes the entire space, with infinite but countable dimensionality. Then, drawing upon Eq. (20), Sect. A.1,

$$P_v = \|v\|^2 = \sum_{k=-\infty}^{\infty} |\alpha_k|^2 \qquad (8)$$

which is Parseval's power theorem. We see, therefore, that signal space concepts provide the theoretical underpinning of the Fourier series.

Nonperiodic Energy Signals

The set of all nonperiodic energy signals having well-defined energy defines a signal space. Similar to Eq. (1), the scalar product is

$$\langle v, w \rangle = \int_{-\infty}^{\infty} v(t) w^*(t) \, dt \qquad (9)$$

and orthogonality means superposition of energy since $\|v\|^2 = E_v$, etc. Although this space lacks a countable basis, we can say that it is spanned by

$$\phi_f(t) = e^{j2\pi ft} \qquad -\infty < f < \infty$$

where f is a continuous variable (frequency) rather than an index. Then $v(t)$ has the co-ordinate function

$$V(f) = \langle v, \phi_f \rangle = \int_{-\infty}^{\infty} v(t) e^{-j2\pi ft} \, dt \qquad (10a)$$

such that

$$v(t) = \int_{-\infty}^{\infty} V(f) e^{j2\pi ft} \, df \qquad (10b)$$

Needless to say, these are the *Fourier transform integrals*.

As remarked in Sect. 2.6, $v(t)$ and $w(t)$ are orthogonal if they are either disjoint (non-overlapping) in time or disjoint in frequency. The latter stems from Eq. (13), Sect. 2.3, written in our present notation as

$$\langle v, w \rangle = \langle V, W \rangle = \int_{-\infty}^{\infty} V(f) W^*(f) \, df \qquad (11)$$

Thus, the time-domain and frequency-domain scalar products are equal.

Bandlimited Signals and Time-Discrete Signals

Consider the space defined by

$$\phi_k(t) = \sqrt{2W} \, \text{sinc} \, (2Wt - k) \qquad k = 0, \pm 1, \pm 2, \ldots \qquad (12)$$

so any $v(t)$ in this space must be *bandlimited* in W because

$$\Phi_k(f) = \mathcal{F}[\phi_k(t)] = \begin{cases} \dfrac{1}{\sqrt{2W}} \, e^{-j2\pi kf/2W} & |f| < W \\ 0 & |f| > W \end{cases} \qquad (13)$$

i.e., the basis functions are bandlimited as well as orthonormal.

Observing that the $\phi_k(t)$ are energy signals, application of Eqs. (11) and (13) yields the coordinates of $v(t)$ as

$$\alpha_k = \langle v, \phi_k \rangle = \langle V, \Phi_k \rangle = \frac{1}{\sqrt{2W}} \, v\left(\frac{k}{2W}\right) \qquad (14)$$

Therefore,

$$v(t) = \sum_{k=-\infty}^{\infty} \alpha_k \phi_k(t) = \sum_{k=-\infty}^{\infty} v\left(\frac{k}{2W}\right) \text{sinc} \, (2Wt - k) \qquad (15)$$

which expands $v(t)$ in terms of its *sample values* at $t = k/2W$. The sampling theorem says that Eq. (15) holds for any bandlimited energy signal, as proved in Chap. 8. Incidentally, note that the space containing such signals has an infinite but countable dimensionality while the space for nonbandlimited energy signals has an uncountable dimensionality.

Having mentioned sampling theory, the case of *time-discrete* signals comes naturally to mind—i.e., signals defined only at discrete points in time. Therefore, consider the set of all sequences $v(m)$, $m = 0, \pm 1, \pm 2, \ldots, \pm M$, for which

$$\frac{1}{K} \sum_{m=-M}^{M} |v(m)|^2 < \infty \qquad K = 2M + 1$$

An appropriate scalar product is

$$\langle v,w \rangle = \frac{1}{K} \sum_{m=-M}^{M} v(m)w^*(m) \qquad (16)$$

and $\|v\|^2$ may be interpreted as the mean-square value of the sequence $v(m)$.

The space so defined has precisely K dimensions and is spanned by

$$\phi_k(m) = e^{j2\pi km/K} \qquad k = 0, \pm 1, \ldots, \pm M$$

The corresponding coordinates of $v(m)$ are

$$\alpha_k = \frac{1}{K} \sum_{m=-M}^{M} v(m)e^{-j2\pi km/K} \qquad (17)$$

which is one form of the *discrete Fourier transform*, the theory behind the fast Fourier transform (FFT).

We have now covered most of the important types of signal spaces—with the exception of random signals—so this section closes with two specific problems that are easily tackled using the concepts developed here. The next section treats a more advanced problem.

Waveform Synthesis

Suppose we desire a system capable of generating any energy signal from a given set $z_m(t)$, $m = 1, 2, \ldots, M$. If the $z_m(t)$ are not linearly independent, the Gram-Schmidt procedure leads to an efficient system design, as follows.

Let $\mathscr{S}_K$ be the space containing all $z_m(t)$, so $K \leq M$ and the equality holds only when the signals are linearly independent. An orthonormal basis $\phi_k(t)$ is found from $z_m(t)$ using Eq. (18), Sect. A.1, such that

$$z_m(t) = \sum_{k=1}^{K} \alpha_{mk} \phi_k(t) \qquad \alpha_{mk} = \langle z_m, \phi_k \rangle \qquad (18)$$

where the formula for α_{mk} follows from Eq. (21), Sect. A.1, and the scalar product is calculated per Eq. (9).

Implementation of Eq. (18) entails an impulse generator, K filters having $\phi_k(t)$ as their impulse responses, and K adjustable gains to provide the coefficients α_{mk}. The complete waveform synthesizer is diagramed in Fig. A.5. If $K \ll M$, this method requires substantially less hardware than building a separate generator for each of the M signals. Equally important, Eq. (18) is a useful signal model in the study of digital communication.

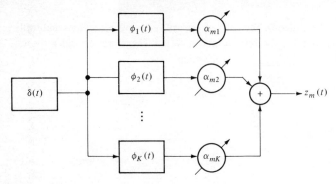

FIGURE A.5
Waveform synthesizer.

Linear Approximations

Given a signal $v(t)$ and a set of K signals $w_k(t)$ over some time interval, say $0 \leq t \leq T$, it is possible to construct a linear approximation to $v(t)$ in the form

$$\tilde{v}(t) = \alpha_0 + \sum_{k=1}^{K} \alpha_k \, w_k(t) \qquad 0 \leq t \leq T \qquad (19)$$

with the property that $\tilde{v}(t)$ is a least-square-error approximation; i.e., $\|v - \tilde{v}\|^2$ is minimized. If it happens that the $w_k(t)$ are orthogonal, the task becomes trivial. If not, one might be inclined to generate an orthonormal set using the Gram-Schmidt procedure. An equivalent but more direct method is presented below.

First we take the scalar product as

$$\langle v, w \rangle = \frac{1}{T} \int_0^T v(t)w^*(t) \, dt$$

so that the average value of $v(t)$ is $\bar{v} = \langle v, 1 \rangle$ and, likewise, $\langle v, \beta \rangle = \beta^* \bar{v}$ for any scalar β. Next we recall that $v(t) - \tilde{v}(t)$ must be orthogonal to every term on the right of Eq. (19) since those terms, in effect, define the approximation subspace—whether or not they are orthogonal. Thus, α_0 must satisfy $\langle v - \tilde{v}, \alpha_0 \rangle = \langle (v - \alpha_0 - \sum \alpha_k w_k), \alpha_0 \rangle = 0$, which yields $\alpha_0 = \bar{v} - \sum \alpha_k \bar{w}_k$. Not surprisingly, the constant α_0 accounts for any nonzero average values, and Eq. (19) becomes

$$\tilde{v}(t) = \bar{v} + \sum_{k=1}^{K} \alpha_k [w_k(t) - \bar{w}_k] \qquad (20)$$

where the α_k are yet to be determined.

Turning to that calculation, we again use the orthogonality condition, this time in the form

$$\langle v - \tilde{v}, \alpha_m w_m \rangle = \left\langle \left[(v - \bar{v}) - \sum_k \alpha_k (w_k - \bar{w}_k) \right], \alpha_m w_m \right\rangle$$

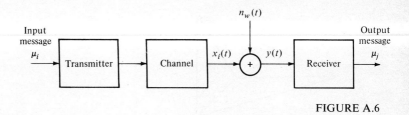

FIGURE A.6

Upon simplification there results a set of K simultaneous equations

$$\sum_{k=1}^{K} \langle w_k - \bar{w}_k, w_m - \bar{w}_m \rangle \alpha_k = \langle v - \bar{v}, w_m - \bar{w}_m \rangle \qquad m = 1, 2, \ldots, K \qquad (21)$$

which can be solved for α_k. In the special case of $K = 1$, the complete approximation is

$$\tilde{v}(t) = \bar{v} + \frac{\langle v - \bar{v}, w - \bar{w} \rangle}{\|w - \bar{w}\|^2} [w(t) - \bar{w}] \qquad (22)$$

The above method also applies to random signals or experimental data, the scalar product being taken as $\langle v, w \rangle = \mathbf{E}[vw^*]$. In that context it is known as *linear regression* analysis.

A.3 DETECTION THEORY

Shannon (1949) exploited signal space concepts to find the capacity of a continuous channel. Subsequently, Arthurs and Dym (1962) and others used similar geometric interpretations to study the detection of digital signals corrupted by noise, obtaining therefrom the implementation of a system whose performance approaches Shannon's limit. This section serves as an introduction to a small but important slice of detection theory based on their original work.

With reference to Fig. A.6, let an information source select a message μ_i from a set of M equiprobable messages. The message is transmitted as a real waveform, producing $x_i(t)$ at the receiver; $x_i(t)$ has duration T, say $0 \le t \le T$, and energy E_i. It is contaminated by additive zero-mean gaussian white noise $n_w(t)$ with $G_{n_w}(f) = \eta/2$. The receiver operates on $y(t) = x_i(t) + n_w(t)$ and determines that message μ_j has been sent, which may or may not be correct. It is assumed that the receiver has available stored copies of the uncontaminated signals and their corresponding messages. The detection problem then is this: How should the receiver operate on $y(t)$ so as to minimize the probability of error P_e?

Observe that we have assumed equiprobable messages and gaussian white noise. Proper source encoding can ensure the former and we will eventually make allowance for nonwhite gaussian noise, so the problem statement is reasonably broad. Moreover, there are no built-in preconceptions about the structure of the receiver aside from the stored-copies assumption. The signal space formulation of the problem ultimately will guide specific receiver implementation.

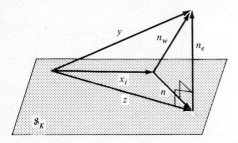

FIGURE A.7
Projection of $y = x_i + n_w$ on $\mathscr{S}_K$.

Signal-Space Formulation

Drawing upon the Gram-Schmidt procedure, there is a space $\mathscr{S}_K$ of dimensionality $K \leq M$ that contains all the possible signal waveforms, $x_i(t)$, $i = 1, 2, \ldots, M$. Let $\mathscr{S}_K$ be spanned by an orthonormal basis such that

$$x_i(t) = \sum_{k=1}^{K} x_{ik} \phi_k(t) \qquad (1a)$$

where

$$x_{ik} = \langle x_i, \phi_k \rangle = \int_{-\infty}^{\infty} x_i(t) \phi_k(t) \, dt \qquad (1b)$$

using the energy scalar product with $\phi_k(t)$ being real in view of the fact that all $x_i(t)$ are real. (Consequently, complex-conjugate terms will not appear anywhere.)

Because the noise is white and not bandlimited, its sample functions $n_w(t)$ are not contained in $\mathscr{S}_K$. However, we can decompose it into two terms

$$n_w(t) = n(t) + n_e(t) \qquad (2)$$

of which $n_e(t)$ is outside $\mathscr{S}_K$, i.e.,

$$\langle n_e, \phi_k \rangle = 0 \qquad k = 1, 2, \ldots, K \qquad (3)$$

so $n_e(t)$ may be termed the extraneous or *irrelevant* noise. The remaining term $n(t)$ is in $\mathscr{S}_K$ and

$$n(t) = \sum_{k=1}^{K} n_k \phi_k(t) \qquad (4a)$$

$$n_k = \langle n, \phi_k \rangle = \langle n_w, \phi_k \rangle \qquad (4b)$$

since, from Eqs. (2) and (3), $\langle n, \phi_k \rangle = \langle n_w, \phi_k \rangle - \langle n_e, \phi_k \rangle = \langle n_w, \phi_k \rangle$.

These manipulations lead us to the vector diagram of Fig. A.7 where, for convenience, $\mathscr{S}_K$ is represented by a plane. The signal vector x_i lies in the plane as does the noise vector n, while n_e is orthogonal to it. We define a new vector

$$z \triangleq y - n_e = x_i + n \qquad (5)$$

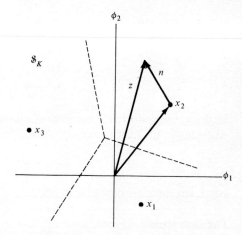

FIGURE A.8
Decision regions in $\mathscr{S}_K$; $K = 2$, $M = 3$.

which is seen to be the *projection* of $y = x_i + n_w$ on the space $\mathscr{S}_K$. This definition is particularly valuable, together with Eq. (2), for it allows us to analyze the detection problem entirely in terms of vectors in $\mathscr{S}_K$.

Figure A.8 illustrates this last point by showing $\mathscr{S}_K$ for the case of $K = 2$ and $M = 3$. The three dots represent the tips of the noise-free signal vectors x_1, x_2, and x_3, and z is a typical projection vector when x_2 is sent and contaminated by noise n. Intuitively, the diagram suggests that the receiver should choose the signal vector whose tip is closest to the tip of z, i.e., choose (or detect) μ_j if

$$\|z - x_j\| < \|z - x_i\| \qquad \text{all} \quad i \neq j \tag{6}$$

It will be shown that this is indeed the optimum detection strategy under the stated assumptions. Corresponding to Eq. (6), $\mathscr{S}_K$ may be divided into M *decision regions* bounded by the dashed lines in Fig. A.8.

The decision rule (6) involves vector lengths or norms. We know that $\|x_i\|^2 = E_i$, but $n(t)$ is a random variable whose properties need to be found before going on.

From Eq. (4a) the norm squared of $n(t)$ is

$$\|n\|^2 = \sum_{k=1}^{K} n_k^2 \tag{7}$$

and, since Eq. (4b) is a linear operation on a gaussian variate, the coordinates n_k are also gaussian with $\bar{n}_k = \langle \bar{n}_w, \phi_k \rangle = 0$. We turn then to the variance and the question of statistical dependence by considering

$$E[n_k n_m] = E\left[\int_{-\infty}^{\infty} n_w(t)\phi_k(t)\, dt \int_{-\infty}^{\infty} n_w(\lambda)\phi_m(\lambda)\, d\lambda \right]$$

$$= \int_{-\infty}^{\infty} \int_{-\infty}^{\infty} E[n_w(t)n_w(\lambda)]\phi_k(t)\phi_m(\lambda)\, dt\, d\lambda$$

Now $E[n_w(t)n_w(\lambda)] = R_{n_w}(t - \lambda)$ and the autocorrelation function of white noise is $R_{n_w}(\tau) = (\eta/2) \, \delta(\tau)$; hence, after some simple manipulations,

$$E[n_k \, n_m] = \begin{cases} \dfrac{\eta}{2} & m = k \\ 0 & m \neq k \end{cases} \tag{8}$$

so the n_k are *statistically independent* gaussian variates with zero mean and variance $\eta/2$. Accordingly, the joint probability density function of the noise vector n is

$$p_n(n) = p_{n_1}(n_1)p_{n_2}(n_2) \cdots p_{n_K}(n_K)$$
$$= (\pi\eta)^{-K/2}e^{-\|n\|^2/\eta} \tag{9}$$

which has spherical symmetry in $\mathscr{S}_K$.

Decision Rule

To analytically support the intuitive decision rule, we note that the detection error probability is minimized if μ_j is the most probable intended message given the received vector z, i.e.,

$$P(\mu_j|z) > P(\mu_i|z) \qquad \text{all} \quad i \neq j \tag{10}$$

Such conditional probabilities can be written using Bayes' mixed rule in the form

$$P(\mu_i|z) = P(\mu_i) \frac{p_z(z|\mu_i)}{p_z(z)} \tag{11}$$

where $p_z(z|\mu_i)$ is the conditional PDF of z given that x_i was sent, etc., and $P(\mu_i) = 1/M$ by prior assumption. Since $z = x_i + n$, $n = z - x_i$ and

$$p_z(z|\mu_i) = p_n(z - x_i) = (\pi\eta)^{-K/2}e^{-\|z - x_i\|^2/\eta} \tag{12}$$

Therefore, inserting Eqs. (12) and (11) into Eq. (10) and taking the logarithm of both sides yields

$$\|z - x_j\|^2 < \|z - x_i\|^2 \qquad \text{all} \quad i \neq j \tag{13}$$

all other terms canceling out. Equation (13) is equivalent to Eq. (6) because norms are non-negative by definition.

  Unfortunately, we cannot design a receiver directly from Eq. (13); the receiver must operate on $y(t) = x_i(t) + n_w(t)$ rather than the projection vector z. However,

$$\|z - x_i\|^2 = E_z - 2\langle z, x_i \rangle + E_i$$

and

$$\langle z, x_i \rangle = \langle y - n_e, x_i \rangle = \langle y, x_i \rangle$$

Substituting these in Eq. (13) and dropping any terms independent of i gives the usable test statistic or *decision function*

$$\mathscr{D}_i = \langle y, x_i \rangle - \tfrac{1}{2}E_i \tag{14}$$

and the decision rule becomes: Choose μ_j such that $\mathscr{D}_j > \mathscr{D}_i$ for all $i \neq j$. This is an optimum decision rule in the sense of minimizing P_e.

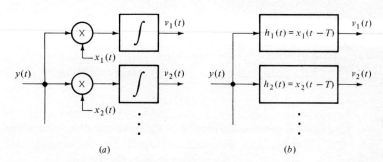

FIGURE A.9
Receiver implementation using: (a) correlators; (b) matched filters.

Receiver Implementation

We implement Eq. (14) by observing that $x_i(t) = 0$ for $t < 0$ or $t > T$ so

$$\langle y, x_i \rangle = \int_0^T y(t) x_i(t) \, dt \qquad (15)$$

Therefore, per Fig. A.9a, the receiver should multiply $y(t)$ by the stored copies of each possible $x_i(t)$ and integrate, producing M parallel outputs $v_i(T) = \langle y, x_i \rangle$. This process is called *correlation detection*. Alternately, the bank of correlators can be replaced by a bank of *matched filters*, the impulse responses being $h_i(t) = x_i(T - t)$, Fig. A.9b. Then

$$v_i(t) = [y(t)] * [h_i(t)] = \int_0^T y(\lambda) x_i(T - t + \lambda) \, d\lambda \qquad (16)$$

and again $v_i(T) = \langle y, x_i \rangle$. Either way, the operation $\langle y, x_i \rangle$ projects y along x_i and strips off the irrelevant noise $n_e(t)$.

Figure A.10 shows a complete receiver utilizing correlators or matched filters. The

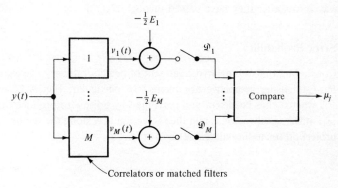

FIGURE A.10
Complete receiver for optimum detection.

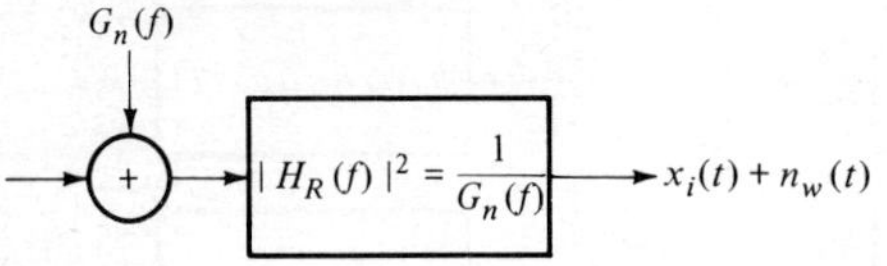

$G_n(f)$

$$|H_R(f)|^2 = \frac{1}{G_n(f)}$$

$x_i(t) + n_w(t)$

FIGURE A.11
Prewhitening filter.

incoming signal is processed in parallel by the correlator/filter bank whose outputs are biased by $-\frac{1}{2}E_i$. (The bias may be omitted if all signals have the same energy.) Sampling at $t = T$ gives $v_i(T) - \frac{1}{2}E_i = \mathscr{D}_i$ and the receiver chooses the message based on the largest $\mathscr{D}_i$.

If the signals $x_i(t)$ are not linearly independent and $K \ll M$, a more efficient design is based on writing

$$\langle y, x_i \rangle = \sum_{k=1}^{K} y_k x_{ik} \qquad y_k = \langle y, \phi_k \rangle \qquad (17)$$

Thus, y_k is generated from $y(t)$ and $\phi_k(t)$ by correlation or matched filtering with K rather than M units. The receiver then calculates

$$\mathscr{D}_i = \sum_{k=1}^{K} y_k x_{ik} - \frac{1}{2}E_i$$

and proceeds as before. Incidentally, only for this implementation do we need to know the $\phi_k(t)$ explicitly.

Finally, for the case of nonwhite (but still gaussian) noise, the above analysis still holds if a *prewhitening filter* is added at the front end of the receiver, Fig. A.11. If $G_n(f) \neq 0$ and the filter has

$$|H_R(f)|^2 = \frac{1}{G_n(f)}$$

then the filtered noise will be white. Note however that $x_i(t)$ must be taken as the signal waveforms after they have passed through $H_R(f)$.

Error Probability

Concluding this abbreviated treatment of detection theory, we examine the error probability P_e—still using geometric arguments. In particular, Fig. A.12 represents the situation in $\mathscr{S}_K$ when x_j has been sent and corrupted by noise n to produce the vector z. Also shown is one other signal vector x_i and the projection of n along the vector $x_i - x_j$. The length of that projection (including algebraic sign) is

$$n_{ij} = \frac{\langle n, x_i - x_j \rangle}{L_{ij}} \qquad (18a)$$

where

$$L_{ij} = \|x_i - x_j\| \qquad (18b)$$

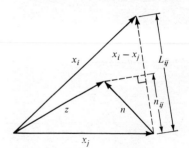

FIGURE A.12

Clearly, a detection error results if n causes z to be closer to x_i than to x_j or, equivalently, if

$$n_{ij} \geq \tfrac{1}{2}L_{ij} \qquad i \neq j$$

From the analysis that led to Eq. (8) one concludes that the projection of n along *any* vector in $\mathscr{S}_K$ is a gaussian variate with zero mean and variance $\eta/2$, so

$$\text{Prob }[n_{ij} \geq \tfrac{1}{2}L_{ij}] = Q\left(\frac{L_{ij}}{\sqrt{2\,\eta}}\right)$$

Hence, accounting for all of the $M-1$ signal vectors x_i, $i \neq j$, the error probability when x_j is sent is upper-bounded by

$$P_{e_j} \leq (M-1)Q\left(\frac{L_j}{\sqrt{2\,\eta}}\right) \qquad L_j = L_{ij}\Big|_{\substack{\min \\ i \neq j}} \tag{19}$$

i.e., L_j is the distance between x_j and its nearest neighbor.

Averaging Eq. (19) over all possible signals gives

$$P_e = \frac{1}{M}\sum_{j=1}^{M} P_{e_j} \leq \frac{M-1}{M}\sum_{j=1}^{M} Q\left(\frac{L_j}{\sqrt{2\,\eta}}\right)$$

$$\leq (M-1)Q\left(\frac{L_{\min}}{\sqrt{2\,\eta}}\right) \qquad L_{\min} = L_j\Big|_{\min} \tag{20}$$

which is a conservative upper bound since $L_{\min}$ is smallest value of L_j. Arthurs and Dym then go on to show that P_e is lower-bounded by

$$P_e \geq Q\left(\frac{L_{av}}{\sqrt{2\,\eta}}\right) \qquad L_{av} = \frac{1}{M}\sum_{j=1}^{M} L_j \tag{21}$$

Figure A.13 illustrates these various distances taking x_1, x_2, and x_3 from Fig. A.8. For a binary system ($M=2$),

$$P_e = Q\left(\frac{\|x_1 - x_2\|}{\sqrt{2\,\eta}}\right) \tag{22}$$

since $L_{av} = L_{\min} = \|x_1 - x_2\|$.

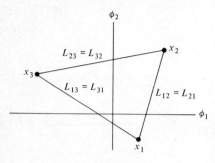

FIGURE A.13
Distances in $\mathscr{S}_K$. Since $L_{12} < L_{13} < L_{23}$, $L_1 = L_2 = L_{12}$, $L_3 = L_{13}$, $L_{min} = L_1$, and $L_{av} = (2L_{12} + L_{13})/3$.

Aside from giving bounds on the error probability with optimum detection, Eqs. (20) and (21) provide valuable guidelines for *signal selection*.† As an example, consider a binary system with an energy constraint $E_i \leq E$; simple vector diagrams prove that $\|x_1 - x_2\|$ is maximized (so P_e is minimized) if $x_2(t) = -x_1(t)$ and $E_1 = E_2 = E$. Moreover, it can be shown that‡ the use of *M orthogonal* signals with equal energy E and the receiver implementations previously discussed yields a system whose performance approaches that of an *ideal* system (in Shannon's sense) having infinite bandwidth; i.e., as $M \to \infty$, $P_e \to 0$ providing that the information rate satisfies $\mathscr{R} = (1/T) \log_2 M \leq 1.44 S_R/\eta$, where $S_R = E/T$—see Eq. (7), Sect. 9.4.

A.4   PROBLEMS

A.1   (Sect. A.1) Consider the vectors v, w, and $z = v + w$ with $\|v\|^2 = \|w\|^2 = 16$ and $\|z\|^2 = 32$. Construct a vector diagram based on this information and use it to find $\|x\|^2$ when $x = 3v + 2w$. (*Ans.*: $\|x\|^2 = 208$.)

A.2   (Sect. A.1) Referring to Prob. A.1, find a vector y in terms of v and w that is in the plane containing v and w and has the property that $\langle y, z \rangle = 0$. Then find the projections y_v and y_w.

A.3   (Sect. A.1) Derive the triangle inequality in the form $\|v + w\|^2 \leq (\|v\| + \|w\|)^2$ by starting with Eq. (9) and applying (10). (*Hint*: Note that $\langle v, w \rangle + \langle v, w \rangle^* = 2 \operatorname{Re}[\langle v, w \rangle]$.)

A.4★   (Sect. A.1) By letting $v = \alpha w + \beta z$, where z is an arbitrary vector, find the relationship between v and w such that $\|v + w\| = \|v\| + \|w\|$. Does your result agree with the vector picture?

A.5   (Sect. A.1) Suppose $v = \alpha_1 z_1 + \alpha_2 z_2$ and $w = \beta_1 z_1 + \beta_2 z_2$ where z_1 and z_2 are not orthonormal. Find an expression for $\langle v, w \rangle$ and compare it with Eq. (19).

A.6   (Sect. A.2) Consider the space spanned by the periodic functions $\phi_1(t)$ and $\phi_2(t)$ where $\phi_1(t)$ is the square wave in Fig. 2.10 with $A = 1$ and $\phi_2(t) = \phi_1(t - T_0/4)$.
(*a*) Show that $\phi_1(t)$ and $\phi_2(t)$ are orthonormal.
(*b*) Find α_1 and α_2 such that $\tilde{v}(t) = \alpha_1 \phi_1(t) + \alpha_2 \phi_2(t)$ is a least-square-error approximation to $v(t) = A \cos(2\pi t/T_0 + 45°)$.

† See Lathi (1968, chap. 6) or Wozencraft and Jacobs (1965, chap. 5).
‡ Lathi (1968, chap. 7) or Wozencraft and Jacobs (1965, chap. 5).

A.7 (Sect. A.2) If $v(t)$ is a real periodic signal, it can be expanded in the form $v(t) = a_0 + \sum_{n=1}^{\infty} (a_n \cos 2\pi nt/T_0 + b_n \sin 2\pi nt/T_0)$, the *sine-cosine Fourier series*. Identify the basis functions, check for orthonormality, and obtain formulas for a_0, a_n, and b_n in terms of $v(t)$.

A.8 (Sect. A.2) Investigate the properties of the energy-signal basis $\phi_f(t) = e^{j2\pi ft}$ by considering $\langle \phi_{f_1}, \phi_{f_2} \rangle = \lim_{T \to \infty} \int_{-T}^{T} \phi_{f_1}(t) \phi_{f_2}^*(t) \, dt$.

A.9 (Sect. A.2) Use Eqs. (11) and (13) to show that the basis functions given in Eq. (12) are orthonormal.

A.10★(Sect. A.2) Taking α_k per Eq. (17), show that $\sum_{k=-M}^{M} \alpha_k \phi_k(n) = v(n)$. (*Hint*: Note that $\exp j2\pi k(n-m)/K = [\exp j2\pi(n-m)/K]^k$ and introduce a new summation index $k' = k + K$.)

A.11 (Sect. A.2) Obtain formulas for α_0 and α_1 such that $\tilde{v}(t) = \alpha_0 + \alpha_1 t$ is a least-square-error approximation to $v(t)$ over $0 \le t \le T$.

A.12★(Sect. A.2) Consider the energy signals $z_1(t) = 1$, $z_2(t) = t$, and $z_3(t) = t^2$ defined over the interval $-1 \le t \le 1$. Use the Gram-Schmidt procedure to generate corresponding orthonormal basis functions. Your results will be proportional to the first three *Legendre polynomials*. (*Ans.*: $\phi_1(t) = 1/\sqrt{2}$, $\phi_2(t) = \sqrt{3/2}\, t$, $\phi_3(t) = \sqrt{5/8}\,(3t^2 - 1)$.)

A.13★(Sect. A.2) Given an energy signal $v(t)$, it is desired to construct the *piecewise-constant approximation* $\tilde{v}(t) = \sum_{k=-\infty}^{\infty} a_k \Pi[(t - k\tau)/\tau]$. Obtain a formula for a_k in terms of $v(t)$ so that $\tilde{v}(t)$ is a least-square-error approximation.

A.14 (Sect. A.3) Obtain a more general version of Eq. (14) by starting with Eq. (10) and dropping the assumption of equiprobable messages, so the $P(\mu_i)$ are arbitrary. (*Ans.*: $\mathcal{D}_i = \langle y, x_i \rangle + [\eta \ln P(\mu_i) - E_i]/2$.)

A.15 (Sect. A.3) Find P_e in terms of $\rho = E/\eta$, where $E = (\|x_1\|^2 + \|x_2\|^2)/2$ is the *average energy*, for each of the following binary-signal pairs. In each case relate α to E, assuming α is real and $\phi_1(t)$ and $\phi_2(t)$ are orthonormal but otherwise arbitrary, and locate x_1, x_2, and the decision region boundary in the ϕ_1-ϕ_2 plane. Compare your results with Eq. (17b), Sect. 4.5.
   (a) $x_1(t) = \alpha\phi_1(t)$, $x_2(t) = 0$;
   (b) $x_1(t) = \alpha\phi_1(t)$, $x_2(t) = \alpha\phi_2(t)$;
   (c) $x_1(t) = \alpha\phi_1(t)$, $x_2(t) = -\alpha\phi_1(t)$.

A.16 (Sect. A.3) Consider a system with $M = 5$ in which $x_1(t) = 0$, $x_2(t) = \phi_1(t)$, $x_3(t) = \phi_2(t)$, $x_4(t) = -\phi_1(t)$, and $x_5(t) = -\phi_2(t)$, where ϕ_1 and ϕ_2 are orthonormal. Draw the vectors and the decision region boundaries in the ϕ_1-ϕ_2 plane, and find L_j, L_{min} and L_{av}.

A.17★(Sect. A.3) Given a set of M equiprobable signal vectors in $\mathscr{S}_K$, the average energy is $E = (1/M) \sum_{i=1}^{M} \|x_i\|^2$. Suppose we construct a new set by subtracting a fixed vector $w = \sum_{k=1}^{K} \alpha_k \phi_k$, i.e., $x_i' = x_i - w$. This does not change the error probability (why?), but the average energy is now $E' = (1/M) \sum_{i=1}^{M} \|x_i - w\|^2$. Assuming all the vectors and scalars are real, show that E' is minimized if the coordinates of w are $\alpha_m = (1/M) \sum_{i=1}^{M} x_{im}$, $m = 1, 2, \ldots, K$. The set x_i' is then called the *minimum-energy equivalent set*. (*Hint*: Expand $\|x_i - w\|^2$ and take the partial derivative of E' with respect to α_m.)

APPENDIX B

RECEIVER NOISE

The study of noise in electrical communication is a vast and multifaceted subject, for noise stems from a variety of mechanisms and enters the system at every point. However, the effects are most serious where the signal level is lowest, at the receiver. Hence, per Fig. B.1, the problem can be broken into three parts: (1) the input or source signal-to-noise ratio $(S/N)_S$ at the antenna terminals (transmission-line terminals in the case of wire systems); (2) the predetection signal-to-noise ratio $(S/N)_R$; and (3) the destination signal-to-noise ratio $(S/N)_D$.

To begin with the input, incoming noise is generally the result of random electromagnetic radiation intercepted by the antenna, this radiation being from both man-made and natural sources. Examples of the former are ignition and commutator sparking, fluorescent lights, and x-ray machines, while the latter includes atmospheric noise (static) and emissions from extraterrestrial bodies.† In addition, the antenna itself may be a noise generator. As a result, the incoming noise power depends on the type of antenna, where it is located and where it is looking, the operating frequency, time of day, and so forth. Clearly, an investigation of all these factors is not possible here; moreover, although prediction formulas do exist, accurate determination of the input noise usually requires on-site measurements. We shall therefore assume that $(S/N)_S$ is known, by one means or another.

---

† Such emissions, known as *cosmic radio noise*, were first discovered by Karl Jansky in 1932, giving birth to the field of radio astronomy. Much has been learned about our universe by studying this noise. Nonetheless, it is a nuisance to the communication engineer.

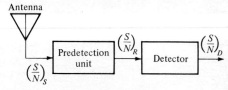

Antenna

FIGURE B.1
Signal-to-noise ratios in a communication receiver.

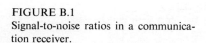

At the other end of the receiver, the detector and any stages thereafter are usually relatively noiseless, so the relation between $(S/N)_R$ and $(S/N)_D$ depends only on the type of modulation system. These relationships were developed in Chaps. 7 and 8.

If the predetection unit is also free of noise, then $(S/N)_R$ equals $(S/N)_S$, and the job is done. But this is seldom the case, since the RF and IF stages, the mixer, etc., often add internally generated noise whose power level is comparable to, or even greater than, the input noise. An accurate assessment of system performance must then include the *receiver noise*. And that is the task at hand.

This appendix discusses receiver noise in terms of the standard measures *noise figure* and *noise temperature*, measures that facilitate system design and evaluation by relating $(S/N)_R$ to $(S/N)_S$. Drawing upon the concepts of thermal noise, available power, and noise equivalent bandwidth from Sect. 3.6 (which the student may wish to review before proceeding), the description of noisy two-port networks will be developed. It is then shown that the first few stages of a receiver are the critical elements in low-noise design. However, discussion of device noise per se is beyond the scope of this text.†

B.1   NOISE FIGURE AND EFFECTIVE NOISE TEMPERATURE

The predetection portion of a receiver consists of several units connected in cascade, each unit having internally generated noise. This section sets forth the description of a single noisy two-port network, Fig. B.2. Let $G_{si}(f) + G_{ni}(f)$ be the signal-plus-noise spectral density at the input and let $H(f)$ be the transfer function. If $G_{nx}(f)$ is the output density of the *excess noise* introduced by the two-port itself, then the output S/N is

$$\left(\frac{S}{N}\right)_o = \frac{\int_{-\infty}^{\infty} |H(f)|^2 G_{si}(f)\, df}{\int_{-\infty}^{\infty} [|H(f)|^2 G_{ni}(f) + G_{nx}(f)]\, df} \tag{1}$$

This formidable expression is greatly simplified if the input noise is white, or at least has uniform density η over the passband of the device, and the amplitude ratio is essentially constant so $|H(f)|^2 = \mathcal{G}$ over the frequency range of the input signal. Under these conditions

$$\left(\frac{S}{N}\right)_o = \frac{\mathcal{G} \int_{-\infty}^{\infty} G_{si}(f)\, df}{\eta \int_0^{\infty} |H(f)|^2\, df + \int_{-\infty}^{\infty} G_{nx}(f)\, df} = \frac{\mathcal{G} S_i}{\mathcal{G}\eta B_N + N_x} \tag{2}$$

SPECTRAL DENSITY/

$G_{si}(f) + G_{ni}(f)$ → | $H(f)$ / $G_{nx}(f)$ | → $|H(f)|^2\, [G_{si}(f) + G_{ni}(f)] + G_{nx}(f)$

FIGURE B.2

† See the selected supplementary reading for references.

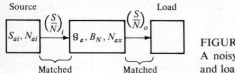

Source | Load

FIGURE B.3
A noisy two-port with matched source
and load.

where S_i is the input signal power and N_x is the total excess noise power at the output. Equation (2) brings out the fact that a two-port amplifies (or attenuates) the input signal and noise by the same amount and then adds noise of its own.

Effective Noise Temperature

Despite the simplifications, Eq. (2) is at best a cumbersome description of a two-port's noisiness. A more tractable measure is obtained if we assume for the moment that all impedances are matched; i.e., looking into the two-port, the source sees a matched impedance, and the output of the two-port sees a matched load, Fig. B.3. Then the source delivers its *available* signal power S_{ai}, and the output signal power is

$$S_{ao} = \mathcal{G}_a S_{ai}$$

where $\mathcal{G}_a$ is the *available power gain* of the device. Similarly, the output noise power is

$$N_{ao} = \mathcal{G}_a N_{ai} + N_{ax}$$

N_{ax} being the available excess noise power at the output. If the input noise is white and represented by a noise temperature $\mathcal{T}_i$, then

$$N_{ai} = k\mathcal{T}_i B_N$$

is the available source noise in the equivalent bandwidth B_N.

Combining these terms gives the output signal-to-signal ratio as

$$\left(\frac{S}{N}\right)_o = \frac{S_{ao}}{N_{ao}} = \frac{\mathcal{G}_a S_{ai}}{\mathcal{G}_a k\mathcal{T}_i B_N + N_{ax}} = \frac{S_{ai}}{k\mathcal{T}_i B_N + N_{ax}/\mathcal{G}_a}$$

and taking the input signal-to-noise ratio as $(S/N)_i = S_{ai}/k\mathcal{T}_i B_N$, we have

$$\left(\frac{S}{N}\right)_o = \frac{(S/N)_i}{1 + (N_{ax}/\mathcal{G}_a k\mathcal{T}_i B_N)} \leq \left(\frac{S}{N}\right)_i \qquad (3)$$

Equation (3) shows that the signal-to-noise ratios can be nearly equal, despite excess noise, providing that $N_{ax} \ll \mathcal{G}_a k\mathcal{T}_i B_N$. Obviously what counts is not the absolute value of the excess noise power but its value relative to the source noise, a conclusion that certainly makes sense.

Pursuing this thought further, we observe that $N_{ax}/\mathcal{G}_a k B_N$ depends only on the parameters of the two-port and has the dimensions of temperature. Therefore, we define the *effective input noise temperature* (also called the *amplifier temperature*) by

$$\mathcal{T}_e \triangleq \frac{N_{ax}}{\mathcal{G}_a k B_N} \qquad (4)$$

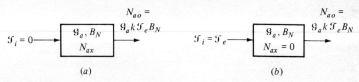

FIGURE B.4
A noisy amplifier with $\mathcal{T}_i = 0$ and its noiseless equivalent with $\mathcal{T}_i = \mathcal{T}_e$.

The meaning of $\mathcal{T}_e$ is illustrated in Fig. B.4, which shows that a noisy amplifier with $\mathcal{T}_i = 0$ can be replaced by a noiseless amplifier with $\mathcal{T}_i = \mathcal{T}_e$. In short, $\mathcal{T}_e$ is a measure of noisiness *referred to the input*. If the device is noiseless, $\mathcal{T}_e = 0$.

Substituting Eq. (4) into Eq. (3) gives

$$\left(\frac{S}{N}\right)_o = \frac{(S/N)_i}{1 + \mathcal{T}_e/\mathcal{T}_i} \tag{5a}$$

$$= \frac{\mathcal{G}_a S_i}{\mathcal{G}_a k(\mathcal{T}_i + \mathcal{T}_e)B_N} \tag{5b}$$

Equation (5b) is particularly informative, for it says that under matched conditions, the available output noise is

$$N_{ao} = \mathcal{G}_a k(\mathcal{T}_i + \mathcal{T}_e)B_N \tag{6}$$

and the output noise temperature is $\mathcal{G}_a(\mathcal{T}_i + \mathcal{T}_e)$.   *OUTPUT NOISE TEMP!!*

If impedances are not matched, all powers will be *less* than the available powers, being reduced by a mismatch factor. Nonetheless, Eqs. (3) and (5) are still valid because they are power *ratios* taken at specific points, and the mismatch factor cancels out. Thus, although an amplifier may not actually be operated with matched impedances, its available power gain and effective input noise temperature are significant parameters. As a bonus, they are relatively easy to measure or calculate. In particular, $\mathcal{G}_a = S_{ao}/S_{ai}$, where S_{ai} is the available power from the source, whether or not the input impedance is matched, while S_{ao} is the power that would be delivered to a matched output load when the source is connected at the input.

Noise Figure

The effective input noise temperature is most useful in describing low-noise amplifiers, devices with $\mathcal{T}_e \ll \mathcal{T}_i$. But when the excess noise is large, the *integrated noise figure F* proves more convenient.

Noise figure is defined as the actual output noise power divided by the output noise power if the two-port were noiseless, the source being at room temperature $\mathcal{T}_0$. The definition is a power ratio and can be written in terms of available powers as

$$F \triangleq \frac{N_{ao}}{\mathcal{G}_a k \mathcal{T}_0 B_N} \tag{7}$$

Now with $\mathcal{T}_i = \mathcal{T}_0$, $N_{ao} = \mathcal{G}_a k(\mathcal{T}_0 + \mathcal{T}_e)B_N$, and hence

$$F = \frac{\mathcal{T}_0 + \mathcal{T}_e}{\mathcal{T}_0} = 1 + \frac{\mathcal{T}_e}{\mathcal{T}_0} \qquad (8a)$$

$$= 1 + \frac{N_{ax}}{\mathcal{G}_a k \mathcal{T}_0 B_N} \qquad (8b)$$

It should be apparent that in general $F \geq 1$ (the actual output noise cannot be less than the amplified source noise) and $F = 1$ for a *noiseless* amplifier.

As to the relationship of input and output signal-to-noise ratios, writing Eq. (8a) as

$$\mathcal{T}_e = (F - 1)\mathcal{T}_0 \qquad (9)$$

and substituting in Eq. (5a) yields

$$\left(\frac{S}{N}\right)_o = \frac{(S/N)_i}{1 + (F - 1)(\mathcal{T}_0/\mathcal{T}_i)} \qquad (10)$$

If, *and only if*, the source temperature is room temperature, Eq. (10) reduces to the simple result

$$\left(\frac{S}{N}\right)_o = \frac{1}{F}\left(\frac{S}{N}\right)_i$$

Prior to the advent of low-noise designs, most source temperatures were essentially $\mathcal{T}_0$ (the noise came from thermal resistance), so the latter expression could be used indiscriminately. For modern systems, in which noise is a crucial factor, Eq. (10) must be used.

Attenuators and Transmission Lines

Although we have been thinking of two-ports as amplifiers, the above results apply equally well to attenuators and other devices characterized by power *loss* rather than gain. Since such devices are almost always impedance-matched, the loss is $\mathcal{L} = 1/\mathcal{G}_a$.

Consider a two-port composed entirely of *resistive* elements in thermal equilibrium at room temperature $\mathcal{T}_0$. (This is a good model for lossy transmission lines and waveguides, as well as for actual networks of resistors.) Assuming the source temperature is also $\mathcal{T}_0$ and that all impedances are matched, looking back into the output terminals we see nothing but thermal resistance and a noise bandwidth. Therefore, the available output noise power is $N_{ao} = k\mathcal{T}_0 B_N$. But from Eq. (6), $N_{ao} = \mathcal{G}_a k(\mathcal{T}_i + \mathcal{T}_e)B_N$ for *any* two-port with matched impedances. The lossy device has $\mathcal{G}_a = 1/\mathcal{L}$ and $\mathcal{T}_i = \mathcal{T}_0$, so $\mathcal{T}_e = (\mathcal{L} - 1)\mathcal{T}_0$, independent of the bandwidth or the source temperature.

Generalizing, if a lossy two-port is at any temperature $\mathcal{T}$, its effective noise temperature is

$$\mathcal{T}_e = (\mathcal{L} - 1)\mathcal{T} \qquad (11)$$

and, using Eq. (8a),

$$F = 1 + (\mathcal{L} - 1)\frac{\mathcal{T}}{\mathcal{T}_0} \qquad (12)$$

More often than not, $\mathcal{T} = \mathcal{T}_0$ so Eq. (12) reduces simply to $F = \mathcal{L}$.

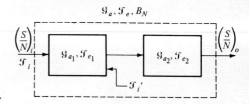

FIGURE B.5
Two noisy amplifiers in cascade.

Example B.1

A simple laboratory technique for measuring $\mathscr{T}_e$ or F requires a "hot" thermal resistance and a relative power meter, both impedance-matched to the device in question, plus a thermometer. The procedure is as follows: First, connect the resistor (at room temperature) to the input of the two-port and record the output-power indication N_1. Let the meter's calibration constant be C_m, so

$$N_1 = C_m N_{ao} = C_m \mathscr{G}_a k(\mathscr{T}_0 + \mathscr{T}_e)B_N$$

Second, heat the resistor until the output-power reading has *doubled* and record the resistor's temperature $\mathscr{T}_R$. The new reading is

$$N_2 = C_m \mathscr{G}_a k(\mathscr{T}_R + \mathscr{T}_e)B_N$$

Now $N_2 = 2N_1$, so $C_m \mathscr{G}_a k(\mathscr{T}_R + \mathscr{T}_e)B_N = 2C_m \mathscr{G}_a k(\mathscr{T}_0 + \mathscr{T}_e)B_N$, and hence

$$\mathscr{T}_e = \mathscr{T}_R - 2\mathscr{T}_0 \qquad F = 1 + \frac{\mathscr{T}_e}{\mathscr{T}_0} = \frac{\mathscr{T}_R}{\mathscr{T}_0} - 1 \qquad (13)$$

Note that we do not have to find $\mathscr{G}_a$ or B_N, nor do we need the calibration constant C_m. However, the resistor will be on the hot side since it must reach a minimum of $2\mathscr{T}_0 = 585°F$!

////

B.2 SYSTEM NOISE CALCULATIONS

Let us now put together a number of two-ports representing the entire predetection unit, thereby relating $(S/N)_R$ to $(S/N)_S$, the signal-to-noise ratio at the antenna terminals. For this purpose we shall find the *overall* receiver noise temperature or noise figure in terms of the properties of the individual stages.

Consider two amplifiers in cascade, as in Fig. B.5, again assuming matched impedances. Clearly the available power gain of the combination is $\mathscr{G}_a = \mathscr{G}_{a_1} \mathscr{G}_{a_2}$. However, the overall noise temperature $\mathscr{T}_e$ requires further thought.

One approach is to examine the situation at the input to the second amplifier, treating all that comes before as a new source with $\mathscr{T}'_i = \mathscr{G}_{a_1}(\mathscr{T}_i + \mathscr{T}_{e_1})$. We could then plug into Eq. (5), Sect. B.1, and turn the crank. But a more instructive method is to follow through the various noise sources and determine their contribution at the output. In particular, N_{ao} will be the sum of three terms:

1 Amplified source noise: $\mathscr{G}_{a_1}\mathscr{G}_{a_2}N_{ai} = \mathscr{G}_{a_1}\mathscr{G}_{a_2}k\mathscr{T}_i B_N$
2 Excess noise from the first stage, amplified by the second stage: $\mathscr{G}_{a_2}N_{ax_1} = \mathscr{G}_{a_2}(\mathscr{G}_{a_1}k\mathscr{T}_{e_1} B_N)$
3 Excess noise from the second stage: $N_{ax_2} = \mathscr{G}_{a_2}k\mathscr{T}_{e_2} B_N$

It has been implicitly assumed that both stages see white noise over their passband and that B_N is the overall noise bandwidth. Actually, good design suggests that the final stage should have the smallest possible bandwidth to minimize unnecessary noise at the demodulator. Thus, as a rule, B_N can be taken as the noise bandwidth of the last stage.

Returning to the calculation, we sum the three terms and factor to yield

$$N_{ao} = \mathscr{G}_{a_1}\mathscr{G}_{a_2}k\left[\mathscr{T}_i + \mathscr{T}_{e_1} + \frac{\mathscr{T}_{e_2}}{\mathscr{G}_{a_1}}\right]B_N$$

But, by definition of $\mathscr{G}_a$ and $\mathscr{T}_e$ for the cascade, $N_{ao} = \mathscr{G}_a k(\mathscr{T}_i + \mathscr{T}_e)B_N$; hence

$$\mathscr{T}_e = \mathscr{T}_{e_1} + \frac{\mathscr{T}_{e_2}}{\mathscr{G}_{a_1}}$$

and therefore

$$F = F_1 + \frac{F_2 - 1}{\mathscr{G}_{a_1}}$$

Iterating this procedure with three or more cascaded two-ports, one obtains for the overall effective input temperature and noise figure

$$\mathscr{T}_e = \mathscr{T}_{e_1} + \frac{\mathscr{T}_{e_2}}{\mathscr{G}_{a_1}} + \frac{\mathscr{T}_{e_3}}{\mathscr{G}_{a_1}\mathscr{G}_{a_2}} + \cdots \tag{1}$$

$$F = F_1 + \frac{F_2 - 1}{\mathscr{G}_{a_1}} + \frac{F_3 - 1}{\mathscr{G}_{a_1}\mathscr{G}_{a_2}} + \cdots \tag{2}$$

The latter is known as *Friis' formula*.

Equations (1) and (2) indicate that the receiver noise may be dominated by the first stage. Suppose, for example, that $\mathscr{G}_{a_1} \gg 1$; then the overall noise temperature is essentially that of the first stage itself, $\mathscr{T}_e \approx \mathscr{T}_{e_1}$. The physical reason is that with large first-stage gain, the amplified source noise (plus N_{ax_1}) will be much greater than any noise added by later stages. On the other hand, if the first stage is an *attenuator* of loss $\mathscr{L} = 1/\mathscr{G}_{a_1} > 1$ — such as a lossy transmission line — the effect is twice cursed since $\mathscr{T}_{e_1} = (\mathscr{L} - 1)\mathscr{T}$ and

$$\mathscr{T}_e = (\mathscr{L} - 1)\mathscr{T} + \mathscr{L}\mathscr{T}_{e_2} + \cdots \tag{3}$$

This situation should be avoided if at all possible.

Clearly, the first few stages are of prime concern in the design of low-noise communication receivers. In particular, the first stage should have a small noise temperature and reason-

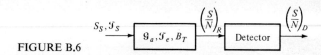

FIGURE B.6

ably large gain. With a good "front end" or preamplifier, the remaining stages merely serve as additional amplification and filtering, amplifying both signal and noise without appreciably changing the ratio.

To complete our calculations, suppose the predetection unit has an overall effective input noise temperature $\mathcal{T}_e$ and a noise bandwidth approximately equal to the modulated signal bandwidth, $B_N \approx B_T$. At the antenna terminals let the signal power be $S_S = S_T/\mathcal{L}$ where $\mathcal{L}$ is the transmission loss, and let the noise temperature (*antenna temperature*) be $\mathcal{T}_s$, Fig. B.6. (Receiving antennas are usually impedance-matched at their terminals, so S_S is the *available* power.) The predetection signal-to-noise ratio is thus

$$\left(\frac{S}{N}\right)_R = \frac{\mathcal{G}_a S_S}{\mathcal{G}_a k(\mathcal{T}_s + \mathcal{T}_e)B_T} = \frac{S_T}{\mathcal{L}k\mathcal{T}_N B_T} \tag{4}$$

where $\mathcal{T}_N = \mathcal{T}_s + \mathcal{T}_e$ is the *system temperature* referred to the antenna terminals. In the past we have written $(S/N)_R = S_R/\eta B_T$. By comparison with Eq. (4) it follows that

$$S_R = \frac{\mathcal{G}_R S_T}{\mathcal{L}} \qquad \eta = \mathcal{G}_R k\mathcal{T}_N$$

where $\mathcal{G}_R$ is the *actual* power gain of the predetection unit.

Example B.2

In adverse locations it is often necessary to put a television receiving antenna on a tall mast. A long and therefore lossy cable connects antenna and receiver. To overcome the effects of the cable, a preamplifier can be mounted at the antenna, as in Fig. B.7. The system parameters are given in decibels, which is standard practice, but must be converted before use in Eq. (1) or (2).

Inserting values in Eq. (2), with $F_2 = \mathcal{L} = 2$, yields for the overall noise figure

$$F = 4 + \frac{2-1}{100} + \frac{20-1}{100 \times \frac{1}{2}} = 4.39 = 6.4 \text{ dB}$$

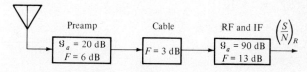

FIGURE B.7
A receiver with preamplification at the antenna terminals.

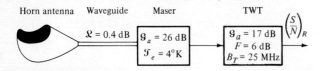

FIGURE B.8
A low-noise receiver for a satellite ground station.

which shows that the noise performance is essentially that of the preamplifier alone. (Note that the RF and IF gain does not enter these calculations.) Thus, if the source temperature is $\mathscr{T}_s = \mathscr{T}_0$, $(S/N)_R$ is 6.4 dB less than the signal-to-noise ratio at the antenna terminals.

If the preamplifier is omitted, $F = 2 + 2(20 - 1) = 40$, and the output noise is about 10 times as large as before.   ////

Example B.3

By space-age standards, the previous example is a very noisy receiver. Low-noise systems, such as the satellite ground station of Fig. B.8, have sufficiently small excess noise for the noise figure to be numerically awkward to handle. Thus, the calculations are usually carried out in terms of temperatures.

The lossy waveguide has $\mathscr{L} = 0.4$ dB $= 1.10$, so $\mathscr{T}_{e_1} = (1.10 - 1)\mathscr{T}_0 = 29°$K. For the traveling-wave tube (TWT), $\mathscr{T}_{e_3} = (F_3 - 1)\mathscr{T}_0 = 870°$K; of course the *physical* temperature of the TWT is much less. Thus

$$\mathscr{T}_e = 29 + 1.1 \times 4 + \frac{1.1 \times 870}{400} \approx 36°\text{K}$$

Note that, despite the small waveguide loss, its noise contribution dominates the system. Interchanging the positions of maser and waveguide would be highly desirable but difficult, since the guide is the flexible connection permitting the horn antenna to be steered. (With a parabolic dish antenna the maser can be mounted directly at the feed, eliminating waveguide loss and noise. However, dish antennas tend to have larger noise temperatures, which cancels out the saving.)

Under typical conditions, the antenna temperature may be $\mathscr{T}_s = 22°$K, giving a system noise temperature of $\mathscr{T}_N = \mathscr{T}_s + \mathscr{T}_e = 58°$K $= 0.2\mathscr{T}_0$. Hence, from Eq. (4) and using $k\mathscr{T}_0 \approx 4 \times 10^{-21}$,

$$\left(\frac{S}{N}\right)_R = \frac{S_S}{4 \times 10^{-21}(\mathscr{T}_N/\mathscr{T}_0)B_T} = \frac{S_S}{2 \times 10^{-14}}$$

A 20-dB predetection signal-to-noise ratio requires an available signal power at the antenna terminals of $S_S = 10^2 \times 2 \times 10^{-14} = 2 \ \mu\mu$W.   ////

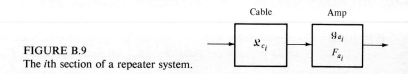

FIGURE B.9
The ith section of a repeater system.

Repeater Systems

Repeater systems were briefly discussed in Sect. 4.1 where, assuming identical units, we found the S/N after M links to be $1/M$ times the S/N for one link. Here we consider the general case where the system consists of M cable/amplifier units, the ith unit being as shown in Fig. B.9. The gain of the amplifier is $\mathcal{G}_{a_i}$ and its noise figure is F_{a_i}; the cable has loss $\mathcal{L}_{c_i}$ so $F_{c_i} = \mathcal{L}_{c_i}$. Applying Eq. (2), the noise figure F_i of the cable/amplifier combination is

$$F_i = \mathcal{L}_{c_i} + \frac{F_{a_i} - 1}{(1/\mathcal{L}_{c_i})} = \mathcal{L}_{c_i} F_{a_i} \tag{5a}$$

and the unit has net gain

$$\mathcal{G}_i = \frac{\mathcal{G}_{a_i}}{\mathcal{L}_{c_i}} \tag{5b}$$

Therefore, for M units in cascade,

$$F = \mathcal{L}_{c_1} F_{a_1} + \left(\frac{\mathcal{L}_{c_1}}{\mathcal{G}_{a_1}}\right)(\mathcal{L}_{c_2} F_{a_2} - 1) + \cdots + \frac{\mathcal{L}_{c_1} \mathcal{L}_{c_2} \cdots \mathcal{L}_{c_{M-1}}}{\mathcal{G}_{a_1} \mathcal{G}_{a_2} \cdots \mathcal{G}_{a_{M-1}}} (\mathcal{L}_{c_M} F_{a_M} - 1) \tag{6}$$

and

$$\left(\frac{S}{N}\right)_R = \frac{1}{F} \left(\frac{S}{N}\right)_S \tag{7}$$

since the input or source noise is almost always thermal noise at $\mathcal{T}_0$.

For the special but important case of nearly identical units, so $\mathcal{L}_{c_1} F_{a_1} = \mathcal{L}_{c_2} F_{a_2} = \cdots$, and a net gain per unit $\mathcal{G}_i = \mathcal{G}_{a_i}/\mathcal{L}_{c_i} = 1$, the noise figure becomes

$$F = M\mathcal{L}_{c_1} F_{a_1} - (M - 1)$$

$$\approx M\mathcal{L}_{c_1} F_{a_1} \qquad \mathcal{L}_{c_1} F_{a_1} \gg 1 \tag{8a}$$

Hence,

$$\left(\frac{S}{N}\right)_R \approx \frac{1}{M\mathcal{L}_{c_1} F_{a_1}} \left(\frac{S}{N}\right)_S = \frac{1}{M}\left(\frac{S}{N}\right)_1 \tag{8b}$$

where $(S/N)_1 = (1/\mathcal{L}_{c_1} F_{a_1})(S/N)_S$ is the signal-to-noise ratio at the end of the first hop. Equation (8a) is the basis for the slogan used by telephone engineers that "doubling the number of repeaters increases the noise figure by 3 dB."

B.3   PROBLEMS

B.1   (Sect. B.1) An amplifier with $\mathcal{G}_a = 50$ dB and $B_N = 20$ kHz is found to have $N_{ao} = 10^{10}k\mathcal{T}_0$ when $\mathcal{T}_i = \mathcal{T}_0$. Find $\mathcal{T}_e$ and calculate N_{ao} when $\mathcal{T}_i = 2\mathcal{T}_0$. (*Ans.*: $4\mathcal{T}_0$, 48 $\mu\mu$W.)

B.2   (Sect. B.1) When the noise temperature at the input to a certain amplifier changes from $\mathcal{T}_0$ to $2\mathcal{T}_0$, the available output noise power increases by one-third. Find $\mathcal{T}_e$ and F.

B.3   (Sect. B.1) Impedance matching between a 300-Ω antenna and a 50-Ω amplifier is sometimes approximated by putting a 300-Ω resistance in series with the antenna and a 50-Ω resistance across the amplifier's input terminals. Calculate the noise figure of this resistive network. (*Hint*: See the discussion regarding $\mathcal{G}_a$ that follows Eq. (6).)

B.4   (Sect. B.1) The *diode noise generator* described in Prob. 3.40 is often used as the "hot resistor" in noise measurements per Example B.1. The diode current I_b is off for the first step and then, in the second step, adjusted until the output power doubles. Show that $F = eI_b R/2k\mathcal{T}_0 \approx 20I_b R$. Hence, if $R = 50$ Ω, then F equals I_b in milliamperes.

B.5★ (Sect. B.1) A sinusoidal oscillator can be used in place of the hot resistor in Example B.1. The oscillator is connected but turned off in the first step, so its internal resistance delivers the source noise. For the second step the oscillator is turned on and its signal power S_i is adjusted to double the total output power. Obtain an expression for F and discuss the disadvantages of this method.

B.6   (Sect. B.2) Derive Eq. (2) for a two-stage cascade by starting with Eq. (5b), Sect. B.1, and treating S_i and $\mathcal{T}_i$ as the output of the first stage.

B.7   (Sect. B.2) Two cascaded amplifiers have the following specifications: $\mathcal{T}_{e_1} = 3\mathcal{T}_0$, $\mathcal{G}_{a_1} = 10$ dB, $F_2 = 13.2$ dB, $\mathcal{G}_{a_2} = 50$ dB. If $B_N = 100$ kHz and $\mathcal{T}_i = 10\mathcal{T}_0$, what value of S_i is required to give $(S/N)_o = 30$ dB? (*Ans.*: 6 $\mu\mu$W.)

B.8   (Sect. B.2) A system consists of a cable whose loss is 2 dB/km followed by an amplifier with $F = 7$ dB. If $\mathcal{T}_i = \mathcal{T}_0$ and it is desired to have $(S/N)_o \geq 0.05(S/N)_i$, what is the maximum possible path length?

B.9   (Sect. B.2) Obtain an expression similar to Eq. (6) when the amplifier is placed before the cable rather than after it. Simplify your result for the case of identical units with $\mathcal{G}_{a_i}/\mathcal{L}_{c_i} = 1$ and compare with Eq. (8a).

B.10★(Sect. B.3) The *Haus-Adler noise measure* is defined as $\mathcal{M} = (F - 1)/(1 - 1/\mathcal{G}_a)$. Show that a cascade of two amplifiers has the lower overall noise figure if the first amplifier has the lower value of $\mathcal{M}$. (*Hint*: Write an expression for the difference $F_{12} - F_{21}$ for the two possible configurations.)

TELEVISION AND FACSIMILE SYSTEMS

Television and facsimile systems are *image* transmission systems; i.e., the message is a two-dimensional pattern and therefore a function of two independent variables. This appendix deals with the means for transmitting an image as an electrical signal, which is a function of just one variable, time. We will concentrate primarily on television, where the images have motion and there is a real-time transmission constraint. Facsimile systems transmit only still pictures, giving the designer more latitude.

C.1 THE VIDEO SIGNAL

To start with the simplest case, consider a motion-free monochrome (black-and-white) intensity pattern $I(h,v)$, where h and v are the horizontal and vertical coordinates. Converting $I(h,v)$ to a signal $x(t)$ — and vice versa — requires a discontinuous mapping process such as the *scanning raster* diagramed in Fig. C.1. The scanning device, which produces a voltage or current proportional to intensity, starts at point A and moves with constant but unequal rates in the horizontal and vertical directions, following the path AB. Thus, if s_h and s_v are the horizontal and vertical scanning speeds, the output of the scanner is the *video signal*

$$x(t) = I(s_h t, s_v t) \qquad (1)$$

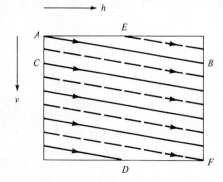

FIGURE C.1
Scanning raster (line spacing grossly exaggerated). Solid lines are the first field; dashed lines are the second field.

since $h = s_h t$, etc. Upon reaching point B, the scanning spot quickly flies back to C (the horizontal retrace) and proceeds similarly to point D, where facsimile scanning would end.

In TV, however, image motion must be accommodated, so the spot retraces vertically to E and follows an interlaced pattern ending at F. The process is then repeated starting again at A. The two sets of lines are called the first and second *fields*; together they constitute one complete picture or *frame*. The frame rate is just rapid enough (25 to 30 per second) to create the illusion of continuous motion, while the field rate (twice the frame rate) makes the flickering imperceptible to the human eye. Hence, interlaced scanning allows the lowest possible picture repetition rate without visible flicker.

Two modifications are made to the video signal after scanning: *blanking pulses* are inserted during the retrace intervals to blank out retrace lines on the receiving picture tube; and *synchronizing pulses* are added on top of the blanking pulses to synchronize the receiver's horizontal and vertical sweep circuits. Figure C.2 shows the waveform for one complete line,

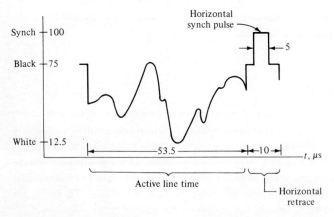

FIGURE C.2
Video waveform for one full line.

Table C.1 UNITED STATES TELEVISION STANDARDS

Aspect ratio (width to height)	4/3
Total lines per frame	525
Line frequency†	15.75 kHz
Line time†	63.5 μs
Horizontal retrace time†	10 μs
Field frequency†	60 Hz
Vertical retrace†	20 lines per field
Video bandwidth	4.2 MHz
Transmission bandwidth	6.0 MHz
Video carrier frequency	54–72, 76–88, 174–216, 470–890 MHz
Audio carrier frequency	4.5 MHz above video carrier
Audio FM deviation	25 kHz

† Nominal values.

with amplitude levels and durations corresponding to United States TV standards. Other standard parameters are listed in Table C.1.

The Video Spectrum

Analyzing the spectrum of the video signal in absence of motion is relatively easy with the aid of Fig. C.3 where, instead of retraced scanning, the image has been periodically repeated in both directions so the equivalent scanning path is unbroken. Now any periodic function of two variables may be expanded as a *two-dimensional Fourier series* by straightforward

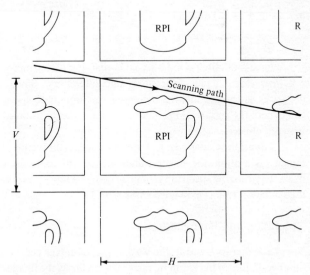

FIGURE C.3
Periodically repeated image with unbroken scanning path.

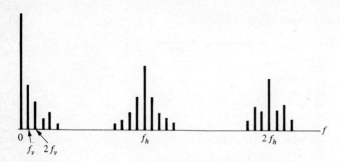

FIGURE C.4
Video spectrum for still image.

extension of the one-dimensional series. For the case at hand with H and V the horizontal and vertical periods (including retrace allowance), the image intensity is

$$I(h,v) = \sum_{m=-\infty}^{\infty} \sum_{n=-\infty}^{\infty} c_{mn} \exp\left[j2\pi\left(\frac{mh}{H} + \frac{nv}{V}\right)\right] \tag{2}$$

where

$$c_{mn} = \frac{1}{HV} \int_0^H \int_0^V I(h,v) \exp\left[-j2\pi\left(\frac{mh}{H} + \frac{nv}{V}\right)\right] dh\, dv \tag{3}$$

Therefore, letting

$$f_h = \frac{S_h}{H} \qquad f_v = \frac{S_v}{V}$$

and using Eqs. (1) and (2),

$$x(t) = \sum_{m=-\infty}^{\infty} \sum_{n=-\infty}^{\infty} c_{mn} e^{j2\pi(mf_h + nf_v)t} \tag{4}$$

so we have a doubly periodic signal containing all harmonics of the *line frequency* f_h and the *field frequency* f_v, plus their sums and differences. Since $f_h \gg f_v$ and since $|c_{mn}|$ generally decreases as the product mn increases, the amplitude spectrum has the form shown in Fig. C.4, where the spectral lines cluster around the harmonics of f_h and there are large gaps between clusters.

Equation (4) and Fig. C.4 are exact for a still picture, i.e., facsimile systems. When the image has motion, the spectral lines merge into continuous clumps around the harmonics of f_h. Even so, the spectrum remains mostly "empty" everywhere else, a fact used to advantage in color TV, as explained in Sect. C.3.

Resolution and Bandwidth

Two basic factors stand in the way of perfect image reproduction: there can be only a finite number of lines in the scanning raster, which limits the image clarity or *resolution* in the vertical direction; and the video signal must be transmitted with a finite bandwidth, which limits horizontal resolution. Quantitatively, we measure resolution in terms of the maximum number

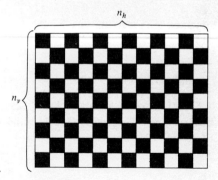

FIGURE C.5
Horizontal and vertical resolution cells.

of discrete image lines that can be distinguished in each direction, say n_h and n_v In other words, the most detailed image that can be resolved is taken to be a checkerboard pattern having n_h columns and n_v rows, Fig. C.5. One usually desires equal horizontal and vertical resolution in lines per unit distance, i.e., n_h/(image width) $= n_v$/(image height), or

$$\frac{n_h}{n_v} = \frac{\text{image width}}{\text{image height}} = \mathscr{A} \qquad (5)$$

and $\mathscr{A}$ is called the *aspect ratio*.

Clearly, vertical resolution is related to the total number of raster lines N; indeed, n_v equals N if all scanning lines are active in image formation (as in facsimile but not TV) and the raster aligns perfectly with the rows in Fig. C.5. Experimental studies show that arbitrary raster alignment reduces the effective resolution by a factor of about 70 percent, called the *Kerr factor*, so

$$n_v = 0.7(N - N_{vr}) \qquad (6)$$

where N_{vr} is the number of raster lines lost during vertical retrace.

Horizontal resolution is determined by the baseband bandwidth B allotted to the video signal. If the video signal is a sinusoid at frequency $f_{\max} = B$, the resulting picture will be a sequence of alternating dark and light spots spaced by one-half cycle in the horizontal direction. It then follows that

$$n_h = 2B(T_{\text{line}} - T_{hr}) \qquad (7)$$

where T_{line} is the total duration of one line and T_{hr} is the horizontal retrace time. Solving Eq. (7) for B and using Eqs. (5) and (6) yields

$$B = \frac{\mathscr{A} n_v}{2(T_{\text{line}} - T_{hr})} = 0.35 \mathscr{A} \frac{N - N_{vr}}{T_{\text{line}} - T_{hr}} \qquad (8)$$

An alternate and more versatile bandwidth expression is obtained by multiplying both sides of Eq. (8) by the frame time $T_{\text{frame}} = N T_{\text{line}}$ and explicitly showing the desired vertical resolution. Since $N = n_v/0.7(1 - N_{vr}/N)$, this results in

$$BT_{\text{frame}} = \frac{0.714 \mathscr{A} n_v^2}{\left(1 - \dfrac{N_{vr}}{N}\right)\left(1 - \dfrac{T_{hr}}{T_{\text{line}}}\right)} \qquad (9)$$

bringing out the fact that the bandwidth requirement (or frame time) is proportional to the square of the resolution.

Example C.1

In United States TV standards,† $N = 525$ and $N_{vr} = 2 \times 20 = 40$ so there are 485 active lines. The line time is $T_{1\text{ine}} = 1/f_h = 63.5$ μs and $T_{hr} = 10$ μs, leaving an active line time of 53.5 μs. Therefore, using Eq. (8) with $\mathscr{A} = \tfrac{4}{3}$,

$$B = 0.35 \times \frac{4}{3} \times \frac{485}{53.5 \times 10^{-6}} \approx 4.3 \text{ MHz}$$

as compared with the specified value of 4.2 MHz. Note that this bandwidth is sufficiently large to ensure that the 5-μs synchronizing pulses suffer little distortion.   ////

Example C.2

Unlike TV, facsimile transmission requires no vertical retrace and the horizontal retrace time is negligible. If a full-size newspaper page (37 by 59 cm) is to be transmitted over a voice telephone circuit ($B \approx 3.2$ kHz) with a resolution of 40 lines/cm, Eq. (9) gives the transmission time as

$$T_{\text{frame}} = \frac{0.714(37/59)(40 \times 59)^2}{3.2 \times 10^3} \approx 780 \text{ s} = 13 \text{ min}$$

Calculations such as this underscore the fact that high-resolution facsimile transmission requires substantial transmission time or a wideband channel.   ////

C.2 TV TRANSMITTERS AND RECEIVERS

The large bandwidth and significant low-frequency content of the video signal, together with the desired simplicity of envelope detection, have led to the selection of VSB + C (as described in Sect. 5.4) for TV broadcasting in the United States. However, since precise vestigial sideband shaping is more easily carried out at the receiver where the power levels are small, the actual modulated-signal spectrum is as indicated in Fig. C.6a. The half-power frequency of the upper sideband is about 4.2 MHz above the video carrier f_{cv} while the lower sideband has a 1-MHz bandwidth. Figure C.6b shows the frequency shaping at the receiver.

The audio signal is frequency-modulated on a separate carrier $f_{ca} = f_{cv} + f_a$, $f_a = 4.5$ MHz, with frequency deviation $f_\Delta = 25$ kHz. Thus, assuming an audio bandwidth of 10 kHz, $\Delta = 2.5$ and the modulated audio occupies about 80 kHz (see Sect. 6.3). TV channels are spaced by 6 MHz, leaving a 250-kHz guard band, with carrier frequencies assigned in the VHF and UHF ranges.

† In Europe, $N = 625$ and $f_v = 50$ Hz.

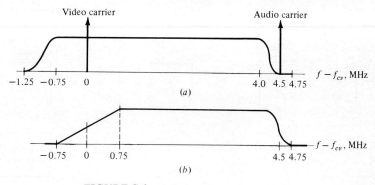

FIGURE C.6

(a) TV spectrum as transmitted; (b) VSB shaping at receiver.

Further details about monochrome TV transmitters and receivers are given below; the modifications for color TV are discussed in the next section. The corresponding electronic circuitry can be found in the literature.†

Transmitters

The essential parts of a TV transmitter are block-diagramed in Fig. C.7. The synchronizing generator controls the scanning raster and supplies blanking and synch pulses for the video signal. The DC restorer and white clipper working together ensure that the amplified video signal levels are in the proportions shown in Fig. C.2. The video modulator is of the high-level AM type, and the power amplifier removes the lower portion of the lower sideband.

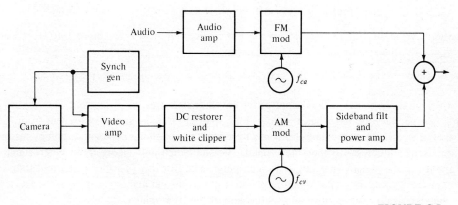

FIGURE C.7
TV transmitter.

† E.g., Terman (1955, chap. 25) or Hansen (1969).

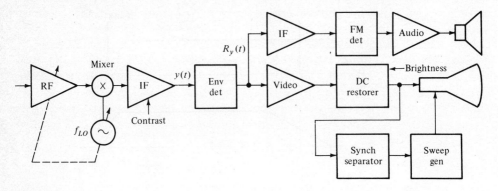

FIGURE C.8
TV receiver.

The antenna has a balanced-bridge configuration such that the outputs of the audio and video transmitters are radiated by the same antenna without interfering with each other. The transmitted audio power is 50 to 70 percent of the video power.

Receivers

As indicated in Fig. C.8, a TV receiver is of the superheterodyne type (Sect. 5.5). The main IF amplifier has f_{IF} in the 41- to 46-MHz range and provides the vestigial shaping per Fig. C.6b. Note that the modulated audio signal is also passed by this amplifier, but with substantially less gain. Thus, drawing upon Eq. (18), Sect. 5.4, the total signal at the input to the envelope detector is

$$y(t) = A_{cv}[1 + mx(t)] \cos \omega_{cv} t - A_{cv} m\zeta(t) \sin \omega_{cv} t + A_{ca} \cos [(\omega_{cv} + \omega_a)t + \phi(t)] \qquad (1)$$

where $x(t)$ is the video signal, $\phi(t)$ is the FM audio, and $\omega_a = 2\pi f_a$. Since $|m\zeta(t)| \ll 1$ and $A_{ca} \ll A_{cv}$, the resulting envelope is approximately

$$R_y(t) = A_{cv}[1 + mx(t)] + A_{ca} \cos [\omega_a t + \phi(t)] \qquad (2)$$

which gives the signal at the output of the envelope detector.

The video amplifier has a lowpass filter that removes the audio component from $R_y(t)$ as well as a DC restorer that electronically clamps the blanking pulses and thereby restores the correct DC level to the video signal. The amplified and DC-restored video signal is applied to the picture tube and to a synch-pulse separator that provides synchronization for the sweep generators. The "brightness" control permits manual adjustment of the DC level while the "contrast" control adjusts the gain of the IF amplifier.

Equation (2) shows that the envelope detector output also includes the modulated audio. This component is picked out and amplified by another IF amplifier tuned to 4.5 MHz. FM detection and amplification then yields the audio signal.

Observe that, although the transmitted composite audio and video signal is a type of frequency-division multiplexing, separate frequency conversion is not required for the audio. This is because the video carrier acts like a local oscillator for the audio in the envelope-detection process, an arrangement called the *intercarrier-sound system* having the advantageous feature that the audio and video are always tuned in together. Successful operation depends on the fact that the video component is large compared to the audio at the envelope detector input, as made possible by the white clipper at the transmitter (which prevents the modulated video signal from becoming too small) and the relative attenuation of the audio by the receiver's IF response, Fig. C.6*b*.

C.3   COLOR TELEVISION

Any color can be synthesized from a mixture of the three additive primary colors, red, green, and blue. Accordingly, a brute-force approach to color TV would involve direct transmission of three video signals, say $x_R(t)$, $x_G(t)$, and $x_B(t)$ — one for each primary. But, aside from the increased bandwidth requirement, this method would not be compatible with existing monochrome systems. A fully compatible color TV signal that fits into the monochrome channel was developed in 1954, drawing upon certain characteristics of human color perception. The salient features of that system are outlined here.†

Luminance and Chrominance Signals

To begin with, the three primary color signals can be uniquely represented by any three other signals that are independent linear combinations of $x_R(t)$, $x_G(t)$, and $x_B(t)$. And, by proper choice of coefficients, one of the linear combinations can be made the same as the intensity or *luminance* signal of monochrome TV. In particular, it turns out that if

$$x_Y(t) = 0.30x_R(t) + 0.59x_G(t) + 0.11x_B(t) \qquad (1a)$$

then $x_Y(t)$ is virtually identical to the conventional video signal previously symbolized by $x(t)$. The remaining two signals, called the *chrominance* signals, are taken as

$$x_I(t) = 0.60x_R(t) - 0.28x_G(t) - 0.32x_B(t) \qquad (1b)$$

$$x_Q(t) = 0.21x_R(t) - 0.52x_G(t) + 0.31x_B(t) \qquad (1c)$$

Here, the color signals are normalized such that $0 \leq x_R(t) \leq 1$, etc., so the luminance signal is never negative while the chrominance signals are bipolar.

Understanding the chrominance signals is enhanced by introducing the *color vector*

$$x_C(t) = x_I(t) + jx_Q(t) \qquad (2)$$

whose magnitude $|x_C(t)|$ is the color intensity or *saturation* and whose angle arg $[x_C(t)]$ is the *hue*. Figure C.9 shows the vector positions of the saturated primary colors in the *IQ*

† Complete specifications and discussion are given in *Proc. IRE*, vol. 42, January 1954, which is devoted entirely to the subject of color television.

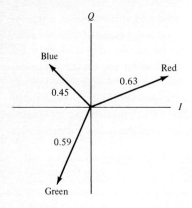

FIGURE C.9
Saturated primary color vectors in the
IQ plane.

plane. A partially saturated (pastel) blue-green, for instance, might have $x_R = 0$ and $x_B = x_G = 0.5$, so $x_C = -0.300 - j0.105$, $|x_C| = 0.318$, and arg $[x_C] = -160°$. Since the origin of the IQ plane represents the absence of color, the luminance signal may be viewed as a vector perpendicular to this plane.

Because $x_Y(t)$ serves as the monochrome signal, it must be allotted the entire 4.2-MHz baseband bandwidth to provide adequate horizontal resolution. Consequently, there would seem to be no room for the chrominance signals. Recall, however, that the spectrum of $x_Y(t)$ has periodic gaps between the harmonics of the line frequency f_h—and the same holds for the chrominance signals. Moreover, subjective tests have shown that the human eye is less perceptive of chrominance resolution than luminance resolution, so that $x_I(t)$ and $x_Q(t)$ can be restricted to about 1.3 MHz and 0.6 MHz, respectively, without significant visible degradation of the color picture. Combining these factors permits multiplexing the chrominance signals in an interleaved fashion in the baseband spectrum of the luminance signal.

Frequency Interleaving and Compatibility

The chrominance signals are multiplexed on a *color subcarrier* whose frequency falls exactly halfway between the 227th and 228th harmonic of f_h, i.e.,

$$f_{cc} = \frac{455}{2} f_h \approx 3.6 \text{ MHz} \qquad (3)$$

Therefore, by extension of Fig. C.4, the luminance and chrominance frequency components are interleaved as indicated in Fig. C.10, and there is 0.6 MHz between f_{cc} and the upper end of the baseband channel. The subcarrier modulation will be described shortly, after we examine frequency interleaving and compatibility.

What happens when a color signal is applied to a monochrome picture tube? Nothing, surprisingly, as far as the viewer sees. True, the color subcarrier and its sidebands produce sinusoidal variations on top of the luminance signal. But because all of these sinusoids are exactly an odd multiple of one-half the line frequency, they reverse in phase from line

FIGURE C.10
Chrominance spectral lines (dashed) interleaved between luminance lines.

to line and from field to field, Fig. C.11. This produces flickering in small areas that averages out over time and space to the correct luminance value and goes essentially unnoticed by the viewer.

By means of this averaging effect, frequency interleaving renders the color signal compatible with an unmodified monochrome receiver. It also simplifies the design of color receivers since, reversing the above argument, the luminance signal does not visibly interfere with the chrominance signals. There is a minor interference problem caused by the difference frequency $f_a - f_{cc}$ between the audio and color subcarriers; this was solved by slightly changing the line frequency to $f_h = f_a/286 = 15.73426$ kHz giving $f_a - f_{cc} = 4,500 - 3,579.545 = 920.455$ kHz $= (107/2)f_h$ which is an "invisible" frequency. (As a result of this change, the field rate is actually 59.94 Hz rather than 60 Hz!)

Chrominance Multiplexing System

Any two signals can be linearly modulated on the same carrier using the system diagramed in Fig. C.12. Known as *quadrature-carrier multiplexing*, this arrangement utilizes carrier phase shifting and synchronous detection to permit two signals to occupy the same frequency band; the analysis is left to the reader. Figure C.13 shows how the quadrature-carrier scheme is incorporated in a color TV transmitter for the chrominance signals.

The three color signals are first matrixed† per Eq. (1) to form $x_Y(t)$, $x_I(t)$, and $x_Q(t)$.

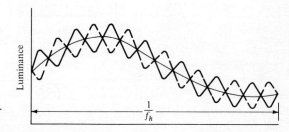

FIGURE C.11
Line-to-line phase reversal of chrominance variations on luminance.

---

† Not shown is the nonlinear *gamma* correction introduced to compensate for the brightness distortion of a typical receiver.

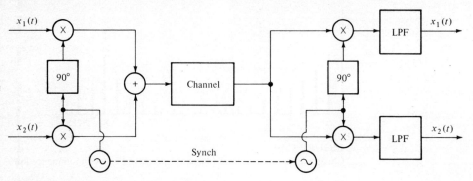

FIGURE C.12
Quadrature-carrier multiplexing.

The chrominance signals are lowpass-filtered (with different bandwidths) and applied to the subcarrier modulators. Subsequent bandpass filtering produces conventional DSB modulation for the Q channel and modified VSB for the I channel—i.e., DSB for baseband frequencies of $x_I(t)$ below 0.6 MHz and LSSB for $0.6 < |f| < 1.3$ MHz. The latter keeps the modulated chrominance signals as high as possible in the baseband spectrum, thereby

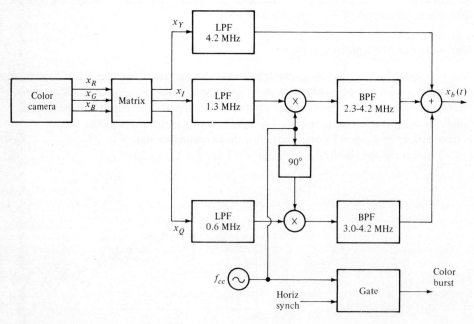

FIGURE C.13
Color subcarrier modulation system.

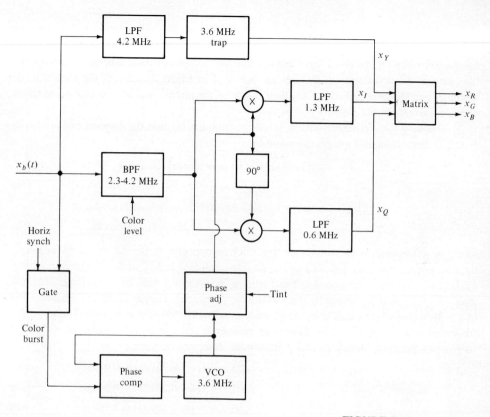

FIGURE C.14
Color demodulation system.

confining the flicker to small areas, while still allowing enough bandwidth for proper resolution of $x_I(t)$. Total sideband suppression cannot be used owing to the significant low-frequency content in $x_I(t)$ and $x_Q(t)$.

Including $x_Y(t)$, the entire baseband signal becomes

$$x_b(t) = x_Y(t) + x_Q(t) \sin \omega_{cc} t + x_I(t) \cos \omega_{cc} t + \hat{x}_{IH}(t) \sin \omega_{cc} t \qquad (4)$$

where $\hat{x}_{IH}(t)$ is the Hilbert transform of the high-frequency portion of $x_I(t)$ and accounts for the asymmetric sidebands. This baseband signal takes the place of the monochrome video signal in Fig. C.7. Additionally, an 8-cycle piece of the color subcarrier known as the *color burst* is put on the trailing portion or " back porch " of the blanking pulses for purposes of synchronization.

Demultiplexing is accomplished in a color TV receiver after the envelope detector, as laid out in Fig. C.14. Since the luminance signal is at baseband here, it requires no further processing save for amplification and a 3.6-MHz trap or rejection filter to eliminate the major flicker component; the chrominance sidebands need not be removed, thanks to frequency interleaving. The chrominance signals pass through a bandpass amplifier and are applied to a pair of synchronous detectors whose local oscillator is a VCO synchronized by phase comparison with the received color burst. Manual controls usually labeled "color level" (i.e., saturation) and "tint" (i.e., hue) are provided to adjust the gain of the chrominance amplifier and the phase of the VCO; their effect on the picture is readily explained in terms of the color vector and Fig. C.9.

Assuming good synchronization, it follows from Eq. (4) that the detected but unfiltered I- and Q-channel signals are proportional to

$$v_I(t) = x_I(t) + 2x_{YH}(t)\cos \omega_{cc} t + x_I(t)\cos 2\omega_{cc} t$$
$$+ [x_Q(t) + \hat{x}_{IH}(t)]\sin 2\omega_{cc} t \qquad (5a)$$

$$v_Q(t) = x_Q(t) + \hat{x}_{IH}(t) + 2x_{YH}(t)\sin \omega_{cc} t + x_I(t)\sin 2\omega_{cc} t$$
$$- [x_Q(t) + \hat{x}_{IH}(t)]\cos 2\omega_{cc} t \qquad (5b)$$

where $x_{YH}(t)$ represents the luminance frequency components in the 2.3- to 4.2-MHz range. Clearly, lowpass filtering will remove the double-frequency terms, while the terms involving $x_{YH}(t)$ are "invisible" frequencies. Furthermore, $\hat{x}_{IH}(t)$ in Eq. (5b) has no components less than 0.6 MHz, so it is rejected by the LPF in the Q channel. (Imperfect filtering here results in a bothersome effect called quadrature color cross talk.) Therefore, ignoring the invisible-frequency terms, $x_I(t)$ and $x_Q(t)$ have been recovered and can then be matrixed with $x_Y(t)$ to generate the color signals for the picture tube. Specifically, from Eq. (1),

$$x_R(t) = x_Y(t) - 0.96x_I(t) + 0.62x_Q(t) \qquad (6a)$$

$$x_G(t) = x_Y(t) - 0.28x_I(t) - 0.64x_Q(t) \qquad (6b)$$

$$x_B(t) = x_Y(t) - 1.10x_I(t) + 1.70x_Q(t) \qquad (6c)$$

If the received signal happens to be monochrome, then the three color signals will be equal and the reproduced picture will be black-and-white. This is termed *reverse compatibility*.

C.4   PROBLEMS

C.1   (Sect. C.1) Explain the following two statements:
   (a) The total number of lines per frame in a TV system should be odd.
   (b) The waveform that drives the scanning path in a TV system should be a sawtooth rather than a triangle or sinusoid.

C.2   (Sect. C.1) Ignoring retracing and the slight slope of the raster, describe the video spectrum when the image consists of alternating black and white vertical bars of width $H/4$. Repeat for horizontal bars of height $V/4$ and compare. [*Hint*: Consider the video signal itself, rather than using Eq. (4).]

C.3   (Sect. C.1) Find $|c_{mn}|$ for an image that is entirely black ($I = 0$) except for a centered white ($I = 1.0$) rectangle αH wide by βV high. (*Ans.*: $\alpha\beta|\text{sinc } m\alpha \text{ sinc } n\beta|$.)

C.4   (Sect. C.1) Referring to Prob. C.3, plot the amplitude spectrum to scale for $f \geq 0$ when $\alpha = 0.6$, $\beta = 0.4$, and $f_h = 20f_v$. Neglect any lines for which $|c_{mn}| < 0.1|c_{00}|$. Repeat with $\alpha = 0.4$ and $\beta = 0.6$, and explain the differences.

.C.5   (Sect. C.1) The *Picturephone®* image is square, the active line time is about 100 μs, and there are about 230 active lines.

(a) Find the video bandwidth requirement.

(b) If the video signal is transmitted via binary PCM (actually DPCM) with $Q = 8$, what is the minimum transmission bandwidth?

C.6   (Sect. C.1) Calculate n_v and B for a TV system with $\mathscr{A} = \frac{4}{3}$, $N = 625$, $N_{vr} = 48$, $f_v = 50$ Hz, and $T_{hr} = 0.16\,T_{line}$. Compare with United States TV standards.

C.7   (Sect. C.1) An image transmission system has fixed values of N_{vr}/N and T_{hr}/T_{line}. It is further specified that the resolution must be n_0 *lines per unit distance* in both directions. Show that $BT_{frame} = 0.714\,HVn_0^2$, which is independent of the aspect ratio.

C.8   (Sect. C.2) Use a phasor diagram to derive Eq. (2) from (1).

C.9   (Sect. C.2) Suppose the scanning process in a TV camera is such that its output signal is $\bar{x}(t) = \int_{t-\Delta}^{t} x(\lambda)\,d\lambda$ where $x(t)$ is the desired video signal and $\Delta \ll T_{line}$. This is known as the horizontal *aperture effect.*

(a) Qualitatively describe what happens to the reproduced image.

(b) Quantitatively, design a filter that compensates for the effect.

C.10   (Sect. C.3) Analyze the *quadrature-carrier multiplex system*, Fig. C.12. In particular, obtain expressions for the output signals when the receiver *LO* has an arbitrary phase error ϕ'.

C.11   (Sect. C.3) Carry out the details leading to Eqs. (5a) and (5b) from (4).

C.12   (Sect. C.3) Using Fig. C.9, describe what happens to the reproduced color image when: the gain of the chrominance amplifier is too high or too low; the phase of the VCO is in error by $\pm 90°$ or $180°$.

C.13★(Sect. C.3) Find expressions equivalent to Eqs. (4) and (5) when all the filters in the x_Q channel (at transmitter and receiver) are the same as the x_I channel. Discuss your results.

TABLE A

FOURIER TRANSFORM PAIRS

Definitions

$$\text{Transform} \quad V(f) = \mathscr{F}[v(t)] = \int_{-\infty}^{\infty} v(t)e^{-j2\pi ft}\, dt$$

$$\text{Inverse transform} \quad v(t) = \mathscr{F}^{-1}[V(f)] = \int_{-\infty}^{\infty} V(f)e^{j2\pi ft}\, df$$

Integral Theorem

$$\int_{-\infty}^{\infty} v(t)w^*(t)\, dt = \int_{-\infty}^{\infty} V(f)W^*(f)\, df$$

Theorems

Operation	Function	Transform
Linearity	$\alpha v(t) + \beta w(t)$	$\alpha V(f) + \beta W(f)$
Time delay	$v(t - t_d)$	$V(f)e^{-j\omega t_a}$
Scale change	$v(at)$	$\dfrac{1}{\lvert a \rvert} V\left(\dfrac{f}{a}\right)$
Conjugation	$v^*(t)$	$V^*(-f)$
Duality	$V(t)$	$v(-f)$
Frequency translation	$v(t)e^{j\omega_c t}$	$V(f - f_c)$
Modulation	$v(t)\cos(\omega_c t + \theta)$	$\tfrac{1}{2}[e^{j\theta}V(f - f_c) + e^{-j\theta}V(f + f_c)]$
Differentiation	$\dfrac{d^n v(t)}{dt^n}$	$(j2\pi f)^n V(f)$
Integration	$\displaystyle\int_{-\infty}^{t} v(\lambda)\, d\lambda$	$(j2\pi f)^{-1}V(f)$
Convolution	$v * w(t)$	$V(f)W(f)$
Multiplication	$v(t)w(t)$	$V * W(f)$
Multiplication by t^n	$t^n v(t)$	$(-j2\pi)^{-1}\dfrac{d^n V(f)}{df^n}$

Transforms

Function	$x(t)$	$X(f)$
Rectangular	$\Pi\left(\dfrac{t}{\tau}\right)$	$\tau \operatorname{sinc} f\tau$
Triangular	$\Lambda\left(\dfrac{t}{\tau}\right)$	$\tau \operatorname{sinc}^2 f\tau$
Gaussian	$e^{-\pi(t/\tau)^2}$	$\tau e^{-\pi(f\tau)^2}$
Exponential, one-sided	$e^{-t/\tau}u(t)$	$\dfrac{\tau}{1+j2\pi f\tau}$
Exponential, two-sided	$e^{-|t|/\tau}$	$\dfrac{2\tau}{1+(2\pi f\tau)^2}$
Sinc	$\operatorname{sinc} 2Wt$	$\dfrac{1}{2W}\Pi\left(\dfrac{f}{2W}\right)$
Constant	1	$\delta(f)$
Phasor	$e^{j(\omega_c t + \phi)}$	$e^{j\phi}\delta(f-f_c)$
Sinusoid	$\cos(\omega_c t + \phi)$	$\tfrac{1}{2}[e^{j\phi}\delta(f-f_c) + e^{-j\phi}\delta(f+f_c)]$
Impulse	$\delta(t-t_d)$	$e^{-j\omega t_d}$
Sampling	$\displaystyle\sum_{k=-\infty}^{\infty}\delta(t-kT_s)$	$f_s\displaystyle\sum_{n=-\infty}^{\infty}\delta(f-nf_s)$
Signum	$\operatorname{sgn} t$	$-j/\pi f$
Step	$u(t)$	$\tfrac{1}{2}\delta(t) + \dfrac{1}{j2\pi f}$

TABLE B

USEFUL MATHEMATICAL RELATIONS

Certain of the mathematical relations encountered in this text are listed below for convenient reference. However, this table is not intended as a substitute for more comprehensive handbooks.

Trigonometric Identities

$$e^{\pm j\theta} = \cos\theta \pm j\sin\theta$$

$$\cos\theta = \frac{1}{2}(e^{j\theta} + e^{-j\theta}) = \sin(\theta + 90°)$$

$$\sin\theta = \frac{1}{2j}(e^{j\theta} - e^{-j\theta}) = \cos(\theta - 90°)$$

$$\sin^2\theta + \cos^2\theta = 1$$
$$\cos^2\theta - \sin^2\theta = \cos 2\theta$$

$$\cos^2\theta = \tfrac{1}{2}(1 + \cos 2\theta)$$
$$\cos^3\theta = \tfrac{1}{4}(3\cos\theta + \cos 3\theta)$$

$$\sin^2\theta = \tfrac{1}{2}(1 - \cos 2\theta)$$
$$\sin^3\theta = \tfrac{1}{4}(3\sin\theta - \sin 3\theta)$$

$$\sin(\alpha \pm \beta) = \sin\alpha\cos\beta \pm \cos\alpha\sin\beta$$
$$\cos(\alpha \pm \beta) = \cos\alpha\cos\beta \mp \sin\alpha\sin\beta$$

$$\tan(\alpha \pm \beta) = \frac{\tan\alpha \pm \tan\beta}{1 \mp \tan\alpha\tan\beta}$$

$$\sin\alpha\sin\beta = \tfrac{1}{2}\cos(\alpha - \beta) - \tfrac{1}{2}\cos(\alpha + \beta)$$
$$\cos\alpha\cos\beta = \tfrac{1}{2}\cos(\alpha - \beta) + \tfrac{1}{2}\cos(\alpha + \beta)$$
$$\sin\alpha\cos\beta = \tfrac{1}{2}\sin(\alpha - \beta) + \tfrac{1}{2}\sin(\alpha + \beta)$$

$$A\cos(\theta + \alpha) + B\cos(\theta + \beta) = C\cos\theta - S\sin\theta = R\cos(\theta + \phi)$$

where

$$C = A\cos\alpha + B\cos\beta$$
$$S = A\sin\alpha + B\sin\beta$$
$$R = \sqrt{C^2 + S^2} = \sqrt{A^2 + B^2 + 2AB\cos(\alpha - \beta)}$$

$$\phi = \arctan\frac{S}{C} = \arctan\frac{A\sin\alpha + B\sin\beta}{A\cos\alpha + B\cos\beta}$$

Series Expansions and Approximations

$$(1 + x)^n = 1 + nx + \frac{n(n - 1)}{2!} x^2 + \cdots \qquad |nx| < 1$$

$$e^x = 1 + x + \frac{1}{2!} x^2 + \cdots$$

$$a^x = 1 + x \ln a + \frac{1}{2!} (x \ln a)^2 + \cdots$$

$$\ln (1 + x) = x - \tfrac{1}{2}x^2 + \tfrac{1}{3}x^3 + \cdots$$

$$\sin x = x - \frac{1}{3!} x^3 + \frac{1}{5!} x^5 - \cdots$$

$$\cos x = 1 - \frac{1}{2!} x^2 + \frac{1}{4!} x^4 - \cdots$$

$$\tan x = x + \tfrac{1}{3}x^3 + \tfrac{2}{15}x^5 + \cdots$$
$$\arcsin x = x + \tfrac{1}{6}x^3 + \tfrac{3}{40}x^5 + \cdots$$

$$\arctan x = \begin{cases} x - \tfrac{1}{3}x^3 + \tfrac{1}{5}x^5 - \cdots & |x| < 1 \\ \dfrac{\pi}{2} - \dfrac{1}{x} + \dfrac{1}{3x^3} - \cdots & x > 1 \end{cases}$$

$$\operatorname{sinc} x = 1 - \frac{1}{3!} (\pi x)^2 + \frac{1}{5!} (\pi x)^4 - \cdots$$

Summations

$$\sum_{m=1}^{M} m = \frac{M(M + 1)}{2}$$

$$\sum_{m=1}^{M} m^2 = \frac{M(M + 1)(2M + 1)}{6}$$

$$\sum_{m=1}^{M} m^3 = \frac{M^2(M + 1)^2}{4}$$

$$\sum_{m=0}^{M} x^m = \frac{(x^M - 1)}{(x - 1)}$$

Definite Integrals

$$\int_0^\infty \frac{x^{m-1}}{1+x^n}\,dx = \frac{\pi/n}{\sin(m\pi/n)} \qquad n > m > 0$$

$$\int_0^\infty \frac{\sin x}{x}\,dx = \int_0^\infty \frac{\tan x}{x}\,dx = \frac{\pi}{2}$$

$$\int_0^\infty \frac{\sin x \cos nx}{x}\,dx = \begin{cases} \dfrac{\pi}{2} & n^2 < 1 \\[2mm] \dfrac{\pi}{4} & n^2 = 1 \\[2mm] 0 & n^2 > 1 \end{cases}$$

$$\int_0^\infty \frac{\sin^2 x}{x^2}\,dx = \frac{\pi}{2}$$

$$\int_0^\infty \frac{\cos nx}{1+x^2}\,dx = \frac{\pi}{2}\,e^{-|n|}$$

$$\int_0^\infty \operatorname{sinc} x\,dx = \int_0^\infty \operatorname{sinc}^2 x\,dx = \tfrac{1}{2}$$

$$\int_0^\infty \sin x^2\,dx = \int_0^\infty \cos x^2\,dx = \frac{1}{2}\sqrt{\frac{\pi}{2}}$$

$$\int_0^\infty x^n e^{-ax}\,dx = \frac{n!}{a^{n+1}} \qquad n \ge 1,\ a > 0$$

$$\int_0^\infty e^{-a^2 x^2}\,dx = \frac{1}{2a}\sqrt{\pi} \qquad a > 0$$

$$\int_0^\infty x^2 e^{-x^2}\,dx = \tfrac{1}{4}\sqrt{\pi}$$

$$\int_0^\infty e^{-ax}\cos x\,dx = \frac{a}{1+a^2} \qquad a > 0$$

$$\int_0^\infty e^{-ax}\sin x\,dx = \frac{1}{1+a^2} \qquad a > 0$$

$$\int_0^\infty e^{-a^2 x^2}\cos bx\,dx = \frac{1}{2a}\sqrt{\pi}\,e^{-(b/2a)^2}$$

TABLE C

THE SINC FUNCTION

Numerical values of sinc $x = (\sin \pi x)/\pi x$ and its square are tabulated below for x from 0 to 3.9 in increments of 0.1.

x	sinc x	sinc^2 x	x	sinc x	sinc^2 x
0.0	1.000	1.000	2.0	0.000	0.000
0.1	0.984	0.968	2.1	0.047	0.002
0.2	0.935	0.875	2.2	0.085	0.007
0.3	0.858	0.737	2.3	0.112	0.013
0.4	0.757	0.573	2.4	0.126	0.016
0.5	0.637	0.405	2.5	0.127	0.016
0.6	0.505	0.255	2.6	0.116	0.014
0.7	0.368	0.135	2.7	0.095	0.009
0.8	0.234	0.055	2.8	0.067	0.004
0.9	0.109	0.012	2.9	0.034	0.001
1.0	0.000	0.000	3.0	0.000	0.000
1.1	−0.089	0.008	3.1	−0.032	0.001
1.2	−0.156	0.024	3.2	−0.058	0.003
1.3	−0.198	0.039	3.3	−0.078	0.006
1.4	−0.216	0.047	3.4	−0.089	0.008
1.5	−0.212	0.045	3.5	−0.091	0.008
1.6	−0.189	0.036	3.6	−0.084	0.007
1.7	−0.151	0.023	3.7	−0.070	0.005
1.8	−0.104	0.011	3.8	−0.049	0.002
1.9	−0.052	0.003	3.9	−0.025	0.001

TABLE D

GAUSSIAN PROBABILITIES

The probability that a gaussian variate with mean m and variance σ^2 will have an observed value greater than $m + \kappa\sigma$ is given by the function

$$Q(\kappa) \triangleq \frac{1}{\sqrt{2\pi}} \int_{\kappa}^{\infty} e^{-\lambda^2/2} \, d\lambda$$

called the area under the gaussian tail. Thus

$$P(X > m + \kappa\sigma) = P(X \leq m - \kappa\sigma) = Q(\kappa)$$
$$P(|X - m| > \kappa\sigma) = 2Q(\kappa)$$
$$P(m < X \leq m + \kappa\sigma) = P(m - \kappa\sigma < X \leq m) = \tfrac{1}{2} - Q(\kappa)$$
$$P(|X - m| \leq \kappa\sigma) = 1 - 2Q(\kappa)$$

Other functions related to $Q(\kappa)$ are as follows:

$$\operatorname{erf} \kappa \triangleq \frac{2}{\sqrt{\pi}} \int_{0}^{\kappa} e^{-\lambda^2} \, d\lambda = 1 - 2Q(\sqrt{2}\,\kappa)$$

$$\operatorname{erfc} \kappa \triangleq \frac{2}{\sqrt{\pi}} \int_{\kappa}^{\infty} e^{-\lambda^2} \, d\lambda = 1 - \operatorname{erf} \kappa = 2Q(\sqrt{2}\,\kappa)$$

$$\Phi(\kappa) \triangleq \frac{1}{\sqrt{2\pi}} \int_{0}^{\kappa} e^{-\lambda^2/2} \, d\lambda = \tfrac{1}{2} - Q(\kappa)$$

It is assumed throughout the above that $\kappa \geq 0$. When the argument of Q is negative, one can use the relation

$$Q(-\kappa) = 1 - Q(\kappa)$$

Numerical values of $Q(\kappa)$ are plotted below for $0 \leq \kappa \leq 7.0$. For larger values of κ, $Q(\kappa)$ may be approximated by

$$Q(\kappa) \approx \frac{1}{\sqrt{2\pi}\,\kappa}\, e^{-\kappa^2/2} \qquad \kappa \gg 1$$

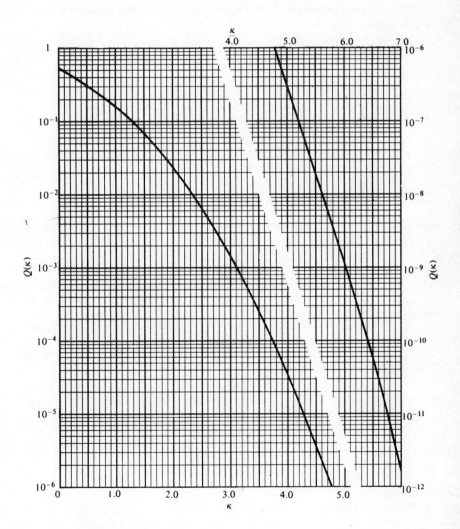

TABLE E

DECIBELS

In communication engineering, decibels are used almost always for *power ratios*. Specifically, if R is a power ratio then

$$R_{dB} \triangleq 10 \log_{10} R$$

and conversely

$$R = 10^{(R_{dB}/10)}$$

A short tabulation of approximate dB conversions is given below for $1 \leq R \leq 10$.

R	R_{dB}	R	R_{dB}
1	0.0	6	7.8
2	3.0	7	8.5
3	4.8	8	9.0
4	6.0	9	9.5
5	7.0	10	10.0

For $R < 1$ or $R > 10$, conversion is simplified by writing

$$R = r \times 10^{\pm N}$$

where $1 < r < 10$; thus

$$R_{dB} = r_{dB} \pm 10N$$

Similarly, for $R_{dB} < 0$ or $R_{dB} > 10$, use the preceding equations in reverse order. Some example conversions follow.

$$6{,}000 = 6 \times 10^3 = (7.8 + 30) \text{ dB} = 37.8 \text{ dB}$$

$$0.02 = 2 \times 10^{-2} = (3.0 - 20) \text{ dB} = -17 \text{ dB}$$

$$49 \text{ dB} = (9 + 40) \text{ dB} = 8 \times 10^4 = 80{,}000$$

$$-4 \text{ dB} = (6 - 10) \text{ dB} = 4 \times 10^{-1} = 0.4$$

Decibels are also used to indicate absolute values of power by adding a third letter, i.e., W for watts and m for milliwatts. For instance:

$$37 \text{ dBW} = 5 \times 10^3 \text{ W} = 5 \text{ kW}$$

$$0 \text{ dBm} = 1 \text{ mW} = 10^{-3} \text{ W}$$

$$-21 \text{ dBm} = 8 \times 10^{-3} \text{ mW} = 8 \ \mu\text{W}$$

Since the decibel is a logarithmic unit, calculations involving multiplication, division, powers, and roots can be carried out directly in decibels, as illustrated by the following example:

$$V = \frac{W X^3 \sqrt{Y}}{Z}$$

$$V_{\text{dB}} = W_{\text{dB}} + 3 X_{\text{dB}} + \tfrac{1}{2} Y_{\text{dB}} - Z_{\text{dB}}$$

Addition and subtraction, however, require converting decibels to numeric values.

TABLE F

GLOSSARY OF SYMBOLIC NOTATION

Operations		Reference section
H^*	Complex conjugate	2.1
$\text{Re}\,[H]$, $\text{Im}\,[H]$	Real and imaginary parts	2.1
$\|H\|$	Magnitude or absolute value	2.1
$\arg\,[H] = \arctan \dfrac{\text{Im}\,[H]}{\text{Re}\,[H]}$	Angle of a complex quantity	2.1
$\langle v(t) \rangle = \lim\limits_{T \to \infty} \dfrac{1}{T} \displaystyle\int_{-T/2}^{T/2} v(t)\,dt$	Time average	2.2
$\mathscr{F}[v(t)] = \displaystyle\int_{-\infty}^{\infty} v(t) e^{-j2\pi ft}\,dt$	Fourier transform	2.3
$\mathscr{F}^{-1}[V(f)] = \displaystyle\int_{-\infty}^{\infty} V(f) e^{j2\pi ft}\,df$	Inverse Fourier transform	2.3
$v * w(t) = \displaystyle\int_{-\infty}^{\infty} v(\lambda) w(t-\lambda)\,d\lambda$	Convolution	2.4
$\langle v(t), w(t) \rangle$	Scalar product	2.6, A.1
$\|v\| = \langle v(t), v(t) \rangle^{1/2}$	Norm	2.6, A.1
$R_{vw}(\tau) = \langle v(t), w(t-\tau) \rangle$	Crosscorrelation	2.6, 3.5
$R_v(\tau) = R_{vv}(\tau)$	Autocorrelation	2.6, 3.5
$G_v(f) = \mathscr{F}[R_v(\tau)]$	Spectral density	2.6, 3.5
$\bar{v}$	Mean value	3.3
$E[v(t)]$	Ensemble average	3.5
$\hat{v}(t) = \dfrac{1}{\pi} \displaystyle\int_{-\infty}^{\infty} \dfrac{v(\lambda)}{t-\lambda}\,d\lambda$	Hilbert transform	5.4

Functions

$$Q(\kappa) = \frac{1}{\sqrt{2\pi}} \int_{\kappa}^{\infty} e^{-\lambda^2/2} \, d\lambda \qquad \text{Gaussian probability}$$

$$\exp t = e^t \qquad \text{Exponential}$$

$$\text{sinc } t = \frac{\sin \pi t}{\pi t} \qquad \text{Sinc}$$

$$\text{sgn } t = \begin{cases} 1 & t > 0 \\ -1 & t < 0 \end{cases} \qquad \text{Sign}$$

$$u(t) = \begin{cases} 1 & t > 0 \\ 0 & t < 0 \end{cases} \qquad \text{Step}$$

$$\Pi\left(\frac{t}{\tau}\right) = \begin{cases} 1 & |t| < \dfrac{\tau}{2} \\ 0 & |t| > \dfrac{\tau}{2} \end{cases} \qquad \text{Rectangle}$$

$$\Lambda\left(\frac{t}{\tau}\right) = \begin{cases} 1 - \dfrac{|t|}{\tau} & |t| < \tau \\ 0 & |t| > \tau \end{cases} \qquad \text{Triangle}$$

Miscellaneous symbols

$\triangleq$	" Equals by definition "
$\approx$	" Approximately equals "
$\displaystyle\int_T$	$\displaystyle\int_{t_1}^{t_1+T}$ where t_1 is arbitrary
$\leftrightarrow$	Denoting a Fourier transform pair
$[a,b]$	The interval from a to b
$\bigstar$	Text material that may be omitted

SELECTED SUPPLEMENTARY READING

Listed below under various subject headings are books and papers for the benefit of those readers who desire an alternate treatment or who wish to pursue a topic in greater depth. All items should be available in a good technical library. Unless otherwise indicated, they are at a level comparable to the corresponding sections of this text. Complete citations are given in the reference section.

Communication Systems in General

Several textbooks have more or less the same coverage of communication systems as this book. The more recent include McMullen (1968), Sakrison (1968), Schwartz (1970), Simpson and Houts (1971), and Taub and Schilling (1971).

Goldman (1948), one of the earliest books on the subject, has numerous examples of spectral analysis in the context of radio engineering. Bennett (1970) gives emphasis to those aspects of communication most pertinent to telephone systems, while Sunde (1969) has extensive treatment of the problems of imperfect channels. Laser communication systems are covered by Pratt (1969).

Signal Analysis

Expanded discussion of signal analysis and Fourier methods will be found in Lathi (1965, chaps. 2 to 6, 10) and Frederick and Carlson (1971, chaps. 4 to 7, 12). Two books dealing exclusively with Fourier transforms and applications are Bracewell (1965) and Papoulis (1962). The former features a pictorial dictionary of transform pairs; the latter strikes a nice balance between rigor and lucidity. More advanced works, not for the casual reader, are Lighthill (1958) and Franks (1969).

Random Signals

Beckmann (1967, chaps. 6 and 7), Lathi (1968, chaps. 2 to 4), and Thomas (1969, chaps. 2 to 4) give short expositions of probability and random-signal theory. More comprehensive and advanced are Cooper and McGillem (1971), Davenport and Root (1958), and Papoulis (1965), in order of increasing sophistication.

Two excellent papers on noise analysis have appeared in the literature: Rice (1944, 1945), a classic reference, and Bennett (1956), a tutorial article.

Electrical Noise

Baghdady (1960, chap. 15) is a concise treatment of noise in communication receivers. One of the best general references is Bennett (1960), which, in addition to receiver noise, discusses noise in electromagnetic radiation, measurement techniques, and the design of low-noise systems.

The paper by Pierce (1956) surveys physical sources of noise. Noise in microwave systems is analyzed by Siegman (1961), using the informative transmission-line approach. Van der Ziel (1970) deals with noise in solid-state devices and lasers, while Jolly (1967) gives a qualitative but illuminating discussion of low-noise electronics.

Modulation

All the aforementioned general texts have chapters on CW and pulse modulation. In addition, Panter (1965) has extensive analyses of FM and PCM supported by abundant literature citations, making it a valuable item for the reference shelf of any communication system engineer.

Taub and Schilling (1971, chaps. 9 and 10) gives a very readable presentation of FM noise and threshold extension. The two classic papers on FM — Carson (1922) and Armstrong (1936) — have withstood the test of time and remain informative reading today.

Though somewhat dated, Black (1953, chaps. 4, 5, 15 to 20) has good overall coverage of sampling and pulse modulation. Linden (1959) is devoted to sampling theory; Rowe (1965, chap. 4) gives the spectral analysis of analog pulse modulation; and Oliver, Pierce, and Shannon (1948) is the landmark article on the philosophy of PCM. The various types of delta modulation systems are surveyed by Schindler (1970).

Statistical Communication Theory

All three main areas of statistical communication theory (i.e., information theory, coding, and detection theory) are treated by Thomas (1969) and Wozencraft and Jacobs (1965). The latter is mathematically demanding but well worth the effort.

The classic papers on information theory are Nyquist (1924, 1928), Hartley (1928), and Shannon (1948, 1949). Shannon (1949) is relatively nonmathematical and highly recommended; among other things, it was the first exposition of sampling theory applied to electrical communication. Abramson (1963), Ash (1965), and Gallager (1968) are graduate-level texts on information theory and coding. On the other hand, Pierce (1961) was written for the layman and includes the implications of information theory on art, music, psychology, etc. Anyone with an interest in these subjects will profit from Pierce's fresh interpretations.

The concise monograph by Selin (1965) outlines detection theory. At a higher mathematical level are Hancock and Wintz (1966) and Brown and Palermo (1969). Turin (1960) is a tutorial paper on matched filters, while the book by Viterbi (1966) deals with coherent detection using phase-coherent equipment.

Digital Data Communication

Bennett and Davey (1965) and Lucky, Salz, and Weldon (1968) are devoted entirely to digital data transmission, the latter being more theoretical. Other works containing appreciable treatment of the subject include Schwartz, Bennett, and Stein (1966), Viterbi (1966), and Wozencraft and Jacobs (1965).

Of the many papers that could be cited here, the following have special merit: Arthurs and Dym (1962), a discussion of digital-signal detection couched in the language of signal space; Salz (1965), which describes digital FM using discriminators; Lucky (1965), the primary article on adaptive equalization; and Jacobs (1967), which compares multilevel systems.

For an introduction to error-control coding, Lin (1970) is among the best. Berlekamp (1968) and Peterson and Weldon (1972) give more inclusive and advanced presentations.

Communication Circuits and Electronics

Everitt and Anner (1956) is one of the standard texts on transmission lines, wave filters, etc., and a convenient tabulation of filter designs has been compiled by Christian and Eisenmann (1966). Numerous aspects of radio engineering hardware are in Terman (1955) and Henney (1959). More recent books on communication electronics are DeFrance (1966), Zeines (1970), Clarke and Hess (1971), and Alley and Atwood (1973). Hansen (1969) is devoted to television electronics.

REFERENCES

ABBOTT, E.: "Flatland," 6th ed., rev., Blackwell, Oxford, 1950.

ABRAMSON, N.: "Information Theory and Coding," McGraw-Hill, New York, 1963.

ALLEY, C. L., and K. W. ATWOOD.: "Electronic Engineering," 3rd. ed., Wiley, New York, 1973.

ARMSTRONG, E. H.: A Method of Reducing Disturbances in Radio Signaling by a System of Frequency Modulation, *Proc. IRE*, vol. 24, pp. 689–740, May 1936.

ARTHURS, E., and H. DYM: On the Optimum Detection of Digital Signals in the Presence of White Gaussian Noise — A Geometric Interpretation and a Study of Three Basic Data Transmission Systems, *IRE Trans. Commun. Systems*, vol. CS-10, pp. 336–372, December 1962.

ASH, R.: "Information Theory," Wiley, New York, 1965.

BAGHDADY, E. J. (ed.): "Lectures on Communication System Theory," McGraw-Hill, New York, 1960.

BAKER, P. A.: Phase-modulation Data Sets for Serial Transmission at 2000 or 2400 Bits per Second, *AIEE Trans.*, pt. I, vol. 61, pp. 161–171, July 1962.

BECKMANN, P.: "Probability in Communication Engineering," Harcourt, Brace & World, New York, 1967.

BELL TELEPHONE LABORATORIES: "Transmission Systems for Communication," revised 4th ed., Bell Telephone Laboratories, Winston-Salem, N.C., 1971.

BENNETT, W. R.: Methods of Solving Noise Problems, *Proc. IRE*, vol. 44, pp. 609–638, May 1956. "Electrical Noise," McGraw-Hill, New York, 1960. "Introduction to Signal Transmission," McGraw-Hill, New York, 1970.

BENNETT, W. R., and J. R. DAVEY: "Data Transmission," McGraw-Hill, New York, 1965.

BERLEKAMP, E. R.: "Algebraic Coding Theory," McGraw-Hill, New York, 1968.

BLACK, H. S.: "Modulation Theory," Van Nostrand, Princeton, N.J., 1953.

BRACEWELL, R.: "The Fourier Transform and Its Applications," McGraw-Hill, New York, 1965.

BRILLOUIN, L.: "Science and Information Theory," Academic, New York, 1956.

BROWN, W. M., and C. J. PALERMO: "Random Processes, Communications and Radar," McGraw-Hill, New York, 1969.

CARSON, J. R.: Notes on the Theory of Modulation, *Proc. IRE*, vol. 10, pp. 57–64, February 1922 (reprinted in *Proc. IEEE*, vol. 51, pp. 893–896, June 1963).

CHAFFEE, J. G.: The Application of Negative Feedback to Frequency-modulation Systems, *Proc. IRE*, vol. 27, pp. 317–331, May 1939.

CHRISTIAN, E., and E. EISENMANN: "Filter Design Tables and Graphs," Wiley, New York, 1966.

CLARKE, K. K., and D. T. HESS: "Communication Circuits: Analysis and Design," Addison-Wesley, Reading, Mass., 1971.

CLOSE, C. M.: "The Analysis of Linear Circuits," Harcourt, Brace & World, New York, 1966.

COOPER, G. R., and C. D. MCGILLEM: "Probabilistic Methods of Signal and System Analysis," Holt, New York, 1971.

CROISIER, A., and J. D. PIERRET: The Digital Echo Modulation, *IEEE Trans. Commun. Technology*, vol. COM-18, pp. 367–376, August 1970.

DAVENPORT, W. B., JR., and W. L. ROOT: "Introduction to Random Signals and Noise," McGraw-Hill, New York, 1958.

DeFRANCE, J. J.: "Communications Electronics Circuits," Holt, New York, 1966.

DOWNING, J. J.: "Modulation Systems and Noise," Prentice-Hall, Englewood Cliffs, N.J., 1964.

DRAKE, A. W.: "Fundamentals of Applied Probability Theory," McGraw-Hill, New York, 1967.

EVERITT, W. L., and G. E. ANNER: "Communication Engineering," 3rd ed., McGraw-Hill, New York, 1956.

FRANKLIN, R. H., and H. B. LAW: Trends in Digital Communication by Wire, *IEEE Spectrum*, vol. 3, pp. 52–58, November 1966.

FRANKS, L. E.: "Signal Theory," Prentice-Hall, Englewood Cliffs, N.J., 1969.

FREDERICK, D. K., and A. B. CARLSON: "Linear Systems in Communication and Control," Wiley, New York, 1971.

FRIEDMAN, B.: "Principles and Techniques of Applied Mathematics," Wiley, New York, 1956.

GALLAGER, R. G.: "Information Theory and Reliable Communication," Wiley, New York, 1968.

GOLDMAN, S.: "Frequency Analysis, Modulation, and Noise," McGraw-Hill, New York, 1948.

HAMMING, R. W.: Error Detecting and Error Correcting Codes, *Bell System Tech. J.*, vol. 29, pp. 147–160, April 1950.

HANCOCK, J. C., and P. A. WINTZ: "Signal Detection Theory," McGraw-Hill, New York, 1966.

HANSEN, G. L.: "Introduction to Solid-State Television Systems," Prentice-Hall, Englewood Cliffs, N.J., 1969.

HARMUTH, H. F.: Applications of Walsh Functions in Communications, *IEEE Spectrum*, vol. 6, pp. 82–91, November 1969.

HARTLEY, R. V.: Transmission of Information, *Bell System Tech. J.*, vol. 7, pp. 535–563, July 1928.

HENNEY, K. (ed.): "Radio Engineering Handbook," 5th ed., McGraw-Hill, New York, 1959.

HOROWITZ, M.: The Dolby Technique for Reducing Noise, *Popular Electronics*, pp. 31–34, August 1972.

JACOBS, I.: Comparison of M-ary Modulation Systems, *Bell System Tech. J.*, vol. 46, pp. 843–863, May–June 1967.

JAHNKE, E., and F. EMDE: "Tables of Functions," 4th ed., Dover, New York, 1945.

JOHNSON, J. B.: Thermal Agitation of Electricity in Conductors, *Phys. Rev.*, vol. 32, pp. 97–109, July 1928.

JOLLY, W. P.: "Low Noise Electronics," American Elsevier, New York, 1967.

JURGEN, R. K.: Untangling the "Quad" Confusion, *IEEE Spectrum*, vol. 9, pp. 55–62, July 1972.

LATHI, B. P.: "Signals, Systems and Communication," Wiley, New York, 1965. "An Introduction to Random Signals and Communication Theory," International Textbook, Scranton, Pa., 1968.

LIGHTHILL, M. J.: "An Introduction to Fourier Analysis and Generalized Functions," Cambridge, New York, 1958.

LIN, S.: "An Introduction to Error-Correcting Codes," Prentice-Hall, Englewood Cliffs, N.J., 1970.

LINDEN, D. A.: A Discussion of Sampling Theorems, *Proc. IRE*, vol. 47, pp. 1219–1226, July 1959.

LUCKY, R. W.: Automatic Equalization for Digital Communication, *Bell System Tech. J.*, vol. 44, pp. 547–588, April 1965.

LUCKY, R. W., J. SALZ, and E. J. WELDON, JR.: "Principles of Data Communication," McGraw-Hill, New York, 1968.

MCMULLEN, C. W.: "Communication Theory Principles," Macmillan, New York, 1968.

NICHOLS, M. H., and L. L. RAUCH: "Radio Telemetry," 2nd ed., Wiley, New York, 1956.

NYQUIST, H.: Certain Factors Affecting Telegraph Speed, *Bell System Tech. J.*, vol. 3, pp. 324–346, April 1924. Certain Topics in Telegraph Transmission Theory, *Trans. AIEE*, vol. 47, pp. 617–644, April 1928. Thermal Agitation of Electric Charge in Conductors, *Phys. Rev.*, vol. 32, pp. 110–113, July 1928.

OLIVER, B. M., J. R. PIERCE, and C. E. SHANNON: The Philosophy of PCM, *Proc. IRE*, vol. 36, pp. 1324–1332, November 1948.

PANTER, P. F.: "Modulation, Noise, and Spectral Analysis," McGraw-Hill, New York, 1965.

PAPOULIS, A.: "The Fourier Integral and Its Applications," McGraw-Hill, New York, 1962. "Probability, Random Variables, and Stochastic Processes," McGraw-Hill, New York, 1965.

PETERSON, W. W., and E. J. WELDON, JR.: "Error Correcting Codes," 2nd ed., M.I.T. Press, Cambridge, Mass., 1972.

PIERCE, J. R.: Physical Sources of Noise, *Proc. IRE*, vol. 44, pp. 601–608, May 1956. "Symbols, Signals and Noise," Harper & Row, New York, 1961.

PRATT, W. K.: "Laser Communication Systems," Wiley, New York, 1969.

REEVES, A. H.: The Past, Present, and Future of PCM, *IEEE Spectrum*, vol. 2, pp. 58–63, May 1965.

RICE, S. O.: Mathematical Analysis of Random Noise, *Bell System Tech. J.*, vol. 23, pp. 282–332, 1944, and vol. 24, pp. 46–156, 1945. Statistical Properties of a Sine-wave plus Random Noise, *Bell System Tech. J.*, vol. 27, pp. 109–157, January 1948. Communication in the Presence of Noise — Probability of Error for Two Encoding Schemes, *Bell System Tech. J.*, vol. 29, pp. 60–93, January 1950.

ROWE, H. E.: "Signals and Noise in Communication Systems," Van Nostrand, Princeton, N.J., 1965.

SAKRISON, D. J.: "Communication Theory: Transmission of Waveforms and Digital Information," Wiley, New York, 1968.

SALZ, J.: Performance of Multilevel Narrow-band FM Digital Communication Systems, *IEEE Trans. Commun. Technology*, vol. COM-13, pp. 420–424, December 1965.

SANDERS, R. W.: Communication Efficiency Comparisons of Several Communication Systems, *Proc. IRE*, pp. 575–588, April 1960.

SCHINDLER, H. R.: Delta Modulation, *IEEE Spectrum*, vol. 7, pp. 69–78, October 1970.

SCHWARTZ, M.: "Information Transmission, Modulation, and Noise," 2d ed., McGraw-Hill, New York, 1970.

SCHWARTZ, M., W. R. BENNETT, and S. STEIN: "Communication Systems and Techniques," McGraw-Hill, New York, 1966.

SELIN, I.: "Detection Theory," Princeton University Press, Princeton, N.J., 1965.

SHANNON, C. E.: A Mathematical Theory of Communication, *Bell System Tech. J.*, vol. 27, pp. 379–423, July 1948, and vol. 27, pp. 623–656, October 1948. Communication in the Presence of Noise, *Proc. IRE*, vol. 37, pp. 10–21, January 1949.

SIEGMAN, A. E.: Thermal Noise in Microwave Systems, *Microwave J.*, vol. 4, pp. 81–90, March 1961, vol. 4, pp. 66–73, April 1961, and vol. 4, pp. 93–104, May 1961.

SIMPSON, R. S., and R. C. HOUTS: "Fundamentals of Analog and Digital Communication Systems," Allyn and Bacon, Boston, 1971.

SLEPIAN, D.: A Class of Binary Signaling Alphabets, *Bell System Tech. J.*, vol. 35, pp. 203–234, January 1956.

SOMMERVILLE, D. M.: "An Introduction to the Geometry of *N* Dimensions," Dutton, New York, 1929.

STILL, A.: "Communication through the Ages," Holt, New York, 1946.

STUMPERS, F. L.: Theory of Frequency-modulation Noise, *Proc. IRE*, vol. 36, pp. 1081–1902, September 1948.

SUNDE, E. D.: "Communication Systems Engineering Theory," Wiley, New York, 1969.

TAUB, H., and D. L. SCHILLING: "Principles of Communication Systems," McGraw-Hill, New York, 1971.

TERMAN, F. E.: "Electronic and Radio Engineering," 4th ed., McGraw-Hill, New York, 1955.

THOMAS, J. B.: "An Introduction to Statistical Communication Theory," Wiley, New York, 1969.

TURIN, G. L.: An Introduction to Matched Filters, *IRE Trans. Inform. Theory*, vol. IT-6, pp. 311–329, June 1960.

VAN DER ZIEL, A.: Noise in Solid-state Devices and Lasers, *Proc. IEEE*, vol. 58, pp. 1178–1206, August 1970.

VITERBI, A. J.: "Principles of Coherent Communication," McGraw-Hill, New York, 1966.

WIENER, N.: "Extrapolation, Interpolation, and Smoothing of Stationary Time Series," Wiley, New York, 1949.

WOZENCRAFT, J. M., and I. M. JACOBS: "Principles of Communication Engineering," Wiley, New York, 1965.

ZEINES, B.: "Electronic Communication Systems," Prentice-Hall, Englewood Cliffs, N.J., 1970.